KARL MARX
FREDERICK ENGELS
COLLECTED WORKS
VOLUME
47

KARL MARX
FREDERICK ENGELS

COLLECTED
WORKS

INTERNATIONAL PUBLISHERS

NEW YORK

KARL MARX
FREDERICK ENGELS

Volume
47

ENGELS: 1883-86

INTERNATIONAL PUBLISHERS

NEW YORK

This volume has been prepared jointly by Lawrence & Wishart Ltd., London, International Publishers Co. Inc., New York, and Progress Publishing Group Corporation, Moscow, in collaboration with the Russian Independent Institute of Social and National Problems (former Institute of Marxism-Leninism), Moscow.

Editorial commissions:

GREAT BRITAIN: Eric Hobsbawm, John Hoffman, Nicholas Jacobs, Monty Johnstone, Jeff Skelley, Ernst Wangermann, Ben Fowkes.

USA: Philip S. Foner, James E. Jackson, Victor Perlo, Betty Smith, Dirk J. Struik.

RUSSIA: for Progress Publishing Group Corporation— Yu. V. Semyonov, Ye. N. Vladimirova; for the Russian Independent Institute of Social and National Problems— L.I. Golman, M.P. Mchedlov, V.N. Pospelova, G.L. Smirnov.

Library of Congress Cataloging in Publication Data

Marx, Karl, 1818-1883
    Karl Marx, Frederick Engels: collected works.

    1. Socialism — Collected works. 2. Economics — Collected works. I. Engels, Friedrich, 1820-1895.
Works, English. 1975. II. Title.
HX 39.5 A 16 1975 335.4 73-84671

ISBN 0-7178-0547-6 (v. 47)

Printed in the USA

V

Contents

FREDERICK ENGELS

LETTERS

April 1883-December 1886

1883

APPENDIX

NOTES AND INDEXES

ILLUSTRATIONS

TRANSLATORS:

PETER AND BETTY ROSS: Letters 3, 4, 8, 9, 11-14,
16, 17, 20, 22, 24, 27, 29-31, 35, 37-40, 42-44, 46,
47, 49, 50, 52, 53, 56, 57, 59, 63, 64, 67, 69, 70, 72,
73, 77, 78, 80-83, 85-89, 91, 94, 95, 97, 99, 101,
103, 104, 107, 109-25, 127-29, 132-34, 136-38,
140, 141, 143-47, 150, 154, 155, 157-59, 161, 163,
166-68, 173, 176, 187, 179-81, 183, 187, 190, 192-
95, 197-99, 201, 203, 204, 206, 209-10, 212-16,
218-19, 221, 223-24, 227, 229, 231, 233, 236, 238,
240, 242-43, 246, 248, 251, 254, 256-58, 261-70,
272-78, 280-83, 285-87, 289, 291-93, 295, 302-05,
308

RODNEY LIVINGSTONE: Letters 1, 25, 36, 51, 54,
58, 65, 66, 68, 75, 79, 90, 93, 106, 108, 148, 153,
165, 169, 202, 208, 211, 217, 220, 225, 234, 239,
249-50, 252, 255, 296

K. M. COOK: Letter 135

STEPHEN SMITH: Letters 10, 76

Preface

Volume 47 of the *Collected Works* of Karl Marx and Frederick Engels contains Engels' letters dated from April 1883 to December 1886.

The letters at the beginning of this volume to the participants of democratic and labour movements in Russia, Germany, Holland, Britain, the United States and Italy on Marx's death reflect the world-wide concern over this sad development.

After Marx's death, the volume of Engels' correspondence increased considerably. The stream of letters from all over the world was evidence of growth of the workers' and democratic movement in Europe and the United States, of Engels' influence on this process and his expanding ties with leaders of socialist parties.

New names appeared among his correspondents, such as those of Hermann Schlüter, John Lincoln Mahon, Pasquale Martignetti, and Florence Kelley-Wischnewetzky. He wrote not only to friends, comrades and followers, but also to strangers who turned to him for advice or with requests (see this volume, pp. 8, 27, 66, 282-83). For Engels maintaining and expanding his international contacts was a most demanding duty. He wrote to August Bebel on 30 April 1883: 'For after all, we wish to maintain intact, in so far as it is in my power, the many threads from all over the world which spontaneously converged upon Marx's study' (p. 17).

Marx named Engels and Eleanor Marx his 'literary executors'. Engels concentrated on completing the publication of Marx's unfinished works, first of all volumes II and III of *Capital*, which he had left in handwritten variants, and of new editions of Volume I of *Capital*

(p. 39). Engels also intended to undertake, but unfortunately did not write, a full biography of Marx on the basis of the existing extensive correspondence and other material from Marx's archive, which would incorporate the history of the German socialist movement from 1843 to 1863 and of the International from 1864 to 1872 (pp. 17, 26). In his letters, Engels referred repeatedly to the history of the International Working Men's Association, stressing the role Marx had played in it. 'Mohr's life without the International,' he wrote (in English) to Laura Lafargue on 24 June 1883, 'would be a diamond ring with the diamond broken out' (p. 40).

Engels completed the preparation for the printer, begun by Marx, of the third German edition of Volume I of *Capital* before the end of 1883. This involved much painstaking labour (as his letter to Friedrich Adolph Sorge of 29 June 1883, among others, shows). He also went out of his way to assure the appearance of *Capital* in other languages (p. 87), choosing translators with great care, and often helping to edit their translations. With Samuel Moore, Edward Aveling and Eleanor Marx, he organised and edited the first English translation of Volume I of *Capital* (pp. 436-37) which took him 'the better part of a year' (p. 492).

Many of Engels' letters refer to his preparation for the printer of the second and third volumes of Marx's *Capital*. They are imbued with respect for his deceased friend and with the wish to make the works of Marx available to the working class and progressive intellectuals. '...Some labour when you're dealing with a man like Marx, who weighed every word,' Engels wrote to Johann Philipp Becker on 22 May 1883. 'But to me it is a labour of love; after all I shall be back again with my old comrade' (p. 26).

Other letters on this score give a fairly good idea of how Engels laboured over *Capital*'s economic manuscripts — how he virtually deciphered Marx's handwriting, how he determined the chronological framework, collated notes, compared separate variants, checked quotations, and finally transcribed the entire volume in order to edit the clean copy (pp. 29, 33, 42-43, 53, 88-89). He could not let anyone else do this because, as he put it, *'there is not another living soul* who can decipher that writing and those abbreviations of words and style' (p. 93).

Preparation of Volume III dragged out and the volume did not appear in print until 1894. In his letters to Karl Kautsky of 21-22 June 1884 and Johann Philipp Becker of 2 April 1885, and elsewhere,

Engels emphasised the scientific significance of the second and third volumes of *Capital* (pp. 154, 267).

Engels followed carefully the dissemination of Marx's ideas. Of particular interest are his letters about the popular summary of *Capital* produced by the French socialist Gabriel Deville. Engels was concerned that the explication of Marxism's basic economic principles should be comprehensible to working people and not overly abstruse (p. 61), and in his letters to Florence Kelley-Wischnewetzky he recommended publishing the popularisations by Deville and Paul Lafargue. This would, he argued, introduce *Capital* and its ideas into the United States (pp. 464-65). Engels also welcomed Kautsky's book, *Karl Marx's Oekonomische Lehren*, which was well received by the public (p. 482).

In the 1880s, economic literature, notably by the so-called 'armchair socialists' (Kathedersozialisten), charged that Marx had borrowed his theory of surplus value from Rodbertus (pp. 138-39). This charge of plagiarism had to be refuted once and for all owing to the influence the armchair socialists were gaining among some Social Democrats. Engels produced a critical analysis of the main works of Rodbertus, whom he vividly described as 'apostle of the careerists of Bismarckian socialism' (p. 139) in letters to Eduard Bernstein and Karl Kautsky (pp. 72, 125-26, 193-94), whose content accords with ideas Engels originally expressed in his prefaces to the first German edition of Marx's *The Poverty of Philosophy* ('Marx and Rodbertus') and the first edition of Volume II of *Capital* (see present edition, Vols. 26 and 36).

The correspondence refers extensively to Engels' work on the translation and republication of a number of other important works by Marx and himself. The letters show that, in choosing these works, Engels was above all guided by the needs of the workers' movement, with an eye to the continuous entry into it of new people unversed in theory.

In some countries, the workers' movement of the 1880s was quite strongly influenced by the anarchists. The focal point of their polemics with Social Democrats was the question of the State. On 18 April 1883, answering the American Philipp Van Patten's question on Marx's attitude to anarchists, Engels elaborated on the historical future of the State. He described anarchist formulae — that the proletarian revolution should begin by abolishing the State — as 'anarchist absurdities', because this would be tantamount to destroying 'the only organism by means of which the victorious working class can exert its newly conquered power' (p. 10). Engels dwelt on the matter also in a letter to Bernstein, this time in connection with the latter's attack in the press on some American socialists who had also failed to understand Marx's doctrine of the State. Engels referred Bernstein to Marx's *The Civil War in France* and cited extracts from *The Poverty of Philosophy* and the *Manifesto of the Communist Party* (pp. 73-74, 86). To bring the Marxist doctrine of the State to those who had newly joined the socialist movement, Engels republished these and other works (Marx's *The Eighteenth Brumaire of Louis Bonaparte* and Engels' *Anti-Dühring* and *The Housing Question*).

Engels examined the nature and class essence of the State in his *The Origin of the Family, Private Property and the State* (see present edition, Vol. 26). He noted that he wrote the book to fulfil Marx's wishes. Marx had read *Ancient Society* by the liberal American scholar, Lewis H. Morgan, and had himself planned to write on the subject (pp.103, 115-16).

The correspondence of the 1880s lifts the veil on Engels' further elaboration of the theory of socialist revolution. He was above all preoccupied by the question of tactics and, in particular, by what he saw as the incorrect evaluation by the German Social Democrats of the character of the expected revolution. Engels examined capitalist world development in the 1880s, and concluded that the socialist revolution in countries with semi-absolutist political survivals and feudal relations in agriculture (for instance, Germany) would necessarily be preceded by a bourgeois-democratic stage. '...In our case ...,' he wrote to Bernstein in 1883, 'the first, immediate result of the revolution can and *must*, so far as *form* is concerned, be nothing other than a *bourgeois* republic'(p. 51). Then and only then would the struggle between the working class and the bourgeoisie follow classical lines, i. e. pave the way to '*direct*, undisguised class struggle between proletariat and bourgeoisie' (ibid.). At the same time, Engels warned against imagining 'the revolution as something that can be achieved overnight. In fact it is a process of development on the part of the masses which takes several years even under conditions that tend to accelerate it' (p. 51).

All his life Engels examined the dynamics of capitalist economics. Like Marx, he noticed the modification of the economic cycle and the appearance of intermediate five-year crises. He associated this with the uneven development of the leading states and the gradual decline of Great Britain in the world market (pp. 23, 82). To be sure, not all of Engels' predictions came true. Among others, this applies to the idea of an economic 'crisis without end' (p. 402) which he predicted in a letter to Nikolai Danielson of 8 February 1886 and Florence Kelley-Wischnewetzky of 3 February 1886 (pp. 396-97). In the 1890s, Engels would elaborate on his views, noting capitalism's considerable stability and expanding sphere of influence (see present edition, Vol. 37).

In many of his letters, Engels touched on various international problems of the mid-1880s which arose owing to the rivalry of the European powers in the Balkans, Germany's aggressive policies, and the views of certain circles in France who wanted back the lands Prussia had seized in 1871 (pp. 353, 483-84, 485-86, 510-11, 513-14). Examining the diplomatic games in Europe, the balance of power and the probable consequences of a military conflict, Engels helped European socialists to work out their tactics in questions of war and peace. In his letters to August Bebel, Johann Philipp Becker and Friedrich Adolph Sorge he stressed that workers of all countries should fight against the militarist system and the war danger. Though Engels admitted that war might create favourable conditions for the victory of the working class, he did not relate revolution and its victory directly to war. On the contrary, he was convinced war would take an incredibly high toll and 'retard our movement' (pp. 353-54, 487).

Special mention should be made of letters to members of the Socialist Workers' Party of Germany which, as Engels put it, was at that time the leading European workers' party (p. 36).

The German labour movement in 1883-86 was exposed to the rigours of Bismarck's Anti-Socialist Law. By combining legal and illegal methods, the party managed to win influence among the mass of the people by the mid-1880s. Engels described its success in Reichstag elections as a trial of strength (p. 198).

He believed that socialist parties should participate in election campaigns and parliamentary activity, but did not regard them as the only or main form of struggle. Looking into the experience of the German Social Democrats, he called their attention to the conditions on which they might come forward with their own bills without prejudicing their principles. In a letter to Bernstein of 11 November 1884, he said such bills could be formulated 'without regard for petty-bourgeois prejudices' and could avoid being utopian (p. 217). He elaborated on this in a letter to Bebel of 20-23 January 1886 (pp. 388-89).

Engels helped the left wing of the German Social Democratic movement in its fight against reformist elements who had a majority in the Social Democratic parliamentary group. He traced the spread of reformism to the influence of the petty bourgeoisie. 'In a philistine country like Germany,' he observed in a letter to Johann Philipp Becker of 15 June 1885 'the party must also have a philistine "educated" right wing' (p. 300). That most of the parliamentary group were men of petty-bourgeois background was traceable to the absence of deputies' salaries, which barred the doors to the Reichstag for many promising worker deputies.

Reacting to differences within the Social Democratic parliamentary group over the bill on State subsidies to shipping companies, Engels set forth his views on party unity in letters to Bebel and others (pp. 239, 269-71, 284 et al). Letting matters reach an open break with the right wing, he felt, was undesirable in the context of the Anti-Socialist Law, and would only weaken the party: in the absence of a forum for public discussion, the rank-and-file would hardly be able to understand the reasons for, and substance of, the split. Engels wrote to Bernstein on 5 June 1884: '*We* ... must steer clear of anything that might lead to a breach, or rather might lay the *blame* for that breach at our door. That is the universal rule when there is a struggle within one's own party, and now it applies more than ever' (p.145).

We see from his correspondence that Engels was a faithful reader of *Der Sozialdemokrat*, the central organ of the Socialist Workers' Party of Germany., and, indeed, was always ready to help its staff headed by Bernstein. His letters were often made the core of editorials, and thus came to be known to the German workers (pp. 139-42, 329-31).

Engels' letters to August Bebel, leader of the party's left wing, touched on an especially broad spectrum of problems. Engels wrote of Bebel: 'There is no more lucid mind in the whole of the German party, besides which he is utterly dependable and firm of purpose' (pp. 201-02).

Engels' letter to Wilhelm Liebknecht of 2 January 1886, first found in 1983, is being published in English translation here for the first time, filling a gap in their correspondence which has reached us incomplete.

During that period, Engels devoted much of his attention to the independent movement of the English working class, especially in connection with 'the sudden emergence' of socialism in Britain (p. 82). He saw the 'secret' of its revival (some decades after Owenism and

Chartism had faded away) in the erosion of Britain's monopoly in the world market by American and German competition, and the impact of the economic depression which had dragged on and on since 1873 (ibid.). More than ten years of slump had increased unemployment, ruined tenant farmers, and speeded up rural migration to the cities, adding to the number of homeless and jobless. The radical-minded intellectuals and politically active workers, disappointed in the Liberals, turned to socialism for relief from economic strains and social contradictions. The word 'socialism' was on everybody's lips. In a letter to Laura Lafargue, who was in Paris, Engels referred to 'the new Socialist "rage" in London' (pp. 94-95).

Engels, as his letters show, was critical of the Democratic Federation formed and headed by Henry Mayers Hyndman in 1881 and renamed the Social Democratic Federation in 1884. His guarded attitude was due to its heterogeneous membership, the young people who had 'emerged from amongst the bourgeoisie'. These elements, he wrote, varied considerably 'morally and intellectually', and had no root in the working class (pp. 54, 82). 'The elements presently active,' he wrote to Bebel on 30 August 1883, 'might become important, now that they have accepted our theoretical programme and thus acquired a basis, but only if a spontaneous movement broke out amongst the workers here and they succeeded in gaining control of it' (p. 54).

After reading the Federation's manifesto, Engels commented that 'these people have now at last been compelled publicly to proclaim our theory as their own, a theory which, at the time of the International, seemed to them to have been imposed upon them from outside' (ibid.). But the incorporation in the programme of a Marxist provision — the socialisation of the means of production — did not mean a mass working-class political party had emerged. Engels, however, had urged English workers to set up such a party as early as 1881, in his contribution to *The Labour Standard* (see present edition, Vol. 24, pp. 404-06). The trade union movement was far removed from socialist ideas. Yet the Social Democratic Federation's leadership, notably Hyndman, renounced contacts with the organised workers. Engels wrote to Laura Lafargue in February 1884: '...The new "respectable" Socialist stir here does go on very nicely, the thing is becoming fashionable, but the working classes do not respond yet. Upon that everything depends' (p. 105).

Engels criticised Hyndman for his lack of scruples, his disregard of political principles, and chauvinism in regard to other nations. He called him to account, too, for his excessive ambition, and his tendency towards political intrigue (pp. 118, 123, 155, 165, 236-37, 247, 366-67). The fact that Marx had broken off relations with Hyndman in 1881 had, of course, contributed to Engels' guarded attitude (see present edition, Vol. 46, pp. 102-04).

Working jointly with Samuel Moore, Edward Aveling and Eleanor Marx on the English translation of Volume I of *Capital*, Engels was sceptical of Hyndman's translation of some of its chapters (pp. 127, 313, 424) printed in *To-Day*. He criticised Hyndman's translation in an article, 'How Not to Translate Marx' (present edition, Vol. 26). Nevertheless the appearance in the socialist press of large fragments of *Capital* before its publication under separate cover in 1887 after Engels' editing had helped the spread of Marx's economic theory among workers and intellectuals.

Engels' letters betray his good knowledge of such socialist periodicals as *Justice* and *To-Day* from which he obtained an idea of the people who had attached themselves to the socialist movement in the early half of the 1880s (pp. 85-86, 114, 122, 424). He was also briefed on the activity of the Social Democratic Federation by Eleanor Marx, Edward Aveling, William Morris, Belfort Bax, and other of its left-leaning members. Towards the close of 1884, Hyndman's sectarian tactics caused profound differences within the Federation, and led to the resignation of those on its left wing who formed a new organisation, the Socialist League. Engels set forth the history of that split in letters to Bernstein and Sorge (pp. 236-38, 245). In the years that followed, he informed his correspondents in Germany and in the United States of the activity of those two socialist organisations.

Although critical of the SDF leadership, Engels approved of its actions in defence of the unemployed (holding demonstrations, sending deputations to MPs, and so forth). However, he described its leaders' attempt at attracting the mass of workers with ultra-left slogans of 'social revolution' as reckless 'revolutionary ranting' (pp. 407-08, 427). In the autumn of 1886 he admitted, however, that the 'Social Democratic Federation is beginning to be something of a power, since the masses have absolutely no other organisation to which they can rally' (p. 529). However, among the active socialists of the SDF, the Radical Clubs in the East End, and the Socialist League, he saw no one who could lead a mass movement of the unemployed (pp. 526, 534). Engels had close contacts with members of the Socialist League and supported their newspaper, *The Commonweal*, and was doubly upset by the symptoms in its ranks of 'teething troubles', sectarianism, and anarchist influence (pp. 438, 446, 471).

Despite some successful actions, the socialist movement in Britain of the early half of the 1880s was divided and had no public backing to speak of. '...The masses,' Engels wrote to Sorge, 'are still holding aloof, although here too *beginnings* of a movement are perceptible. But it will be some time before the masses are in full spate, which is a good thing because it means that there will be time for proper leaders to emerge' (p. 492).

In a series of letters Engels referred to specific features in the history of France and its labour movement. Ever since 1789, he pointed out, the political struggles in France had followed classical lines, with the governments that succeeded each other 'moving ever further to the Left' (pp. 149, 342). In 1885 Engels welcomed the collapse of Jules Ferry's cabinet which had ruled on behalf of the big bourgeoisie and stock exchange speculators with a big stake in colonial conquest, and had predicted the imminent victory in elections of the Radicals. This, he hoped, would provide favourable conditions for class struggle (pp. 270, 364). What might hamper the growth of the French labour movement, he maintained, was its low theoretical level and the surviving influence of various types of pre-Marxian socialism (pp. 183, 342). In his view, it had not yet fully recovered from the defeat of the Paris Commune (p. 211).

The correspondence is an important source of information about the processes that were underway in the French socialist movement of the early half of the 1880s. In 1882 the movement broke up into separate organisations of reformists (Possibilists) and collectivists, the latter comprising the Workers' Party, by and large an adherent of scientific socialism. Engels' letters clarify his outlook and that of the leaders of the Workers' Party on two crucial issues that had a bearing on the party's future: the relationship with the Possibilists, and use of the bourgeois parliament in the workers' interests.

At a complicated time, with the Workers' Party locked in struggle with the Possibilists, Engels urged its leaders to study theory. Some of his letters to Lafargue were printed as articles in the French socialist press (pp. 235-36, 255-56). He commended Lafargue and Deville for lecturing on Marx's teaching in France and for coming to grips with the opponents of Marxism in the press (pp. 107, 134-35, 171, 179-83).

Engels welcomed the independent labour faction in the Chamber of Deputies. For the first time, the voice of labour resounded publicly in defence of the striking miners of Decazeville. The workers' deputies edged away from the Radicals, which Engels considered as 'a great event' (pp. 409, 414, 418, 441-42). Although the faction was small, the Workers' Party had now acquired a public political tribune.

Time and again, in letters to Bebel, Liebknecht, and Paul and Laura Lafargue, Engels offered his view of bourgeois radicalism in France whose influence had risen in the autumn of 1885. Some of his statements were over-emphatic. This applied first of all to his ideas about the historical possibilities of the Radicals, and also to over-optimistic predictions of the imminent emergence of the French socialists onto the political foreground (pp. 300, 314, 343, 470).

A conspicuous place in the volume is taken up by Engels' correspondence with his old friend, the American socialist Friedrich Adolph Sorge, and with Florence Kelley-Wischnewetzky, who translated some of Engels' works. His letters show how profoundly he understood the specificity of the United States, a country that had had no feudal past and was the 'ideal of all bourgeois: a country rich, vast, expanding, with purely bourgeois institutions unleavened by feudal remnants or monarchical traditions, and without a permanent and hereditary proletariat' (p. 452). Still, the emergence of large-scale industry there resulted in the appearance of an indigenous working class.

A powerful workers' action for an eight-hour working day was mounted in 1886, with 11,500 enterprises being engulfed in strikes. This and the success of the French socialists Engels described as 'the two events of world historic importance' of the year (p. 470). The strikes demolished the image of a non-antagonistic America to which the European bourgeoisie had resorted in the election campaign. 'What has completely stunned these people is the fact that the movement is so strongly accentuated as a labour movement, and that it has sprung up so suddenly and with such force' (p. 533).

The socialist movement in 19th-century America was strongly influenced by German immigrants. Nor was this influence all positive. The Lassalleans, advocates of essentially political struggle, had all too often caused a weakening of local unions which confined themselves to economic demands only. The Socialist Labor Party founded in 1876 consisted almost exclusively of German immigrants. It had its newspapers, *New-Yorker Volkszeitung* and *Der Sozialist*, both of which appeared in German. At times, the German socialist movement in the United States was perceived by its members as a branch of the German socialist movement in Europe. Engels referred scathingly to the bookwormish dogmatism of the German socialists in the USA (p. 531). In a letter to Florence Kelley-Wischnewetzky in December 1886, he deplored their sectarianism and non-participation in the 1886 movement of the American workers (pp. 541-42). He was troubled by the lack of cohesion and unity in the US labour movement, and referred to the subject at length in his letters, emphasising its importance (pp. 470, 525).

The letters show that Engels saw the Noble Order of the Knights of Labor, an organisation of chiefly unskilled white and black workers, as the point of departure in the drive for a true working-class party in the USA. Not that he was blind to the mistakes of its leaders. He considered it a real force, stating in no uncertain terms that the Order should be revolutionised from within, that it was necessary 'to work in their midst, to form ... a nucleus of men who know the movement and its aims' (pp. 532, 541). Neither the Knights of Labor nor the United Labor Party, whose founding Engels welcomed in his letter to Laura Lafargue of 24 November 1886, however, proved viable.

When Kelley-Wischnewetzky asked for Engels' permission to translate and publish his book, *The Condition of the Working-Class in England*, he gave his consent and promised to edit the translation. In lieu of a preface, he wrote an article, 'The Labour Movement in America' (see present edition, Vol. 26), where he raised the problems he had discussed in his correspondence with Kelley-Wischnewetzky (pp. 82, 525, 530, 540-41), and made an incisive analysis of the popular US economist Henry George.

Engels' correspondence reflects his keen interest in the social-economic and political history of Russia and the Russian revolutionary movement. His chief Russian correspondents in 1883-86 were Nikolai Danielson, Pyotr Lavrov, and Vera Zasulich. Their letters, along with the periodicals and other literature, were for him a continuous source of information about life in Russia.

Engels saw the specificity of Russia in that there every degree of 'social development is represented, from the primitive commune to modern big industry and high finance, and ... all these contradictions are forcibly pent up by an unheard-of despotism' (p. 281). He predicted an imminent financial crash and stressed the disaffection among all social groups over the internal situation. He observed that 'the so-called emancipation of the peasants' in 1861 had not entirely liberated the peasants, with left-overs of feudal relations surviving in the countryside. As in the 1870s, one of the central subjects in the correspondence between Engels and the Russian revolutionaries was that of the prospects for revolution in Russia. Engels clearly overestimated the revolutionary sentiment in Russia when he wrote that the Tsar's government was 'at bay' and that the country would soon have its own 1789 (pp. 112, 338). His optimism was partly stimulated by the activity of Narodnaya Volya (People's Will) revolutionary organisation (pp. 256, 338).

His letter to Vera Zasulich of 23 April 1885 contains his conception of the character and motive forces of the impending revolution in Russia. He discusses possible revolutionary scenarios, from a palace coup to a people's revolution, which he compares to the Jacobinic dictatorship of 1793 . When he gave both main dates of the French Revolution, 1789 and 1793, he evidently had in mind the succession of stages in the revolutionary cycle, from the bourgeois to the bourgeois-democratic revolution (pp. 112, 281).

Like Marx, he was certain that the Russian revolution would tear down tsarism, that 'last stronghold of reaction' (pp. 488-89), and thereby influence the political situation in the rest of Europe, ending tsarism's policy of conquests (pp. 338, 515-16).

The letters show that Engels welcomed the growth of revolutionary forces in Russia and that he established close ties with the first Russian Marxists in the Emancipation of Labour group.

Nor did he ever deny support to Russian socialists who had translated into Russian such works as: K. Marx, *The Poverty of Philosophy* (1886), Volume II of *Capital* (1885), and his *Socialism: Utopian and Scientific* (1884), and so forth. He commended their professional skill. In a letter to Sorge of 29 June 1883 he wrote, 'Translating the *Manifesto* is awfully difficult; by far the best renderings I have seen are the Russian' (p. 42).

The correspondence of 1883-1886 is a valuable source of information about Engels' life and offers evidence of his boundless respect for Marx. To perpetuate the memory of his friend, often to the detriment of his then shaky health, he worked from eight to ten hours at his desk, editing Marx's manuscripts (pp. 197, 202, 456, 492). Conscious of the pressure of his obligations, he wrote to Johann Philipp Becker on 15 October 1884: '...My misfortune is that since we lost Marx I have been supposed to represent him. I have spent a lifetime doing what I was fitted for, namely playing second fiddle, and indeed I believe I acquitted myself reasonably well. And I was happy to have so splendid a first fiddle as Marx. But now that I am suddenly expected to take Marx's place in matters of theory and play first fiddle, there will inevitably be blunders and no one is more aware of that than I' (p. 202).

The letters produce a vivid and most attractive portrait of Engels, a revolutionary internationalist, theorist, sensitive and responsive friend, a man brimming with energy and optimism. They testify to his touching affection for Marx's daughters, and his warm concern for such veterans of the labour movement as Friedrich Lessner, Johann Philipp Becker, George Julian Harney, and others.

*　*　*

Volume 47 contains 310 letters by Frederick Engels. Of these 180 are published in English for the first time; 130 letters have been published in English before, 65 of these in part only. All previous publications are indicated in the notes.

Letter No. 310 of 25 March 1886, the use of which was kindly granted by University College Library, London, shortly before the deadline, was included in the volume at the last moment on p. 543, so that the chronological order had to be disregarded.

Eleanor Marx-Aveling's letter to Horatio Bryan Donkin of 8 February 1886, the use of which was kindly granted by University College Library, London, is included in the Appendix and is being published in English for the first time.

Obvious errors in the text of the letters have been silently corrected. Abbreviated proper and place names, and individual words are given in full, except when the abbreviations were made for reasons of secrecy or cannot be deciphered. Defects in the originals are indicated in the footnotes, and passages with lost or illegible words are denoted by omission marks. Wherever their hypothetical reconstruction was possible, it is given in square brackets. Any text crossed out by the author is reproduced in footnotes only if it has a substantive bearing on the sense. The special nature of certain letters which were drafts or fragments reproduced in other documents is indicated either in the text itself or in the notes.

Foreign words and expressions in the text of the letters are retained in the form in which they were used by the authors, with a translation where necessary in the footnotes and italicised (if they were underlined by the authors they are italicised and spaced out). English words and expressions used by Engels in texts written in German and French are printed in small caps. Longer passages written in English in the original are placed in asterisks.

The numbers of notes relating to the same facts and events in the texts of different letters, are repeated.

The texts of letters and notes were prepared for publication by Irina Shikanyan (April 1883 to November 1885), Yelena Kofanova (November 1885 to January 1886), and Natalia Sayenko (January to December 1886). The Preface was written by Irina Shikanyan. Editors of the volume are Valeria Kunina and Velta Pospelova. The name index and the index of periodicals are by Andrei Pozdnyakov with the assistance of Yelena Kofanova, and the index of quoted and mentioned literature is by Yelena Kofanova (Russian Independent Institute of Social and National Problems).

The translations were done by Peter and Betty Ross, and Rodney Livingstone (Lawrence & Wishart), K. M. Cook and Stephen Smith (Progress Publishing Group Corporation) and edited by K. M. Cook, Stephen Smith, Maria Shcheglova, Anna Vladimirova (Progress Publishing Group Corporation) and Vladimir Mosolov, scientific editor (RIISNP).

The volume was prepared for the press by Svetlana Gerasimenko (Progress Publishing Group Corporation).

KARL MARX
FREDERICK ENGELS
COLLECTED WORKS
VOLUME
47

1883

1

ENGELS TO PYOTR LAVROV [1]

IN PARIS

London, 2 April 1883

My dear Lavrov,

I hasten to acknowledge receipt of your letter enclosing a postal order for 124.50 frs. I shall not be able to cash it until Wednesday [a] at the earliest, as tomorrow I have to examine the manuscripts left by Marx. [2] On completion of the commission I shall announce the fact in the *Sozialdemokrat* of Zurich, and shall ask the editorial department to send you one or two copies of that particular number. It goes without saying that no mention will be made of Citizen Krantz's's [b] name. [3]

I have found the manuscript of the *Zirkulation des Kapitals* [c] and of the third book: *Die Gestaltungen des Gesammtprozesses* [d] — some 1,000 in-folio pages. [4] So far it's impossible for me to say whether the manuscript as it stands is in a fit condition to go to press. In any case I shall have to copy it out as it is in rough draft. Tomorrow I shall at last have time enough to devote several hours to going through all the manuscripts that Moor has left us, in particular an outline of dialectics which he had always intended to do. [5] But he always refrained from telling us how far his work had progressed, for he was aware that, once people realised something was ready, he would be pestered until he consented to its publication. All this is between you and me; I have no right to publish anything without Tussy who is my literary co-executrix.

---

[a] 4 April - [b] a pen-name for Pyotr Lavrov - [c] *Circulation of Capital* - [d] *The Process of Capitalist Production as a Whole*

We were all delighted and surprised to hear that our good, brave —
to the point of madness — Lopatin had so happily regained his
freedom.[6] Let us hope that, while retaining his bravery, he has left
his madness behind him in Russia. I hope to see him here one of these
days. Please give him my warm regards.

Yours ever,

F. Engels

First published in: Marx and Engels,
Works, First Russian Edition, Vol. XXVII,
Moscow, 1935

Printed according to the original

Translated from the French

Published in English in full for the
first time

2

ENGELS TO LAURA LAFARGUE

IN PARIS

London, 11 April 1883

My dear Laura,

I do indeed think, along with you, that Paul ought to go and see his
mother and I have told him so many a time and many a year ago. As
to the extra expense, that will not be much and I can soon find you
that, if informed in time. Only, if things are as you describe, it will require some considerable diplomacy on Paul's part, not to spoil his
own game — that Christian sister of charity ought not to be made an
enemy of [7] — she is *always* there and Paul *not*, and if only her suspicions are aroused, be sure she will never cease to beguile the old
woman into a will as much in her favour as the law will permit. So
that point I suppose is settled — you'll have to look after the execution.

We all of us have had a hearty laugh at your account of the Argenteuil adventures. [8] It is so like him [a] from beginning to end. To-day it

---

[a] Charles Longuet

is a week that Tussy sent him a very categorical letter: when is the boy [a] to come? Not a line in reply. *Il est toujours en train de réfléchir.* [b]

Paul is sure of six months at least. [9] He was awfully funky about it when here, and amused Liebknecht out of all measure with his *horror carceris.* [c] But if he does not now start in earnest to learn German, I shall consider him to be nothing but *un enfant gâté.* [d] Imagine he writes to me that he *will* learn it — '*comme vous le dites très bien* (!) *il pourra* (!) *devenir nécessaire que je le sache pour des traductions!*'. [e] As if the perfection of his own accomplishments, bright as they are, did not entirely depend on his reading certain German things, published and unpublished! He rejoices in the prospect of the 2nd volume [of] *Capital* being published, but will he ever be able to read it?

If M-me Gendre will translate the *Manifest* [f] into French and let me revise the translation (it's no child's play, you know) I will write her a preface sufficient to explain the historical circumstances, etc. [10] But as I know nothing much of the lady, I am bound to say at present: no revision, no preface. A *right* to stop any proceedings of hers in that direction I have not. This notabene is for Paul. So is this: What speech of Giffen he writes about I don't know, nor where it was published.

Pumps is still 'expectant', or was so at least last night. Percy's mother told him the other day that really he ought to be a little better informed in a case like that.

Jollymeyer is here for a few days. Since then (as some days before he left 10 days ago) we have every evening a bobby promenading before the house, when I let Carlo out about 12. The imbeciles evidently think we are manufacturing dynamite, when in reality we are discussing whisky.

Kind regards from him and myself to both of you.

Yours affectionately,
F. Engels

First published, in the language of the original (English), in: F. Engels, P. et L. Lafargue, *Correspondance*, t. I, Paris, 1956

Reproduced from the original

---

[a] Jean Longuet - [b] He is still thinking it over. - [c] fear of imprisonment - [d] a spoilt child - [e] 'As you say *very aptly* (!) it may (!) prove necessary for me to know it for translations!' - [f] K. Marx and F. Engels, *Manifesto of the Communist Party.*

3

ENGELS TO FERDINAND DOMELA NIEUWENHUIS [1]
IN THE HAGUE

London, 11 April 1883
122 Regent's Park Road, N. W.

Dear Comrade,

You must understand that, since the death of my old friend, I have been so taken up with correspondence, business matters, the perusal of his writings, etc., that I have been able to attend only to what was absolutely imperative. [2] Today I have at last found a minute or two in which to thank you for your letter of condolence [11] and for your excellent obituary in *Recht voor Allen*. [a] That obituary was undoubtedly one of the best we have seen, and was unanimously acclaimed as such among our circle of intimates here.

Many thanks, too, on behalf of his surviving daughters [b] and of myself, to the Dutch workers' party [12] for their participation, at least in spirit, in our friend's last rites. In this they were at one with our German, French, Spanish, Russian and American comrades.

Should fate or the urge to travel—in our case sadly curbed—bring me to Holland, I shall consider myself under an obligation to look you up, just as I would urge you to look me up should you come to England.

Marx has left a great wad of manuscript for the second part of *Capital*, the whole of which I must first read (and what handwriting!) before I can tell to what extent it is printable and to what extent it requires complementing from subsequent notebooks. [4] At all events, *the main substance is there*. Since I cannot as yet say anything more definite, however, I would ask you not to put anything in the papers about it just now, as this might lead to misunderstandings. Besides, Marx's youngest daughter Eleanor is my literary co-executrix, I can do nothing without her and the ladies, as you know, are sticklers for form.

---

[a] F. D. Nieuwenhuis, 'Karl Marx', *Recht voor Allen*, No. 4, 24 March 1883.-
[b] Laura Lafargue and Eleanor Marx

Excuse me *dat ik niet op hollandsch schrijf*[a]; in recent years I have had no practice in the use of your language.

Very sincerely yours,
F. Engels

I enclose my photograph and beg you to send me yours. As soon as we have got new ones of Marx I shall send you one.

First published, in Russian, in *Istorik-marksist*, No. 6, Moscow, 1934

Printed according to the original

Published in English in full for the first time

4

ENGELS TO EDUARD BERNSTEIN

IN ZURICH

London, 14 April 1883

Dear Mr Bernstein,

Dr Aveling, editor of *Progress*, wrote to *The Republican* with a view to purchasing the wood block of Marx's portrait which appeared in that paper. [13] Came the reply: THAT BLOCK HAS BEEN SENT TO GERMANY FOR THE *Sozialdemokrat*, SO IT IS IMPOSSIBLE FOR YOU TO HAVE IT. Aveling now enjoins me to write forthwith, asking if he could have the block as soon as possible. If not, then perhaps a cliché of it. There may also be some misunderstanding, the block having, perhaps, gone to the *Neue Welt*. Please let me know at once by postcard. [14]

The report of the Congress [15] most edifying. [16]

In great haste,

Yours,
F. E.

----

[a] for not writing in Dutch

The 2nd volume of *Capital* is there — but I can't tell you what a state it's in — 1,000 pages of ms. to go through. [17] However, don't put anything in the paper yet; as soon as I can say anything for sure, I'll let you have something authoritative.

First published, in Russian, in *Marx-Engels Archives*, Book I, Moscow, 1924

Printed according to the original

Published in English for the first time

5

ENGELS TO THOMAS JAMES KNOWLES [18]

IN LONDON

[Draft]

[London,] 17 April 1883

Dear Sir,

There exists a manuscript — a critical résumé of *Das Kapital* by me [a] — among the papers of the late Dr Marx, but up to to-day we have been unable to find it amongst the mass of papers left by him.

However, even if found, I should hesitate to send it to you at least for the purpose you indicate. [b] I am not aware that it is usual, in the literature of this or any other country, for one author to lend his manuscripts to another.

As to our experience of English review-writers it has not been very encouraging. With the exception of a few clergymen of the Church of England, they have invariably distorted our views and disfigured our actions. Their utter ignorance of our theory and practice has been equalled only by their presumption. The *XIX Century* I believe, in July 1878, published an article of George Howell on the International [c]

---

[a] F. Engels, *Synopsis of Volume One of 'Capital' by Karl Marx.* - [b] See this volume, p. 12. - [c] G. Howell, 'The History of the International Association', *The Nineteenth Century*, No. XVII, July 1878.

brimfull of untruths and inaccuracies. Marx sent you a reply[a] but you refused to insert it.

I am afraid, if you want to acquaint yourself with Marx's views you will have to read the German, Russian or French edition of *Das Kapital.*

I know but one living Englishman capable of giving a correct account of the contents of *Das Kapital.* It is a barrister in Manchester.[b] If you desire I shall be glad to ask him whether he is willing to undertake the task for you.

Yours faithfully

Jos. Knowles Esq.
the Hollies, Clapham Common
          S. W.

First published in: Marx and Engels, *Works*, First Russian Edition, Vol. XXVII, Moscow, 1935

Reproduced from the original

Published in English for the first time

6

ENGELS TO PHILIPP VAN PATTEN [19]

IN NEW YORK

[Draft]

London, 18 April 1883

Philipp Van Patten,
57 2nd Avenue, New York

Esteemed Comrade,

My statement in reply to your inquiry of the 2nd April as to Karl Marx's position with regard to the Anarchists in general and Johann Most in particular shall be short and clear.

---

[a] K. Marx, 'Mr George Howell's History of the International Working-Men's Association'. - [b] Samuel Moore

Marx and I, ever since 1845, have held the view that *one* of the final results of the future proletarian revolution will be the gradual dissolution and ultimate disappearance of that political organisation called *the State*; an organisation the main object of which has ever been to secure, by armed force, the economical subjection of the working majority to the wealthy minority. With the disappearance of a wealthy minority the necessity for an armed repressive State-force disappears also. At the same time we have always held, that in order to arrive at this and the other, far more important ends of the social revolution of the future, the proletarian class will first have to possess itself of the organised political force of the State and with its aid stamp out the resistance of the Capitalist class and re-organise society. This is stated already in the *Communist Manifesto* of 1847, end of Chapter II.[a]

The Anarchists reverse the matter. They say, that the Proletarian revolution has to *begin* by abolishing the political organisation of the State. But after the victory of the Proletariat, the only organisation the victorious working class finds ready-made for use, is that of the State. It may require adaptation to the new functions.[b] But to destroy that at such a moment, would be to destroy the only organism by means of which the victorious working class can exert its newly conquered power, keep down its capitalist enemies and carry out that economical revolution of society without which the whole victory must end in a defeat[c] and in a massacre of the working class like that after the Paris Commune.

Does it require my express assertion, that Marx opposed these anarchist absurdities from the very first day that they were started in their present form by Bakunin? The whole internal history of the International Working Men's Association is there to prove it. The Anarchists tried to obtain the lead of the International, by the foulest means, ever since 1867[20] and the chief obstacle in their way was Marx. The result of the five years' struggle was the expulsion, at the Hague Congress, September 1872, of the Anarchists from the International,[21] and the man who did most to procure that expulsion was Marx. Our old friend F. A. Sorge of Hoboken, who was present as a delegate, can give you further particulars if you desire.

---

[a] See present edition, Vol. 6, pp. 505-06. - [b] In *Der Sozialdemokrat* this sentence reads: 'This State may require very important changes before it can fulfil its new functions.' - [c] In *Der Sozialdemokrat*: 'another defeat'.

Now as to Johann Most. If any man asserts that Most, since he turned anarchist, has had any relations with, or support from Marx, he is either a dupe or a deliberate liar. After the first No. of the London *Freiheit* had been published,[a] Most did not call upon Marx and myself more than once, at most twice. Nor did we call on him or even meet him accidentally anywhere or at any time since his new-fangled anarchism had burst forth in that paper.[b] Indeed, we at last ceased to take it in as there was absolutely 'nothing in it'. We had for his anarchism and anarchist tactics the same contempt as for that of the people from whom he had learnt it.[c]

While still in Germany, Most published a 'popular' extract of *Das Kapital.*[d] Marx was requested to revise it for a second edition. I assisted Marx in that work. We found it impossible to eradicate more than the very worst mistakes, unless we re-wrote the whole thing from beginning to end, and Marx consented his corrections being inserted on the express condition only that his name was never in any way connected with even this revised form of Johann Most's production.[e]

You are perfectly at liberty to publish this letter in the *Voice of the People*,[f] if you like to do so.

Yours fraternally,

F. E.

First published, slightly abridged, in *Der Sozialdemokrat*, Nr. 21, 17 Mai 1883 and in full, in Russian, in *Marx-Engels Archives*, Vol. I (VI), Moscow, 1932

Reproduced from the original, checked with the newspaper

---

[a] on 4 January 1879 - [b] The words 'since his new-fangled anarchism had burst forth in that paper' are omitted in *Der Sozialdemokrat*. - [c] See letters of K. Marx to J. Ph. Becker of 1 July 1879 and to F. A. Sorge of 19 September 1879, and of F. Engels to J. Ph. Becker of 1 April 1880 (present edition, Vols. 45, 46). - [d] J. Most, *Kapital und Arbeit. Ein populärer Auszug aus 'Das Kapital' von Karl Marx*, Chemnitz [1873]. - [e] See this volume, p. 14. - [f] In *Der Sozialdemokrat*, the words 'in the *Voice of the People*' are omitted.

7

ENGELS TO THOMAS JAMES KNOWLES [22]

IN LONDON

[Draft]

[London,] 20 April 1883

Dear Sir,

If we do find the ms. in question I shall be glad and give you the refusal of it, on two self-understood conditions but which I may as well mention 1) that in case of refusal you do not communicate it to anybody else, and 2) that in case you print it, it appears as a separate article out of all connection with any other.

Yours faithfully,

F. E.

Allow me to say that I am no 'Dr' but a retired cotton-spinner. [23]

First published in: Marx and Engels, *Works*, First Russian Edition, Vol. XXVII, Moscow, 1935

Reproduced from the original

Published in English for the first time

8

ENGELS TO EDUARD BERNSTEIN [24]

IN ZURICH

[London,] 23 April 1883

Herewith also the proofs. [25] Your letter received; shall answer it this week with an article about Marx for the *Sozialdemokrat*. I still have all sorts of matters to deal with before I can finish it off properly. [26]

The little piece about the good Marx being led astray by the evil Engels has been performed countless times since 1844, alternating with the other little piece about Ormuzd-Engels being lured away from the path of virtue by Ahriman-Marx. Now, however, the eyes of the worthy Parisians will at last be opened.

Yours,
F. E.

First published, in Russian, in *Marx-Engels Archives*, Book I, Moscow, 1924

Printed according to the original

Published in English for the first time

9

ENGELS TO FRIEDRICH ADOLPH SORGE [27]

IN HOBOKEN

London, 24 April 1883

Dear Sorge,

Enclosed a line or two for Gartman from his friend Brocher, a muddle-headed anarchist but a sterling chap. Perhaps you would be good enough to send it on.

The *Volkszeitung* has perpetrated follies enough, though still not as many as I expected. Nevertheless they have all contributed their share, Schewitsch, Cuno, Douai, Hepner. Here was a quartet performed by would-be know-alls who, JOINTLY AND SEVERALLY, knew damned little. However I felt impelled to write a line to the editors, [a] pointing out that they had printed my telegram to you [b] as though it had been addressed to *them* and had, in my second to *them*, [c] inserted a false statement to the effect that Marx had died in Argenteuil. [d] We did not, I told them, stand for that sort of thing over here; as a result they had

---

[a] F. Engels, 'To the Editors of the *New Yorker Volkszeitung*' (18 April 1883). - [b] of 14 March 1883 - [c] F. Engels, 'To the *New Yorker Volkszeitung*' (16 March 1883). - [d] Marx died in London.

made it impossible for me to send them any further reports and, in the event of their again venturing to make such misuse of my name, I should be compelled to ask you to announce at once in public that the whole thing was a falsification on their part. Those gentlemen ought to confine their Yankee HUMBUG to themselves. Besides, the Americans are far more honest; according to the *Volkszeitung*, I was sent a telegram [28] which I never received and I was almost inclined to believe that the gentlemen on the *Volkszeitung* had pocketed the money for themselves. Now Van Patten writes to say that there hadn't been any money in the first place. I am now compelled to make this publicly known over here, for otherwise it would be said that I had withheld the telegram from the Paris press and the *Sozialdemokrat*. The answer re Most, which I sent Van Patten in response to his enquiry,[a] will doubtless have already been published by him by the time this arrives.

At the Copenhagen Congress [15] it was resolved that Liebknecht's and Bebel's trip to America should take place next spring. [29] It has to do with money for the election campaign in 1884-85. (All this is *between ourselves*.) Liebknecht has proposed to Tussy that she should accompany him as his secretary and she is very keen to go; so it might easily be that you see her there before long. Generally speaking we have not made any plans yet. The literary work (third edition, Volume I of *Capital*, editing of Volume II, the ms. of which has been found though as yet there is no knowing to what extent it is ready for printing or requires supplementing, [17] biography based on the enormous correspondence, [30] etc.) takes up all my spare time, besides which Tussy has a mass of literary ENGAGEMENTS to get through.

You are, of course, fully entitled to print the passages on Henry George in Marx's letters. [31] The question is, however, whether it might not be better to wait until I am able to sort out for you the marginal notes made by Marx in his copy of George's book and then do the whole lot at one go. Résumés of the kind Marx provides, theoretically acute but brief and unaccompanied by examples, are surely still above the head of your average American and after all there is no hurry. I shall take a closer look at the things as soon as I have time. If, in the meanwhile, you send me a copy of the relevant passage in Marx's letter, it will make the job simpler.[b]

---

[a] See this volume, pp. 9-11. - [b] Ibid., p. 42.

Pamphlet herewith. I have only received a few copies myself; the 2nd edition is in the press. [25] *Does Weydemeyer know English now?* [32] His earlier translations were grammatically and stylistically quite unprintable; they would have made us look appalling asses and at the same time exposed the author to ridicule. Anyhow I should like to see a specimen.

Your
F. E.

First published abridged in *Briefe und Auszüge aus Briefen von Joh. Phil. Becker, Jos. Dietzgen, Friedrich Engels, Karl Marx u. A. an F. A. Sorge und Andere*, Stuttgart, 1906 and in full in: Marx and Engels, *Works*, First Russian Edition, Vol. XXVII, Moscow, 1935

Printed according to the original

10

ENGELS TO EDUARD BERNSTEIN

IN ZURICH

London, 28 April 1883

Dear Bernstein,

(I think we should discard the boring 'Mr'.) The continuation of what follows will contain some correspondence, i. a. with Americans over Most.[a]

It is unforgivable that you are not returning via London,[33] I had quite counted on it. Well, perhaps you'll come in summer and we'll take a swim in the sea together. You can always be sure of a bed at my home.

Mayall, the leading London photographer always to work for Marx, has the principle: WE DO NOT TAKE MONEY FROM EMINENT PEOPLE. So we can't now press the man for copies (he is extremely muddled), except by a roundabout route. Hence we have given him an order,

---

[a] Ibid., pp. 9-11.

claiming it was for a German bookseller, for 1,000 *cartes de visite* ($£12 = M240 = 24d$. each) and 200 CABINET PORTRAITS ($^3/_4$ figure) à $£8 = M160 = 80d$. each. It is the last and best picture to depict Moor at his sprightly Olympian ease, confident of victory. I am offering them to you, and to Liebknecht and Sorge in New York after deducting those we need ourselves. How many do you want? You don't have to sell them all at once. They will be better in any case than any made there.

Yours,

F. E.

First published, in Russian, in *Marx-Engels Archives*, Book I, Moscow, 1924

Printed according to the original

Published in English for the first time

11

ENGELS TO AUGUST BEBEL

IN BORSDORF NEAR LEIPZIG [34]

London, 30 April 1883

Dear Bebel,

There is a very simple answer to your question as to whether I might remove to Germany or Switzerland or somewhere else on the Continent, namely that I shall not go to any country from which one can be expelled. But that is something one can only be safe from in England and America. I should at most go to the latter country on a visit, unless otherwise compelled. Hence I shall remain here.

Moreover England has another great advantage. Since the demise of the International there has been no labour movement whatsoever here, save as an appendage to the bourgeoisie, the radicals and for the pursuit of limited aims *within* the capitalist system. Thus, only here does one have the peace one needs if one is to go on with one's theoretical work. Everywhere else one would have had to take part in practical agitation and waste an enormous amount of time. As regards practical agitation, I should have achieved no more than anyone else; as regards theoretical work, I cannot yet see who could take the place of Marx and myself. What younger men have attempted in this line is worth little, indeed, for the most part less than nothing. Kautsky, the only one who applies himself to study, has to write for a living and for that reason if no other can achieve nothing. And now, in my sixty-third year, up to my eyes in my own work and with the prospect of a year's work on the second volume of *Capital* and another year's work on Marx's biography,[30] along with the history of the German socialist movement from 1843 to 1863 and of the International from 1864-72,[35] it would be madness for me to exchange my peaceful retreat here for some place where one would have to take part in meetings and newspaper battles, which alone would be enough to blur, as it necessarily must, the clarity of one's vision. To be sure, if things were as they were in 1848 and 1849, I would again take to the saddle if need arose. But now — strict division of labour. I must even withdraw as much as possible from the *Sozialdemokrat*. You have only to think of the enormous correspondence, formerly shared out between Marx and myself, which I have had to conduct on my own for over a year now. For after all, we wish to maintain intact, in so far as it is in my power, the many threads from all over the world which spontaneously converged upon Marx's study.

As regards a monument to Marx,[36] I do not know what ought to be done. The family is against it. The simple headstone made for his wife, which now also bears his and his little grandson's[a] names, would be desecrated in their eyes if replaced by a monument which, here in London, would be scarcely distinguishable from the pretentious philistine monuments surrounding it. A London cemetery of this kind looks quite different from a German one. The graves lie closely side by side, not room for a tree between them, and a monument is not allowed to exceed the length and breadth of the small plot that has been bought.

Liebknecht spoke of a complete edition of Marx's writings. All very well, but Dietz's plan for Volume II has made people forget that that Volume was long since promised to Meissner and that an edition of the other, shorter works would likewise have to be offered to Meissner first, and then could *only* appear *abroad*. After all, even *before* the Anti-Socialist Law[37] it was always said that not even the *Communist*

---

[a] Henri Longuet

Manifesto could be printed in Germany save in the document read out at your trial.[38]

The manuscript of Volume II was completed prior to 1873, probably even prior to 1870.[17] It is written in German script; after 1873 Marx never used anything but Latin characters.

It is too late for registration, so this letter must go off as it is; however, I shall seal it with my seal.

A letter this evening to Liebknecht in Berlin.[39]

Your

F. E.

First published in: A. Bebel, *Aus meinem Leben*, Th. III, Stuttgart, 1914

Printed according to the original

Published in English for the first time

12

ENGELS TO FRIEDRICH ADOLPH SORGE

IN HOBOKEN

London, 1 May 1883

Dear Sorge,

So as to obtain a good photograph of Marx, we have ordered from Mayall, the leading photographer here, who took the last ones of him,

1,000 *cartes de visite*   £12

i. e. approx. 3d. apiece;

200 CABINET SIZE, $^3/_4$ figure, *à* £8

i. e. approx. 9d. apiece

of the last nice one.

You can have some of these at cost price — I have also offered them to Liebknecht and Bernstein in Zurich.[a] If the above quantity does not

---

[a] See this volume, pp. 15-16.

suffice, no doubt we shall be able to get hold of more, but a quick decision is necessary.

Your

F. Engels

First published in: Marx and Engels, *Works*, First Russian Edition, Vol. XXVII, Moscow, 1935

Printed according to the original

Published in English for the first time

13

ENGELS TO WILHELM LIEBKNECHT

IN BORSDORF NEAR LEIPZIG [34]

London, 10 May 1883

Dear Liebknecht,

If you carry on in this way, causing me unnecessary expenditure of ink by the schemes you keep hatching and the ill-considered actions you perform off your own bat, our correspondence would assuredly cease.

All I asked you for originally was a *reply*, telling me what my legal position was in regard to Wigand. The 1845 contract envisages a 2nd edition and lays down the fee to be paid for it. [40] Question:

1. Am *I* still bound by this?

2. If *so*, and if Wigand refuses to print a 2nd edition on the conditions of payment agreed, does that release me *outright*?

I have *never* been able to get an answer from you to these simple questions and, since you promised to obtain one for me, I can only describe it as 'neglect on your part'.

Never have I instructed you either personally or via a third party to act on my behalf, and I cannot conceive why, at this moment, you took it into your head to set such a thing in motion off your own bat and without even reflecting. *I would expressly request* that you make no move whatever; I should at once write to Wigand and *disclaim everything*.

Meissner has written today; makes no mention at all of publication instalments.[a] The contract does not entitle us to interfere here. But if Dietz can show Meissner that it is to his own advantage, he may do it after all.

Lafargue's address:

66 Boulevard de Port-Royal, Paris (close to Ste-Pélagie, handy for a chap going to quod).[9]

Photographs will be delivered in batches and sent to Dietz as soon as possible.[b]

First published, in Russian, in *Marx-Engels Archives*, Vol. I (VI), Moscow, 1932

Printed according to the original

Published in English for the first time

14

ENGELS TO AUGUST BEBEL[41]

IN BORSDORF NEAR LEIPZIG[34]

London, 10-11 May 1883

Dear Bebel,

That you would sooner *not* sit in the Reichstag, I am ready to believe. But you can see what your absence has made possible. Some years ago Bracke wrote to me saying: Bebel is, in fact, the only one of us possessed of real parliamentary tact.[42] And I have found this constantly confirmed. So there's probably no alternative but for you to return to your post at the first opportunity and I should be delighted were you to be elected in Hamburg so that necessity relieved you of your doubts.[43]

Certainly, agitational and parliamentary work becomes very bor-

---

[a] This refers probably to the third German edition of Volume I of *Capital*. - [b] See this volume, pp. 15-16.

ing after a time. It is much the same thing as advertising, puffing one's wares and travelling around are in business: success is slow in coming, and some never achieve it. But there's no other alternative, and once you are in it you've got to see the thing through to the end, if all your trouble is not to have been for nothing. And the Anti-Socialist Law [37] means that this, the only course to have remained open, simply cannot be dispensed with.

Despite the way it was written, the report on the Copenhagen Congress [15] enabled me to read sufficiently between the lines to amend Liebknecht's, as always rosy, version of things.[a] At all events I perceived that the half-and-halfs [44] had suffered a severe defeat and this, I admit, led me to believe that they would now draw in their horns. Yet such does not seem to be the case, or not to that degree. We have never been under any illusions about these men. Neither Hasenclever nor, for that matter, Hasselmann, should ever have been admitted, but Liebknecht's undue haste over unification — against which, at the time, we protested for all we were worth — has landed us with a jackass and also, for a while, with a rascal.[45] In his day, Blos was a lively, courageous chap but after his marriage, etc., the stuffing was soon knocked out of him by the difficulty of making both ends meet. Geiser always was an indolent, self-opinionated fellow and Kayser a big-mouthed *commis-voyageur*.[b] Even in 1848 Rittinghausen was a nonentity; he's only a socialist *pro forma*, in order to enlist our help in achieving his direct government by the people. But we have better things to do.

What you say about Liebknecht is something you have doubtless long been thinking.[46] We have known him for many years. Popularity is the very stuff of life to him. Hence he has *got to* conciliate and conceal in order to postpone the crisis. Besides, he's an optimist by nature and sees everything through rose-tinted spectacles. That's what keeps him so lively and is the main reason for his popularity, but it also has its disadvantages. So long as I corresponded only with him, not only did he report everything in accordance with his own rosy views, but also withheld everything that was unpleasant and, upon being questioned, replied in such an airy and off-hand way that, more than by anything else, one was unfailingly needled by the thought 'Can the man suppose us so stupid as to be taken in by it?'

---

[a] Cf. this volume, pp. 7 and 32.-[b] commercial traveller

Add to that his incessant busyness, an undoubted asset in day-to-day agitation but involving us over here in a mass of useless letter-writing; a perpetual stream of projects whose only outcome was to burden *other people* with extra work—in short, as you will understand, all this made a really businesslike and down-to-earth correspondence of the kind I have conducted for years with you as well as with Bernstein a sheer impossibility. Hence the constant bickering and the honorary title he once jokingly conferred upon me here of being the rudest man in Europe. My letters to him were, it is true, often rude, but the rudeness was conditioned by the contents of his own. No one knew that better than Marx.

Again, for all his valuable qualities, Liebknecht is a born schoolmaster. If a working man in the Reichstag happens to say me instead of I, or pronounce a short Latin vowel as a long one, and the bourgeois laugh, he's in despair. Hence he has to have 'eddicated' men, like that weakling Viereck who, with a *single* speech, would make us look more foolish in the Reichstag than would two thousand wrong 'mes'. And then, he can't wait. A momentary success, even if it means the sacrifice of a subsequent, far greater one, takes precedence over everything else. You people will discover that in America, when you go there in the *wake* of Fritzsche and Viereck.[47] Their mission was a blunder as great as the over-hasty unification with the Lassalleans who, six months later, would have come to you of their own accord—but as a disorganised gang without their bankrupt leaders.

As you see, I speak to you quite frankly—in confidence. But I also believe that you would do well firmly to resist Liebknecht's persuasive blandishments. Then he's bound to yield. If really confronted by a decision, he will certainly adopt the right course. But he would rather do so tomorrow than today, and in a year's time rather than tomorrow.

If a few deputies were in fact to vote for Bismarck's Bills,[48] thus planting a kiss on his backside in return for having theirs kicked, and if the parliamentary group[49] failed to expel these people, I too would, of course, be capable of publicly disassociating myself from a party prepared to tolerate such a thing. To the best of my knowledge, however, that would be impossible, having regard to existing party discipline whereby the minority has *got to* vote with the majority. But you are better informed than I.

Any split that took place while the Anti-Socialist Law is in operation I should look upon as a misfortune, since all means of communicating with the masses have been cut off. But it may be forced on us and then we shall have to look facts in the face. So if anything of the sort should happen — no matter where you are — I should be glad if you could inform me and do so at once, for my German papers always arrive very belatedly.

Blos, when he went to Bremen after being expelled from Hamburg, did indeed write me a very plaintive letter [50] to which I sent a very firm reply. [39] Now, my papers have for years been in the most shocking muddle, and finding this particular one would be a day's work. But some time I shall have to put them in order and, if needs be, shall send you the letter in the *original*.

Your view of the business conditions is being corroborated in England, France and America. [51] It is an intermediate crisis like that of 1841-42, but on a much vaster scale. Generally speaking, it is only since 1847 (because of Californian and Australian gold production which resulted in the world market becoming fully established) that the ten-year cycle has clearly emerged. Now, when America, France and Germany are beginning to break England's monopoly of the world market and when, therefore, overproduction is beginning, as it did before 1847, to assert itself more rapidly, the quinquennial intermediate crises are also recurring. Proof of this is the complete exhaustion of the capitalist mode of production. The period of prosperity no longer reaches its full term; overproduction recurs after only 5 years and, even during those 5 years, things in general go downhill. Which, however, is very far from proving that, between 1884 and 1887, we shan't have a period of pretty brisk trade, as happened between 1844 and 1847. But then the great crash will quite surely come.

11 May. I had wanted to write and tell you more about the general state of trade, but meanwhile it is time for the registered mail. Till next time, then.

Your
F. E.

First published abridged in: A. Bebel, *Aus meinem Leben*, Th. III, Stuttgart, 1914 and in full, in Russian, in *Marx-Engels Archives*, Vol. I (VI), Moscow, 1932

Printed according to the original

Published in English in full for the first time

15

ENGELS TO ACHILLE LORIA [52]

IN MANTUA

London, 20 May 1883
122 Regent's Park Road, N. W.

Dear Sir,

I have received your pamphlet on Karl Marx. You are entitled to subject his doctrines to the most stringent criticism, indeed to misunderstand them; you are entitled to write a biography of Marx which is pure fiction. But what you are not entitled to do, and what I shall never permit anyone to do, is slander the character of my departed friend.

Already in a previous work[a] you took the liberty of accusing Marx of quoting in bad faith. When Marx read this he checked his and your quotations against the originals and he told me that his were all correct and that if there was any *bad faith* it was on your part. And seeing how you quote Marx, how you have the audacity to make Marx speak of profit when he speaks of *Mehrwerth*,[b] when he defends himself time and again against the error of identifying the two (something which Mr Moore and I have repeated to you verbally here in London) I know whom to believe and where the bad faith lies.

This however is a trifle compared to your 'deep and firm conviction... that *conscious sophistry* pervades them all' (Marx's doctrines); that Marx 'did not baulk at paralogisms, while *knowing them to be such*', that 'he was often a sophist who wished to arrive, *at the expense of the truth*, at a negation of present-day society' and that, as Lamartine says, '*il jouait avec les mensonges et les vérités comme les enfants avec les osselets*'.[c][53]

In Italy, a country of ancient civilisation, this might perhaps be taken as a compliment, or it might be considered great praise among armchair socialists,[54] seeing that these venerable professors could never produce their innumerable systems except 'at the expense of the truth'. We revolutionary communists see things differently. We re-

---

[a] A. Loria, *La teoria del valore negli economisti italiani*. - [b] surplus value - [c] 'he played with lies and truth like children with marbles'

gard such assertions as defamatory accusations and, knowing them to be lies, we turn them against their inventor who has defamed himself in thinking them up.

In my opinion, it should have been your duty to make known to the public this famous '*conscious sophistry*' which pervades all of Marx's doctrines. But I look for it in vain! *N a g o t t!*[a]

What a tiny mind one must have to imagine that a man like Marx could have 'always threatened his critics' with a second volume which he 'had not the slightest intention of writing', and that this second volume was nothing but 'an ingenious pretext dreamed up by Marx in place of scientific arguments'. This second volume *exists* and it will shortly be published. Perhaps you will then learn to understand the difference between *Mehrwerth* and profit.

A German translation of this letter will be published in the next issue of the Zurich *Sozialdemokrat*.

I have the honour of saluting you with all the sentiments you deserve.

F. E.

First published in *Der Sozialdemokrat*, Nr. 21, 17. Mai 1883

Printed according to the original, checked with the newspaper

Translated from the Italian

Published in English for the first time

16

ENGELS TO JOHANN PHILIPP BECKER [55]

IN GENEVA

London, 22 May 1883

Dear Old Man,

How can you suppose that *I* might somehow be able to find paid literary work for a young party member[b]? After all, it is years since

---

[a] The following words were added in the newspaper: (Lombardic swear-word for: nothing at all).- [b] Ludwig Klopfer; see next letter.

I had any sort of contact with German publishers apart from Meissner (on account of *Capital*), let alone with newspapers and periodicals. So what could I do? Even if the man could translate the other way round, from German into French or English, I should be unable to help him find work. You would certainly do better to approach Liebknecht who after all has the *Neue Zeit* and connections in plenty.

We shall be saddled with Marx's house until next March, so there is no need to be over-hasty about the removal or plans for the future. Moreover a tremendous amount of work is involved in getting these papers in order. What surprises me is that Marx has actually saved papers, letters and manuscripts from the period prior to 1848, splendid material for the biography which I shall of course be writing and which, inter alia, will also be the history of the *Neue Rheinische Zeitung* and of the movement of 1848-49 on the Lower Rhine, as well as the history of the rascally emigration in London between 1849 and 1852 and of the International.[30] The first task is the editing of Volume II of *Capital*[4] and that is no joke. There are in existence 4 or 5 revisions of Book II, of which only the first is complete, the others having been merely started on[17]; some labour when you're dealing with a man like Marx, who weighed every word. But to me it is a labour of love; after all I shall be back again with my old comrade.

For the past few days I have been sorting letters from 1842-62. As I watched the old times pass before my eyes they really came to life again, as did all the fun we used to have at our adversaries' expense. Many of our early doings made me weep with laughter; they didn't, after all, ever succeed in banishing our sense of humour. But there were also many very serious moments in between whiles.

This is in confidence; mind you, don't let a word of it get into the papers. Such information as is ripe for imparting will be published by me from time to time in the *Sozialdemokrat*. Bernstein is getting on very well, he is eager to learn, is witty and has an open mind, can put up with criticism and is quite free of all petty-bourgeois moralisings. But our lads in Germany have also been truly magnificent, ever since the time that the Anti-Socialist Law[37] liberated them from the 'eddicated' gentlemen who, in their ignorant academic muddle-headedness, had attempted prior to 1878 to instruct the workers from on high, an attempt that was, alas, condoned by all too many of the 'leaders'. This worthless lumber has not yet been entirely cleared away, but the movement has again taken a decidedly revolutionary turn. That is precisely what is so splendid about our lads, the fact that the masses are far better than almost any of the leaders; and now that the Anti-Socialist Law is compelling the masses to take care of the movement *themselves*, now that the influence of the leaders is reduced to a minimum, the movement is better than ever.

Your old friend
F. Engels

First published in: F. Engels, *Vergessene Briefe (Briefe Friedrich Engels' an Johann Philipp Becker)*, Berlin, 1920

Printed according to the original

Published in English in full for the first time

17

ENGELS TO LUDWIG KLOPFER

IN GENEVA

London, 22 May 1883

Dear Mr Klopfer,

I should be only too glad to help you if I possibly could. However I have *absolutely no* publishing or literary connections in Germany and should not know whom to approach.[a] The party, however, still has various periodicals, etc., in Germany, e. g. Liebknecht's and Kautsky's *Neue Zeit* in Stuttgart (Dietz Verlag); you should get Becker to give you letters for them. If anything can be done for you, it is over there; we here are as cut off from everything as you are in Geneva.

Your letter of the 9th bears the Geneva postmark of the 13th. I hope that this will at least partly explain my delay in replying.

---

[a] See previous letter.

Trusting that the adoption of the above course will enable you to achieve your object, I remain,

Yours truly,

F. Engels

First published in: Marx and Engels, *Works*, Second Russian Edition, Vol. 39, Moscow, 1966

Printed according to the original

Published in English for the first time

18

ENGELS TO LAURA LAFARGUE

IN PARIS

London, 22 May 1883

My dear Laura,

I had not, as Paul suggests, forgotten his five pd. note, but having Sam Moore here, could not get a free moment when to get it ready and register the letter. Yesterday evening Sam returned to Manchester and the note would have left here to-day, but for Paul's letter which alters his directions to me. The cheque is enclosed, £ 10.-

So *ce cher* Paul is while I write this, a prisoner. [9] He has just (5.45) been debarred from receiving visitors and can now in all rest and peace discuss with Guesde the chances of *la révolution révolutionnaire*. We drank his health last Sunday[a] in a bowl of splendid *Maitrank*[b] and wished him any amount of pluck and patience.

Well, for a long time I thought you might profit of Paul's involuntary seclusion, to come over to London, and would have at once placed the whole of 122 Regent's Park Road at your disposal, but from all I learnt I was afraid I might hurt someone's feelings by such a proposal. Even Nim when she returned, never mentioned a word about it, that you had spoken of showing your bright face in this dull climate; and when Paul wrote he expected you to lunch with him

---

[a] 20 May - [b] Wine flavoured with sweet woodruff, May wine.

every morning in St-Pélagie I lost heart altogether. Now however it is all right, and I hope to hear soon from you that you accept my invitation, to make this place your headquarters for a couple of months at least, which of course will not exclude trips to the sea-side, etc. If Paul has to be under lock and key, so much the more reason for you to look after your own health.

While Sam was here, we found out, through him, the very unpleasant fact that Mohr never had, nor have we, the right to stop unauthorised translation of the *Kapital*. The right was lost as soon as the first year elapsed without a *commencement* of translation being published. So as there are several fellows in the field,[56] we have to dodge and to use the unpublished 2nd volume as a means to bring them round.

The 2nd volume will give me an awful deal of work — at least the II book.[4] There is one *complete* text, of about 1868, but a mere *brouillon*.[a] Then there are at least three, if not four, *Ueberarbeitungen*[b] belonging to various later periods, but none of them completed. That will be a job to select from them a definitive text! The 3rd book is complete since 1869-70 and has never been touched since. But here, where the rent of land is treated, I shall have to compare his Russian extracts[57] for notes, facts and instances. Maybe I shall be able to concoct even a bit of a 3rd volume from the ms. of 1858-62[58] (the beginning of which appeared in Berlin [in] 1859[c]) and which at the end of every chapter contains the critical history of the theoretical points discussed in it.

Lately I have been occupied with sorting the correspondence. There is a large box full of most important letters [from] 1841 (nay 1837 from your grandfather Marx[d]) to 1862. It is nearly sorted, but it will take me some hours more to complete it. I can assure you it is great fun to me to stumble over these old things most of which concern me as much as they did Mohr and there is such a deal to laugh over. Nim helps me — awful lot of dusting required! and we have many a good laugh over old times. The correspondence since 1862 he has sorted, in a passable way, himself. But before we fathom all the mysteries of that garret full of boxes, packets, parcels, books, etc., some time must elapse. And I have to prepare for the 3rd edition sundry additions from the French translation[59] which I know Mohr intended inserting; and that must be done in 3-4 weeks.

---

[a] draft - [b] revised versions - [c] K. Marx, *A Contribution to the Critique of Political Economy. Part One.* - [d] Heinrich Marx

But now it's post-time and so good-bye for to-day.

Yours affectionately,

F. Engels

First published, in the language of the original (English), in: F. Engels, P. et L. Lafargue, *Correspondance*, t. I, Paris, 1956

Reproduced from the original

19

ENGELS TO LAURA LAFARGUE

IN PARIS

London, 2 June 1883

My dear Laura,

Herewith cheque £ 10.- for Paul as desired. To judge from his letter, he seems to be pretty cheerful for his condition, but of course the *grincement des clefs et des verroux*[a] must be something awful. [9] What is comparative liberty by day when one is reduced to solitary confinement by night, and how is he to sing:

Singet nicht in Trauertönen
Von der Einsamkeit der Nacht,
Denn sie ist, o holde Schönen,
Zur Geselligkeit gemacht. [b]

As Paul is going to work up his German in prison, you might give him that to translate.

Now, by this time the two heroic martyrs[c] ought to be pretty well

---

[a] clinking of keys and bolts
[b] Sing no more in strains of sadness
Of the loveliness of night!
Darksome hours were made for gladness,
Social joy, and love's delight.
Goethe, *Wilhelm Meister's Apprenticeship*, translated by R. Dillon Boylan, London, Henry Bohn, 1861.
[c] Paul Lafargue and Jules Guesde

settled down and don't you think you might come over, say by Thursday or Friday next[a]? The fact is I expect Jollymeier to-night who will be able to stay here till Monday week, 11th June, and he would so like to see you. Moreover, Tussy talks very much about your coming and seems very anxious to have you here and to consult you about the disposal of the things in the house, etc., etc., the sole responsibility seems to weigh very much upon her. So that your journey would be to some extent *on business*. If you will come and if you write at once, I shall send you the funds by return, I should have added them to the cheque to-day, only my balance is low and I have money to come in next week.

Among Mohr's papers I have found a whole lot of mss, our common work, of before 1848.[60] Some of these I shall soon publish.

There is one I shall read to you when you are here, you will crack your sides with laughing. I read it to Nim and Tussy, Nim said: *jetzt weiss ich auch, warum Sie Zwei damals in Brüssel des Nachts so gelacht haben, dass kein Mensch im Hause davor schlafen konnte.*[b] We were bold devils then, Heine's poetry is childlike innocence compared with our prose.

There is a chance of a translation of the *Kapital* being published by Kegan Paul and Co., they would be the best men.[56] Tussy is going to see them on Monday[c]; if anything practicable comes of it, we shall then go together afterwards. S. Moore will translate, and I shall revise. There are other people at it, but if we can arrange the thing, they will soon be out of the field. S. Moore was here in Whitweek, and we settled the matter with him, as far as he is concerned. He is by far the best man, slightly heavy, but that can be mended. He has been of immense use to us as our legal adviser. Indeed I have still to write to him by first mail upon a legal question.

Pumps is going on very well and her two babies too, the boy is awfully big and fat, very near the size of his sister! at least so says the proud Mamma. If you are here next Sunday (to-morrow) week, we shall have a grand bowl of *Maitrank*,[d] it is just in its prime now, I mean the Waldmeister, we have had two bowls here on Sundays and two at Tussy's in the week, and plenty of Moselle left!

If you say you will come, the same day I shall write to Dublin for a case of the best and of the *super* best Claret which we will finish quietly betwixt us.

---

[a] 7 or 8 June - [b] Now I know why you two laughed at night in Brussels at that time so that no one could sleep in the building. - [c] 4 June - [d] Wine flavoured with sweet woodruff, May wine.

A few lines to Paul in a day or two. In the meantime affectionally yours,

F. Engels

First published, in the language of the original (English), in: F. Engels, P. et L. Lafargue, *Correspondance*, t. I, Paris, 1956

Reproduced from the original

20

ENGELS TO EDUARD BERNSTEIN [61]

IN ZURICH

London, 12-13 June 1883

Dear Bernstein,

It is half past eleven at night and having just read the proof of the second sheet of the third edition of *Capital*[a] (no small task), and sent it off, I shall try and utilise what is left of the evening at least to begin a letter to you.

As regards internal matters, I had more or less read between the lines of the official report[b] and, soon after, also received a short exposé from Bebel. Some while previously I had written and told Bebel that there must ultimately be a break with the ninnies of the right wing,[c] but that in my view it was not in our interests to force it before we were again in a position to consort directly with the masses; i. e. not so long as the Anti-Socialist Law remained operative.[37] Should they *force* our hand, then we should see to it that it was *they*, not us, who rebelled against party discipline, in which case the game would already be ours. And they should be brought to do this if they refused to keep quiet. So far as Liebknecht is concerned, he will do everything in his

---

[a] the third German edition of Volume I of *Capital*.- [b] *Protokoll über den Kongreß der deutschen Sozialdemokratie in Kopenhagen*. See also this volume, p. 21.- [c] See Engels' letter to August Bebel of 21 June 1882 (present edition, Vol. 46).

power to put off the crisis, but when it does come and he realises that it can no longer be postponed, he will be in the right place.

Let me briefly sum up what I have to do:

1) Put the papers in order [2]; here almost everything has to be done by myself since no one except me knows about the old stuff, and there's an enormous pile of it in a fine state of disarray. Much is still missing and a lot of packages and boxes haven't even been opened yet.

2) See to the third edition, with sundry alterations and a few addenda from the French edition. [59] On top of that, read the proofs.

3) Take advantage of an opportunity that has presented itself to bring out an English translation — in connection with which I today called on one of the big publishers here [a] — and then revise the translation myself [56] (Moore, who will be doing it, is first-rate, a friend of ours for twenty-six years, but slow).

4) Collate the 3 or 4 versions of the beginning of Volume II and prepare them for the press, besides *making a fair copy* of the whole of the second volume. [17]

5) Spend a week every now and again tippling with Schorlemmer who returned to Manchester yesterday — he always brings some work with him, but *o, jerum!*[b]

Voilà la vie![c]

The jackass in the *Vossische* (I've been sent the thing [d] *four times*) would certainly seem to have disseminated a lot of despondency in good old Germany respecting the despondent Marx. I might, some time when in really jolly mood, take a kick at him. Were these oafs to get the chance of reading the correspondence between Moor and myself, they'd be speechless with rage. Heine's poetry is trifling by comparison with our impudent, mocking prose. Moor was capable of becoming furiously angry, but down-in-the-mouth — *jamais!*[e] I was convulsed when I reread the old stuff. This correspondence is, by the way, also historically memorable and, in so far as it is in my power, it will end up in the right hands. Unfortunately I only have the letters Marx wrote after 1849, but those are complete.

---

[a] Kegan Paul - [b] *O, jerum, jerum, jerum! O, quae mutatio rerum!* (Oh, dear me, dear me, dear me. A crazy world. Lord, hear me!) — part of the refrain from a student song attributed to Eugen Höfling. - [c] That's life! - [d] 'Zur Beurteilung von Karl Marx', *Königlich privilegirte Berlinische Zeitung von Staats- und gelehrten Sachen*, No. 235, 1st supplement, 24 May 1883. - [e] never!

Herewith part of the original draft from the last part of the *Communist Manifesto* which you want to keep as a memento. The first two lines were dictated, and were taken down by Mrs Marx.[62]

I would have sent you the enclosed poem by Weerth in time for the feuilleton, had you not so contrived matters that your letter arrived twelve hours too late — as it was, I had to wait and see whether you printed the feuilleton *tel quel*.[a] Anyhow, you can put it in somewhere else.[63] If only by contrast with the solemn Freiligrath, all of Weerth's stuff is ironical and humorous. Never any question of 'sherioushness' here.

As regards the repeal of the Anti-Socialist Law, the chaps in Germany can never see beyond their own noses. By disappointing Russia (and things are far more acute there) with his proclamation in Moscow just as Frederick William IV disappointed the Prussians in 1841,[64] Alexander III has done more towards that end than all your Geisers, Bloses and Co. could ever do with their lamentations. If, one fine morning, he is riddled with bullets — as he surely will be — Bismarck's *internal* régime won't be worth a brass farthing. Then they'll change their tune. Even if old William[b] merely (I don't mean Wilhelm Blos[c]) kicks the bucket, there will of necessity be changes. The men of today have never experienced, nor can they possibly imagine, what a crown prince,[d] grown up in what has in the meantime become a revolutionary situation, is capable of. And a fool, what's more, as vacillating and weak-willed as 'our Fritz'. Nor, for that matter, can the possibility be excluded that the crazy French government may fall foul of all the world in such a way as to incite violent action in Paris. Tunis, Egypt, Madagascar, Tonkin[65] — and now they are actually seeking to contest England's possession of a few rocky islands, with barely 50 inhabitants, off the coast of Normandy. I only hope that nothing happens in Paris, for the stupidity that prevails among the masses there is exceeded only here, in London.

And on top of that the ingenuous Bismarck works for us like the very devil. His latest theory — that the imperial constitution is nothing but a contract made by governments for which they can substitute another one any old day, without consulting the Reichstag — is a real godsend to us. Just let him try. Add to which the manifest intention to bring about a conflict, his stupid, impertinent Bödikers & Co. in the Reichstag — all this is grist to our mill. True, this

---

[a] as it stood - [b] William I - [c] In Engels' text the parenthesis was a footnote. In German 'merely' = *bloss*. - [d] Frederick William

means the end of the catch-phrase about 'one reactionary mass', [66] a phrase generally appropriate only for declamation (or, again, for a *truly* revolutionary situation). For it is precisely in this that the quirk of history — one operating in our favour — consists, namely that the *different* elements of that feudal and bourgeois mass erode, fight with and devour one another, to *our* advantage and are, therefore, the very opposite of that uniform mass which your *lout* imagines he can dismiss by dubbing the whole lot 'reactionary'. On the contrary. All these diverse scoundrels must first mutually destroy, utterly ruin and discredit each other, and pave the way for us by proving their ineptitude, each lot in turn. It was one of Lassalle's greatest mistakes, when engaged in agitation, wholly to lose sight of what little dialectics he had learned from Hegel. Thus, just like Liebknecht, he never saw more than one side and, since the former, for certain reasons, happened to see the right side, he ultimately proved superior to the great Lassalle after all.

The one regrettable thing about the present German bourgeois movement is precisely that the chaps constitute no more than 'one reactionary mass', and this has got to stop. We can make no progress until at least part of the bourgeoisie has been forced over onto the side of a *genuine* movement, whether by internal or external events. That is why we have now had enough of Bismarck's régime *in its present form*, why he can only benefit us by provoking a conflict or resigning and also why the time will come for the Anti-Socialist Law to be done away with by semi-revolutionary or wholly revolutionary means. All those arguments as to whether the 'Lesser' [67] alone should go, or the Law as a whole, or whether the ordinary penal law should be tightened up, seem to me like arguments about the virginity of Mary *in partu* and *post partum*.[a] What is crucial is the wider political situation both at home *and abroad*; and this changes, does not remain as it is today. In Germany, by contrast, the case is discussed solely on the assumption that present conditions in Germany will persist *eternally*. And running parallel with this is an idea, related to that of one reactionary mass, namely that, with the subversion of the present state of affairs, we shall come to the helm. That is nonsense. A revolution is a lengthy process, cf. 1642-46 and 1789-93[68]; and in order that circumstances should be ready for us and we for them, all the intermediate parties must come to power in turn and destroy themselves. And

---

[a] during and after parturition

then we shall come — and may, perhaps, once more be momentarily routed. Not that I think this very probable in the normal course of events.

I have today despatched to 'Volksbuchhandlung, Hottingen-Zurich',[a] freight forward per CONTINENTAL PARCELS EXPRESS (correspondent of the German and Swiss parcel post), a parcel containing the photographs ordered,[b] invoice enclosed. Of the money you should retain the £17/- credited to my account over there, against 4 frs for snifters transmitted by proxy, subscriptions, etc. (If, when remitting the balance, it would be more convenient to include a little more or a little less, that would, of course, be ALL RIGHT.) Over here 500 cartes [c] and 280 CABINETS are still available — first come, first served. Not that you have any competitors as yet, save for Dietz. Just how much is pushed on to me you will realise when I tell you that I have today had to attend, single-handed, to all the details of checking and repacking the photographs for you and Dietz, and have likewise had to take them to the office (2 $\frac{1}{2}$ English miles from here). And then I'm expected to work!

Borde is a jackass whom we have known for years; at Marx's house there are a hundred or more of the notebooks he sent him, lying about unopened. Envoyez-le au diable.[d]

I shall not come to Switzerland until the continental routes are safer. After all, there was no certainty of Marx's being able to travel to, or through, France unscathed this summer. Once one has been expelled, that is that, unless one is prepared to take steps such as I should find impossible. Don't I know it!

You do not, by the way, bore me in the least with internal matters. Anyone who's abroad can never hear enough about the details of this sort of internal struggle in a workers' party which, despite everything, is the leading one in Europe. And that kind of thing is withheld from me on principle by friend Liebknecht, all of whose reports are rosy red, dawn pink, sky-blue and green as the tender leaves of hope.

For the anniversary of the June battle of 1848, I am sending you a Neue Rheinische Zeitung article by Marx,[e] who was the only man in

---

[a] a Social Democratic publishing house- [b] See this volume, pp. 15-16. - [c] Cartes de visite; small photographic portraits mounted on a card. - [d] Consign him to the devil.-
[e] 'The June Revolution'

the whole of the European press to back up the insurgents after they had fallen.

Kindest regards,

Yours,

F. E.

13 June 1883

Do you think the time is ripe for the *Sozialdemokrat*'s feuilleton to print an *excessively* impudent piece Marx and I wrote in 1847,[69] in which the 'true socialists', who are now also members of the Reichstag, are pulled to pieces? The most impudent thing ever to have been written in the German language.

First published, in Russian, in *Marx-Engels Archives*, Book I, Moscow, 1924

Printed according to the original

Published in English in full for the first time

21

ENGELS TO PASQUALE MARTIGNETTI

IN BENEVENTO

London, 19 June 1883
122 Regent's Park Road, N. W.

Dear Sir,

I was very pleased to receive your fine Italian translation of my *Socialism: Utopian and Scientific*.[70] I have been through it and I have suggested minor alterations in a number of places, although I am diffident and aware that my Italian is imperfect and that I am out of practice. I hope that despite this you can understand the translation (into Italian or French) of the additions to the first German edition which I have inserted at the corresponding points in your manuscript.

I am enclosing a copy of the recently published German edition, and a copy of the 2nd edition, which is going to press at the moment, will follow.[25] I am sorry that the translation could not have been made from the German text, since Italian is much better suited than French to the dialectical mode of presentation.

Thank you for your kind offer to send me several copies of the translation; six, or at most a dozen, will be enough.

Yours respectfully,

Fred. Engels

I am sending by the midday post a *registered* parcel containing
1) your manuscript,
2) the copy of the German edition.

First published in *La corrispondenza di Marx e Engels con italiani. 1848-1895*, Milano, 1964

Printed according to the original

Translated from the Italian

Published in English for the first time

22

ENGELS TO EDUARD BERNSTEIN

IN ZURICH

London, 22 June 1883

Dear Bernstein,

When you go to Paris, you must certainly cross the water and spend a day or two here. The trip both ways will cost you less than the amount you would fritter away in Paris in that time. A room has already been prepared for you here. I can then also show you the impudent ms. I mentioned, as well as the other mss.[69] Madame Lafargue will advise you about the best way to make the journey.

Yours,

F. E.

Regards to Liebknecht.

First published, in Russian, in *Marx-Engels Archives*, Book I, Moscow, 1924

Printed according to the original

Published in English for the first time

23

ENGELS TO LAURA LAFARGUE

IN PARIS

London, 24 June 1883

My dear Laura,

When you spoke of your knowledge of what poor Moor's views and wishes had been at Vevey,[71] it was in connection with dispositions of a more or less testamentary nature, and I therefore naturally concluded that you alluded to similar subjects. And as those might comprise wishes as to what should be done with some mementos of your Mama, etc., books and so forth, and as here we are bound to come to some conclusion or other, and Tussy moreover seems to shun responsibility of acting on her own hook, I thought it my clear duty to inform you, so that, in case you had anything to communicate, it could be done in time.

After poor Mohr's death, on my inquiry, Tussy informed me that he had told her, she and I were to take possession of all his papers, and procure the publication of what was to be published, especially the 2nd volume[a] and the mathematical works.[72] The 3rd German edition[b] is in hand, I am looking after that too. If you wish to have Mohr's exact words, Tussy will no doubt give them to you if you ask her to do so.

This matter was talked about here when Paul was here, and I am almost certain he is aware of it.

As to the expression, literary executors, I am alone responsible for it. I could not find another at the time, and if by it I have in any way offended you, I humbly ask your pardon.[73]

How the disposition itself can wound you, I cannot see. The work must be done *here on the spot*. The real work, that you know as well as Tussy does, will mostly have to be done by me. But as Mohr had one daughter living in London, I find it but natural that he should associate her to me in such work as she could do. Had you been living here instead of in Paris, all the three of us would have been jointly appointed, no doubt about that.

---

[a] of *Capital* - [b] of the first volume of *Capital*

But there is another view of the case. According to English law (which we had explained by Sam Moore) the only person living which is the legal representative of Mohr, in England, is Tussy. Or rather the only person who can become his legal representative by taking out letters of administration. This must be done by the *next of kin living in England* — Tussy; unless she declines and proposes someone else, who also must reside in the United Kingdom. So that legally I too am out of it. For various reasons these letters of administration *have* to be taken out.

Of the projects Mohr discussed with you at Vevey I was of course utterly ignorant and only regret you did not come over since the 14th March, when we should have known and complied with them as much as possible. But here is how the matter stands with regard to the English translation.[a] We find (from Sam. Moore as well as from Meissner) that we have *no right* to stop anyone from publishing an unauthorised translation. That right, in the best of cases, lasts but three years after first publication and lapsed finally in 1870. Now there were several people in the field and a well-meaning but poor and unbusinesslike publisher, Reeves, the most undesirable man of all, told Radford he had found a translator and was going to publish his translation. There was then no time to lose. We must find someone willing and able to do the work — we could think of no one but Sam. Moore and of Kegan Paul and Co. as publishers. The two entered into correspondence, then Tussy saw Kegan Paul, then I. Nothing is concluded, but very probably we shall come to some agreement. The question is: would you, under the altered circumstances, have undertaken to do the translation and bind yourself to a given time, say 6 months?

As to the History of the International, I am perfectly willing, as far as *I* am concerned, that all papers, etc., relating to the International be handed over to you for that purpose. But my plan was to write a full biography of Mohr,[30] and if you take those papers, that falls to the ground. Mohr's life without the International would be a diamond ring with the diamond broken out.

I have said nothing to Tussy about your letter, as I do not wish to interfere in any way between two sisters. Therefore, if you require any explanations from her, you will please write direct to her. But I think

---

[a] Of the first volume of *Capital*; see this volume, p. 29.

the best thing you could do, is to come over and have the matter mutually explained. You know very well there is on my part no other desire but to consider your wishes as much as possible and in every respect. And I am the same in the case with Tussy. If you wish to have your name associated to ours in the common work, and if you wish to share this work, and means can be found how, I for one shall only be glad of that. As it is we shall want your assistance often enough for information, etc., and nothing could throw greater obstacles in our way than fresh unpleasantness between you and Tussy. What we all of us are desirous of seeing carried out, is a befitting monument to the memory of Mohr, the first portion of which will and must be the publication of his posthumous works. Let us then all contribute what we can towards that end.

The only person to whom I have spoken about this matter is Nim and she is quite of the opinion expressed above.

As to our two martyrs,[a] they seem happy and contented enough, and even afraid of Grévy's putting an end to their prison-bliss on the 14th July.[9] What a fine sentence that on Louise Michel![74] Fortunately nobody knows who will rule France a couple of years hence. A shell between the legs of Alexander III, and all prison doors in Europe and Asia fly open except — the Irish ones.

Now I must conclude. I have to read proof-sheets No. 4 of 3rd edition[b] which arrived here on Saturday[c] and I have bound myself to return them in 48 hours. Then I have to work at the alterations for 3rd edition (done up to page 404) partly upon an annotated copy,[75] partly upon the French edition,[59] which must be done quick so as not to give excuse for delay. So no more at present.

Ever yours affectionately,

F. Engels

First published in: Marx and Engels, *Works*, Second Russian Edition, Vol. 36, Moscow, 1964

Reproduced from the original

Published in English for the first time

---

[a] Paul Lafargue and Jules Guesde - [b] the third German edition of Volume I of *Capital* - [c] 23 June

24

ENGELS TO FRIEDRICH ADOLPH SORGE [76]

IN HOBOKEN

London, 29 June 1883

Dear Sorge,

My evening's work has been disrupted by callers and this has given me a bit of spare time in which to write to you.

The critique of Henry George, which Marx sent you, is essentially a work of such extraordinary skill and stylistically so much all of a piece, that it would be a pity to tone it down by including the desultory marginal comments that appear in English in Marx's copy.[a] These will always be to hand in case of need later on. Every word of the letter he sent you was written, as was usually Marx's custom on such occasions, with an eye to the subsequent publication of the text. So you will not be guilty of any indiscretion if you have it printed. If it is to come out in English, I will translate it for you, since the translation of the *Manifesto*[b] has again shown that there seems to be no one over there who can translate *our* German, at any rate, into literary, grammatical English.[77] This calls for a writer with practice in both languages, practice, what's more, that is not merely confined to the daily press. Translating the *Manifesto* is awfully difficult; by far the best renderings I have seen are the Russian.[78]

The 3rd edition of *Capital*[c] is causing me a tremendous amount of work. We have one copy in which Marx follows the French edition[59] when indicating the emendations and additions to be made,[75] but all the detailed work remains to be done. I have got as far as 'Accumulation',[d] but here it is a case of revising almost completely the entire theoretical section. On top of that there is the responsibility. For to some extent the French translation lacks the depth of the German text; Marx would never have written in German in that way. Moreover the publisher keeps pressing me.

Until I finish this there can be no question of my going on to Vol-

---

[a] See this volume, p. 14. - [b] K. Marx and F. Engels, *Manifesto of the Communist Party.* - [c] the third German edition of Volume I of *Capital* - [d] i. e. Part VII of the first volume of *Capital*

ume II. There are in existence at least four versions of the beginning, thus often did Marx apply himself to the task, the editing of the definitive work having been interrupted on each occasion by illness. How the arrangement and conclusion of the last, dating from 1878, will agree with the first, which goes back to before 1870, I cannot yet say.[17]

Practically everything has been saved from the period up to 1848. Not only virtually all of the mss he and I worked on at the time (in so far as they haven't been eaten by mice), but also the correspondence. Everything after 1849 is also complete, of course, and, from 1862 on, is actually in some sort of order. Also extensive written material on the International, sufficient, I imagine, for a full history, though I have not yet been able to take a closer look at it.

There are also 3 or 4 notebooks of mathematical studies. I once showed your Adolf[a] an example of Marx's new explanation of differential calculus.[79]

Had it not been for the mass of American and Russian material[80] (there are over two cubic metres of books of Russian statistics alone), Volume II would have long since been printed. These detailed studies held him up for years. As always, everything had to be brought right up to date and now it has all come to nothing, apart from his excerpts which will, I trust, include many of his customary critical commentaries for use as notes to Volume II.

The photographs are here[b]; as soon as I can find time to pack them I shall send them to you. But how? BOOK POST precludes any stout packing, no parcel post exists as yet,. and to send a small package like this per parcels agency would cost a mint of money. Perhaps you would let me know how best to go about it.

I have already read five sheets of the final proof of the 3rd edition; the man has promised to send three sheets a week.

Your
F. Engels

I haven't possibly got time to answer little Hepner's many long letters just now. His reports are always of interest to me, intermingled though they are with a great deal of personal gossip and written with the sense of superiority of the newly disembarked. Meanwhile you had better convey my apologies to him.

---

[a] Adolf Sorge jun.- [b] See this volume, p. 18.

Schewitsch has sent me a 'dignified' reply and regrets my 'small-mindedness'.[a] Dignity becomes him. He won't get an answer.

Nor will Most, who is, of course, bound to confirm everything I have said,[b] which is exactly what has made him so furious. I believe he will find support in sectarian America and sow confusion for a time. But it is precisely in the nature of the American movement that all mistakes must be experienced in practice. If America's energy and vitality were backed by Europe's theoretical clarity, you would get everything fixed up within ten years. But that is, after all, an historical impossibility.

First published in *Briefe und Auszüge aus Briefen von Joh. Phil. Becker, Jos. Dietzgen, Friedrich Engels, Karl Marx u. A. an F. A. Sorge und Andere*, Stuttgart, 1906

Printed according to the original

Published in English in full for the first time

25

ENGELS TO GABRIEL DEVILLE

IN PARIS

London, 12 August 1883
122 Regent's Park Road, N. W.

Dear Citizen Deville,

I have received your letter and your manuscript, for which I thank you.[81] Next week I shall be leaving London for a seaside resort.[82] There I shall have sufficient leisure to look over your work which will be returned to you as soon as possible.

Your manuscript arrived at an opportune moment. Only yesterday I completed the final editing of the 3rd German edition of *Capital*,[c] and have undertaken to begin editing the 2nd volume immediately on my return from the seaside. So your work reached me precisely at the moment when I happened to have a short interval of time.

---

[a] See this volume, pp. 13-14 and 91.- [b] Ibid., p. 11.- [c] the first volume

I have read the section you sent to Marx a little while ago; it seems to me very clear and very accurate. And, since it comprises the most difficult part of the work, there would appear to be no reason to anticipate any misapprehensions in the remaining sections.

Yours ever,
F. Engels

First published, heavily abridged, in: M. Dommanget, *Karl Marx et Frédéric Engels,* Paris, 1951 and in full in: Marx and Engels, *Works,* Second Russian Edition, Vol. 36, Moscow, 1964

Printed according to the original

Translated from the French

Published in English for the first time

26

ENGELS TO LAURA LAFARGUE

IN PARIS

Eastbourne, 19 August 1883
4 Cavendish Place

My dear Laura,

At last out of London.[82] As soon as I saw my way clear, I sent Percy (last Wednesday[a]) over here to look out for apartments. He did his business well, and found excellent accommodation, not without difficulty. Two doors from the Parade, facing the Pier, fine rooms, no sun more than is wanted, good sea-view, good cooking, the only thing we are sorry for is that it could not be arranged in time for you to go with us. On Friday we arrived here, Pumps, babies and girl, Nim, Jollymeier (who felt a little out of sorts again but has picked up here at once and will soon leave us) and myself. First-class Scotch mist on arrival, fine rain off and on all night, very encouraging! But next day splendid, so that we could take our walks under the trees and show Nim a little of the place. To-day, Sunday, fine morning but

---

[a] 15 August

becoming foggy, well we must take our chance, but anyhow so far the place looks quite different to what it did in the rainy weather when last here.[83] There has been an immense deal of building, the lodging part of the town has about doubled in size, all the fields towards Beachy Head and a good deal of the slope are built over. Pilsener Beer is flourishing and better even than in London. Nim and Pumps find things cheaper and better here than at home.

Emily Rosher's little *avorton*[a] died yesterday, best thing it could do.

I wrote to Deville at once announcing arrival of his ms.[b] At the same time or a little after I got also Sam Moore's translation[c] — so I shall have plenty to do here, besides working off my colossal arrears of correspondence.

The place is very full, but the style of the people seems to be more 'free and easy' than formerly. Even on Sunday morning the chimney-pot hat plays but a very poor part, and 'athletic' costumes run about pretty free.

Just now the whole party throng in again, awfully thirsty, Jolly-meier has to open the Pilsener, and you conceive that it is no use struggling against the difficulties crowding upon me and stopping not only rational but even irrational correspondence. The second bottle has just been opened, the little girl is crawling about my knees, and so I give it up in despair. The whole colony send their kindest regards to you and Paul whose half-term we shall celebrate the day after tomor-row[9] in an extra draft of Pilsener.

Nim wishes you, literally, 'to have a good look-out about her for-tune, as she expects it soon to come in'.[84]

And so, dear Laura,

Yours most affectionately,

F. Engels

First published, in the language of the original (English), in: F. Engels, P. et L. Lafargue, *Correspondance*, t. I, Paris, 1956

Reproduced from the original

---

[a] abortion - [b] See previous letter.- [c] Part of the English translation of the first volume of *Capital* (see Note 56).

27

ENGELS TO WILHELM LIEBKNECHT

IN BORSDORF NEAR LEIPZIG [34]

[Eastbourne,] 21 August 1883

Dear Liebknecht,

Your letter [85] has remained unanswered because of final work on the 3rd edition,[a] after which I came to stay here at

4 Cavendish Place, Eastbourne, England where I intend to remain until about 12 September.[82]

Mrs Marx died on 2 December 1881, Jenny on 9 January 1883. Both deaths were reported in the *Sozialdemokrat*.[b]

The Paris *Vorwärts!* was a little sheet which is now being accorded more importance than it deserves; the editors were a dilatory lot. Marx's main concern was to keep it on the right lines and from time to time he also wrote polemical articles and reviews attacking the Prussians.[c] Heine sent Marx some of the advance proofs of the *Wintermärchen* from Hamburg for publication in the *Vorwärts!* before the book appeared in Germany.[86]

I actually only set eyes on a few numbers and the little paper did not survive for long, so I cannot let you have any further details.

Marx wrote quite a lot of things for the *Deutsche-Brüsseler-Zeitung*, including a polemical discourse against Heinzen.[d]

Bebel's letter safely received; will be answered from here[e]; along with all the other correspondence, have been unable to attend to it because of overwork. Tell Bebel that Schorlemmer, who is here, will be going to Darmstadt shortly and staying there until about the middle of September. If Bebel is visiting those parts before then, Schorlemmer would like him to let him know (Prof. Schorlemmer, Darm-

---

[a] the third German edition of Volume I of *Capital*.- [b] F. Engels, 'Jenny Marx, née von Westphalen'; 'Jenny Longuet, née Marx'.- [c] K. Marx, 'Critical Marginal Notes on the Article "The King of Prussia and Social Reform. By a Prussian"'; 'Illustrations of the Latest Exercise in Cabinet Style of Frederick William IV'.- [d] K. Marx, 'Moralising Criticism and Critical Morality. A Contribution to German Cultural History. Contra Karl Heinzen'.- [e] See this volume, pp. 52-55.

stadt is sufficient address) and tell him where Schorlemmer can meet him; in which case he will do his utmost to look him up.

Lafargue finished half his time today.[9]

Your

F. E.

First published, in Russian, in *Marx-Engels Archives*, Vol. I (VI), Moscow, 1932

Printed according to the original

Published in English for the first time

28

ENGELS TO PASQUALE MARTIGNETTI

IN BENEVENTO

England, Eastbourne, 22 August 1883
4 Cavendish Place

Dear Citizen,

Please excuse my delay in replying to your letter of 25/6 and your postcard of 30/7.[87] The need to finish in a short time the text of the 3rd German edition of *Capital*[a] forced me to suspend all correspondence.

I do not know much about Ahn's method, and the dictionary you mention is entirely unknown to me. In order to learn a language the method I have always followed is this: I do not bother with grammar (except for declensions and conjugations, and pronouns) and I read, with a dictionary, the most difficult classical author I can find. Thus I began Italian with Dante, Petrarch and Ariosto, Spanish with Cervantes and Calderon, Russian with Pushkin. Then I read newspapers, etc. For German, I think the first part of Goethe's *Faust* might be suitable; it is written, for the most part, in a popular style, and the things which would seem difficult to you would also be difficult, without a commentary, for a German reader.

---

[a] the first volume

For the works of Marx, etc., you could approach the offices of the *Sozialdemokrat*, Hottingen-Zurich, Switzerland; it is the official organ of the German workers' party.

Thank you for the copies of the translation, which reached me in good condition, and also for kindly sending your photograph, in return for which I enclose mine.

Yours with regards,

F. Engels

The normal London address is fine; I am here at the seaside for a few weeks.

First published in *La corrispondenza di Marx e Engels con italiani. 1848-1895,* Milano, 1964

Printed according to the original

Translated from the Italian

Published in English for the first time

29

ENGELS TO EDUARD BERNSTEIN [88]

IN ZURICH

Eastbourne, 27 August 1883
4 Cavendish Place

Dear Bernstein,

Herewith money order for £4 for old Becker.[a] I am still hoping that the news — and it wouldn't be the first time — is being exaggerated by his family. But he is, of course, very old, has been through a great deal and, or so I was told by Mme Lafargue, looked considerably older last year in Geneva by comparison with his hearty appearance at The Hague.[89]

I shall not be able to write a great deal today. The post leaves here at one o'clock in the afternoon and here beside me, for proof-reading, lies sheet 19 of *Capital*,[b] which also has to go off.

---

[a] Johann Philipp Becker - [b] of the third German edition of Volume I of *Capital*

Many thanks for your suggestion about Kaler-Reinthal,[90] but I cannot, unfortunately, take advantage of it. With the exception of trifles, all my extra jobs are of a kind that call for my *personal* attention. And in so far as I could pass anything on, it would have to be to a man who spoke *coulant*[a] English and was intimately acquainted with London and local conditions, thus being able to save me running errands.

I am staying here until about 12 September,[82] until when the above address holds good; then back to London.

Besides proofs and arrears of correspondence, I must, while here, attend to:

1) Deville's ms., French popularisation of *Capital*.[81]

2) Ms., part of the English translation,[b] both of them sorely in need of revision. So you see, no peace here either. Luckily I live right next to the sea and sit besides an open window through which the sea air comes wafting in.

I was very sorry that you didn't come over here. I had a number of things to discuss with you. We have in any case got to resign ourselves to the fact that *some* of Marx's unpublished works will have to appear abroad[c] and you alone could give me practical information or suggestions relating to this; it is, however, something that has to be discussed verbally — by letter it would be endless. But please say nothing about this, otherwise it might arouse false hopes in the people who run the printing works out there; my experience of party presses is such that I would *think twice* before entrusting a major and important work to any of them.

I shall retain the money order here, it being expressly stated thereon that it is of no use to the recipient. I gave your address, 137 alte Landstraße Riesbach, from memory; if wrong, please put this right at the *main* post office in Zurich.

My suggestion about the impudent ms. was, as it were, a bad joke.[d] So long as the Anti-Socialist Law is in force,[37] and the *Sozialdemokrat* is the only possible organ, it is imperative not to sow discord among the party merely for the sake of such secondary issues, and that is what would happen if one sought to make a 'question of principle' out of this issue.

---

[a] fluent - [b] of the first volume of *Capital* (see Note 56) - [c] See this volume, p. 17.- [d] Ibid., p. 37.

It would seem to me that, in the treatment of the 'republic', especially in France, the most important aspect did not emerge clearly enough in the *Sozialdemokrat*,[91] namely this:

In the class struggle between proletariat and bourgeoisie, the Bonapartist monarchy (the characteristics of which have been expounded by Marx in the *Eighteenth Brumaire* and by myself in *The Housing Question*, II, and elsewhere) adopted a role similar to that of the old absolute monarchy in the struggle between feudalism and bourgeoisie. But just as that struggle could not be fought out under the old, absolute monarchy but only under a constitutional one (England, France 1789-92 and 1815-30) so, too, that between bourgeoisie and proletariat can only be fought out in a republic. Inasmuch, then, as the French were helped by favourable conditions and revolutionary antecedents to overthrow Bonaparte and establish a bourgeois republic,[92] they have the advantage over us, who remain stuck in a farrago of semi-feudalism and Bonapartism, of already possessing the form in which the struggle must be fought out and which we must first *master* for ourselves. Politically they are a whole stage ahead of us. Hence, the inevitable consequence of a monarchist restoration in France would be that the struggle for the restoration of the *bourgeois* republic would again appear on the agenda; continuance of the republic, on the other hand, means mounting intensification of the *direct*, undisguised class struggle between proletariat and bourgeoisie until a crisis is reached.

Similarly in our case the first, immediate result of the revolution can and *must*, so far as *form* is concerned, be nothing other than a *bourgeois* republic. But in this instance it will be no more than a brief, transitional period since fortunately we do not possess a purely republican bourgeois party. A bourgeois republic with, perhaps, the Party of Progress [93] at the helm, will serve us at first *to win over the great mass of the workers to revolutionary socialism* — which will have been effected in a year or two — and will be conducive to the thorough erosion and self-destruction of all possible intermediate parties but not ours. Only then can we successfully take over.

The great mistake made by the Germans is to imagine the revolution as something that can be achieved overnight. In fact it is a process of development on the part of the masses which takes several years even under conditions that tend to accelerate it. Every revolution that has been achieved overnight has merely ousted a reactionary regime doomed from the outset (1830) or has led directly to the exact opposite of what was aspired to (1848, France).

Yours,

F. E

What do you think of this:

'The last so-called *red number of the "Rheinische Zeitung"* [a] (third edition) of 19 May 1849, which carried the *Neue Rheinische Zeitung*'s farewell message by Ferdinand Freiligrath at the top of its front page, was again confiscated by the police here not long ago. A second-hand dealer had bought as waste paper a number of copies of this last farewell issue of the sometime organ of democracy and was selling them at 10 pfennigs a piece. The police put a stop to this by confiscating such of the papers as the dealer still had left. If the confiscation was effected on the grounds that the sheet's wretched pale red print was bound to harm its readers' eyes, the public has cause to thank the police; today, the text would be most unlikely to inflame anyone's feelings.' [b]

First published abridged in *Le Mouvement socialiste*, Paris, t. IV, No. 45, novembre 1, 1900 and in full, in Russian, in *Marx-Engels Archives*, Book I, Moscow, 1924

Printed according to the original

Published in English in full for the first time

30

ENGELS TO AUGUST BEBEL [94]

IN BORSDORF NEAR LEIPZIG [34]

Eastbourne, 30 August 1883
4 Cavendish Place

Dear Bebel,

I am taking advantage of a moment's peace to write to you. In London numerous jobs, down here numerous interruptions (three grown-ups and two small children in one room!); on top of that proof-reading [c] and the revision of an English specimen translation [56] as also of a popularised French version of *Capital*.[81] How's a chap to write letters!

I have corrected up to sheet 21 of the 3rd edition which contains

---

[a] *Neue Rheinische Zeitung* - [b] See *Kölnische Zeitung*, No. 119, 20 July 1883. - [c] of the third German edition of Volume I of *Capital*

voluminous addenda; by the end of the year the thing will be out. As soon as I am back I shall get down to Volume 2 in real earnest and that is an enormous task. Alongside parts that have been completely finished are others that are merely sketched out, the whole being a *brouillon*[a] with the exception of perhaps two chapters. Quotations from sources in no kind of order, piles of them jumbled together, collected simply with a view to future selection. Besides that there is the handwriting which certainly cannot be deciphered by anyone but *me*, and then only with difficulty.[17] You ask why I of all people should not have been told how far the thing had got. It is quite simple; had I known, I should have pestered him night and day until it was all finished and printed. And Marx knew that better than anyone else. He knew besides that, if the worst came to the worst, as has now happened, the ms. could be edited by me in the spirit in which he would have done it himself, indeed he told Tussy as much.[95]

As regards the photograph,[b] the head is quite excellent. The pose is stiff, as in all his photographs; he was a bad 'sitter'. It does not irritate me in any way but, because of the stiffness of the pose, I prefer the smaller one to the larger.

The election in Hamburg[96] has also created a great sensation abroad. But then the behaviour of our chaps could not have been more exemplary. Such tenacity, perseverance, flexibility and ready wit, such waggish confidence of winning in the struggle with the greater and lesser miseries of the Germany of today, is unprecedented in recent German history. Especially splendid is the contrast it presents to the corruption, flabbiness and general decay of all other classes of German society. The very extent to which these classes demonstrate their inability to rule brings out in brilliant relief the ruling mission of the German proletariat, its ability to overturn the whole sordid old mess.

The 'jets of cold water' directed by Bismarck on Paris[97] are becoming ridiculous, even in the eyes of the French bourgeois. Even a paper as stupid as the *Soir* has discovered that nothing more is involved than the new appropriations in the Reichstag for the military (this time the field artillery).[c] As for his alliances (he has descended to Serbia, Romania and now Spain of all places[98]), all these are houses built of cards that will be blown down by a puff of wind. If he's lucky he won't need them and if he's unlucky they will land him in

---

[a] draft - [b] of Marx - [c] *Le Soir*, 29 August 1883.

the cart. The greater a blackguard a man is, the more he believes in the uprightness of others and that, in the end, is his undoing. It is unlikely to get to that stage with Bismarck so far as his foreign policy is concerned, for the French won't do him the favour of picking a quarrel. Only the Tsar[a] might try something of the kind out of desperation and come to grief in the process. But I hope he will come to grief at home before that.

The manifesto of the Democratic Federation in London[99] has been issued by some 20-30 little societies which, under various names (always the same people), have been persistently trying to look important for the past 20 years at least and always with the same lack of success. All that is important is that these people have now at last been compelled publicly to proclaim our theory as their own, a theory which, at the time of International, seemed to them to have been imposed upon them from outside, and further that a number of young people have lately emerged from amongst the bourgeoisie who, to the shame, be it said, of the English workers, understand these things better and embrace them more enthusiastically than do the workers. For even in the Democratic Federation the workers have accepted the new programme for the most part no more than reluctantly and outwardly. Hyndman, the head of the Democratic Federation, is an ex-Conservative, an ambitious man, hopelessly jingoistic but not stupid. He behaved pretty shabbily[b] towards Marx (to whom he had been introduced by Rudolf Meyer), and for that reason has been personally ignored by us.[100] On no account whatever allow yourself to be bamboozled into believing that a real proletarian movement is afoot here. I know that this is what Liebknecht would have himself and the rest of the world believe, but it is not so. The elements presently active might become important, now that they have accepted our theoretical programme and thus acquired a basis, but only if a spontaneous movement broke out amongst the workers here and they succeeded in gaining control of it. Until then they will continue to be so many isolated individuals with, behind them, an omnium-gatherum of muddle-headed sects, the remnants of the great movement of the forties,[101] but nothing more. A really universal labour movement will come about here—barring the unexpected—only when the workers become sensible of the fact that England's world

---

[a] Alexander III - [b] The words 'ziemlich schofel' ('pretty shabbily') were crossed out in the original and 'nicht schön' ('not nicely') written above them in an unknown handwriting.

monopoly has been broken. Participation in the domination of the world market was and is the economic basis of the English workers' political nullity. As the appendage of the bourgeois in the economic exploitation of this monopoly, though nevertheless participating in the advantages that accrue from the said exploitation, they are, in the nature of things, a political appendage of the 'Great Liberal Party' which, for its part, courts them in minor matters, acknowledges TRADES UNIONS and STRIKES as legitimate factors, has abandoned the struggle for an unlimited working day, and enfranchised most of the better paid workers.[102] But once America and the combined competition of the other industrial nations have made a sizeable breach in this monopoly (imminent in the case of iron, less so, unfortunately, in that of cotton), just wait and see what happens here.

I asked Liebknecht to tell you[a] that, if you happened to be in the neighbourhood of Darmstadt between now and 12 September, you should advise Schorlemmer who is staying there, so that he can look you up somewhere in that region. It is probably too late now. Regards to Liebknecht.

Your
F. E.

First published, in Russian, in *Marx-Engels Archives*, Vol. I (VI), Moscow, 1932

Printed according to the original

Published in English in full for the first time

31

ENGELS TO KARL KAUTSKY[103]

IN STUTTGART

London, 18 September 1883

Dear Mr Kautsky,

As regards the Geiser business, I do not believe the time has yet come for me to intervene.[104] The chaps must first compromise them-

---

[a] See this volume, pp. 47-48.

selves a bit more in the eyes of the public. The paltry little flysheet and the failure of the motion on the right to work are not enough; they must express themselves in yet stronger terms if we are to get a proper hold on them and if they are not to lie their way out by pleading false excuses. Meanwhile it would be most helpful if you would gather together material in this connection, for the moment will come when we shall have to have a go at these gentlemen. There's no immediate hurry.[a] Bebel and the *Sozialdemokrat*, as you say yourself, have got the masses behind them, and there is, after all, an antidote to hand. That you have a great deal of this sort of thing to put up with in that Swabian hole, I can well believe, considering that Stuckert[b] and Munich are the worst places in Germany. And then, I definitely have not got the time to become embroiled in a dispute that would demand a great deal of toil and trouble. If it has *got* to be — well and good. I return the flysheet herewith.

Lack of time precludes my engaging in further detailed discussion of the articles on marriage.[105] In any case, primitive hetaerism is so remote in time and has been so much overlaid by later developments, whether progressive or otherwise, that nowadays we can nowhere expect to find examples in their pristine form. But all subsequent forms lead back to those primitive origins. Of this much I am certain,— until you have completely dropped the element of jealousy as a *determining social factor* (in primitive times), it will not be possible to give a correct account of the way things have developed.

Generally speaking, in the case of all those scientific researches which embrace so wide a field and such a mass of material, nothing can really be achieved except by dint of many years of study. Individual aspects that are both new and accurate — and these are, of course, to be found in your articles — present themselves more readily; but to survey the whole and to order it anew is something that can only be done after it has been fully explored. Otherwise there would be many more books like *Capital*. So I am glad to see that you have turned to themes — for immediate literary treatment — such as early biblical history[c] and colonisation,[d] which make it possible to achieve something without so exhaustive and detailed a study, and yet at the same time strike a topical note. I liked the colonisation article very much. Unfortunately almost all the material you've got is

[a] See this volume, p. 64.- [b] Stuttgart - [c] K. Kautsky, 'Die Entstehung der biblischen Urgeschichte', *Kosmos...*, Vol. XIII, June 1883. - [d] K. Kautsky, 'Auswanderung und Kolonisation', *Die Neue Zeit*, Nos. 8 and 9, 1883.

German which, as usual, is toned down and fails to present either the lurid hues of tropical colonisation or its most recent mode. The latter is colonisation, directly and wittingly carried out in the interest of stock-market manipulations, as now by France in Tunisia and Tongking.[65] Of this there is a new and striking instance in the South Seas slave trade; that trade was the immediate purpose of the attempted annexation of New Guinea, etc., by Queensland. Almost on the same day as the expedition set out to annex New Guinea, a Queensland vessel, the *Fanny*, left for the same island and others further east in order to seize LABOUR, returning, however, *without* LABOUR but with wounded as well as other unpleasant signs of an encounter.[106] *The Daily News* reports this and, in a leading article,[a] remarks that the British can hardly censure the French for such practices while doing the same thing themselves! (Beginning of September.)

Last week, at the TRADES UNIONS CONGRESS sitting at Nottingham, Adam Weiler's proposal to press for international factory legislation was thrown out by 26 votes to 2 on the motion of the 'Labour' parliamentarian Broadhurst.[107] So much for Liebknecht's much-vaunted TRADES UNIONS![108]

Why doesn't Fritz Denhardt write for the *Neue Zeit* any more?[109] He had a very nice cheery style. The journal itself, of course, has to content with appalling difficulties: the censorship it has to impose upon itself is a thousand times worse than the old, official censorship used to be. You still have some pretty odd contributors and you yourself must often enough long for better ones. At all events, this business has for you the advantage of enabling you at the same time to pursue your scientific studies and let them come to gradual fruition.

Incidentally, Java provides proof of the fact that nowhere and at no time does a population increase so rapidly as under a not unduly oppressive system of bondage: 1755—2 mill.; 1826—$5^1/_2$ mill.; 1850—9 mill.; 1878—19 mill.; — an almost tenfold increase in 125 years — the only example of anything like Malthusian growth. Were they to send the Dutch blood-suckers packing the population would become fairly stable.

Adler turned up just as I was off to the seaside and likewise on my return; he is a man of some promise. He saw much here that might be of use to him.[110]

---

[a] *The Daily News*, 12 September 1883.

I yesterday received a money order from Stuttgart for £ 6 3/ - for the photographs,[a] but there was no accompanying letter. Will you ask Dietz to be so kind as to drop me a note informing me what name (Christian name) and address (in Stuttgart) he gave at the post office on taking out the order? The post office here is very pedantic in such matters, and if the particulars I give differ in the slightest respect I shall not get the money.

The 2nd volume of *Capital* will provide me with work and to spare. The bulk of the ms. dates back to *before 1868* and is in places no more than a *brouillon*.[b][17] The second book will greatly disappoint the vulgar socialists, it contains virtually nothing but rigorously scientific, very minute examinations of things that take place within the capitalist class itself, and nothing at all out of which to fabricate catch-words and orations.

Pumps has already got two offspring. Tussy Marx has taken rooms near the British Museum. Lenchen is keeping house for me.

Kindest regards.

Yours,
F. E.

First published, in Russian, in *Marx-Engels Archives*, Vol. I (VI), Moscow, 1932

Printed according to the original

Published in English in full for the first time

32

ENGELS TO LAURA LAFARGUE

IN PARIS

London, 19 September 1883

My dear Laura,

At last returned from Eastbourne,[82] where correspondence was rendered difficult and almost impossible by circumstances. When proof-sheets[c] arrived — 3 times a week — my company left me to my

---

[a] See this volume, pp. 15-16.- [b] draft - [c] of the third German edition of Volume I of *Capital*

work, but on the silent understanding that I was not to exact anything further—and how indeed could I have asked for peace and
quietness in the one sitting room allotted to us all, especially when the
thirst for Pilsener drove them in at certain times of the day?

I was besides busy with Sam Moore's specimen translation[a] the
greater part of which is very good and lively; the beginning—rather
a difficult chapter[b]—wanted a deal of 'look after', on account of his
not having been exact enough in rendering the terminology, but that
could be easily settled. I am certain from what I have seen that he
will do the job well.

I also began revising Deville's pamphlet,[81] it requires more work,
especially in the beginning where great precision is necessary, but is
wanting here and there. However I shall have no difficulty in setting
that right, only it will take a week or a fortnight. I shall set to work seriously to-morrow. As far as I have gone, I am much pleased with his
work, he has well understood everything (except small details) and it
is written in a more lively style than I thought it would be.

As soon as that is shaken off I begin with the 2nd volume [of]
Kapital.

I hope you received my post-card[111] with the information you had
asked me for. It was sent the day after I received your letter.

We came back last Friday,[c] Pumps and Percy stayed here over
Sunday, their house not being in order. Since then we had a thunderstorm and fearful rain in parts of London which flooded their back
drawing-room. Otherwise they are flourishing. The little boy is getting on wonderfully well, he was five months yesterday, and is extremely intelligent for his age.

Nim declares she must reduce her allowance of beer. She thinks she
is getting too fat with it.

This morning Lopatin walks in, his adventures have ripened him
considerably.[112] He will be here again directly and have dinner with
us. He says he saw Paul lately and found him well and content, all
things considered.[9]

Tussy I have not seen yet, I believe she is not in town, I wrote her
a line but she did not turn up on Sunday. As soon as Nim can get off
she'll call on her.

---

[a] the English translation of the first volume of *Capital* (see Note 56) - [b] the first
chapter of Volume I of *Capital*—'Commodities'. - [c] 14 September

Of my little pamphlet *Entwicklung etc.* two editions are already sold, the third is in the press.[25] That shows anyhow that it is not too difficult for the mass of the working people in Germany.

When this letter arrives, Paul will have 'done' $^2/_3$ rds of his time— I hope he will keep his pluck up for the two last and most trying months.

Of the 3rd edition [of] *Kapital*[a] I have read proofs up to page 448, so if they go on at this rate, the whole will be completed by December. I am sorry Mohr has not lived to see how well this time the thing is done: no delay, no trouble with the printers, no trifling complaint but is at once set right, and excellent proofs with very few mistakes. Leipzig[113] seems at last, and at least in this one respect of printing, to become '*ein klein Paris*'.[b] High time it was.

So now I conclude this budget of miscellaneous news in order to set a few little jobs right before Lopatin drops in again. Kind regards for[c] Paul and a hearty kiss for yourself from

Yours affectionately,

Le général pour rire[d]

First published, in the language of the original (English), in: F. Engels, P. et L. Lafargue, *Correspondance*, t. I, Paris, 1956

Reproduced from the original

33

ENGELS TO LAURA LAFARGUE

IN PARIS

London, 3 October 1883

My dear Laura,

Herewith cheque for £ 14.- of which £ 4.- are your $^1/_3$ share of £ 12.- sent by Meissner on account of 2nd edition [of] *Kapital*,[e]

---

[a] the third German edition of Volume I of *Capital* -[b] 'a little Paris' -[c] In the original mistakenly: 'from'. -[d] The general, in a manner of speaking. -[e] the second German edition of Volume I of *Capital*

£ 4.- for Tussy and £ 4.- for Longuets children, which Tussy has banked for the present until a little more money accrues to them, when we can consider, along with you, what is to be done in their interest.

Jollymeier left here yesterday, highly enchanted with Paris. He says you will come over at Christmas—hope it will turn out true!

Today I sent to you, registered, pages 1-123 of Deville's ms.[81] I cannot find his letter with his address. The defect of the thing is that many parts of it have been done rather too hurriedly. This is principally the case with the descriptive portions (especially *manufacture* and *grande industrie*[a]). The points do not at all come out as they ought to do. It is not sufficient to express them, as much as possible, in Marx's own words; these cannot be torn from the context without giving rise to misinterpretation or leaving many things in comparative obscurity. Deville would do well to revise these two chapters throughout and to complete them by some of the exemplifications of the original without which they have become very abstract and to working-men-readers obscure. In the theoretical parts there are also many slight inaccuracies (some too, as his definition of *marchandise*,[b] very serious) and *des choses faites à la hâte*,[c] but these it was mostly not very difficult to set more or less right. Then many portions, of interest and importance for theoretical economic science, but without immediate *portée*[d] on the question between capital and labour, might be omitted. One or two I have indicated.

Now then I close. Though a good deal better I am ordered to lie down as much as possible quietly for a few days longer and so with kind regards to the prisoners[9] and sincere love from Nim and myself remain

Ever yours affectionately,

F. Engels

First published, in the language of the original (English), in: F. Engels, P. et L. Lafargue, *Correspondance*, t. I, Paris, 1956

Reproduced from the original

---

[a] Cf. this volume, p. 76.- [b] commodity - [c] things done in haste - [d] bearing

34

ENGELS TO LAURA LAFARGUE

IN PARIS

London, 15 October 1883

My dear Laura,

My last letter was awfully rough. But I was not allowed to sit long at the desk, and *had* to write — as you will allow — to Deville first.[39] So I could only say a few words to you and these must have looked very unkind indeed. Pardon me.

Well, I have made up my mind *d'en finir avec cette sacrée maladie chronique.*[a] Since last Wednesday night[b] I have stayed in bed, in order to do away with any excuse for the constant cause of all my relapses, want of rest and temptation for moving about. To-day I feel quite well, and inclined for a dance. But that is just the time when absolute rest is most needed, and therefore I shall not stir out of bed until bed will do me more harm than good. If nothing unexpected occurs, I think I shall be *en pleine guérison*[c] before the week is out. So now, that will satisfy you I hope as far as my health is concerned.

I perfectly understand what Jollymeier meant by his letter to you. Gumpert had given him the note of warning — *awfully exaggerated,* though, for my case — but Gumpert could not interfere in my treatment by another doctor. Still I think Jollymeier might have found another way to save Gumpert's scruples as to medical étiquette without frightening *you.* As it is, I have used your letter to stir up my doctors a bit, and with success. *Ich hab' ihnen Beine gemacht,*[d] and energetic treatment is now all the rage.

But enough of that. All I am sorry for, and very sorry, is that I responded in such an unkind way to your letter and to the kind feeling which had dictated it. It has weighed on my mind all the time, and yet I would not again write to you until I could indicate a decided improvement and good reasons for an approaching final cure.

Fortin has written, he wants a preface[e] and asks about 20 questions which it would take a year to answer thoroughly. Tussy was here when his letter came, I read it to her and I wish you could have heard

---

[a] to get rid of this accursed chronic ailment - [b] 10 October - [c] fully fit - [d] I made them get a move on - [e] to the French edition of Marx's *The Eighteenth Brumaire of Louis Bonaparte*; see also this volume, p. 358.

us laugh at that never ending series of inquiries, each requiring a volume to answer it completely. I shall ask him to send me the manuscript[a] and put off the rest for better times.

Read to-day proof-sheet[b] up to page 600.

Tussy has promised to look up the American reports for Paul.[114]

It is getting post-time and dinner-time too. But before concluding: Deville writes to say he has no time to recast the 3 chapters indicated by me.[81] Please do, you and Paul, as much as you can, to get him to revise them as much as possible. Such as they are, they are not intelligible but to those who know the original. He says the publisher will give no time. But the whole cannot be printed at once!! A fortnight will do it and it will be a *wonderful improvement*.

Kind regards to the prisoner[c] now soon to be free.

A kiss from Nim and from your affectionate

F. Engels

First published, in the language of the original (English), in: F. Engels, P. et L. Lafargue, *Correspondance*, t. I, Paris, 1956   Reproduced from the original

35

ENGELS TO EDUARD BERNSTEIN

IN ZURICH

London, 8 November 1883

Dear Bernstein,

I have been keeping to my bed for the past few weeks in order to rid myself of a chronic ailment, mild in itself but tiresome and long neglected; I shall be up again in a few days. Hence my silence. Please accept my apologies and also convey them to Kautsky; I don't know whether he is still in Stuckert.[d]

---

[a] See Engels' letter to Laura Lafargue, 21 March 1887 (present edition, Vol. 48). -
[b] of the third German edition of Volume I of *Capital* - [c] Paul Lafargue - [d] Stuttgart

The article on the right to work was very good and very much *à propos*.[a] Kautsky had already bombarded me about the same subject[b] and I shall be perfectly willing as soon as it becomes *necessary*, but I think one should first let these gentlemen compromise themselves a little more; they ought first to formulate more precisely what they mean by it; one must never stop people from giving 'complete and full' expression to their nonsense; only then does one get something really tangible. I hope your article will commit the chaps to this course.

If the Germans in Paris have not had their eyes opened to Malon & Co. *now*, there's no helping them. Their open alliance with the *traitors* of the English labour movement, the official representatives of the TRADES UNIONS, has earned them the applause of the entire English bourgeois press from *The Times* and *The Daily News* to *The Standard*.[115] A good thing that Guesde and Lafargue were doing time,[9] thereby enabling this magnificent performance to be put on with no interruptions whatever!

Apropos. Do you know a Dr Moritz[c] Quarck (sic!) In Rudolstadt? This man, with whom I am totally unfamiliar, has referred me to a pamphlet,[d] with which I am equally unfamiliar, attacking one Fleischmann[e] with whom I am even less familiar, and wants to translate *The Poverty of Philosophy* into German.[f] I have my misgivings.

Well, let me know sometime soon what is going on in the world. I have become so stupid, lolling about in bed, that I can no longer marshal my thoughts.

Yours,

F. E.

First published, in Russian, in *Marx-Engels Archives*, Book I, Moscow, 1924

Printed according to the original

Published in English for the first time

---

[a] [E. Bernstein,] 'Das Recht auf Arbeit', *Der Sozialdemokrat*, No. 44, 25 October 1883. - [b] See this volume, p. 56. - [c] A mistake; should be Max. - [d] [M. Quarck,] *Kommerzienrath Adolf Fleischmann als Nationalökonom und die Thüringer Hausindustrie*. - [e] A. Fleischmann, *Die Sonneberger Spielwaaren-Hausindustrie und ihr Handel*. - [f] See this volume, pp. 66 and 67.

Engels in his sickbed working on the manuscript of Volume II of Marx's *Capital*
(October 1883-June 1884)

36

ENGELS TO VERA ZASULICH

IN GENEVA

London, 13 November 1883
122 Regent's Park Road, N. W.

Dear Citizen,

I am not really in a position to answer the questions you have been so good as to put to me.[116] The publication of the second volume of *Capital*, in the original text, continues to be delayed. Up till now I have had to confine my attention mainly to the 3rd edition of the first volume.[a]

So far I have heard nothing at all from St Petersburg in regard to a Russian translation of the 2nd volume. Nor, for that matter, do I believe that, as things are now, there could be any question of publishing a work of this kind in the Russian capital; no doubt they would first want to take a look at the German text.

On the other hand, the political situation in Russia is now so tense that a crisis might supervene any day. I even think it probable that the press will be free in Russia before it becomes so in Germany. And in that case the translator of the first volume, Германъ Лопатинъ,[b] could, with some reason, claim the right to translate the second.[117]

I do not, therefore, believe that the time is yet ripe for an attempt to arrive at a final decision on this matter, but must thank you sincerely for your kind offer which I shall bear in mind. Perhaps we shall be able to see things more clearly in a month or two, and then we can renew our discussion on the subject.

It pleases me very much to hear that it is you who have undertaken to translate my *Entwicklung etc.*[c]; I look forward eagerly to seeing your work and fully appreciate the honour you have done me.

---

[a] in German - [b] (Russ.) Hermann Lopatin - [c] *Socialism: Utopian and Scientific*

I am, my dear and courageous citizen,

Yours ever,

F. Engels

To Citizen Vera Zasulich

First published, in Russian, in *Gruppa* '*Osvobozhdeniye truda*', No. 1, Moscow, 1924

Printed according to the original

Translated from the French

Published in English for the first time

37

ENGELS TO MAX QUARCK

IN RUDOLSTADT

London, 13 November 1883

Dear Sir,

I have kept you waiting a long time for an answer.[a] Firstly because I had to keep to my bed on account of a mild but tedious indisposition and, secondly, because you are not the first to have approached me about the matter in question. Hence, before I could reply to you, I had to make further inquiries.

The result is that Mr Eduard Bernstein of Zurich has now definitely expressed his intention of translating *The Poverty etc.* into German and has enlisted my support.[118] This I cannot possibly refuse, since he was the first to speak to me about the matter, his qualifications for the task are known to me, and immediate printing in Zurich is assured, should it become apparent that publication in Germany itself might meet with difficulties.

Under the circumstances, and in the knowledge that neither I nor anyone else is legally empowered to prevent you or others from publishing a translation of that work, I have nothing further to say other

---

[a] See this volume, p. 64.

than to express my thanks to you for having thought fit to approach me in the first place.

I remain,

Yours very truly,

F. Engels

First published in: Marx and Engels, *Works*, Second Russian Edition, Vol. 36, Moscow, 1964

Printed according to the original

Published in English for the first time

38

ENGELS TO EDUARD BERNSTEIN

IN ZURICH

London, 13 November 1883

Dear Bernstein,

Encl. for Vera Zasulich.[a]

As to Quarck,[b] you have taken a load off my mind.[119] I have written telling him that *you* were the first to apply and that you would be translating *The Poverty etc.*[118] The man has thus been disposed of. His pamphlet[c] is 'Quarck'.[d] Marx would wring my neck were I to agree to his being translated by this boastful Hohenzollern-worshipper and conservative state socialist.

But it behoves us to make a proper job of it. Nothing pedestrian; the thing is by no means so easy. You might, if you have got as far, send me the ms. of the first sheet; that would give us an opportunity to agree upon the whole *modus operandi*.

I have not been sent Plekhanov's pamphlet[e]; only the *Manifesto* and *Wage Labour and Capital*.[f] From this I learn that it has appeared in a *German* edition.[120] Why has no one deigned to send me and Marx's heirs a copy?

Nor have I ever received a copy of the new edition of the *Manifesto*

----

[a] See this volume, pp. 65-66. - [b] Ibid., p. 66. - [c] [M. Quarck,] *Kommerzienrath Adolf Fleischmann als Nationalökonom...* - [d] In German 'Quark' = curd or cottage cheese; fig. rubbish. - [e] G. V. Plekhanov, *Социализмъ и политическая борьба* (Socialism and Political Struggle). - [f] by Marx

(German).[a] Nor yet of the 3rd edition of *Entwicklung*.[b] And I have never heard a word of what became of 'The Mark', which had been trimmed to size expressly for a separate edition.[121] This, of course, only happens to one when 'easy-going' Germans are involved.

Of the portraits of me in existence there is only one that you have got; I don't imagine that the man (in Brighton) would quote a cheap price for prints in bulk, but I shall do what I can. So you see, *I* bear no grudge against your office,[c] but their worships could well be a little less touchy about a bad joke, especially since they devote a full half column of every number to that kind of thing.

Beware of the *Droit à la paresse*.[122] Parts of it were too much even for the French and it was much exploited by Malon and Brousse at Lafargue's expense. You must certainly see to it that the wailers[123] are not provided with an easy excuse just now; even friend Bebel is still somewhat Germanic in this respect. Which reminds me of the poem about the 'arse'. If the author is responsible for all the heroic deeds enumerated therein, he is entitled to celebrate them in song. Besides, I am speaking of the sex organs, and it is difficult for me to enter into discussion with people who include their bottoms under that heading.

It certainly must have been hard for our friend Lavrov to have set his hand to a document saying that he and his Russians 'had definitively broken with their anarchist traditions'.[124] Not that he set much store by them, but all the same there was about them something attractively 'Russian'. Besides, he is a thoroughly honest old fellow who is, however, invariably the hen that hatches out ducks' eggs in the form of 'Russian youth' and watches aghast as the ducklings set out across the HORRIBLE water. This has happened to him umpteen times.

Kautsky's visit[125] will give me much pleasure; I trust I shall be up to the mark again by then.

Yours,
F. E.

First published, in Russian, in *Marx-Engels Archives*, Book I, Moscow, 1924

Printed according to the original

Published in English for the first time

---

[a] K. Marx and F. Engels, *Manifesto of the Communist Party*. - [b] F. Engels, *Socialism: Utopian and Scientific*. - [c] i. e. *Der Sozialdemokrat*

39

ENGELS TO JOHANN PHILIPP BECKER

IN GENEVA

London, 30 November 1883

Dear Old Man,

I can't tell you how glad I was to see your own handwriting again. Nowhere had I been able to learn anything definite about how you were getting on, and am now glad to know that you are at least to some extent back on your feet again.

I, too, have been in bed for a good month now, in order to rid myself of a mild but most tiresome and prolonged ailment, and can only write very briefly since any position but the horizontal is forbidden me. But no doubt I, too, will soon be up again and able to tackle the large accumulation of work.

As soon as I can resume the task of putting Marx's papers in order, I shall look out the things you want,[126] but everything is still in the utmost disorder since I have to attend to everything myself. Mme Lafargue has been living in Paris for a year or more now, and the youngest sister[a] has furnished a couple of rooms nearby — nearby being half an hour's walk from here, and since it is I alone who must decide what is important and what is not among the vast mass of papers, etc., it is understandable that, considering her many literary activities, she should leave the sorting out to me.

I, too, hope that I shall see you again, my old comrade-in-arms, somewhere some day — who knows whether it might not be, as once before, at Durlach and Vöhrenbach in mid-campaign[127]? How wonderful that would be! And, after all, the present swindle can't go on for very much longer, provided Mr Bismarck does not again hold up or temporarily obstruct revolutionary developments by unleashing a general war, as is clearly his intention.

You will be getting from the post office a money order for £5 sterling.

---

[a] Eleanor Marx

But now I must lie down flat on my back again. Goodbye, old man.
See that you get fit again, and write sometimes to your old, trusty

F. Engels

First published in: F. Engels, *Vergessene
Briefe (Briefe Friedrich Engels' an Johann
Philipp Becker)*, Berlin, 1920

Printed according to the original

Published in English for the first
time

40

ENGELS TO KARL KAUTSKY

IN LONDON [128]

[London, 1 December 1883]

Dear Kautsky,

What can be the matter? Not a sign of you either at Tussy's or at
my house!

Yours,
F. E.

First published in *Aus der Frühzeit des Marxismus. Engels Briefwechsel mit Kautsky*,
Prag, 1935

Printed according to the original

Published in English for the first
time

41

ENGELS TO LAURA LAFARGUE

IN PARIS

London, 13 December 1883

My dear Laura,

I did not intend to write to you until I should be able to inform you
that I was 'up and doing' again. To-day it is eight weeks that I went

to bed for good (or rather bad) and although I feel considerably better, and keep in bed more for safety's sake than anything else, I am still far from able to use my legs as I ought to. These poor 'lower extremities' to use the language of respectability, are woefully shrunk, and what is quite as bad, have left scarcely anything 'behind them'. The worst is I am quite at ease only when laid flat on my back and writing has to be done in a constrained position and soon becomes a torture, so this must excuse my short and unfrequent letters.

Paul's article in *Progress* [a] I read with much pleasure, it hits more than one nail on the head. Let us hope the 'Blé' will come out soon after the period of *étrennes*, [b] [114] and be followed soon by that novel [c] which I am most anxious to see. Paul in Balzac's slippers it will be good! By the bye I have been reading scarcely anything but Balzac while laid up and enjoyed the grand old fellow thoroughly. *There* is the history of France from 1815 to 1848, far more than in all the Vaulabelles, Capefigues, Louis Blancs and *tutti quanti*. [d] And what boldness! What a revolutionary dialectic in his poetical justice!

But alas, we always drop back from the blooming field of romance into the dreary sick-bed of reality. This bids fair to be a poor Christmas! In the best of cases I may be allowed to spend it on the first floor, with order to go to my bedroom when one ought to begin to enjoy oneself! And no tipple, or at all events wine to be taken by the spoonful, as medicine! Well it can't be helped.

Percy is now partner of 'Garman and Rosher, Chartered Accountants' Walbrook House, E. C. Hope he will prosper. His father has at last forked out the needful and set him up though with the sourest face and in the unpleasantest way possible.

Tussy has got neuralgia again, she will call here to-night, but only after this letter has gone. The Jutas (he, she, [e] and Willa) arrived here last week, so Tussy will have plenty on her hands.

Kapital, 3rd edition [f] now fully printed, will be issued very soon; as soon as we get copies we shall send you one.

Pumps and Percy were in Manchester last week, say Jollymeier is not quite well yet. When we are all on our legs again, we must have a continuation of last summer's sprees, and you must then bring Paul

---

[a] P. Lafargue, 'Socialism and Darwinism', *Progress*, Vol. 2, December 1883, pp. 343-49. - [b] Christmas presents - [c] The novel which Lafargue was trying to write was entitled *Jugement de Paris*. - [d] all the rest - [e] Johann Carl and Louise - [f] the third German edition of Volume I of *Capital*

too, unless he is clever enough to get himself locked up again. In the meantime *mille saluts* to him and to you too from

Your affectionate

F. Engels

First published, in the language of the original (English), in: F. Engels, P. et L. Lafargue, *Correspondance*, t. I, Paris, 1956

Reproduced from the original

42

ENGELS TO EDUARD BERNSTEIN [24]

IN ZURICH

[London, 22 December 1883]

If you have still got *The Labour Standard*, will you please send it to *Lafargue straight away*; he gave Shipton's remarks a lambasting in the *Cri du Peuple*, and wants to have the original as the thing is creating a furore.[129] I wouldn't be able to get hold of another copy before Monday, not to say Thursday[a] (and perhaps not even then).

Have been up again since Saturday[b] but still very wobbly.

You gave von der Mark his deserts all right! The fool imagines people should take account of what *he* understands by 'State'![130] Just as Rodbertus criticised Marx for supposing capital to be *real* capital, rather than Rodbertus' 'notion of capital'.[131] German to the core.

Kautsky back?

Regards, yours,

F. E.

First published, in Russian, in *Marx-Engels Archives*, Book I, Moscow, 1924

Printed according to the original

Published in English for the first time

---

[a] 24 and 27 December accordingly - [b] 15 December

1884

43

ENGELS TO EDUARD BERNSTEIN[94]

IN ZURICH

London, 1 January 1884

Dear Bernstein,

First a Happy New Year to you, Kautsky and the whole newspaper office.[a]

Then a request to send me last week's *Sozialdemokrat*. It should have arrived on Saturday, 29 December, but hasn't reached me yet.

A fortnight ago I was at last able to get up again, have improved steadily and hope to be fit for work in a week's time. And a damned good thing too!

I trust you were not too much infuriated by the number of amendments I made to your ms.[118] As I once said to Kautsky, while we cannot imitate Marx's style, our own ought to be such as not to be wholly out of keeping with Marx's. Provided you don't lose sight of this altogether, we may well produce a work that is presentable.

The note on American slavery[b] shall be done, and various others besides. I shall also be able to include a fair amount in the preface.[c] How true the passage on slavery was is still evident today: capitalist production in the cotton states is not prospering — through not having any *coolies*, Chinese or Indian, i. e. slaves disguised as free labour; whereas in Cuba, Mauritius, Réunion, etc., it flourishes in so far as, and only in so far as, it has coolies at its disposal.

As regards your earlier inquiry about the passage from *The Civil War in France* in the preface to the *Manifesto*,[132] you will, no doubt,

---

[a] *Der Sozialdemokrat* - [b] See present edition, Vol. 6, pp. 167-68. - [c] F. Engels, 'Marx and Rodbertus'.

concur with the answer that is given in the original (*The Civil War,*
pp. 19 ff.).[a] I am sending you a copy in case you have not got one
there. It is simply a question of showing that the victorious proletariat
must first reshape the old, bureaucratic, administratively centralised
state machine before they can use it for their own purposes; whereas,
since 1848, *all* bourgeois republicans, so long as they were in opposition, have heaped abuse on that machine but, no sooner in office,
have taken it over intact and made use of it, partly against reaction
but to an even greater extent against the proletariat. That the Commune's *unconscious* tendencies should, in *The Civil War,* have been
credited to it as more or less deliberate plans was justifiable and perhaps even necessary in the circumstances. The Russians have very
properly appended the passage from *The Civil War* to their translation of the *Manifesto.*[133] If there hadn't been such a great
rush over getting it out, we could have done this and one or two other
things.

Apropos. You once spoke of Guesde's disreputable past, or something of the sort. I know absolutely nothing about that. Undoubtedly just a pack of lies on Malon's part, but I should be glad if
you would enable me to clear the matter up.

I shall shortly be sending you one pound sterling from Schorlemmer for his subscription, the balance for party purposes. It's too late
to take out a money order today.

At last things have got moving again in Russia. The affair of the
sledge and the Tsar is most suspect,[134] that of Sudeikin, on the other
hand, crystal clear.[135] We should like to send Alexander[b] a telegram
wishing him 'a happy holiday'.

Has Tussy Marx sent you *To-Day* and the last numbers of *Progress?*
If not I shall attend to this. These two are *completely divorced* from
the TRADES UNIONS movement and are in fact run by a *very motley* society. Bax is very honest but still somewhat green, Aveling is good but
has little time in which to familiarise himself with economics, a subject utterly foreign to him. Joynes is an unreliable chap (once
a schoolmaster at the big doss house at Eton, travelled to Ireland with
Henry George, was arrested with him and lost his post; is therefore
looking around to see what's doing) and Hyndman, an ambitious
party leader *in partibus infidelium,*[c] provisionally in search of a party

---

[a] See present edition, Vol. 22, pp. 328-35. - [b] Alexander III - [c] It means literally:
in parts inhabited by unbelievers; here: nominally.

and meanwhile issuing orders into the blue,—come to that a pretty shrewd fellow.[a] One's best course is to do justice to the aspirations without identifying oneself with the persons. At all events, the publication of *To-Day* and the transformation of *Progress* into a socialist journal is of great significance at this particular juncture, now that the poor in the East End OF London are beginning to find their voice. On top of that, all over the country we have chronic overproduction which now seems to be hastening on the crisis. Circumstances are favourable, but whether the people who have taken the matter in hand are a match for those circumstances remains to be seen. This time it's hardly likely to remain without a sequel, as have so many previous curtain-raisers.

Now *basta*. I haven't written a letter as long as this for the past three months. Schorlemmer and I send our cordial regards to all our friends.

Yours,

F. E.

First published, in Russian, in *Marx-Engels Archives*, Book I, Moscow, 1924

Printed according to the original

Published in English in full for the first time

44

ENGELS TO KARL KAUTSKY

IN ZURICH

London, 9 January 1884[b]

Dear Kautsky,

(Why must we continue to bore each other with 'Mr'?) The news about the coronation scenery is absolutely typical and has aroused much mirth; at the same time we have taken care that it does not leak

---

[a] See this volume, p. 54. - [b] 1883 in the original

out prematurely over here; i. e. before the scenery has been delivered and paid for.[136] Not a soul knows about it apart from Schorlemmer, Lenchen and Tussy.

Many thanks for Frankel's address.

So far as purely theoretical matters are concerned, Deville's summary[a] is the best that has yet appeared. He has understood everything aright, though his use of terminology has been very lax and this I have amended in the manuscript. On the other hand the descriptive part is treated far too cursorily, with the result that some of it is totally incomprehensible to anyone unfamiliar with the original. Again, what would make for much greater ease of comprehension, particularly in a popular account, namely the *historical* emergence of manufacture and large-scale industry as *consecutive historical periods*, is pushed much too much into the background. (We aren't even told that 'factory legislation' does not operate at all in France, but only in England!) And, finally, he gives a full summary of the entire contents, including stuff which Marx had had to bring in if his account of scientific developments was to be complete, but which is not necessary to an understanding of the theory of surplus value and its consequences (and this alone is what counts in the case of a popular summary). Similarly as regards the number of coins in circulation, etc.[b]

But then he also quotes verbatim from Marx's recapitulatory propositions, having given no more than an incomplete account of the assumptions upon which they were based. Consequently these propositions are frequently so distorted that in the course of my perusal I often found myself wanting to contest a proposition of Marx's, the limitations of which are made plain in the original by what goes before; in Deville, however, they are accorded absolutely universal, and hence false, validity. I can't change this without redoing the whole ms.

Now as to your translation of this,[137] my position vis-à-vis Meissner compels me to adopt an entirely neutral position. As soon as you write and tell me definitely that you will take the thing on, I propose, and I have already discussed this with Tussy who shares my view entirely, to act as follows: I shall write to Meissner saying that someone intends to publish Deville's piece (which I shall send Meissner) in German and that I can see nothing in this that might damage the sales of *Capital* — boost them, more likely; I shall then add that I can-

---

[a] G. Deville, *Le Capital de Karl Marx. Résumé et accompagné d'un aperçu sur le socialisme scientifique.* - [b] See *Capital*, Vol. I, Part I, Ch. III, Sect. 2b (present edition, Vol. 35).

not stop it but that, if he intends to take preventive action, he might let me know and I shall then pass this on.

Seen in the abstract (i. e. disregarding Meissner), a new popular and *short* account (*half* the size of Deville) of the theory of surplus value is much needed, and Deville's work is, so far as theory goes, far better than the rest. What should be dropped are 1) detailed references to the individual chapters and subsections of *Capital* and, 2) anything that is not necessary to an understanding of the theory of surplus value. This will involve rewriting the descriptive part from the beginning, and also considerable abridgement. It would allay the worst of Meissner's misgivings, especially if we changed the title to e. g. *Unpaid Labour and Its Transformation into Capital* or something of the kind.

At worst the thing could be printed by Dietz and published in Switzerland, like Bebel's *Frau*.[138]

So give the matter some thought and drop me a line.

I enclose the two photographs[a] for you and Motteler.

The business of the missing no. of the *Sozialdemokrat* has since been cleared up — the greatest success scored by Social Democracy to date is to have contrived *to put 53 weeks into a year*,[139] — a real miracle. Just let them carry on like that and we'll all live two per cent longer.

Kindest regards to Bernstein and yourself from

Yours,

F. E.

I had intended to enclose a one pound money order from Schorlemmer but it is now too late; must do so in my next. When does Tussy's and my subscription expire? Up till yesterday she had not received her *Sozialdemokrat* either. Might it have been forgotten? Kindly look into it.

First published, in Russian, in *Marx-Engels Archives*, Vol. I (VI), Moscow, 1932

Printed according to the original

Published in English for the first time

---

[a] of Engels

45

ENGELS TO LAURA LAFARGUE

IN PARIS

London, 14 January 1884

My dear Laura,

Herewith cheque £15.- which I hope will stop the landlord's cravings. The same dearth of news of which you complain, reigns supreme here, and old Nim and I have the house much to ourselves, of which I at least do not much complain, being still rather shaky and progressing only slowly. Percy is very busy in his new concern, and has had very poor health lately, rheumatism, erysipelas of the nose, and to wind up, catarrh of the stomach. Tussy and Aveling called yesterday. 'Yesterday' reminds me of *To-Day* which I suppose you have got. A rather motley society[a] of most of which lot Heine said: *Viel dunklere Wolke war die Idee, die ihr im Herzen getragen.*[b] Well, it's a beginning, and they will weed each other out in time.[c]

Do you receive the *Sozialdemokrat?* If not, let me know. There ought to be an exchange of publications between Zurich and Paris which you might organise, it will prevent such blunders and misunderstandings as were current some time ago. Kautsky wishes to translate Deville's *Capital*,[137] has a copy been sent to Zurich? If not please see to it (address Redaktion *Sozialdemokrat*, Volksbuchhandlung, Hottingen-Zurich, Suisse). If this translation be done, I shall require another copy to be sent to Meissner, to prevent unpleasantness hereafter. I shall let you know, as soon as it is settled.

Herewith 5 photos of Mohr and 4 of mine. Of Mohr's you can have as many as you like, large or small.

Paul's examples of victorious German 'goût' are mostly as old as the hills.[140] That German *gravures pour enfants (Bilderbogen)*[d] are generally good, is simple enough. For more than 50 years they have been made chiefly at Düsseldorf, Munich, etc., and the designs are by young and often rising artists who do this work to earn a little money. 40 years ago however I recollect that French *gravures* of that sort came

---

[a] See this volume, p. 74. - [b] The thought you carried in your heart was a much darker cloud. - [c] Cf. this volume, p. 82. - [d] pictures for children (picture-sheets)

to Germany, a good many by Adam the horse- and soldier-painter, and they were immensely superior to the German ones in chic and life. If that has not been continued by French artists, they must have found no market.

As to *toys*, the German superiority is 1) cheapness, domestic industry at starvation level (described lately by Dr Emanuel Sax, *Die Hausindustrie in Thüringen*, very good) and 2) in that they are invented by *peasants*; townspeople never will be fit to invent for children, least of all French townspeople who hate their own children.

For *furniture* Paul gives the reason himself: the stupid fiscal policy of the French government.

Flowers similar: division of labour and low wages: who can compete against the East End of London and Germany in cheapness? Generally speaking, bourgeois taste is getting so much out of taste that even the Germans may hope to be able to satisfy it. And if any trade has become broken down enough to make 'cheap and nasty' its market-rule, then you may be sure the Germans will step in and defeat all competition by starving their own workpeople. And as this is the rule generally now for all trades, it explains the appearance of German goods in all trades and all markets.

I sent Lavroff last Thursday's *Standard* containing a report of an interview of their correspondent with a Petersburg police chief and in which Lavroff is blamed for all — the whole thing of course got up for the benefit of the philistine, but so stupidly that the effect aimed at is visible plainly in every word.[135]

Jollymeier left here last Monday,[a] better a good deal, but not yet himself again. Sam Moore did not come at all, he had a bad catarrh of the stomach and is now busy at the court of chancery in Manchester and Liverpool. He is doing very well indeed in law-business, for a beginner.

Had a letter from Meyer[b] this morning informing me that he will not be here till March, and asking from me nothing less than to forward to him all the material I have for the history of German Socialism up to 1852! which of course I want myself for Mohr's biography.[30] Of course I shall decline.

---

[a] 7 January - [b] Rudolf Hermann Meyer

Nim sends her love to you and Paul, and to use the sacramental philistine British phrase, I 'join' her.

Very affectionately yours,

F. E.

First published, in the language of the original (English), in: F. Engels, P. et L. Lafargue, *Correspondance*, t. I, Paris, 1956

Reproduced from the original

46

ENGELS TO AUGUST BEBEL [94]

IN BORSDORF NEAR LEIPZIG [34]

London, 18 January 1884

Dear Bebel,

At last I have recovered sufficiently to spend at least a few hours a day at my desk and thus fulfil my obligations in regard to letter-writing. The thing was neither serious nor painful, but damned tedious and *gênant*,[a] and I shall have to take great care of myself for some little while yet.

You will have received my letter about Miss Issleib written in bed in pencil. Since I have heard nothing more, I can only suppose the matter has been dropped.[141] — I dictated to Kautsky, who happened to be on the spot,[125] a letter to Liebknecht[39] which I hope he has received and shown to you as requested. From it you will have seen that I am under no illusions as to the American business,[b] nor was I in any way inclined to give you the impression that I regarded the thing as absolutely essential. But I still maintain that, if it is to succeed, you two must go and no one else. Whether you can do so, I have absolutely no idea — you will know best. But this much is certain — no amount of American money will make good the damage that will infallibly be done if, after the manner of Fritzsche and Viereck, the emissaries again water down the party's viewpoint into a semblance

---

[a] inconvenient - [b] See this volume, p. 14.

of vulgar democracy and homespun philistinism.[47] And your presence would certainly be the best guarantee that nothing of the sort would happen.

I was delighted by the good news you sent me about the movement's progress. The government could not, in fact, have hit on any better means of keeping the movement going and intensifying it than by everywhere involving our chaps in these violent local struggles with the police, particularly when the police in Germany is made up of such worthless characters that our lads can turn the enemy's own weapons against him and take the offensive. And if, on top of that,— as recently in Berlin—the police are confused by constantly changing instructions from above, so much the better.

Should there be any repetition of the attempt to bring 'the right to work' back into fashion,[142] I would write something about it in the *Sozialdemokrat*. I have discussed this with Kautsky[a]; but first I should like Geiser and Co. to commit themselves a bit, to produce something tangible for us to go on, though Kautsky maintains that they won't. These ne'r-do-well students, shop assistants, etc., are the bane of the movement. They know less than nothing and are, for that very reason, reluctant to learn anything at all; their so-called socialism is nothing but philistine hot air.

Whether you will rid yourselves of the emergency article,[67] I cannot say; there will always be the pretext that only in this way is it possible to protect the person of old William,[b] a phrase before which all Philistia will grovel on their bellies.

Many thanks for your book *Die Frau*.[138] I read it with great interest and there is much in it that is very good. What you say about the development of industry in Germany is particularly good and clear. This is a matter to which I, too, have again been turning my attention of late and I would, given the time, write something about it for the *Sozialdemokrat*. Odd, how the philistines fail to realise that the 'plague of vagabonds' they so lament is, in the present state of agriculture and handicrafts in Germany, the inescapable consequence of the rise of large-scale industry, or that, because Germany is always the last to arrive on the scene, the development of this selfsame large-scale industry can only take place there under the constant pressure of poor business conditions. For the Germans are only able to com-

---

[a] See this volume, p. 55. - [b] William I

pete by paying lower wages, depressed to starvation level, and by regularly exploiting to the utmost the cottage industry that forms the background to manufacturing industry. The transformation of handicrafts into cottage industry and the gradual transformation of cottage industry, in so far as this pays, into manufacturing and machinery—such is the present trend in Germany. So far, the only large-scale industry proper we have is iron; in the textile industry—thanks to starvation wages and the fact that weavers possess potato plots—the hand-loom still prevails.

In this country, too, industry has taken on a different character. The ten-year cycle would seem to have been disrupted since 1870, when American and German competition began to destroy England's monopoly of the world market. Since 1868 business has been slack in the main branches, while production has been gradually increasing; and now, here and in America, we appear to be on the eve of another crisis which has not, in England, been preceded by a period of prosperity. That is the secret behind the sudden emergence of the socialist movement over here—sudden, although it has been slowly maturing for the past 3 years. Organised labour—TRADE UNIONS—has, as yet, no sort of connection with it; the movement proceeds under 'educated' elements of bourgeois origin, some of whom seek to make contact with the masses and occasionally succeed in so doing. Morally and intellectually, these elements vary considerably and it will be some time before they sort themselves out and the position becomes clear. But the thing is hardly likely to fizzle out again altogether. Henry George and his nationalisation of land [143] may well play a meteoric role because this issue is of traditional significance over here—of real significance, too, owing to the vast dimensions of the big estates. But in the long run this by itself must cease to have any pull in what is the world's leading industrial country. Besides, George is a bourgeois born and bred, and *his* plan of meeting all state expenditure out of rent is merely a second edition of the *Ricardian* school's plan, i. e. purely bourgeois.

If you wish to study a model of state socialism, then take a look at *Java*. There the Dutch government has, on the basis of the old, communistic village communities, organised production as a whole along such nicely socialist lines, and so neatly assumed control of the sale of all produce that, apart from some 100 million marks for army and civil service pay, there remains each year a clear profit of some 70 million marks for payment of interest to the luckless creditors of the Dutch state.[a] Bismarck is a mere child by comparison!

One way or another, we shall have a Russian constitution in the course of this year, and then the fun will begin.

Your
F. E.

First published, in Russian, in *Marx-Engels Archives*, Vol. I (VI), Moscow, 1932

Printed according to the original

Published in English in full for the first time

47

ENGELS TO AUGUST BEBEL

IN BORSDORF NEAR LEIPZIG [34]

London, 23 January 1884

Dear Bebel,

I forgot to say in Saturday's letter[b] that you and Liebknecht should on no account order copies of the third edition of *Capital*[c] since we shall be sending one for each of you as soon as we get any. A third will go to the party archives in Zurich.[144]

Tussy will have written to you regarding a translation of *Die Frau*.[145] It's unlikely that you'll get any royalties from it, though there's no harm in trying—at most 3 PENCE = 0.25 mark per copy sold; that is the usual form here. The actual book could, I believe, only fetch, say, 2 à 2.50 marks here, of which 30% at least would go to the retail booksellers. Moreover, the kind of publishers who deal in such books are very few and far between and also *pauvres*.[d] We ourselves shall have to invest something like £200 in cash in the English edition of *Capital*,[56] and may also have to advance the translator's fee,

---

[a] See this volume, pp. 102-03. -[b] See previous letter. -[c] the third German edition of Volume I of *Capital* -[d] poor

and then work on a fifty-fifty basis; it probably couldn't be done in any other way.

Kindest regards to Liebknecht and yourself from

Your

F. E.

First published, in Russian, in *Marx-Engels Archives*, Vol. I (VI), Moscow, 1932

Printed according to the original

Published in English for the first time

48

ENGELS TO CHARLES FITZGERALD [146]

IN LONDON

[Draft]

[London, between 26 and 28 January 1884]

Enclosed I beg to hand you post office order 10[sh.] 10 for my year's subscription to *Justice*.

I am so overcharged with work, not only for the immediate future, but for a considerable period of time to come, that it would be folly on my part to promise contributions to your paper. I have been disabled from active work for the last six months and am only now slowly regaining the strength necessary to accomplish my most urgent task — to prepare for the press the manuscripts left by my late friend Marx. So that I am bound to devote all my time. I did promise an article to *To-Day* but that was in better days and I am afraid they too will have to wait.

First published in: Marx and Engels, *Works*, First Russian Edition, Vol. XXVII, Moscow, 1935

Reproduced from the original

Published in English for the first time

49

ENGELS TO EDUARD BERNSTEIN [94]

IN ZURICH

London, 28 January 1884

Dear Bernstein,

You\will have got my letter of the 1st, as will Kautsky that of the 9th.[a] I am in some doubt about the latter, being unsure of the number of the house (38?); I also sent him the photographs he wanted.[b]

My inquiry today concerns the following:

Various things among Marx's papers will be suitable for the party archives [144]; just now I am in process of sorting his books, etc., and am glad to be again in a condition to do so. Besides these, however, there is a good deal of superfluous stuff which would be very useful to an editorial library for the party organ[c] and is superfluous here, as we have *in duplo*.[d] Firstly dictionaries: 1) the big French-German Mozin-Peschier, 5 volumes quarto, binding very dilapidated, 2) the old Italian Jagemann, also very good, 3) Spanish, Dutch, Danish, perhaps even more. I can't yet be sure whether Tussy might not want to keep one thing or another; if not shall I send them to Zurich with the remainder? Besides these, one thing or another will continue to turn up and could be offered to you, once I know that you are interested.

Further, as regards *Justice*. This paper has suddenly been launched upon the world by Hyndman with insufficient financial and absolutely *no* literary preparation. *To-Day* might survive and within 6 to 12 months pave the way for a weekly. But as it is the two of them are bound to sap each other's strength. Hyndman, however, cannot wait and will probably burn his fingers yet again. They have asked me to contribute, but I refused on the grounds of lack of time. One can send stuff to *To-Day* without hesitation; but this won't do in the case of a weekly purporting to be a party organ until one knows the whys

---

[a] See this volume, pp. 73-75 and 75-77. - [b] of Engels - [c] i. e. *Der Sozialdemok-rat* - [d] duplicate copies

and wherefores. It is apparent from the complete dearth of ideas in the first two numbers that the chaps are at their wits' end and are looking to new contributors for further material. In short it has misfired and only an unexpectedly favourable turn of events can put it on its feet.

In case Mr von der Mark or anyone else should again speak of our 'concessions' to the anarchists,[130] the following passages prove that we had proclaimed the cessation [Aufhören] of the state before the anarchists even existed: *Misere de la philosophie*, page 177:

'*La classe laborieuse substituera, dans son développement, à l'ancienne société civile une association qui excluera les classes et leur antagonisme, et il · n'y aura plus de pouvoir politique proprement dit, puisque le pouvoir politique est précisément le résumé officiel de l'antagonisme dans la société civile.*'[a]

Manifesto, end of Section II:

'When, in the course of development, class distinctions have disappeared ... *the public power will lose its political character. Political power, properly so called, is merely the organised power of one class for oppressing another.*'[b]

The last issue of the *Sozialdemokrat*[c] was again very good. Cheerful and plenty of meat in it. Admittedly this last does not always depend upon the editors. Your rendering of Lafargue is truly delightful; the German substitutions cheered me up enormously.[122]

Regards to Kautsky.

Yours,

F. E.

First published, in Russian, in *Marx-Engels Archives*, Book I, Moscow, 1924

Printed according to the original

Published in English in full for the first time

---

[a] 'The working class, in the course of its development, will substitute for the old civil society an association which will exclude classes and their antagonism, *and there will be no more political power properly so-called, since political power is precisely the official expression of antagonism in civil society*' (K. Marx, *The Poverty of Philosophy*, present edition, Vol. 6, p. 212). - [b] See present edition, Vol. 6, p. 505. - [c] No. 4, 24 January 1884.

50

ENGELS TO LUDWIK KRZYWICKI

IN BORSDORF NEAR LEIPZIG [34]

[Draft]

London, 28 January 1884
122 Regent's Park Road, N. W.

Dear Comrade,

In reply to your kind note of the 23rd inst.,[147] we shall be only too happy to welcome the appearance of a Polish translation of Karl Marx's *Capital* and are perfectly willing to assist, in so far as this lies in our power, in the removal of any obstacles that stand in the way of its publication.

Accordingly, in our capacity as the author's literary executors, we [a] hereby give you our express permission to publish this translation [b] and we wish you every success.

First published in: Marx and Engels, *Works*, First Russian Edition, Vol. XXVII, Moscow, 1935

Printed according to the original

Published in English for the first time

51

ENGELS TO PYOTR LAVROV [1]

IN PARIS

London, 28 January 1884
122 Regent's Park Road, N. W.

My dear Lavrov,

Some three weeks ago I sent you a *Standard* containing an article I thought might be of interest to you [c]; I hope it reached you safely.

[a] Frederick Engels and Eleanor Marx - [b] In the original the following words are deleted: 'in so far as we are empowered to give such permission'. - [c] See this volume, p. 79.

I am at present engaged — as my health at long last permits — in
sorting out the books, etc., left by Marx. Amongst other things they
comprise, thanks to the kindness of Danielson, an entire library of
Russian books, with some very important material on present social
conditions in Russia; it contains almost everything that has been
brought out on the subject. At my age, and overburdened as I am
with work, it would be impossible for me to resume a novo[a] the
thorough-going survey of Russia so unfortunately interrupted by the
death of our friend.[57] So it seemed to me, and Tussy is of the same opinion, that it was our duty to place these books at your disposal. In
your capacity as the acknowledged representative of the revolutionary Russian emigration and as an old friend of the deceased, you have
clearly more right than anyone else to the collection of books so devot-
edly provided by friends, both yours and ours, in Russia — either for
your personal use or to form the nucleus of a library for the revolutionary Russian emigration. If you accept, I could send them either
to your own address or to any other you might indicate this February. The only books I should keep here would be those from which
Marx had made extracts, along with one or two others which I might
need for the second volume of *Capital*[4]; the remainder when all deductions have been made, would amount to a hundred or so volumes
at the outside.[148]

As for the second volume, I am at last beginning to see daylight. For
the most important parts — i. e. the beginning and the end of the second book, *Circulation of Capital*,— we have a version dating from
1875 and later. To this nothing needs to be added save quotations in
accordance with the indications supplied. For the middle section
there are no fewer than four versions dating from before 1870, and
therein lies the only difficulty.[17] The third volume, *Capitalist Production as a Whole*, exists in two versions dating from before 1869; subsequent to that there is nothing but a few notes and a notebook full of
equations, the purpose of which is to arrive at the many reasons why
the *Mehrwertsrate* becomes the *Profitrate*.[b][149] But the extracts from books
both on Russia and on the United States[80] contain a vast amount of
material and copious notes on land rent, while others relate to money
capital, to credit and to paper money as an instrument of credit, etc.
As yet I do not know what use I shall be able to make of this for the
third book; it might perhaps be better to combine them in a separate

---

[a] anew - [b] the rate of surplus value becomes the rate of profit

publication, and I shall certainly do so if the difficulty of incorporating them into *Capital* proves too great. My chief concern is that the book should come out as soon as possible, and also and above all that the book I publish should be unmistakably a work by *Marx.*

Any day now we should receive copies of the 3rd edition of Volume I, [a] and one will be sent off to you as soon as they arrive.

The Russian publications from Geneva—the *Manifesto*, etc.[78]—gave me much pleasure.

I have just had a letter from two Poles, Krzywicki and Sosnowski, requesting our [b] consent to a Polish translation of *Capital* which, of course, we gave.[c] Sosnowski is in Paris; do you, by any chance, know these citizens? [150]

Yours ever,

F. Engels

First published in: Marx and Engels, *Works*, First Russian Edition, Vol. XXVII, Moscow, 1935

Printed according to the original

Translated from the French

Published in English in full for the first time

52

ENGELS TO KARL KAUTSKY

IN ZURICH

London, 4 February 1884

Dear Kautsky,

A quick line before the post goes.

Please write and tell me by return *what* sort of version you propose to do of Deville [137]—word for word, including all the titles, or abridged, as I suggested? [d] As soon as I know this, I can put the matter to Meissner; I must have something definite to tell him. A copy has been ordered for Meissner in Paris; by the time it arrives, your answer may have got here as well.

---

[a] of the third German edition of Volume I of *Capital* - [b] Engels' and Eleanor Marx's - [c] See previous letter. - [d] See this volume, pp. 76-77.

I shall be glad to look over the *theoretical* part, although I can hardly suppose it is necessary. There's no point in my looking over the descriptive part, as you won't have any difficulty in avoiding Deville's mistakes. Of these the chief is his presenting as absolute, Marxian propositions which, in Marx, hold good only with qualifications (omitted by Deville) and which therefore appear false.

All other matters in a day or two.

Yours,

F. E.

First published, in Russian, in *Marx-Engels Archives*, Vol. I (VI), Moscow, 1932

Printed according to the original

Published in English for the first time

53

ENGELS TO EDUARD BERNSTEIN [61]

IN ZURICH

London, 5 February 1884

Dear Bernstein,

You can set your mind at rest about one thing: I could wish for no better translator than you yourself.[118] In attempting, in the first sheet, to give an accurate and precise rendering of the sense, you have paid rather too little attention to the syntax, *voilà tout*.[a] Moreover I wanted to incorporate Marx's idiosyncratic syntax which is unfamiliar to you; hence the many emendations.

If, having once put the sense into German, you go through the ms. again with an eye to readable syntax, at the same time bearing in mind that you should wherever possible avoid the wearisome syntax of the schoolroom which always puts the verb of the subordinate clause right at the end — and which was drummed into all of us —, you will have little difficulty and be perfectly capable of putting everything right yourself.

---

[a] that's all

You would do best to send me the ms. *by sections*, each of them ± [a] a whole, 1, $1^1/_2$ or 2 printed sheets at a time. In which case I shall also supply the notes for it straight away. I should also like to see the proofs; many things look quite different in print.

Please send me the article on Proudhon in the old *Social-Demokrat*.[151] I had overlooked it; the *whole thing* might have to go into the preface. You will get it back, of course.

As regards von der Mark and the *Volkszeitung*, I am entirely of your opinion.[130] When Marx died, Schewitsch *falsified* my telegram to Sorge and printed it as though it had been sent to the *Volkszeitung*. I protested.[b] He glossed over the falsification with the lie that the first word had been illegible — though he copied it *correctly*! while the other he had 'considered necessary in the interests of the paper'! Moreover he thought it 'petty' of me to have drawn his attention to it. Petty it certainly was not, *magnanimous* rather, considering the way those gentlemen took advantage of Marx's death to draw attention to themselves and proclaim their semi-alliance with Most. However, Schewitsch is the last Russian socialist aristocrat; such men must always 'go further than anyone else' and are accustomed to use the world at large as a means to serve their own ends. The article on tolerance was downright silly.[152] Russians have set about one another *con amore*,[c] as have the Irish.

I don't know whether you get the *Travailleur*, etc.; I receive a few copies from time to time and shall send them to you. Also two *Sozialdemokrats* with scorings by Marx which might interest you.

I shall keep Schorlemmer's pound here then; will you debit me with this, in return credit Schorlemmer with his annual subscription, and pay the balance (inserting an announcement to this effect in the *Sozialdemokrat*) into the election fund.[d] Similarly, will you debit me with Tussy's and my subscriptions, supposing that she doesn't decide to send you *To-Day* in exchange. Finally, will you alter Tussy's address and send items to

Miss Marx,
32 Great Coram St., London, W. C.

As to what is to be done with the money for Marx's memorial, I have absolutely no idea.[e] How much is there altogether? If you wish,

---

[a] more or less - [b] F. Engels, 'To the Editors of the *New Yorker Volkszeitung*' (18 April 1883); see also this volume, pp. 13-14. - [c] Here: with a will. - [d] 'Allgemeiner Wahlfonds', *Der Sozialdemokrat*, No. 9, 28 February 1884. - [e] See this volume, p. 17.

I shall write an article for your issue of 14 March. Let me know roughly what it should be about so that it fits into your scheme.[153]

Meissner, then, will doubtless still have copies of the *18th Brumaire*[a]; his failure to push it is doubtless attributable to timidity. Marx sold him the *entire* edition, so there is nothing we can do.[b]

Tussy has taken the best of the dictionaries—French and Italian—but there are still plenty left and I have made certain that you get one particularly nice item—the editorial copy of the *Neue Rheinische Zeitung*. The parcel will go off in the course of this month.

I don't know of any poems—*König Dampf*, perhaps, from my *Condition of the Working-Class*[c]? A search is being made here for the English original, but it seems to have fallen into oblivion, like the Serbian of Goethe's lament of Hassan Aga's noble wife, only still more so, since the latter does after all still exist in black and white.

What wouldn't Bismarck give to have the 'Viennese in Berlin', namely the anarchists! A perfect caricature of the Russians—though obviously *bred by the police*![154]

Yours,

F. E.

First published, in Russian, in *Marx-Engels Archives*, Book I, Moscow, 1924

Printed according to the original

Published in English in full for the first time

54

ENGELS TO PYOTR LAVROV[1]

IN PARIS

London, 5 February 1884

My dear Lavrov,

So I shall send you the books; that is agreed.[d]

The 2nd volume[e]—ah! If you only knew, my old friend, how it

---

[a] K. Marx, *The Eighteenth Brumaire of Louis Bonaparte.* - [b] See Marx's letter to Engels of 29 January 1869 (present edition, Vol. 43, p. 211).- [c] E. P. Mead, 'The Steam King'; see present edition, Vol. 4, pp. 474-77. - [d] See this volume, p. 88.- [e] of Marx's *Capital*

weighs on me! But then six months have gone to waste, thanks to my infernal illness. And, even so, I shan't be able to set about things seriously before the middle of March. It will take me up till then to get all the books, papers, periodicals, etc., in order, and I can't work on them for more than a few hours a day without becoming overtired. It weighs on me all the more heavily for the knowledge that *there is not another living soul* who can decipher that writing and those abbreviations of words and style. As to publication by instalments,[155] that will depend to some extent upon the editor and upon legislation in Germany; hitherto I have not thought such a method particularly useful for a book of this kind. I shall try and do what Лопатинъ[a] wants in regard to the proofs. But then Въра Засуличъ[b] wrote to me a couple of months ago asking whether I would allow her to do the translation. I told her that I regarded Лопатинъ as having first refusal and that it was still too soon to talk about the matter.[c] What could be discussed at once, however, would be the possibility of publishing the translation *in Russia*. Do you think that might be done? The 2nd book is purely scientific, dealing solely with questions *as from bourgeois to bourgeois*, but the 3rd will contain passages which make me doubt the very possibility of their being published in Germany under the Anti-Socialist Law.[37]

The same difficulty applies to the publication of Marx's complete works, and that is only one of the many difficulties to be overcome. I have some 60 sheets (each of 16 printed pages) of old manuscripts by Marx and myself dating from between 1845 and 1848. Of this material only extracts could be published, but I shan't be able to get down to it until I have finished with the manuscript of the 2nd volume of *Capital*. So all we can do is wait.

The article you speak of,[156] and which we no longer have here, will amount to between 3 and 5 printed sheets; it is a detailed summary of the political development of France from 24 February 1848 up till 1851. It is summed up in the *18th Brumaire*[d] but all the same it is worth translating. I myself am on the lookout for a complete set of the *Neue Rheinische Zeitung Revue*,[e] only ²/₅ths of which are in my possession.

---

[a] (Russ.) Lopatin - [b] (Russ.) Vera Zasulich - [c] See this volume, p. 65. - [d] K. Marx, *The Eighteenth Brumaire of Louis Bonaparte.* - [e] *Neue Rheinische Zeitung. Politisch-ökonomische Revue*

Deville sent me his manuscript [81] for revision. Being indisposed, I confined myself to the theoretical part where I found little that needed correcting. However the descriptive part has been done in too great haste. To begin with, it is at times unintelligible to anyone who has not read the original and, what is more, he frequently presents Marx's conclusions while passing over the conditions under which those conclusions alone hold good; at times that gives a somewhat false impression. I have drawn his attention to this, but they were much too eager to publish the book.

Yours ever,

F. Engels

First published in: Marx and Engels, *Works*, First Russian Edition, Vol. XXVII, Moscow, 1935

Printed according to the original

Translated from the French

Published in English in full for the first time

55

ENGELS TO LAURA LAFARGUE

IN PARIS

London, 5 February 1884

My dear Laura,

I knew he[a] would turn up again. Received the *Travailleur*. Much amused that Paul and Guesde had '*manqué train*'.[b][157] Hope soon to receive good news about the children,[c] Tussy is rather anxious about them; and hope you got over your cold. Nim has caught one just as bad as yours can be, I wanted her last night to take a hot whisky night-cap, but she declined, so you may think. Pumps is below, she called yesterday with Elsa, who looks as *plain* as ever (and quite as *angular* at the same time), they met Tussy and Aveling here, who called on business; Bradlaugh and Mrs Besant are furious at the new

---

[a] Paul Lafargue - [b] 'missed the train' - [c] Jean, Edgar, Marcel and Jenny Longuet

Socialist 'rage' in London which threatens to cut short their vittles, and so have opened an attack or two on Tussy and Aveling. Bradlaugh throws about the most mysterious innuendos about Mohr's having preached assassination and arson and having been in secret league with Continental governments,—but nothing tangible.[158] I want to get him to come out a bit more, before I unmask *my* batteries.

Nim and I are now busy among the books at Maitland Park.[159] There are a good many that would be uselessly heaped up in my place or at Tussy's, indeed there will be no room here for more than half. Now there is a lot of good French books and valuable, which we thought might be more useful in your and Paul's hands than anywhere else, for instance:

Mably, *Oeuvres complètes.*

Adam Smith in French (capital edition bound).[a]

Malthus—ditto.[b]

Guizot, *Histoire de la civilisation en France.*

All the books about the French Revolution (Loustalot,[c] *deux amis de la liberté,*[160] etc., etc.).

Now if you will have them we will send them to you free of charge. I cannot make out a complete list. Also if Paul wants any more American official publications, there are lots—I shall require but a few. There are some other books of yours here (*Old England Dramatists* etc.) which can be sent same time.

Please let me know soon, as time becomes pressing and we are in an awful *embarras de richesses.*[d] The Russian books we have promised to Lavroff, he is I think positively entitled to them, being Danielson's next friend outside Russia. Another lot of duplicates, etc., we intend sending to Zurich—part for the *Partei-Archiv,*[144] part for a *bibliothèque de rédaction.* The Blue Books[161] mostly to Sam Moore for use with the translation.[e] And a few 'popular' things to the *Arbeiterverein* here.[162]

Now if you or Paul should wish for any particular books besides, please say so, and we will forward everything not absolutely required here.

---

[a] A. Smith, *Recherches sur la nature et les causes de la richesse des nations.*-
[b] T. R. Malthus, *Essai sur le principe de population...* -[c] Élisée Loustalot published a weekly *Révolutions de Paris.* -[d] difficulty over the sheer amount -[e] of the first volume of *Capital* into English (see Note 56)

Yesterday I received a letter from a certain Nonne,[a] *Kandidat der Philologie*, was here some time ago, now in Paris, resides 56 Boulevard de Port-Royal. He is a leading man amongst the German workmen in Paris who you recollect had a few years ago been coaxed round by Malon's soft sawder, and were further pushed in that direction by some stupid blunders of the *Citoyen*. They are now furious anti-Broussists since the 'international Conference'[115]; but still thick with Adhémar Leclère and his *Cercle international*.[163] I have asked Paul several times to get into connection with the Paris Germans. They are not worth much, but they *influence the German party as to Parisian affairs*. Since the Socialist Law,[37] these societies abroad have naturally recovered an influence much above their merits, as they are the only bodies remaining in possession of a public organisation. It will be difficult for the *Sozialdemokrat* to go direct against them in its judgment of Parisian internal quarrels. So they are worth coaxing a bit, which will not be difficult, and as the man is your neighbour, I thought best to send him my card '*pour introduire M. Nonné auprès de M. et M-me Lafargue*'.[b] Whether anything will come of it I don't know, anyhow I hope you will excuse the liberty I have taken.

Sorry I could not see much of *citoyen* Robelet — he came, was seen and vanished again.

Will Paul favour us with a few words about his mysterious adventures in *la Province*?[157]

What has become of the *citoyenne* Paule Mink[164]? The last reports were '*qu'elle se multipliait dans le midi*'[c] and, what after this is not so much to be wondered at, '*qu'elle développait son sujet*'.[d] The outcome??

Yours affectionately,

F. Engels

Would you please forward as soon as ever possible another copy of Deville's *Capital*? Kautsky is to translate it, but Meissner's permission is necessary and I cannot expect to get it unless I send him the original.[e]

---

[a] For Engels' reply see next letter. - [b] 'to introduce Mr Nonne to Mr and Mrs Lafargue' - [c] 'that she *was being torn to pieces* in the south' - [d] 'that she *was elaborating her subject*' - [e] See this volume, p. 76.

How about the new edition of the *Misère de la philosophie*? People keep bothering me about it. Has anything been done?[165]

First published, in the language of the original (English), in: F. Engels, P. et L. Lafargue, *Correspondance*, t. I, Paris, 1956

Reproduced from the original

56

ENGELS TO HEINRICH NONNE [166]

IN PARIS

[Draft]

[London, between 9 and 21 February 1884]

I cannot say anything definite about the plan outlined by you, so long as I do not know what persons are involved and what your intentions are. All I can say is that I could, in certain circumstances and provided they were worth the trouble, enter into a *cartel*, but never form an/*alliance*, with people who have not comlpetely and unreservedly adopted the revolutionary communist standpoint. Besides my time is completely taken up with work that it is absolutely imperative I should do, and my international correspondence is, in any case, already extensive enough. Clemenceau would certainly have to be induced to go considerably further before we could ally ourselves with him; whether, as the immediate ministerial candidate of the extreme Left, he would wish to be on more than ordinarily 'good terms' with us would seem to be debatable. One can remain thus on good terms with socialists of the most diverse shades of opinion until a difference of principle or tactics crops up, whereupon sympathy turns into antipathy. Accordingly, it is now for you to decide whether I am a man who would suit your book.

First published in: Marx* and Engels, *Works*, First Russian Edition, Vol. XXVII, Moscow, 1935

Printed according to the original

Published in English for the first time

57

ENGELS TO JOHANN PHILIPP BECKER [55]

IN GENEVA

London, 14 February 1884
122 Regent's Park Road, N. W.

Dear Old Man,

There is no reason for you to worry about my health; the thing
was a long drawn-out but not at all dangerous, and is steadily
abating.

I have sent Laura a copy of the note with the New Year's
greetings.

I have also taken out a money order for five pounds to enable you,
old chap, to cosset yourself and your wife a bit. I hope that the comparatively mild winter and the better time of year now approaching
will put you both on your feet again.

I have found a few things that emanated from you but cannot yet
say whether there are any more. There's a whole big hamper full of
letters, etc., to be looked through. As soon as I've sorted it out, I shall
send you everything that turns up.[126]

Now, as regards your plan,[167] it is the circumstances presently prevailing in Germany that are the first consideration. From time to time
I get information on the subject direct from Germany and, according
to this, the despotism of the police is unrestrained and the government is determined to put a stop to *any* public agitation by our party,
no matter what the pretext for that agitation or under what name it is
conducted. The fact that Social Democrats are at the back of it is
enough for any meeting to be dispersed, any attempt to have a say in
the press smothered and any participant expelled from a locality subject to the state of emergency.[67] The experience of the past six years
cannot leave us in any doubt as to that.

Now I am of the view that the appropriateness, timing and object
of a renewed attempt at mass agitation are things we who live abroad
are utterly incapable of deciding, and that this must be left entirely to
those in Germany who have to endure the pressure there and who
know best what is possible and what is impossible. So if you approach

Bebel or Liebknecht, and they deliberate the matter there, it would, in my view, be for them to decide the pros and cons, and for us to abide by their decision.

Come to that, things aren't going too badly in Germany where agitation is concerned, although the bourgeois papers suppress most of it and only sometimes and despite themselves emit an anxious moan about the rapidity with which the party is gaining ground instead of losing it. The police have opened up for our men a quite splendid field — the omnipresent and unremitting struggle with the police themselves. It is being conducted everywhere and continuously with great success and, better still, with great humour. The police are defeated and — ridiculed into the bargain. And, in the circumstances, I consider this struggle to be more useful than any other. Above all, it keeps contempt for the enemy alive in our lads' minds. No worse troops could be sent into action than those of the German police; even when they have the upper hand they suffer moral defeat, and our lads' confidence in victory grows from day to day. The effect of this struggle will be such that, as soon as the pressure at last lets up (and that will happen on the day things get cracking in Russia) we shall not be numbered in our hundreds of thousands but in our millions. Among the so-called leaders there may be plenty of rotten stuff, but in our masses I have unmitigated faith, and what they lack in revolutionary tradition, they will increasingly be taught by their guerilla war with the police. And, say what you will, we have never yet seen a proletariat learn in so short a time to act collectively and march shoulder to shoulder. Hence, although nothing may appear on the surface, we can, I think, confidently look to the day when the alarm is sounded. Then just watch them stand to!

Fraternal greetings from your old friend

F. Engels

First published in: F. Engels, *Vergessene Briefe (Briefe Friedrich Engels' an Johann Philipp Becker)*, Berlin, 1920

Printed according to the original

Published in English in full for the first time

58

ENGELS TO PYOTR LAVROV

IN PARIS

London, 14 February 1884

My dear Lavrov,

I have noted what you say about the Russian translation of the 2nd volume of *Capital*. I shall revert to this at the appropriate moment.[168]

As to the German edition, you will be aware that over there we are under threat from absolute despotism and that *anything* is liable to be suppressed. Marx never allowed himself to be inhibited by the legislation of the day; he always spoke his mind and it would be truly miraculous if the 2nd volume did not contain enough confiscable and suppressible material to fall foul of the law of 1878.[37] But that is a risk we must run and, as for myself, I certainly have no intention of watering anything down.

When Германъ Лопатинъ [a] was here [b] he told me that Nikolai Danielson wanted me to return him a book entitled *Труды Комиссіи для изслѣдованія хлѣбной промышленности въ Россіи*.[c] I have now found several books on the marketing and production of grain: the title most closely resembling the one he quotes is *Труды экспедиціи, снаряженной императорскими Вольнымъ экономическимъ и Русскимъ географическимъ обществами, для изслѣдованія хлѣбной торговли и производительности въ Россіи*,[d] Volume 2, 1870.

Might that be the book he is referring to? If so I shall return it to 27 Мойка,[e] St Petersburg as soon as I have your confirmation.

I hope to send off your books [f] next week; I have kept some of them.

---

[a] (Russ.) Hermann Lopatin.- [b] See this volume, p. 59.- [c] *Proceedings of the Committee of Inquiry into Bakeries in Russia*.- [d] (Russ.) *Trudy...* (Papers of an Expedition Sponsored by the Imperial Free Economic and Russian Geographical Societies for Studying Grain Cultivation and the Grain Trade in Russia).- [e] (Russ.) Moika St.- [f] See this volume, p. 88.

If I find I don't need them for the 2nd volume, I shall despatch them to you later.

Yours ever,

F. Engels

First published in: Marx and Engels, *Works*, First Russian Edition, Vol. XXVII, Moscow, 1935

Printed according to the original

Translated from the French

Published in English for the first time

59

ENGELS TO KARL KAUTSKY [88]

IN ZURICH

London, 16 February 1884

Dear Kautsky,

I happen to have an hour or two to spare today, hence my prompt reply.

Not only Deville's *historical* section, but also his descriptive one (working day, cooperation, manufacturing, large-scale industry, etc.) will require revision, of which you may assure yourself by going through a couple of chapters. All I shall do for the present, so far as Meissner is concerned, is to send him the French text and inform him that revision is under way [137] and that I shall let him have further details in due course.

The *Poverty* is also coming out in a new French edition in Paris. I am writing a preface to it [169]; in the one to the German edition, I shall dispose of the myth of Rodbertus.[a] This stemmed from Rudolf Meyer [170] and has been so widely hawked around in Germany, this country and even America, that the thing has got to be scotched once and for all. I shall show, 1) that in 1850 we had had no opportunity of learning anything whatsoever from Mr Rodbertus, 2) that he was

---

[a] F. Engels, 'Marx and Rodbertus'.

quite unknown to us, 3) that his great discoveries had already been commonplaces in 1848, 4) that the remedies he specifies for use in socialist therapy had already been criticised in the *Poverty, prior to* Rodbertus' discovery of them.

So as you see, there's plenty left for you to do; but the above matters can only be attended to, because experienced, *by me*, while I am also the only person to possess the necessary material from the years 1840-50.

Rodbertus' theory of rent is nonsense; the first 1861-63 manuscript of *Capital* contains a detailed and somewhat ironical critique of it by Marx, in a very long section, *Theories of Surplus Value*, which I shall probably publish at the end of the 2nd volume or as a 3rd volume.[171]

What I require for my preface, however, is Rodbertus' *Offener Brief an das Comité des Deutschen Arbeitervereins*, Leipzig, 1863. Could you or Ede get hold of the thing and let me have it for a few days? As soon as I have made extracts, you shall have it back.

I have not yet received the Proudhon article from the old *Social-Demokrat*[151] promised me by Ede — might arrive this evening. I shall probably translate it for the French edition.

If Ede were suddenly to turn up here it would please me no end; I could join him in a drink, being now once again able to indulge in a very modest way.

Let us now return to your last letter but one.[172] Dietz asked for the *Condition of the Working-Class* long ago, and I virtually promised he should have it as soon as I had found out how I stood with *Wigand*, its former publisher. For the past 15 years Liebknecht has been promising to ascertain this through Freytag (i. e. what my legal position is vis-à-vis *Wigand*), and still I'm in the dark.[a] At all events, Dietz has first refusal, and ultimately I shall myself take steps to find out what I am entitled to do.

It would be a good thing if someone were to take the trouble to throw light on the proliferation of state socialism, drawing for the purpose on an exceedingly flourishing example of the practice in *Java*. All the material is to be found in *Java, How to Manage a Colony*, BY J. W. B. Money, BARRISTER AT LAW, London, 1861, 2 VOLS. Here one sees how the Dutch have, on the basis of the communities' age-old communism, organised production for the benefit of the state and ensured that the people enjoy what is, in their own estimation, a quite com-

---

[a] See this volume, pp. 19-20.

fortable existence; the consequence is that the people are kept in a state of primitive stupidity and the Dutch exchequer rakes in 70 million marks a year (now probably more). It's a most interesting case, and conclusions as to its practical application are easy to draw. It also shows how there, as in India and Russia today, primitive communism (provided no modern communist element comes to stir it up) supplies the best and also the broadest basis for exploitation and despotism, and survives in the midst of modern society as an anachronism (to be eliminated or, one might almost say, turned back on its course) no less glaring than the Mark communities of the original cantons.[173]

There is a *definitive* book — as definitive as Darwin's was in the case of biology — on the primitive state of society; once again, of course, Marx was the one to discover it. It is Morgan's *Ancient Society*, 1877. Marx mentioned it, but my head was full of other things at the time and he never referred to it again which was, no doubt, agreeable to him, wishing as he did to introduce the book to the Germans *himself*[174]; I can see this from his very exhaustive extracts. Within the limits set by his subject, Morgan rediscovers for himself Marx's materialist view of history, and concludes with what are, for modern society, downright communist postulates. The Roman and Greek gens is, for the first time, fully elucidated in the light of that of savages, in particular the American Indians, thus providing a firm basis for the history of primitive times. If I had the time to spare, I would work up the material, together with Marx's notes, for the feuilleton of the *Sozialdemokrat* or for the *Neue Zeit*, but it's out of the question. All the impostures — endogamy, exogamy and whatever else the balderdash is called — of Tylor, Lubbock and Co. have been demolished once and for all.[175] These gentry are doing all they can to suppress the book in this country; it is printed in America and I ordered it 5 weeks since but cannot get hold of it, although the name of a London firm figures as co-publisher on the title-page!

Kindest regards.

Yours,

F. E.

First published, in Russian, in *Marx-Engels Archives*, Vol. I (VI), Moscow, 1932

Printed according to the original

Published in English in full for the first time

60

ENGELS TO LAURA LAFARGUE

IN PARIS

London, 16 February 1884

My dear Laura,

To-morrow is Sunday and on Monday we shall have to rummage in Maitland Park again,[159] so if I don't write to-day to you there is no telling how long it may be delayed. We have got the old '*Speicher*'[a] at last cleared out, found a whole lot of things that have to be kept, but about half a ton of old newspapers that it is impossible to sort. I think next week we can begin to clear out and the week after sell up the remainder for what it will fetch. I was afraid at one time I should have to give it up again, but fortunately I am getting better every day, I can walk again for half an hour as fast as ever and with Nim's help get through two bottles of Pilsener and a fair allowance of claret every 24 hours.

Amongst the manuscripts there is the first version of the *Kapital* (1861-63) and there I find several hundred pages: *Theorien über den Mehrwert*[171] partly worked up into the text of the later versions,[176] but there will be quite enough left to swell the 2nd volume into a 2nd and a 3rd.

Bernstein is sending me an article of Mohr's on *Proudhon*, published in the Berlin *Social-Demokrat* of 1865. Very likely the whole of it will have to be translated for the French edition of the *Misère*.[165]

By the bye Bernstein will be in Lyons to-morrow and may come to Paris while once on the road, and even extend his trip to London. If he does come to Paris, pray engage him to come here too, I want to see him about a good many things; he knows he finds a bed here ready to receive him and if he is a little short of cash, that should not stop him, we can arrange about that.[177]

Paul tells me I can take my time about the preface to the *Misère*[169] but I don't believe in that sort of thing, I have too much experience of publishers. I want to know by what time Oriol will require it, though I won't undertake that I shall deliver it to the day or even the week; but I ought to have *some* idea. The house in Maitland Park has to be

---

[a] 'storehouse'

Helene Demuth

delivered up on the 25th March, and I have plenty of other things to do besides; I must be able to arrange my plans beforehand to some extent at least.

What Paul thinks is an article of Mohr's on Proudhon's *la propriété c'est le vol*,[a] is in the *Heilige Familie* which I have got.[b]

I cannot much share Paul's enthusiasm about the London *Justice*, I find the paper awfully dull. But what can you expect of a set of people who take in hand the task of instructing the world about matters of which they themselves are ignorant? There is not a single burning question which they know how to tackle; Hyndman combines internationalist phraseology and jingo aspirations, Joynes is a muddled ignoramus (I saw him a fortnight ago), Morris is all very well as far as he goes, but it is not far, poor Bax gets himself fast in German philosophy of a rather antiquated character—all that might do for a monthly where they have time to get themselves into harness, but for a weekly, with all sorts of *questions d'actualité* to be tackled, it is blamable.

Anyhow the new 'respectable' Socialist stir here does go on very nicely, the thing is becoming fashionable, but the working classes do not respond yet. Upon that everything depends. And this is why it was so stupid to hurry on the bringing out of *Justice*. Articles like these will never stir up the masses. Six months' intercourse with working people would have prepared a public and taught the writers how to write for it. But what's the use of grumbling? *Les petits grands hommes veulent absolument faire leur petit bonhomme de chemin!*[c]

I hope the children[d] are better. Nim is rather anxious about them. Do please let us know how they are going on.

Best love from Nim and from

Your affectionate

F. Engels

First published, in the language of the original (English), in: F. Engels, P. et L. Lafargue, *Correspondance*, t. I, Paris, 1956

Reproduced from the original

---

[a] property is theft - [b] K. Marx and F. Engels, *The Holy Family*, Ch. IV (see present edition, Vol. 4, pp. 23-54). - [c] Petty great people always want to follow their own path! - [d] Jean, Edgar, Marcel and Jenny Longuet

61

ENGELS TO JOHN DARBYSHIRE [178]

IN MANCHESTER

[Draft]

[London, not earlier than 17 February 1884]

Cannot do anything myself in that line, shall I hand their principles to the Democratic Federation,[99] to *Justice* or *To-Day?*

First published in: Marx and Engels, *Works*, Second Russian Edition, Vol. 36, Moscow, 1964

Reproduced from the original

Published in English for the first time

62

ENGELS TO LAURA LAFARGUE

IN PARIS

London, 21 February 1884

My dear Laura,

Your news about the children's [a] health is more or less reassuring — except poor Wolf[b] who, however, seems the strongest of the lot and, we hope, will have got over the worst when you next give us some news.

As to what is to be done in case anything happens to Longuet, well, that will have to be considered if that event should occur; I do not see what much should be gained if we 'speculated' on that now — I mean speculating in the philosophical sense — at any rate I do not see either what we can do under present circumstances with such a paternal father as Longuet, but if you do, I shall be most happy to hear from you on the subject.

We have arranged with Gittens about packing and forwarding the books, etc., for you and Lavroff[c] and as they have not come for them for two days, Nim has gone to stir them up.

---

[a] Jean, Edgar, Marcel and Jenny Longuet - [b] Edgar Longuet - [c] See this volume, p. 95.

Herewith the preface to the *Misère* by — Mohr himself! [151] Bernstein has re-discovered this old article which I have at once translated. Please, you and Paul, to turn my translation into proper French and return it along with the original which belongs to the *Partei-Archiv* [144] at Zurich. There will only a few more words be required. But what will the French public say to the rather unceremonious manner in which Mohr speaks of them? And will it be wise to have this true and impartial judgment at the risk that the Brousses say: *voilà le Prussien* [a]? Anyhow, I should be very loth to soften the article down to suit *le goût parisien* [b] but it is worth considering. There is no denying that the *bas empire* [c] has been there for 18 years.

Paul's *bon dieu* [d] is charming, so is the introduction to his *conférence*. [179] The *exposé* too is quite taking for his public and I am not astonished at his success. But he might now and then give them a *new* illustration from the *Kapital* besides the old quotation of Liebig about the size of recruits [e]; and not treat 1) *la concurrence* and 2) *l'offre et la demande*, [f] which is but *la concurrence* over again. If I am strict with him, it's because I see it does him good and he improves considerably by hammering a bit now and then; his last performances certainly show great progress, and if he would only be a little more attentive to certain theoretical points (mostly of detail) he would be a great light in Paris, *ville-lumière* [g] as it is.

Now I must conclude. Nim has come back and we must make up book-packets for Russia and America, in time for registering. She says Gittens cannot come before Tuesday or Wednesday [h] — so she sends you a kiss, I the same, and *une bonne poignée de main* [i] to Paul

From your affectionate

F. Engels

First published, in the language of the original (English), in: F. Engels, P. et L. Lafargue, *Correspondance*, t. I, Paris, 1956

Reproduced from the original

---

[a] here you have a Prussian - [b] the Parisian taste - [c] Lower Empire (designation of the late Roman, or Byzantine Empire, and also of any empire on the decline); here, the Second Empire in France. - [d] God - [e] K. Marx, *Capital*, Vol. I, Part III, Ch. X, Sect. 2 (see present edition, Vol. 35). - [f] 1) competition and 2) supply and demand - [g] illuminating city - [h] 26 or 27 February - [i] a firm handshake

63

ENGELS TO HEINRICH NONNE

IN PARIS

[Draft]

[London, about 26 February 1884]

What I wrote and told you about Malon [39] are the simple facts of which I have been given proof and which are in no way altered by Paris gossip. Malon did indeed quit the Peace Congress [180] in company with Bakunin and 15 others, and he was a co-founder of the secret Alliance.[20] The document of March 1870 has actually been in my possession [181]; what the lies are that Malon has recently been concocting about the International are of no interest to me; I am unlikely so much as to look at them. In my view the fact that he is self-taught does not give him the right to falsify history. If *he* is fit to play a leading role among the French, I am sorry for the French proletariat.

As regards your propagation of international relations,[a]

1) the aims are so vague that I really cannot give up any time on the strength of your general prospects;

2) virtually all the people you mention are unknown to me (the only one I know at all *well* is precisely the one you fail to name). But one cannot be active in the international movement for 40 years without having everywhere old friends and allies to whom one is politically and morally committed. I should therefore first have to obtain information from them about many of your people and about the attitude of one side to the other. I cannot very well do that, however, without giving some inkling of your scheme;

3) but I cannot possibly embark on an alliance without having the least idea of where and into what further associations it will lead me. Some kind of central committee would presumably be set up in Paris, which would decide on the admission of new members and on possi-

---

[a] See this volume, p. 97.

ble action, and it might so happen that I found myself in the same association as people whom I should be compelled to oppose outright or that I became responsible for an action I disapproved of. That is an eventuality I cannot expose myself to at all.

Do not, however, let this deter you. If you are able to achieve something worthwhile, it will please me nonetheless. I am grateful to you for your confidence and remain, etc.

First published in: Marx and Engels, *Works*, First Russian Edition, Vol. XXVII, Moscow, 1935

Printed according to the original

Published in English for the first time

64

ENGELS TO KARL KAUTSKY

IN ZURICH

London, 3 March 1884

Dear Kautsky,

Ede Bernstein has assumed the responsibility of drinking a fraternal pledge[a] with me in your name and on your behalf. I hereby take the liberty of putting this into immediate effect in the hope that you will not disavow his action.

Apart from that, he left this evening for Paris [177] where he will spend tomorrow, departing the same night; no doubt he will reach Zurich at the same time as this letter.

Enclosed the sale of Russia to Bismarck for Bismarck to invest with Bleichröder with a view to a new Russian loan.[182] Ferry and Gladstone were the first to be taken in but, if Bleichröder supplies the

---

[a] A little ceremony which precedes the use of *Du* (thou), the familiar form of address.

money, the same thing may happen to Bismarck and, once the fun begins in Russia, it will be all up with the lot of them.

Your

F. Engels

First published, in Russian, in *Marx-Engels Archives*, Vol. I (VI), Moscow, 1932

Printed according to the original

Published in English for the first time

65

ENGELS TO PYOTR LAVROV [183]

IN PARIS

[London,] 3 March 1884
122 Regent's Park Road [N. W.]

My dear Lavrov,

Last Friday[a] I sent you through the agency of Messrs Flageollet frères, 27 rue Paul Lelong, Paris a case containing the books you know about.[b] *Carriage has been paid over here*; if they charge you for it, let me know. In case of non-arrival you should make enquiries at the above address.

It was despatched from here per Messrs Gittens & Co.

Yours ever,

F. Engels

First published in: Marx and Engels, *Works*, First Russian Edition, Vol. XXVII, Moscow, 1935

Printed according to the original

Translated from the French

Published in English for the first time

---

[a] 28 February - [b] See this volume, p. 88.

66

ENGELS TO VERA ZASULICH [184]

IN GENEVA

London, 6 March 1884
122 Regent's Park Road, N. W.

Dear Citizen,

For me, as also for Marx's daughters, it will be a great day when the Russian translation of *The Poverty of Philosophy* appears.[185] I need hardly say that I shall be glad to place at your disposal any material that might be useful to you. This is what I propose to do.

In addition to the German translation, a new French edition is at present being printed in Paris.[165] For these two editions I am preparing a few explanatory notes, the text of which I shall send you.

For the preface there is in existence an article by Marx on Proudhon in the Berlin *Social-Demokrat* (1865), which contains virtually all that is necessary. It will be printed at the beginning of the two new French and German editions. The only copy in existence is in our party archives at Zurich [144]; if a second one doesn't turn up amongst my own or Marx's papers (I shall know about this in a few weeks), you will easily be able to get hold of a copy of it through Bernstein.

For the German edition I shall have to do a separate preface^a rebutting the absurd contention by reactionary socialists [186] that in *Capital* Marx plagiarised Rodbertus, and proving that, on the contrary, Marx had produced his critique of Rodbertus in the *Poverty* before Rodbertus wrote his *Social Letters*.[187] To my mind this is of no interest to a Russian public as yet unpenetrated by our pseudo-socialists. But you are the best judge; the thing is at your disposal should you think it suitable.

What you tell me about the increase in the study of books on socialist theory in Russia gives me much pleasure. The theoretical and critical spirit, which has virtually disappeared from our German schools, would indeed appear to have taken refuge in Russia. You ask me to suggest some books for translation. But you have already translated, or promised to translate, almost all of Marx's works and you have taken the best of mine. The remainder of our German books are ei-

---

^a F. Engels, 'Marx and Rodbertus'; see also this volume, pp. 101-02.

ther weak on theory or concerned with matters more or less restricted to Germany. The French have latterly produced some pretty good stuff, but this is still in its infancy. Deville's summary of *Capital* [81] is good as regards the theoretical part, but the descriptive part was done in too great haste and is virtually unintelligible to anyone not familiar with the original; moreover it is too long for a summary. However I believe something worthwhile might be made of it if it were rewritten, and a summary of *Capital* would always be of use in a country where the book itself can only be obtained with difficulty.

It is true that, when I spoke of the situation in Russia,[a] I was also thinking, inter alia, specifically of her finances—but not exclusively. For a government at bay, like the one in Petersburg, and a captive Tsar, like the hermit of Gatchina,[b] the situation cannot continue without becoming ever more tense.[188] Nobility and peasantry both ruined, the army ruffled in its chauvinism and shocked by the daily spectacle of a государь,[c] who hides himself away; the necessity for an external war as a safety-valve for 'evil passions' and for general discontent—at the same time the impossibility of embarking upon one for lack of money and of favourable political conjunctures; a powerful national intelligentsia impatient to break the fetters that bind it and, on top of all this, a total absence of money and an authority with the knives of the дъятели[d] at its throat [189]—it seems to me that with every month the situation must become more impossible and that, were a bold and constitutionally minded grand duke to turn up, Russian 'society' itself must see that a palace coup would be the best way out of this impasse. Will Bismarck and Bleichröder now come to the rescue of their new friends? [182] I doubt it. Rather, I wonder which of the two contracting parties will be cheated by the other.

Enclosed a manuscript of Marx's (copy) for you to use as you think fit. I no longer know whether it was in *Слово*[e] or in *Отечественныя записки*[f] that he found the article 'Karl Marx Before the Tribunal of Mr Zhukovsky'.[g] This is the reply he wrote; it bears the stamp of a piece done for publication in Russia, but he never sent it to Peters-

---

[a] See this volume, p. 65. - [b] Alexander III - [c] (Russ.) tsar - [d] (Russ.) activists - [e] (Russ.) *Slovo* (The Word), a journal. - [f] (Russ.) *Otechestvenniya zapiski* (Fatherland's Notes), a journal. - [g] N. [K.] M[ikhailovsky]. 'Карлъ Марксъ передъ судомъ г. Ю. Жуковскаго', *Отечественныя записки*, No. 10, October 1877.

burg for fear that the mere mention of his name might compromise the existence of the review which published his reply.[190]

Yours very sincerely,
F. Engels

Your translation of my pamphlet[a] strikes me as excellent — what a beautiful language Russian is. All the advantages of German but without its ghastly coarseness.

First published, in Russian, in *Gruppa* '*Osvobozhdeniye truda*', No. 1, Moscow, 1924

Printed according to the original

Translated from the French

67

ENGELS TO FRIEDRICH ADOLPH SORGE[191]

IN HOBOKEN

London, 7 March 1884

Dear Sorge,

After suffering continuously throughout the whole autumn and winter from a minor if very tiresome disorder, and spending 2 months resting in bed, I am at last sufficiently recovered to be able to work regularly and to pay off the letters I owe. I trust that you and your wife will also gradually get over the after-effects of your far more serious illness and then gradually resume your old way of life.

Since I am not yet completely mobile and my excursions are limited to the immediate neighbourhood, and not having anyone to send out on errands, I carried out your commission in rather a different way. Your copy of *Capital*, 3rd edition,[b] and likewise one of Deville's *Le Capital*, were despatched to you in 2 parcels per BOOK POST; I shall send the photographs in the same manner, having now found out how to pack them. No doubt you will be able to obtain the other 2 copies of *Capital* easily enough over there.

---

[a] *Socialism: Utopian and Scientific* - [b] the third German edition of Volume I of *Capital*

I have taken out a year's subscription to *To-Day* for you and you will, no doubt, be getting it regularly. The chaps are very well-intentioned but damnably ignorant; which may be all right for *To-Day*, but now the DEMOCRATIC FEDERATION [99] is bringing out a weekly journal, *Justice*, which is conspicuous for the exceeding boredom of its invariably repetitive contents and for its total inability to get hold of the right end of the stick even when dealing with a question of the day. I shall send you a couple of issues; it's not worth taking. All in all, the DEMOCRATIC FEDERATION cannot simply be taken on trust; it harbours all manner of dubious elements. Hyndman, who sets himself up as a party leader *in partibus infidelium*,[a] is a pretty unscrupulous career-ist, and only a few years ago stood unsuccessfully as a Conservative candidate for Parliament [192]; moreover, he treated Marx very shab-bily.[100] I will have nothing whatever to do with the DEMOCRATIC FEDE-RATION, a handy excuse being want of time, and am on closer terms only with *To-Day*, more notably Bax. The latter is a very good chap, save only that he is most unseasonably swotting up on *Kant*. *If you have no objection*, I shall publish in *To-Day* an English version of the letter Marx wrote to you about Henry George.[31] Then you will be able to make further use of it over there.

I shall hardly have time to enter into a debate with Stiebeling.[193] Such little tin gods can safely be left to their own devices. In any case, it will be years before anything can be done to inhibit sectarianism in America. Thus the great Most will, no doubt, eventually end up as Karl Heinzen II. I get the *Wochen-Volkszeitung*,[b] but there's not much in it.

What the position is as regards Bebel's, Liebknecht's or anyone else's going to America, I don't know.[29] When they asked me, I told the chaps that it probably wouldn't do to go tapping America for election funds every third year. In Germany, by the way, the position is very good. Our lads are conducting themselves really splendidly. Everywhere the Anti-Socialist Law [37] is involving them in local struggles with the police, to the accompaniment of all manner of jokes and dirty tricks, struggles which usually turn out in our favour and are a source of the best propaganda in the world. Every now and again one or other of the bourgeois papers vents a sigh about the enormous progress made by our people, and they all of them dread the coming elections.[194] A fortnight ago one of my nephews from

---

[a] It means literally: in parts inhabited by unbelievers; here: nominally. - [b] *Wochen-blatt der N. Y. Volkszeitung*

Barmen was over here — a liberal conservative. 'In Germany,' I told him, 'we have got to the stage when we can sit with our hands in our laps and let our opponents do the work for us. No matter whether you repeal, renew, tighten up or moderate the Anti-Socialist Law, whatever you do plays into our hands.' 'Yes,' said he, 'it is remarkable how circumstances are working for you.' 'To be sure they are,' I said, 'but they wouldn't be if we hadn't diagnosed them aright forty years ago, and acted accordingly.' No reply.

In France, too, things have been going better since Lafargue, Guesde and Dormoy were released from prison.[9] They are very active, spend much time in the provinces where, luckily, their chief strength lies, possess little news-sheets in Rheims and St Pierre-les-Calais,[a] and will be holding a congress at Roubaix in a month's time.[195] Every Sunday, what is more, they give a very well-attended lecture in Paris, when Lafargue speaks on the materialist view of history, and Deville on *Capital*.[179] I shall write and ask them to send you the things, all of which are printed. It's fortunate that they haven't got a daily in Paris just now, since it's much too early for that. A new edition of *The Poverty of Philosophy* is coming out in Paris.[165] Likewise a German one in Zurich and a Russian in Geneva. I don't believe I have yet sent you a copy of my *Entwicklung*,[b] never having received more than one or two myself. (The oafs!) Now the thing has come out in a 3rd edition, as well as in French, Italian, Russian and Polish. Aveling wishes to translate it into English.[c] He, too, is an admirable young man, but he has TOO MANY IRONS IN THE FIRE and is currently engaged in time-consuming strife with his former friend Bradlaugh; the socialist movement here is cutting the ground from under the latter's feet — and with it his livelihood. That means he must fight for it, but it isn't easy for that narrow-minded and rascally fellow.

So far, all is well with Tussy who generally comes here on Sundays. Lenchen is, as you know, keeping house for me. In a fortnight's time I shall be able to settle down in real earnest to Volume II of *Capital* — another huge task, but I look forward to it.

You should read Morgan (Lewis H.), *Ancient Society*, published in America in 1877. A masterly exposé of primitive times and their com-

---

[a] *La Défense des travailleurs* and *Le Travailleur* - [b] *Socialism: Utopian and Scientific* -
[c] See this volume, p. 394.

munism. *Rediscovered Marx's theory of history all on his own,* and concludes by drawing communist inferences in regard to the present day.

Kindest regards to Adolf.[a]

Your
F. E.

First published in *Briefe und Auszüge aus Briefen von Joh. Phil. Becker, Jos. Dietzgen, Friedrich Engels, Karl Marx u. A. an F. A. Sorge und Andere,* Stuttgart, 1906

Printed according to the original

Published in English in full for the first time

68

ENGELS TO PAUL LAFARGUE [196]

IN PARIS

[London,] 11 and 15 March 1884

My dear Lafargue,

In complete agreement with almost all your alterations, [197] except for the following:

p. 6, wrong ideas about ... exchange value—you can't continue with an 'and'; what follows, his utopian interpretation, is *caused* by those wrong ideas; that causation must be shown.

p. 6, bottom: he deafens us, etc., has been unduly shortened; what is lacking is the *false* or *spurious* science. You must try to stick closer to the original.

p. 7, same objections; and also: 'but who, having to forego some of his pretensions to originality'—this corrupts the text. Marx says: 'There is in addition the clumsy repugnant show of erudition of the self-taught, whose natural pride in his original reasoning has already been broken' [b]; he has, in fact, been an original thinker and is proud so to have been, but is so no longer, having discovered that what he be-

---

[a] Adolf Sorge jun. - [b] K. Marx, 'On Proudhon', present edition, Vol. 20, pp. 30-31; here and below Engels quotes Marx's article in German.

lieved to be original and new had already been said by others before him; then he goes on to spurious science, etc. Your text *denies* the originality of Proudhon.

ibid. Cabet. You have no right to make Marx say more than he actually said: 'Cabet — worthy of respect for his practical attitude towards the French proletariat'.[a] Marx says nothing of devotion, a word he abhorred, as you must know, — it might run: worthy of respect for the rôle he played amongst the French proletariat (or in the political movement of the French proletariat), etc., or something of the sort.

ibid. Can you say: to preach *throughout all 3 volumes?*

Ibid. bottom, *Thiers*: if you abridge in the way you do, you ought to add what the original says: 'Thiers, by his reply opposing Proudhon's proposals, *which was then issued as a special booklet*'.[b] This is, I think, the famous book *De la propriété*, but I am not sure.

p. 8, *credit* ... *might accelerate* — not credit, but the application thereof; you should therefore say: might *serve* to accelerate, or some such turn of phrase.

p. 9, displays the cynicism of a moron to the greater glory of the Tsar? 'For the greater glory of the tsar he expresses moronic cynicism'.[c] The extreme cynicism with which Proudhon addresses himself to the misfortunes of Poland pays court to the policy of the Tsar.[198] This is what needs to be brought out.

ibid. bottom. *On the one hand*, etc. — the *two contradicting tendencies* which govern the interests of the petty bourgeois, should not be omitted; your text appears to do away with them.

p. 10, rowdy would be better than scandalous.

15 March

Well, now! Try to be more faithful to the original; Marx isn't a man with whom one can afford to take liberties. I hope that Laura will insist upon the text's being well and faithfully rendered.

Herewith the £ 10.

We have all the books and BOOK-CASES [d] here and, for the past 3 days, have been busy amalgamating the two libraries and setting them in

---

[a] Ibid., p. 31. - [b] Ibid. - [c] Ibid., p. 32. - [d] from Marx's library

order. It's the very devil of a task and Nim and I are both tired, so WITH LOVE TO Laura FROM Nim AND MYSELF NO MORE AT PRESENT

FROM YOURS TRULY,

F. E.

First published in: Marx and Engels, *Works*, First Russian Edition, Vol. XXVII, Moscow, 1935

Printed according to the original

Translated from the French

69

ENGELS TO EDUARD BERNSTEIN [94]

IN ZURICH

London, 24 March 1884

Dear Ede,

In great haste, a bit of gossip. We have at last wound things up to-day at Maitland Park [159] and handed back the old house to its owner. [a] I, on the other hand, am still in the throes of sorting out the books and papers nor, until this has been done, shall I be able to embark on any regular work.

The demonstration of the 16th [199] caused two people to make fools of themselves—Hyndman and Frohme.

Hyndman, without having actually given his assent, had been proposed as speaker—by, it is said, Rackow. Not being convinced of success, he declared in *Justice* that 'a working man' must speak and that as for *him*, he would merely listen. [b] The same issue of *Justice* contained an extremely impertinent notice on the last number of *To-Day*—amounting to a veiled declaration of war. [200] Hyndman next proceeded to intrigue against the despatch of delegates to the Roubaix congress, [195] alleging that those responsible were in a minority and that one ought not to go meddling in internal French disputes. [201] But at a committee meeting of the DEMOCRATIC FEDERATION [99] the following Tuesday, [c] he was well and truly defeated; his most

---

[a] Edwin Willis - [b] H. M. Hyndman, 'A Sad Anniversary. To the Editor of *Justice*', *Justice*, No. 8, 8 March 1884. - [c] 18 March

trusty followers took the floor against him, nor could he confess the real motives for his intervention; it was enthusiastically resolved to participate in both demonstration and congress, and Hyndman, who would *now* have gladly spoken in Highgate, had cut off his own line of retreat, the invitation to speak having passed to Aveling and been gladly accepted. That's what invariably befalls these clever-clever cliquists—they are hoist with their own petard.

Frohme apparently spoke very well in Highgate and, by contrast, quite atrociously at the Society. [162] I am sending you the *Deutsche Londoner Zeitung* in which the philistine reporter naively betrays his delight at the way Frohme had, with his atrocious platitudes, voiced his inmost thoughts for him. [a] This, apparently, was altogether too much of a good thing and gave rise to a tremendous row in the Society; Frohme was given a dressing-down and is said to have declared that he hadn't met a single socialist, let alone a *human being*, in London. He's unlikely to reappear for some time to come. He has left me alone, I'm glad to say.

Many thanks for the *Deutsches Tageblatt* which I return herewith. To reply to Bernhard Becker's balderdash would be doing him too great an honour. What the ex-president of mankind [202] writes and the *Tageblatt* prints is a matter of complete indifference, and even in Berlin it has long been forgotten. This kind of impotent malice chokes on its own bile. But what sort of press must it be to print such stuff? Even the Parisian Figaristes were more adept liars, albeit only during the period of general alarm immediately after the Commune.

All things considered, the March article was very good, with the right emphasis on essential points. So, too, was the one in the next issue, about the People's Party [203] man preaching to the peasants, its only fault being to invoke the 'concept' of democracy. [b] That concept changes according to the *demos* and hence does not get us one step further. What in my view should have been said is this: For the seizure of political power, democratic *forms* are also necessary to the proletariat for whom, however, like all political forms, they are only a means. But if, today, you want democracy as an *end*, you have to look for support to the peasants and petty bourgeoisie, i. e. to classes which are in decline and which, from the moment they try to preserve

---

[a] 'Die Märzfeier in London', *Londoner Zeitung. Hermann*, No. 1316, 22 March 1884. -

[b] [E. Bernstein,] 'Zum Gedenktage der Märzkämpfe', *Der Sozialdemokrat*, No. 11, 13 March 1884 (leader); 'Zur Naturgeschichte der Volkspartei', *Der Sozialdemokrat*, No. 12, 20 March 1884 (leader).

their existence by factitious means, are *reactionary* in their relations with the proletariat. Another thing that should not be forgotten is that the *logical* form of bourgeois rule is, precisely, a democratic republic which, however, has become too much of a risk only because of the progress already made by the proletariat, but which, as France and America go to show, is still feasible simply as bourgeois rule. Regarded, therefore, as 'definite, historically evolved', the 'principle' of liberalism is really just an illogicality; a liberal constitutional monarchy is an adequate form of bourgeois rule 1) at the beginning, when the bourgeoisie has not yet quite done with absolute monarchy, and 2) at the end, when the proletariat has already rendered a democratic republic too much of a risk. And yet a democratic republic is still the *final* form assumed by bourgeois rule, the form in which it comes to grief. And here I conclude this rigmarole.

Nim sends her regards. I didn't see Tussy yesterday.

Your
F. E.

First published, in Russian, in *Marx-Engels Archives*, Book I, Moscow, 1924

Printed according to the original

Published in English in full for the first time

70

ENGELS TO KARL KAUTSKY

IN ZURICH

London, 24 March 1884

Dear Kautsky,

You'd do best to order Morgan's book in America; the few copies printed for England in association with the firm of MacMillan appear to be sold out or unavailable—I got mine *second-hand* and then only with difficulty. I don't know the American publisher. Mine cost me 13/4d.

When I can find time I shall get out something on it for you for the

Neue Zeit, provided you are willing to print a separate copy in pamphlet form (it would be approx. 3 sheets); actually I am indebted to Marx for it and can incorporate his notes. [174]

I have now agreed with Meissner that the 2nd book of *Capital* should appear separately at first; the 3rd, [4] and the *Theories of Surplus Value*, [171] will then follow on as the second half of Volume II. This will get the thing moving more quickly. Time for the post.

Your
F. E.

The Morris affair is of no significance; they are a muddle-headed lot. [204]

First published, in Russian, in *Marx-Engels Archives*, Vol. I (VI), Moscow, 1932

Printed according to the original

Published in English for the first time

71

ENGELS TO LAURA LAFARGUE

IN PARIS

London, 31 March 1884

My dear Laura,

Even if it had not been for Paul's letter this morning, this afternoon was set apart for a letter to you. I am so bothered and pestered just now that not only my time, but also my room and my desk are not my own. On Monday last [a] we got clear of 41 Maitland Park Road, paid Willis and gave him the key. [159] What furniture there was left, is in Gittens' hands, they offered £12.10.- but advised a sale—we are trying to get £15.- out of them to have done with it; this will be attended to this week. Then I have been busy with the books, and was getting clear—two more days would have settled the heavy work—when lo! the landlord sends the painters to do the house outside, and

---

[a] 24 March

here we are, three dawdling fellows in the house, all windows open, every room invaded at the most unexpected hours, and to crown all, a bleak east-wind blowing inside as well as outside. That I got as fine a specimen of rheumatism as could be wished for, was only natural. Fortunately, if the dawdlers keep possession of the house even now, the east-wind has left us and so has, more or less, the rheumatism; and I am promised possession of my room for to-day,— on condition of giving it up to-morrow. So let us enjoy the present while it lasts.

Nim says there is such a weight off her mind now since the old house is done with that she at last can sleep again, it was a nightmare for her which even an occasional nightcap of 'Irish' could not drive away. Our place has much changed, two of my book-cases have gone below, the piano is in the corner between the fire-place and folding door (in the front room), the other corner filled up by one of Mohr's book-cases, while his large book-case (that behind his sofa) now takes the place where the piano stood in the back room. As soon as the painters will have cleared out, I shall finish the sorting of the last heap of books, and then try and get off the last box of books, for you, there is a nice little lot of things relating to the French Revolution, Lousta-lot, *Feuille Villageoise, Prisons de Paris pendant la Révolution,*[205] etc., etc.

I have settled with Meissner that the 2nd book (*Zirkulationsprozess des Kapitals*[a]) is to be published first separately; as soon as the *gross* work is finished, I can begin. The 3rd book will follow, along with *Theorien über den Mehrwert,*[b] a long critical work forming part of the *first* ms. of the *Kapital* (1862) which I have discovered.[171] The English translation is going on slowly, Sam has too much law-work to attend to, and is too conscientious to hurry on with it, 'regardless of quality'.[56]

The movement here is showing more and more of its emptiness every week. *Justice* drives me to despair by its utter incapacity of tackling even one single question. *To-Day* will live this next month entirely by Davitt and Paul who you will have been glad to learn from *Justice* is the first living authority on French peasant property.[206] These fellows cannot even give a man his due without trying to make him look ridiculous. Bax and Aveling are the only two, as far as I can see at present, of whom something can be made; but Bax has Kant on the brain and Aveling in order to live, has to keep a good many irons

---

[a] *The Process of Circulation of Capital* - [b] *Theories of Surplus Value*

in the fire and is a perfect novice in everything relating to political economy. Paul will no doubt see Bax at Roubaix [195]; he and a workingman[a] have been delegated by the Democratic Federation, [99] much against Hyndman's will who has lately made several attempts at forcing his personal plans and dodges upon them, but was ignominiously defeated: so he opposed sending delegates to Roubaix as he wanted to keep open the chance of a connexion with Brousse and Co. That fellow will not go far: he cannot bide his time.

I am afraid Paul will be disappointed with regard to a German delegate to Roubaix; unless Liebknecht does come[b]; but as he has promised to do so, it is not likely. The others do not speak French, except perhaps Bernstein, and him the deputies are sure not to send, as they mostly hate him, and would replace him in Zurich if they could and dared. Thanks to the great accession of petit bourgeois — *gebildete Schafsköpfe*,[c] our 'leaders' in Germany have become a sorry lot. Anyhow I hope Roubaix will be a great success *devant le public*, [d] it will help on enormously; in the meantime I enclose the cheque £10.- and send you plenty of kisses from Nim and your affectionate old cripple

F. Engels

First published, in the language of the original (English), in: F. Engels, P. et L. Lafargue, *Correspondance*, t. I, Paris, 1956

Reproduced from the original

72

ENGELS TO KARL KAUTSKY

IN ZURICH

London, 11 April 1884

Dear Kautsky,

Have got yours and Ede's letter. I hope to be done with Morgan next week [174]; cannot do much at the moment as Schorlemmer and

---

[a] Harry Quelch - [b] See this volume, pp. 125 and 129. - [c] educated numbskulls - [d] in public

Moore are here. This will be my last job for some time; it is no joke making a résumé of so meaty and ill-written a book. If Tussy can find the letter, I shall also include an assessment of Richard Wagner by Marx [207]; what the connection is you must find out for yourselves.

Thereafter work will proceed uninterruptedly on Volume II [a] as well as on revisions of: 1) your *Poverty*, [118] 2) notes and preface [169] to the French ditto, [165] 3) revision of the English translation [56] which ought now to forge ahead. Besides that, 4), more *Dühring* [208] and whatever else may be sent me from France for revision.

Fabian has been going for me with a persistence he would be quick to drop if he knew how much entertainment we over here derive from it. Some years ago he had suggested that we should write for a periodical to be founded by him and another great thinker, [b] and this on the basis of a philosophical programme they had laid down ready cut and dried and consisting in a crabbed and misconstrued fourth generation Kantianism. After that he went for my dialectical approach to mathematics and complained to Marx that I had defamed $\sqrt{-1}$. [209] And now the fun is beginning all over again. Let him roam the world arm in arm with von der Mark; he will not be read by me.

The Condition of the Working-Class. The last news *I* had about it from Liebknecht was that Freytag had told him that I was still bound by my contract with Wigand. You can't go by what Liebknecht *says*, and what he has done in this matter amounts to nil. [c] I shall write to Freytag myself; it is the only thing to do. [39]

However much Geiser may abuse the atheists, Bismarck certainly won't do him the favour of repealing the Anti-Socialist Law. [37] Whoever may have harboured any illusions on this point hitherto will doubtless now be rid of them, Bismarck having thrown in his last reserve, that old jackass Lehmann, in order to preserve it. [210]

How delicious that the parliamentary group should have *forbidden* Liebknecht to write for a paper. [d][211] That beats the old Prussian censorship. Well, if Liebknecht stands for that, things have come to a pretty pass.

Rodbertus, [e] etc., received, many thanks; will be returned next week. The relevant note in *Capital* is in the 2nd edition, p. 552 [f] and

---

[a] of *Capital*.- [b] Wilhelm Ludwig Rosenberg.- [c] See this volume, pp. 19-20 and 102.- [d] *Berliner Volksblatt*.- [e] K. Rodbertus, *Offener Brief an das Comité des Deutschen Arbeitervereins zu Leipzig*.- [f] See K. Marx, *Capital*, Vol. I, Part V, Ch. XVIII (present edition, Vol. 35).

will, in the 3rd edition, be considerably qualified by me in an addendum; kindly attend to this.

You must now excuse me, as I still have to write to Ede.

Your

F. E.

First published, in Russian, in *Marx-Engels Archives*, Vol. I (VI), Moscow, 1932

Printed according to the original

Published in English for the first time

73

ENGELS TO EDUARD BERNSTEIN [1]

IN ZURICH

London, 11 April 1884

Dear Ede,

Like you, I think it would be better to allow Frohme's massive tome[a] to die a natural death.

A delegation to Roubaix would have done a great deal of harm at a moment when the Anti-Socialist Law [37] was under discussion. The wailers [123] would have apportioned the blame for its renewal — in any case inevitable — to that delegation alone; this had to be avoided. Congresses are demonstrations and an occasion for useful personal encounters, and as such are of secondary importance, nor should more weighty considerations be sacrificed to them. I shall try to make this clear to the Parisians. In the circumstances, the address was the only thing possible and quite adequate. [195] The very thought of an international congress in London [212] appals me. I should go away.

As regards the Rodbertus stuff, you would do best to wait until you have my preface to the *Poverty*[b]; you can't possibly be aware of the most important works, namely those concerning England (alluded to

---

[a] K. Frohme, *Die Entwicklung der Eigenthums-Verhältnisse.* - [b] F. Engels, 'Marx and Rodbertus'.

in *Poverty*, p. [...]^a) from which it is plain that the socialist *application* of Ricardo's theory of value—Rodbertus' great hobby-horse—had been an economic commonplace in England since 1820 and one universally known to socialists since 1830. As I have, I believe, already written and told you,^b I shall show, on the same occasion, that, far from purloining the least thing from Rodbertus, Marx had, in the *Poverty*, unwittingly criticised in advance all the said Rodbertus' works, both written and unwritten. I think we had best withhold our attack until the *Poverty* has come out in German, and then go it hot and strong (i. e. the main attack I mean; no harm at all in skirmishes to draw Rodbertus' fire).

I look forward to seeing the ms. [118] Notabene, should you have difficulty over the Hegelian expressions in the 2nd chapter, simply leave blanks in the ms. and I will fill them in; the German version must contain the terminology proper to that school, otherwise it will be incomprehensible.

There were *three* copies of the 3rd edition.^c I racked my brains a bit over the *Dühring* that came with them and then simply laid it on one side, imagining it had got in by accident. That it might be a hint about a 2nd edition never occurred to me. I am delighted to find that this is so, more especially since I have learnt from various sources that the thing has been more influential—particularly in Russia—than I would ever have expected. So after all the tedium of a polemic with an inconsiderable opponent has not prevented the attempt to present an encyclopaedic survey of our view of the problems pertaining to philosophy, natural science and history from taking effect. I shall make virtually no changes but stylistic ones and, perhaps, add something to the section on natural science.— Its earlier publication in 2 parts was due to the way the thing came out (as a separate edition), otherwise there would have been absolutely no sense in it. [208]

The cards for Nim you ask about have not yet turned up.

Your

F. E.

First published, in Russian, in *Marx-Engels Archives*, Book I, Moscow, 1924

Printed according to the original

Published in English in full for the first time

---

^a A blank in the original. Apparently Engels had in mind pp. 49-50 of the first edition of Marx's *The Poverty of Philosophy* (see present edition, Vol. 6, p. 138). - ^b See this volume, p. 101. - ^c of the first volume of *Capital* in German

74

ENGELS TO LAURA LAFARGUE

IN PARIS

London, 18 April 1884

My dear Laura,

Best thanks for your news about the children[a] which were very grateful to all of us. Will hope the new arrangement may work at least for some time and without too much friction, though she[b] looks, from what you say, a rough subject enough to create any amount of that.

As to our 'Socialist' group here, I too am of opinion and said so, that Bax and Aveling are the only ones worth having, they at least study with a will, though not always a well directed one. But the worst is, this little clique of *public* 'mutual admirators' and at least partially *secret* 'mutual detractors' (especially Hyndman) are getting a regular nuisance through their mischievous gossip. First we hear from Sam Moore that he has heard in Manchester that Hyndman was busy translating the *Kapital*. This mystery we have as yet not been able to sift thoroughly but it will probably turn out a *canard*. Now, before we are well over that, those two busybodies in Paris[c] spread the report that Aveling was at it! The long and the short of this is as follows. Aveling, who studies the German text, has translated a few pages for his own benefit. When Hyndman was named as a possible competitor in the field, Sam at the same time declared that his own translation was getting on very slow, and he would be glad of some help. So Aveling was mentioned; I looked over his work and found it utterly useless. He was however very eager, and so, on his meeting Sam Moore here last week, it was arranged that he should try his hand at the chapter 'Der Arbeitstag',[d] this being chiefly descriptive and free, comparatively, from difficult theoretical passages for which Aveling is totally unfit *as yet*, that is to say until he has worked himself through the whole book and understands it. But at

---

[a] Jean, Edgar, Marcel and Jenny Longuet - [b] a new housekeeper of the Longuets - [c] Ernest Belfort Bax and James Leigh Joynes - [d] 'The Working Day'

the same time I said to Sam that I made it a condition that you should be asked also to take a share in the work, of which Sam was very glad, and now I come to ask you to choose one. The matter stands at present as follows:

Sam is now doing the 1st *Abschnitt*[a] from the beginning, we have gone over part of his 1st chapter and it is very good, though we shall revise it again. He intends going on to the end, page 127 (2nd edition) and the most difficult parts (p. 22-44) we shall each do independently and then compare.— From p. 128 to 221 (2nd *Abschnitt* and 3rd *Abschnitt*, chapters 5, 6 and 7) all is completed. Chapter 8th we will let Aveling try. All the rest is open to you to choose from. I do not think you will like to take the next 4th *Abschnitt, Kooperation, Teilung der Arbeit..., Maschinerie etc.*[b] p. 318-529, this being rather technical, and so is the 6th *Abschnitt: der Arbeitslohn.*[c] The 7th: *die Akkumulation,*[d] I should suppose, would suit you best. But choose for yourself. Any technical terms for which it might be difficult to find the English equivalent in Paris, you might leave room for, we could hunt them up here or in Manchester and fill them in. As all parts of the translation pass through my hands, I can easily restore the unity of expression (the application of the same technical terms throughout the book). If you accept our proposal, as I hope you will, and choose a section for yourself, we shall have fulfilled at least partially Mohr's wish and have your name and your work associated with this translation which I am convinced more and more every day is an absolute necessity, if the present movement here is not to collapse like a pricked ball by its own inanity; and we shall also be able to hasten the publication. Tussy has undertaken to hunt up all the quotations from Blue Books [161] and to transcribe the original passages so as to avoid re-translation and errors unavoidably connected with it. She will also see Kegan Paul as soon as possible, may be to-day (the Easter holidays stopped action in that direction), and arrange an interview for me with him when we hope we may be able to settle business matters; we shall then also know whether there is any truth in the Hyndman report.

So if you do say yes, at least something good will have to be connect-

---

[a] part - [b] 'Cooperation', 'Division of Labour...', 'Machinery etc.' - [c] 'Wages' - [d] 'Accumulation'

ed with the gossiping reports of Bax and Joynes; for to tell you the truth I have no great faith in Aveling's *present* attempts.

Of Mohr's photographs there are about 450 small ones (*cartes*[a]) 24/-per 100 and 250 large ones (cabinets) 50/-per 100 cost price. I shall send you a good parcel of them if you like as soon as I shall have time to pack them. At present I have still heaps of books to stow away. Sam left on Wednesday, Schorlemmer is still here till Monday.[b] He sends kindest regards by the million.

The copy [of the] 3rd edition[c] I sent to Danielson direct on 5th April, *registered*, and should be glad if Paul would mention this in his next letter to him. Lopatine had asked me to send it and given me the address.

Now I shall have to write to Paul. So until next time I remain

Your very affectionate

F. Engels

First published, in the language of the original (English), in: F. Engels, P. et L. Lafargue, *Correspondance*, t. I, Paris, 1956

Reproduced from the original

75

ENGELS TO PAUL LAFARGUE [196]

IN PARIS

London, 18 April 1884

My dear Paul,

A quarter to 5 — so must hurry!

My congratulations on the success of your Congress,[195] a success that is evident from the different way in which the earlier and later meetings are reported in the *Journal de Roubaix*. The Germans did right in not sending a delegate, for had they done so it would have

---

[a] *Cartes de visite*; small photographic portraits mounted on a card - [b] 21 April -
[c] of the third German edition of Volume I of *Capital*

unduly facilitated the further retention of the Exceptional Law [37] by the government and the bourgeoisie; the *moderates* in our party (very numerous among the leaders, very few among the masses, who are first-rate) would have exploited this; such a mistake would have been impermissible. In cases of this kind, demonstrations, even international ones, must be foregone.

When shall I get back the ms. of the translation [a]? This time you really must try harder, I beg of you. It is essential that the thing should either be done well or not at all. And when will it be possible to begin printing? I ask this so that I can make arrangements to write a few notes and a short preface [b]—if you like you can do a preface and send it to me here. You asked that you be given precedence over the German edition; but I have got a complete ms. of the first part of the latter and the Zurich people will begin printing the moment a manuscript reaches them.

What with this German text and the English *Capital* to revise,[56] my hands are full, and accordingly I wish ho know how to arrange things so as to avoid unnecessary loss of time. For it's essential that I get down to the 2nd volume [c]—and now Zurich has to inform me of the need for a 2nd edition of my *Anti-Dühring* [208] and a 4th of the *Peasant War*,[213] which means further revisions and further prefaces to be done! And that's what I—and Mr Bismarck—have gained from the banning of my books in Germany!

Old William [d] is more or less *in extremis*.[e] He no longer recognises those who come to see him, nor can he repeat the phrases he has been taught to say by rote in reply to deputations.

Nim has just come back from shopping, she sends you her '*amours*' (LOVES) and as much as you want of them.

Yours ever,
F. E.

Twenty minutes past five.

First published in: F. Engels, P. et L. Lafargue, *Correspondance*, t. I, Paris, 1956

Printed according to the original

Translated from the French

---

[a] of the French translation of Marx's 'On Proudhon' - [b] for the second French edition of Marx's *The Poverty of Philosophy* (see Note 165) - [c] of *Capital* - [d] William I - [e] near death

76

ENGELS TO KARL KAUTSKY

IN ZURICH

London, 22 April 1884

Dear Kautsky,

Letters and ms.[118] received, similarly cards for Nim. More anon. Hard at work on Morgan,[174] having been able to return to it only today.

The purpose of this is the following:

Please inform the printers that I have *very major revisions* to make right at the beginning both of *Anti-Dühring*[208] and the *Peasant War*[213] and so must insist that *no new edition is tackled before receipt of my manuscript.* I shall write at further length to Ede as soon as he can get back,[a] i. e. in about a week, for he, after all, is the one who has to take care of these things.

So please see that not one line is set *under any circumstances.* I wouldn't be able to acknowledge it.

In haste,

Your
F. Engels

First published in: Marx and Engels, *Works*, Second Russian Edition, Vol. 50, Moscow, 1981

Printed according to the original

Published in English for the first time

77

ENGELS TO KARL KAUTSKY [88]

IN ZURICH

London, 26 April 1884

Dear Kautsky,

I had made up my mind and told everyone here that I would play a trick on Bismarck and write something (Morgan)[174] that he would

---

[a] See this volume, pp. 135-36.

positively be unable to ban. But with the best will in the world I found it impossible. The chapter on monogamy and the final chapter on private ownership as the source of class antagonisms and also as the detonator that exploded the old communal system I find absolutely *impossible* to couch in such a way as to comply with the Anti-Socialist Law.[37] As Luther said: Let the devil come and fetch me, I cannot do otherwise.[214]

Nor would there be any point in the thing if I intended to write merely an 'objective' review and not deal with Morgan critically, if I did not try to evaluate the results recently achieved or present them in the light of our views and of what has already been achieved. Our workers would get nothing out of it. So — good and necessarily banned, or — permitted and execrable. The latter I cannot do.

I shall probably (Schorlemmer is here again until Monday[a]) be finished next week. It will amount to a full 4 sheets or more. If you are then *willing* to risk publishing it in the *Neue Zeit* (after you have read it) may any blood that is spilt as a result be on your own heads and don't blame me afterwards. If you are sensible, however, and do not wish to jeopardise the whole periodical for the sake of one article, you will do better to print it as a pamphlet either in Zurich or in the same way as *Frau*.[138] But that is your own look-out.

I think the thing will have a particularly important bearing on our general view. Morgan enables us to present entirely new aspects by providing us, in the shape of prehistory, with a factual basis we have hitherto lacked. Whatever doubts you may still entertain about individual primitives and 'savages', with the gens the case has been largely resolved and prehistory elucidated. And that is why the thing should be thoroughly worked on, properly weighed up and presented as a coherent whole — but also dealt with *without regard for the Anti-Socialist Law*.

And there's another most important point: I must show how brilliantly Fourier has anticipated Morgan in so many things. It is thanks to Morgan that for the first time the brilliance of Fourier's critique of civilisation really comes across. And that will mean a lot of work.[b]

I hope you got the letter I wrote on Monday on the subject of the

---

[a] 28 April - [b] See present edition, Vol. 26, p. 276 (footnote).

new editions.[a] Will you make sure that *absolutely nothing* is set up in type before my ms. arrives. The *Peasant War* is being *completely* re-written.[213] In the case of *Dühring*, the alterations, etc., made to the *Socialism: Utopian and Scientific* have to be inserted right at the beginning, there's a great deal· to be corrected and some more stuff to be put in.

Apropos. I have here approx. 50 copies of *Dühring*. If you can use them I shall send them off at once, but you must tell me by what route, so that they don't go via Germany and get seized. They will certainly know about that over there. Let me have as full details as possible.

Your

F. E.

First published, in Russian, in *Marx-Engels Archives*, Vol. I (VI), Moscow, 1932

Printed according to the original

Published in English in full for the first time·

78

ENGELS TO LUDWIG KUGELMANN

IN HANOVER

London, 4 May 1884
122 Regent's Park Road, N. W.

Dear Kugelmann,

My health is ALL RIGHT; it was a tedious and inconvenient affair though in no way serious, but to describe it to you would take pages. I received your card and also send my thanks for the Leibnitziad[215]; unfortunately I cannot embark on incidental studies of this kind, as I have my hands full attending to Volume II[b] and revising translations of Marx's things into German,[118] English[56] and French.[165] On top of that there are new editions of two of my works.[c] The 2nd book

---

[a] The reference is probably to the previous letter which Engels sent on Tuesday, 22 April. - [b] of *Capital* - [c] *Anti-Dühring* and *The Peasant War in Germany*; see also this volume, pp. 130 and 131.

will probably appear separately, but, having lost so much time during the autumn and winter, I am very behindhand with everything and, as I am being solicited from so many quarters, I have resolved to make no more promises.

Your

F. Engels

First published in: Marx and Engels, *Works*, First Russian Edition, Vol. XXVII, Moscow, 1935

Printed according to the original

Published in English for the first time

79

ENGELS TO PAUL LAFARGUE [196]

IN PARIS

London, 10 May 1884

My dear Lafargue,

Herewith cheque for £14.

Since I do not see any of the Paris papers, it is only from *The Standard* and from yourself that I know what is going on; your electoral tactics are just what I myself would have recommended [216] — these people will do themselves in if left to their own devices; GIVE THEM PLENTY OF ROPE AND THEY ARE SURE TO HANG THEMSELVES. However, Bernstein wrote and told me that you had put up a candidate [a] in opposition to Joffrin, and that he thought this ill-advised; let me know what the circumstances are so that I can answer him.

Thank you for the article — it is only the first one and I cannot now remember if I wrote the sequel. [217]

I have only seen the first number of Vaillant's translation. It is good and accurate, save that he does not always appear to be conversant with military terminology.

Your lectures and those of Deville are excellent [179] but, at least for the published version, you should develop more exhaustively the con-

---

[a] Louis Simon Dereure; see this volume, p. 141.

clusions of your second one on Darwinism. That part seems overwhelmed by the mass of premisses leading up to the conclusion, nor is the latter self-evident enough, while its detail is inadequately developed. I have not yet read the third one. As soon as the translation of *The Poverty of Philosophy* has been completed in Zurich,[118] I shall suggest that they bring out the lectures in German.

I shall now withdraw, having a rather important piece of work to complete: *The Origin of the Family, Private Property and the State*,[174] which I hope to have rid myself of by the end of next week. Until then I must soldier on.

Give Laura a kiss from me and from Nim, who also sends one to you.

Yours ever,
F. E.

First published in: F. Engels, P. et L. Lafargue, *Correspondance*, Vol. I, Paris, 1956

Printed according to the original

Translated from the French

80

ENGELS TO EDUARD BERNSTEIN

IN ZURICH

[London,] 17 May 1884

Dear Ede,

The ms.[a] will be finished today; there remains the checking and the polishing, which will take a day or two. Then you shall have it. I think that Kautsky is arranging for the *Neue Zeit* to print the chapter on the family (minus monogamy[b]) as a sample and that the whole will be printed separately. You can let me have your suggestions about ways and means when you get it.

A word on the Paris elections[c] and other matters as soon as I have time. At the moment I am impatient to be done with the ms. and

---

[a] F. Engels, *The Origin of the Family, Private Property and the State*. - [b] See present edition, Vol. 26, pp. 170-82. - [c] See this volume, p. 141.

have left everything else, however urgent, on one side. It will be long—approx. 130 closely written octavo pages and is called *Die Entstehung der Familie, des Privateigentums und des Staats.*[a] Time for the post and a meal. Regards to Kautsky.

Your
F. E.

Amongst other vicissitudes, Pumps' little boy is very dangerously ill; I am very anxious about him.

First published, in Russian, in *Marx-Engels Archives*, Book I, Moscow, 1924

Printed according to the original

Published in English for the first time

81

ENGELS TO EDUARD BERNSTEIN AND KARL KAUTSKY

IN ZURICH

London, 22 May 1884

My Dear Fellows,

Herewith the ms.[a] with the exception of the final chapter which still needs revising. You will find that it is not suitable for the *open* market in Germany, so consider whether it ought to be printed in Stuttgart under a false style or then and there in Zurich, and let me know in writing. Since the Prussian schnapps affair,[218] *everything bearing my name has been banned.* If it goes to Stuttgart I shouldn't want it to be revealed beforehand to the Wise Men who hold sway there.[219] In any case I must read the *proof* myself and would ask you for the sheets *in duplicate*, on good paper with a wide margin, otherwise one cannot make proper corrections. Perhaps you would be good enough to send a postcard acknowledging receipt. I shall answer your letters tonight or tomorrow; I have put everything on one side in order to

---

[a] F. Engels, *The Origin of the Family, Private Property and the State.*

get the enclosed finished and must presently set off for the funeral of Pumps' little boy who died on Sunday.[a]

Your old friend
F. E.

First published, in Russian, in *Marx-Engels Archives*, Vol. I (VI), Moscow, 1932

Printed according to the original

Published in English for the first time

82

ENGELS TO KARL KAUTSKY [1]

IN ZURICH

[London,] 23 May 1884

Dear Kautsky,

I trust you will have received the ms. of chapters 1-8 [b]; it went off to you yesterday by *registered mail*. As I have already suggested, I think the best thing to do, if you want to use some of it for the *Neue Zeit*, would be to take the chapter on the family with the exception of monogamy.[c] It anticipates the latter to the extent necessary to produce a fairly well rounded whole.

As to the ban, I have already written and told you that everything by me is banned on principle [d]; 'Prussian Schnapps' was a personal insult to Bismarck and, now that Richter has used it to concoct a policy of his own for schnapps,[220] the schnapps and wrapping-paper man will henceforward give me no rope at all. Anyhow all your arguments [221] fall to the ground with the successful endorsement of the Anti-Socialist Law [222] and with the banning of the *Süddeutsche Post* that immediately ensued.[223] And the government can afford to be harsh when letting fly with its bans; proof of this is provided by the liberal press which is literally clamouring for vigorous action against us. You, as an Austrian, cannot possibly follow the reasoning that

---

[a] 18 May - [b] of Engels' *The Origin of the Family, Private Property and the State* - [c] See this volume, p. 135.- [d] See previous letter.

goes on in the minds of people like Bismarck, Puttkamer & Co.; for that you would have to be familiar with the Prussian police regime before 1848; to restore *this* to full bloom by means of the Anti-Socialist Law is the prime motive of these Junker bureaucrats. Everything else — at home — is secondary.

I have not yet heard anything further about the *Dührings* that are stored here.[a]

I have Rodbertus' *Kapital*. Seems to be nothing in it. A repository of the most meagre material, endlessly repeated.

The things from the archives are being carefully looked after at my house and I shall be punctilious about returning them.[224] As soon as I have polished off the final chapter and put various other things — books, etc.— in the house in order, I shall tackle the 2nd volume of *Capital* — in the *daytime*; in the *evenings* I shall first of all revise your *Poverty of Philosophy*[118] and do the notes and preface for it.[b] This apportionment is not only useful but absolutely essential, since one does not study Marx's handwriting by lamplight for any length of time unless one is intent on going blind. Moreover my critique of Rodbertus will be confined in the main simply to the accusation of plagiarism [225] and all the rest — his social salvationist utopias, rent, mortgage relief for the landed aristocracy, etc., only mentioned in passing. So you will have sufficient material to administer a sound thrashing to this little Pomeranian exploiter of cottagers,[226] who might have become a second-rate economist had he not been a Pomeranian. Now that the milksops, who cling to us on the one hand and to the armchair socialists [54] on the other with the intention of protecting both their flanks, have, *à la* Freiarsch Thüringer,[c] played off the 'great[d] Rodbertus' against Marx, and now that Adolph Wagner and other Bismarckians have actually elevated the same to the rank of prophet of careerist socialism,[227] we have absolutely no cause to spare this prodigy invented by Rodbertus himself and loudly extolled by Meyer (who knows nothing about economics and, in the former, possessed his own secret oracle). The man achieved absolutely nothing in the field of economics; he had much talent, but always remained a dilettante and, above all, an ignorant Pomeranian and arrogant Prussian. The most he ever

---

[a] See this volume, p. 133. - [b] F. Engels, 'Marx and Rodbertus'. - [c] Freiwald Thüringer (Max Quarck) - [d] In the original: 'grauβen' (South-German dialect).

achieved was to present a number of neat and correct points of view, but he was never able to turn them to good account. How can a decent chap actually come to be regarded as the apostle of the careerists of Bismarckian socialism? It is history's revenge upon this artificially inflated 'prodigy'.

Your news from Germany about internal matters is always very · welcome.

But now I must write to Ede.

Your
F. E.

First published, in Russian, in *Marx-Engels Archives*, Vol. I (VI), Moscow, 1932

Printed according to the original

Published in English in full for the first time

83

ENGELS TO EDUARD BERNSTEIN [88]

IN ZURICH

London, 23 May 1884

Dear Ede,

I trust your business trip was eventually crowned with success. All that is necessary to begin with, I think, is for the gentry to be thrown off the scent; once you have managed to do that, the old route, or parts of it, can again be made use of. The stupidity of the police will see to the rest. [228]

I ordered Rodbertus' *Normal-Arbeitstag*, but it was out of print. I should be grateful if you could let me have the thing — on loan, of course, — since it contains the only authentic version of his proposed labour reforms. — I am now returning the issues of the old *Social-Demokrat* by REGISTERED MAIL, [224] having discovered that Lessner possesses them. The translation to be agreed with Lafargue is still pending,[a] which is why I had to have the original here; now, of course, it can be returned.

___
[a] See this volume, pp. 116-17.

Singer has been over here and I informed him, amongst other things, of my views regarding the tactics to be adopted in the case of final ballots. For I consider it nonsensical to try and set up universally applicable rules for these which, when it actually comes to the point, are never adhered to. We have great potential power of which no use at all will be made if abstention from the polls is prescribed in all cases where none of our people are involved in the final ballot. As it happens, in all such cases electoral pacts — e. g. with the Centre [229] — invariably come into being automatically: We shall vote for you *here* if you vote for us *there*, and many a seat have we acquired thus. Blunders may result of course, but blunders will always be made, nor is this any reason for committing an even greater one. I therefore told him that, in places like Berlin, for instance, where the electoral campaign is virtually confined to ourselves and the men of Progress, [93] pacts *before* the general election were not out of the question — you cede us that constituency and in return we cede you this one — but only, of course, if one can count on their being observed. What I consider inept is, in effect, the attempt by congresses to formulate in advance universally valid rules for as yet non-existent tactical cases.

Au fond,[a] I am glad that the Anti-Socialist Law has been renewed and *not* repealed forthwith. [222] The liberal philistine would have secured a tremendous electoral victory for the Conservatives [230]; in order to preserve the Anti-Socialist Law he would not only go through fire and water, but wade through the deepest of cess-pits. And it would only have resulted in another, more draconian law. As it now stands, it has probably been renewed for the last time and will, once old Wilm[b] succumbs to his nephritis, soon cease to exist in practice. And the thorough discrediting of the German Free Thinkers [231] and of the Centre Party in the course of the division [232] is also of some value, though not as much as Bismarck's right to work. [233] Now that that addle-pate has taken this up there's a chance of our ridding ourselves of the wailers [123] *à la* Geiser. Come to that, no one but a Bismarck could perpetrate such a blunder in the face of a workers' movement that cannot be kept down even by means of emergency laws. For the present our people are right to press for implementation and thus implicate him as deeply as possible; the moment the man has committed himself a bit more (though he is not likely to do so very soon), the whole imposture will resolve itself — into Prussian police

[a] On the whole - [b] William I

chicanery. *Qua* electoral programme, the slogan by itself will do him damn' all good.

The right to work was Fourier's idea but realised in his case only in the *phalanstère*, [234] and thus presupposes the adoption of the latter. The Fourierists — peace-loving philistines of *Démocratie pacifique*, as their paper was called — disseminated the slogan precisely because it sounded safe. The Parisian workers of 1848 swallowed it whole — it being something theoretically utterly unclear — because it seemed so practical, so non-utopian, so readily realisable. The government realised it — in the only way it could be realised in a capitalist society — in the form of preposterous national workshops. [235] Similarly in this country, during the 1861-64 cotton crisis, the right to work was realised in Lancashire in the form of municipal workshops. And in Germany it is likewise being realised in those hunger and cudgel workers' colonies about which your philistine is now enthusing. Advanced as a *separate* demand, the right to work *cannot* be realised in any other form. The demand for its realisation by capitalist society can only be met by the latter within the terms of its *own* existence, but if the demand for the right to work be made of *that society*, then it is made on these specific terms and hence is a demand for national workshops, workhouses and [workers'] colonies. But if the demand for the right to work is to comprise *indirectly* the demand for the subversion of the capitalist mode of production, it is, in regard to the present state of the movement, a dastardly piece of tergiversation, a concession to the Anti-Socialist Law, a slogan whose only purpose can be to bemuse and befuddle the workers as to the aims they ought to pursue and the only terms upon which they can attain them.

In the Paris municipal elections, our people have in fact pursued the tactics recommended by you, only putting up Dereure against Joffrin because there was at first no Opportunist [236] standing against him, so that in this instance opposition was pretty well obligatory. Simoneau did not come upon the scene until later, whereupon Guesde immediately demanded that Dereure withdraw; but at this point Dereure's courage failed him and thus he suffered a resounding defeat. Vaillant, on the other hand, triumphed over the Possibilists [237] in his *arrondissement*, for Retiès was a tosspot (*poivrard*) of the worst repute and was deservedly defeated. And if Joffrin was defeated in the final ballot, it was not our people but his who were to blame. It will, by the way, be necessary to go on opposing the Possibilists until they deign to come to an agreement with our chaps at election time; so long as they simply go on making themselves out to be the *parti ouvrier par excellence*, [a] they will force our chaps into direct opposition. So either — or; it's for those gentlemen to decide.

As regards Joffrin in particular, his programme was so lousy and lukewarm that even the Radicals refrained from putting up a rival candidate, Joffrin's programme being, in essence, *their own!*

Over here *Justice* gets more wretched by the week.

Your
F. E.

I shall also set to work on the *Dühring*. [208] When roughly do you want to start printing? Once I have begun, I shall be able to knock off some 6 to 8 sheets straight away, although it is precisely at the beginning that there is much revision to be done.

The Peasant War will be completely rewritten save for the account of military events. [213] I have learned a great deal about the subject in recent years and shall be including quite a lot of German history. This as soon as *Dühring* is ready!

First published abridged, in Russian, in *Marx-Engels Archives*, Book I, Moscow, 1924 and in full in *Die Briefe von Friedrich Engels an Eduard Bernstein*, Berlin, 1925

Printed according to the original

Published in English in full for the first time

84

ENGELS TO LAURA LAFARGUE

IN PARIS

London, 26 May 1884

My dear Laura,

Since the receipt of your letter of the 15th we have had sorrowful times. On the 18th Pumps' little boy died and was buried on the 22nd.

---

[a] workers' party *par excellence*

The child suffered from whooping-cough, bronchitis, convulsions and croup, there was but little hope a week before he died. I was under the impression Pumps or Percy had written to you, and they it seems relied on me for letting you know; well, I was busy finishing my pamphlet[a] to which I postponed even the most pressing letters — and finishing it, as you may conceive, under difficulties of every sort. Well, it's done, the last sheets go off tomorrow. How long they will be over the printing of it, I don't know.

I am sorry you won't go in for the 'Akkumulationsprozess des Kapitals'.[b] Think it over again. I am afraid we cannot do without help from without, and to tell you the truth I have deuced little confidence in what assistance I may get here. Aveling has *den besten Willen*[c] but he is to translate strange matter *aus einem ihm unbekannten Deutsch in ein ihm unbekanntes Englisch*[d]; if it was natural science it would be easy enough, but political economy and industrial facts where he is not acquainted even with the commonest terms. And Sam[e] who is doing the first chapter far better than I expected, takes such a time over it. And yet it is daily becoming a greater necessity to have it out, and Kegan Paul and Co. with whom I expect to come to terms soon, are pressing, but unless I can promise the ms. by say November, complete, I cannot well conclude anything. You might try a few pages and see how you get on. A German-English dictionary would be useless; the words *you* would have to look for, you would not find there; you could leave space for them, and I could fill them in, they will mostly be technical or philosophical terms.

Paul's *conférences*[f] are a great success,[179] the *New Yorker Volkszeitung* brings them regular, their own translation, I believe. If the French had two or three people who could and would assimilate German publications in the same manner, it would help them on immensely. I foresee that when my *Ursprung der Familie etc.*[g] comes out, Paul will be mad after translating it, there are things in it just in his line,[h] but if he begins he will have to take the German words in their own sense and not in the sense he pleases to impart to them, because I shall have no time whatever to work at it. I shall now start with the 2nd volume [of] *Kapital* and work at it during daylight, the evenings

---

[a] *The Origin of the Family, Private Property and the State* - [b] The reference is to Part VII of the first volume of *Capital*, see also this volume, p. 128 and Note 56. - [c] best intentions - [d] from unfamiliar German into unfamiliar English - [e] Samuel Moore - [f] lectures - [g] *The Origin of the Family etc.* - [h] See this volume, p. 293.

will be for the revision of the various translations in hand and threatened. This pamphlet I just finished will be the last independent work
for some time to come. Will you please tell Deville that I have not as
yet had the time to read his last *conférence*, but shall do so before the
week is out and hope it is as good as its predecessors.

Now I must conclude, it is past eleven and Nim is moving for bed,
she has got 'pains all over', *id est* slight muscular rheumatism in consequence of cold, and she must stand at the door while I post this letter,
as Annie is in bed, so in order to keep Nim no longer from her much
needed rest (she has slept a bit in her arm-chair already) I hope you
will excuse the blank space at the foot of this.

By the way, it appears Liebknecht has been in Paris, the German
papers tell the most extraordinary things about his mysterious proceedings, [238] also that he spoke at a banquet together with that muff
Lecler. [a]

Kisses from Nim and

From yours affectionately,

F. Engels

First published, in the language of the   Reproduced from the original
original (English), in: F. Engels, P. et L.
Lafargue, *Correspondance*, t. I, Paris, 1956

85

ENGELS TO EDUARD BERNSTEIN

IN ZURICH

London, 5 June 1884

Dear Ede,

Have spent a week at the seaside. [239] While there I got a nasty cut on
my right index finger and hence can only write briefly and badly. So
Kautsky will have to wait, the *Sozialdemokrat* being more important

---

[a] Henri Leclère

than the *Neue Zeit* and, in the latter's case, the circumstances are such
that it makes no difference anyway whether I stick my oar in or not.
Besides I consider that all Kautsky's moves, in so far as he has told me
about them and in so far as I am able to judge the situation, have
been absolutely correct. [240]
As regards the *Sozialdemokrat*, it is a rather different matter. Now
that their worships, the wailers, [123] have formally combined into
a party and constitute a majority in the parliamentary group, [49] now
that they have recognised, and are exploiting, the power they have
acquired thanks to the Anti-Socialist Law, [37] I consider it to be more
than ever our duty to defend all *our own* vantage points to the utmost,
especially our vantage point on the *Sozialdemokrat*, which is the most
important of all.

These people *live* off the Anti-Socialist Law. Were there to be free
discussion tomorrow, I should be all for letting fly at once, in which
case they would soon come to grief. But so long as there is no free discussion, so long as they control all the papers printed in Germany and
their numbers (as the majority of the 'leaders') enable them to make
the very most of gossip, intrigue, whispering campaigns, *we*, I believe,
must steer clear of anything that might lead to a breach, or rather
might lay the *blame* for that breach at our door. That is the universal
rule when there is a struggle within one's own party, and now it
applies more than ever. The breach must be so contrived that we
continue to lead the old party while they either resign or are chucked
out.

Then the timing. Just now everything is in *their* favour. We cannot,
after the breach, stop them from slandering and reviling us in Germany, from posing as the representatives of the masses (for the masses
do *elect* them after all!). We have only the *Sozialdemokrat* and the
foreign press. They can gain a hearing, we can only do so with difficulty. So if *we* precipitate a breach at this moment, the great mass of
the party will claim not without justification that we have sown discord, have disorganised the party at the very time when, beset by
dangers, it is laboriously reorganising itself. If we can avoid it, the
breach ought to be postponed, and this is still my view, until some
change in Germany gives us rather more elbow room.

If a breach becomes inevitable nevertheless, it must not be of the
personal kind, it must not involve any rows (or what could be represented as such) between e. g. you and the Stuttgarters [219]; rather the
occasion for it must be a quite specific point of principle, i. e. in this

case of an infringement of the programme. Rotten though the programme may be, a cursory perusal of it will enable you to find enough in it to support your argument. [241] The programme, however, is not subject to the jurisdiction of the parliamentary group. The breach must be prepared in advance to the extent that Bebel, for one, agrees to it and at once goes along with you. And, thirdly, you must know what you want and are *able* to do once the breach has been made. To allow the *Sozialdemokrat* to pass into the hands of these people would be to make the German party the laughing-stock of the entire world.

The worst thing of all in such a case is impatience; decisions made on the spur of the moment and dictated by passion always seem to oneself tremendously noble and heroic, but they regularly lead to blunders, as I know only too well from a hundred examples from my own practical experience.

So: 1) postpone the breach for as long as possible, 2) if it becomes inevitable, make sure that it emanates from *them*, 3) get everything ready in the meantime, 4) do nothing without Bebel, for one, and possibly also Liebknecht, who will again be good for something (possibly *too* good) once he sees that the thing is inevitable and, 5) defend your vantage point on the *Sozialdemokrat envers et contre tous*,[a] down to your last cartridge. That is my view.

You could certainly repay the 'condescension' of these gentlemen a thousand times over. You're certainly never at a loss for a ready answer in other respects and can certainly confront those jackasses with enough irony as well as disdain to make them rue this behaviour. There can be no serious discussion with ignoramuses like these who glory in their own ignorance; rather, they must be derided, hoist with their own petard, etc.

Don't forget either that, should things come to a head, my hands are very much tied by the vast amount of work ahead of me and I shan't be able to join in the fray to the extent I might wish to do.

I should also be grateful if, instead of general complaints about the philistines, you could give me a few details of *what* they object to and *what* they demand. *Nota bene*, the longer you negotiate with them, the greater the amount of self-incriminating material they must inevitably supply you with!

Write and tell me how far I ought to go into these matters when

---

[a] against all-comers

corresponding with Bebel; I shall have to write to him shortly and intend to put off doing so until Monday the 9th inst., by which time I may have had a reply from you.

Regards to Kautsky.

Your

F. E.

First published in *Die Briefe von Friedrich Engels an Eduard Bernstein*, Berlin, 1925

Printed according to the original

Published in English for the first time

86

ENGELS TO AUGUST BEBEL [88]

IN BORSDORF NEAR LEIPZIG [34]

London, 6 June 1884

Dear Bebel,

Have received your letter of the 4th inst. and shall attend to the enclosure. You do not say whether you got my registered letter of 21 April, [39] in which I returned the *envelope*, its seal *broken*, of your letter of the 18th of that month. If it has been intercepted, then the Stieberising of letters has been doubly proven. [242]

If everything were to go according to the wishes of the Conservatives [230] and Liberals, [243] and likewise accord to the secret yearnings of the progressist philistines, [93] there can be no doubt that the Anti-Socialist Law [37] would long since have been perpetuated as an institution in Germany and that it would so remain. But that can only happen if nothing happens elsewhere in the world, and everything remains as it is now. Despite all these philistine desires, the Law was on the very brink of disaster when friend Bismarck applied his two last and most powerful levers—Lehmann's direct intervention [210] and the threat of dissolution. [244] Hence it would not even require a particularly violent convulsion of the present status quo, peaceful as it is, to put an end to the whole caboodle. And in my opinion this will surely happen before two years are out.

True, Bismarck has, for the first time, played a *really* nasty trick on us by procuring 300 million marks for the Russians. [182] That will give the Tsar [a] a couple of years' respite from an *acute* financial emergency and thus temporarily eliminate the danger that looms largest — the necessity of having to convene the Estates for the voting of subsidies, as in France in 1789 and Prussia in 1846. If the revolution in Russia is not to be put back by several years, there must either be some unforeseen complications or else a couple of nihilistic thunderbolts. [b] Neither of these can be counted on to happen. All we may be sure of is that the recent borrowing operation cannot be repeated.

At home, on the other hand — as you yourself say — a change of monarch is imminent and is bound to make everything totter. Here again it is as it was in 1840, before the death of old Frederick William III. So many interests are bound up with the old familiar state of political stagnation that there is nothing the heart of Philistia as a whole desires more fervently than its perpetuation. But with the old monarch [c] the keystone disappears and the whole artificial structure collapses. The afore-mentioned interests, faced with an entirely new situation, suddenly discover that the world of today looks completely different from that of yesterday, and that they will have to look round for new mainstays. The new monarch [d] and his new entourage have plans that have long been suppressed; the whole body of those who govern or are capable of governing expands and changes; officials are perplexed by the new conditions, and the insecurity of the future, the uncertainty about who will be at the helm tomorrow or the day after, causes the action of the entire government machine to falter. That, however, is all we require. But we shall get more. For in the first place we may be sure that while, at the start, the new government may have liberalising aspirations, it will soon become frightened at its own daring, will vacillate hither and thither and eventually grope its way hither and thither, living from hand to mouth, from instance to instance, each decision conflicting with the next. Aside from the general effect of this vacillation, what will become of the Anti-Socialist Law if it is administered under these conditions? The slightest attempt to administer it 'fairly' would be enough to render it ineffective. Either it has to be operated as at present, purely at the whim of the police, or it

[a] Alexander III - [b] Cf. this volume, pp. 256, 275.- [c] William I - [d] Crown Prince Frederick William

will everywhere be broken.— That is one aspect. But there is another, namely that then, at last, some animation will return to the bourgeois political scene, the official parties will cease to be the one reactionary mass they now are (which is no gain to us, but rather a dead loss), and again begin seriously combatting one another and likewise struggling for political supremacy. It will make a tremendous difference to us whether, on the one hand, both National Liberals and Crown Prince Free Thinkers [231] have a chance of coming to the helm, or whether, as now, the ability to govern is confined to the liberal Conservatives. We shall never be able to lure the masses away from the liberal parties so long as the latter are not given an opportunity of discrediting themselves in practice, of taking the helm and demonstrating their ineptitude. As in 1848, we are still the opposition of the future and must, therefore, have the most extreme among the existing parties at the helm before being able to confront it as the opposition of the present. Political stagnation, i. e. aimless and purposeless struggle between the official parties, as at present, can be of no service to us in the long run. What could, however, is a progressive struggle between those parties, with the centre of gravity gradually shifting to the Left. That's what is currently happening in France where, as always, the course of the political struggle has assumed a classical form. The successive governments are moving ever further to the Left, and a Clemenceau government is already in sight; it will not be the most extreme bourgeois government. With every shift to the Left, concessions accrue to the workers (cf. the recent strike at Denain in which, for the first time, the military did *not* intervene [245]) and, more important still, the field is being increasingly cleared for the decisive battle, while the position of the parties becomes more distinct and well-defined. This slow but inexorable progress of the French Republic towards its logical conclusion— the confrontation between radical would-be socialist bourgeois and genuinely revolutionary workers— I consider to be a manifestation of the utmost importance, and I hope that nothing will happen to stop it. And I am glad that our people are not yet strong enough in Paris (but all the stronger for that in the provinces) to be misled by the force of revolutionary phrases into attempting a putsch.— In muddle-headed Germany, needless to say, progress is not being made along the same purely classical lines as in France; we have lagged much too far behind for that, and everything we experience has already had its day elsewhere. But despite the rottenness of our official parties, political life of some description would be of far greater advantage to us than the present political death in which action is confined to the secret intrigues of foreign policy.

Sooner than I expected, friend Bismarck has lowered his trousers and shown the assembled people the posterior of his right to work [233] — an amalgam of the Poor Act of the 43rd year of the reign of Elizabeth and the Bastille amendment of 1834.[246] What bliss for Blos, Geiser and Co. who have, after all, been riding the hobby-horse of the right to work for some time now[a] and who already seem to imagine that it was *they* who had roped in Bismarck! And, having once embarked on this topic, I feel impelled to tell you that the performance of these gentry, both in the Reichstag — in so far as one can judge from the inadequate newspaper reports — and in their own press, has increasingly convinced me that *I*, at least, do not even remotely share their standpoint or have anything at all in common with them. These allegedly 'educated' but in fact utterly ignorant and obstinately ineducable philanthropists, who were not only admitted in the face of Marx's and my long and oft reiterated warnings, but were actually shepherded into the Reichstag, would seem to me to be becoming increasingly aware that they are in a majority in the parliamentary group and that it is precisely they who, with their time-serving attitude towards every crumb of state socialism tossed to them by Bismarck, more than any one else, are concerned that the Anti-Socialist Law should remain in force and that it should be applied leniently, if at all, to well-meaning persons like themselves — again something which only people like you and I prevent the government from doing, for if these, the afore-mentioned philanthropists, were rid of us it would be easy for them to prove that there was no call for an Anti-Socialist Law where they were concerned. Their abstention as well as their general performance in connection with the Dynamite Bill was likewise typical.[247] But what's going to happen at the next election [194] if, as seems probable, the safest constituencies fall to these chaps?

It is a great pity that, during the next few critical months, you will be so far away; now, with the elections upon us, we should certainly have had occasion to tell each other a great deal. Could you not let me have an address from which my letters could be forwarded to you? I also hope you may sometimes be able to send me some interesting information about your trip.

---

[a] See this volume, pp. 55-56.

Apart from what seems to me steady progress and increasing cohesion on the part of the eddicated bourgeois elements of the party, I am not at all anxious about the course things are taking. I would, if possible, rather see a split avoided so long as we have no freedom of action. But if it has to be—and it is for you people to decide, then so be it!

A work of mine on the origin of the family, property and the state is about to appear. As soon as it comes out I shall send it to you.

Your old friend
F. Engels

First published, in Russian, in *Marx-Engels Archives*, Vol. I (VI), Moscow, 1932

Printed according to the original

Published in English in full for the first time

87

ENGELS TO JOHANN PHILIPP BECKER

IN GENEVA

London, 20 June 1884

Dear Old Man,

I hereby notify you that I have today taken out a £5 money order on your behalf and hope the post office will have advised you of its receipt by the time this letter arrives—it goes off by the next post. I have long looked forward to being able to make the above available and am glad that the moment has now come.

However, I cannot, alas, write you a long letter since, in my particular condition, prolonged sitting at my desk is bad for me and consequently prohibited. Unfortunately I have again knocked myself up a bit by doing so, for I have had a great deal of work to get through; but resting in a prone position, as I have again been doing most assiduously for the past few days, will soon put me to rights again. I am now dictating the 2nd volume of *Capital*,[a] and so far it has been go-

---

[a] Presumably to Oskar Eisengarten (see this volume, p. 153).

ing quite quickly, but it's the devil of a job and will demand a great deal of time and, in parts, much brain-racking. Luckily my brain is in pretty good shape and quite up to the mark where work is concerned as you will, I hope, be able to see from a little book on the origin of the family, private property and the state soon to be published. The second book of *Capital* will also, I think, come out before the end of the year, and the third next year.

At Whitsuntide I spent a week with Borkheim [239]; he is still laid up, with one side half paralysed, gets up three times a day for meals and to do some writing, is writing his biography,[248] and is in good spirits and surprisingly cheerful for one in his condition, but sometimes suffers terribly from boredom. Moreover, he cannot read anything that demands much effort — not that he ever really has done. I send him books and the like every so often. He asked fondly after you and, in fact, we talked a great deal about you and about the old days.

Amongst Marx's papers I have found a few military campaign journals and the like relating to German columns in Switzerland which, no doubt, form part of the papers you mention.[126] Some more may turn up. Everything is safely here, but is still in a state of complete disorder. For the time being I shall have to lock away all correspondence, etc., in a large trunk until I have time to sort the stuff out and put it in order. But now it is absolutely essential that a text, both printable and written in a legible hand, be produced of the final volumes of *Capital*. Neither of these things can be done by any one now alive save for myself. If I were to kick the bucket first, no one else could possibly decipher the things which Marx himself was often unable to read, although his wife and I could do so. The letters, on the other hand, are written in such a way that others can read them.

In three or four months' time we shall be having elections in Germany.[194] I am extremely optimistic. There are many milksops amongst the leaders, but my faith in the masses is unshakable.

Your old friend

F. Engels

First published in: F. Engels, *Vergessene Briefe (Briefe Friedrich Engels' an Johann Philipp Becker)*, Berlin, 1920

Printed according to the original

Published in English for the first time

88

ENGELS TO KARL KAUTSKY [249]

IN ZURICH

London, 21-22 June 1884

Dear Kautsky,

I hope you are now back from your trip to Salzburg [250] and will soon be able to tell me something about the outcome of the Stuckert [a]-on-the-Neckar affair over the *Neue Zeit*. [240] According to what I hear from Ede and also from August, [b] something of a damper has since been put on the passions of the Wise Men. [219] It is high time, too, that I heard something definite concerning the fate of my ms. [c] Ede dropped me a pencilled note and promised something more, but did = 0.

Your ms. [118] still reposes here and has not yet been attended to for the following reason. After having completed the ms. [c] I was like a cat on hot bricks until I could begin work on Volume II of *Capital*. I did so. Next, I proposed to set about revising your work, as also the English translation (of the 1st volume of *Capital*), [56] in the evenings. But I had reckoned without my host. I had been hard at it since Easter, often spending 8 or 10 hours at my desk and, as a result of the posture this involved, my former indisposition partially reappeared — this time in chronic, not in its previous sub-acute, form. So desk work was again forbidden, *sauf quelques exceptions*. [d] I therefore took the heroic step of engaging Eisengarten so that I might dictate the ms. to him and, since the beginning of the week, he and I have been slogging away from 10 to 5 every day, during which time I lie on the sofa, recovering visibly (idiotic word — nothing to be seen, only felt) but, of course, slowly. The thing's going far better than expected. Eisengarten is intelligent and hard-working and puts his heart into the thing, the more so since he is just working his way through the 3rd edition of the 1st volume. But most of the mss. are such that I have to spend every evening going through what I have dictated if I am to produce a text that is even provisionally valid. At the moment this takes up all my available time. But I believe that things will improve, as we are

---

[a] Stuttgart - [b] Bebel - [c] *The Origin of the Family, Private Property and the State* - [d] save for a few exceptions

now coming to the original gospel written before 1870, which means that there will be less re-editing.[17] Anyway, I couldn't very well have revised your ms. *lying down*. But if you are in a hurry, I shall find the time and do it all at one go. There could be no question of this, however, nor for that matter, any necessity for it, unless you had got almost all of it done. I shall then — if not before — also let you have the preface about Rodbertus.[a]

For the rest, I shall not discuss in detail your complaints about the eddicated chaps; I have known these worthies in this guise or that for 40 years now and have already given Ede my opinion of them at some length.[b] The main thing is not to let oneself be browbeaten and, at the same time, retain one's composure.

The dynamiters have at long last discovered just what to do. They are concerned with striking at the root of the old social order, and now it transpires that the root in question is in fact the tail. This profound truth with which they are imbued eventually enabled them to discover how best to set about it, and they went and blew up a pissoir.[251]

Which reminds me that the man behind the Geneva-Carouge *Explosion* is none other than the Italian *mouchard*,[c] Carlo Terzaghi, who had already been unmasked by us in *The Alliance of Socialist Democracy*.[252]

The expelled Austrian anarchists[253] purport to be connected with the regular German charities which have long existed over here. One of them touched me for alms but was unmasked and, upon his returning today, was chucked out at top speed.

The 2nd book of *Capital* will give us even more headaches, at least to start off with, than the first one. But it contains quite admirable analyses that will, for the first time, show people what is money and what capital and much else.

But now it is time to lie down again. All things considered, and apart from the localised trouble, I'm as fit as a fiddle, and my brain is in first-class condition.

Regards to Ede.

Your

F. E.

---

[a] F. Engels, 'Marx and Rodbertus'.- [b] See this volume, pp. 144-47.- [c] police spy

Sunday 22nd.

Postscript. Hyndman intends to *buy up* the whole of the little movement here. He has done everything he can think of to ruin *To-Day*. Bax, who advanced the money for the purpose, got his sums wrong and was soon cleaned out. Hyndman, who is rich and also has access to the resources of Morris, a very rich but politically inept art lover, will either take *To-Day* under his wing or let it perish. Either way, he believes, he will reign supreme. I am glad that I have remained aloof from the whole caboodle. Hyndman is shrewd and a good business man, but superficial and STOCK-JOHN-BULL; moreover his ambition far outruns his talents and achievements. Bax and Aveling have the best of intentions and are, besides, learning by degrees, but everything's at sixes and sevens, nor can these literati do anything on their own. The fact is that the masses are not yet going along with them. Once the chaps have sorted themselves out a bit it will be better.

First published, in Russian, in *Marx-Engels Archives*, Vol. I (VI), Moscow, 1932

Printed according to the original

89

ENGELS TO KARL KAUTSKY [184]

IN ZURICH

London, 26 June 1884

Dear Kautsky,

The anti-Rodbertus ms. [254] goes back tomorrow by registered mail. I found little that called for comment and have made a few pencilled notes. Apart from these I would add the following:

1) Roman Law is the consummation of the law of *simple*, i. e. of precapitalist, *commodity production*, though the latter also embodies much of the legal system of the capitalist period. Exactly, that is, what our burghers *needed* at the time of their rise and, in accordance with local common law, did *not* get.

On p. 10 there are several things I object to: 1. Surplus *value* is the exception only in the case of production by slaves and serfs. It ought to read surplus *product*, most of which is directly consumed but not *valorised*.

2) As regards the means of production, the matter is not quite as you say. In all societies based on a division of labour that has evolved naturally, the product, and hence also to some extent the means of production, dominates the producer — on occasion at any rate — as did, in the Middle Ages, the soil the peasant who was simply an appurtenance of the land and the tool the guild handicraftsman. Division of labour is the direct domination of the instruments of labour over the worker, although not in the capitalist sense.

Much the same applies to the concluding bit on the means of production.

1) You should not separate *agriculture* any more than *technology* from political economy, as you do on pp. 21 and 22. Rotation of crops, artificial fertilisers, the steam engine, the power loom, cannot be separated from capitalist production any more than the tools of the savage and the barbarian from *his* production. The tools of the savage condition *his* society just as much as do more modern ones capitalist society. What your view boils down to is that, while produc- *j* tion does indeed determine the social institution *today*, it did not do so before capitalist production existed, because tools had not as yet been guilty of original sin.

The moment you say means of production, you say society and a society *determined* by, amongst other things, those means of production. Means of production *as such*, extraneous to society and without influence over it, exist no more than does capital *as such*.

But how the means of production, which, at earlier periods, including that of simple commodity production, exercised only a very mild domination compared with now, came to exercise their present despotic domination, is something that calls for proof and yours strikes me as inadequate, since it fails to mention one pole, namely the creation of a class which no longer had any means of production of its own, or, therefore, any means of subsistence, and hence was compelled to sell itself piecemeal.

In the case of Rodbertus' positive proposals, emphasis ought to be laid on his Proudhonism — after all he proclaimed himself Proudhon I, the forerunner of the French Proudhon. Constituted value, invented by Rodbertus as early as 1842,[255] is to be established. His proposals here are lamentably retrograde by comparison with Bray and with Proudhon's exchange bank. The worker is to get only $^1/_4$ of the product, but that is assured! We can discuss this later.

Repose (physical) is suiting me splendidly; I get better every day and this time the cure will be complete. The dictation of the 2nd book of *Capital* is going ahead splendidly. We[a] have already reached Part II — but there are big gaps. The editing is only provisional, of course, but that too will get done. I can see my way ahead, *cela suffit.*[b]

Ede's letter received with thanks. You will have to be patient with my letter-writing; I mustn't get run down again and a frightful amount of work and correspondence is piling up.

My regards to you both,

Your
F. E.

Wage Labour and Capital[c] will go off as soon as the comparison is done, perhaps tomorrow.[d]

First published, in Russian, in *Marx-Engels Archives*, Vol. I (VI), Moscow, 1932

Printed according to the original

90

ENGELS TO EVGENIA PAPRITZ

IN LONDON

[London,] 26 June 1884
122 Regent's Park Road, N. W.

Dear Madam,

The lithographed journal to which you have been so good as to draw my attention is already known to me by repute, although I have not yet been fortunate enough to see a copy of it.[256]

Are you not, perhaps, being a trifle unjust towards your compatriots? Marx and I have not, for our part, found any cause for complaint in them. While certain schools may have been more noted for

[a] Engels dictated Marx's ms. to Oskar Eisengarten; see this volume, p. 153.- [b] that's enough - [c] by Marx - [d] See this volume, p. 159.

their revolutionary zeal than for their scientific studies, and while, here and there, some degree of trial and error may have been and may still be in evidence, we have, on the other hand, witnessed a critical spirit and a devotion to research, even in the field of pure theory, wholly worthy of a nation capable of producing a Dobrolyubov and a Chernyshevsky. And here I speak, not only of the active revolutionary socialists, but of the historical and critical school in Russian literature, which is infinitely superior to anything of the kind produced in Germany and France by way of official history. And even among active revolutionaries our ideas, and the science of economics as remodelled by Marx, have always met with an intelligent and sympathetic response. As you are doubtless aware, a number of our works have quite recently appeared in Russian translation, and are to be followed by others, notably Marx's *Poverty of Philosophy*. His short work dating from before 1848, *Wage Labour and Capital* (Наемный трудъ и капиталъ), has also appeared under that title in this series.[257]

I am exceedingly flattered by your suggestion that a translation of my *Outlines etc.* might prove useful. Although still a little proud of this, my first work on social science, I am all too aware that it is now completely out of date and replete, not only with mistakes, but also with 'howlers'. The misapprehensions it could hardly fail to engender would, I fear, quite outbalance such good as it might do.

I shall be sending you by post a copy of *Dühring's Revolution etc.*[a]

As for our old newspaper articles, it would be difficult to lay hands on them just now. Most of them have little relevance today; as soon as the publication of the manuscripts left by Marx allows me sufficient leisure, I intend to bring them out as a collection with explanatory notes, etc. But that will not be for some time to come.

I am not quite sure what you mean by the manifesto addressed to *English* working men. Might it be The Civil War in France, the International's manifesto on the Paris Commune [b]? That I could send you.

If my health permitted, I should ask your permission to come and call on you; unfortunately I am not allowed to go out and about, though I feel reasonably well when *at home*.—Should you be willing

---

[a] F. Engels, *Anti-Dühring. Herr Eugen Dühring's Revolution in Science.*- [b] K. Marx, *The Civil War in France. Address of the General Council of the International Working Men's Association.*

to do me the honour of dropping in on me here, you would always find me at your service round about seven or eight o'clock in the evening.

I am, Madam,

Yours very truly,

F. Engels

First published in: Marx and Engels, *Works*, First Russian Edition, Vol. XXVII, Moscow, 1935

Printed according to the original

Translated from the French

91

ENGELS TO EDUARD BERNSTEIN [61]

IN ZURICH

London, 29 June 1884

Dear Ede,

1. I return *Wage Labour and Capital*[a] herewith. The Silesian edition has certainly required a great deal of revision.[258] I did not, it is true, have time to compare it with the original throughout, but only those passages that worried me most. However, you chaps have got it there and will be able to attend to that when correcting the proofs.

2. I shall get another portrait of Marx done by the same man who did mine, and let you have it. It is not a chalk drawing but an enlarged photograph. But how will a colour-print turn out if the chap has never seen Moor and his singularly dark complexion?[259]

3. A parcel of 40 *Revolutions*[b] went off from here yesterday addressed to Volksbuchhandlung, 3 Kasinostraße, Hottingen-Zurich, Switzerland, 'Books, Value £3 Carriage forward' (i. e. not prepaid) per Continental Parcels Express, which is the correspondent of the German Imperial Post Office and of the Swiss Post Office, and likewise of the French parcels offices. The association stuff [*Vereinssachen*] from Zurich also comes here by the same route. There is no parcel post be-

---

[a] by Marx - [b] F. Engels, *Anti-Dühring. Herr Eugen Dühring's Revolution in Science*; see this volume, p. 133.

tween England and the Continent, hence no 'postal packages *à* 5 kilos', or not, at any rate, for this country; splitting them up would mean doubling the cost *over here*. Not splitting them up into 2 parcels surely wouldn't raise the cost of consignment *there* as much as would splitting them up over here.

4. Schorlemmer writes to say that his brother Ludwig in Darmstadt has not yet received a single number of the *Sozialdemokrat* despite the fact that receipt of his subscription was acknowledged in the paper. Is this an isolated misfortune or general one? Please look into it.

5. I can't get hold of any socialist poems specifically by Weerth. There are some in Moses Hess' old *Gesellschaftsspiegel* of 1845, but I believe you have already seen those. I once heard something about a collection of his verse but have never set eyes on it.[260] In any case, *he* never published such a thing any more than *we* did.

6. The archivist will have to wait; I haven't the time to get my own things in order. If I do get round to it, you may be sure he won't be overlooked.[261] But now the prime consideration is the completion of the 2nd volume of *Capital*. The thing's going swimmingly, the preliminary edition of about $^1/_3$ having been done, and is progressing by something like $^1/_2$ a printed sheet a day, or a little under. As soon as we get to the last part ('The Circulation of the Aggregate Social Capital'),[a] Eisengarten can, with my help, copy out the existing ms. of 1878,[17] while I can get on with the final editing of what has already been done. In this way we shall finish before so very long, and then go on to the 3rd, most important book.

Only then will it be possible to consider putting the old pre-'48 mss. in order and preparing extracts thereof for the press. It's not that I am unwilling, but this requires work, i. e. time.

So you, too, have finally come round to the view that we shall end up by coping quite successfully with the 'Wise Men'.[219] I sent for a few numbers of the *Neue Welt*, so as to meet the gentlemen *chez eux*[b] for once. So far have only read the correspondence column. German schoolboy cheek which presupposes a very tame readership.

You should not, by the way, allow yourself to get worked up about pin-pricks; that is the golden rule in this struggle. And remember that

---

[a] See K. Marx, *Capital*, Vol. II, Part III: 'The Reproduction and Circulation of the Aggregate Social Capital'. - [b] on their own ground

Nothing gives one more delight
Than one's antagonists to bite,
Than making scurvy jokes about
This uncouth clod, that clumsy lout.[a]

Regards to Kautsky.

Your
F. E.

First published, in Russian, in *Marx-Engels Archives*, Book I, Moscow, 1924

Printed according to the original

Published in English in full for the first time

92

ENGELS TO SARAH ALLEN [262]

IN LONDON

[Draft]

[London, about 6 July 1884]

Madam,

In reply to your note of the 5th arrived to hand yesterday and an answer to which was retarded by my absence from town, I beg to say that I consider Mr E. Aveling quite a desirable tenant and have no doubt that you will not regret having let your premises to him.

Yours, etc.

First published in: Marx and Engels, *Works*, Second Russian Edition, Vol. 36, Moscow, 1964

Reproduced from the original

---

[a] G. Weerth, *Nichts Schönres gibt es auf der Welt...*

93

ENGELS TO GABRIEL DEVILLE

IN PARIS

London, 8 July 1884

My dear Citizen Deville,

Thank you for sending me your lectures [179] — the last one reached me yesterday and I have not yet had time to read it. I have no doubt that it is no less excellent than its predecessors. I shall suggest to our friends that they translate them into German and publish them in the same way as you are doing in Paris; it's precisely what we need for propaganda just now.

Would you be so kind as to pass on the enclosed note to Lafargue *without Mme Lafargue's knowledge*? He'll tell you the reason for this — perfectly innocent, by the way.

Yours ever,
F. Engels

First published abridged in: M. Dommanget, *L'introduction du marxisme en France*, Lausanne, 1969 and in full in: Marx and Engels, *Works*, Second Russian Edition, Vol. 50, Moscow, 1981

Printed according to the original

Translated from the French

Published in English for the first time

94

ENGELS TO KARL KAUTSKY

IN ZURICH

London, 11 July 1884

Dear Kautsky,

I trust Ede will get over his feverish attack; give him my regards and tell him that I, too, shall be drinking to his health.

To have let Auer have the Hamburg stuff is perfectly all right so far as I'm concerned. I suggested Bebel and Dietz merely because I had to tell the man to *whom* I intended to mention his name; needless to say this does not in any way restrict your freedom of action.

The matter of Dietz is becoming a bore. If he won't say either yes or no, then we can't go on waiting for him. My chief concern is that the thing[a] should come out and, secondly, that it should not be instantly confiscated *en masse*. I. e. two things that are to be had simultaneously only in Switzerland. Printing in Austria should be considered only in *case of need*; 1) it would mean fresh delays and negotiations and 2) the thing would be banned *all the same*, you need be under no illusions as to that[b]; and 3) not only could it be banned in Austria, but also seized (remember the Viennese affair you told me about last autumn). So do get something positive done at last.

There must still be something peculiar going on in the *Neue Zeit*, otherwise that wise man Schippel would certainly not have been allowed to talk of a 'Rodbertusian-Marxian theory', or of things that '*one* has come to recognise since Rodbertus'; and without editorial comment at that.[c] The Germans must have fallen low indeed if they have still not discovered that what Marx has in common with Rodbertus is nothing more than the *application égalitaire de la théorie ricardienne*[d] mentioned by Marx on p. 49 of the *Poverty*[e] and which has been a commonplace among English socialists since 1827! But that is very far from being surplus value as defined by Marx and applied by him to every aspect of the science of economics. Which is why the good English, and likewise Rodbertus, for all their borrowings from Ricardo, have made no headway at all in the matter of economics; the first advance in this field was made by Marx, who demolished all previous political economy.

Incidentally, if I am to tackle Rodbertus *properly*, I must have his piece of 1842,[f] *Zur Erkenntniss unsrer Zustände*, or whatever it is called. You quoted from it.[g] Could you let me have it for a day or two or, better still, buy it for me? To judge by some of the quotations, it

---

[a] F. Engels, *The Origin of the Family, Private Property and the State*. - [b] Cf. this volume, pp. 131-32. - [c] M. Schippel, 'H. M. Hyndman. *The Historical Basis of Socialism in England*, London, 1883', *Die Neue Zeit*, No. 7, 1884. - [d] equalitarian application of Ricardian theory - [e] See K. Marx, *The Poverty of Philosophy*, present edition, Vol. 6, p. 138. - [f] 1841 in the original. - [g] K. Kautsky, 'Das *Kapital* von Rodbertus', *Die Neue Zeit*, Nos. 8-9, 1884, pp. 343, 389.

would seem to be the best, because the first thing that he wrote, his later stuff being a mere rehash, hence increasingly flimsy.

Your

F. E.

First published, in Russian, in *Marx-Engels Archives*, Vol. I (VI), Moscow, 1932

Printed according to the original

Published in English for the first time

95

ENGELS TO KARL KAUTSKY [263]

IN ZURICH

London, 19 July 1884

Dear Kautsky,

Did not get the letter from you and Ede until this morning, although postmarked Zurich 17/7.

I agree to your proposals, provided the thing now goes ahead. If our workers can read Roman just as easily as German characters, I would myself, of course, prefer Roman. Format about the same as *Entwicklung*[a] — Bebel's *Frau* [138] was too large. If you believe you can sell 5,000, I am quite agreeable. So just get on with it and let me have the proofs soon. The arrangement with Schabelitz is also quite satisfactory. [264]

So the only reward we get for the consideration we have shown Dietz is his regarding us all as his enemies!

That the *Neue Zeit* is to cease publication [265] is no misfortune for the party. It is becoming increasingly clear that the great majority of *literary* party men in Germany belong to the ranks of those opportunists and pussy-footers whom the Anti-Socialist Law,[37] adversely though it may affect their pockets, has placed in exactly the right *literary* atmosphere; they can express themselves uninhibitedly, whereas we are prevented from giving them a piece of our mind. Thus the very fact of having to fill up such a review every month demands considerable forbearance, and entails the gradual encroachment of philanthropy, humanism, sentimentality — in short all the anti-revolutionary vices

---

[a] F. Engels, *Socialism: Utopian and Scientific.*

of your Freiwalds,[a] Quarcks, Schippels, Rosuses[b] et al. People who refuse on principle to learn anything and who turn out nothing but literature about literature and à propos of literature ($^9/_{10}$ of all German
writing today consists of writing about other writing) will, needless to
say, produce more sheets per year than those who mug up a subject
and attempt to write about other books only when 1) they have mas-
tered those other books, 2) the latter contain anything that is worthwhile. The preponderance of these gentlemen in literature published
in Germany, a preponderance created by the Anti-Socialist Law, is unavoidable so long as that Law endures. On the other hand, we have
a weapon of altogether different calibre in the shape of the literature
appearing abroad.

It would be delightful if you were to come to this country. But
I don't know whether you ought to count with such certainty on the
New Yorkers. Over 3 months ago Aveling was taken on as London
correspondent[c] and, though he has written regularly, he has not yet
had a penny. Here on the spot there's nothing to be earned. Neither
Justice nor *To-Day* pay, and if there's anything to be picked up elsewhere in the press, everyone is on to it like a pack of wolves.

The clairvoyance in the *Neue Welt*[266] is the best thing that could
have happened. That sort of 'erudition' regularly degenerates into
such-like nonsense. The cruder the better — it will be over all the
sooner. I did so laugh when I got your postcard. A few more such au-
dacious Geiseriads and the chap will have to pack his bags.

Hyndman's book,[d] like the man himself, is a pretentious, impertinent jumble in which he, too, continually tries to pick holes in Marx
(for not being an Englishman; Hyndman is the most jingoistic John
Bull imaginable) and yet is so ignorant of English history that it's all
w r o n g except for what he has learnt from the Germans. But Hyndman is about to come a cropper here; true he has, with his own and
Morris' money, now bought up the entire movement, financially
speaking (likewise *To-Day* which Bax is unable to carry on for want of
resources, and which has now been transferred lock, stock and barrel
to Hyndman), but his eagerness to play the dictator, his envy of all
potential rivals and his persistent self-promotion, have rendered him
suspect to even his surest friends, and his position in the Democratic
Federation[99] is growing shaky. *Cet homme n'ira pas loin, il ne sait pas*

---

[a] Freiwald Thüringer — pen-name of Max Quarck - [b] Robert Schweichel - [c] to the
New Yorker Volkszeitung - [d] H. M. Hyndman, *The Historical Basis of Socialism in England*.

attendre.[a]On top of that, *Justice* is becoming ever sillier, and I hope that this *initial* phase of the movement here will very soon be over[b]; it is becoming dreadfully unedifying.

With your bacillu*m*, you have given Geiser an opening [267] which, however, he may with any luck be too stupid to exploit. Both forms, *baculus* and *baculum*, are current, hence either gender so far as the derivation is concerned. But bacillus has long since been exclusively adopted in biology.

As I shall probably be going to the seaside for a bit at the end of this or the beginning of next month, I should be grateful if I could have Rodbertus' *Zur Erkenntniss now.*[c] I shall return it immediately, along with the *Normal-Arbeitstag*, etc., but it is necessary for me to have seen the thing because *he himself* maintained in 1879 that Marx had made use of it without due acknowledgment.[187] No such accusation could ever be brought against Marx save by people without any idea of the hair-raising ignorance it requires so much as to assert anything of the kind. Anyone who has read Ricardo — and even in Adam Smith there are passages enough to this effect — must after all know what is the 'source' of surplus value without having to read the great[d] Rodbertus first.

Your
F. E.

First published, in Russian, in *Marx-Engels Archives*, Vol. I (VI), Moscow, 1932

Printed according to the original

Published in English in full for the first time

96

ENGELS TO LAURA LAFARGUE

IN PARIS

London, 22 July 1884

My dear Laura,

'*La suite à demain!*' ... *mais je l'attends encore, cette suite*[e] which was to explain to me the many otherwise inexplicable things in your last let-

---

[a] This man will not go far; he does not know how to bide his time. - [b] See this volume, p. 236. - [c] Ibid., p. 163. - [d] In the original: 'graußen' (South German dialect). - [e] 'More tomorrow!' ... but I am still waiting for this continuation

ter. Why, I thought you lived in one of the finest, airiest, healthiest, etc., quarter of Paris, at an elevation sufficient to raise you above all earthly things, and now all at once you are going to move, and that at this blessed hot time of the year, and Paul is going to Bordeaux, and the whole world is all sixes and sevens and the long and the short of it is that you are not coming [268] but must spend the hot season in Paris, and will only leave Paris at that season when Heine admired it most:

> die Sterne
> sind am schönsten in Paris
> Wenn sie eines Winterabends
> Dort im Strassenkot sich spiegeln.[a]

Well, Nim and Jollymeier who came on Friday,[b] and myself have given this matter our most serious consideration and we have come to the unanimous, but so far not very satisfactory conclusion: that something must be wrong somewhere.

Anyhow: As *La Suite*[c] won't come, I hope you will after all come yourself and let all these considerations go to the wind. If you wait for Paul's going to Bordeaux to start a paper, that may or may not come off these next 100 years. If he does not go, and it is absolutely necessary that you should move from 66 Boulevard de Port-Royal, well, then let *him* hunt for apartments and do the moving. So I do not see what should stop you from coming over—if only for 3 weeks say—and as soon as you tell me that you are coming, we will make the road as smooth for you as we can.

Tussy and Edward are off on honeymoon No. I, if not back already again—the grand honeymoon is to come off next Thursday.[d] Of course, Nim, Jollymeier and I have been fully aware of what was going on for a considerable time and had a good laugh at these poor innocents who thought all the time we had no eyes, and who did not approach the *quart d'heure de Rabelais* [269] without a certain funk. However we soon got them over that. In fact had Tussy asked my advice before she leaped, I might have considered it my duty to expati-

---

[a] The stars
Are at their prettiest in Paris,
When they are reflected in the street filth
On a winter's evening.
Engels quotes from memory Heine's *Atta Troll*, Ch. II.-[b] 18 July-[c] continuation-
[d] 31 July

ate upon the various possible and unavoidable consequences of their step—but when it was all settled, the best thing was for them to have it out at once before other people could take advantage of its being kept in the dark. And that was one of the reasons why I was glad that we knew all about it—if any wise people had found it out and come up to us with the grand news, we should have been prepared. I hope they will continue as happy as they seem now, I like Edward very much, and think it will be a good thing for him to come more into contact with other people besides the literary and lecturing circle in which he moved, he has a good foundation of solid studies, and felt himself out of place amongst that extremely superficial lot amongst whom fate had thrown him.

Jollymeier is very well and lively now—while I work he takes long walks—he is off now on one of them. Pumps has at last got over her bronchitis, etc., and will move to-day into her new house in Kilburn—beg pardon, 'West Hampstead' (I never knew Hampstead to reach as far as Edgware Road, but so it seems).

Nim is very well and lively—next week I suppose we shall have to move towards the sea, but where to? that grand question remains still to be solved. As to myself I am right enough on condition of keeping—for the present—within very narrow bounds both as to exercise, work and enjoyment—I hope the change of air will finally set me right.

And now for 'la suite', and let it be a good one, a suite that brings you over!

Paul's Blé has arrived this morning. What a pity he does not follow the wise counsels of la rédaction du[a] Journal des économistes! [270]

Very affectionately yours,
F. E

First published, in the language of the original (English), in: F. Engels, P. et L. Lafargue, Correspondance, t. I, Paris, 1956

Reproduced from the original

---

[a] the editorial board of

97

ENGELS TO EDUARD BERNSTEIN

IN ZURICH

[London, not earlier than 25 July 1884]

Dear Ede,

You may send the enclosed to Auer if you wish; I have contrived it with that in view.

As regards the apportionment of constituencies,[271] I assure you that I, too, have often been annoyed about it, but it is due to the desire to proceed, in purely tactical matters, in accordance with general principles and this always happens at congresses where everything is made to look so nice and simple. Dual candidatures are, of course, useless as a rule; but if you reckon that in the doubtful constituencies the best people are more likely to get in than the others and you therefore put them up there, you must either tolerate dual candidatures in their case or run the risk of their not being elected at all. So if you're totally opposed to dual candidatures, you must put up the best people in the safest constituencies. But then it is odd that this relegation to doubtful constituencies never happens to Liebknecht but only to Bebel, and that e. g. at the last election Liebknecht had, if I am not mistaken, *two* quite good constituencies.[a] *Enfin*[b] such things cannot be avoided. Nor must one forget that a battle always has its ups and downs and hence not be put out if the downs sometimes tend to predominate.

At all events, this much is certain: so long as we have the *Sozialdemokrat*, their worships the opportunists may do as they wish; and even if they gained control of the parliamentary group (which is after all only possible if Bebel is not re-elected), they wouldn't have won, not by a long chalk. What are their intentions towards the masses? The latter keep pressing these same people onwards whether they like it or not. And if the Wise Men[219] also succeeded in gaining command of the *Sozialdemokrat*, this would be of shorter duration than the *Sozialdemokrat*'s first weak-kneed period which at the outset also met with

---

[a] See Engels' letter to Bernstein of 30 November 1881 (present edition, Vol. 46). -
[b] Well

support, even among the better of the 'leaders', but was utterly rejected by the masses.

As to the Vast Erudition of the celebrated non-atheist,[272] I shall be highly delighted if it takes every possible opportunity to parade itself. An equally mysterious savant[a] crops up in Paul de Kock's *Amant de la lune*; when, having gone to the utmost trouble, people finally get the measure of his erudition, they discover that it consists in a couple of conjuring tricks with corks. Think of all the trouble we went to before this celebrated man finally consented to provide us with just a *few* samples of his erudition! And how pretty they are! And he has actually got as far as clairvoyance.[266] What more could we want? — *cela marche!*[b]

Regards to Karl Kautsky, also from Schorlemmer.

Your
F. E.

Tell Manz, who has written to me, that a portrait just like mine is now being done for him and that he shall have it as soon as it is ready[c]; in a sprawling city like London, however, I can't chase after things personally and must therefore depend on other people.

First published, in Russian, in *Marx-Engels Archives*, Book I, Moscow, 1924

Printed according to the original

Published in English for the first time

98

ENGELS TO LAURA LAFARGUE

IN PARIS

London, 26 July 1884

My dear Laura,

La suite, la suite de la suite et la conclusion par[d] Paul Lafargue to hand. I have just sent my *amanuensis*[e] home and have a few minutes

---

[a] Saucissard - [b] He's doing well. - [c] See this volume, p. 159. - [d] The continuation, continuation of the continuation and the conclusion by; see this volume, pp. 166-68. -
[e] secretary (Oskar Eisengarten)

left to say that I shall be very glad not only to revise Paul's article but also to offer suggestions as to points of attack.[273] But for that I must have the book[a] and to get it I must know the *exact title*—please let me have that at once so that I can order it.

It appears, then, that after all we shall have to do without you at the seaside.[268] Well, I don't know—if this weather continues, whether France is not preferable. We have now, 5 p. m., hardly 17° Centigrade and plenty of rain so that poor Jollymeier has not been able to take his walk.

Pumps and Percy are just coming in for dinner so I must conclude. Love from all.

Yours affectionately,
F. E.

First published, in the language of the original (English), in: F. Engels, P. et L. Lafargue, *Correspondance*, t. I, Paris, 1956   Reproduced from the original

99

ENGELS TO HERMANN SCHLÜTER

IN HOTTINGEN-ZURICH

[London,] 28 July 1884

Dear Mr Schlüter,

Proofs[b] returned herewith. Shall continue to return them promptly. But I would ask you to be rather more indulgent with my spelling; I have no cause in my advancing years to let myself be either *c*ivilised or *c*entralised, let alone *c*ited.[c] Supposedly 'consistent' spelling is usually far less consistent and far less historical than the good old casualness.

I am in full agreement with your suggestions. However these are things you know more about than I do.

---

[a] P. Leroy-Beaulieu, *Le Collectivisme. Examen critique du nouveau socialisme.* - [b] F. Engels, *The Origin of the Family, Private Property and the State.* - [c] At that time *zivilisieren*, *zentralisieren* and *zitieren* were customarily spelt with a 'c'. In this letter Engels spells them with a 'z'.

I would now ask you to be good enough to let me have the final proofs and, when the book is ready, 25 copies of the deluxe edition and 5 of the other; I shall not be able to manage with less.[264]

To save postage, the ms. can be sent *with* the proofs in a stiff, strong wrapper; over here mss. and proofs are both charged as book post. They must, however, carry the *full* amount of stamps, otherwise they won't arrive here.

Yours faithfully,

F. Engels

First published in: Marx and Engels, *Works*, First Russian Edition, Vol. XXVII, Moscow, 1935

Printed according to the original

Published in English for the first time

100

ENGELS TO JAMES LEIGH JOYNES

IN LONDON

[Draft]

[London,] 30 July 1884

Dear Sir,

I am sorry I cannot at present give you my consent to a translation of my *Entwicklung etc.*[a] for *To-Day*, as I am bound by a previous engagement to another gentleman.[b]

As to my promise of an article for *To-Day*, that promise was given to Mr Bax and as far as I know Mr Bax is no longer one of the Editors of *To-Day*.[c]

Yours faithfully,

F. E.

First published in: Marx and Engels, *Works*, First Russian Edition, Vol. XXVII, Moscow, 1935

Reproduced from the original

Published in English for the first time

---

[a] *Socialism: Utopian and Scientific* - [b] Edward Aveling - [c] See this volume, p. 177.

101

ENGELS TO EDUARD BERNSTEIN

IN ZURICH

[London, July 1884][274]

[...][a] By way of self-sacrifice I looked through a few numbers of the *Neue Welt*. It was so deadly dull that it couldn't be done for long. As regards Mr Geiser, his 'erudition' is unassailable *there*. The very fact of a person's parading his erudition in a penny paper of this kind is proof enough that he has failed to take in anything at all. Even had he not invariably written cholera ba*cc*illus for bacillus, as though the word stemmed from *bacca* and not *baculus*. Besides, it's to be found in any Latin dictionary. The assertion that both materialism and idealism are one-sided and must be synthesised in a higher entity[b] is a hoary one and ought not to worry you; again, that atheism merely expresses a negation is an argument we ourselves had already advanced against the philosophers 40 years ago, only with the corollary that atheism, as the *mere* negation of, and referring only to, religion, would itself be nothing without it and is thus itself another religion. Typical of the·remaining erudition is an article by Blos on the Greek and German gods[c] in which alone I noted the following serious bloomers:

1. The *Epistolae obscurorum virorum* are said to be by Reuchlin. While they did originate from his entourage, he had less of a hand in them than Ulrich von Hutten.[275]

2. The Greek gods '*feast* on nectar and *quaff* ambrosia'!

3. 'Mead', alias 'Meed',[d] he explains in brackets, is 'beer', when every child knows that it is, and always has been, made, not with malt, but with honey.

4. Blos does not even know the names of the German gods; [he][e] gives them now in early Nordic, now in German. Alongside the early Nordic Odin whose German name (early Saxon Wodan, Old High German Wuotan) he doesn't know, we find the Old High German Ziu. Odin is also said to have a wife called Freia; but in early Nordic

---

[a] The first part of the letter is missing.- [b] A reference to the article by Bruno Geiser, 'Das Innere der Erde', *Die Neue Welt*, Nos. 14 and 15, 1884.- [c] W. Blos, 'Die Götter in der Dichtung', *Die Neue Welt*, No. 10, 1884. - [d] In the original: 'Met', alias Meth.- [e] The manuscript is damaged here.

she is called Frigg, Old High German Fricka, something even Richard Wagner could have told him. There you have a little nosegay culled rapidly in the space of 10 minutes! Not even the meanest cur could be frightened by erudition of *that* sort. Just let them strut like peacocks in their penny paper; you only have to look behind their fans to see where the droppings come from!

Your
F. E.

Regards to Karl Kautsky.

First published in *Die Briefe von Friedrich Engels an Eduard Bernstein*, Berlin, 1925

Printed according to the original

Published in English for the first time

102

ENGELS TO LAURA LAFARGUE [276]

IN PARIS

London, 1 August 1884

My dear Laura,

Leroy-Beaulieu duly arrived.[a] Thanks. Have not had much time yet to look at it, but shall do now,[b] Schorlemmer has gone to Germany yesterday.

We shall probably start on Monday[c] for Worthing near Brighton — it's Percy's choice, and from all other people's reports a horridly dull place.[277] All the same to me, but if Pumps does not like it, she will have to settle that with the husband of her bosom. Shall let you have exact address as soon as possible.

Have had a bad cold in consequence of the heat and exposure to drafts — have not smoked or tasted beer for nearly a week, but am on the right side of both again since yesterday.

[a] P. Leroy-Beaulieu, *Le Collectivisme. Examen critique du nouveau socialisme.*-[b] See this volume, pp. 179-83.-[c] 4 August

As Paul's article on the *blé*[a] is not complete yet and they are almost sure to have a month between that and the attack on Leroy-Beaulieu, [273] so that this latter article will only appear in the *October* No., there will be a bit of breathing time—at least I hope so. I do want a bit of rest, and shall have, besides this affair, plenty of translations to revise while at the seaside. The great thing for Paul will have to be—*conciseness*, limitation of the question *strictly to Leroy-Beaulieu's criticisms on Mohr*, leaving entirely out Lassalle, etc.—except perhaps when Leroy-Beaulieu gives occasion to show his glaring ignorance. However as soon as I have looked the book over I shall be able to judge better. Anyhow as the book is big and the place for reply small, the limitation to what is strictly necessary will be unavoidable.

Now I must conclude—it's blazing hot, I have written already five letters and have still to write to 'Mrs Aveling' and to Zurich.

Nim too has a bit of the cough and what I almost feel inclined to call a whooping-cough sometimes—but it is not bad. You know that Tussy caught a *regular whooping-cough* from little Lilian Rosher! It's positively true.

Tell Paul to give you a kiss each for Nim and me.

Very affectionately yours,

F. E.

First published in *Économie et politique*, No. 11, Paris, 1955   Reproduced from the original

103

ENGELS TO KARL KAUTSKY

IN ZURICH

London, 1 August 1884

Dear Kautsky,

Have today returned Rodbertus' *Zur Erkenntniss* by *registered mail*, and trust it will arrive safely. After receipt of this, don't send any

---

[a] wheat; Engels is referring to Paul Lafargue's article 'Le blé en Amérique; production et commerce'.

more *letters* here. I shall be going to the seaside [277] on Monday[a] and might even be able to send you my new address *pro tempore* tomorrow.

Rodbertus' book is indeed by far the best thing he ever wrote—youthful work in both the good and the bad sense—the original version of subsequent flimsier ones—shows how close he came to the thing, if he had only followed it up instead of setting his sights on Utopias. I am *very glad indeed* to have seen it. Time for the post and lunch.

Your

F. E.

Regards to Ede, the ex-epididymitician.

First published, in Russian, in *Marx-Engels Archives*, Vol. I (VI), Moscow, 1932

Printed according to the original

Published in English for the first time

104

ENGELS TO EDUARD BERNSTEIN [263]

IN ZURICH

Worthing, 6 August 1884
48 Marine Parade

Dear Ede,

After all manner of vagaries I have at last landed up here, on the South coast, where I hope to stay for a good 3 weeks.[277] At our door we have the whole expanse of the Channel, though at low tide it recedes a good 300 paces; on the whole a quiet, boring little spot where, between bouts of idleness, I shall probably find enough time to look through your and Kautsky's translation of the *Poverty*.[118]

Perhaps you would be so kind as to arrange for the proof-sheets[b] to

---

[a] 4 August - [b] F. Engels, *The Origin of the Family, Private Property and the State*.

Laura Lafargue. Latter half of the 1880s

be sent me here until further notice. Eisengarten will arrange for the *Sozialdemokrat* to be forwarded from London.

The weather here is fine and hot and I still have to notify umpteen people of my new address. So no further news (in any case damned scarce) save that Hyndman has now succeeded in buying *To-Day* as well. Bax, who invested in it what little money he had — I warned him as early as October that it wouldn't be enough — was *au bout de ses finances*,[a] at which juncture Hyndman interposed his attendant page, Champion, through whom he offered additional funds if he, Champion, became editor in place of Bax. Thus seized by the throat, Bax accordingly resigned, the result being that Hyndman now controls the whole of the so-called socialist press. But as in the case of all such little fellows whose ambition is disproportionate to their character and talents the moment of victory was also the moment of defeat. Outward success is matched by failure within his own faction. To an increasing extent Hyndman's following is coming to consist only of those he has bought outright, and/or people who are financially dependent on him. He is daily losing ground in the Democratic Federation. The day before yesterday there was a conference of delegates[278]; what transpired there I cannot say since Aveling, though he attended it, is at present in Derbyshire. For he and Tussy have got married without benefit of registrar, etc., and are now revelling in each other's company amidst the Derbyshire hills. Nota bene: No publicity should be given to this; it will be time enough when, perhaps, some reactionary puts something into the papers about it. The fact is that Aveling has a lawful wife whom he cannot get rid of *de jure* although he has for years been rid of her *de facto*. The matter is fairly common knowledge over here, and has, on the whole, been taken well, even by literary philistines. My London is almost a Paris in miniature and it educates its people.

But enough for now. Regards to Karl Kautsky.

Your
F. E.

First published, in Russian, in *Marx-Engels Archives*, Book I, Moscow, 1924

Printed according to the original

Published in English in full for the first time

---

[a] at the end of his finances

105

ENGELS TO LAURA LAFARGUE

IN PARIS

Worthing, 6 August 1884
48 Marine Parade

My dear Laura,

Here we are and here is our address in as primitive a place as the British sea-side will admit of[277] — the first lodgings we took we had to leave because the old Madam objected to smoking!!

No Lager Beer as yet, but Percy is hunting some up at Brighton — as soon as that is to hand I will try whether I can digest Leroy-Beaulieu[273]; it is blazing hot but fine continental heat and sea-breeze, the Channel is right before our noses but at ebbtide about $1/4$ mile away. Pumps and Nim just come in for beer, they say it is so hot they cannot stand it outside any longer and the house is indeed cooler.

Why, after all *ces pauvres parisiens*[a] will be done out of their share of cholera! What a shame after all their preparations.

Nim just says she hopes she has come into a fortune on July 31st in that grand drawing in Paris. If so, you are to telegraph at once to the Baroness de Demuth at the above address, as she wants to come out with a grand treat.

I am lazy and have so many letters to write! So I hope I shall have good news from Paul, that is to say that the great Leroy-Beaulieu is not in such a hurry to pocket his thrashing.[b]

Anyhow, I must take *beneficium caloris*[c] and conclude.

The whole lot send any amount of loves, ditto

Yours affectionately,
F. E.

First published, in the language of the original (English), in: F. Engels, P. et L. Lafargue, *Correspondance*, t. I, Paris, 1956

Printed according to a photocopy of the original

---

[a] those poor Parisians - [b] See this volume, pp. 174-75 and 179-83.- [c] beneficial heat

106

ENGELS TO PAUL LAFARGUE [196]

IN PARIS

[Worthing, about 11 August 1884] [279]

p. 1. Beaulieu always writes Schoeffle: the gentleman's name is *Schäffle*.

p. 3, *nascent* capitalist system — ? about 1780-1800? The *birth* of that system dates back to the 15th century, whereas nascent big industry merely led to its apogee.

pp. 1 and 4. Maine does not in any way deserve to be cited in the same breath as Maurer; he discovered nothing and is merely a disciple of the disciples of Maurer; long before his day, the communal ownership of land in India had been known about and described by Campbell, etc.; that in Java by Money, that in Russia by Haxthausen.[a] His only merit is to have been the first Englishman to have accepted and vulgarised Maurer's discoveries.

p. 5, must be entirely recast. The examples you give do not apply to the point under discussion. The peasant's plot which turns into capital would be *land as capital*, a very complex matter not discussed by Marx until the *3rd book*.[b] Your slave-owner producing for the New Orleans market is no more a capitalist than the Romanian boyar who exploits forced peasant labour. No one can be a capitalist unless he owns the means of labour and *exploits* the f r e e w o r k i n g m a n!

Rather you should say: the loom of the small peasant of pre-revolutionary times, which was used to weave clothing for his family, was not capital, nor yet is it capital when the peasant sells to the merchant the cloth he has been able to make during the long winter evenings; but if he employs a paid hand to weave those commodities for the merchant, and if he pockets the difference between the cost of production and the price of the sale of the cloth, then the loom is transformed into capital. — The object of production — to produce commodities — *does not impart* to the instrument the character of capi-

---

[a] G. Campbell, *Modern India: a Sketch of the System of Civil Government*; J. W. B. Money, *Java; or, How to Manage a Colony*; A. Freiherr von Haxthausen, *Die ländliche Verfassung Rußlands*. - [b] of *Capital*

tal. The production of commodities is one of the preconditions for the existence of capital; but so long as the producer sells only *what he himself produces*, he is not a capitalist; he becomes so only from the moment he makes use of his instrument *to exploit the wage labour of others.* This also applies to p. 6. How can you possibly have failed to draw that distinction?

In place of your impossible slave-owner (don't be so *Réache!*), you might say: a feudal lord whose fields are cultivated by tenants subject to labour-rent, and who, moreover, collects tribute from them in the form of eggs, poultry, fruit, cattle, etc., is not a capitalist. He lives on the surplus labour of others, but he does not transform the product of that surplus labour into surplus value; he does not sell, but consumes, spends and dissipates it. But if the said lord, as he so frequently did in the 18th century, rids himself of some of those tenants, if he combines their plots into one big farm and rents it out to one big industrial farmer of the kind so beloved of the Physiocrats; if, in the cultivation of his farm, the said big farmer employs as wage labour those formerly subject to labour-rent, then agriculture is transformed from feudal into capitalist agriculture, and the farmer becomes a capitalist.

p. 6. The *direct* form taken by the circulation of commodities is, of course, its *primitive* form [280]; this clearly has to exist before the 2nd form can come into being. Compared with simple *barter* it is *not* primitive; but the circulation of commodities presupposes the existence of money; barter creates only fortuitous exchanges, not the circulation of commodities.

p. 7. Capitalist production is not some form or other, whether direct or indirect, of the circulation of commodities. Production and circulation are two different things. All capitalist production presupposes the circulation of commodities, this being the element in which it moves, but it is not itself circulation, any more than digestion is the circulation of the blood. You can delete the whole of that sentence, which contributes nothing whatever to the sense.

p. 11. The passage you underline, I find incomprehensible as well as wrong on all counts. Your average capitalist *does sell* and *can sell* for more than 10 frs what is produced at a cost of 10 frs.— Where you go wrong is over 'the *costs of production*'. But the costs of production, in the sense used by economists,[a] include profit; they consist 1) of the amount the product has cost the capitalist and 2) of the

---

[a] Engels is actually referring to the price of production.

profit; in other words: 1) of the amount which replaces the constant capital spent, 2) of the amount which replaces the wages paid, 3) of the surplus value, either as a whole or in part, created by the surplus labour of the wage earners. You should therefore take Beaulieu's sentence, his definition of value (p. 9, bottom), and compare the two expressions of value one with the other: either the cost price includes the profit, in which case the commodities are paid for 'in accordance with the social labour they contain'. In which case the price (or value) includes a *surplus value* created by living labour, over and above the wages paid, and appropriated by the capital. Or else the cost price does not cover the profit; in which case the value is determined, not by the social labour comprised in the object, but by the wages, whether high or low, paid for that labour—an outworn concept refuted at some length by Ricardo.

pp. 12 and 13. The *whole* value of the machine and of the cotton, *and even that of the waste*, is transmitted to the product; and therein lies the true nub of your argument. If the 115 lbs of cotton yield only 100 lbs of yarn, the price[a] of the 115 lbs of raw cotton is added to the value of those 100 lbs of yarn. Perhaps it is this, the value of the 15 lbs which have disappeared *qua* material but have reappeared *qua* value, that Mr Beaulieu calls *surplus value?*

p. 13. If the capitalist were to *lend* his machinery, etc., to the workman, the product would belong to the latter—which is never the case.

pp. 13 and 14, 'engenders a gain called profit': cf. para. 1, p. 270, where Mr Beaulieu demonstrates that it is not the capitalist but rather the consumer who is the beneficiary of technical progress. He criticises Marx for forgetting competition; yet all through the chapter on manufacture and big industry, Marx demonstrates that machinery merely helps to lower the price of the products, and that it is competition which accentuates that effect[b]; in other words, the gain consists in manufacturing a greater number of products in the same length of time, so that the amount of work involved in each is correspondingly less and the value of each proportionally lower. Mr Beaulieu forgets to tell us in what respect the wage earner benefits from seeing his productivity increase when the product of that increased

---

[a] In this context Marx uses 'value', not 'price' (*Capital*, Vol. I, Part III, Ch. VIII, present edition, Vol. 35). - [b] See K. Marx, *Capital*, Vol. I, Part IV, Ch. XV (present edition, Vol. 35).

productivity does not belong to him, and when his wage is not determined by the productivity of the instrument.

pp. 14 and 15. The justification of profit here proffered by Beaulieu contains what is the quintessence of vulgar economics, namely its justification of the exploitation of the working man by the capitalist. The *creator of capital* demands his 'due' return for that creation (that is to say, the 'wages of abstinence' — see Marx [a]), and that return has to be paid by the exploited working man in the form of unpaid labour. This you commend on the grounds that 'profit is the legitimate offspring of living labour'! 'The *managerial salary*' is represented and assessed in terms of the salary paid to a salaried manager, a salary with which no capitalist would rest content. Cf. *Capital*, 3rd German edition, pp. 171 and 172 (the French edition is not to hand), where you will find all these statements refuted in a few words.[b] The insurance premium against '*risk*' is indeed taken out of surplus value, but it is reckoned *over and above* the profit; every year the capitalist sets aside a sum amounting to ... as a reserve for what he calls the '*ducroire*'[c] (from the Italian *del credere*, that is, to cover himself against bad faith or bad debts). Finally, *rewards for greater efficiency*, for inventions not yet generally exploited, occur only in exceptional cases and may then yield an *extra* profit; but here we are concerned with ordinary, average profit such as is common to all industrialists. Come to that, you will find this type of profit discussed in *Capital*, 3rd German edition, pp. 314-17.[d]

By taking these statements of Beaulieu's in earnest, by declaring that profit thereby becomes 'the legitimate offspring of living labour' (*not of the working man*, but *of the labour of the capitalist!*), you endorse, on Marx's behalf and in Marx's name, those doctrines of vulgar economics which he combatted always and everywhere. You must, therefore, completely change your mode of expression so as to exclude even the semblance of such a meaning. Otherwise it will be you who falls into the trap.

Your assertion on p. 16 that 'when the products ... capitalist profit is nil or all but nil', runs completely contrary to the facts. For in that case, where is the exploitation of the workers? What are you complaining about? And what do the capitalists live and grow fat on, or dissipate? Where the deuce did you light on such an idea, never expounded even by vulgar economists and which, furthermore, is not

[a] Ibid., Part VII, Ch. XXIV, Sect. 3. - [b] Ibid., Part III, Ch. VII, Sect. 2. - [c] guarantee - [d] K. Marx, *Capital*, Vol. I, Part IV, Chs. XII-XIV (present edition, Vol. 35).

even to be found in Beaulieu? And you call it a general law! What is true is that, with machines making 100 metres of cloth with the same expenditure of labour as manual labour on its own would require for 1 metre, the capitalist can spread his profit over 100 metres instead of concentrating it on only one; the result being that, while every metre carries only $^1/_{100}$ of the profit, the profit on the sum total of labour expended may stay the same, if not actually increase.

p. 16. Marx would protest against 'the political and social ideal' attributed to him by you. When one is an economist, 'a man of science', one does not have an ideal, one elaborates scientific results, and when one is, to boot, a party man, one struggles to put them into practice. But when one has an ideal, one cannot be a man of science, having, as one then does, preconceived ideas.

In short, the article will have an effect if you eliminate the chief errors I have indicated. But for the purpose of your riposte,[281] which must be of a far more serious nature, I am firmly of the opinion that you must seriously re-read *Capital*, from cover to cover, with Beaulieu's book beside you; and that you should mark all the passages relating to vulgar economics. I say *Capital* rather than Deville's book[a] which would be wholly inadequate because of grave defects in the descriptive section.

Again, you must not forget that these gentry, Beaulieu and others, are far better versed than you are in the ordinary literature of economics, and that this is a field in which you will not be able to combat them on equal terms; it is their business to know such things, not yours. So do not venture too far into that field.

I have spoken frankly and hope you will not take it amiss. It is too serious a matter and, if you were to put a foot wrong, the whole party would suffer as a result.

We are dying of heat here, but are pretty well, nonetheless. Everyone sends a thousand greetings to Laura and yourself. Unfortunately our stock of Pilsener is nearly exhausted and takes two days to be replenished from Brighton! We are right out in the wilds here.

Yours ever,

F. E.

First published in *Économie et politique*, No. 11, Paris, 1955

Printed according to the original

Translated from the French

---

[a] G. Deville, *Le Capital de Karl Marx* (see also Note 81).

107

ENGELS TO GEORG HEINRICH VON VOLLMAR

IN MUNICH

Worthing, England, 13 August 1884
48 Marine Parade

Dear Comrade,

It was not till yesterday that your esteemed letter was sent on to me from London, hence my delay in replying.

The question you put to me [282] is difficult, or rather only to be answered in the negative. No science is so botched today as economics, and this at every university in the world. Not only is there no one anywhere who expounds the old classical economics along the lines of Ricardo and his school; it would actually be difficult to find any one who expounded common-or-garden free trade, i. e. so-called Manchesterism à la Bastiat,[283] in unadulterated form. In England and America, as in France and Germany, the pressure of the proletarian movement caused bourgeois economists, almost without exception, to acquire an armchair-socialist cum philanthropic complexion,[54] while an uncritical, benevolent eclecticism is everywhere in evidence — a soft, elastic, gelatinous substance that can be compressed into any desired shape and, for that very reason, exudes an excellent nutrient fluid for the culture of careerists just as does real gelatine for the culture of bacteria. The effect of this insubstantial, enervating, intellectual pap has made itself felt in Germany, at any rate, as also here and there among German Americans, even within the very confines of our party, while on the periphery it luxuriates unchecked.

Such being the case, I would find it difficult to discover any appreciable difference between the various universities. Independent and thoroughgoing study of classical economics, from the Physiocrats and Smith to Ricardo and his school, as also of the Utopians Saint-Simon, Fourier and Owen and, finally, of Marx, combined with the constant use of one's own judgment, would probably yield the best results. I am assuming that your friend would study the actual sources and not let herself be led astray by text-books and other secondary sources. In *Capital* Marx has indicated the most important sources of information on actual economic conditions. How the official statistics of the various countries should be evaluated, and to what extent they are or are not useful, can best be learnt from an actual study and comparison of them. And in just the same way, one's individual studies, the more advanced they become, provide the best guidance as to the ways and means of learning more, always supposing one has started off with genuinely classical texts and not with the most worthless of all — German economic text-books and/or the lectures of their authors.

That is about all I can say on the subject. And I shall be delighted if Miss Kjellberg finds anything here that can be of use to her.

I look forward, by the way, to the general elections [194] and remain

Very sincerely yours,

F. Engels

First published, abridged, in: G. Mayer, *Friedrich Engels. Eine Biographie*, Bd. II, Haag, 1934 and in full in: Marx and Engels, *Works*, Second Russian Edition, Vol. 36, Moscow, 1964

Printed according to the original

Published in English for the first time

108

ENGELS TO MARYA JANKOWSKA (S. LEONOWICZ) [284]

IN GENEVA

[Draft]

[Worthing, mid-August 1884]

Yes. The only condition I must impose on you — and this categorically — is that you should publish *nothing* in Polish before the German edition has been completed. The work would be instantly banned in Germany and the least indiscretion or premature allusion could only result in alerting the German police and in hampering the circulation of the original, if not in causing a large part of the edition to be confiscated. Perhaps you would be so kind, then, as to acknowledge receipt

of this letter and to give me your assurance that you will abide by
a condition which, unfortunately, cannot be dispensed with.

First published in: Marx and Engels,
Works, First Russian Edition, Vol. XXIX,
Moscow, 1946

Printed according to the original

Translated from the French

Published in English for the first
time

109

ENGELS TO KARL KAUTSKY [1]

IN ZURICH

(please *omit Brighton* from
the address, makes the post
office here do silly things)

Worthing, England, 22 August 1884
48 Marine Parade

Dear Kautsky,

Have just received your letters which were somewhat delayed, as
you did not put the number of the house; also the mental faculties of
our postal drudges over here are of the very lowest order.

Poverty.[118] The manuscript I have here has now been revised.
Apart from slight misinterpretations of those niceties of French that
can only be properly learnt in France itself, there was not much to alter. For *rapports*[a] I usually put *Verhältnis* rather than '*Beziehungen*'
because the latter is too indefinite and also because Marx always rendered the German *Verhältnis* as *rapport* and vice versa. Moreover in
rapport de proportionnalité, for instance, *rapport*, being *quantitative*, can
only be rendered as *Verhältnis*, since *Beziehung* has primarily
a qualitative meaning. I must make a few more notes on this subject.
I await your next manuscript. The passages relating to Hegel and
things Hegelian can only be gone through in London, as I shall need
my Hegel for the purpose. I shall do all I can to finish it as quickly as
possible. But *Capital*, Book II, ought also to be finished at the same

---

[a] relations

time and there is a hell of a lot still to be done to it; and in *this* particular clash of interests the latter must, after all, take precedence! However I shall do my utmost. But when must you have the preface? I shall reply twice to Rodbertus, once in the preface to *Capital*, Book II,[a] and again in that to the *Poverty*.[b] There is no other way, since both works will be appearing more or less simultaneously and Rodbertus' accusation was couched in such formal terms.[187] In *Capital* I must assume an air of dignity, whereas in the preface to the *Poverty* I shall be more at liberty to speak my mind.

If you leave Zurich, you would certainly do better to come here rather than go anywhere else, with the possible exception of Paris. Obviously the material aspect enters into it since you, having been duly installed as a married man, can no longer afford to take the risks a bachelor would. Besides, Paris is said to be just as expensive a place to live in as here. And for study the BRITISH MUSEUM is, after all, incomparably better; the Paris library cannot hold a candle to it so far as people like us are concerned, partly because of the difficulty of using the place, shortage of catalogues, etc., etc. I trust the matter can be arranged.

As to what you want to do in regard to my pamphlet, you are bound to be a better judge than I; so do what you think appropriate.[285] However I'm prepared to bet that the thing will be banned.

Like Ede, I believe that in regard to Bebel you have allowed yourself to be much too much influenced by first impressions. True, his last letter also evinced a certain lassitude and a desire to rest. If there is no other way he ought to be allowed to do so for a time; but would he be able to, even if he were temporarily to absent himself from the Reichstag? This much is certain: he is irreplaceable in Germany and must be kept going, must, if necessary, spare himself, so as to be fit for action at the crucial moment.

It also seems to me that you are too censorious about the people in Germany—i.e. the masses. Since time immemorial, progress has been damned slow in the case of the new blood; most of them were *à la* Geiser and Viereck. That the Anti-Socialist Law[37] does more harm than good in this case in certainly not in doubt. However so long as so much forbidden literature gets into the country, the ground will be prepared nevertheless and, when the air has cleared again, it should be possible to speed things up in this respect also, and to do so

---

[a] See present edition, Vol. 36.- [b] F. Engels, 'Marx and Rodbertus'.

more quickly than would have been the case had there been no interruption.

But now I must write to Ede. It is one o'clock and the post goes at two!

Your
F. E.

First published, in Russian, in *Marx-Engels Archives*, Vol. I (VI), Moscow, 1932

Printed according to the original

Published in English in full for the first time

110

ENGELS TO EDUARD BERNSTEIN [1]

IN ZURICH

[Worthing, 22 August 1884]

[...][a] index for *Capital* would be highly desirable.[286] But why not all at one go when the whole thing is done? That will be next year for sure, provided I don't collapse, of which there is no prospect at present. For your own information, *The History of Theory* has also been largely completed. The ms. of *A Contribution to the Critique of Political Economy* of 1860-62 contains, as I think I showed you when you were here, approx. 500 quarto pages on *Theories of Surplus Value*, a great deal of which must, it is true, be deleted because it has since been rewritten, but there will still be enough of it.[171]

In his *Schulze-Bastiat*, Lassalle cited Rodbertus in a connection that might in anyone else's case have earned him intense hostility, i. e. as the authority for and/or discoverer of a trifle. The *Briefe*[b] may, it is true, have contributed to the Rodbertus cult. But what has done so more than anything else is, firstly, the desire among non-communists to set alongside Marx a rival who is himself a non-communist and, secondly, those people's unscientific confusion. To all those who loiter on the state socialist fringes of our party, make sympathetic speeches

---

[a] The first part of the letter is missing.- [b] The reference is probably to Rodbertus' *Briefe und Socialpolitische Aufsaetze*.

but nevertheless want to avoid the hostility of the police, His Excellency Rodbertus is a godsend.

The move of the *Neue Zeit* to Hamburg may after all be only the prelude to its end.[265] Of course I know nothing about those presently in charge of the Hamburg office.

Last Tuesday[a] we had a revolution here in Worthing. A shop belonging to a Salvation Army fanatic was attacked and broken up; the man fired his revolver, wounding three people. Next day windows were smashed in the lock-up; that same evening 40 dragoons and 50 police moved in (the little place has about 10,000 inhabitants) to clear the streets, whereupon the good citizens, knowing themselves to be innocuous, refused to budge and in several instances received a merciless beating; now all is calm. Really, the tomfoolery one witnesses. *Both sides*, SALVATIONISTS and ANTI-SALVATIONISTS, *are secretly in the pay of the bourgeoisie.*

Your
F. E.

First published, in Russian, in *Marx-Engels Archives*, Book I, Moscow, 1924

Printed according to the original

Published in English in full for the first time

111

ENGELS TO KARL KAUTSKY[287]

IN ZURICH

[Worthing, 30 August 1884]

Letters received. Have ordered G. Adler's little pamphlet: will doubtless be able to get hold of it in London.[288] Thank you for the particulars. The man shall be dealt with. Am busy with the *Poverty*[118] and hope to finish it while still here. A good deal of the philosophical part needs to be translated into the appropriate Hegelian jargon.

There is no hurry about Bachofen's *Antiquarische Briefe*. Meleager

---

[a] 19 August

has already figured in his *Mutterrecht*; this aspect is of importance to me in the present instance only in conjunction with the view I have put forward.[a]

Over here 4 musicians, with the help of misleading music, are making propaganda for Bismarck by informing the English in a brand of Rhenish-Franconian totally incomprehensible, even to me, that they pledge their souls and bodies to live for thee alone, etc., and that Strasbourg is a city wondrous fair.[b] Regards to Ede.

Your
F. E.

Send things to London from now on. We go back on Tuesday.[277]

First published, in Russian, in *Marx-Engels Archives*, Vol. I (VI), Moscow, 1932

Printed according to the original

Published in English for the first time

112

ENGELS TO EDUARD BERNSTEIN

IN ZURICH

London, 13-15 September 1884

Dear Ede,

I have been back here a fortnight (all but).[277] During my absence Eisengarten was supposed to be making a fair copy of that part of the ms. of Part II[c] that was ready. The great heat, however, led him, now to dawdle, now to write so beautifully, if so slowly and so little, that I dare not send what has been done to Meissner because I would not be able to follow it up quickly enough. So that puts paid for the present to early publication; what Meissner will do now, I don't know. In some respects I'm not sorry, for in this way I can be

---

[a] See present edition, Vol. 26, p. 238.- [b] An allusion to two traditional German airs. - [c] the second volume of *Capital*

all the more certain that nothing will have to be done in too much of a hurry.

What you say about the translation of my pamphlet[a] is all very well. But *how* does Lafargue translate? He consults neither his wife nor the dictionary; he does everything on his own, decrees that such and such a German word is so and so in French, and then, proud of his masterpiece, sends me the ms. I could do it just as well myself. He, of course, wants to set to at once — however, *nous verrons ce que nous verrons*.[b] As for an English version, Aveling has enough on his hands for the time being,[c] and also proposes to translate my *Entwicklung*.[d] But what publisher will pay for it? And in his position he can't do more unpaid work than he already does. Nor is there any particular hurry about this. Our prime concern must be to put *Capital* into English, and that will give us work and to spare.

I was greatly tickled by the way you took Bahr and Fabian, not to mention friend Gumbel, to task over the stock exchange taxes [289] (I always know my Gumbel, whether he's vindicating his respectable toping companions, the Heilbronn philistines, or whatever). In Bahr and Fabian you have two fine examples of German 'erudition', something I am always glad to see harshly taken to task. One aims at Bahr the blow intended for Geiser. What particularly pleased me, however, was the way you struck home, putting emphasis on essential points, and also your verve.

Now I must break off; I can only spend a short time sitting at my desk. I took some cold sea-baths that did me more harm than good. Till tomorrow then.

14 September. I returned the ms. of *Poverty* [118] to you last week, 4 September, by registered post, together with my comments. I presume you received it. When you [and Kautsky] compare my amendments with the original you will find that certain turns of speech had not, in fact, been correctly understood (in some cases I have made comments), but that is inevitable unless one has spent a good deal of time in the country concerned.

I have at last been able to get hold of a copy of my enlarged photograph for the artist[e]— I forget his name and have mislaid his letter—

---

[a] Clearly *The Origin of the Family, Private Property and the State*.- [b] we shall see what we shall see - [c] Aveling was translating into English the first volume of *Capital* (see also Note 56).- [d] *Socialism: Utopian and Scientific* - [e] Karl Manz-Schäppi

who wishes to make a colour-print of Marx.[a] I shall send it to you to-morrow or the day after.

Since the present elections will have a major impact[194] we must all make an effort and so I am sending you herewith a money order for £25 for the election fund.

Sorge has sent me Gronlund's *The Cooperative Commonwealth*; his exposé of theory rather flat after Marx's, but comprehensible to philistines; the main object is, apparently, to present his model of the future as true GERMAN SOCIALISM, but I found it too boring to read. Marx is not quoted, the only reference to him being SUCH NOBLE JEWS AS MARX AND LASSALLE! Crikey!

Under Hyndman's direction *To-Day* gets worse and worse. To make it more interesting they accept anything and everything. The editor has written to me saying that the October issue will contain a critique of *Capital*!!,[b] and invites me to reply — which I refused with thanks.[290] Thus a socialist organ has turned into an organ in which the pros and cons of socialism are discussed by every Tom, Dick and Harry.

I am sending you a *Kölnische* from which you may see what methods are used in Africa even by Stanley-Leopold of Belgium's humane, civilising Association Internationale.[291] Then what may we not expect of the Portuguese and French,— not to speak of our flog 'em-and-shoot 'em Prussians — when they get going? Come to that, Bismarck has pulled off a thundering good electoral coup with that colonial racket of his.[292] Not a philistine will be spared, they'll fall for it *en masse*. No doubt he will again succeed in obtaining a double majority of his own choosing — Conservatives[230] + National liberals[243], or should the latter again prove peevish, Conservatives + the Centre.[229] It's all one to us.

If I have the time, I shall enclose a line or two for Karl Kautsky.

Your
F. E.

15 September. No time, K. K. will have to wait a bit.

First published, in Russian, in *Marx-Engels Archives*, Book I, Moscow, 1924

Printed according to the original

Published in English for the first time

---

[a] See this volume, p. 170.- [b] Ph. H. Wicksteed, '*Das Kapital*. A Criticism', *To-Day*, No. 10, October 1884.

113

ENGELS TO KARL KAUTSKY [1]

IN ZURICH

London, 20 September 1884

Dear Kautsky,

I return the mss.[293] herewith by registered post.

Your article on Rodbertus was very good in regard to economics; what I would take issue with here again are your apodictic assertions in fields where, as you yourself know, you are not on firm ground, and in which you also lay yourself open to attack by Schramm who has been astute enough to seize on that opportunity.

This applies particularly to 'abstraction' which you undoubtedly come down on far too heavily in a general way. The distinction here is as follows:

Marx reduces the common content shared by things and circumstances to the most general conceptual expression, hence his abstraction merely reproduces in conceptual form the content already inherent in things.

Rodbertus, on the other hand, concocts what is a more or less imperfect conceptual expression and measures things against that concept to which they must conform. He is looking for the true, *eternal* content of things and of social conditions of which, however, the content is essentially transient. Hence *true* capital. This is not capital *as it is today*, which is only an imperfect realisation of the concept. Instead of deducing the concept of capital from capital as it is today — the only sort, after all, that really does exist — he seeks to arrive at true capital from present-day capital by the device of taking an isolated individual, and asking what might figure as capital in that individual's production. Namely, the simple means of production. In this way *true* capital is simply lumped together with the means of production which, depending on circumstances, is or is not capital. In this way all the *bad* properties of capital, namely all the *real* properties, are eliminated therefrom. He can now demand that real capital should conform to this concept, i. e. merely continue to function as a simple, social means of production, discard everything that makes it capital, and yet remain capital, indeed become true capital precisely as a result of this.

You do the same kind of thing in the case of *value*. Present value is that of the production of commodities, but with the suppression of the production of commodities, value 'changes' or rather, *value as such* remains and merely changes its form. But in fact economic value is a category that appertains to the production of commodities, *disappearing* with it (cf. *Dühring*, pp. 252-62[a]), just as it did not exist before it. The relation of labour to product prior to and after production of commodities no longer expresses itself in the form of *value*.

Fortunately Schramm is also a bit shaky in the matter of philosophy, and lays himself open to attack, as you have perfectly well apprehended and demonstrated.

Further:

1) Schramm recognises material interests that do not derive—either directly or indirectly—from the mode of production. On this, cf. Marx, *A Contribution to the Critique*, preface,[b] where the matter is presented concisely and cogently in 20 lines.

2) Long before Rodbertus, the English and French Utopians had criticised existing society just as well as, if not better than, he, as had the post-Ricardian school of socialist economists on the basis of Ricardo's theory of value; Marx cites some of these in the *Poverty*, pp. 49 and 50.[c]

3) The Robinson mentioned by Marx[d] is Daniel Defoe's *genuine*, original Robinson Crusoe, whence the attendant circumstances—the objects salvaged from the shipwreck, etc.—are also taken. Later on he, too, has his Freitag (FRIDAY); he was also a shipwrecked merchant who, unless I am mistaken, likewise engaged from time to time in the slave trade. A proper 'bourgeois', therefore.

4) To talk of the Marxian *school of history* was certainly most premature. I should curtail that part of your reply and refer primarily *to Marx himself,*— the above-mentioned passage from *A Contribution to the Critique*, and also *Capital* itself, in particular primitive accumula-

---

[a] F. Engels, *Anti-Dühring*, present edition, Vol. 25, pp. 286-98.- [b] Ibid., Vol. 29, pp. 263-64. - [c] Ibid., Vol. 6, p. 138.- [d] See K. Marx, *Capital*, Vol. I, Part I, Ch. 1, Sect. 4 (present edition, Vol. 35).

tion,[a] in which Schramm can find out for himself about the chicken and the egg.

In other respects it's really fortunate that all the bourgeois elements should now be rallying to Rodbertus. We could ask for nothing better.

You will have got your *Poverty* ms.[118] As will Ede my letter of last Sunday containing the contribution to the election fund.[b]

Tussy asks that in future the *Sozialdemokrat*, etc., be sent to her at the following address:

> Mrs Aveling
> 55 Great Russell Street, London, W. C.

Your

F. E.

I return Bebel's letter herewith.

So we can expect you here in January or February.

To-Day has simply become a 'symposium', i. e. a review in which anybody can write for or against socialism. In the next number there's to be a critique of *Capital*![c] The idea was that I should answer this anonymous piece but I politely refused.[290] Dr Drysdale has also written for the paper, invoking you.[294] There's a reply from Burrows asking about you. I attended to this, but somewhat cautiously, not knowing whether Drysdale mightn't have your book.

First published, in Russian, in *Marx-Engels Archives*, Vol. I (VI), Moscow, 1932

Printed according to the original

Published in English in full for the first time

---

[a] See K. Marx, *Capital*, Vol. I, Part VIII (present edition, Vol. 35).-[b] See previous letter.-[c] Ph. H. Wicksteed, 'Das Kapital. A Criticism', *To-Day*, No. 10, October 1884.

114

ENGELS TO HERMANN SCHLÜTER [295]

IN HOTTINGEN-ZURICH

[London, 1 October 1884]

Dear Mr Schlüter,

Proofs[a] received with thanks and returned. I now only àwait clean proofs 8-9. Should they contain no mistakes to speak of, a list of printing errors will not be necessary.

Rodbertus' *Erkenntniss etc.*[b] is advertised by Fock of Leipzig à 4.20 marks. I should be glad to buy a copy at this price, if not less.

There does exist a *French* speech by Marx on the subject of free trade[c] but none, so far as I am aware, on protective tariffs. It would hardly be suitable for translation as a book on its own, but if Ede wishes to use it as an appendix to the German *Poverty*,[118] it wouldn't be a bad idea and I could send my copy.

Yours sincerely,
F. E.

First published in: Marx and Engels, *Works*, First Russian Edition, Vol. XXVII, Moscow, 1935

Printed according to the original

Published in English for the first time

115

ENGELS TO HERMANN SCHLÜTER [296]

IN HOTTINGEN-ZURICH

[London,] 3 October 1884

Dear Mr Schlüter,

Everything gratefully received.[a] Just the following misprints:

---

[a] F. Engels, *The Origin of the Family, Private Property and the State.*- [b] J. K. Rodbertus-Jagetzow, *Zur Erkenntniss unsrer staatswirthschaftlichen Zustände*, Berlin, 1885.- [c] K. Marx, 'Speech on the Question of Free Trade'.

p. 134, line 8 from top *Gesellschaft*[a] for *Lesellschaft*
  line 9   "   " *Lebensbedingungen*[b] for *Gebensbedingungen*
p. 144, line 2   "   " *platte*[c] for *glatte*.
You will have had my postcard.[d]
In haste,

Yours ever,
F. E.

First published in: Marx and Engels, *Works*, First Russian Edition, Vol. XXVII, Moscow, 1935

Printed according to the original

Published in English for the first time

116

ENGELS TO AUGUST BEBEL[263]

IN PLAUEN NEAR DRESDEN

London, 11 October 1884

Dear Bebel,

I really must apologise for not having got round to answering your two letters of 8 June and the 3rd inst. until today. But since the beginning of June I have been able to sit at my desk and write only at the cost of some pain and in defiance of doctor's orders. For almost 18 months now, my movements have been hampered by a peculiar ailment which somewhat mystifies the doctors; I have had to abandon completely my old way of life, which entailed much movement, and have, in particular, been prevented from writing. Only for the past 10 days or so have I been enabled by mechanical appliances to move about with a certain amount of freedom and I believe that, once these appliances have been properly adjusted, I shall be more or less my old self again; apart from the discomfort I have suffered, the thing is of no great significance and will, I hope, gradually disappear altogether.

However, if I could not write, I could at least dictate — I dictated the whole of the 2nd book of *Capital* from the ms., and practically got

---

[a] society - [b] conditions of existence - [c] outright - [d] See previous letter.

it ready for the press, as well as revised the first $^3/_8$ of the English translation[a] and have, besides, perused all kinds of other things, so that I have got through quite a fair amount of work.

At the same time as this, you will be getting a copy of my newly published work[b]; I shall make sure it goes off.

All day my head has been full of electoral agitation.[194] Our great triennial trial is an event of European significance by comparison with which the anxious journeyings of no matter how many emperors [297] are as nothing. I well remember how thunderstruck Europe was in 1875 by our people's electoral victories [298] and how Bakuninist anarchism was banished from the scene in Italy, France, Switzerland and Spain. And just now another such result is urgently required. In Europe, at any rate, those caricatures of anarchists à la Most, who have already sunk from the level of a Rinaldo Rinaldini to and below that of a Schinderhannes[c] if not lower, would in their turn — at least so far as Europe was concerned — succumb to a similar knock-out blow, and thus save us a deal of toil and trouble. In America, where sects continue to proliferate, these could then simply be allowed to die off gradually; after all, did not Karl Heinzen manage to remain alive there for 25 years after he was dead and buried in Europe?[d] The French in the provinces, who are forging ahead most manfully, would be considerably encouraged and the Parisian masses be given a further impulse towards emancipating themselves from their position as appendage of the extreme Left. Here in England, where the Reform Bill has given new power to the workers,[299] the impulse would come just in time for the next elections in 1885 and might provide the Social Democratic Federation [300]— which merely consists on the one hand of literati, on the other of the remnants of old sects and, thirdly, of a sentimental public — with the opportunity of becoming a *real* party. In America, it only requires an event of this kind to make the English-speaking workers at last realise what power is theirs if they choose to make use of it. And in Italy and Spain it would deal a fresh blow to the doctrinaire anarchist rhetoric which still continues to flourish there. In short, the victories you achieve will take effect, from Siberia to California, and from Sicily to Sweden.

But how will the new 'parliamentary group' turn out? Many of the new prospective candidates are quite unknown to me and what

---

[a] of the first volume of *Capital* (see Note 56) - [b] *The Origin of the Family, Private Property and the State* - [c] Johann Bückler - [d] Cf. this volume, p. 114.

I know of the majority of 'educated' ones is not altogether to their credit. The Anti-Socialist Law [37] makes it all too easy for bourgeois and bourgeois-inspired socialists to satisfy the electorate and to indulge their own urge for self-advancement. Not that it isn't perfectly in order for such men to be put up and elected in comparatively backward constituencies. But they are likewise invading the old constituencies, which deserve better representatives, and in this they are supported by people who ought to know better. I am not at all sure how the new parliamentary group will turn out, and still less what it will do. The division into proletarian and bourgeois camps is becoming ever more pronounced and, once the bourgeois elements have plucked up the courage to outvote the proletarian, a breach might be provoked. This is a possibility which should, I think, be kept in view. If *they* provoke the breach — something that will call for a bit more Dutch courage — it won't be too bad. I am still of the opinion that, so long as the Anti-Socialist Law continues in force, the breach should not be provoked by us; but if it does come, then you should go to with a will, in which case I shall also put my shoulder to the wheel.

I am glad to hear that the colonial racket is not proving attractive.[292] It is the best card Bismarck has played, nicely calculated to appeal to the philistine and replete, not only with illusory hopes but also with horrendously heavy costs, which will be recovered only by degrees. Bismarck and his colonies remind me of the crazy (really idiotic) last Duke of Bernburg[a] who remarked in the early forties: I am going to have a railway, even if it costs me a *thousand talers*. What 1,000 talers are to the cost of a railway, so the colonial budget adumbrated by Bismarck and his fellow-philistines is to the actual costs involved. For in this case I consider Bismarck fool enough to believe that Lüderitz and Woermann would bear the costs.

Apropos Bismarck. At a conference of engineers, a friend of ours met Bismarck's partner in the Varziner Paper Mill (Behrens), and from him learned a good deal about Bismarck's uncouth behaviour. A true Prussian Junker, on rare occasions and by a painful effort capable of good manners at most in the drawing-room, but who otherwise allows his brutality free rein. You know all about that, however. Having asked a factory inspector what his salary was and learned that it was 1,000 talers, he remarked: 'In that case you are dependent on bribes.' But the really interesting thing was Bismarck's telling the afore-mentioned Behrens that the only speaker in the Reichstag

---

[a] Alexander Karl

worthy of the name, and one to whom everyone always listened, was August Bebel.

The more often you write and tell me about the situation in Germany, and in particular about industrial developments, the better pleased I am. If I do not always reply in detail it is because, in this instance, I am merely your pupil — the more gladly in that the only information I can regard as wholly reliable is that provided by you. On the whole, German industry remains what it has always been: it manufactures those articles which the British consider too insignificant, and the French too common, but does so on a very large scale; German industry still depends for its subsistence on 1) the theft of patterns from abroad and 2) the free gift of ordinary surplus value to the purchasers, whereby it is alone enabled to compete, and the exaction of inordinate surplus value by forcing down wages, which alone enables it to exist. This means, however, that while the struggle between worker and capitalist may stagnate in some places (where abnormal wages have already become the norm), in most it is growing more acute by reason of ever-rising pressure. At all events, 1848 marked the beginning of an industrial revolution in Germany which will yet give the worthy bourgeois pause for thought. Goodbye for now.

Your old friend

F. E.

First published abridged in: F. Engels, *Politisches Vermächtnis. Aus unveröffentlichten Briefen*, Berlin, 1920 and in full, in Russian, in *Marx-Engels Archives*, Vol. I (VI), Moscow, 1932

Printed according to the original

Published in English in full for the first time

117

ENGELS TO KARL KAUTSKY [287]

IN ZURICH

[London,] 13 October 1884

In great haste. The sheets have been returned to Dietz after restoration of h, tz and the botched foreign words.[301] Wrote telling

Dietz [39] that both of you[a] had protested and that I had concurred and had made the above-mentioned reinstatements in agreement with you. I would, I said, no more have spelling imposed upon me than I would a woman and hence if the proofs were not corrected in accordance with my demands, I should 1) call for the deletion of all my notes and 2) not provide a preface,[b] as I couldn't possibly have two kinds of spelling for my stuff.

Do you really not wish to put your names on the title page as translators? The title should in any case be so worded that I simply appear as the author of the notes and preface unless you expressly insist on the revision mentioned, though I consider this quite unnecessary.

Another whole day has been wasted thanks to these asininities. Right in the middle of election time,[194] what's more.

Your
F. E.

First published, in Russian, in *Marx-Engels Archives*, Vol. I (VI), Moscow, 1932

Printed according to the original

Published in English for the first time

118

ENGELS TO JOHANN PHILIPP BECKER

IN GENEVA

London, 15 October 1884

Dear Old Man,

I sent off to you yesterday my little book on the origin of the family, etc.,[c] and have today taken out a money order for five pounds. I trust you will get both very shortly.

I was glad to hear from you that Bebel had visited you during the summer. Your opinion of him is exactly the same as mine. There is no

---

[a] Karl Kautsky and Eduard Bernstein - [b] F. Engels, 'Marx and Rodbertus'. - [c] *The Origin of the Family, Private Property and the State*

more lucid mind in the whole of the German party, besides which he is utterly dependable and firm of purpose. What is unusual is that his great oratorical talents—all the philistines recognise these and do so readily, while Bismarck told Behrens, a partner in his paper mill, that Bebel was the only orator in the whole of the Reichstag—have not trivialised him in any way.[a] Nothing of the kind has happened since Demosthenes. All other orators have been shallow-pated.

Don't worry about my health; it is a localised and sometimes troublesome complaint but there are no general after-effects whatever and it is not even necessarily incurable; at worst it renders me unfit for active service though I may be able to mount a horse again in a few years' time. Having been incapable of writing for the past 4 months I have dictated instead, and am now pretty well done with the 2nd book of *Capital*; have also gone through the English translation (as far as it has got—about $^3/_8$ths of the whole) of the 1st book.[56] Moreover I have now discovered a device which is helping me to get more or less back on my feet again and I hope to make still further progress before long. Rather, my misfortune is that since we lost Marx I have been supposed to represent him. I have spent a lifetime doing what I was fitted for, namely playing second fiddle, and indeed I believe I acquitted myself reasonably well. And I was happy to have so splendid a first fiddle as Marx. But now that I am suddenly expected to take Marx's place in matters of theory and play first fiddle, there will inevitably be blunders and no one is more aware of that than I. And not until the times get somewhat more turbulent shall we really be aware of what we have lost in Marx. Not one of us possesses the breadth of vision that enabled him, at the very moment when rapid action was called for, invariably to hit upon the right solution and at once get to the heart of the matter. In more peaceful times it could happen that events proved me right and him wrong, but at a revolutionary juncture his judgment was virtually infallible.

Marx's youngest daughter[b] has married a really excellent Irishman, Dr Aveling; they come here every Sunday. The other daughter,[c] whom you know, is also with me just now and sends you her kindest regards. She still talks a lot and fondly about the day she spent with you in Geneva.

I trust your health is still progressing satisfactorily. But if anything should happen to you again, you must let me know at once, on the

---

[a] Cf. this volume, pp. 199-200. - [b] Eleanor - [c] Laura Lafargue

last occasion a great deal of time elapsed before I knew the least thing about it and you must not err in that way again.

I shall hunt out your letters, etc.,[126] as soon as I can really get at the papers. Since May I have been physically incapable of doing so and just now there is so much urgent work to be attended to that I can't even consider it. There are over 6 large boxfuls to be sorted out and not even the books are arranged in such a way as to enable me to make full use of them.

Well, take care of your health (there's no need to tell you to keep your chin up) and be assured of the good wishes

Of your old friend

F. Engels

Borkheim sends his regards. He wrote to me a week ago — it's always the same old story with him. No change.

First published abridged in *Prosveshcheniye*, Nos. 7-8, St Petersburg, 1913 and in full in *Der Kampf*, Nr. 12, Wien, 1913

Printed according to the original

Published in English for the first time

119

ENGELS TO KARL KAUTSKY

IN ZURICH

London, 15 October[a] 1884

Dear Kautsky,

You will have got my postcard.[b] If possible I shall set to work on the preface[c] tomorrow; there are interruptions every day; today, for example, the whole of my time will be spent on correspondence and I'm still not allowed to sit for too long at my desk. Once I settle down to it I shall be done in a day or two.

---

[a] August in the original.- [b] See this volume, pp. 200-01.- [c] F. Engels, 'Marx and Rodbertus'

So Geiser is the inventor of this marvellous spelling! Another feather in his cap. I must confess that my aversion to this procrustean bed was to some extent responsible for my failing to get a move on with contributions to the *Neue Zeit*. But do tell me whether this splendid system was obligatory in the case of other *books* published by Dietz — in that of Bebel's *Frau* [138] it was not; it is important that I should know this in the event of my replying to Dietz.

Having protested to Dietz [39] about Geiserianism so categorically, I cannot now submit to it in the *Neue Zeit* — nor yet where the printing of the preface is concerned. Elsewhere I have no objections, of course.

For Ede: Wehner writes to say that the person did not *demand* the money on behalf of our people, he having sent it of his own free will; however the said person says that they had *accepted* it. This amounts to the same thing.

I have not read Rodbertus' *Creditnoth* [a] either; however it can only contain what we know already, namely that mortgages are not redeemable, not repayable in capital, but merely intended to establish a claim to 'rent', i.e. regular payments of interest; if these payments are not forthcoming, an order may be made for the sale of the property; the mortgagee has no further claim. This is Rodbertus' 'principle of rent', intended to enable the Junkers to produce, bourgeois-fashion, 5,000 talers per annum and expend, aristo-fashion, 10,000 talers and still not ruin themselves. How it's done remains a mystery. I had to laugh when I saw Schramm trying to find something significant in it. [b]

Marx's photograph went off to Manz today. [c] I understand he wants to know about the colour. You will be able to help him there of course. As swarthy as any southern European might be, not much red about the cheeks (when you saw Marx he was already a very sickly yellow; that wasn't normal), moustache jet black, streaked with white but without a trace of brown; save for grizzled hairs, hair and beard snow white. The picture — a retouched photographic enlargement — is a speaking likeness, and he will get it per the Swiss post office.

Apart from the Polish translation of the *Origin*, Vera Zasulich has applied to do the Russian and Anderfuhren (from Meiringen), a law

[a] [J. K.] Rodbertus-Jagetzow, *Zur Erklärung und Abhülfe der heutigen Creditnoth des Grundbesitzes*.- [b] C. A. S[chramm], 'K. Kautsky und Rodbertus', *Die Neue Zeit*, No. 11, 1884.- [c] See this volume, pp. 191-92.

student in Berne, the Italian.[302] Do you know anything about this man? Dr Cerioli, his teacher, an Italian and socialist, will go over the translation.

I sent copies [a] to you and Ede yesterday. Over 30 have already gone off to all parts of the world. I have sent it to *To-Day* and *Justice* and no doubt you will attend to the other review copies. My sincerest thanks to you and Ede for all the trouble you've taken over the thing.

Your
F. E.

What news of your coming here [b]? I am speaking not of *origo* [c] but of *adventus*.[d]

First published, in Russian, in *Marx-Engels Archives*, Vol. I (VI), Moscow, 1932

Printed according to the original

Published in English for the first time

120

ENGELS TO KARL KAUTSKY [287]

IN ZURICH

[London,] 17 October 1884

Dietz tells me that the spelling has been changed.[301]

'Had Kautsky,' he writes, 'added a brief comment when sending the ms., you and I would have been spared the task of alteration.'

Not a word about the thing being kept quiet until 3 whole sheets had been printed (though this may not have been Dietz's fault).

Is old Bachofen still alive and is he still in Basle? I should like to inscribe a copy to him.

---

[a] F. Engels, *The Origin of the Family, Private Property and the State.*- [b] The word used is *Herkommen* which can mean either 'coming here' or 'origins'.- [c] origins - [d] arrival

The preface[a] is in course of preparation, i.e. I am first of all ploughing through the whole of *Zur Erkenntniss*[b] again. It will repay the trouble; only by a really close investigation does one properly appreciate the stupendousness of the nonsense preached here, nonsense that literally overwhelms the few flashes of insight which, though admittedly not new, are nevertheless accurate and, for Germany, commendable. *Capital*, Book II, will be *very* illuminating on this point. Regards to Ede.

Your

F. E.

First published, in Russian, in *Marx-Engels Archives*, Vol. I (VI), Moscow, 1932

Printed according to the original

Published in English for the first time

121

ENGELS TO KARL KAUTSKY [263]

IN ZURICH

London, 20 October 1884

Dear Kautsky,

Have sent you by *registered mail* proofs and pp. 49-96 of the *Poverty* ms.[301] I did no more than skim through them, nor was I able to compare them with the ms. Please get this done at once. I am asking Dietz to send the remainder to you and only the proofs of the *preface*[a] to me; I should have begun this today had I not again been robbed of my best working time by the afore-mentioned proof-correcting. But tomorrow I shall get down to it; my preface will, I think, come first, then Marx's article from the old *Social-Demokrat* as locum tenens for *his* preface.[151]

I was on the point of asking you about Nonne, Mme Lafargue being anxious to know something about this neighbour whom they regard-

---

[a] F. Engels, 'Marx and Rodbertus'.- [b] [J. K.] Rodbertus-Jagetzow, *Zur Erkenntniss unsrer staatswirthschaftlichen Zustände.*

ed with suspicion. Then came the 'Execution' in the Paris press.[303] Everyone is astonished that the Prussians should have appointed and paid (?) such a clumsy brute.

Joynes of *To-Day* has just been to see me. They have been wanting for some time to publish an English version of the *Entwicklung*,[a] the rights to translate which I had long since conceded to Aveling.[b] They don't want him, however, he and Hyndman being ± [c] rivals, and tried to insist upon my accepting Shaw, who does not know German and proposes to translate from the French. This I took the liberty of declining and referred him to Aveling whom, in any case, I like better every day. These little literary intrigues make up the greater part of the internal history of the movement in this country. Nor is this their only trouble. A week ago last Tuesday[d] Mme Lafargue attended a meeting of the Council of the Social Democratic Federation [300] during which they were bickering about some trifle or other to such good purpose that the air was buzzing with cries of DAMNED LIAR. Great fun, it seems. The only men in whom I have any confidence are Bax and Aveling, both thoroughly good chaps, intelligent and sincere, but in need of a great deal of help. I don't give much for the others, in so far as I have had the opportunity to judge them.

I have now also got Mr Mommsen just where I want him. In his *Römische Forschungen* he wrote a lot of nonsense about *enuptio gentis*[e]; I went into the matter and have now extracted all the relevant passages.[f] If anyone of the Mommsen school should try to fault me in regard to Roman history (quite possible in regard to *form*, but not substance), I shall be able to oblige.

Hirsch has sent me the *Frankfurter Zeitung* with a feuilleton on Lippert's *Geschichte der Familie*.[g] The book is obviously barefaced plagiarism from Morgan and Bachofen, with a few trimmings from other easily discoverable sources.

Warmest regards to Ede.

Your
F. E.

---

[a] F. Engels, *Socialism: Utopian and Scientific*.- [b] See this volume, p. 400.- [c] more or less - [d] 14 October - [e] exogamy - [f] See F. Engels, *The Origin of the Family, Private Property and the State* (present edition, Vol. 26, pp. 225-28).- [g] H. Kaltenboeck, 'Familie und Ehe', *Frankfurter Zeitung und Handelsblatt*, No. 278, 4 October 1884 (morning edition).

Another thing I haven't yet seen is your feuilleton in the *Frà`nkfurter Zeitung*.[a] Have you still got it? I will send it back.

First published, in Russian, in *Marx-Engels Archives*, Vol. I (VI), Moscow, 1932

Printed according to the original

Published in English in full for the first time

122

ENGELS TO EDUARD BERNSTEIN

IN ZURICH

London, 22 October 1884

Dear Ede,

I am laying aside my preface[b] to inform you:

1. That I am sending you herewith, by registered mail, Marx's 'Speech on the Question of Free Trade'. This irreplaceable copy, acquired with much difficulty at second-hand, must be returned to me after use.

2. That I consider it necessary to print in the form of an appendix at the end of the *Poverty* the passage from *A Contribution to the Critique of Political Economy* concerning *John Gray, the first precursor of Proudhon and Rodbertus*, from p. 61, 'the theory that labour time', etc., up to the end of the section on p. 64.[301] Would you be so kind as to send it to Stuttgart forthwith? I refer to this appendix in the preface. *Between us* we shall have *completely* demolished the whole of this aspect of petty-bourgeois socialism and disposed at the same time of the reply to Rodbertus' Utopia, for I shall use the preface to make good any other deficiencies.

Whether or not you use the *'libre échange'*[c] as an appendix is for you to decide; I can't think where else to put it, and can hardly imagine it would be effective simply as a pamphlet — as to which you are better judges than I.

If Dietz should raise any difficulties regarding the Gray appendix, it might be included after the preface and the article on Proudhon

---

[a] K. Kautsky, 'Aus dem Nachlasse von Carl Marx', *Frankfurter Zeitung und Handelsblatt*, No. 263, 19 September 1884 (morning edition). - [b] F. Engels, 'Marx and Rodbertus'.- [c] 'free trade'; Engels is referring to Marx's 'Speech on the Question of Free Trade'.

from the *Social-Demokrat* (the old one). But included it must be, as you yourselves will find.

Your
F. E.

First published, in Russian, in *Marx-Engels Archives*, Book I, Moscow, 1924

Printed according to the original

Published in English for the first time

123

ENGELS TO EDUARD BERNSTEIN

IN ZURICH

London, 23 October 1884

Dear Ede,

Herewith the preface.[a] If you are going to add the '*libre échange*'[b] to it, include what I have appended on the last page, otherwise alter it.[c]

I have also taken out a money order for £1 in your favour, this being Schorlemmer's contribution to the election fund. You are probably already aware that Schorlemmer was charged in Darmstadt. When the arrest was made at Haug's house in Freiburg, they also found a copy of the *Sozialdemokrat* addressed to his brother[d] — ergo domiciliary search, resulting in the discovery of letters from Schorlemmer which contained indifferent jokes about Bismarck — resulting in further inquiries about him at his mother's house and at Höchst where he then happened to be. To spare his mother unpleasantness he took his departure. Caused a great furore in Darmstadt.[304]

At Bebel's suggestion I have sent Schumacher some information about Rittinghausen in 1848.

What has by now, alas, become a very lengthy preface does not see the end of Mr Rodbertus; in the preface to the 2nd book of *Capital*[e] I shall mount another attack on his 'discoveries' about surplus

---

[a] F. Engels, 'Marx and Rodbertus'.- [b] 'free trade' - [c] See previous letter.- [d] Ludwig Schorlemmer - [e] See present edition, Vol. 36.

value. Odd that Ricardo should be so completely forgotten in Germany! Regards to Karl Kautsky.

Your
F. E.

Should Dietz send the manuscript and proofs of the preface to Zurich, kindly send them on here.

First published, in Russian, in *Marx-Engels Archives*, Book I, Moscow, 1924

Printed according to the original

Published in English for the first time

124

ENGELS TO AUGUST BEBEL [305]

IN PLAUEN NEAR DRESDEN

London, 29 October 1884

Dear Bebel,

Your telegram arrived here a minute or two after six and was hailed with cries of delight.[306] I at once sent off postcards to people here and in the provinces to make its contents known and also advised Paris [39] where the first news they hear of anything is invariably garbled and contradictory. Very many thanks for sparing me a thought in the midst of the electoral hurly-burly. I have also informed [39] the Society.[162]

It is more than I expected. I am less concerned just now with the number of seats that will eventually be won; the obligatory fifteen are assured [307] and the main thing is the proof that the movement is marching ahead at a pace that is as rapid as it is sure, that constituency after constituency has been carried away by it and has ceased to be a safe seat for the other parties. But what is also splendid is the way our workers have run the affair, the tenacity, determination and, above all, humour with which they have captured position after position and set at naught all the dodges, threats and bullying on the part of government and bourgeoisie. What Germany could damned well do with is reinstatement in the world's esteem; Bismarck and Moltke can make her feared; respect, genuine esteem, such as is only accorded to free, self-disciplined men — that respect will only be exacted by our proletarians.

The effect on Europe and America will be enormous. I have hopes that in France it will provide fresh impetus for our party. Over there people are still suffering from the aftermath of the Commune. Great though its influence on Europe may have been, it has also seriously set back the French proletariat. To have been in power for three months — and in Paris at that — and not to have radically altered the world but rather have come to grief through their own incompetence (such being the biassed fashion in which the matter is understood today) — is proof that the party is not viable. That is the specious argument usually advanced by people who fail to realise that, while the Commune was the grave of *early* specifically French socialism, it was, for France, also and at the same time the cradle of a new international communism. And this last will be duly set on its feet by the German victories. Mme Lafargue, who is here and sends you her warm regards, is also of this opinion.

Similarly the news will make a strong impact on the English-speaking proletariat in America.

You will have received my registered letter[39] as also my postcard[111] of the day before yesterday.

My main worry just now is whether you yourself have pulled it off in your doubtful constituencies.[308] In view of the many new elements who are in any case joining the parliamentary group, it is precisely at the beginning that you are so urgently needed, lest you find yourself subsequently presented with *faits accomplis* in which you had no part. I also know you are not in the best of health and you must at all costs conserve yourself for the party and the more critical times that lie ahead of it. But no doubt everything will work out satisfactorily.

I wanted to tell you more about the Rodbertus business, but it's no longer possible this evening. As for Schramm himself, he will already have had an adequate dressing-down from Karl Kautsky.[a] In the preface to the *Poverty*[b] I have already clarified Rodbertus' attitude towards us and this will, I think, suffice until I am able to deal with him more thoroughly in the preface to *Capital*, Book II.[c] Should it prove

---

[a] See this volume, pp. 193-95.- [b] F. Engels, 'Marx and Rodbertus'.- [c] See present edition, Vol. 36.

necessary to do so in the interim, I can step in again. More about this anon.

Your

F. E.

First published, in Russian, in *Marx-Engels Archives*, Vol. I (VI), Moscow, 1932

Printed according to the original

Published in English in full for the first time

125

ENGELS TO KARL KAUTSKY [263]

IN ZURICH

London, 8 November 1884

Dear Kautsky,

Between the time your letter arrived and today the elections — i. e. five years — have supervened.[309] So I shall revert to it only briefly.

Herewith Liebknecht's letter — typical. Why you should not be able to edit the *Neue Zeit* just as well from London as from Zurich is inconceivable. Equally so, why your being in London should mean that you'll be lost to the German party. However, this letter provides no proof that Liebknecht — under the influence of different surroundings and a different frame of mind — might not very soon think and write quite differently. The fact that he was only partially successful at Offenbach — we over here don't yet know the results of the second ballot — may have given him reason to pause.[310] The bit about the 'impregnable' position in Stukkert[a] is killing. Like the NCO in the French revolutionary army telling his bare-footed squad about the speech made by the people's representative: *Le représentant a dit: Avec du fer et du pain on va jusqu'en Chine. Il n'a pas parlé de chaussures.*[b] Impregnable — if there were no police!

I am writing to Dietz [39] telling him to send me the proofs of the preface[c] *in galley form* since a number of alterations will be neces-

---

[a] A reference to the editorial offices of *Die Neue Zeit* in Stuttgart.- [b] The representative said: With iron and bread we can get as far as China. He didn't mention *boots*. - [c] F. Engels, 'Marx and Rodbertus'.

sary. With this sort of thing, one cannot be too careful about one's mode of expression if one is not to find oneself pinned down to some ill-chosen or ambiguous word.

The elections will elicit an echo throughout Europe and America. And what a triumphant day it was! The *Kölnische* concedes us $^3/_4$ of a million votes and, in the hope of obtaining their support in the second ballot, is grovelling before the 4,000 who voted for Bebel in Cologne.[311] To me the *Kölnische* is more important than any other paper because the Rhenish bourgeois are still the most advanced bourgeois in Germany and the *Kölnische* is their mirror. And hence this complete volte-face, this sudden respect for a new power, is all the more significant.

But how truly splendid it is! For the first time in history a strong, coherent workers' party exists as a real political power, evolved and come of age amidst the harshest persecution, irresistibly capturing one position after another, free of all philistinism in the most philistine, free of all chauvinism in the most cock-a-hoop country in Europe. A power the existence and rise of which is as incomprehensible and mysterious to governments and the old ruling classes as was the rising tide of Christianity to the authorities of the declining Roman Empire, but which is working its way to the fore as certainly and inexorably as once Christianity — so certainly that the rate at which its velocity will increase, and hence the actual time of its ultimate victory, already permits of mathematical calculation. Helped on its way rather than suppressed by the Anti-Socialist Law,[37] it deigns only to spurn Bismarck's social reform[312] and the last desperate measure to suppress it momentarily — by fomenting a premature coup — would elicit nothing but immortal laughter.

It's strange. The best aid to our progress is precisely the backwardness of Germany's industrial position. In England and France the transition to large-scale industry is pretty well complete. The conditions in which the proletariat now finds itself have already become stable; agricultural districts and industrial districts, large-scale industry and cottage industries have become separated and, as far as is in fact possible in modern industry, firmly established. Even the fluctuations inseparable from the ten-year cycle of crises have become habitual conditions of existence. The political, if not actually socialist, movements that arose during the period of industrial revolution — immature as they were — have failed, leaving behind them discouragement rather than encouragement. Bourgeois capitalist development has proved stronger than revolutionary counter-pressure; if there is to be another revolt against capitalist production there must be another, more powerful impulse, such as the ousting of England from the dominant position she has hitherto occupied in the world market, or some special revolutionary opportunity in France.

In Germany, on the other hand, large-scale industry goes back no further than 1848 and is the greatest legacy of that year. The industrial revolution is still going on, and doing so under the most unfavourable conditions. Cottage industries, based on small-, free- or lease-holdings, still continue to struggle against machinery and steam; the foundering smallholder looks to a cottage industry as his last sheet anchor, but no sooner is he industrialised than he is again subjected to pressure from machinery and steam. Subsidiary income from the land, the domestic potato plot, provides the capitalist with the most powerful pretext for depressing wages; he can now present his foreign customers with the entire normal surplus value—the only way he can compete in the world market—the whole of his profits being derived from what he deducts from the normal wages. Alongside this there is the complete subversion of all living conditions in the industrial centres as a result of the enormous strides made by large-scale industry. Thus the whole of Germany, with perhaps the exception of the Junker-dominated North-East, is becoming swept into the social revolution, the smallholder drawn into industry, and patriarchal circles being precipitated into the movement, and thus is far more fundamentally revolutionised than England or France. This social revolution of which the eventual outcome is the expropriation of the smallholder and handicraftsman is, however, taking place at the very time when a German, Marx, was destined to make a theoretical analysis of the results of historical developments, both theoretical and practical, in England and France, to elucidate the whole nature of capitalist production and hence its ultimate historical fate, and thus provide the German proletariat with a programme such as the English and the French, its precursors, have never possessed. A more fundamental revolutionising of society on the one hand, greater lucidity of intellect on the other—that is the secret of the irresistible progress made by the German workers' movement.

I had meant to write to Ede as well, but it has grown too late— moreover Pumps has arrived with her little girl with whom I shall have to play. Aveling and Tussy are arriving at 5 and at 7. Morris wants to hold a grand consultation with me. So for the time being Ede will have to content himself with my good wishes.

Your

F. E.

First published, in Russian, in *Marx-Engels Archives*, Vol. I (VI), Moscow, 1932

Printed according to the original

Published in English in full for the first time

126

ENGELS TO PASQUALE MARTIGNETTI

IN BENEVENTO

London, 8 November 1884
122 Regent's Park Road, N. W.

Dear Sir,

On receiving your kind letter of 27th last [313] I sent you a copy of my pamphlet *The Origin etc.*,[a] and I would have sent it sooner had I known for certain that your last address was still valid.

I congratulate you on the splendid progress you have made in your study of the German language. I entrust you with the Italian translation of *The Origin* with pleasure and confidence. I have received in the meantime an earlier and similar offer from another quarter,[b] which I have not yet accepted. In order to reject it definitively, it would be useful for me to know whether you have at your disposal a publisher who will print and publish your translation without delay.[314]

I remain with respect your devoted

F. Engels

First published in *La corrispondenza di Marx e Engels con italiani. 1848-1895*, Milano, 1964

Printed according to the original

Translated from the Italian

Published in English for the first time

---

[a] *The Origin of the Family, Private Property and the State.* - [b] See this volume, pp. 204-05

127

ENGELS TO EDUARD BERNSTEIN

IN ZURICH

London, 11 November 1884

Dear Ede,

The inquiry in your letter about Marx's article on Proudhon[a] has been dealt with in my preface[b] where I made direct reference to it. You must now let me know how you propose to arrange the whole[301]; I may receive the proofs of the preface any day and shall proceed accordingly in regard to the above article, the excerpt from *A Contribution to the Critique*[c] and possibly the 'Speech'.[d]

You did right to stress in the *Sozialdemokrat*[e] that we are the only serious opponents of the Centre.[229] Only by penetrating the strongholds of the Centre—Munich, Mainz, Cologne, Aachen, Düsseldorf, Essen, etc.—shall we be able to disperse this artificially united omnium-gatherum of opposing views and compel every one of them to show their true colours. And then it will transpire that the *genuinely* Catholic group is simply the Catholic wing of reaction, just as in Belgium and France it constitutes the *whole* of reaction. And no one would suffer more from this dispersal of the Centre than Mr Bismarck, who can darned well do with a hotchpotch of a party like that.

I get little news of how the second ballots are going and then only belatedly.[306] I hope that at this juncture a good many will turn out well, for the more new elements there are in the parliamentary group just now the better. The worst of them (the eddicated) have already been elected; those still to come are most of them working men and they can only improve the company.

Judgment has been passed on the Anti-Socialist Law.[37] State and bourgeoisie have been made to look fearful asses vis-à-vis ourselves. But they are nevertheless going merrily on their way and anyone who thinks that the Law will necessarily receive its quietus as a result of

---

[a] K. Marx, 'On Proudhon'.- [b] F. Engels, 'Marx and Rodbertus'.- [c] K. Marx, *A Contribution to the Critique of Political Economy*.- [d] K. Marx, 'Speech on the Question of Free Trade'.- [e] 'Unsere Bilanz', *Der Sozialdemokrat*, No. 45, 6 November 1884 (leader).

this could be badly mistaken. Over here old John Russell carried on as Prime Minister for 20 years after his political demise. To abolish the Law does, after all, require a decision, and they are unlikely to make the necessary effort. At best there would be penal clauses which would cause us heavier casualties than would the Anti-Socialist Law.

We must now put forward positive proposals in regard to legislation.[307] If they are couched emphatically, i.e. without regard for petty-bourgeois prejudices, then they will be very good. But if they are Geisered and Vierecked, then they will be bad. Normal working day (10 hours gradually reducing to perhaps 8), domestic and international factory legislation (in which the domestic could go further than the international), radical revision of the legislation affecting employers' liability, accident, sickness, disabled workmen, etc.— these will provide enough and more to go on with. *Nous verrons.*[a]

The 1884 elections are for us what those of 1866 were for the German philistine. Then, all of a sudden, he became a 'great nation' without having had anything to do with it and, indeed, against his will.[b] Now we have become a 'great party', but by our own hard work and at the cost of heavy sacrifices. *Noblesse oblige.* We cannot bring the mass of the nation over to our side unless that mass undergoes a gradual process of development. Frankfurt, Munich, Königsberg, cannot suddenly become as pronouncedly proletarian as Saxony, Berlin, the industrial Ruhr. Just now the petty-bourgeois elements among the leaders may find here and there among the masses the backing they have hitherto lacked. What has hitherto been a reactionary tendency in the case of individuals may now reproduce itself as a necessary developmental element—localised—in the case of the masses. That would call for a change of tactics if the masses are to be helped on their way without, at the same time, allowing the bad leaders to gain the ascendant. Here again we shall have to wait and see.

Tomorrow I shall attend to the very tricky final editing of Part III of the 2nd book of *Capital.*[c] As soon as I have finished I hope to find time to rewrite the *Peasant War*[213] which this time will appear as a turning-point for the whole of the history of Germany and hence calls for important historical additions both at the beginning and the end. Only the account of the actual war will remain more or less as it stands. I feel that it is more important to print the *Peasant War* first rather than the *Dühring* which I shall alter little, simply adding notes

[a] We shall see.- [b] See this volume, pp. 221-22.- [c] See present edition, Vol. 36.

or appendices. What arrangements do you propose to make about the printing?

Whatever becomes of the Anti-Socialist Law, the paper[a] and the press in Zurich must, in my view, continue to operate. They will never restore freedom to us, even of the pre-1878 variety. Your Geisers and Auerbachs will be allowed complete freedom and they in turn will trot out the pretty excuse that they went as far as they could. But in our case, the requisite freedom of the press is only to be had abroad. Come to that, it is even possible that attempts will be made to curtail universal suffrage; cowardliness makes people stupid and the philistine is *capable de tout*.[b] Admittedly we shall receive compliments from left, right and centre and they won't in every case fall on stony ground. For friend Singer might feel inclined to show proof that, despite or because of his paunch, he is no ogre.

Karl Kautsky will have received my letter of yesterday.[c]

Your
F. E.

First published, in Russian, in *Marx-Engels Archives*, Book I, Moscow, 1924

Printed according to the original

Published in English for the first time

128

ENGELS TO HERMANN ENGELS[315]

IN BARMEN

London, 11 November 1884

Dear Hermann,

The sad news of Emil's[d] illness brought to me by your letter of 25 September did not come as a complete surprise. He himself had written to me from time to time about the state of his health and about the necessity he was in of spending the winter in the south; moreover

---

[a] *Der Sozialdemokrat* - [b] capable of anything - [c] See this volume, pp. 212-15. -
[d] Emil Engels, Frederick Engels' brother

your earlier letters also contained a number of allusions that gave me cause for anxiety. If tubercles have now finally appeared—not exactly common at our age—it is certainly a very bad sign, but I trust he will still be able to remain among us for a time and in a condition that does not make life too much of a burden to him. Nevertheless one pleasure he has still been able to experience, as I saw not long ago in the paper, is the opening of the Aggertal railway[a] to which he devoted so many years of incessant toil. Even though this little branch line may be far from what he had in mind, it is nevertheless better than nothing and will bring quite a different kind of life into the valley and Engelskirchen than has been the case hitherto.

I should have written to you sooner had not Hermann's[b] wedding intervened, at which time I wasn't absolutely sure where you were; since then there have been numerous interruptions and, on top of that, I have been up to my eyes in work. Moreover, for the past 18 months I, in my own person, have been sharply reminded of the frailty of the human body. What was actually wrong I shall probably never discover, but suffice it to say that the thing now seems to be righting itself and developing into some kind of hernial trouble (what is involved is not the prolapse of a piece of gut, but water in the abdomen). Besides, I have found a very efficient bandage-maker who has treated many cases of this kind, which are pretty rare as a rule, and has constructed a highly practical but in no way uncomfortable appliance for it. After lengthy experiments I can now manage it pretty well and am at last able to move about again and, what had hitherto proved a virtual impossibility, work at my desk. If things carry on like this, I shall be content; apart from relaxed muscles and ligaments, which is only natural after one has lain motionless on a sofa for so long, I no longer feel anything and am gradually becoming my old self again.

I trust you are all keeping well otherwise. Rudolf[c] would also seem to be on the mend again. He seems to have inherited father's constitution in many respects, for he too had constant trouble with his stomach until his forties but was then perfectly all right and would doubtless still be alive had not typhoid reft him away.

---

[a] See 'Lübeck-Büchenbahn', *Kölnische Zeitung*, No. 314, 11 November 1884 (second edition).- [b] Hermann Friedrich Theodor Engels.- [c] Rudolf Engels

Please let me know soon how Emil and the rest of you are getting on and what Hedwig[a] is doing. No doubt Hermann will soon be returning from his honeymoon.

Fondest regards to all of you, brothers, sisters, Emma,[b] your children and you yourself.

Your
Friedrich

First published in *Deutsche Revue*, Jg. 46, Bd. 3, Stuttgart-Leipzig, 1921

Printed according to the original

Published in English for the first time

129

ENGELS TO AUGUST BEBEL[316]

IN PLAUEN NEAR DRESDEN

London, 18 November 1884

Dear Bebel,

I had meant to write to you about the Rodbertus business but, now that my preface to *The Poverty of Philosophy*[c] is to appear in the *Neue Zeit*, you will find the essentials set forth better there than could be done in a letter. The rest will follow later, in the preface to *Capital*, Book II.[d]

There is, however, another point about which I should like to give you my opinion, and which seems to me more urgent.

Such is the respect we have inspired in liberal philistines generally that they all exclaim with one voice: 'All right, only let the Social Democrats place themselves on a *legal* footing and abjure *revolution* — then we shall support the immediate repeal of the Anti-Socialist Law.[37]' Hence there can be no doubt that this insolent proposal will be put to you forthwith in the Reichstag. The reply you make is of importance, not so much to Germany where our stalwart lads have already given it at the polling booths, as to other countries.

---

[a] Hedwig Boelling, née Engels - [b] Emma Engels - [c] F. Engels, 'Marx and Rodbertus'.- [d] See present edition, Vol. 36.

A *tame* reply would immediately destroy the tremendous impression created by the elections. [306]

As I see it, the case is as follows:

The political situation now obtaining throughout Europe is the result of revolutions. Everywhere the fundamental laws, historical laws, legitimacy, have been infringed a thousand times over, if not actually subverted. It is, however, in the nature of all parties and/or classes that have come to power by revolutionary means to demand that the fundamental laws newly created by the revolution be unconditionally recognised and held sacrosanct. The right to revolution *has* existed — otherwise those who now rule would, after all, not be entitled to do so — but from now on it is to cease to exist.

In Germany the present situation is based on the revolution that began in 1848 and ended in 1866. 1866 saw a complete revolution. Just as Prussia became what it is only by betraying and making war on the German Empire in alliance with other countries (1740, 1756, 1795 [317]), so, too, it was only by the forcible subversion of the German Confederation and by civil war that it brought into being the Prusso-German Empire. [318] Its assertion that it was the others who broke the federal treaty in no way alters the fact. The others maintain the contrary. No revolution has ever yet lacked a pretext of legality — vide France in 1830 when King [a] and bourgeoisie each claimed to be in the right. In short, Prussia fomented civil war and, with it, revolution. After its victory, it overthrew *three thrones 'by the grace of God'* and annexed their territories, together with the once free city of Frankfurt. [319] If that was not revolutionary, then I don't know what the word means. Not content with that, it confiscated the private property of the princes it had driven out. That this was not legal, hence revolutionary, it admitted when it induced an assembly — the Reichstag — to approve the deed in retrospect, though the said assembly had no more right than the government to dispose of those funds. [320]

The Prusso-German Empire, as the consummation of the North German Confederation forcibly created by the events of 1867, [b] [321] is a wholly revolutionary creation. I am not complaining about that. What I do reproach the chaps for — the ones responsible for it — is for having been no more than pusillanimous revolutionaries, for not hav-

---

[a] Louis Philippe - [b] 1866 in the original.

ing gone much further and annexed the whole of Germany to Prussia straight away. But anyone whose instruments are blood and iron, who overthrows monarchies, engulfs entire states and confiscates private property, should not damn other people as revolutionaries. Should the party merely retain the right to be neither more nor less revolutionary than the imperial government has shown itself, it will have obtained all it requires.

Not long since, it was officially stated that the imperial constitution was not a compact between the princes and the people, but only a compact between the princes and the free cities for which a new one could at any time be substituted. Thus, the government organs that expounded this were demanding for the governments the right *to subvert the imperial constitution.* They were not subjected to an emergency law, nor were they prosecuted. Very well — neither do we demand for ourselves, in the most extreme case, more than is demanded for the governments in this one.

The Duke of Cumberland is the rightful, undisputed heir to the throne of Brunswick. The King of Prussia has no more right to reign in Berlin than is claimed by Cumberland in Brunswick. Anything else that is wanted of him can only be laid claim to after Cumberland has taken possession of his rightful, legitimate throne. This the revolutionary German imperial government is forcibly preventing him from doing. Yet another revolutionary act.

And what is the position as regards the parties?

In November 1848 the Conservative Party did not hesitate to infringe the legality constituted in March of that year. [322] In any case, it accords only provisional recognition to the present constitutional state of affairs and would joyfully acclaim any feudal and absolutist coup d'état.

The Liberal Party of all shades participated in the revolution from 1848 to 1866, nor would it today allow anyone to deny it the right to counter the forcible subversion of the constitution with force.

The Centre [229] recognises the Church as the supreme power transcending the state; a power, that is, which might, in certain circumstances, make revolution a *duty.*

And these are the parties which demand of us that *we* and *we alone out of all the rest* should declare that we would *in no circumstances* resort to force, would submit to any pressure, any outrage, not only when these have a veneer of legality — *are* legal in our opponents' view — but also when they are downright illegal.

No party, unless it was lying, has ever denied the right to armed resistance *in certain circumstances*. None has ever been able to renounce that ultimate right.

But once the debate begins to turn on the *circumstances* in which a party may reserve that right, the game is already won. The whole thing becomes progressively more nonsensical. Particularly in the case of a party that has been declared illegal and is thus actually reduced by higher authority to resorting to revolution. And such a declaration of illegality, having been made once already, might recur any day. To demand an unconditional statement of this kind from such a party is utterly preposterous.

Nor, for that matter, have the gentlemen anything to worry about. The military position being what it now is, we shall not go into action so long as we have a military power against us. We can bide our time until that military power ceases *to be a power against us*. Any revolution prior to that, even a victorious one, would bring to power, not *ourselves*, but the most radical elements of the bourgeoisie and/or petty bourgeoisie.

In any case, the elections have shown that we can expect to gain nothing by submissiveness, i. e. concessions to our opponents. It is only defiant resistance that has gained us their respect and turned us into a power. Only power is respected and only so long as we remain a power will your philistine respect us. Anyone who makes concessions and is therefore no longer a power, he will despise. You can let them feel the iron fist in the velvet glove, indeed you must. The German proletariat has become a powerful party — may its representatives be worthy of it!

> Your
> F. E.

(Time for the post.)

First published abridged in: F. Engels, *Politisches Vermächtnis. Aus unveröffentlichten Briefen*, Berlin, 1920 and in full, in Russian, in *Marx-Engels Archives*, Vol. I (VI), Moscow, 1932

Printed according to the original

Published in English in full for the first time

130

ENGELS TO LAURA LAFARGUE

IN PARIS

London, 23 November 1884

My dear Laura,

Glad you arrived safe and well [268] and Paul liked his cake — but Nim can't get over his insisting to eat cheese along with it. Nim has suffered much from tooth-ache — a sound tooth, but loose. Yesterday she took an old pair of small tongs which she brought from Maitland Park and wrenched it out with it, rewarding her courage with a drop of brandy, and is now quite lively again.

Friday last[a] the Social Democratic Federation [300] had a benefit. Tussy and Edward played in a piece — I did not go, as I do not as yet see my way to sitting three hours consecutively in a stiff chair. Nim says they played very well — the piece was more or less, she says, their own history. Mother Wright read — very well — Bax played the piano — rather long — Morris who was here the other night and quite delighted to find the Old Norse Edda [323] on my table — he is an Icelandic enthusiast — Morris read a piece of his poetry[b] (a 'refonte'[c] of the Eddaic *Helreid Brynhildar*[d] — the description of Brynhild burning herself with Sigurd's corpse), etc., etc.; it went off very well — their art seems to be rather better than their literature and their poetry better than their prose.

Paul's reply to Block is excellent, not only in style but in subject-matter. [281] People have different ways of learning things, and if he learns political economy by fighting, it's all right so that he does learn it. He was quite right in bearing out the question of the equal price of corn which costs different amounts of labour — that is too complicated and is solved only in Book III, *Kapital*. But what he may return to, when he has an opportunity, is the stupid calumny of Block, page 131, note: that Mohr *insiste surtout sur le capital employé dans le commerce, tant sous la forme a r g e n t (espèces) que sous la forme m a r-*

---

[a] 21 November - [b] W. Morris, *The Story of Sigurd the Volsung and the Fall of the Nibelungs.-* [c] 'variant' - [d] Brynhild's raid into the hell

c h a n d i s e s. [a] This is a direct lie or a proof that he does not know what he is writing about. Mohr mentions interest-bearing capital and merchants' capital only as historical *facts*, but expressly *excludes* them from all economical discussion in Book I, where capital is only considered in its simplest form as industrial capital.

A slip of the pen of Paul's p. 285: *la grandeur de la plus-value est en rapport d i r e c t avec la longueur de la journée de travail, mais en rapport i n v e r s e avec le taux du salaire.* [b]

Du reste, [c] you know that my only objection to Paul's replying to Block was the fear that it might 'block' his ultimate reply to Leroy-Beaulieu. [d]—If he has *eingeseift* [e] Molinari to that extent, that he allows Paul to reply anything to anybody, all the better.

The report of the meeting in favour of the Germans in the *Sozialdemokrat* as well as the extracts from *Lyon-Socialiste* [324] given there will have a capital effect in Germany and everywhere. Nothing can strike the philistine and also the workmen of other countries more than this cordiality and working hand in hand of the proletarians of the two *'erbfeindliche Nationen'* [f]. It ought to be *mis en avant* [g] as much and as often as possible.

As to poor Brousse, the man without a programme, being in doubt about the programme on which our people have been elected, the proclamation of Müller in Darmstadt which I was glad Guesde worked up in the *Cri du Peuple* will have answered him. Better still is the Hanoverian programme in this week's *Sozialdemokrat* No. 47. [325] I wish Guesde would make use of that. These two proclamations, and the fact that they were issued in *new* districts—Darmstadt and Hanover, where our people might be expected to coax votes, have given me quite as much pleasure as the elections themselves. They show how thoroughly the revolutionary spirit has been evoked by Bismarck's persecutions. I was almost expecting that the new districts might send 'moderate' men, but no fear of that now. Also Sabor the Jewish schoolmaster from Frankfort belongs to the *Bebel* wing of the party.

Bernstein's letter to Paul about Lassalle [326] finds its explanation in this, that in *Paris*, as in London and New York, the old Lassalle set is still strongly represented among the Germans. They have mostly

---

[a] especially insists on commercial capital both in its *money* form (coinage) and in its *commodity* form - [b] The amount of surplus value is in a *direct* ratio to the length of the working day and in an *inverse* ratio to the size of wages.- [c] Besides - [d] P. Lafargue, 'La théorie de la plus-value de Karl Marx et la critique de M. Paul Leroy-Beaulieu'.- [e] cheated - [f] 'traditionally hostile nations' - [g] emphasised

emigrated, Germany is too hot for them and won't listen to them. But as they are comparatively harmless abroad, and form a useful international cement, besides finding funds for the Germans at home, *on les ménage un peu.*[a]

Loria takes good care not to send me his expectorations.[b] As a true '*Kathedersocialistischer*[54] *Streber*'[c] he robs us right and left. By the bye, what Paul intends doing if he should reply to him, *donne de côté.*[d] Loria knows that as well as ourselves, *why* capitalists go as well into one branch of industry as another. But the real question is as I stated it, and one which is not so easy, in fact, it broke down classical economy which could not solve it. The *déroute*, as Mohr's manuscript calls it,[e] of the Ricardian school on this very question[f] opened the door to vulgar economy.

My walks with you have done me a deal of good—I extend them every day, and my muscles are hardening again.

Kind regards to Paul. Love from Nim.

Yours affectionately,
F. E.

Poor old Mother Hess!

'Wir waben, wir waben!'[g]

Hope she is suited at last.

Now before concluding I want to ask you a favour. Paul has from me: 1) Darwin's *Origin of Species*, 2) Thierry, *Histoire du tiers état*, 3) Paquet, *Institutions provinciales et communales de la France*, 4) Buonarotti, *Conspiracy of Babeuf*. Now, Jenny had from me: 1) *Die 'Edda', poetische und prosaische*, and 2) *Beowulf*, both in Simrock's New High German translation. The latter two books and Darwin I am in especial want of. Could you get them together if they can be found (Thierry and Paquet I also have use for and Buonarroti is not to be had now) and send them in a parcel to me? The agents of the Continental Parcels Express (*agence Continentale*), are

E. d'Odiardi, 18 rue Bergère and

P. Bigeault, 23 rue Dunkerque, opposite the station du Nord.

The carriage *not* to be paid, as the delivery will be all the safer; and

---

[a] they are spared a little - [b] A. Loria, 'La théorie de la valeur de Karl Marx', *Journal des Économistes*, No. 10, October 1884. - [c] 'armchair-socialist careerist' - [d] stand aside - [e] disintegration - [f] See present edition, Vol. 32, pp. 258-373. - [g] 'We weave, we weave' (South German dialect); Engels quotes from Heine's *Die schlesischen Weber*.

mind, I am not in such a hurry that you should rush off post haste to Argenteuil to look the books up.

Clemenceau seems to be going down morally while going up politically — this appears unavoidable in French bourgeois politics. His visit to Gladstone and the rubbish he talked there is one symptom, the other is his silence in the chamber with regard to the *Socialistenhetze* [a] and the atrocious judgments of Lyon, Montluçon, etc.

As to Paul's wish to have an Irish paper, there is none that can be recommended. Besides if the *Égalité* writes up every murder, be it ever so stupid, as *une exécution*, Havas' telegrams are quite sufficient. For other things the *Daily News* Irish correspondence will be found sufficient.

If Paul sees that the *Égalité* is regularly forwarded to the *Sozialdemokrat* at Zurich, that paper will be duly sent in return, but I shall write to Bernstein to send it to *your* address, so that *you* get it, and not those that do not understand it.

Kind regards to Paul.

Yours very affectionately,
F. E.

First published, in the language of the original (English), in: F. Engels, P. et L. Lafargue, *Correspondance*, t. I, Paris, 1956

Reproduced from the original

131

ENGELS TO JOHN LINCOLN MAHON [327]

IN LONDON

[London,] 28 November 1884
122 Regent's Park Road, N. W.

Dear Sir,

I received your note only this morning owing to the No. being stated wrong on the address (132 instead of 122).

---

[a] persecution of socialists

If you will be good enough to call on me to-morrow Friday night from 7 to 8, I shall be glad to hear what you have to communicate to me. [328]

Yours truly,

F. Engels

First published in: Marx and Engels, *Works*, First Russian Edition, Vol. XXVII, Moscow, 1935

Reproduced from the original

132

ENGELS TO CHARLOTTE ENGELS

IN ENGELSKIRCHEN

London, 1 December 1884

Dear Lottchen,

Your telegram arrived this morning shortly before ten. I had been prepared for this news for some time, ever since Hermann wrote to me in some detail about Emil's condition [a] and especially since the week before last when your brother-in-law Colsman visited me. We talked a great deal about Emil, Colsman being fully conversant with the medical circumstances of the case. There was, I gathered, no more hope, the verdict had been given and the consummation could only be a matter of weeks. And yet I had not expected that it would be so quick. It has happened, and we must resign ourselves to it.

It has been a period of your life, dear Lottchen, such as you will never again experience; a line has been drawn through a whole chapter of happiness, now irrevocably brought to an end. I know how bleak and empty the world must seem to you at this moment, and I know that in your heart of hearts you wish that chance may enable you presently to be laid to rest beside your Emil. That is natural and is what anyone who stands beside the bier of a beloved spouse would

---

[a] See this volume, pp. 218-19.

wish. But remember that my mother had to endure this too. She had 41 years of happiness and then was widowed. And there are few women who loved their husbands more ardently than she my father. And yet with her children and among their children and children's children she acquired a new lease of life and lived among us, at any rate not unhappily, for the next 14 years. And she was older than you are and all her children were grown-up and provided for, whereas you still have several for whom there are duties to fulfil of a kind only a mother can fulfil and which weigh all the more heavily for their now being fatherless.

I always had a particularly intimate relationship with Emil and, however far our views may have diverged, one thing we still had in common was our preoccupation with scientific matters, irrespective of whether or not they had any immediate practical application. One episode I shall never forget. When, after father's death, I had to cope with a most difficult state of affairs while physically so indisposed that I was incapable of making one single urgent decision in a sound frame of mind and with faculties unimpaired, there was Emil, clear of eye, firm of resolve and in full command of the situation, to extricate me and bring the negotiations in Manchester, upon which my whole future depended, to a successful conclusion. [329] If I now live here in London, a man of independent means, this is thanks not least to Emil.

Nor would my uncertain state of health deter me from leaving tonight to pay my dear brother my last respects. But there is the possibility, indeed probability, that my presence would lead to harassment by the police and nothing in the world would induce me to expose you and the others to such a thing at this particular moment. After all, was not a universally renowned chemist, [a] naturalised Englishman and member of the British Royal Society, harassed in Darmstadt, his native city, a few months ago simply because he had attended Marx's funeral, harassed to the extent that he at once departed? [b] What might I not expect? Once again I shall doubtless have to regard myself as a political refugee for the time being.

Well, dear Lottchen, one thing I do know and that is that you women are stronger and pluckier than we men. Whatever you endure, if endure it you must, you do so better than we do. You, yourself, with the marvellous self-control that I have often envied, will be able

---

[a] Carl Schorlemmer - [b] See this volume, p. 209.

to overcome even this most grievous blow, the grief we all of us share with you and of which you must bear the brunt.

A kiss from me for the children. With all my love.

Your trusty old

Friedrich

First published in *Deutsche Revue*, Jg. 46, Bd. 3, Stuttgart-Leipzig, 1921

Printed according to the magazine

Published in English for the first time

133

ENGELS TO KARL KAUTSKY [330]

IN VIENNA

[London, 9 December 1884]

Dear Kautsky,

It goes without saying that you can have your letters addressed to 122 Regent's Park Road as often and for as long as you wish. I hope this will still catch you in Vienna; in my haste I had overlooked your inquiry and for the past week I have had many interruptions.

Why you and the others do not settle the matter of the 'Speech' [a] when you yourselves are certainly better able to decide such matters than I am, is more than I can understand. I am writing to Dietz to tell him to attend to it himself.

Your

F. E.

First published, in Russian, in *Marx-Engels Archives*, Vol. I (VI), Moscow, 1932

Printed according to the original

Published in English for the first time

---

[a] K. Marx, 'Speech on the Question of Free Trade'.

134

ENGELS TO AUGUST BEBEL [316; 331]

[IN BERLIN]

London, 11-12 December 1884

Dear Bebel,

The point of my last letter[a] was as follows:

Among the newly elected members some were known to me, who, by education and temperament, would throw in their weight with the *right*, bourgeois wing of the parliamentary group. In view of the tremendous blandishments suddenly extended to us after our victories by all the other parties, it seemed to me not impossible that the said gentlemen might fall for the bait and be prepared to make a statement such as that demanded of us by, for instance, the *Kölnische Zeitung* as a condition of the repeal of the Anti-Socialist Law [311] — a statement would only have to go a hair's breadth further to the right in surrendering the party's revolutionary character than did, for instance, Geiser's speech during the Anti-Socialist Law debate, which Grillenberger printed alongside yours.[332] The gentlemen of the Liberal Party are soft and would be content with very little; a small concession on our part would have satisfied them, and it was that small concession I feared since it would have discredited us beyond all measure abroad. I knew, of course, that it would not be made by you. But you, i. e. we, might have been outvoted. Indeed, the least sign of a split — in speeches — would have done enormous harm. That is the reason — and the only reason — I thought it my duty to provide you with support against such an occasion by supplying you with a few handy historical arguments which, perhaps, might not be so fresh in your mind as in mine. And so that you might show the letter to others if you thought fit, I omitted all allusions to those for whom it was, ultimately, intended.

Nobody is gladder than I that my fears have proved unfounded and that the power of the movement should have been such as to carry away even the bourgeois elements of the party and that the parliamentary group had kept abreast of the electorate. And I must con-

[a] See this volume, pp. 220-23.

fess that I find Singer, who spent a short while here this Sunday[a] and will be coming to see me again next Sunday, a completely changed man. He is beginning to believe (quite literally) that he might yet experience something in the nature of a social transformation. I trust that it will last and that our 'eddicated' chaps will ultimately resist the temptation of showing the other parties that they're not ogres.

I have never been mistaken about our proletarian masses. The progress of their movement — assured, confident of victory and, for that very reason, cheerful and good-humoured — is exemplary and beyond compare. No European proletariat could have stood the test of the Anti-Socialist Law so splendidly nor, after six years of oppression, have responded by demonstrating how greatly its power had increased and its organisation been consolidated. None could have brought that organisation into being, as was done here, without any pretence at conspiracy. And, now that I have seen the electoral manifestos of Darmstadt and Hanover,[325] I have ceased to worry about the possibility of having to make concessions in the new districts (constituencies). If, in both those towns, they could speak in such revolutionary and proletarian terms, then all is won.

It is greatly to our advantage that in Germany the industrial revolution should not really have got going until now, whereas in France and England it is for the most part complete. In those countries, the division into town and country, industrial districts and agricultural districts, is complete to the extent that such further change as there is will be very gradual. The bulk of the people grow up in the conditions in which they will subsequently have to live; they are so used to them that even fluctuations and crises come to be regarded almost as a matter of course. Added to which is the memory of earlier, unsuccessful movements. In Germany, by contrast, everything is still in a state of flux. What remains of the old, self-sufficient rural industrial production is being superseded by capitalist cottage industries, while elsewhere capitalist cottage industries are in their turn making way for the machine. And it is the very nature of our industry, lagging as it does far behind all the rest, that makes the revolution[b] such a fundamental one. Since large mass-produced articles, for the popular as well as the luxury trades, are already monopolised by the British and French, pretty well all that is left for our export industry is the insignificant stuff which, however, also runs into very large quantities, and is first manufactured by cottage industries, not being machine-made

---

[a] 7 December - [b] Altered in an unknown hand to 'social revolution'.

until later when it is produced in bulk. In this way cottage industries (capitalist) are introduced into far wider fields and make an even cleaner sweep. If I except the Prussia of the Eastern Elbe area, i. e. East and West Prussia, Pomerania, Posen and the larger part of Brandenburg, as well as Old Bavaria,[a] there are now few districts where the farmer is not being increasingly caught up in cottage industries. The area thus[b] revolutionised will,[c] in Germany, be larger than anywhere else.

Furthermore, the fact that the worker in a cottage industry usually goes in for a bit of agriculture makes it possible to depress wages to an extent unknown elsewhere. What used to be the small man's good fortune — the combination of agriculture and industry — has now become the most effective means of capitalist exploitation. The potato plot, the cow, the little bit of husbandry, makes feasible the sale of labour power below its proper price, indeed *necessitates* this because it binds the worker to the soil which, after all, provides part of his nourishment. Hence, in Germany, industry becomes capable of exporting because the customer, more often than not, is presented with the entire surplus value, while the capitalist's profits derive from deductions made from the normal working wage. This applies to pretty well all rural cottage industries, more so in Germany than anywhere else.

Moreover, our industrial revolution, set in train by the revolution of 1848 and its bourgeois advances (puny though these were), was enormously speeded up 1) by the removal, between 1866 and 1870, of internal obstacles[d] and 2) by the French milliards, destined as these were for capitalist investment.[333] In this way we have achieved an industrial revolution that is more thorough-going and fundamental, more extensive and comprehensive than in any other country; we have done so with a completely fresh, intact proletariat, undemoralised by defeat and, finally — thanks to Marx — with an insight into the causes of economic and political developments and into the prerequisites for the impending revolution such as none of our predecessors possessed. But for that very reason we are *under an obligation* to win.

As regards pure democracy and its future role, I am not of your opinion. That it plays a far more subordinate role in Germany than in countries long since industrialised, goes without saying. But that will not prevent it *qua* extreme *bourgeois* party — which, after all, it

[a] Old Bavaria: Upper and Lower Bavaria and Upper Palatinate. - [b] 'industrially' inserted in an unknown hand - [c] 'hence,' inserted in an unknown hand - [d] See this volume, pp. 221-22.

had already made itself out to be at Frankfurt — from acquiring, at the moment of revolution, a temporary significance as the last sheet-anchor of the bourgeois and, indeed, feudal economy generally.[334] At such a moment the entire reactionary mass will align itself behind it and swell its ranks, whereupon all erstwhile reactionaries will act as though they were democrats. It was thus that, from March to September 1848, the entire feudal-bureaucratic mass swelled the ranks of the Liberals in order to keep down the revolutionary masses and, having done so, kick out the Liberals as a matter of course. It was thus that in France in 1848, from May until Bonaparte's [a] election in December, the purely Republican party of *Le National*,[335] the very weakest of them all, was able to hold sway thanks only to the forces of reaction, all of which rallied to its defences. It has always been thus in every revolution: The tamest party still capable of governing takes its turn at the helm precisely because the vanquished look to it as their last hope of salvation. Now we cannot expect to have the majority of the electorate, i. e. of the nation, already at our backs when the crucial moment comes. The whole of the middle and the residue of the feudal, land-owning class, and the better part of the petty bourgeoisie as of the rural population, will then rally round the most extreme bourgeois — in word by now the most extreme revolutionary — party which will, I think, most probably be represented in the provisional government, indeed might actually form its majority for a time. How, as a minority, one ought *not* to act in such a case was demonstrated in Paris in 1848 by the Social Democratic minority in the February government.[336] However, for the moment this question remains an academic one.

Now in Germany matters might take a different course, and this for military reasons. As things are at present, an impulse from without would be unlikely to come from anywhere but Russia. Should it fail to come, and the impulse emanate from Germany, the revolution could only emanate from the army. An unarmed population confronted by a modern army is militarily an altogether infinitesimal quantity. In that event — when our reserves of 20- or 25-year-olds, who do not vote, but train, would go into action — pure democracy might be given a miss. But here again the question is, at present, still academic although I, as representative, so to speak, of the party's Great General Staff, am obliged to bear it in mind. At all events, on the crucial day and the day after that, our only adversary will be *collective reaction centred round pure democracy* and this, I think, ought never to be lost from view.

---

[a] Napoleon III

If you people table motions in the Reichstag, there is one thing you should not forget. State-owned land is for the most part rented out to big farmers, only very little being sold to smallholders whose plots, however, are so diminutive that these new smallholders are reduced to hiring themselves out by the day to the large farms. What should be demanded is the *leasing of large, undivided estates to cooperatives of agricultural workers to be farmed communally*. The Empire possesses no estates and this will presumably provide a pretext for throwing out any such motion. But I believe that this firebrand ought to be cast among the agricultural day labourers, which is quite possible in view of the many debates about state socialism. This and this alone will enable you to rope in the agricultural workers. It is the best way of showing them that they are ultimately destined to run the big estates of those who are now their lords and masters, and to run them for the common weal. And with this friend Bismarck and his demand that you make positive proposals ought to be satisfied for a while.

Warmest regards.

Your
F. E.

12 December 1884

First published abridged in: F. Engels, *Politisches Vermächtnis. Aus unveröffentlichten Briefen*, Berlin, 1920 and in full, in Russian, in *Marx-Engels Archives*, Vol. I (VI), Moscow, 1932

Printed according to the original

Published in English in full for the first time

135

ENGELS TO PAUL LAFARGUE [337]

IN PARIS

[Excerpt]   [London, mid-December 1884]

In Germany there are far too many soldiers and non-commissioned officers belonging to the party for one to be able to preach a riot with the slightest chance of success. They know that it is in the ranks of the army itself that the *demoralisation* (from' the bourgeois point of view) must take place; given modern military conditions (rapid-firing arms, etc.), the revolution is bound to begin in the army. At any rate it will begin there in our country. No one knows better than the government how the number of socialist conscripts is growing year after year. Our universal suffrage does not begin until the age of twenty-five; if the great reserve of the 21- to 25-year-olds does not figure in the voting, it is present in the army.

First published in *Lyon-Socialiste*, No. 15, 21 décembre 1884

Printed according to the newspaper

Translated from the French

136

ENGELS TO EDUARD BERNSTEIN [338]

IN ZURICH

London, 29 December 1884

Dear Ede,

From Kautsky I learn that you have lost not only your sister but also your father. Let me assure you of my warmest sympathy. It is one of the more sombre aspects of exile which I, too, have come to know. The fatherland as such is something one can easily dispense with, but—

Now for events over here. On Saturday the SOCIAL DEMOCRATIC FEDERATION [300] happily disintegrated. The bubble burst somewhat sooner than I had expected, but it was bound to come.

Hyndman, a political adventurer with aspirations to a *carrière* in Parliament, had long since gained control of the whole business. When, a year ago, Bax launched *To-Day*, there was not enough literary talent to keep the little affair going, let alone a weekly, but a weekly Hyndman must needs have. Hence *Justice* was founded— with money given by two enthusiasts, Morris and Carpenter; it was edited by Hyndman with the aid of a few young literati who were on the look-out for some new movement capable of paying them (Fitzgerald and Champion) and one Joynes, a teacher dismissed from Eton

for agitation conducted in company with Henry George,[a] and hence
a socialist, willy-nilly. These men were paid, directly or indirectly —
Hyndman is rich but tight-fisted —, the rest had to contribute gratis.
All the FEDERATION's papers went to Hyndman, Fitzgerald and Champion, who placed before the Council only what they thought fit, and
corresponded off their own bat in the FEDERATION's name; in short,
Hyndman treated the Council as Bismarck treats the Reichstag.
Loud complaints; they even reached me. I said: 'Give the man
his head. He's a petty-minded chap and won't last long, *for he
cannot wait.*'[b] And he has come a cropper sooner than I thought he
would.

Morris, who was in Scotland a fortnight ago, uncovered there such
intrigues on Hyndman's part that he said he could no longer continue
to work with the fellow. He had long had his suspicions. An interview
with Andreas Scheu in Edinburgh brought matters to a head.[339]
Hyndman had defamed Scheu by calling him an anarchist and dyna-
miter — Scheu was able to provide Morris not only with proof to the
contrary, but also of the fact that Hyndman knew this. Similar machinations of Hyndman's in Glasgow, where the branch had received
letters from the secretary, Fitzgerald, bearing the FEDERATION's stamp
but which had not only not been written at the behest of the Council,
but actually in defiance of its resolutions. Furthermore, Hyndman
had told several people that a somewhat mysterious letter to the
Council in Paris was a forgery concocted by Mme Lafargue and
Tussy with a view to laying a trap for him. However, he had withheld
the actual letter from the Council. Finally, in addition to having repeatedly stirred up strife between members of the Council, he was
shown to have fabricated a provincial branch which did not exist at
all.

In short, last Tuesday[c] things came to a head. Hyndman was attacked from every side, Scheu himself was there, documents in hand.
Tussy had a letter from her sister about the alleged forgery. There
was a row. Meeting adjourned till Saturday. Morris and Aveling
came to see me beforehand, when I was able to give them some
further advice. Big debate on the Saturday. None of the facts could be
denied, either by Hyndman or by the supporters he had drummed
up. Motion of censure on Hyndman adopted. Whereupon the majority resigned from the FEDERATION. The grounds for this were, 1) that

---

[a] See this volume, pp. 74-75. - [b] Ibid., pp. 165-66. - [c] 23 December

at a congress, Hyndman might fabricate a majority with the aid of his BOGUS branch, while they would be unable to prove the non-existence of that branch, or at any rate not until it was too late, 2) — and this was the main reason — *because the* entire FEDERATION *was, after all, no better than a racket.*[340]

Those who resigned were Aveling, Bax and Morris, the only honest ones amongst the literati, but also three as unpractical men — two poets and a philosopher — as it is possible to find. Also, the cream of the better-known working men. They intend to do the rounds of the London branches in the hope of winning over the majority, whereupon they will let Hyndman and his non-existent provincial branches go whistle. Their organ is to be a little monthly.[a] At last they are going to operate modestly and in accordance with their powers, and not go on pretending that the English proletariat must instantly jump to it the moment the trumpet is sounded by a few literary converts to socialism. (In London, according to Morris' admission, they were 400 strong at the outside and barely 100 in the provinces.) The circulation of *Justice* is about 3,500.

Hyndman is retaining *Justice* and *To-Day*, together with his speculative literati Fitzgerald, Champion, Burrows, Shaw and possibly also Sketchley who, as a former Chartist, presumably considers himself entitled to a pension. Add to that what remains of the old democratic or socialist sects. Whose prize the other remnants of the FEDERATION will be, remains to be seen. But since Hyndman will no longer be getting any money either from Morris or from Carpenter for his unprofitable organs, he will either have to pay up himself, or sell himself, his organs and the remnants of his faction to the CHRISTIAN SOCIALISTS or — to Lord Randolph Churchill and Tory DEMOCRACY. He'll have to look sharp if he wants to stand for Parliament in the elections next autumn.

I have the satisfaction of having seen through the whole racket from the outset, correctly sized up all the people concerned and foretold what the end would be, and similarly that the said racket would eventually do more harm than good.

Your
F. E.

First published, in Russian, in *Marx-Engels Archives*, Book I, Moscow, 1924

Printed according to the original

Published in English in full for the first time

---

[a] *The Commonweal*

137

ENGELS TO WILHELM LIEBKNECHT [341]

[IN BERLIN]

[Excerpt]

[London, 29 December 1884]

Should the parliamentary group not wish to adopt a merely negative attitude, they can, or so it seems to me, *only give their consent* to state aid for the bourgeoisie,[342] from which the workers might *conceivably* derive some indirect advantage (something that still remains to be proved, however) *if the workers are assured of similar state aid.*[a] 'If you give us 4 to 5 millions a year for *workers' cooperatives* (not a loan but a gift, as for the shipowners), then we're prepared to discuss the matter. If you give us guarantees to the effect that in *Prussia state-owned land* will be leased, not to big farmers or to peasants who cannot exist without hiring day labourers, but to *workers' cooperatives,* and that *public works* will be put out to *workers' cooperatives* instead of to capitalists, very well, we'll see what we can do. But not otherwise.'

Provided the parliamentary group makes proposals of this sort for which, of course, the right wording must first be found, no one will be able to reproach the Social Democratic deputies with neglecting the present needs of the workers for the sake of the future.

First published in *Der Sozialdemokrat,* Nr. 2, Zurich, 8. Januar 1885

Printed according to the newspaper

Published in English for the first time

---

[a] See this volume, pp. 241-42

138

ENGELS TO AUGUST BEBEL

IN PLAUEN NEAR DRESDEN

London, 30 December 1884

Dear Bebel,

I hasten to reply to your letter.

Friend Singer would seem to have digested only such of my remarks as accorded with his own views: one soon learns how to do this in business where it may sometimes help, but in politics as in science one should, after all, learn to take an objective view of things.

To begin with, I told Singer that I had not yet by any means given the matter adequate thought (my attention having been drawn to it only the evening before by the *Sozialdemokrat*),[342] and that what I was saying could *by no means* be regarded *as my final verdict*.

Next, I went on to say that, *under certain circumstances and on certain conditions*, it might be *admissible* to vote for it, i. e. if the government were to *undertake* to accord to the workers the same state aid it was now prepared to accord to the bourgeoisie. In particular, that is, the leasing of state-owned land to workers' cooperatives, etc. Since I know very well that the government will not do so, this is another way of saying that those who *would like* to vote for it should be shown how they *can* vote against it with a semblance of decency and without doing violence to themselves.

I further told Singer — and this seemed news to him — that in parliamentary life one may often find oneself in the position of having to vote *against* something which one would privately like to see carried.

Well, yesterday I wrote to Liebknecht about other matters and took the opportunity of giving him what was now, after long reflection, a considered view of the case.[a] In many respects it tallies almost word for word — get him to read you that bit of my letter some time — with what you say, although your letter did not arrive until this morning. Where I diverge from you is, briefly, as follows:

1. You are above all a party versed in economics. You, or some of you, have at various times made a great show of the party's superi-

---

[a] See previous letter.

ority in this field, yet as soon as you were confronted in practice with your first economic question, you fell out — over protective tariffs.[343] But if the same thing is going to happen each time an economic question crops up, what is the point of having a parliamentary group at all?

2. On principle, you ought to vote against it. I told Liebknecht so plainly enough. But suppose the majority want to vote for it? In that case, the only thing to do is to persuade them to attach such conditions to their vote as will excuse it, at any rate to the extent that no odium attaches to them in the eyes of Europe, as would otherwise inevitably happen. Those conditions, however, are, and can only be, such that the government cannot agree to them, i. e. that the majority of the parliamentary group, should they attach those conditions to their vote, will not be able to vote for it.

Needless to say, I could never have considered an unconditional vote in favour of presenting the bourgeoisie with working men's pennies. But neither, for that matter, could the cardinal question — the disruption of the parliamentary group — have been envisaged in this context.

To my mind, your best way of dealing with all such questions, if you want to take account of the voters' petty-bourgeois prejudices, is to say: 'On principle we're against it. But since you wish us to make positive proposals and since you maintain that these things would also be of benefit to the workers, which we contest in so far as anything more than a microscopic advantage is concerned — well and good. You must place workers and bourgeoisie on an equal footing. For every million you take from the worker's pocket and give to the bourgeoisie, directly or indirectly, you must give the workers a million; the same applies to loans made by the state.' I. e. more or less as follows (only by way of an example and without regard for the particular form it would have to assume for Germany, since I am too little acquainted with the details of existing legislation):

1) The granting of subventions and advances to workers' cooperatives, not for the purpose, or not so much for the purpose, of starting up new businesses (which would be no better than Lassalle's proposal, with all its deficiencies) as, in particular, in order to

a) take on lease and farm cooperatively state-owned land (or other types of landed property);

b) purchase for their own or the government account and operate as cooperatives factories, etc., which, at a time of crisis or, perhaps, due to bankruptcy, have been shut down by their owners or have otherwise come on the market, and thus pave the way for the gradual transition of all production to cooperative production.

2) Preference to be given to cooperatives over capitalists and the latters' associations in all public contracts, and on the same terms; i. e. as a general principle, contracts for public works to be accorded wherever possible to cooperatives.

3) The removal of all legal obstacles and difficulties that still stand in the way of free cooperatives, i. e. above all the reinstatement of the working class within the common law — pitiful though this may be — by the repeal of the Anti-Socialist Law [37] which, after all, is the ruin of all trade associations and cooperatives.

4) Complete freedom for trade associations (TRADE UNIONS) and their recognition as *legal persons* with all the latters' rights.

By demanding this, all you demand is that equal consideration be accorded to workers and bourgeois alike; and if gifts to the bourgeois will allegedly boost industry, will not gifts to the workers boost it far more? *Without* any such quid pro quo, I fail to see how a Social Democratic parliamentary group could vote for anything of the sort. If you confront the people with such demands, the electorate, too, would soon stop pestering you about state aid for industry in the shape of gifts to the bourgeoisie. All these are matters which could be initiated here and now and actually set in train within the year, being obstructed only by the bourgeoisie and the government. And yet, as things now are, these are important measures whose impact upon the workers would be a very different affair from that made by steamship subsidies, [342] protective tariffs, etc. And the French are demanding essentially the same.

But now for something else which has only just come to light. The outcome of the division will, as likely as not, be determined by the Social Democrats. And what utter asses you would look in the eyes of the whole world if this business of donations to the bourgeoisie were to be the work *of your votes!* And without any quid pro quo! I really do not know what, in that case, I should tell the French and the people over here. And what a triumph for the anarchists, who would say exultantly: 'There you are — they're out-and-out philistines!'

I shall go into the other matters another time, since I am anxious that you should not for a moment be in doubt as to my views on this point. I trust that the change in your business affairs [344] will above all be beneficial to your health. With all good wishes to you and your family for the New Year.

Your
F. E.

That there won't be enough money is clear as day. And another thing I told Singer was that anyone who votes for it must, if he is to be consistent, also vote for colonies. As regards the point about money, see my letter to Liebknecht. [a]

First published abridged in: F. Engels, *Politisches Vermächtnis. Aus unveröffentlichten Briefen*, Berlin, 1920 and in full, in Russian, in *Marx-Engels Archives*, Vol. I (VI), Moscow, 1932

Printed according to the original

Published in English in full for the first time

139

ENGELS TO PASQUALE MARTIGNETTI

IN BENEVENTO

London, 30 December 1884

Dear Sir,

Unfortunately it is not till now that your latest letter dated 18 November has received a reply from me. [345] Please excuse me; I am overwhelmed with work and things to be done.

My *Peasant War* is a pamphlet which is only of interest to Germany. Besides, I must prepare a completely reworked edition, [213] and I cannot begin before February or March. The book would be published around July (I know what to expect from our party press). Finally, what it deals with has nothing to do with the subject of *The Origin etc.* [b]

I think therefore that it will be better to publish the latter separately; as for the way in which it is published, I leave the decision entirely in your hands.

[a] See previous letter. - [b] F. Engels, *The Origin of the Family, Private Property and the State*.

As soon as *The Peasant War* is published, I shall be honoured to send you a copy. You can then judge whether it is worth the trouble of translating. I doubt it.

I remain with respect your devoted

F. Engels

First published in *La corrispondenza di Marx e Engels con italiani. 1848-1895*, Milano, 1964

Printed according to the original

Translated from the Italian

Published in English for the first time

140

ENGELS TO FRIEDRICH ADOLPH SORGE [263]

IN HOBOKEN

London, 31 December 1884

Dear Sorge,

I trust that your health has improved, as mine has, although I am not yet quite my old self again,— very nearly, however.

Capital, Book II (some 600 pages of print) will go to press in January. The editing will have been completed in about 10 days' time, after which all that will remain to be done is the revision of the fair copy. It's been quite a task—there were 2 complete and 6 partial texts! [17]

Then, as soon as I have attended to a few urgent intermediate jobs, it will be the turn of Book III. [a] There are 2 complete texts and a notebook of calculations [b]; this, too, will run to some 600 or 700 pages.

Finally, Book IV, *Theories of Surplus Value*, from the earliest manuscript of 1856-61. [171] It is still in limbo and cannot be taken in hand until everything else has been completed. There are about 1,000 closely written quarto sheets.

I am completely revising my *Peasant War* [213] and making it the

---

[a] See this volume, pp. 88-89.- [b] See present edition, Vol. 37 (Engels' Preface).

pivot for my whole history of Germany. It will be some task. But the preliminary studies are as good as finished.

The English translation of *Capital* is coming along slowly, more than half having been finished. Tussy's husband, Aveling, is helping with it, but doesn't do it as thoroughly as Sam Moore, who is doing the main part. [56]

This summer Schorlemmer was subjected to a domiciliary search in Darmstadt for suspected distribution of the *Sozialdemokrat*. [304] Great uproar amongst the philistines has earned us some 500 votes.

On Saturday the DEMOCRATIC FEDERATION here was disrupted. [300] Hyndman, an adventurer who had gained control of the whole affair, was unmasked as a fomenter of strife between the members, a with-holder of correspondence intended for the COUNCIL and a founder of BOGUS BRANCHES in the provinces so that meetings and congresses might be packed with his own creatures. Though a vote of censure was passed on him, the majority resigned, mainly on the grounds that the whole organisation was simply a *racket*. And it's true. They haven't got 400 paid-up members, and their readers consist of sentimental bourgeois. They now intend to start a new organisation (Morris, Bax, Aveling, etc.) [346] and leave *Justice* and *To-Day* to Hyndman and his lot (Fitzgerald, Champion, Burrows, etc.), while they themselves, having at last recognised the weakness of their own effectives, will start off with a little MONTHLY. [a] As the capitalists who provided the money have also resigned (they, more than anyone else, were sensible of their exploitation by Hyndman) he, Hyndman, will either have to pay for his own unprofitable papers himself or else sell the entire party, in so far as it adheres to him (this will transpire in a week's time), to the highest bidder. And, being intent on getting into Parliament at the next elections, he will have to hurry.

Petty-bourgeois prejudice of every kind is to be found among the German deputies, as, for instance, the desire of the majority to vote for the steamship subsidies 'in the interests of industry'. [342] Which provides me with correspondence and to spare. Luckily we have Bebel there who invariably gets hold of the right end of the stick, and I therefore hope that the whole thing will go off without our being discredited. Ever since I have conducted the 'official' correspondence with Bebel instead of with Liebknecht, not only does all go smoothly, but something actually comes of it, and my views are presented to the

---

[a] *The Commonweal*

chaps in their entirety. Bebel is a really splendid fellow and I hope he won't ruin his health which is none too good.

But now here's to a Happy New Year and an improvement in your own health — regards to Adolf.[a]

Your
F. E.

Thank you for the *Volkszeitung* in which the wise man expresses his reservations about the abolition of the state. If I were to try and reply to such doubts, I would simply have to shelve my other work. Apropos, the *Volkszeitung* is no longer sending me its weekly edition.[b] So if there's anything interesting in it, I should be obliged if you could possibly let me have it.

First published in *Briefe und Auszüge aus Briefen von Joh. Phil. Becker, Jos. Dietzgen, Friedrich Engels, Karl Marx u. A. an F. A. Sorge und Andere*, Stuttgart, 1906

Printed according to the original

Published in English in full for the first time

141

ENGELS TO JOSEPH DIETZGEN[347]

IN NEW YORK

[Excerpt]

[London, 31 December 1884]

So for the time being I can hold out no prospect of being able to contribute to your paper. But should I happen to take a holiday, and should something then turn up, or if events were to take place which would render my assistance of real use, it goes without saying that I should at once make myself available.

First published in *Der Sozialist*, Nr. 4, New York, 24. Januar 1885

Printed according to the newspaper

Published in English for the first time

---

[a] Adolf Sorge jun. - [b] *Wochenblatt der N. Y. Volkszeitung*

1885

142

ENGELS TO LAURA LAFARGUE

IN PARIS

London, 1 January 1885

My dear Laura,

In all haste a few lines. Moore and Jollymeyer are off to Tussy's and so I have profited of the occasion to shake off a lot of business letters — a few moments remain before 5.30.

I had paid for your *Justice* up to 31 December, but as I had no proper receipt, could not do much — besides every letter of mine to anybody at that office was followed by an application from them for an article of mine, so that I really could not write to them even on business. However Edward says he pays to the Modern Press and so I have sent the money today for both you and myself for 6 months' *Justice* and *To-Day* and hope you will get it. What we can get of back numbers you shall also have, but there is not much in it worth your notice, the leaning towards the Possibilists is of quite recent date and not at all pronounced, except last No. [with] a letter from Adolphe Smith.[348] Now however it's sure to bloom out.

Last night we were at Pumps', she is uncommonly well but overdoes it a little — the baby all right.

I am sorry the crisis in the Social Democratic Federation[a] could not be retarded a little longer; Hyndman would have got deeper into the mud, and the personal element would have been thrown more into the background. However it could not be helped. The reason why the majority, instead of following up their victory, *resigned*, and starts a new organisation[346] was this chiefly, as Morris said to me:

---

[a] See this volume, p. 245.

that the old organisation was not *worth having*. The London branches
are about 300 strong in all and those they hope mostly to get, and as
to the provinces, it's all bosh and bogus.
Well we'll see what they will make. There is this to be said in their
favour: that three more unpractical men for a political organisation
than Aveling, Bax and Morris are not to be found in all England. But
they are sincere.
Again Happy New Year to both of you and to the poor little ones[a]
at Argenteuil when you see them, from Nim and myself.

Your

F. E.

First published in: Marx and Engels,
Works, Second Russian Edition, Vol. 36,
Moscow, 1964

Reproduced from the original

Published in English for the first
time

143

ENGELS TO HERMANN SCHLÜTER

IN HOTTINGEN-ZURICH

London, 1 January 1885

Dear Mr Schlüter,

I have received your esteemed note of the 10th as well as Mrs Kelley-Wischnewetzky's ms. [349]: I have advised her of its receipt and told
her I hope to be able to revise it next week.
The Condition of the Working-Class has not as yet been entirely prised out of Wigand's hands. From what Freytag the lawyer
said, the old contract, which envisaged a second edition, was still in
force about 10 years ago. [40] Since then I have on several occasions
tried to find out from Freytag how I stood with Wigand under Saxon law but have never received an answer. So long as I remain in

---

[a] the Longuets' children

doubt on this point I shan't know what steps I can take. I have also told Dietz as much [39] but heard nothing further after that; he spoke of bringing out a new edition but I was not told anything definite.

However a new edition would not be possible without various notes by me, which in turn would involve consulting sundry works of reference and, in places, call for study and this I cannot take on at the moment as I have more than enough to do. I might consider it towards the middle of the year. So I think the best thing would be simply to let the matter rest till then.

Now, however, Ede tells me that my *Anti-Dühring* ought to be reprinted. [208] After considerable thought I have decided that it should be brought out *unaltered*. I owe this to my opponent and shall simply provide a new preface, [a] also appendices to some of the chapters, which can go together at the end. Then a new preface. This, too, I shall find time for. So if you want work for the press, I would suggest you start with that. Besides, the thing is not particularly urgent and can therefore be printed at your convenience.

I hope to finish Marx's *Capital*, Book II, in January and then proceed at once to rewrite the *Peasant War*. [213] That will take a good 6 weeks. But I must be quit of it so as to get on with *Capital*, Book III. To begin with, this will be a purely daytime occupation, leaving my evenings to some extent free, when I can attend to the *Condition of the Working-Class* — if, that is, the revision of sundry translations, attending to proofs, etc., leaves me time for it.

So think the matter over and let me know what you have decided. I shall gladly do all I can to help you.

Kindest regards and a Happy New Year to the colony at large.

Yours,
F. Engels

First published in: Marx and Engels, *Works*, First Russian Edition, Vol. XXVII, Moscow, 1935

Printed according to the original

Published in English for the first time

---

[a] See present edition, Vol. 25, pp. 8-15.

144

ENGELS TO KARL KAUTSKY

IN VIENNA

London, 13 January 1885

Dear Kautsky,

I trust this will still catch you in Vienna.

It was only a day or two ago that I received the 1st number of the *Neue Zeit*. Can you get hold of about 2 or 3 more copies for me? Having promised Rudolf Meyer my critique of Rodbertus,[a] I can hardly send him a copy — the poor conservative social muddle-head is on tenterhooks — without also doing Mme Lafargue and Tussy the same service.

I would also ask you to send me copies of the *Poverty of Philosophy* for the above. The thing is advertised as having 'appeared'.

Groß would appear to be a blockhead, though an honest one. I have nothing against the biography; if you intend to lambast him for his confusion over theory, I don't envy you your task.[350]

Give Frankel my kind regards. No doubt you will tell me what he is in fact up to.

The New Year's card he and the others sent me gave me much pleasure.

Well, that's all until you come over here.

Your
F. E.

With an editor like □[b] you wouldn't have stuck it even for a fortnight. Better to come over here, rather than make yourself yet another deadly enemy in the parliamentary group.[351]

First published, in Russian, in *Marx-Engels Archives*, Vol. I (VI), Moscow, 1932

Printed according to the original

Published in English for the first time

---

[a] The first issue of *Die Neue Zeit*, 1885, carried Engels' preface to the first German edition of Marx's *The Poverty of Philosophy*, entitled 'Marx and Rodbertus'. - [b] Louis Viereck (*Viereck* = square in German)

145

ENGELS TO HERMANN SCHLÜTER

IN HOTTINGEN-ZURICH

London, 13 January 1885

Dear Mr Schlüter,

By all means start with the *Anti-Dühring* as soon as convenient. [208] I have not read the philistine's reply,[a] nor do I wish to do so. Reply he cannot and he's welcome to lay about him with as much insolent verbiage as he wishes.

I have long been searching in vain for the *Rheinische Zeitung Revue.* I only have numbers 3, 5 and 6; 1, 2 and 4 are missing. [352] There are virtually no articles in them worth reprinting. Numbers 1-4 contain Marx's history of the French Revolution from 1848 to 1850[b] (comprised in the *18th Brumaire*) and my account of events in May 1849 in the Rhineland and Baden-Palatinate.[c] Then the *Peasant War*[d] (5 and 6) and short critical essays, as also a review of daily events.[e] The right to work is not touched on other than very briefly in, I think, Number I[f]; Marx wasn't much interested in catchphrases.

It would be quite a good idea for you to inquire from Wigand in your own name about a new edition of the *Condition etc.*,[40] but that won't get us very much further. I have got to know how I stand with him in law and shall inquire again from Freytag. N. B. I am assuming that, as soon as the matter is sufficiently advanced, you will come to an understanding with Dietz, as he does in fact have, or might assert, a prior claim.

Regards to Ede.

Yours faithfully,

F. Engels

First published in: Marx and Engels, *Works*, First Russian Edition, Vol. XXVII, Moscow, 1935

Printed according to the original

Published in English for the first time

---

[a] E. Dühring, *Kritische Geschichte der Nationalökonomie und des Socialismus.* - [b] K. Marx, *The Class Struggles in France, 1848 to 1850.* - [c] F. Engels, *The Campaign for the German Imperial Constitution.* - [d] F. Engels, *The Peasant War in Germany.* - [e] K. Marx and F. Engels, 'Review, January-February 1850'; 'Review, March-April 1850'; 'Review, May to October 1850'. - [f] See K. Marx, *The Class Struggles in France, 1848 to 1850* (present edition, Vol. 10, pp. 55-56).

146

ENGELS TO HERMANN SCHLÜTER

IN HOTTINGEN-ZURICH

London, 17 January 1885

Dear Mr Schlüter,

As regards the *Anti-Dühring*, I would further advise you that 1) the old preface is followed by another to the 2nd edition which, however, I can't really do as yet; so doubtless you will, as usual, begin with the actual text and leave preface and title to the last; 2) such additions as there are will appear as an appendix.[a]

I have heard from Bonn[b] that the *Origin of the Family etc.* is not obtainable in the bookshops; according to the booksellers they have had word from Switzerland—from the publisher—that the book has been *banned* and various friends have been bombarding me with inquiries as to where the book may be obtained. Since there has, to my knowledge, been no *public* ban, while a *secret* ban would be nonsensical, and since the assumption that Zurich has been spreading rumours of a ban is even more nonsensical, I find the matter puzzling. Could it be that the government, to spare itself the ridicule that would come of a public ban, has persuaded Schabelitz's agents in Leipzig to spread such things about and thus make sales more difficult? Perhaps you would be good enough to start inquiries over there and let me know the result; I shall also try to find out whether the same tactics are being pursued elsewhere.

What is Ede doing? I have had neither sight nor sound of him.

Yours faithfully,

F. Engels

First published in: Marx and Engels, *Works*, First Russian Edition, Vol. XXVII, Moscow, 1935

Printed according to the original

Published in English for the first time

---

[a] See present edition, Vol. 25, pp. 630-42. - [b] in a letter Hagen wrote to Engels

147

ENGELS TO AUGUST BEBEL

IN BERLIN

London, 19 January 1885

Dear Bebel,

I hope you have had my last registered letter concerning the matter of the Steamship Bill (of 30 or 31 December).[a] Today I must trouble you with an inquiry. Mr Franz Mehring has now written to me for the second time asking me to place at his disposal material for a biography, etc., of Marx and, amongst other things, has the nerve to presume that I send him 'on loan' to Berlin irreplaceable editions of ours which he is unable to procure over there! I shall not reply, but send a message via Hirsch. But if I am to strike the right note, I ought to know something more definite about his past and present and about his attitude towards the party. Generally speaking, all I know is that, some time before 1878, he was pretty roundly taken to task in the *Volksstaat* and the *Vorwärts* for being a reptile [353] and a defector from the party and, from the few writings of his which have fallen into my hands, I have seen that he was making literary use of such intimate knowledge as he had of the movement to dole out liberal portions of 'truth and fiction'[b] about it to your philistine, and to pass himself off as an authority in such matters. If he has done anything especially underhand that might single him out from the rest of the literary rabble, it would be most helpful for me to know it.[354]

Then there's another thing. I am being strongly urged to bring out a new edition of my *Condition of the Working-Class*. I can do absolutely nothing about it before finding out what my legal position is in regard to Wigand, the previous publisher.[40] I have asked Liebknecht about this umpteen times, and on each occasion he has undertaken to obtain the information for me from Freytag, but none has ever been forthcoming. And who was the first to express surprise that nothing had been settled? Why, Liebknecht, of course. Now since it would be

---

[a] See this volume, pp. 240-43. - [b] 'Wahrheit und Dichtung' in the original, which is a paraphrase of the title of Goethe's autobiographical book *Dichtung und Wahrheit*, 'Dichtung' meaning 'poetry, fiction'.

folly to entrust him with any further errands, I must once again bother you, and ask you to obtain for me from Freytag, or some other *Saxon* advocate, a reply to the enclosed questions. As soon as I have that reply I can, and intend to, proceed.

To return to Germany's industrial position, I readily concede that enormous progress has been made since 1866, and more especially since 1871. But the contrast with other countries still remains, nonetheless. England had had the monopoly of mass-produced articles and France that of the *finer* luxury and fashion goods, and in this respect there has not, after all, been any change worth mentioning. In iron, it is true, Germany is, together with America, second only to England; but she is very far from attaining the level of English mass-production and can only hope to compete by selling *at a loss*. In cotton, Germany manufactures only subsidiary articles for the world market. The massive quantities of yarn and other woven goods (SHIRT-INGS and other mass-produced articles) for the Indian and Chinese market are still an English monopoly, and such competition as there may be in this sphere comes, not from Germany but from America. In woollen goods, too, England still dominates the world market, ditto in linen (Ireland). Birmingham is still the centre for hardware for domestic use, etc., as Sheffield is for cutlery, and the greatest threat of competition is still posed by America, not Germany. Machinery (with the exception of locomotives), England and America.

In the matter of fashion goods, France has lost a lot of ground. Here, too, fashion has changed considerably, and this certainly applies to Germany also. Both countries, however, and Germany in particular, produce in the main 2nd, 3rd and 4th class goods and still to a large extent depend on the Paris fashions. Meanwhile it is obvious that, in the case of buyers who consist almost exclusively of parvenus, 2nd and 3rd class articles play a considerable role and can be sold to these boors as 1st class goods.

One thing, however, is certain: the large bulk of German exports is composed of a mass of what, seen individually, are more or less insignificant articles, the manufacture of which, in so far as fashion comes into it, depends largely on the theft of Parisian patterns — e. g. the women's coat trade in Berlin — as is openly admitted in the *Kölnische Zeitung*. Moreover, foreign cloth is largely used for the purpose.

I believe the world market can be more accurately sized up from this country than from over there; but in doing so I have regularly followed the specialised German trade reports and hence see both sides of the picture. I wish I could sometime spare a moment to write something from this standpoint on the subject of protective tariffs in Germany. They are completely cock-eyed. German industry developed and became capable of exporting under a system of free trade more comprehensive than in any other industrial country save England — and it is being restricted by protective tariffs in the very sphere in which it is capable of exporting! That the *exporters* should be demanding protective tariffs is characteristic of Germany — we must have them so as to be able to sell to other countries at a loss and yet show a profit at the end of the year! What we give to other countries must be paid back to us at home, just as we present other countries with the surplus value and make our profits from deductions made on wages!

N. B. That worthy citizen Mehring is the author of the 'leading articles' in the *Demokratische Blätter*, which he sends me as an earnest of his principles.

Your
F. E.

First published abridged in: Th. Höhle, *Franz Mehring*, Berlin, 1956 and in full in: Marx and Engels, *Works*, Second Russian Edition, Vol. 36, Moscow, 1964

Printed according to the original

Published in English for the first time

148

ENGELS TO PAUL LAFARGUE [196;355]

IN PARIS

[Excerpt]

[London, about 25 January 1885]

You know what efforts the Russian government has been making for years past to wrest from England and France — but from England in particular—their assent to the extradition of the heroic nihilists.[356] Once these two countries had been won over to such a cause, the rest of Europe was bound to follow suit. There was even reason to hope that America might also be moved to act in similar fashion.

Now, *The Pall Mall Gazette* of 15 January contained an article by Mme Novikov, devil's advocate of tsarism, appealing yet again to England to desist from giving asylum to the Gartmans, the Stepnyaks and all those who 'organise assassination in Russia'.[a] The English, she goes on, are now threatened with similar chemical attacks; the refuge they afford to the Russian dynamiters is likewise afforded by America to the Irish dynamiters. What England is asking of America is precisely what Russia is asking of England.

All this is plain enough. But there is better to come. On the morning of 24 January all the newspapers carried the text of an agreement, concluded through diplomatic channels, between St Petersburg and Berlin whereby the extradition of political offenders was to be extended to Germany and thence to the rest of Europe.[357]

And on the afternoon of that same day, the 24th of January, London was terrorised by a threefold explosion, one in the House of Commons, directed against the legislature, one in Westminster Hall directed against the judiciary, and one in the Tower, directed against the executive. This time it was no longer a matter of blowing up public lavatories or of frightening travellers on the underground railway.[358] Rather it was a concerted attack upon the three great powers of state, symbolised by the buildings in which they assemble.

Is this no more than an act perpetrated by a handful of Fenian hotheads? Might it not rather be the great coup tsarism needed to bring off if it was to compel England to join the ranks of its anti-revolutionary league? If the dynamite was of Russian origin, and handled by Russian agents, could it, I ask, have exploded at a time better calculated to prostrate a terrified and repentant John Bull at the feet of Alexander III?

First published in *Cri du Peuple*, No. 461, Paris, 31 janvier 1885

Printed according to the newspaper

Translated from the French

---

[a] O. Novikova, 'The Russification of England'.

Engels' correspondents:
Paul Lafargue, Edward Aveling, Florence Kelley-Wischnewetzky,
Friedrich Adolph Sorge

Vera Zasulich, Nikolai Danielson,
Pyotr Lavrov

149

ENGELS TO FLORENCE KELLEY-WISCHNEWETZKY

IN HEIDELBERG

London, 4 February 1885
122 Regent's Park Road, N. W.

Dear Madam,

I hope you have received the letter I wrote to you about the time of the New Year.[39]

I now forward to you, *registered*, the ms. you sent to me, and only regret that press of work prevented my returning it earlier.[349] I have looked it over carefully, and entered some corrections and suggestions in pencil, in order to show you how I should like it translated. Here and there you may find that my suggestions, taken together with the rest of the sentence, will not turn out to be correct English; in these cases I left it to you to set that right.

As for the technical terms, if you will be good enough to forward me from time to time a list of them with the pages on which they occur, I shall be glad to give you the English equivalents.

The German preface (as well as the English dedication)[359] I would, in your place, leave out entirely. They contain nothing of interest *now*. The first part of the preface refers to a phase of intellectual development in Germany and elsewhere which is now almost forgotten, and the second part is in our days superfluous.

As to translations of my other writings you will understand as a matter of course that I cannot now take any positive engagements. There are people here who wish to translate one thing or another, and I have consented conditionally, that is to say if they find a publisher and really undertake the work.

The English preface I shall write[360] when things are a little more advanced.

In the meantime I remain

Yours very truly,
F. Engels

First published, in the language of the original (English), in *Briefe und Auszüge aus Briefen von Joh. Phil. Becker, Jos. Dietzgen, Friedrich Engels, Karl Marx u. A. an F. A. Sorge und Andere*, Stuttgart, 1906

Reproduced from the original

150

ENGELS TO WILHELM LIEBKNECHT

IN BORSDORF NEAR LEIPZIG [34]

London, 4 February 1885

Dear Liebknecht,

So you have sent me that literatus after all; I trust it is the last of its kind. Surely you can see for yourself how these impudent rascals are misusing you. The man is quite incorrigible, just like his friend Quarck — they're both *Quark* [a] —, and if they fall into line with you people and you accept them, I shall fall somewhat out of line. Won't you ever get it into your head that this semi-educated pack of literati can only spoil and adulterate the party? From what you say, Viereck ought never to get into the Reichstag either! The petty-bourgeois element in the party is increasingly gaining the upper hand. They want to suppress Marx's name as much as possible. If things go on like this, there will be a split in the party, on that you may depend. You blame it all on their worships the philistines having been affronted. But there are moments when that must be done or else they get above themselves. Is then the subsection on German, or true, socialism [b] to become applicable again 40 years later?

For the rest I am keeping well, though I have a hellish lot to do and cannot write long letters.

Your
F. E.

First published, in Russian, in *Marx-Engels Archives*, Vol. I (VI), Moscow, 1932

Printed according to the original

Published in English for the first time

---

[a] 'Quark' = curd or cottage cheese; fig. rubbish in German. - [b] K. Marx and F. Engels, *Manifesto of the Communist Party* (see present edition, Vol. 6, pp. 510-13).

151

ENGELS TO FLORENCE KELLEY-WISCHNEWETZKY

IN HEIDELBERG

London, 10 February 1885
122 Regent's Park Road, N. W.

Dear Madam,

I herewith return Mr Putnam's letter — of course it would be a splendid success if we could secure publication [a] by that firm — but I am afraid Mr Putnam will stick to his objections, the great strength of which, from a publisher's standpoint, I fully recognise. Perhaps the fact that a new German edition of my work is in actual preparation, may shake him a little. My friends in Germany say that the book is important to them just now because it describes a state of things which is almost exactly reproduced at the present moment in Germany; and, as the development of manufacturing industry, steam and machinery and their social outcrop in the creation of a proletariate, in America corresponds at the present moment as nearly as possible to the English status of 1844 (though your go-ahead people are sure to outstrip the old world in the next 15-20 years altogether) the comparison of industrial England of 1844 with industrial America of 1885 might have its interest too.

Of course in the new preface to the English translation [360] I shall refer as fully as space will permit to the changes in the condition of the British working class which have taken place in the interval; to the improved position of a more or less privileged minority, to the certainly not alleviated misery of the great body, and especially to the impending change for the worse which must necessarily follow from the break-down of the industrial monopoly of England in consequence of the increasing competition in the markets of the world, of Continental Europe and especially of America.

Very sincerely yours,
F. Engels

First published, in the language of the original (English), in *Briefe und Auszüge aus Briefen von Joh. Phil. Becker, Jos. Dietzgen, Friedrich Engels, Karl Marx u. A. an F. A. Sorge und Andere*, Stuttgart, 1906

[a] of Engels' *The Condition of the Working-Class in England*

152

ENGELS TO NIKOLAI DANIELSON

IN ST PETERSBURG

London, 11 February 1885

My dear Sir,

I shall be glad to send you the proof-sheets of Volume II as soon as you let me know whether I shall send them '*sous bande*' (per book-post) or in a closed envelope as a letter.[361] The fact is, that if one gets lost, it will be impossible to replace it until the work is completed. By the time your answer arrives I expect to have two or three for you.

I thank you very much for the offer you made me some time ago to place at my disposal the letters you have from Mr Williams.[a] At present the manuscripts claim all my time and attention, but the moment is sure to come when I shall take advantage of your kind offer.

Have you any news from our mutual friend[b] since the accident which happened to him some time ago?[362]

Be kind enough to address in future as stated at foot.

Yours very sincerely,

P. Rosher[363]

Mrs Rosher
6 Richmond Villas, Messina Avenue,
West Hampstead,
N.W. London

First published, in Russian, in *Minuvshiye gody*, No. 2, St Petersburg, 1908

Reproduced from the original

Published in English for the first time

---

[a] Marx's pseudonym - [b] Hermann Lopatin

153

ENGELS TO PYOTR LAVROV [1]

IN PARIS

London, 12 February 1885

My dear Lavrov,

I hasten to reply to your questions.[364] The item about the *Neue Rheinische Zeitung. Revue*, edited by Karl Marx, Hamburg and London, 1850, is absolutely correct. It appeared in *Heft*[a] I-VI and was published by Schuberth in Hamburg. You yourself asked me a few months ago for information about the articles by Marx which appeared in the *Revue* on the subject of the February revolution and the events that followed it.[156] I possess only 3 of the instalments and have tried in vain to get hold of the complete set. The other facts provided by Groß are also correct, if memory serves me aright (Tussy has got my copy, so I can't compare it). Needless to say, I in no way agree with his silly strictures on Marx's theories. He was recommended to me by the Viennese socialists and, in reply to some biographical questions he put to me, I gave him the facts.

The German translation of the *Poverty* contains just a few explanatory notes by me,[118] but also an article written by Marx in 1865 on Proudhon and his speech of 1847 on free trade.

The 2nd volume of *Capital* is now being printed; yesterday I corrected the 4th sheet. The rest of the manuscript goes off from here in a fortnight's time. The 3rd volume will be the most important one, and I shall get to work on it as soon as the 2nd has been well and truly launched.— The English edition is dragging its feet, the two translators[b] being too busy with other matters to work at it with the proper ardour. It will be finished, I hope, come the summer.[56]

I had already heard that you were having trouble with your eyes. Would it not be wise to give up working for a time so as not to tire your eyesight unduly? I find that, at our age, it is always best to tackle morbid symptoms when they first occur. Let's hope that you will be able to let me have better news before too long.

_____
[a] issue - [b] Samuel Moore and Edward Aveling

In the preface to the 2nd volume of *Capital*, I again revert to Rodbertus in order to show that the objections he raises against Marx result from his quite unbelievable ignorance of classical political economy.[a]

Yours ever,

F. Engels

(Фёдоръ Фёдорычъ [b])

First published in: Marx and Engels, *Works*, First Russian Edition, Vol. XXVII, Moscow, 1935

Printed according to the original

Translated from the French

Published in English in full for the first time

154

ENGELS TO KARL KAUTSKY

IN LONDON [365]

[London,] 14 February 1885

Dear Kautsky,

I forgot to remind you day before yesterday that we are, as usual, expecting you and your wife to a meal this Sunday (tomorrow the 15th inst.), i. e. if you have nothing better to do, and you are hereby given a standing invitation to take potluck with me on Sundays.

Your

F. Engels

First published in *Friedrich Engels' Briefwechsel mit Karl Kautsky*, Wien, 1955

Printed according to the book

Published in English for the first time

---

[a] See present edition, Vol. 36; see also F. Engels, 'Marx and Rodbertus'. - [b] (Russ.) Fyodor Fyodorych

155

ENGELS TO HERMANN SCHLÜTER

IN HOTTINGEN-ZURICH

London, 22 February 1885

Dear Mr Schlüter,

I look forward to seeing the proof-sheets of the *Anti-Dühring*.[208]
In Wigand's case[40] matters stand thus: it had already been noted in Leipzig in 1875 or 1876 that no more copies of the *Condition* were available and I possess the original invoice marked 'last copies'. However no harm can be done if confirmation of this is once again provided by the other party. I have at long last been given a legal opinion from which I gather that the matter is by no means as simple as had appeared at first glance. Now that I know how I stand, I shall take further steps and advise you as soon as I receive a positive reply from Wigand.

I knew Schabelitz even before 1848 when he was here in London and belonged to the Communist Society.[162] Give him my kindest regards when you see him. Your explanation re the alleged 'ban' was just what I wanted[366]; it is quite typical of the German book trade. Obviously nothing can be done about it so long as not one agent can be found who is possessed of pluck. But the bulk of bourgeois readers don't buy our stuff, so in this case pluck is not a particularly paying proposition. It was a different matter when banned books were merely liberal or radical, or even when, prior to 1848, communism was still a cause with which the bourgeoisie flirted.

The last ms. of the 2nd book of *Capital* goes off tomorrow, and day after tomorrow I shall start on the 3rd book. So long as I have it on my conscience, I shall be unable to give serious thought to anything else.

Please tell Ede that I shall write to him as soon as I have a spare moment.

Kindest regards from

Yours,

F. Engels

First published in: Marx and Engels, *Works*, First Russian Edition, Vol. XXVII, Moscow, 1935

Printed according to the original

Published in English for the first time

156

ENGELS TO LAURA LAFARGUE

IN PARIS

London, 8 March 1885

My dear Laura,

Somehow or other I have to-night a few free moments and so sit down to write to you — hoping that nobody will drop in. For evening calls are getting rather frequent of late, more than is desirable sometimes, when there is work to do. And the dictated portions of the *Capital*[a] I am obliged to look over while the thing is fresh in my mind and the original at hand ready to correct mistakes. Moreover, there are still translations to revise (last week part of a Danish one of my *Ursprung*[b] — very fair) and Russian pamphlets to decipher (Vera Zasoulitch has sent me one of Plechanoff, polemical against Lavroff and Tichomiroff,[c] and wants me to give her my opinion,[d] and besides these Russian quarrels are not uninteresting) and such like, so that besides the current small fry I have not had time to read a book for months.

The 3rd book [of] *Capital* is getting grander and grander the deeper I get into it, and I am only (having passed over entirely about 70 pages, more or less superseded by a later manuscript) at page 230 out of 525. It is almost inconceivable how a man who had such tremendous discoveries, such an entire and complete scientific revolution in his head, could keep it there for 20 years. For the ms. I am working at, has been written either before, or at the same time as the *first volume*; and the essential part of it is already in the old manuscript of 1860-1862.[171] The fact is, first the intricacies of the 2nd book (which he wrote last and which alone he touched after 1870) kept him fast, as he of course would have to publish his 3 books in regular order; and then, his Russian and American material for the theory of the rent of land[80] would have required working up into the old manuscript and would probably have nearly doubled its size.

---

[a] of the third volume - [b] *The Origin of the Family, Private Property and the State* - [c] [Plekhanov] Г. Плехановъ, *Наши разногласiя* (Our Differences). - [d] See this volume, pp. 279-81.

Here the two socialist bodies [346] are so far jogging on alongside each other without collision, but the foreign department will very likely embroil them. You may have seen in No. 9 of the *Sozialdemokrat* a letter from Varenholz, dictated by Hyndman. This rather *schnoddrige* [a] effusion required a reply which we have concocted and which will come, if possible, in next Saturday's *Sozialdemokrat*. This time, of course, Aveling had to speak out, and that strong enough to stop Hyndman's game once for all. [367]

We have Kautsky here [365] whom I think you saw before, with a young Viennese wife, a nice little body. [b] They intend settling down here for the present — and live in Maitland Park; just out of the Crescent. So there is always some connection going on with the old place. [368]

Pumps and Percy are getting on as usual. On Sundays there is here now a great cardplaying company, some play whist if there are 4 to be got for that, the rest 'Mariage' and 'Nap', games introduced by the noble Percy. His firm had a law-suit which they lost but it is nothing serious, only I hope that it will damp poor Percy's ardent faith in English law. The little ones are getting on very well upon the whole; Lily is very amiable and jolly. She has an extremely sharp ear and retentive memory for *des jurons*, [c] and you may be sure, that she finds many an opportunity to catch them.

On Saturday [d] Nim and Tussy as well as Pumps will go to Highgate. [369] I cannot go, I am still very changeable with respect to capacity for movement, and have just had a little bit of notice to keep quiet. Anyhow I shall continue working at the book which will be a monument to him, made by himself, grander than any that other people could set for Mohr. Two years already on Saturday! And yet I can truly say that while I work at this book, I am in living communion with him.

The 2nd book is getting on well. 13 sheets corrected. Will you please ask Paul *to send* me at once the address under which he writes to Danielson. I have had a letter from him and want to send the proof-sheets, [361] but am not certain as to address which may besides have been changed.

How is the Montceau Brenin Thévenin affair going on? [370] And has the *Cri du Peuple* cried his last?

---

[a] shabby - [b] Louise Kautsky - [c] swear-words - [d] 14 March

Amitiés à Paul.

Yours affectionately,

F. Engels

Nim's love!

First published, in the language of the original (English), in: F. Engels, P. et L. Lafargue, *Correspondance*, t. I, Paris, 1956   Reproduced from the original

157

ENGELS TO RICHARD STEGEMANN

IN TÜBINGEN

[Draft]

[London,] 26 March 1885

Dear Sir,

I hardly imagine that I would be capable of acceding to your request. [371] You might, it is true, be able to produce a fairly clear portrait of Marx the man from all the activities, both literary and political, Marx engaged in; information on these activities is of course freely available to the world at large, with the single exception of Germany, most of the requisite material having appeared abroad. On the other hand, a character sketch by me would necessarily be brief, hence not only inadequate but ±[a] dogmatic and likewise 'belletristic', hence worse than nothing at all. Besides I cannot presume that my assessment should be taken by you for gospel, and so could not tell what would ultimately become of my contribution, even having regard to your indisputable bona fides. If, however, you proceed on the assumption that Marx was the exact opposite of the German philistine in every conceivable respect, you can't go far wrong.

Whether this is now the precise moment for a critique of Marx,

---

[a] more or less

what with the 2nd book of *Capital* due to appear in a month or two and with work proceeding on the 3rd, is for you to decide. At all events you are right in saying that criticism and so-called 'scholarship' have disclosed nothing hitherto save a 'general lack of judgment', and no one was more amused by that than Marx himself. I can still see him laughing over the despairing sighs of Mr Schäffle who had studied *Capital* for ten years and still hadn't understood it. [a]

First published in: Marx and Engels, *Works*, First Russian Edition, Vol. XXVII, Moscow, 1935

Printed according to the original

Published in English for the first time

158

ENGELS TO JOHANN PHILIPP BECKER [1]

IN GENEVA

London, 2 April 1885

Dear Old Man,

So that you shouldn't think you had been forgotten, I have taken out a money order for five pounds for you and trust you will get the money at once. So far I am pretty well, though not, it is true, as yet fit for active service, nor am I likely ever to be able to mount a horse again, but I am still perky enough for peacetime work. $^2/_3$ of the second volume of *Capital* have been printed and the book will be appearing in some 2 months' time, while work on the third volume is well advanced. This last, which contains the final conclusions and, indeed, some quite brilliant stuff, will revolutionise economics once and for all and create a tremendous sensation.

In the meantime things are beginning to liven up again. Ferry's fall [372] opened the proceedings, now it's Gladstone's turn, and Bismarck's will follow as soon as that jackass William [b] kicks the bucket.

---

[a] See [A. Schäffle,] *Die Quintessenz des Socialismus*, Gotha, 1875, p. 5; see also Engels' letter to Eduard Bernstein of 12 March 1881 (present edition, Vol. 46, p. 74). -
[b] William I

For us, the most favourable situation will arise when, at the moment of revolution, the most radical elements of the bourgeoisie are everywhere at the helm — Clemenceau in France, Dilke and Chamberlain in this country and Richter in Germany — so that when they have ruined themselves, the revolution will be carried out against them and not for their benefit. It looks as though this might come about, provided no premature action is taken in Paris.

As was inevitable in the circumstances of the Anti-Socialist Law, [37] a number of thoroughgoing philistines have been returned to the Reichstag by our people and are beginning to give themselves airs because they constitute a majority in the parliamentary group. [373] We shall now have to wait and see how far they go; they can be tolerated for a time if in tow, but not when in the lead. They know that they haven't got the masses behind them, but they also know that, at the moment, the hands of the masses are very much tied. Of one thing we may be certain. If they gain the upper hand, I shall continue to cooperate up to a certain point, but beyond that it will be *bon jour, messieurs.* [a] Being overwhelmed with work, I cannot unfortunately go into the attack as I should like to do, but perhaps it is a good thing to allow these gentlemen a little latitude. The matter of the Steamship Subsidies [342] went off pretty smoothly on the whole, after several of them had made real fools of themselves. Now they are out for the blood of the Zurich *Sozialdemokrat,* [374] which is rather more serious. For it's bad enough to be made to look a fool in the eyes of the gentlemen in the Reichstag, but in the eyes of the whole of Europe — that really is a bit thick! If Bebel were in good health, none of this would matter a great deal, but he is nervy and debilitated, on top of which he has to work himself to the bone on his family's account.

But everything will come right when old William pegs out. The Crown Prince[b] is a weak, irresolute fellow, as if destined for decapitation, his wife[c] ambitious, with a clique of her own — in short, there will be all manner of changes that will play havoc with the existing order of things and bemuse and unsettle the civil service, while the bourgeoisie will at last be compelled to clear away some of the old lumber and play a political role — as it damned well ought. Only let the political scene at home come to life again and we shall need nothing more. But the rotten bourgeoisie has so greatly deteriorated that

---

[a] good day, gentlemen - [b] Frederick William - [c] Victoria

what it should do voluntarily and in its own interests as a class, it will do only under compulsion — the compulsion of the historical circumstances imposed upon it. And so long as the old jackass lives, it will be under no compulsion to get moving, which is why I hope that he will kick the bucket and do so in the way of nature, thus leaving his successor free to choose what stupidity to indulge in first. And with this pious wish, it being almost time for the post, I shall now conclude. Borkheim was rather less well during the winter, but has now improved again, i. e. he's much as before.

Fraternal greetings,

From your old friend
F. E.

First published in: F. Engels, *Vergessene Briefe (Briefe Friedrich Engels' an Johann Philipp Becker)*, Berlin, 1920

Printed according to the original

Published in English in full for the first time

159

ENGELS TO AUGUST BEBEL

IN PLAUEN NEAR DRESDEN

London, 4 April 1885

Dear Bebel,

Since you happen to be at home now and I, too, am granting myself a bit of a holiday, I shall take advantage of the opportunity to remind you of my existence.

So those gentlemen who form the majority of the parliamentary group are intent on setting themselves up as a 'power' to judge by their statement in today's *Sozialdemokrat*. [374] The endeavour as such is feeble, and is basically an admission of their own ineptitude. 'We are,' they say, 'annoyed by the paper's attitude; it conflicts with ours, we are to be held responsible for an opinion that is the opposite of our own, and we really don't know what to do about it. Are we not to be pitied?' But it is their first step towards the establishment of the petty bourgeoisie as the dominant, official element in the party, and the relegation of the proletariat to the status of one that is barely tolerated. How far along this road they will dare to travel remains to be seen. If they gain control of the *Sozialdemokrat*, it will no longer be possible for me to vindicate the party abroad through thick and thin as single-mindedly as I have always done. And their committee of inquiry would seem to betray a certain desire to take over the organ. Come to that, their main grievance would seem to lie in having been compelled in the end to vote against the Steamship Bill upon which they had set their hearts.

For the rest, things in general are going very well. The year 1885 has got off to an excellent start. In France, Ferry topples, colonial policy, dictated by stock-market speculators, collapses, [372] new elections in the offing consequent upon new electoral legislation. [375] In Paris, what's more, a state of ferment, provoked by the rapacity and inefficiency of the ruling middle class and exacerbated by the infamies of the police (everything they do, however base, is condoned, provided they keep the masses at bay); we can only hope that things won't come to a head there in the form of attempted coups. If they take a peaceful course, radicalism — i. e. Clemenceau — is bound to come to the helm before very long. Should he come to power peacefully and not as the result of rioting, and thus be compelled to keep his promises and put his radical *panacée* into practice, the Parisian workers will quickly be cured of their belief in radicalism. In addition, there will be the new elections consequent upon the new electoral legislation, and thus stagnation will again give way to activity.

In England, with her thoroughly effete government, [376] there will also be new elections consequent upon the new electoral legislation. [299] And in Germany, a change of monarch that may occur any day now and which, in a country as chockful of traditions as Prussia-Germany, always ushers in a new period of activity; in short, things will begin to liven up everywhere, and this on the economic basis of universal and incurable overproduction, a state of affairs that is gradually leading up to an acute crisis.

Kautsky has just arrived with a long letter from Ede about his conflict with the parliamentary group. I have told Kautsky that in my view it was in fact Ede's duty to let the party at large have their say in the paper, and that the parliamentary group has no right to prevent this. If he adopts this standpoint, the group won't be able to touch him. Secondly, he mustn't let the group press him into posing the cardinal question; to be rid of him is exactly what the chaps are after, and he could do them no greater service. In the third place, he should not take upon himself responsibility for other people's articles unless he reserves the right to name them. You know whom I mean and who it was that wrote most of the articles about the steamship affair — the ones that so enraged the majority and for which Ede appears to have assumed responsibility. [377] After all, he has long had to do battle with the petty-bourgeois lot; now the struggle has simply assumed a different form, but the cause is still the same and, like you, I think it improbable that these gentlemen will take things to extremes, much though they would like to exploit the position the Anti-Socialist Law [37] affords them, namely immunity to official and genuine opposition or criticism on the part of their voters.

The matter would, in my view, take a smoother course were the *Sozialdemokrat* to discard the *official* character that has been attached to it. Though not undesirable at one time, this no longer serves any purpose. Whether and how such a thing can be done, you will know better than I.

25 sheets (out of 38) of *Capital*, Book II have been printed. Book III is in hand. It is quite extraordinarily brilliant. This complete reversal of all previous economics is truly astounding. Our theory is thereby provided for the first time with an unassailable basis while we ourselves are enabled to hold our own successfully against all comers. Directly it appears, the philistines in the party will again be dealt a blow that will give them something to think about. For it will again bring general economic questions to the forefront of the controversy.

Time for the post. Unless I send this off, it won't leave till Monday[a] and, perhaps, no longer find you at home. My warm regards, then, and mind you keep well and look after yourself; we don't just need a Bebel, but a Bebel sound in wind and limb.

Your

F. E.

First published, in Russian, in *Marx-Engels Archives*, Vol. I (VI), Moscow, 1932

Printed according to the original
Published in English for the first time

---

[a] 6 April

160

ENGELS TO PASQUALE MARTIGNETTI

IN BENEVENTO

London, 11 April 1885
122 Regent's Park Road, N. W.

Dear Sir,

I am writing these few lines just to tell you that I have received the translation[a] and am dealing with it. I hope to be able to return it with my comments and suggestions in ten to fifteen days' time. What I have managed to read so far seems very well done.

Thanking you cordially, I remain your devoted

F. Engels

First published in *La corrispondenza di Marx e Engels con italiani. 1848-1895*, Milano, 1964

Printed according to the original

Translated from the Italian

Published in English for the first time

161

ENGELS TO KARL KAUTSKY

IN LONDON

[London,] 16 April 1885

Dear Kautsky,

Lenchen has a touch of bronchitis and has been ordered to bed by the doctor, so our usual Sunday dinner must, alas, be given a miss.

---

[a] The Italian translation of Engels' *The Origin of the Family, Private Property and the State* (see also this volume, p. 215).

I trust your wife is at last rid of her headache.
Kind regards.

Your

F. Engels

First published, in Russian, in *Marx-Engels Archives*, Vol. I (VI), Moscow, 1932

Printed according to the original

Published in English for the first time

162

ENGELS TO LAURA LAFARGUE

IN PARIS

London, 16-17 April 1885

My dear Laura,

It has struck me, since I wrote last,[a] that something might be done in the matter of Lawroff's Russian friends, if they are willing to risk some money on preliminary expenses. 1) If the man died in London and the date of his death, locality, etc., is approximately known, these particulars might enable some one to trace the authentic record of the death. 2) Having that, it will be easy to ascertain at the Court of Probate whether there was a will proved, or whether some one, and who, took out letters of administration and appropriated the gold the man is supposed to have left.

These two steps will in any case be the first two steps that have to be taken, and will put the inquiring parties in a position where they can better judge whether it is worth while proceeding any further. I think Percy might be entrusted with this preliminary part of the matter, and I would see that his charges are no more than what is usual. They would depend, of course, upon the amount of trouble he would be put to.

---

[a] See this volume, pp. 264-66.

How is poor old Lawroff getting on with his eyesight? It must be terrible for him to be debarred from the use of his books.

Here is another patient: old Harney has been hovering about all parts of England and Scotland ever since July last and everywhere persecuted by articular rheumatism and bad weather — and now at last turned up in London. He has gone through all sorts of semi-quack treatments — Turkish baths, brine-baths, magnetic belts, etc., and all of course no use, and now has put himself again in the hands of an advertising 'specialist' who exploits the uric-acid-gout theory (which in itself is quite correct) in what looks to me an extremely quackish way. However I'll hope the best, and the poor old fellow is much in want of it. He is shaky enough in arms, hands, legs and feet, and of course much reduced by the treatment he has undergone. I saw him this afternoon (he stays somewhere near the Brecknock) and he speaks of nothing but his sufferings, though here and there with a dash of his old dry humour. His treatment has of course cost him an awful lot of money and he seems to dread the necessity of returning to America. From all this you see how much eight months of continuous pains and gradually sinking hopes of relief have brought the old chap down. I hope the spring weather which anyhow must come sometime, will bring him at least some relief.

It's nothing but patients today. Tussy may have informed you that Edward fell ill about 10 days ago and that Donkin says it is a calculus in the kidney — he is at Ventnor at present and rest, we hope, will allay the irritation. Of course, there are a good many people loafing about with such a thing in their kidney but it is not pleasant certainly.

The next patient is not so bad, but it is Nim, she had a severe cold, and as one could not keep her out of the kitchen, it turned into a — so far slight — attack of bronchitis. Anyhow I got her to consult the doctor today who told her the shortest way to get over it at once was to go to bed, so there we got her with a fire in the room and 64 degrees Fahrenheit and hope she will be able to get up about Monday.

So now I have come to an end of my sick-list, it is the longest I have had for some time and a mighty pleasant subject to write about, and more pleasant still for the reader!

Paul's article for Kautsky goes in German into the *Neue Zeit*[a] and in

---

[a] [P. Lafargue, 'Die Krisis in Frankreich. Der Krieg in Tongking',] *Die Neue Zeit*, No. 5, 1885.

English into next *Commonweal.*[a] I do not know whether you get this regularly. The business arrangements are as usual awfully defective, everything is put upon Edward's shoulders and as he cannot supervise every detail, nobody knows whether the paper is really forwarded to all those people abroad who ought to have it. The whole Socialist League[346] is now in an awful excitement about the Afghan scare—they see not only war, but England defeated, India in revolt and last, revolution at home, Socialism triumphant—hooray! Poor Bax was going to write in this style but Tussy told him he had better see me about it, and I have done my best to cool him down a bit.[378] Whenever an Englishman does get free of Jingoism thoroughly, he seems to get a positive hatred of his own nationality. This is not such a bad quality, only rather misplaced in the case of a war with the Russian Tsar.[b] The Socialist League will not as yet set England in a blaze, but the Russian Nihilists[356] may Russia—with the help of an unsuccessful war.

You will have seen the stupid proclamation of the German deputies in the *Sozialdemokrat.*[374] The petit-bourgeois element has decidedly got the majority among the deputies, as I feared from the beginning. This is owing to the Socialist Law[37] which gives them exceptional facilities in pushing their candidatures. But they will soon find out their mistake, if they have not already done so. I am rather glad they have come out so soon and so stupidly. The separation from this element which has been pushed and cajoled principally by friend Liebknecht—with the usual best intentions, of course—will come, but I do not want to provoke it while the Socialist Law is in force, because that prevents us from fighting it out. It gives these people a certain advantage but that we must put up with for the time being. And I do not think they will push things to a crisis.

Now a word for Paul.[379] No doubt *lex*[c] is derived from *legere*[d] and νόμος[e] from νέμω,[f] and so a certain connection can be established between agricultural and political terms. And this cannot be otherwise. The first social regulations which were put in force, necessarily referred to production and the means of getting the livelihood. That this is confirmed by the development of the language, *rien de plus naturel.*[g] But now to go further, and to work the derivation of *legere* and νέμω into a complete system, cannot lead but to fanciful

[a] P. Lafargue, 'The Tonkin War and Socialism', *The Commonweal*, No. 4, May 1885.-[b] Alexander III-[c] law-[d] to gather-[e] pasture-[f] tending grazing cattle-[g] nothing more natural

results — if only for the reason that we do not know at what time each particular derivate was formed and still less at what time it received the meaning at which it was handed down to us. And moreover, old etymologists like Vico are bad guide, *ilex* has the root *il*, and nothing to do with *lex*. Etymology like physiology and any other -ology must be learned, cannot be invented. And this leads me to the Roshers. You recollect Charley went in for a new railway carriage by which in case of a collision you could get smashed in a new way. Well, that is exploded. But Charley's younger brothers (one 20, the other 18) have invented a new carriage, have patented it, and old Rosher does not seem much disinclined to go in for this thing! What a family of geniuses!

Sur ce,[a] I shut up. Kind regards to Paul.— Hope 'better news next time'.

Affectionately yours,
F. E.

17th April. The doctor has been. Nim is better, and can get up in a couple of days.

First published in: Marx and Engels, *Works*, Second Russian Edition, Vol. 36, Moscow, 1964

Reproduced from the original

Published in English for the first time

163

ENGELS TO EDUARD BERNSTEIN

IN ZURICH

[London, after 16 April 1885]

Dear Ede,

Thanks. Letter from August[b]: the parliamentary group, whose authority August contested, resolved *unanimously* after a 3 days' debate

---

[a] And here - [b] August Bebel

that the *personal* controversy be dropped and the non-personal be postponed until *after* the Reichstag sitting, and with this August concurred. [380] So the news of a defeat was false; we have won all along the line.

Your
F. E.

First published in: Marx and Engels, *Works*, First Russian Edition, Vol. XXVII, Moscow, 1935

Printed according to the original

Published in English for the first time

164

ENGELS TO NIKOLAI DANIELSON

IN ST PETERSBURG

London, 23 April 1885

Dear Sir,

I have received your kind letter of the 9/21 last month and am very much obliged for the very interesting information it contains. [381] That the law of wages being in inverse proportion to the length of working time should also be verified in Russia is a very interesting fact indeed. So also is the rapid disintegration of the мiръ[a] by the progress of modern industry and financing, as shown in the increasing number of the безхозяйственные хозяева. [b] All such facts are of the highest importance to me, and I shall feel very much obliged if you will communicate to me, from time to time, what you may know about the economical condition and development of your great country. Unfortunately at present all my time is taken up with the publication of the manuscripts, [c] so much so that I have to interrupt not only independent work but even my studies, and can scarcely find

---

[a] (Russ.) rural community - [b] (Russ.) farmless peasants - [c] of the third volume of *Capital*

time for correspondence; so you see I cannot take advantage just now of your kind offer to send me original Russian works on economical subjects, I should really not have the time to make use of them. But I hope you will not blame me, if hereafter at the first opportunity I take the liberty of reminding you of your kind promise. In the meantime these inestimable manuscripts are to me a source of the highest scientific *Genuss*,[a] and no doubt so will the proofs be to you.[361] Of these I forwarded to you Nos. 5-9 about 3 weeks ago 27th March and yesterday Nos. 10-14. I shall again forward a set shortly, always *registered*. The whole of No. II will be about 37 sheets and will be out by end of May. I am now busy with No. III which is the concluding and crowning part, and will eclipse even No. I. I dictate from the original, which is positively illegible to any living man except myself, and shall have no rest until it is all transferred to a manuscript which at all events will be legible to others. Then I can take my time with the final redaction, which will be no easy task, seeing the imperfect state of the original. But anyhow, even if I should not be spared to finish that, it would be saved from being utterly lost, and could be published as it is in case of need. This No. III is the most astounding thing I ever read, and it is a thousand pities that the author did not live to work it out and publish it himself and see the effect it is destined to create. After this lucid exposition, no candid opposition is any longer possible. The most difficult points are cleared up and disentangled as if they were a mere child's play, and the whole system acquires a new and simple aspect. I am afraid this No. III will fill two volumes. Besides that I have an old manuscript which treats the history of the theory and will also require a good deal of work.[171] So you see I have my hands full.

Very sincerely yours,
P. W. Rosher[363]

First published, in Russian, in *Minuvshiye gody*, No. 2, St Petersburg, 1908

Reproduced from the original

Published in English for the first time

---

[a] enjoyment

165

ENGELS TO VERA ZASULICH [316; 382]

IN GENEVA

London, 23 April 1885

Dear Citizen,

I still owe you an answer to your letter of 14 February. Below you will find the reasons for my tardiness, which can certainly not be attributed to idleness on my part.

You ask me to give you my opinion of Plekhanov's book *Наши разногласiя.*[a] To do this I should have to have read it. I find little difficulty in reading Russian when I have spent a week devoting myself to it, but six months or more may go by without my having any opportunity to do so; then, having lost the habit of it, I am compelled to learn the language all over again, as it were. And that is what has happened with the *Разногласiя.* Marx's manuscripts, which I dictate to a secretary,[b] take up the whole of my day; in the evening people come to call who cannot, after all, simply be shown the door. Also there are proofs to be read, a great deal of correspondence and, finally, translations (into the Italian, Danish, etc.) of my *Origin etc.,*[c] which I am asked to look over and whose revision sometimes turns out to be neither easy nor superfluous. Well, all these interruptions have prevented my progressing further than page 60 of the *Разногласiя.* If only I could have three days to myself, the job would be done and, what is more, I should have brushed up my Russian.

However, the little I have read is, I think, enough to put me more or less *au fait* with the dispute[d] in question.

To begin with, let me repeat how proud I am to know that there exists among the younger generation in Russia a party which frankly and unreservedly accepts the great economic and historical theories evolved by Marx, and which has broken for good with all the anarchic and to some extent Slavophil traditions of its predecessors.[383] And Marx himself, had he lived a little longer, would have been no less proud than I. It marks a step forward which will be of the utmost

---

[a] See this volume, p. 264. - [b] Oskar Eisengarten - [c] *The Origin of the Family, Private Property and the State*; see also this volume, pp. 264 and 272. - [d] Crossed out in the draft: 'between your group and the Narodnaya Volya members[356]'.

importance to the revolutionary development of Russia. In my eyes, Marx's historical theory is fundamentally essential to revolutionary tactics, if these are to be *consistent* and *logical*; to discover what those tactics ought to be, all one has to do is to apply the theory to economic and political conditions in the country concerned.

But to do so demands familiarity with those conditions, and I, for my part, am too ignorant of the present situation in Russia to suppose myself competent to assess in detail the tactics that might be required at any given moment. Again, the internal and intimate history of the Russian revolutionary party, in particular that of the last few years, is to me a closed book. My friends among the Narodnaya Volya members have never discussed it with me. Yet this is an element which, if one is to form an opinion, cannot be ignored.

What I know, or believe I know, of the situation in Russia leads me to think that that country is nearing its 1789. Revolution is *bound* to break out some time or other; it *may* break out any day. In conditions such as these the country is like a charged mine, all that is needed is to apply the match. Especially after what happened on 13 March. [188] It is one of those special cases where it is possible for a handful of men to *effect* a revolution, that is, to bring about at one stroke the collapse of an entire system whose equilibrium is more than labile (to use Plekhanov's metaphor [a]),[384] and to release, by a single and intrinsically insignificant act, explosive forces which later become uncontrollable. Well, if ever Blanquism, the fantasy of subverting the whole of a society through action by a small group of conspirators, had any rational foundation, it would assuredly be in St Petersburg. [b] Once the match has been applied to the powder, once the forces have been unleashed and the national energy has been converted from potential to kinetic (another of Plekhanov's favourite and, indeed, excellent metaphors) [385] — the men who have sprung the mine will be swept off their feet by an explosion a thousand times more powerful than they themselves, one which will seek whatever outlet it may find in accordance with the prevailing economic forces and resistances.

Suppose that these men imagine they will be able to seize power, what of it? Providing they make the hole which causes the dam to collapse, the resulting torrent of water will soon put paid to their illusions. But what if those illusions succeeded in endowing them with an ex-

---

[a] The draft had 'pet metaphor'. - [b] Crossed out in the draft: 'I do not say "in Russia" because in the provinces, far from the administrative centre, it [such action] is not necessary.'

ceptional strength of will? Would that be any cause for complaint? Men who have boasted of having *effected* a revolution have always found on the morrow that they didn't know what they were doing; that once *effected*, the revolution has borne no resemblance at all to what they had intended. That is what Hegel calls the irony of history, [386] an irony which few historical дъятели [a] can escape. [b] You have only to look at Bismarck, a revolutionary in spite of himself, and Gladstone, who ended up by falling out with his beloved Tsar. [c]

What, in my view, is important in Russia is that the impulse should be given, that revolution should break out. Whether it is this or that group that gives the signal, whether it be under this flag or that, is of little concern to me. Even if it were [d] a palace plot, its instigators would be swept away on the morrow. In a place where the situation is so tense, where revolutionary elements have accumulated to such a degree, where the economic situation of the vast mass of the people becomes daily more impossible, where every degree of social development is represented, from the primitive commune to modern big industry and high finance, and where all these contradictions are forcibly pent up by an unheard-of despotism — a despotism increasingly unacceptable to a younger generation in which are combined the nation's intelligence and dignity — in such a place 1789, once launched, will before long be followed by 1793.

I say 'good-bye', dear Citizen. It is half past two in the morning. Tomorrow before the departure of the courier I will hardly have time to add anything. If you prefer, do write to me in Russian, but please bear in mind that Russian *handwriting* is something I do not read every day.

Your devoted
F. Engels

First published, in Russian, in *Gruppa 'Osvobozhdeniye truda'*, No. 3, Moscow, 1925

Printed according to the original, checked with the draft

Translated from the French

Published in English in full for the first time

---

[a] (Russ.) Here: figures. - [b] Crossed out in the draft: 'Maybe the same thing will happen to us all.' - [c] Alexander III - [d] Crossed out in the draft: 'a clique of the nobles or of money-bags — well, all the best ... until'.

166

ENGELS TO RICHARD STEGEMANN

IN TÜBINGEN

[Draft]

[London,] 5 May 1885

Dear Sir,

Mature reflection has shown that I cannot possibly comply with your request.[387]

Either the work you want must be *short*, in which case it could contain nothing but asseverations on my part, and thus merely be assertive and belletristic.

Or I should have to supply documentary evidence, in which case it would turn into a book, and that would not suit your purpose; moreover, I could not write it in so off-hand and casual a manner, for which my material is far too abundant.

A further consideration is that I should be more or less committing myself to co-editing a work about which I know nothing save the brief account provided by you.

In addition, the thing would — within the limits prescribed — be utterly useless. However vigorous my protestations, they would utterly fail to move the semi-educated vulgarian whose prejudices you wish to combat. People who say that Marx 'died friendless' must, presumably, harbour the belief that I do not exist at all. In which case, what magical effect could asseverations on my part be expected to have?

The old fairy-tales invented by the vulgar democratic emigration of 1850-59, and further elaborated by Bonaparte's paid agent, Karl Vogt, — *il lui a été remis en* 1859[a] 40,000 frs, according to the Tuileries papers,[388] may perhaps be more in vogue in your district than elsewhere because the Swabian People's Party[203] is the direct descendant of that same democratic emigration, certain of its leaders having been on intimate terms with the afore-mentioned Vogt. Since all this was dealt with by Marx in *Herr Vogt*, there would seem to be

---

[a] in 1859 he was paid

no reason for me to hark back to it at this particular juncture. Vast numbers of lies were told about Marx to which he never saw fit to reply. The time may, perhaps, come when it will behove me to do so on his behalf, but the choice of time, place and modus operandi will be my affair. Which will, of course, only serve to revive my reputation for 'callousness'.

In any case, I haven't got time just now to do anything along these lines that would either be to the purpose or satisfy my own requirements in regard to such a work. My entire time is taken up with editing Marx's manuscripts, and I shall be acting wholly in his spirit if, in view of this obligation, I treat all this philistine carping with contempt.

I remain, Sir, very sincerely

First published in: Marx and Engels, *Works*, First Russian Edition, Vol. XXVII, Moscow, 1935

Printed according to the original

Published in English for the first time

167

ENGELS TO EDUARD BERNSTEIN

IN ZURICH

London, 15 May 1885

Dear Ede,

I think it's about time to drop you a line or two again, otherwise you will grow far too melancholy. You and Kautsky seem to evoke from one another so many doleful laments that a complete concert in the minor key could be produced therefrom; it's like the trombone in Wagner that always sounds forth whenever something dire is going to happen. Each time you get bad news, the pair of you always forget the old adage about a dog's back being worse than its bite.

The general and inescapable impression left by the whole shindy between 'parliamentary group and editors' is that the parliamentary group have made fools of themselves. And should the parliamentary group insist on doing it again, they ought not to be prevented. Had you immediately published the first written communication,[389] as they demanded, they would have made complete and utter fools of themselves, and a 'storm of indignation' would have broken out on all sides. Not, of course, that this could very well have been asked of you at the start, but there can be no doubt at all that it is not in our interests to prevent the parliamentary group from *showing themselves in their true colours*. As things are, 'parliamentary group and editors' confront each other as equals—in the eyes of the public—, this being the result of the last, lengthy middle-of-the-road statement,[390] and what happens next, we shall have to see.

I had Singer here on Sunday,[a] and cut short all his speechifying. The parliamentary group's first statement, he said, was directed not so much against the articles in the paper,[377] as against the (alleged) attempt to try and arouse a storm of indignation against the parliamentary group. That, I said, was something the public couldn't have known; if you make a public statement, it can only refer to publicly available facts. But if you hit out at the paper on account of things that have never appeared in it, the public may justifiably ask: 'What are these gentlemen after, if not the suppression of free speech?' This he had to admit. Next I said that, to judge by what was to me a very familiar style, most of the objectionable articles had been by Liebknecht.— Singer: 'Quite right, and we gave Liebknecht a proper dressing-down for it in the parliamentary group.' I: 'But to censure the paper in public for printing things that actually emanated from the parliamentary group simply won't do. You ought to have settled the matter amongst yourselves. Instead, you publicly attack the editors for matters that are solely the private concern of the parliamentary group. To whom, then, are the editors to look?' Here again he could raise no objection. 'In short, you have, by your ill-considered action, made fools of yourselves, and if anyone has come off best in the eyes of the public, it is the editors.' This, too, he had to concede indirectly. Since I stuck to the main points and disregarded all his personal tittle-tattle, of which he had ample store, we concluded our business in ten minutes.

That's not the end of the matter, of course. But we now know what the gentlemen's weak side is. If I were editor of the *Sozialdemokrat*, I should, from the editorial point of view, let the parliamentary group

---

[a] 10 May

stew in its own juice, i. e. in the Reichstag, entrust any criticism thereof to the members of the party, on the strength of the oft-cited 'free expression of opinion', and tell Liebknecht once and for all that he must himself be answerable to the parliamentary group for his articles, thus putting an end to his double-dealing, in this respect at any rate. Then, provided the paper continues to be edited along the lines already laid down, that is enough for us. It is far more important for us to maintain our theoretical standpoint in the face of the rubbish that is printed in Germany than to criticise the parliamentary group's mode of action. For after all, those who have been elected are themselves doing everything in their power to enlighten the electorate as to the character of the elected. And for that matter, day to day events provide opportunity enough to make clear what our standpoint is, even if we leave it to the parliamentary group and party members to take care of the parliamentary group. It is, however, that very standpoint that vexes them most of all, and it is something they dare not publicly attack.

The Reichstag will soon be going home. In the meantime the gentlemen — although almost all of them are secret protectionists — will have seen what havoc is wrought by a policy of protective tariffs.[391] That is but the first of many disappointments that lie in store for them. Not that it will change their philistine character, but it will probably shake their confidence and cause them to fall out over philistine questions that necessitate their declaring themselves for or against. Only give such types a little rope, and they'll hang themselves.

In short, our policy is, I believe, to temporise. The Anti-Socialist Law[37] is working in their favour and if, while it remains in force, they can only find an opportunity to show themselves in their true colours, that is really all we need for the present. In the meantime we must defend every position to the utmost, particularly in the press, and this will not always call for active resistance. To outflank an enemy is also a defensive manoeuvre but one that has offensive connotations. At the moment we have much against us. Bebel is ill and has, so it seems, lost heart. Nor shall I be able to help as much as I would like until I have finished with Marx's manuscripts. So you and Kautsky must bear the brunt of the battle. But don't forget the old rule — never to allow the actualities of the movement and of the struggle to make you forget the movement's future. And that belongs to us. The third volume of *Capital* will do in all these chaps at one blow.

Your

F. E.

First published, in Russian, in *Marx-Engels Archives*, Book I, Moscow, 1924

Printed according to the original

Published in English for the first time

168

ENGELS TO HERMANN SCHLÜTER [392]

IN HOTTINGEN-ZURICH

London, 15 May 1885

Dear Mr Schlüter,

As regards the poems [393]:

The *Marseillaise* of the Peasants' War was *Ein feste Burg ist unser Gott* [394] and, vainglorious though its words and tune may be, it neither should nor need be taken in the same spirit today. Other songs of that time are to be found in anthologies of folk songs, *Des Knaben Wunderhorn,*[a] etc. You might perhaps find something there. But even at that time the *Landsknecht*[b] exercised a virtual monopoly over our popular poetry.

Of foreign songs, the only one I know is the beautiful old Danish song about Herr Tidmann, which I translated for the Berlin *Social-Demokrat* in 1865.[c]

There were all kinds of Chartist songs, but they are now no longer to be had. One began:

> * Britannia's Sons, though slaves you be,
> God your creator made you free;
> To all he life and freedom gave,
> But never, never made a slave.*

---

[a] compiled by L. A. von Arnim and C. Brentano - [b] mercenary soldier - [c] See present edition, Vol. 20, pp. 34-35.

I don't know how it goes on.

All that stuff has been forgotten and in any case wasn't up to much as poetry.

In 1848 two popular songs were current and were sung to the same tune.

1) Schleswig-Holstein.

2) The Hecker song [395]:

> Hecker, may thy name resound
> Up and down the German Rhine,
> Thy generous heart nay, e'en thy look
> Inspired confidence in mind.
> Hecker, a German man and free
> Who'd give his life for liberty.

That, I think, suffices. Then there's another version:

> Hecker, Struve, Blenker, Zitz and Blum
> Slay the German princes.

In general, the poetry of past revolutions (always excepting the *Marseillaise* [396]) seldom has much revolutionary impact later on because, if it is to influence the masses, it must reflect the mass prejudices of the day — hence the religious nonsense found even in the Chartists.

Now as to Marx's shorter pieces, this is a matter upon which others beside myself have to decide, while I for my own part must make quite sure that nothing is done that might interfere with the proposed edition of the *Complete Works*. The things appertaining to the International, the *Inaugural Address, Civil War, Hague Report*,[a] etc., like the *Manifesto*,[b] I do not regard as forming part of these, though I should like to reserve the right to provide a few words of introduction. As regards the articles from the *Neue Rheinische Zeitung*, you must first find out which were written by Marx. For instance, only one, an outstanding article on the June insurrection was by Marx,[c] while the account of the struggle, etc., was entirely mine.[d] Likewise the anti-Bakunin and anti-Pan-Slavism articles.[e] The things Marx and I wrote at that time are on the whole almost indistinguishable owing to our systematic division of labour.

---

[a] K. Marx, *Report of the General Council to the Fifth Annual Congress...* - [b] K. Marx and F. Engels, *Manifesto of the Communist Party*. - [c] K. Marx, 'The June Revolution'. - [d] F. Engels, 'Details about the 23rd of June'; 'The 23rd of June'; 'The 24th of June'; 'The 25th of June'; 'The June Revolution (The Course of the Paris Uprising)'. - [e] F. Engels, 'Democratic Pan-Slavism'.

As I have said, I shall certainly not place unnecessary obstacles in your way, but I should be glad all the same if you could let me have a rather more detailed idea of your plan before I say anything definite about it. At all events, it would hardly do to publish stuff from the *Neue Rheinische Zeitung* and on the International side by side, i. e. in one volume; there was an interval of some 15 or 20 years in between.— The *Cologne Trial*[a] would run to a goodly volume on its own, and I would write you an introduction to it.[b] But please note that in that case I must know when it is *really needed* and, what with the luckless *Dühring*,[c] you have after all enough to print just now. You will have received the two sheets, 4 and 5.

Apropos, my intention is that the chapter 'Theoretical' from the section *Socialism* should be printed according to the revised text of *Socialism: Utopian and Scientific*. When it has got to that stage I shall send you what is necessary. This is merely to notify you in advance.

For the rest, warm regards from

Yours,

F. Engels

First published abridged in *Die Neue Zeit*, Bd. 1, Nr. 11, Stuttgart, 1918 and in full in: Marx and Engels, *Works*, First Russian Edition, Vol. XXVII, Moscow, 1935

Printed according to the original

Published in English in full for the first time

169

ENGELS TO PAUL LAFARGUE

IN PARIS

London, 19 May 1885

My dear Lafargue,

The Lissagaray affair pleased me greatly and I trust he will be chucked out of the *Bataille*.[397] The irony of history is without mercy, even to revolutionary stink-bugs.

---

[a] K. Marx, *Revelations Concerning the Communist Trial in Cologne*. - [b] F. Engels, 'On the History of the Communist League'. - [c] F. Engels, *Anti-Dühring*.

> I must repent, must repent me,
> Where my sins were most committed[a]

as good king Don Rodrigo said while snakes devoured his vital parts. Brousse at the head of a daily paper would be too comical, he would never last. It would be all he needed to cut his own throat.

The idea that life is simply the normal mode of existence of albuminous bodies and that as a result the protein of the future, if the chemists ever contrive to manufacture it, must display signs of life, appears in my anti-Dühring book where it is developed to some extent on page 60, etc.[b] By assuming responsibility for it Schorlemmer did a bold thing, for if it falls flat, the blame will be his, whereas if it catches on, he will be the first to give me the credit.[398] Moreover your Grimaux must be an imbecile if he really said that

'we have nothing to show us how this initial movement is acquired whereby an albuminoid *is organised into a living cell*'.[c]

So the good man appears to be unaware that there is a whole army of living things which are still very far removed from the organisation of a cell, being no more than '*plasson*', as Haeckel has it,[d] albuminoids that have no trace of organisation, yet are alive—for example protamoebas, siphonales, etc. The poor albuminoid has probably worked for millions of years in order to organise itself into a cell. But your Grimaux doesn't even see the point at issue. Moreover he betrays his ignorance of physiology still further by comparing with a primitive protoplasm, the source of all life on earth, a product as specialised as the egg of a vertebrate.

We have had poor Harney here for the past 10 days. He suffers badly from chronic rheumatoid arthritis of a $\pm$[e] gouty nature. Nim has had her work cut out looking after him. If the weather improves he hopes to set off for Macclesfield on Saturday.[f] On that same Saturday we are expecting Sam Moore with his translation[g]—alas, as yet uncompleted.

The 2nd volume has been printed with the exception of my preface, the proofs of which should arrive any day. The consignments sent to Danielson have so far all arrived and 7 sheets have been translated.[361] I have dictated more than half of the 3rd volume, but two

---

[a] Engels quotes in Spanish. - [b] F. Engels, *Anti-Dühring*, present edition, Vol. 25, pp. 75-77. - [c] É. Grimaux, 'Les substances colloïdales et la coagulation', *Revue scientifique*, No. 16, 18 April 1885, p. 500. - [d] E. Haeckel, *Die Perigenesis der Plastidule...*, Berlin, 1876, pp. 76, 77. - [e] more or less - [f] 23 May; see also this volume, p. 292. - [g] of the first volume of *Capital* (see Note 56)

sections [399] are going to give me a fine old time. The one on bank capital and credit is in such disorder as to strike terror into the heart of a better man than me, but that is how it is. I am now at land rent. It is quite superbly done. But this will entail even more work, for the manuscript dates from 1865 and I shall have to consult his extracts made between 1870 and 1878 both for the banks and for landed property in America and Russia. And there are not a few of them. This means that the 3rd volume will have to wait another year at least.

The storm in a teacup that has disrupted our ranks in Germany [374] will doubtless calm down for the time being. Now that the Reichstag has been sent about its business, the gents of the 'socialist group' have dispersed. The Social Democrats have won a moral victory over the 'group'. But that is not the end of the matter and there may be a recurrence. Were it not for the Anti-Socialist Law, [37] I should have been in favour of an outright split. But so long as it is in force, it deprives us of all our weapons while enabling the party's petit-bourgeois section to reap all the benefit. And, in any case, it is not our business to provoke it. The thing was inevitable; it was bound to come sooner or later. But it would have come either later or under circumstances more favourable to ourselves had it not been for the incredible stupidities of Liebknecht, who has not only wavered between the two sections and invariably protected the petit bourgeois, but has also been prepared on more than one occasion to sacrifice the proletarian nature of the party for a simulacrum of unity that is credible to no one. It would appear that his own protégés, the representatives of the petit-bourgeois side, have now had enough of his double dealing. Liebknecht always believes what he says when he is saying it, but believes something quite different whenever he speaks to someone else. Over here he is all for revolution, over there all for circumspection. That won't prevent his being on our side on the crucial day and telling us: Didn't I always tell you so! *This is between ourselves.* A kiss for Laura.

Yours ever,

F. E.

First published in: Marx and Engels, *Works*, Second Russian Edition, Vol. 36, Moscow, 1964

Printed according to the original

Translated from the French

Published in English for the first time

170

ENGELS TO PASQUALE MARTIGNETTI [400]

IN BENEVENTO

[Draft]

[London, 19 May 1885]

Dear Citizen,

...on the etc. I sent you, by registered mail, the translation[a] with my comments. I am very sorry that my limited practice of Italian has not enabled me to do them better, but I hope they will be intelligible nonetheless. I am amazed that, without having lived in Germany and learned the language there, you have been able to render my thoughts so well. I only found a few abbreviated, idiomatic and proverbial expressions where there was an error; and even these are impossible to understand properly for someone who has not spoken the everyday language and even the dialects of the country — things which are not to be found in grammars and dictionaries. And in several cases when you have understood the meaning well, I think you could be a little freer and more adventurous.

I fear that the note about 'Mark' is not very clear. It is the only note which I think should be printed. The others are for your information only. If therefore you have any doubts about that note, please let me know and I shall try and rewrite it.[401]

Please excuse the long time it has taken me to do the revision. But my days are taken up with dictating Marx's manuscripts, and my evenings are not always free. In addition, I have had a Danish translation[b] to check at the same time, not to mention the English translation of *Capital*.[56]

Thanking you again for the considerable work you have done on my behalf, I remain

Your devoted

First published in: Marx and Engels, *Works*, First Russian Edition, Vol. XXVII, Moscow, 1935

Printed according to the original

Translated from the Italian

Published in English for the first time

---

[a] the Italian translation of Engels' *The Origin of the Family, Private Property and the State* - [b] of *The Origin of the Family, Private Property and the State*

171

ENGELS TO LAURA LAFARGUE

IN PARIS

London, 29 May 1885

My dear Laura,

So then at least one thing is settled, and that is poor Paul in his *Kittchen*[a] in Ste Pélagie.[402] Hope it will not be for four months — the four best of the year too! Anyhow, what a consolation it is for him, to be no longer crucified between the *braconnier*[b] on one side and the *vol avec effraction (de puanteur)*[c] on the other! And to consider it a hard-fought victory that he can have his old *Kittchen* again in company with a spouting anarchist. Well let us hope Révillon and a few more deputies will make it hot for the Liberal ministry and procure his release.

Harney is gone to Macclesfield yesterday, and arrived safely. He is a good deal better, intrinsically, but of course the pains do not go all at once, and as soon as he is a bit better, he begins stirring about in cabs; he did so for two days before he left, then the journey, and of course arrived worse. I am afraid he will never get quite over it, partly because the complaint is too inveterate and partly on account of his inconsistency and listening to everybody who has a remedy to propose. It has been a hard time for poor Nim, and I am glad for her sake it has come to an end. Sam Moore had to go to Pumps', I think he rather liked it this time as he was bent on exhibitions, picture galleries, Royal Academies and the like, and so he and Pumps have a fine time of it. Today they are gone to see a cricket match at Lords.[d]

I had this morning the last proof-sheet of my preface to Second Volume,[e] so from that you see that the report of its being out is another canard. You may be sure that as soon as it is out and we get copies, you have one sent the same day. The 3rd edition of the *18th Brumaire*[f] is in the press, two sheets printed.

---

[a] jail (slang) - [b] poacher - [c] burglar (stinking) - [d] Lords Cricket Ground in London - [e] of *Capital* - [f] K. Marx, *The Eighteenth Brumaire of Louis Bonaparte.*

The Italian translation of the *Ursprung* is also in the press. But you will at once see that it will be hardly possible to translate from that into French. [403] If Paul uses it merely to facilitate to him the comprehension of the original, well and good; otherwise it would only enable him to give a very enfeebled *Abklatsch*[a] and poor *rechauffé*,[b] and I have no ambition to appear before the French public in that shape. The man[c] has done his best and some passages are really good. But it is not to be expected from him, who learnt German without assistance in Benevento, that he should put idiomatic German into equally idiomatic Italian. And that defect I could not remedy, as my idiomatic Italian is not Italian but only Milanese, and that, too, nearly forgotten.

I hope there will not be much more of that fighting about red flags, etc., in Paris — the police *want* a few barricades, and if they get them, there will be a jolly massacre — the people have not a ghost of a chance of victory. [404] Even if the government should show hesitation, the reactionary military chiefs will take care to be ready for action and to act.

There is one consolation for Paul — that he will be virtually 'out of Paris' on the day of the French Grand Old Man's[d] funeral.

What with proof-sheet, and writing to Harney [39] and making parcels up for him and writing to a confectioner from Colmar[e] [39] who asked my advice as to his finding work in London (answer: certainly not) and one thing and another, it has become 5.20, and so I must close if I want to catch this post. So with hopes that Paul will not be too unhappy, nor too long where he is, and that you will keep up, in spite of all, your state of, in Paris, *abnormal* health, here is the conclusion.

Love from Nim.

Yours affectionately,

F. Engels

First published in: Marx and Engels, *Works*, Second Russian Edition, Vol. 36, Moscow, 1964

Reproduced from the original

Published in English for the first time

---

[a] copy - [b] concoction - [c] Pasquale Martignetti - [d] Victor Hugo - [e] Wegmann

172

ENGELS TO NIKOLAI DANIELSON [405]

IN ST PETERSBURG

London, 3 June 1885

Dear Sir,

I have received your letter of the 24 [April]/6 May and hope you will have received the sheets 21/26 forwarded to you 13th May. [361] To-day I forward 27/33, the conclusion. In a few days I hope to be able to send you the preface, etc. From that preface you will see that the ms. of Volume III has been written as early as 1864/66, and thus before the period when the author, thanks to your kindness, became so intimately acquainted with the agricultural system of your country: I am at present working at the chapter on the rent of land, and have so far not found any allusion to Russian conditions. [406] As soon as the whole manuscript shall have been transcribed into a legible handwriting, I shall have to work it out by comparison with what other materials have been left by the author, and there are, for the chapter on rent, very voluminous extracts from the various statistical works he owed to you — but whether these will contain any critical notes that can be made use of for this volume, I cannot as yet tell. Whatever there is, shall be used most conscientiously. At all events the mere work of transcription will occupy me far into autumn, and as the manuscript is nearly 600 pages in folio, it may again have to be divided into two volumes.

The analysis of rent is theoretically so complete that you will necessarily find therein a good deal of interest for the special conditions of your country. Still this ms. excludes the treatment of the pre-capitalistic forms of landed property; they are merely alluded to here and there for the sake of comparison.

Yours very sincerely,
P. W. Rosher [363]

First published, in Russian, in *Minuvshiye gody*, No. 2, St Petersburg, 1908

Reproduced from the original

173

ENGELS TO FRIEDRICH ADOLPH SORGE [407]

IN HOBOKEN

London, 3 June 1885

Dear Sorge,

I was sorry to hear that you have been incapable of writing and trust that the thing has subsided. The Gronlunds and Elys,[a] as also the newspapers, gratefully received. Ely is a well-meaning philistine and does at least take more trouble than his German fellow-sufferers and fellow-blockheads which, after all, deserves recognition. Gronlund, on the other hand, strikes me as being speculative: his boosting of our stuff, in so far as he does or does not understand it, is clearly aimed at palming off his own utopian fiddle-faddle as REAL LIVE GERMAN SOCIALISM. A symptom at any rate.

As regards *To-Days* and *Commonweals*, I am sending you the former from March onwards and the latter from the beginning.[b] However their administrative side is not particularly efficient; should the paper (*The Commonweal*) fail to reach the *Sozialist* regularly, I should be *very grateful* if you would advise me so that I can provide *proof* of inefficiency, this being invariably denied by the secretary, though it undoubtedly exists.

You would do best to ignore Fabian completely; the man feels a need to get himself talked about and there is no necessity to encourage that.[c] His chief grievance against me is that I maliciously defamed $\sqrt{-1}$ in the *Anti-Dühring*, a point on which he complained to Marx by letter. [209]

You have had the same correct presentiment about the Reichstag laddies as I have — the case of the Steamship Subsidies [342] has revealed the immensity of their philistine aspirations. It almost came to a split, which would not be desirable at present, so long as the Anti-Socialist Law [37] remains in force. As soon as we get a bit more ELBOW-ROOM in Germany, the split will doubtless come and can then only do

---

[a] L. Gronlund, *The Cooperative Commonwealth in Its Outlines*; R. T. Ely, *French and German Socialism in Modern Times* (see also this volume, p. 192). - [b] See this volume, pp. 298, 312. - [c] Ibid., p. 124.

good. A petty-bourgeois-socialist parliamentary group is inevitable in a country like Germany where philistinism, even more than historical right, 'doesn't have no date'. [408] It will also be useful once it has constituted itself a body separate from the proletarian party. However such a split could only do harm just now if it were provoked by *us*. But if they do in fact renounce the programme, so much the better; we shall then be able to let fly.

You in America also suffer from various great savants of the kind possessed by Germany's philistine socialists in the persons of Geiser, Frohme, Blos, etc. The historical digressions in the *Sozialist* by your Stiebelings, Douais, etc., on the subject of Völkerwanderung [a] amused me greatly, for these people have studied the whole thing far better and far more thoroughly than I have. Douai, in particular, gives himself colossal airs. For instance in No. 13 of the *Sozialist*, apropos the German conquests in Italy, etc., he tells us that the King acquired $^1/_3$ of the land and the officers and soldiers $^2/_3$, of which $^2/_3$ passed in turn to the former slaves, etc. '*This we learn from Jornandes and Cassiodorus.*' [409] When I read that I was completely bowled over. '*Precisely similar accounts,*' he goes on, '*are provided about the Visigoths. Nor was it otherwise* in France.' Well, the whole thing is an invention from start to finish and you *won't find a word of it either in Jornandes or in Cassiodorus or in any other contemporary source.* It reveals at once colossal ignorance and impudence to confront me with such utter rubbish and to say that I am 'demonstrably in the wrong'. The sources, and I know practically all of them, state precisely the opposite. I have let it pass this time, as it was written in America where one can hardly make an issue of that kind of thing. But Monsieur Douai had better watch out in future; I might well lose patience some day.

The 2nd volume of *Capital* will be out shortly; all I am awaiting is the last half proof-sheet of the preface where Rodbertus receives a further broadside. The 3rd book is going ahead merrily, but will take a long time. Not that that matters, as the 2nd volume must be digested first. The 2nd volume will cause great disappointment, being a purely scientific work with little in the way of agitation. By contrast the third volume will again have the effect of a thunderbolt, since the

---

[a] G. C. Stiebeling, 'Reform oder Revolution', *Der Sozialist*, No. 7, 14 February 1885; A. Douai, 'Eine Entgegnung auf Dr. Stiebeling's Artikel', *Der Sozialist*, No. 13, 28 March 1885.

whole of capitalist production is dealt with in context for the first time and all official bourgeois economics rejected out of hand. But it will be quite a task. Since the New Year I have dictated more than half of the final version and expect to finish this preliminary work in about 4 months. But after that there will be the actual job of editing, which won't be easy as the most important chapters are in some disorder — so far as form is concerned. However everything will work out all right, though it will take time. As you can imagine, I shall have to leave everything else on one side until I have finished, and hence neglect my correspondence; nor can there be any question of writing articles. But you would oblige me if you would see to it that nothing of what I have said about the 3rd volume gets into the *Sozialist*. That would inevitably give rise to unpleasantnesses in Zurich and elsewhere. Whatever the readers need to know will appear in my preface to the 2nd volume.

All is well with Tussy so far. The two of them[a] are very happy together, though unfortunately they are not always in good health. Lafargue must now do another 4 months on account of the same old fine and costs. [402] The police were intent on fomenting a riot in Paris on 24 May, but nothing came of it and the ministers took fright. [404] So the Victor Hugo business went off quietly after all, and that is just as well. As there is no Garde Nationale, no weapons are to be had and any attempted coup would inevitably be crushed. One just has to adapt one's tactics to the circumstances. Regards to Dietzgen and Adolf.[b]

Your
F. E.

First published in *Briefe und Auszüge aus Briefen von Joh. Phil. Becker, Jos. Dietzgen, Friedrich Engels, Karl Marx u. A. an F. A. Sorge und Andere*, Stuttgart, 1906

Printed according to the original

Published in English in full for the first time

---

[a] Eleanor Marx-Aveling and Edward Aveling - [b] Adolf Sorge jun.

174

ENGELS TO JOHN LINCOLN MAHON [410]

IN LONDON

[Draft]

[London, between 10 and 12 June 1885]

Postage	- - 6d.
Stamps enclosed	- 3.2

Please *forward me the 2nd copy at once* Nos. 1 to 5,[a] they are for a friend in America.[b]

If the above be not correct please let me know what else there may be to pay.

Yours truly,
F. Engels

First published in: Marx and Engels, *Works*, Second Russian Edition, Vol. 50, Moscow, 1981

Reproduced from a copy of the draft

Published in English for the first time

175

ENGELS TO PASQUALE MARTIGNETTI

IN BENEVENTO

London, 13 June 1885

Dear Sir,

Kindly send me *six* copies of your translation.[c] These will be enough.

---

[a] of *The Commonweal* - [b] Friedrich Adolph Sorge - [c] the Italian translation of Engels' *The Origin of the Family, Private Property and the State*

I hope you have received the letter I sent about ten days after the translation. [a]

Your devoted

F. Engels

I am also sending you a copy of the *Manifesto of the Communist Party* of 1847 (by Marx and Engels). [b] Old as it is, I believe it still deserves to be read.

First published in *La corrispondenza di Marx e Engels con italiani. 1848-1895*, Milano, 1964

Printed according to the original

Translated from the Italian

Published in English for the first time

176

ENGELS TO JOHANN PHILIPP BECKER [263]

IN GENEVA

London, 15 June 1885

My Dear Old Fellow,

I was delighted to get your letter; it is indeed a damned shame that we should be so far apart. However the time will doubtless come when the likes of us will again be able to travel about untroubled by too great a pressure of work or the harassments of the continental police. Then I shall pack my bags and pay you a visit.

Meanwhile the world goes very gently on its way, though it may well speed up a bit shortly. Old William[c] would long since have kicked the bucket had he not been informed from on high that the angels' drill still left something to be desired and, in particular, that when ordered to goose-step they were still failing to throw their legs in the air as prescribed in the regulations. Accordingly he could not yet be re-

---

[a] See this volume, p. 291. - [b] written in December 1847-January 1848 - [c] William I

ceived with the appropriate honours. That is why he has now despatched Frederick Charles to carry out an inspection. [411] It is hoped he will be able to report that Field-Marshal Michael Archangel has succeeded in training the heavenly host to the standard of perfection sought by the Prussians, in which case old William will doubtless make haste to take the heavenly guard-mounting parade in person.

You are quite right, radicalism in France is rapidly becoming more and more threadbare. There is only one man left who has yet to become so and that is Clemenceau. If he gets in he'll shed a whole mass of illusions, above all the illusion that nowadays a bourgeois republic can govern in France without thieving and causing others to thieve. It is just possible that he will then go further. But that is not necessary. All that is necessary is that this last sheet-anchor of the bourgeoisie should show what he is capable of—which, given his present point of view, is nothing.

Here in England the cause is progressing pretty well, even if not in the form that is customary at home. Since 1848 the English parliament has unquestionably been the most revolutionary body in the world and the next elections will mark the beginning of a new epoch, even though it may not necessarily manifest itself as quickly as all that. [a] Workers will appear in Parliament in growing numbers, each one worse than the last. But that is necessary over here. All the scoundrels who at the time of the International played at being bourgeois-radical philistines must appear in Parliament for what they are. Whereupon the masses will become socialist here too. Industrial overproduction will do the rest.

The rumpus in the German party came as no surprise to me. [374] In a philistine country like Germany the party must also have a philistine 'educated' right wing [373] which it will shed when the time comes. In Germany philistine socialism dates back to 1844 and was criticised in the *Communist Manifesto*. It is as immortal as your German philistine himself. So long as the Anti-Socialist Law [37] remains in force, I am not in favour of *our* provoking a split, since there is no parity of weapons. Should these gentlemen, however, themselves bring about a split by attempting to suppress the proletarian nature of the party and replace it with a crudely aesthetic form of sentimental philanthropy

---

[a] See this volume, p. 367.

without guts or substance, then we shall just have to take it as it comes. I am still engaged in dictating the third volume of *Capital*. It is a magnificent book and as a work of science puts even the first one in the shade. As soon as I have it in a ms. other people can also read, I shall be able to devote some time to sorting the papers. I shall then look out your things. [126] Until that time—round about the autumn—I shall have absolutely no chance to turn my hand to anything else. The second volume has been printed and I shall probably be able to send you a copy in a fortnight or so.

Marx's daughters have been keeping well so far. Mme Lafargue's husband is back in jail for another 4 months (for non-payment of a fine), [402] while Mrs Aveling is working hard at propaganda over here, though it may be some time before there is any great success.

I have taken out another five pound money order for you, of which you have doubtless already been advised. I trust it will prove welcome. Well then, take care of your health so that you can join in the little bit of fun that is bound to come pretty soon. I have been keeping well so far, though the doctors say I'm unlikely to be able to mount a horse again—hence unfit for active service, dammit!

For the rest I remain

Ever your old friend

F. Engels

First published abridged in: F. Engels, *Vergessene Briefe (Briefe Friedrich Engels' an Johann Philipp Becker)*, Berlin, 1920 and in full in: Marx and Engels, *Works*, First Russian Edition, Vol. XXVII, Moscow, 1935

Printed according to the original

Published in English in full for the first time

177

ENGELS TO EDUARD BERNSTEIN

IN ZURICH

London, 16 June 1885

Dear Ede,

Last week I returned to you *by registered mail* Rodbertus' two pamphlets from the archives, which I trust you have received. [a] Yesterday

---

[a] One of these was apparently Rodbertus' *Briefe und Socialpolitische Aufsaetze* which Engels asked to be sent in a letter to Bernstein of 8 February 1883 (see present edition, Vol. 46, pp. 431-34).

Karl Kautsky received the complete set of *Frankfurter Zeitungs* containing the various statements. [412] Most amusing. But I'm prepared to bet that even so they will let all this fuss die down again, and that the majority in the parliamentary group will reassure themselves by pointing out that there were mistakes on both sides. The whole thing is primarily just another flash in the pan, but that, too, is a symptom.

Today Frederick Charles inspected the heavenly host and grumbled about the slovenliness of their goose-step. [411]

Your
F. E.

First published, in Russian, in *Marx-Engels Archives*, Book I, Moscow, 1924

Printed according to the original

Published in English for the first time

178

ENGELS TO LAURA LAFARGUE

IN PARIS

London, 16 June 1885

My dear Laura,

Well, you have the same troubles as I have myself! Visitors, on the whole agreeable in themselves, but damned in the way when you have more work to do than they. Here I have been settling down every evening for the last week to write to you, and either visitors or urgent business correspondence steps in. And even now, at half past one in the morning, I have to snatch a few moments to write to you a few lines which will cut a sorry figure alongside of your amiable and lively letters! Well it cannot be helped and you must put up with my scrimmage.

The particulars about Lawroff's dead man might be found out, I think, without much difficulty. But what am I to do in the matter?

Percy is as good as anybody to find that out, but of course he must be paid for his work at the common London price.[a]

Tussy was not here last Sunday[b] — they[c] went on the river somewhere with a chap who has a boat and a tent and they both want as much fresh air as they can get. The British Museum is a nice place enough but not to live opposite to. So I shall not see them before next Sunday.

Kautsky has received and translated Paul's article about *le coeur du coeur du monde, qui vient de cesser de battre (coeur* No. 1 I mean).[d]

Very glad the Germans send some money for the French elections. Though I am sorry that it is the Hamburgers who have done it; because this is intended as a bribe for Liebknecht, to induce him to take *their* side (the *kleinbürgerliche Seite*[e]) in the present storm in a — pot now going on amongst the German parliamentarians.[413] I believe this storm will blow over, for the present at least, but it's a symptom. If the Socialist Law[37] was abolished and we had elbow-room, and if the 3rd book of the *Kapital* was finished I should not care a bit to have it out at once. As it is, I am for a temporising policy. But the split will come some day, and then we shall give the *Spiessbürger*[f] the necessary kick. By the bye I see also from the New York *Sozialist* that there too money has been collected for the French elections.

Poor Paul! I am afraid he will have to pass *la belle saison*[g] in *quod*. Once nailed,[402] I do not see how anything but an *acte de grâce* of old Grévy could get him out. At all events he has now had about one month of it and his elasticity must carry him over the rest.

From Petersburg I hear that the whole of the proof-sheets have arrived and that 18 sheets out of 33 are already translated.[361] This work is almost too quick to be good.

You have no idea how comfortable John Bull feels under his ministerial crisis.[414] Not a bit of excitement. Evening papers, special editions, etc., do not sell at all. The Grand Old Man, as they call Gladstone, disappears from the political foreground quite unnoticed. The ingratitude of this world is shocking indeed. The fact is, Whigs and Radicals have found out, just before the new elections by a revolu-

---

[a] See this volume, p. 273. - [b] 14 June - [c] Eleanor Marx-Aveling and Edward Aveling - [d] the heart of hearts of the world which has ceased to beat (the heart...); see P. Lafargue's obituary on the death of Victor Hugo published anonymously in *Die Neue Zeit*, No. 8, 1885. - [e] petty-bourgeois side - [f] philistines - [g] the fine season

tionised constituency,[299] that they cannot get on together any longer.[415] So there is hope that after the autumn elections Tories and Whigs will coalesce.[a] And then we have *all* landed property on one side, *all* industrial capital on the opposite side, and the working class compelled to face them both — the basis of a revolutionary situation.

Today there is a grand review in heaven. Frederick Charles is inspecting the hosts of the Lord of hosts.[411] I am afraid he will find very great fault with their *Parademarsch*,[b] and send word to old William[c] that they are not yet fit to parade before him. If the Archangel Michael could only have been sent to do duty for a few years with the Prussian Guards!

Nim complains of rheumatism and threatened to drop beer but I told her that was rubbish, and I think she will believe me. Pumps and her children are very well. Percy has the usual rows with his parents. The cheque £ 10.- is enclosed. And herewith — *sur ce* — I remain your old affectionate

F. Engels

First published in: Marx and Engels, *Works*, Second Russian Edition, Vol. 36, Moscow, 1964

Reproduced from the original

Published in English for the first time

179

ENGELS TO HERMANN SCHLÜTER

IN HOTTINGEN-ZURICH

London, 16 June 1885

Dear Mr Schlüter,

1) The two trials at Assizes — that of the *Neue Rheinische Zeitung* and that of the democratic committee — of 1849 both appeared at the time as *Zwei politische Prozesse* and were based on the newspaper report. If you wish to republish one or both, it could be quite effective, and I should write you a foreword to it.[416]

---

[a] See this volume, p. 317. - [b] goose-step - [c] William I

2) It might also be a good thing to republish the *Communist Trial*[a]; for one thing, it will once again show the old Lassalleans that something was already afoot in Germany before the great Ferdinand's[b] time and, for another, the proceedings of the Prussians did, in fact, even then set the pattern for what the Anti-Socialist Law [37] has now made the norm. A preface[c] will be available for this as well, the moment printing is actually in progress; unfortunately my time does not permit me to work in advance and on spec. Again, I haven't got a copy of the Leipzig edition with Marx's later notes.[d] It is typical of the way they used then to conduct their affairs that neither Marx nor I should ever have been sent a copy!

Do you have in your archives Stieber and Wermuth, *Die Communisten-Verschwörungen des 19. Jahrhunderts*[e] (Berlin, Hayn, 1853, 2 parts) — the so-called 'black book'? It contains two addresses from the Central Committee to the League[f] which you might print as an appendix.

3) If I understand you aright, you are thinking of publishing the series of articles from the *Neue Rheinische Zeitung* on the Paris battle in June 1848.[g][417] It's not a bad idea. I could arrange the relevant passages for you, interspersed with a few notes to provide a context, and also whatever is needed from Marx's article in the *Revue der Neuen Rheinischen Zeitung*,[h] etc. Being the *only* contemporary account of the Paris proletariat's battle to take the side of the June fighters, the thing has a certain importance. Nor can the masses be reminded too often of the event. But it's a task that would take at least a week, and I cannot embark on it until the autumn.

4) Various other things from the *Neue Rheinische Zeitung* might follow, but just now I simply haven't got the time to look them out; if you could make some suggestions, we might be able to see. The same applies to other, lesser works of that period by Marx and myself. As soon as the rough ms. of the 3rd volume of *Capital* has been transposed into a legible one — in the autumn, that is — I shall have to put

---

[a] K. Marx, *Revelations Concerning the Communist Trial in Cologne*. - [b] Ferdinand Lassalle - [c] F. Engels, 'On the History of the Communist League'. - [d] K. Marx, 'Epilogue to *Revelations Concerning the Communist Trial in Cologne*'. - [e] Wermuth/Stieber, *Die Communisten-Verschwörungen des neunzehnten Jahrhunderts*. - [f] K. Marx and F. Engels, 'Address of the Central Authority to the League, March 1850'; 'Address of the Central Authority to the League, June 1850'. - [g] 1849 in the original. - [h]K. Marx, *The Class Struggles in France, 1848 to 1850*.

the papers[a] in order. Only then shall I once more obtain a general idea of what is in fact available and be able to look out some suitable stuff. Up till then I shall be more or less working in the dark. So long as the dictation of *Capital*, Book III remains incomplete, my days will be taken up from 10-5, while in the evenings, apart from visitors, I not only have to deal with an ever-increasing volume of correspondence, but also to read over what I have dictated, in addition to revising the French, Italian, Danish and English translations of our things (including the English one of *Capital*[56]), and how, I should like to know, am I to find time for anything else? Hence — as you must realise — I cannot let myself in for anything, unless it is of the utmost urgency.

Besides the afore-mentioned edition of the *Communist Trial*, I would ask you to send me:

3 copies of Marx's *Wage Labour and Capital*.

6 *Communist Manifestos*, Zurich edition, and charge them up to me. I should also be grateful to have a statement of account so that I may know how we stand. We still have copies of Marx's photograph here in both sizes.

Kindly give the enclosed to Ede.

Most cordially yours,

F. Engels

First published in: Marx and Engels, *Works*, First Russian Edition, Vol. XXVII, Moscow, 1935

Printed according to the original

Published in English for the first time

180

ENGELS TO AUGUST BEBEL[1]

IN PLAUEN NEAR DRESDEN

London, 22-24 June 1885
122 Regent's Park Road, N. W.

Dear Bebel,

I hasten to answer your letter of the 19th, received this morning, so that my reply may reach you before you set off on your long journey.

---

[a] Marx's manuscripts

Generally speaking I have been kept informed about recent events, at least so far as public pronouncements are concerned, and have thus been able to read the various effronteries of Geiser and Frohme, as also your short, trenchant replies.[412]

All this mud-slinging is largely attributable to Liebknecht, with his predilection for educated know-alls and for men in bourgeois occupations who can be used to impress your philistine. Nor can he resist a literary or business man who flirts with socialism. But in Germany these are the very people of whom one should most beware, and it is they whom Marx and I have ceaselessly combatted since 1845. Once you've let them into the party, in which they everywhere push themselves to the fore, dissimulation becomes the rule, either because their petty-bourgeois standpoint is in perpetual conflict with that of the proletarian masses, or because they try to vitiate this latter standpoint. Nevertheless, I am convinced that, if things ever really come to a head, Liebknecht will be on our side,—asserting, what's more, that he had never said anything else and that it was we who had stopped him from letting fly any sooner. However, a little object-lesson will have done him no harm.

The split will come as sure as eggs is eggs, but I still maintain that we must not provoke it while the Anti-Socialist Law [37] is in operation. If it is forced upon us, then there'll be nothing for it. But we must be prepared. And that, I think, means hanging on for all we're worth to three positions: 1) the Zurich press and bookshop, 2) the management of the *Sozialdemokrat* and 3) that of the *Neue Zeit*. These are the only positions still in our hands and, notwithstanding the Anti-Socialist Law, they suffice to keep us in touch with the party. All the other positions in the press, though held by philistines, count for very little by comparison with these three. You should be able to foil many of the plots against us. In my opinion, you ought to do everything you can to ensure that, by hook or by crook, these 3 positions remain in our hands. How to set about it you will know better than I. Not surprisingly Ede and Kautsky feel very insecure in their editorial seats and are in need of encouragement. That people are busily intriguing against them is obvious. And they're a couple of competent and really first-rate chaps. In matters of theory, Ede is a very clear-sighted man and, what's more, is witty and has a gift for repartee, but he is still somewhat lacking in self-confidence—nowadays a most unusual trait and, if you consider the megalomania common to even the most insignificant lettered nitwits, a very fortunate one, relatively speaking. Kautsky has picked up a frightful lot of rubbish at university but is doing his utmost to unlearn it again, and both men are reliable, able to tolerate honest criticism and have a correct grasp of essentials. In view of the appalling new generation of literati that has attached itself to the party, two such people are pearls beyond price.

I entirely agree with what you say about our parliamentary representation generally and about the impossibility—in time of peace, as at present—of creating any really proletarian representation. The necessarily more or less bourgeois parliamentarians are an evil no less unavoidable than the professional agitators foisted upon the party from amongst those workers boycotted by the bourgeoisie and hence unemployed. This was a phenomenon already strongly in evidence among the Chartists during the 1839-48 period, and was apparent to me even at that time. If remuneration for deputies is introduced, these fellows will range themselves alongside the predominantly bourgeois and petty-bourgeois, i.e. the 'educated', representatives. But all this will be overcome. My confidence in our proletariat is as absolute as my mistrust of the utterly abject German philistines is unlimited. And when things liven up a bit, the struggle will similarly become keen enough to be conducted *con amore*,[a] while the irritation caused by the pettiness and philistinism with which you now have to contend *en détail* and with which I am familiar from long experience, will evaporate in the wider dimensions of the struggle and then, too, we shall get the right sort of men in parliament. But it's all very well for me to talk—I'm over here, while you are having to do the dirty work, and that is certainly no joke. Anyhow, I am glad that you are physically fit again. Spare your nerves for better times; we shall need them.

The greater part of *Capital*, Book III, has now been dictated from the manuscripts and set out in a legible hand. This preliminary work will be pretty well complete in 5 or 6 weeks' time. Then there will be the very difficult final editing which will require a considerable amount of work. But the thing's brilliant and will have all the impact of a thunderbolt. I daily await the first copies of Book II,[b] one of which will instantly be forwarded to you.

Your old friend
F. E.

---

[a] Here: with enthusiasm. - [b] of *Capital*

23 June. Too late to register this today, so won't go off till tomorrow.

24 June. Berlin papers received with thanks.

First published, in Russian, in *Marx-Engels Archives*, Vol. I (VI), Moscow, 1932

Printed according to the original

Published in English in full for the first time

181

ENGELS TO HERMANN SCHLÜTER

IN HOTTINGEN-ZURICH

London, 1 July 1885

Dear Mr Schlüter,

Herewith the preface to the *Trial*.[a] I have made a note of the other items. It is unlikely that I can do a preface[b] and notes for the *Communist Trial*[c] before the beginning of September. In July I shall not have a moment to spare and in August I must relax at the seaside for a while.

After which I shall also be able to tackle the *June Insurrection*.[417]

I should be *delighted* to see the *Schlesische Milliarde* republished. In addition, you should reprint my biographical note on Wolff from the *Neue Welt* (about 1873 I think), to which I should also do an introduction.[418]

I am still waiting for Volume II of *Capital*. I can't really do anything for you where Meissner is concerned; I have no right to meddle in these matters, and the chap is meticulous.[419]

There are still several hundred portraits of Marx available, in both sizes.

On the whole, everything is going quite well in Germany; our working men will see to it that everything turns out all right.

Yours sincerely,

F. E.

---

[a] F. Engels, 'Preface to the Pamphlet *Karl Marx Before the Cologne Jury*'. - [b] F. Engels, 'On the History of the Communist League'. - [c] K. Marx, *Revelations Concerning the Communist Trial in Cologne*.

Please let me have clean sheets of the *Dühring* [208] so that I can draw up a list of printer's errors. I would also ask that in future you let me have 2 clean proofs, as is customary and, indeed, essential.

If you wish to call the things 'From the *Neue Rheinische Zeitung*', Vols. I, II, etc., I am quite agreeable, of course.

First published in: Marx and Engels, *Works*, First Russian Edition, Vol. XXVII, Moscow, 1935

Printed according to the original

Published in English for the first time

182

ENGELS TO LAURA LAFARGUE

IN PARIS

London, 4 July 1885

My dear Laura,

Herewith the cheque £ 15.- as desired by Paul who I hope does not suffer too much from the heat which ought to be rather trying in Ste Pélagie [402] by this time.

Your adventure with the Russians vividly recalled to me the times when one was never sure that Dupont would not drop in about half past one in the morning with one or two *citoyens* [a] (something in a lightly elevated state) whom he then and there deposited for the night.

Justice announces, as you may have seen, that Reeves (a rather impecunious small man of Fleet St.) is going to publish a translation of Deville's extract of the *Capital* in 'numbers'. This is a dodge against our translation. [420] If it comes out I shall have to declare that Deville's extract is anything but faithful or rather too faithful in the second half, giving all the conclusions and leaving out most of the premises and all the qualifications.

Fortin of Beauvais sends me the beginning of his translation of *The 18th Brumaire*. [b] I have not yet had time to look at it.

I have nearly done dictating of the 3rd volume [c] —what can be dictated. Then, after my return from the seaside (end of August) [421] comes first the sorting of the letters, etc. (and also of the books), and

---

[a] citizens - [b] See this volume, pp. 62-63. - [c] of *Capital*

then the real work with the 3rd volume. Of the 2nd volume no news. If it does not come next week I shall write. These publishers always have some business pretext why a thing should not be brought out at once.

Mohr's trial at Cologne[a] is being reprinted in Zurich.

Of the Russian translation [of] 2nd volume 18 sheets out of 33 are already done.[361]

Now I must go to town on urgent private affairs (cash), so no more today from

Yours ever affectionately,

F. Engels

First published in: Marx and Engels, *Works*, Second Russian Edition, Vol. 36, Moscow, 1964

Reproduced from the original

Published in English for the first time

183

ENGELS TO GERTRUD GUILLAUME-SCHACK[184]

IN BEUTHEN

[Draft]

[London, about 5 July 1885]

Dear Madam,

In reply to your inquiry, I can only say that I am not entitled to provide any information ultimately intended for publication with regard to Marx's and my collaboration on those political writings which we were asked to do *in confidence*. Nor can I accept any responsibility, either in my own or Marx's name, for the French programme as a whole[b] the very nature of which meant that[c] we were at most acting in an advisory capacity. I can, however, tell you *in confidence*, that the *Preamble* of the programme of the *Parti ouvrier*, of the *Roanne* trend, originated with Marx.[422]

If the French are less inclined than the Germans to demand the li-

---

[a] *Karl Marx vor den Kölner Geschwornen. Prozeß gegen den Ausschuß der rheinischen Demokraten...* - [b] 'Programme électoral des travailleurs socialistes', *L'Égalité*, No. 24, 30 June 1880. - [c] Crossed out in the draft: 'we were only represented as advisers'.

mitation of female labour, this is because in French industry, more especially in Paris, female labour plays a comparatively subordinate role. Equal wages for equal work regardless of sex are, so far as I know, demanded by all socialists until such time as wages are totally abolished. That the working woman, because of her particular physiological functions, requires special protection against capitalist exploitation seems clear to me. Those Englishwomen who championed a women's formal right to allow themselves to be as thoroughly exploited by capitalists as men are, have, for the most part, a direct or indirect interest in the capitalist exploitation of both sexes.[a] As for myself, I must confess that I am more interested in the health of the coming generation than in absolute, formal equality between the sexes during the final years of the capitalist mode of production. True equality between men and women can, or so I am convinced, become a reality only when [b] the exploitation of both by capital has been abolished, and private work in the home been transformed into a public industry.

First published in: Marx and Engels, *Works*, First Russian Edition, Vol. XXVII, Moscow, 1935

Printed according to the original

184

ENGELS TO JOHN LINCOLN MAHON [423]

IN LONDON

[Draft]

[London, not earlier than 11 July 1885]

6d. stamps enclosed. Will feel obliged if you send the one copy to America as per address herewith:

F. A. Sorge
Hoboken, N. J.
U. S. America

1 copy 'Commonweal' from July 1st.[c]

Published for the first time

Reproduced from a copy of the draft

[a] This refers to members of the National Society for Women's Suffrage. - [b] Crossed out in the draft: 'capital that has evolved on the basis of male predominance'. - [c] See this volume, p. 298.

185

ENGELS TO LAURA LAFARGUE

IN PARIS

London, 23 July 1885

My dear Laura,

Very glad to learn that our prisoner[a] is going soon again to breathe *l'air pur de la liberté (sans égalité et fraternité)*[b] and [...]^c Of course Deville is quite innocent of the trick of Hyndman and Co.[420] — for it is said that the 'John Broadhouse' who figure-heads as translator, is the immortal Hyndman himself — and I hope the thing may blow over. Perhaps it was merely concocted between Hyndman and Kegan Paul to set us on, for Kegan Paul has not heard from me for a long time, considering that I cannot as yet fix a date when we shall be ready. At all events we cannot have anything about this pretended publication. Of course it would be best if it turned out a mere *Schreckschuss*.[d] But if not, I am bound to declare publicly that the latter half of the résumé does *not* render the original correctly. I told Deville so, before it was printed,[e] and yet it was printed in the old shape, 'because the publisher would not wait'. That could be allowed to pass unnoticed in France, where the French edition is in the market. But it will never do here, so long as there is no English translation out,[56] or so long as it is brought out in competition to that.

The little squabble amongst the German deputies has on the whole had excellent effects. The workingmen have everywhere shown such an energetic front against these ridiculous pretensions that the big men in Parliament are not likely to repeat their attempt at domineering.[374] This our men have done in the most unmistakable way and in spite of all the trammels of the Socialist Law.[37] In the meantime poor Liebknecht is hurrying from one end of Germany to the other preaching concord and telling everybody that there are no differences of principle, that it's all personal squabbles, that both sides have com-

---

[a] Paul Lafargue - [b] fresh air of freedom (without equality and brotherhood) - [c] The next two lines in the original are crossed out by an unknown person and cannot be deciphered. - [d] false alarm - [e] See this volume, pp. 61, 63.

mitted faults, etc.— the hen that has hatched ducklings. He has been hatching 'heducated' socialists for the last twenty years and now obstinately refuses to see that the chickens are ducklings, the socialists are philanthropic *Spiessbürger*.[a]

Most happy am I to see that the *scrutin de liste*[375] invented to perpetuate Opportunist government, is likely to smash up Opportunism altogether.[236] If Clemenceau keeps only one half of what he promises, if he merely *initiates* the break-up of the vast French bureaucracy, it will be an immense progress. On the other hand, even supposing him to really intend being sincere and a man of his word, he will find so many real obstacles, he will so soon be brought to a standstill, that to the Paris electors he will always appear as a traitor. It is a delusion to think that in France Anglo-Saxon, especially American local self-government can be introduced without upsetting the whole bourgeois régime. So, very soon he will have to choose: either drop his reforms and remain bourgeois *avec les bourgeois*[b] or go on and revolutionise himself. I think he will remain bourgeois, and then our time may come.

Schorlemmer is here, has as yet no definite projects for Continental tours, but keeps his mind's eye on Paris. He is out at present, may return before I close this.

Here too we shall have a peaceable revolution in November. The new electorate is sure to change the whole basis of old parties.[299] The Whigs have already declared through their great mouthpiece *The Edinburgh Review* that there must be now 'a parting of the waters': the Radicals are to shift for themselves and the Whigs intend joining the Tories who, they find, are not so bad after all.[424] Whether the Tories will accept them, and on what terms, remains to be seen. The fact is that this alliance has been on the tapis for the last 10 years, but always broke down on the question of the division of the spoil. Another progress: we shall very likely get all the rotten 'representative working men' into Parliament. That is just the place where we want them.

Pumps wants us to go Jersey this year; if we do, and Paul is out, will you come and join us there, and then come over to London? Steamers from *St Malo*— or will you wait in Paris till Jollymeier comes and brings you over? You might ruminate that a bit and let me know. We

---

[a] philistines - [b] with the bourgeois

cannot leave before 8th or 10th August on account of Percy's business.[421]

Love from Nim and Jollymeier.

Yours affectionately,
F. Engels

First published in: Marx and Engels, *Works*, Second Russian Edition, Vol. 36, Moscow, 1964

Reproduced from the original

Published in English for the first time

186

ENGELS TO AUGUST BEBEL [263]

IN ZURICH

London, 24 July 1885

Dear Bebel,

I shall try and see whether this letter finds you in Zurich on the 26th, as you lead me to suppose.

So far as I can see from here, the row in the party is taking just the course we wanted. Frohme has got his comrades into as nasty a fix as possible, which cannot but please us, but luckily Liebknecht is there to save their bacon; he has notified the Society over here that *he* will now go to Frankfurt and put everything to rights [425] but that should this fail, Frohme will have to be thrown out. The part being played by Liebknecht in all this business is the entertaining one of the hen that has hatched out ducklings: he had thought he was rearing 'eddicated' socialists and lo! what emerged from the eggs but a clutch of cits and philistines! And now the worthy hen would have us believe that it's chickens after all, and not ducks, swimming about out there in bourgeois waters. Not that there's anything we can do except take him for what he is, illusions and all, but at Offenbach, if one is to believe the newspaper account, he really has gone a bit too far.[426] Well, little will come of the whole affair save the party's awareness that it harbours two tendencies, *one* of which determines the course taken by the masses, the other that taken by the majority of the self-styled leaders, and that these two courses must increasingly diverge. This will pave the way for an eventual split, and that is no bad thing. Our friends of the Right will think twice before promulgating another ukase.

You have put your finger unerringly on Kautsky's principal weakness. His youthful tendency to make hasty pronouncements has been further reinforced by the lousy methods of teaching history at universities — particularly those in Austria. There, students are systematically taught to produce historical papers with material which they know to be inadequate but are *expected to treat as adequate*, i. e. to write things they themselves must be aware are wrong but yet are supposed to regard as right. Kautsky, of course, began by doing this with considerable brashness. Then came literary life — writing for money, and copiously at that. So that he had absolutely no idea what is meant by really learned work. He thus burnt his fingers badly on a couple of occasions, first with his demographic thing and later with his articles on marriage in primitive times. Indeed in the friendliest possible manner and without mincing my words, I told him as much, nor do I spare him in this regard, mercilessly criticising all his stuff from *that* point of view.[427] Luckily I am able to add by way of consolation that in my callow youth I did exactly the same thing, and that it was only from Marx that I learnt how one ought to work. In fact, it would already seem to have helped quite a lot.

The articles in the Berlin *Zeitung* are undoubtedly by Mehring; I, for one, don't know of anyone else in Berlin who writes so well.[428] The chap has a great deal of talent and a lucid brain, but he's a calculating scoundrel and a born traitor. I hope you will bear this in mind should he return to our midst, as he surely will the moment times have changed.[354]

Walther and his wife came to see me, bringing with them papers with news of the row in the party. They are coming again on Sunday.[a]

I sent off *Capital* II to you in Dresden as soon as it arrived. I have finished dictating the manuscript of III in so far as this was possible, and in the autumn, as soon as I have had a bit of a holiday and attended to all manner of other urgent work, I shall embark on the final editing. However, my mind is at rest, the ms. is now available in a legible hand and can, if the worst comes to the worst, be printed as it stands, even if I were to kick the bucket in the meantime. Until this

---

[a] 26 July

had been done I was constantly on tenterhooks. Not that the editing of 3 very important parts, i. e. $^2/_3$ of the whole, won't involve a hell of a lot of work. But it will all come right in the end, and I look forward to the hullaballoo it will create when it appears. In the autumn we shall see two peaceful revolutions—the elections in France and over here.

In France, the *scrutin de liste* [375] invented by the out-and-out Republicans and introduced by the Gambettists so as to make sure of remaining perpetually in power by means of the enforced election of lawyers and journalists, especially Parisians, will probably lead to the wholesale ejection of the Gambettists and will almost certainly bring Clemenceau and the Radicals [429] to power, if not immediately, then in the near future. Of the bourgeois parties that now exist, they are the only *remaining possibility*. Clemenceau's panacea is departmental and communal self-government, i. e. decentralisation of the administration and abolition of bureaucracy. The very fact of embarking on this would, in France, be a revolution greater than any that has happened since 1800. But government by the Radicals in France means above all the emancipation of the proletariat from the *old* revolutionary tradition and a direct struggle between proletariat and bourgeoisie, i. e. the establishment of an ultimate, unequivocal state of hostilities.

In this country the new suffrage [299] will completely upset the old state of the parties. The alliance between Whigs and Tories [430] to form one big Conservative party, having for its basis landed property *as a single whole* rather than divided into two camps as hitherto, and comprising all the conservative elements of the bourgeoisie—banks, high finance, trade and some of the industries; alongside this, on the other hand, the radical bourgeoisie, i. e. the bulk of large-scale industry, the petty bourgeoisie and the proletariat as a tail for the time being, awakening once more to political life—that is a revolutionary starting-point such as England has not seen since 1689. [431]

And on top of all that, old William,[a] now on his last legs. It promises great things. You'll see.

Your

F. E.

First published, in Russian, in *Marx-Engels Archives*, Vol. I (VI), Moscow, 1932

Printed according to the original
Published in English in full for the first time

---

[a] William I

187

ENGELS TO EDUARD BERNSTEIN

IN ZURICH

[London, 24 July 1885]

Dear Ede,

Bebel has written to say he will be in Zurich on or about the 26th inst.— the enclosed lines are for him [a]; if he doesn't turn up, you will know how to deal with it.

Schorlemmer sends his regards.

The coming autumn elections in France [b] and England [299] will be the beginning of the end, and I trust we shall also see the end of old William.[c] Now that the Russians seem to have come to a standstill, we shall doubtless have to make a start ourselves. And, if the three great Western nations begin to move, that will also do.

Your
F. E.

First published, in Russian, in *Marx-Engels Archives*, Book I, Moscow, 1924

Printed according to the original

Published in English for the first time

188

ENGELS TO NIKOLAI DANIELSON [1]

IN ST PETERSBURG [432]

London, 8 August 1885

Dear Sir,

I have considered your proposal to write a special preface for the Russian edition, but I do not see how I could do so in a satisfactory way. [433]

---

[a] This probably refers to the previous letter. - [b] See this volume, pp. 320 and 330. -
[c] William I

If you consider that it will be better not to refer to Rodbertus at all, then I would propose that you leave out the whole of the second part of the preface. As an exposition of the author's [a] place in the history of economical science, it is far too incomplete, unless justified by the special circumstances under which it was written, viz. the attacks of the Rodbertus clique. This clique is extremely influential in Germany, makes a deal of noise, and will no doubt soon also be heard of in Russia. It is such a very cheap and convenient way of settling the whole question, to say that our author merely copied Rodbertus, [225] that it is sure to be repeated everywhere where our author is read and discussed. But of all these matters you are the best judge, and so I leave the matter entirely in your own hands, the more so as I have not the remotest idea what your censorship would allow to pass and what not.

There are some favourable rumours spread here about our mutual friend [362]; can you give me any news?

Yours faithfully,

P. W. Rosher [363]

First published, in Russian, in *Minuvshiye gody*, No. 2, St Petersburg, 1908

Reproduced from the original

Published in English in full for the first time

189

ENGELS TO LAURA LAFARGUE

IN PARIS

London, 8 August 1885

My dear Laura,

To my astonishment I find that in all copies [b] I can lay my hands on, the index has been omitted in the binding. I have at once written to Meissner for explanations and shall send you a copy as soon as received.

---

[a] Marx's - [b] of the second volume of *Capital*

It is quite right that you should go to see Mother Vaillant at Villerville but that is no reason why you should not see us. We intend leaving here on Tuesday 11th, and shall be back September 11th at latest.[421] Schorlemmer will leave about same time for Germany and return via Paris about middle of September, and we cannot see any reason why you should not then come over with him. If Paul cannot go to Bordeaux *now*, he may manage to go *then* and so everything would be for the best.[434]

Your letter reminds me that indeed Deville's publisher can stop the translation for *one* year after publication of the original.[435] But that year has passed, as it is now two years since I had the manuscript at Eastbourne,[a] after which time it was brought out almost immediately. The man who is to bring out the translation is William Reeves, 185 Fleet St., but we cannot either procure a copy or hear anything more about it.

Tussy and Edward were to leave yesterday for Deal, but I have not yet had a note from them with their address. They intend staying from 10-14 days. The Kautskys have gone to Eastbourne. The mother Kautsky is a singularly unaffected woman for a German authoress. I have read one of her novels,[b] it is not at all bad. However I advised her to study Balzac and she has taken a few volumes, but will her French be up to that sort of reading?

The *scrutin de liste*[375] is no doubt at first against our people, but that does not matter so long as our people are not more numerous. If they succeed in making a decent show in Paris and some great provincial centres, there will be a necessity for the Radicals next time to make a combined list with them in some places, and then some may get in; besides by that time, they will be a good deal stronger, and a good many of the outside sects, Possibilists,[237] etc., will be broken up. If this next election[c] brings Clemenceau into office, I shall be quite satisfied. He is the last man, as far as I can see, that the bourgeoisie has to put forward. After him *le déluge*.[436] And at the same time the elections here with an entirely new electorate[299] which must be the beginning of the end; and old William[d] on his last legs (he fell upstairs again yesterday at Gastein) — we shall see what we shall see.

After the elections here — which will, I hope, carry all the Potters, Cremers and other *faux frères*[e] into Parliament — the basis for a so-

---

[a] See this volume, p. 46. - [b] M. Kautsky, *Stefan vom Grillenhof*. - [c] See this volume, p. 330. - [d] William I - [e] false brothers

cialist movement here will become broader and firmer. And therefore I am glad to see that Hyndmanite movement will not take serious roots anywhere and that the simple, clumsy, wonderfully blundering, but *sincere* movement of the Socialist League [346] is slowly and apparently surely gaining ground. *Justice* is of an increasing vacuousness, and *To-Day* is dying, if not dead.

Good-bye — I have to write a heap of letters yet — love from all of us.

Yours affectionately,

F. Engels

First published in: Marx and Engels, *Works*, Second Russian Edition, Vol. 36, Moscow, 1964

Reproduced from the original

Published in English for the first time

190

ENGELS TO KARL KAUTSKY [437]

IN EASTBOURNE

[Jersey,] Sunday [16 August 1885]

Dear Kautsky,

After sundry vagaries we landed here the day before yesterday morning and, after some difficulty, found accommodation. [421] The little place has not changed much in 10 years and is still quite pleasant when the weather is fine. We had a very good passage, though towards morning Nim, Pumps and Lily were somewhat overcome, or rather only the last two; Nim lay down and felt better. In Guernsey we unloaded some 10 calves and 20 sheep, a pitiful sight, for all of them were sea-sick. A supply of Pilsener beer has been discovered and is being rapidly consumed; there is also very good red wine at 10d. a bottle. I shall now leave the party to its own devices, but if you have anything of interest to tell me I shall be glad to hear about it. Address

2 Royal Crescent, Jersey. Kind regards from us all to you, your wife and your mother. [a]

Your
F. E.

First published, in Russian, in *Marx-Engels Archives*, Vol. I (VI), Moscow, 1932

Printed according to the original
Published in English for the first time

191

ENGELS TO NIKOLAI DANIELSON

IN ST PETERSBURG

Jersey, 25 August 1885
31 Roseville Street

Dear Sir,

I have received your letters 6/18 and 9/21 August to which I shall reply on my return to London. [421] In the meantime herewith the letter for the Editor of the *Сѣверный вѣстникъ*. [438] The reply you have, I suppose. If not, please write as before to London, when on my return in 14 days hence I will send a fresh copy.

Yours truly,
P. W. Rosher [363]

First published, in Russian, in *Minuvshiye gody*, No. 2, St Petersburg, 1908

Reproduced from the original
Published in English for the first time

192

ENGELS TO HERMANN SCHLÜTER [439]

IN HOTTINGEN-ZURICH

Jersey, 26 August 1885
31 Roseville Street

Dear Mr Schlüter,

Sheets 16 and 17[b] arrived in London after I had left — the Kaut-

---

[a] Louise and Minna Kautsky - [b] of the second edition of Engels' *Anti-Dühring*

skys and Avelings were also away so there was no one there capable of sending on the large quantity of incoming printed matter in some semblance of order. It was not until Monday that Mrs Aveling arrived at my house and posted me the sheets. These went back to you corrected yesterday, Wednesday. A lot of words had been inserted that do not appear in the original and they completely distort the sense. And on sheet 17 in particular the pages are in a complete muddle: 257, 262, 263, 258, 259, 264, etc., which is totally inadmissible in this, the most important chapter of the book, and that is why I have taken the precaution of writing to you.

I shall be staying here for another fortnight.[421] *After Saturday, 3 September* everything had best be sent to London again.— We are literally stifling here during the present spell of fine weather, for the lack of rain has led to a serious water shortage on this pretty little island. I neither see nor hear anything of the party, which, if the latest storm in the parliamentary tea cup[374] is anything to go by, is no calamity. Kindest regards to Ede.

Yours,

F. E.

First published in: Marx and Engels, *Works*, First Russian Edition, Vol. XXVII, Moscow, 1935

Printed according to the original

Published in English for the first time

193

ENGELS TO KARL KAUTSKY

IN LONDON

[Jersey,] 6 September 1885

Dear Kautsky,

We leave here[a] on Thursday[b] and therefore hope to see you both at our house on Sunday as usual. The *Volks-Zeitung* and □[c] received

[a] See this volume, p. 325.-[b] 10 September-[c] This may refer to one of Louis Viereck's articles (Viereck = square in German).

with thanks. The chap wants to ingratiate himself with his papa. [440] The latter, however, has better things to do. Not content with having created a French republic in 1870, [92] he must now do his utmost to create a Spanish one. [441] I hope he succeeds. What jackasses these great men are!

Kindest regards to your wife and yourself from all of us.

Your
F. E.

First published, in Russian, in *Marx-Engels Archives*, Vol. I (VI), Moscow, 1932

Printed according to the original

Published in English for the first time

194

ENGELS TO HERMANN SCHLÜTER [439]

IN HOTTINGEN-ZURICH

Jersey, 9 September 1885

Final *Dühring* proof received yesterday. [208] I shall be going home tomorrow [421] and hence can do nothing with it here, especially as sheet 18 is in London, still to be corrected. The re-direction to this address of stuff sent to London has been handled very badly this year, hence the delay. My first task will be to see to these corrections as well as the preface. [a] The rest has been taken note of and will follow. Please send the Wolff biography from the *Neue Welt* to London straight away; it, too, will then be promptly dealt with. [418] Kindest regards.

Yours,
F. Engels

First published in: Marx and Engels, *Works*, First Russian Edition, Vol. XXVII, Moscow, 1935

Printed according to the original

Published in English for the first time

---

[a] F. Engels, 'On the History of the Prussian Peasants. Introduction to Wilhelm Wolff's Pamphlet *The Silesian Milliard*'.

195

ENGELS TO KARL KAUTSKY

IN LONDON

[Jersey,] Thursday [10 September 1885]

Dear Kautsky,

We are still here thanks to a violent storm and while it lasts I cannot be responsible for allowing the children to sail. Nor is it likely that we shall be able to leave tomorrow. [421] So that puts paid to the prospect of seeing you both again at my home on Sunday.[a] Kindest regards to your wife.

Your
F. E.

First published, in Russian, in *Marx-Engels Archives*, Vol. I (VI), Moscow, 1932

Printed according to the original

Published in English for the first time

196

ENGELS TO LAURA LAFARGUE

IN PARIS

London, 22 September 1885

My dear Laura,

Yesterday when I was going to write to you, people came in and made one miss the post. So I can only today send you the cheque £ 10. - which is all I can spare until I get some more money in which I hope won't be long. I have not heard from Schorlemmer but sup-

---

[a] 13 September; see also this volume, p. 323.

pose you must as you expect him, and this being the case I naturally pass a step further and give expression to the expectation that he will bring you over with him which will be some time next week. We are quite ready for you.

While you had a fine row in Paris last Sunday,[442] Tussy and Aveling had one here in the East End, I will forward you *The Daily News* which has the best report and a leading article.[443] They were here this morning, my opinion is that unless they can, get the Radicals[415] who are very eager, apparently, on their side, to take the matter up, *le jeu ne vaut pas la chandelle.*[a] The Socialists are nowhere, the Radicals are a power. If the question can be made one for which a dozen Radicals will have themselves arrested, the government will give way — if only in view of the elections.[b] If only Socialists are the victims, they will go to prison without any effect.

I like the systematic and theoretically correct way in which the French go about working the *scrutin de liste.*[375] Each party makes a complete list of its own. The consequence will be that everywhere the relatively strongest party will get all their own men in, the rest none. But at the same time each party will count itself and know its strength. And at the next elections, the necessary result will come out: that the parties nearest to each other will combine for a joint list according to their relative strength — unless indeed this is not already done now on the eve of the voting. *Scrutin de liste* compels Radicals[429] and Socialists to have a joint list, as it will gradually compel Opportunists and Monarchists to join in a common list, at least in sundry departments. But it is characteristic of the *génie français*[c] that this can only come out as the result of actual experience. It is this ideological, absolute character which gives to French political history its classical form, as compared to the muddled politics of other nations.

I am overwhelmed with proof-sheets, revisions, prefaces to write, etc., etc., so that I have not had the time yet to look seriously at your translation of the *Manifest.*[444] As soon as the most urgent business is off, end of this week I hope, I shall go at it and then we can discuss the matter here. I am glad you are at last taking the bushel off your light and helping us to get some good things translated into French, our own native Frenchmen being apparently unable to understand Ger-

---

[a] The game is not worth the candle. - [b] See this volume, p. 361. - [c] French mind

man. When you are once at it, you will continue by the law of the force of inertia, and gradually begin to like the treadmill.

Now the post-time is up and so good-bye until we see you here when I hope you will bring the rest of your translation.

Nim sends her love.

Yours affectionately,

F. Engels

First published in: Marx and Engels, *Works*, Second Russian Edition, Vol. 36, Moscow, 1964

Reproduced from the original

Published in English for the first time

197

ENGELS TO HERMANN SCHLÜTER

IN HOTTINGEN-ZURICH

London, 23 September 1885

Dear Mr Schlüter,

I. You will have received all the proofs of the *Dühring*.[208] They were sent off from here on the 13th and 14th. If anything is missing kindly let me know; the type-setting was such that there could be absolutely no question of its being printed unless corrected by me.

The last clean proof to arrive here was No. 14. I await the remainder for the list of printing errors. Enclosed a provisional list which corrects a great deal of nonsense, much of which I myself had doubtless allowed to stand. However I shall go through the whole thing once again.

Herewith also and at long last the preface[a] which caused me much toil and sweat. In the first place there were numerous interruptions. But then again my knowledge of natural science was very rusty and there was much I had to look up.

---

[a] Engels' preface to the second edition of *Anti-Dühring*.

II. Please send me if possible (along with the preface) proofs (in duplicate) of *Marx vor den Geschwornen*,[a] or at any rate clean proofs for the list of printing errors. The original edition is not devoid of bad errors; indeed, the worthy compositors sometimes exercise their minds more than the author would wish.

III. 'Preface',[b] etc., to the *Communist Trial*[c] will follow this week provided there are no interruptions.

IV. Immediately after that I shall put Lupus'[d] biography to rights for the *Schlesische Milliarde* as well as anything else appertaining to it.[418] This will follow in a few days.

Please send me clean proofs of everything as well as proofs of my prefaces, etc. Also 12 copies of each of the above.

I am also seeing to Marx's photograph.

Then I shall get on with re-writing the *Peasant War*[213] as soon as I have got the revision of the French[444] and English translations[e] off my back.

Now that I am back home[421] the correction of proofs will be attended to speedily and punctually.

I have had a good few bones to pick with Mr Meissner about the get-up of the 2nd volume of *Capital*. In the preface and text the type is all jumbled up, although I had already gone a long way towards sorting this out in the proofs, so far as it was possible to do so. No excuse for that. Moreover, there are 500 copies with no index at all. I enclose one copy for the archives.[144]

□[f] is incorrigible.[g] His appeal to his papa is touching[440]; the old man will take a stick to him.

With best wishes,

Yours,

F. Engels

First published in: Marx and Engels, *Works*, First Russian Edition, Vol. XXVII, Moscow, 1935

Printed according to the original

Published in English for the first time

---

[a] *Karl Marx vor den Kölner Geschwornen* - [b] F. Engels, 'On the History of the Communist League'. - [c] K. Marx, *Revelations Concerning the Communist Trial in Cologne*. - [d] Wilhelm Wolff's - [e] of the first volume of *Capital* (see also Note 56) - [f] Louis Viereck (Viereck = square in German) - [g] See this volume, pp. 323-24.

198

ENGELS TO EDUARD BERNSTEIN

IN ZURICH

London, 8 October 1885

Dear Ede,

I enclose herewith the introduction[a] to the *Revelations Concerning the Trial in Cologne*.[b] If you want to print it initially as a feuilleton in the *Sozialdemokrat*, I should have no objection. Only you must come to some arrangement with Schlüter, who is probably awaiting it anxiously. Tell him he will be getting the notes and the proofs of Marx's text tomorrow, as also instructions about what to print of the enclosures[c] from Stieber.[d]

Karl Kautsky will be sending you a few *Kölnische Zeitungs* containing the first rational report on events in Bulgaria.[445] The correspondent is in Belgrade and is well-informed, and since as yet Bismarck's interests have not provoked a hushing-up order, the report can, in fact, be regarded as an honest one. So the Russians have fallen into their own trap. They forgot that, as a lieutenant in the Prussian Guards, Alexander Battenberg is rightly relying on his 'comrade' William.[e]

You worry too much about someone 'succeeding' you on the *Sozialdemokrat*. But the best of it is that they couldn't really put anyone in your place; any attempt on the part of those gentry to put one of their milksops would fail because 1) no one of that ilk would voluntarily go into exile, 2) the party would soon put a stop to it, nor would they continue to support such a paper. If you go, the *Sozialdemokrat* goes with you, and this coincidence is all to the good. August[f] is likewise of the opinion that the Zurich establishments[g] should in all circumstances remain in our hands, as indeed they probably will, since they would only be a burden to others. It is up to you, I believe, to ensure that we retain the press and bookshop, in which case the matter of the

---

[a] F. Engels, 'On the History of the Communist League'. - [b] K. Marx, *Revelations Concerning the Communist Trial in Cologne*. - [c] K. Marx and F. Engels, 'Address of the Central Authority to the League, March 1850' and 'Address of the Central Authority to the League, June 1850'. - [d] Wermuth/Stieber, *Die Communisten-Verschwörungen des neunzehnten Jahrhunderts*. - [e] William I - [f] Bebel - [g] the editorial board, bookshop and the press of the newspaper *Der Sozialdemokrat*

Sozialdemokrat will resolve itself—if the worst comes to the worst—through the issue of a new paper after the demise of the present one. But you rate these gentlemen's offensive power too high.

The acquittal in Chemnitz is splendid. [446] So it was too much of a good thing even for a Saxon judiciary.

The French elections mark a great advance. As I had previously said,[a] the *scrutin de liste* [375] has eliminated the Opportunists. [447] But that it would eliminate them so thoroughly, that the upper, middle and part of the lower middle classes would take refuge with the Monarchists, and do so *en masse*, was something that could not have been foreseen—not, at any rate, outside France. The Opportunists played at being a 'Directory' and such was their corruption that it far outstripped even that of the Second Empire. But they didn't guarantee your bourgeois the peace and quiet that would be guaranteed him by a monarchy. The relapse into monarchism, here dubbed *Orleanism*, was all the more natural in that the entire *Centre gauche*[b] (Ribot, *Journal des Débats*, etc.) are simply Orleanists disguised as Republicans; so that people prefer genuine Orleanists, and are even content, if there is no other alternative, with Bonapartists and Legitimists. The second ballots may already witness a setback, the bourgeois having taken fright at his own electoral victory, and hence a swing to radicalism. If not there will soon be a set-to. [448]

This much, at any rate, has been won—the ousting of the parties of the Centre, Monarchists versus Radicals, the few Centre Party deputies compelled to choose between joining one or the other. The situation is thus a *revolutionary* one. No one in France seriously believes in the monarchy as such, if only because of the vast number of Pretenders. But there is some possibility of the Orleanists attempting a coup, in which case there would be a show-down. At all events, this is how the question is presented: either *la république en danger*,[c] or the setting up of a 'radical' republic. There would seem to be every probability that the latter will prevail. But then the Radicals [429] will not only have to abide by their promises[a] and replace Napoleon's centralised administration with the kind of self-government exercised by the departments and communes between 1792 and 1798; they will also have to rely on the support of the Socialists. We could wish for no more favourable situation. France remains faithful to her own logico-dialectical course of development. Contradictions are never sup-

---

[a] Cf. this volume, p. 317. - [b] left centre - [c] Here: endanger the Republic.

pressed for very long, but are constantly being fought out. And we can wish for nothing better.

That the Socialists have so few votes (a source of considerable chagrin to Lafargue) is perfectly natural.[449] The French working man does not chuck away his ballot paper. And since in France there are still *living* parties and not, as in Germany, only dead or dying ones, it is far from politic to vote for a Socialist who has no prospects, if by so doing one puts a Radical in the minority and an Opportunist in the majority. The fact is that there are considerable drawbacks to the practice of nominating candidates as a measure of strength in France, as there may be in some parts of Germany as soon as life returns to the political scene there. When once the course of things in France enables the Socialists to become a political opposition, i. e. when Clemenceau finally comes to the helm, we shall instantly gain millions of votes. But one shouldn't try and insist upon the French developing along *German* lines, although that is what many of our best men in Germany are doing.

A final verdict will not, of course, be possible until the second ballot is over.

Your

F. E.

First published, in Russian, in *Marx-Engels Archives*, Book I, Moscow, 1924

Printed according to the original

Published in English for the first time

199

ENGELS TO HERMANN SCHLÜTER

IN HOTTINGEN-ZURICH

London, 9 October 1885

Dear Mr Schlüter,

Yesterday I sent the introduction[a] to the *Cologne Trial*[b] to Ede in case he wished to print it beforehand in the *Sozialdemokrat*, in which

---

[a] F. Engels, 'On the History of the Communist League'. - [b] K. Marx, *Revelations Concerning the Communist Trial in Cologne*.

case he would have to arrange matters with you. [a] Herewith now the list of contents to show you how it has been arranged; also printing errors in, and notes on, the Leipzig edition of 1875. [450] I have included only the London Central Authority's two Addresses of March and June [b]; the *Cologne Address* of December 1850 [c] offers nothing new in the way of theory, being a detailed account of the party's break-up which today would be of importance only in a *circumstantial* history of the movement of those days.

The thing has got badly behindhand—through no fault of my own. *La bravoure, c'est dans le ventre,* [d] as Marshal Davout once said to his host, Marx's father-in-law, [e] when the latter congratulated him on his appetite. *L'esprit, c'est dans le ventre* [f] is what I say, after discovering to what depths of stupidity and incapacity one can be reduced by catarrh of the stomach. To sweat away for five hours at one page and then furiously consign what one has written to the flames — WELL, it's all over now, not to return for a very long time, or so I hope.

Tomorrow I shall tackle the introduction to the *Schlesische Milliarde.* [418]

As regards the June battle, however, there's nothing doing yet. I have become convinced that the things from the *Neue Rheinische Zeitung* can't be printed on their own without a *real* history of events. [417] But this would call for specialised studies which can't be done until I have sorted out the piles of Marx's pamphlets, because only then shall I know *what* stuff I have yet to procure for the purpose. And only then could I embark on my studies. So for the time being this will have to be shelved.

With kindest regards,

Yours,

F. Engels

First published in: Marx and Engels, *Works*, First Russian Edition, Vol. XXVII, Moscow, 1935

Printed according to the original

Published in English for the first time

---

[a] See this volume, p. 329. - [b] K. Marx and F. Engels, 'Address of the Central Authority to the League, March 1850'; 'Address of the Central Authority to the League, June 1850'. - [c] 'Proposal from the London District of the Communist League to the Central Authority in Cologne'. - [d] Bravery begins in the stomach. - [e] Ludwig von Westphalen - [f] Thinking begins in the stomach.

200

ENGELS TO LAURA LAFARGUE
IN PARIS

London, 13 October 1885

My dear Laura,

I return you by this post the first ten leaflets of the *Manifest* [444] — I was compelled to break off, firstly because it is 5 o'clock and secondly because there is a *lacune* of considerable extent which I cannot fill up. Paul I hope will send me what is wanting at once, and I will return it if possible same day. For I see now that it will not take me long. To tell you the truth, a translation of the *Manifest* always frightens me — it reminds me of weary hours spent in vain on that most untranslatable of documents. But you have hit the nail on the head. There are only two passages where you evidently were interrupted and did not catch the exact meaning. Otherwise the work is excellently done, and for the first time the pamphlet will appear in French in a form that we can be proud of and that will give the reader an idea of what the original is. As you go on towards the end, practice will make you still more perfect, and you will more and more, not translate, but reproduce in the other language. You will therefore take my notes — where the meaning is not in question — as mere suggestions on the value of which you will have to decide. I am so out of practice in speaking and writing French that positively an hour's chat with Johnny [a] acts upon me as a refresher upon a German Counsel, and really revives my capacity of thinking in French more than ever I should have dreamt.

I am glad indeed that you have taken this job in hand; that you would succeed if you once put your shoulder to the wheel, I never doubted, but I am glad to read the *thing done*. Now we have got you in harness and will do our best to keep you in it. It will be of infinite use to the movement in France, for you may be sure the learning of German will not make much progress for some time amongst them, and even those that do learn it, learn it like schoolboys and without perhaps ever speaking to a native. Poor Fortin's translation [b] do give me trouble enough — the German words are mere skeletons to him, no

_____
[a] Jean Longuet - [b] the French translation of Marx's *The Eighteenth Brumaire of Louis Bonaparte*

flesh and blood—how can he reproduce them in French! And Mohr's vigorous German too!

Well here's to your health and success, after the *Manifest* anything you may tackle will appear child's play!

Dinner bell—so good-bye,

Yours ever,

F. E.

First published in: Marx and Engels, *Works*, Second Russian Edition, Vol. 36, Moscow, 1964

Reproduced from the original

Published in English for the first time

201

ENGELS TO KARL KAUTSKY

IN LONDON

[London, 14 October 1885]

The latest act is called:
* 'The Factory and Workshops Act, 1878, 41. Victoria, Chapter 16' *—and is obtainable from
* P. S. King & Son
Canada Building
King St., Westminster. *
Published with commentary in:
* 'The Factory & Workshops Act 1878'—by Alex Redgrave, Her Majesty's Inspector of Factories. 2nd ed., London, Shaw & Sons, Fetter Lane and Crane Court, Law Printers and Publishers. * 1879. 238 pages small octavo. *5 shillings.*
The act itself costs a shilling at most.

Your

F. E.

First published in *Aus der Frühzeit des Marxismus. Engels Briefwechsel mit Kautsky*, Prag, 1935

Printed according to the original

Published in English for the first time

Das Kapital.

Kritik der politischen Oekonomie.

Von

Karl Marx.

Zweiter Band.

Buch II: Der Cirkulationsprocess des Kapitals.

Herausgegeben von Friedrich Engels.

Das Recht der Uebersetzung ist vorbehalten.

A mon ami P. Lavroff
London, 11 Julai 1885. *F. Engels*

Hamburg
Verlag von Otto Meissner.
1885.

Зак. 674 офс. 70 г. контур Рогова Светогорка

Title page of the first edition of Marx's *Capital*, Volume II, with Engels'
dedication to Pyotr Lavrov

202

ENGELS TO PYOTR LAVROV [451]

IN PARIS

[London,] 20 October 1885

My dear Lavrov,

Greatly to my annoyance I am unable to help you with sources for a history of Chartism. [452] All my papers, books, journals, etc., which date back to that period went astray during the upheavals of 1848-49. The chief source, *The Northern Star*, is nowhere to be found, even in the north of England (Harney, its former editor-in-chief, is seeking in vain to get hold of a set). What the bourgeois have written on the subject is for the most part false; nor have I ever concerned myself with such literature. It's unfortunate, for if Harney doesn't write his memoirs, the history of the first great workers' party will be lost for ever. [453]

Yours ever and with regret,

F. E.

First published in: Marx and Engels, *Works*, First Russian Edition, Vol. XXVII, Moscow, 1935

Printed according to the original

Translated from the French

Published in English for the first time

203

ENGELS TO SALO FAERBER

IN BRESLAU

London, 22 October 1885

Dear Sir,

I have received your esteemed note of the 15th, [454] though the seal was badly damaged; this I enclose herewith to the greater glory of Mr Stephan. [455]

Since 1848 I, too, have frequently maintained that Russian tsardom is the last refuge and chief military reserve of European reaction. However there have been many changes in Russia over the past 20 years. The so-called emancipation of the peasants has created a thoroughly revolutionary situation in that it has placed the peasants in a situation in which they can neither live nor die. The rapid development of large-scale industry and its means of communication, the banks, etc., have merely aggravated this situation. Russia is faced with its own 1789. The Nihilists, [356] on the one hand, and a financial crisis on the other are symptomatic of this situation. Prior to the last loan, things had got to such a pitch that the Russian government was unable to raise money even in Berlin unless the loan was guaranteed by a representative assembly. Even Mendelssohn imposed this condition. At this point, when tsardom was in dire straits, Bismarck stepped in and authorised a loan, admittedly of a paltry 15 million pounds, a drop in the ocean, but enough to provide a few years' respite. [182] By doing so, Bismarck subjugated Russia, which even today cannot get money without him, but by the same token he also put off the Russian revolution and that certainly did not suit his book either. It is the first time Bismarck has done something that has not indirectly and contrary to his will turned out to our advantage and if he carries on in the same way we may no longer have any use for him.

So whether the Russians are to get any more money depends primarily on Bismarck and, if he consents, the financial philistines of Germany will be only too delighted to fall into the trap set for them. The fact that they will lose their money in the process concerns me not at all; on the contrary, it will serve them right, nor will the so-called German national capital suffer much in the process, since the portion we are interested in consists of ironworks, factories and other instruments of production, which can hardly be loaned to the Russians. The so-called money capital that is being lent is to a great extent bogus capital, lines of credit, and this is of little consequence. What would be of far greater consequence would be to make it difficult, if not impossible, for the Russians to obtain credit, but on this score your typical German punter has more faith in Bismarck than in us. At the moment it's quite impossible for me to spend time on an attempt to reduce the question of Russian state credits to the size it deserves; a work of that kind, however timely and worthwhile, would nevertheless call for a study of Russian conditions from Russian sources. As regards the actual financial side, a table showing the Russian national debt for the past few years together with lists of stock market prices would suffice, but in the case of economic conditions within the country itself a great deal of study would be necessary if one was to form an accurate opinion. One of the main works is a survey carried out by the Russian War Ministry under the title *Военно-статистическій сборникъ IV. Россія*,[a] St Petersburg, 1871. Also:

А. Скребицкій, *Крестьянское дѣло въ царствованіе Императора Александра II*,[b] Bonn, 1862-68, 4 volumes, about 5,000 pages in all.

Also the сборники статистическихъ свѣдѣній[c] of the individual *gouvernements*,[d] in particular Moscow and Tver, and Янсонъ, *Сравнительная статистика Россіи и западно-европейскихъ государствъ*,[e] St Petersburg, 1880, several volumes.

The Russian budgets aren't worth the paper they are written on. Sheer lies and invention, more so even than those presented in Prussia prior to 1848.

As to an evaluation of the armies now reorganised along Prussian lines, this is a sheer impossibility. We do know, however, that Austria and, to an even greater extent, Russia, lack the large educated class which alone can supply an adequate number of officers suitable for employment in armies of this size, and that, according to the account of their own General Kuropatkin,[f] the Russians' conduct of operations in 1878 in Turkey was inferior to that of the Prussians in 1806.[456]

Liebknecht's letter returned herewith.[457]

I am, Sir,

Your obedient servant,

F. Engels

First published in: Marx and Engels, *Works*, First Russian Edition, Vol. XXVII, Moscow, 1935

Printed according to the original

Published in English for the first time

---

[a] *Military Statistical Miscellany IV. Russia* - [b] A. Skrebitsky, *Peasants' Question during the Reign of Emperor Alexander II*. - [c] statistical miscellanies - [d] gubernias - [e] Yanson, *Russia and West European States: Comparative Statistics*. - [f] [Kuropatkin] А. Куропаткинъ, *Ловча, Плевна и Шейново. (Изъ исторіи русско-турецкой войны 1877—1878 гг.)* (Lovech, Pleven and Sheinovo. (From the History of the Russo-Turkish War of 1877-78)); idem, *Дѣйствія отрядовъ генерала Скобелева въ русско-турецкую войну 1877—1878 годовъ. Ловча и Плевна* (Actions of General Skobelev's Detachments during the Russo-Turkish War of 1877-78. Lovech and Pleven).

204

ENGELS TO AUGUST BEBEL [263]

IN PLAUEN NEAR DRESDEN

London, 28 October 1885

Dear Bebel,

Liebknecht's defeat in Saxony makes me feel sorry for him as a man, but in other respects it can do him no harm. He sets far too much store by popularity, to which he is prepared to sacrifice more than is proper, and it will therefore do him good to see for once that no amount of concessions to the Right will be of any avail, particularly when suffrage is qualified by age and property, in which case they won't even earn him the vote of the petty bourgeoisie. [458]

Your news about the independent spirit of the masses gave me much pleasure. However, the gentlemen of the right wing will refuse to credit it until some of them have been made an example of; they live within the orbit of small cliques and what they hear they assume to be the voice of the people. The scales will soon fall from their eyes.

Chronic pressure on all the crucial branches of industry continues without remission, not only in this country, but also in France and America. Particularly in iron and cotton. It is an unprecedented state of affairs, for all that it is the inevitable consequence of the capitalist system: overproduction on such an enormous scale that it can't even manage to produce a crisis! The overproduction of disposable capital seeking investment is so great that the discount rate here actually fluctuates between 1 and $1^1/_2\%$ per annum, while for money invested in short-term loans which can be paid off or called in any day (MONEY AT CALL) barely $^1/_2\%$ per annum is obtainable. But the very fact that the financial capitalist prefers to invest his money thus rather than in new industrial enterprises amounts to an admission that the economy is, in his eyes, rotten to the core. And this fear of new investment and any kind of speculation, already a feature of the 1867 crisis, is the main reason for the inability to bring about an acute crisis. But sooner or later it is bound to come and then, with any luck, it will put paid to the old trades unions over here. These cheerfully retain the same old guild character which has attached to them from the start and becomes daily more unbearable. You might suppose that any worker would be admitted without more ado by the engineers, carpenters, masons, etc., if he practised the relevant trade. Not a bit of it. Anyone seeking admission must have been bound apprentice for a number of years (usually 7) to a workman belonging to the trades union. This was supposed to restrict the number of workers, but served no other purpose, unless to bring in money to the master, in return for which he in fact did nothing at all. This may have been all right up till 1848. But since that time the tremendous growth of industry has created a class of workers as, if not more, numerous than their 'skilled' counterparts in the TRADES UNIONS, and who do as much, if not more, work than they, yet can never be admitted as members. These people have been *virtually brought into being* by the guild regulations of the TRADES UNIONS. But do you suppose the UNIONS have ever thought of doing away with this antiquated rubbish? Not on your life! I cannot remember ever reading about a proposal of that kind at a TRADES UNIONS Congress. The idiots want to reform society in accordance with their own set-up, not their own set-up in accordance with society's process of development. They cleave to their traditional superstitions, which harm only themselves, instead of getting rid of the lumber and thus doubling their numbers and strength to become in fact what they daily resemble less and less, namely anti-capitalist associations of all the workers of a particular trade. This will, I think, help you to understand much in the behaviour of these privileged working men.

What is really essential here is for the official labour leaders to get into Parliament *en masse*. That would speed things up all right; they'd quickly show themselves for what they were. The elections in November should prove a great help since 10 or 12 of them are sure to get in, provided their Liberal friends don't play some trick on them at the last moment.[a] The first elections under a new system [299] are always a kind of lottery and reveal only the least part of the revolution they usher in. But universal suffrage—and its recent introduction here will, in view of Britain's industrial lead and the absence of a peasant class, lend the workers as much power as it did in Germany—is today the best lever a proletarian movement can have, and so it will prove in this country also. That's why it is so important to smash the SOCIAL DEMOCRATIC FEDERATION [300] at the earliest opportunity, for its leaders are nothing but adventurers, literati and political careerists.

---

[a] See this volume, p. 361.

Hyndman, their boss, is doing all he can to further this end; he can hardly wait for the little bell to strike twelve, as the folk song has it, [a] and makes more of an ass of himself every day, so frantically does he pursue success. He's a wretched caricature of Lassalle.

I don't believe your opinion of the French is altogether fair. The masses in Paris are 'socialist' in the sense of a neutral middle-of-the-road socialism distilled over the course of years from Proudhon, Louis Blanc, Pierre Leroux, etc. The only experience they have had of communism was that of Cabet's utopia, which culminated in a model colony in America, i.e. in flight from France and discord and semi-bankruptcy in America. [459] Anything over and above that they derive from Germany, nor is it surprising that France which, from 1789 to 1850, was in every case the first country, not only to give clear expression to political ideas, but also to put them into practice, should be somewhat reluctant to endorse her own abdication as leader in matters of revolutionary theory; particularly after the glorious Commune and, what is more, vis-à-vis a Germany that was, to all intents and purposes, defeated by the Paris workers in 1870, seeing that the German army did not dare occupy Paris — a case, be it noted, unprecedented in the history of warfare. Then again, you should ask yourself how the French workers are to increase their discernment. Even the French edition of *Capital* is to them a sealed book; and not to them alone, but to a large part of the educated class as well. The only thing they are familiar with is my *Socialism: Utopian and Scientific* [460] which, in fact, has proved surprisingly influential. None of the leaders know German, except Vaillant whom I don't count because being a Blanquist, his tactics are totally different from our own. Mme Lafargue is now at last translating the *Manifesto* into good French. [444] Even the leaders' knowledge of theory still leaves something to be desired and, if you knew Paris, you would realise how easy it is to live and agitate, as opposed to doing any serious work there. So whence is discernment to come to the French workers?

And now a further word about the elections. In Germany it is easy to vote for a Social Democrat because we are the only real opposition party and because the Reichstag has no say in things, so that ultimately it doesn't matter whether one votes at all, or for which of the 'dogs that we all are' [461] one does vote. The only other party to have

---

[a] Engels refers to the poem *Kurzweil*, published in *Die Volkslieder der Deutschen*, Vol. 4, Mannheim, 1835, pp. 174-75.

a policy of its own is, perhaps, the Centre. [229] But in France, things are altogether different. There, the Chamber is the effective power in the land and there can be no question of chucking away one's ballot paper. Besides which it must be remembered that every time the Gambettists pit themselves against the Monarchists, and the Radicals [429] against the Gambettists, a step forward is made. And indeed practice proves this to be the case. In Germany Junker-style reaction has flourished since 1870 and everything is retrogressing. In France, they have the best schools in the world with compulsory education to match, and whereas Bismarck cannot get rid of the clergy, [462] the French have already ousted them completely from their schools. Our German army, apart from the growing Social Democratic element, is a more infamous tool of reaction than ever before. In France, general conscription has brought the army infinitely closer to the people, and *it is primarily the army* that makes monarchy impossible (cf. 1878). [463] And if the Radicals come to the helm and are compelled to implement their programme, there will be decentralisation of the administration, self-government for departments and communes, as in America and in the France of 1792-98, and separation of Church and State, every man to pay his own parson. We are not yet in a position to direct historical developments either in Germany or in France. This does not mean that those developments are standing still, however, but only that in the German Empire they are temporarily retrogressing, while in France they are for all that advancing. But our turn will not come — such is the slow but sure course of history — until the bourgeois and petty-bourgeois parties, having demonstrated, publicly and in practice, their inability to govern the country, find themselves up a gum tree. (After a French revolution we might, somewhat *anticipando*, [a] come to power in Germany but *only if carried there by a European tidal wave*.) That is why the instinct of the Paris workers in always supporting the most radical party *possible* is right from one point of view. As soon as the Radicals come to the helm, the same instinct will drive the workers into the arms of the Communists, for the Radicals are pledged to their *old*, muddled, socialist (*not* communist) programme and this will be their undoing. And then instinct and reason will coincide; the most radical party possible will then be the party of the proletariat as such, and things will happen fast. But the

---

[a] before our time

fact is that the English and the French have long since forgotten their pre-revolutionary state of virginity, whereas we Germans, not having had a revolution *of our own*, are still trailing around with this some-times very awkward encumbrance. Both conditions have their ad-vantages and disadvantages; but it would be most unjust to use the same one-sided standard in assessing the varying attitudes of the wor-kers in those three countries.

Kautsky has given me Adler's very superficial book[a] which is largely based on Stieber.[b] I shall help him write the review.[c]

Won't you come over here some time? Should business take you to the Rhine, you could be here in no time.

Your

F. E.

First published, in Russian, in *Marx-Engels Archives*, Vol. I (VI), Moscow, 1932

Printed according to the original

Published in English in full for the first time

205

ENGELS TO LAURA LAFARGUE

IN PARIS

London, 7 November 1885

My dear Laura,

I have no objection whatever to write a short introduction to the *Manifesto*. But in order to enable me to do so, I ought to know what passages in the old preface[d] would appear objectionable to the deli-cate ears of your Parisian public. I confess I cannot find them out, un-less it is one about the Commune which was put in by Mohr himself and on which he particularly insisted.[464] Although in my opinion our Paris friends give way by far too much to these susceptibilities, which ought to be put down as much as possible, I am quite willing

---

[a] G. Adler, *Die Geschichte der ersten sozialpolitischen Arbeiterbewegung in Deutschland...* - [b] Wermuth/Stieber, *Die Communisten-Verschwörungen des neunzehnten Jahrhunderts.* - [c] See this volume, p. 362. - [d] K. Marx and F. Engels, 'Preface to the 1872 German Edition of the *Manifesto of the Communist Party*'.

um des lieben Friedens willen[a] to please them as much as I can, without thereby falsifying history or strengthening the belief that all light necessarily comes from Paris. It is in my opinion utterly impossible for the *Manifesto* to go out in any language without stating how it originated. The conclusion of II, and the whole of III and IV are utterly incomprehensible without that.

'Mr Broadhouse' has actually had the impudence of having Aveling asked — through Reeves, the publisher — whether I would not collaborate with him in the translation of the *Capital!*[b] I suppose you have received the last No. of the *Commonweal?* If you will let me know what Nos. you are short of, I'll see that you get them.

Nim is as jolly as ever, we have just had a bottle of Pilsener together. She was last night at the Lyceum with Pumps to see 'Olivia',[465] says it is a regular *Rührstück*,[c] Irving no great shakes, Ellen Terry very good.

Lavigne says he sent his translation of the *18 Brumaire* to Paul but nothing came of it, what was the reason? I have the thing here, but as I am under an engagement with Fortin,[d] dare not look at it, otherwise I might be accused of having made undue use of it, so I cannot form a judgment as to its merits.[466]

Next week the grand political spree begins. On the 10th the French Chambers, on the 19th or thereabouts the German Reichstag, and a week later the elections here.[e] Whatever they may turn out in the shape of a Parliament, two things are certain: the Irish will command the whole by their 80-90 votes, and the Great Liberal Party will come, at last, to an end by the separation of the Whigs from the Radicals and the preparation if not the completion, of the Union between Whigs and Tories.[415]

Kind regards to Paul (11,500 votes)[467] which I hope have not quite crushed him. He'll have better luck next year.

Yours affectionately,
F. Engels

First published in: Marx and Engels, *Works*, Second Russian Edition, Vol. 36, Moscow, 1964

Reproduced from the original

Published in English for the first time

---

[a] for the sake of peace - [b] See this volume, p. 313. - [c] melodrama - [d] See this volume, pp. 358-59. - [e] Ibid., p. 361.

206

ENGELS TO HERMANN SCHLÜTER

IN HOTTINGEN-ZURICH

London, 11 November 1885

Dear Mr Schlüter,

Have received clean sheets of *Dühring* up to 20 incl. [208]; ending and prefaces are still to come. As soon as these arrive you will be sent the list of printing errors.

The introduction to the *Schlesische Milliarde*[418] is in hand and would have been finished long ago but for a series of interruptions of all kinds. It has been lying heavily on my conscience, so you may be sure that it will not be held up for a moment longer than is absolutely necessary.

You will have received the corrected proofs of the *Communist League*.[a] You might be good enough to tell Ede that I had already received via Kautsky the book by a sparrow calling itself 'Adler',[b] and had deliberately not mentioned it because it, too, draws on Stieber[c] as the final authority. The passage about Buttermilch-Born was worded in that way precisely because the book left me in no doubt that Born had surreptitiously poured out some buttermilk[d] for Adler but had refused (see preface) to allow his name to appear.[468] Hence he had to be given a kick or two in the pants.

Dietz has written to Kautsky saying he wants to take over publication of my *Origin*[e] now and asking whether I would have any objection. I have told him I have no objection provided he comes to an agreement with you and Schabelitz. So you should act in whatever way you think best. All being well, Dietz promises to place the work in the bookshops, which would of course be most acceptable to us, but then, too, Zurich[f] is also entitled to a say now that it has been circulating for

---

[a] F. Engels, 'On the History of the Communist League'. - [b] Adler = eagle in German; this refers to G. Adler, *Die Geschichte der ersten sozialpolitischen Arbeiterbewegung in Deutschland...*; see also this volume, p. 344. - [c] Wermuth/Stieber, *Die Communisten-Verschwörungen des neunzehnten Jahrhunderts.* - [d] Born's real name was Buttermilch = buttermilk in German. - [e] *The Origin of the Family, Private Property and the State* - [f] The editorial board and the press of *Der Sozialdemokrat* were located in Zurich, as well as the bookshop (Volksbuchhandlung).

a year without being banned. On the other hand it was his shilly-shallying which caused the printing to drag on for months; it's all very well for him to talk after arriving belatedly on the scene when others have already taken the risks. Moreover I'm not acquainted with the actual details of what was discussed at the time and hence have no alternative but to refer him to you. So please settle the affair in any way you think fit.

I have found another whole mass of printing errors in the *Dühring* — all of which I myself had allowed to stand. I have become so accustomed to correcting *two* proofs — one for the meaning, the other for individual errors — that when there isn't an opportunity of doing so I allow utter nonsense to stand. Hence most of them were in the first 11 sheets which were, moreover, corrected in difficult circumstances.

Kindest regards.

Yours,

F. E.

First published in: Marx and Engels, *Works*, First Russian Edition, Vol. XXVII, Moscow, 1935

Printed according to the original

Published in English for the first time

207

ENGELS TO NIKOLAI DANIELSON

IN ST PETERSBURG

London, 13 November 1885

Dear Sir,

I received your two letters 6/18 and 9/21 August while I was in Jersey[a] and immediately sent you the letter you desired for the *Сѣверный вѣстникъ*.[438] Since then I have been prevented by press of work from replying more fully to these letters as well as that of the 25 August/5 September.

---

[a] See this volume, p. 322.

I had no doubt that the 2nd volume[a] would afford you the same pleasure as it has done to me. The developments it contains are indeed of such a superior order that the vulgar reader will not take the trouble to fathom them and to follow them out. This is actually the case in Germany where all historical science, including political economy, has fallen so low that it can scarcely fall any lower. Our *Kathe-der-Sozialisten*[54] have never been much more, theoretically, than slightly philanthropic *Vulgärökonomen*,[b] and now they have sunk to the level of simple apologists of Bismarck's *Staats-Sozialismus*.[c] To them, the 2nd volume will always remain a sealed book. It is a fine piece of what Hegel calls *die Ironie der Weltgeschichte*,[d][386] that German historical science, by the fact of the elevation of Germany to the position of the first European power, should be again reduced to the same vile state to which it was reduced by the deepest political degradation of Germany, after the Thirty Years' War.[469] But such is the fact. And thus, German 'Science' stares at this new volume without being able to understand it; only, a wholesome fear of the consequences prevents them from criticising it in public, and so, official economic literature observes a cautious silence with regard to it. The 3rd volume[c] will however compel them to speak out.

Of that 3rd volume, I have completed the first transcript from the original into a legible manuscript. Three-fourths of it are almost fit for publication as they are; but the last fourth, or perhaps third, will require a great deal of work: the first section (relation of *Mehrwertsrate* to *Profitrate*[f]) and then the subsequent sections on credit and partly also on *Grundrente*[g]; besides certain portions of almost all the other sections. For the last two months I have been compelled to attend to a good deal of other work which had been neglected by my exclusive attention to the 2nd and 3rd volumes.[4] This will continue for some time yet, and then, maybe, the revision of the English translation of Volume I[56] which is nearly completed, will occupy me for a month longer, but then I shall start with the 3rd volume and carry it out to the end. Maybe it will be published in 2 sections, as it will contain about 1,000 pages.

I thank you very much for your extracts from the author's letters from 1879 to 1881.[470] I could not read them without a sorrowful

---

[a] of *Capital* - [b] vulgar economists - [c] state socialism - [d] the irony of world history - [e] of *Capital* - [f] rate of surplus value to rate of profit - [g] ground rent (or rent of land)

smile. Alas, we are so used to these excuses for the non-completion of the work! Whenever the state of his health made it impossible for him to go on with it, this impossibility preyed heavily upon his mind, and he was only too glad if he could only find out some theoretical excuse why the work should not then be completed. All these arguments he has at the time made use of vis-à-vis *de moi*[a]; they seemed to ease his conscience.

After completing the 3rd volume and selecting from the other ms. the portions fit for publication, I shall very likely try to collect such of the author's correspondence as is scientifically important, and there his letters to you rank amongst the first. When that time comes, I shall therefore avail myself of your kind offer of placing at my disposal copies of these letters.

I am often in the case of forwarding to you pamphlets, etc.—republications of the author's and my own writings, etc., but do not know whether it would be safe to send them direct to you. I should be much obliged if you would tell me what to do.

I hope our mutual friend's[b] health is improving, notwithstanding the bad prognosis of his doctors. [362] Any news with regard to him will always be welcome.

That crisis of which the author speaks in his letter, was indeed an exceptional one. [471] The fact is it continues still, all Europe and America suffer under it to this day. The absence of the financial crash is one cause of it. But the principal cause is undoubtedly the totally changed state of the *Weltmarkt*.[c] Since 1870, Germany and especially America have become England's rivals in modern industry, while most other European countries have so far developed their own manufactures as to cease to be dependent on England. The consequence has been the spreading of the process of overproduction over a far larger area than when it was mainly confined to England, and has taken—up to now—a chronic instead of an acute character. By thus delaying the thunderstorm which formerly cleared the atmosphere every ten years, this continued chronic depression must prepare a crash of a violence and extent such as we have never known before. And the more so as the agricultural crisis of which the author speaks, has also continued up to now, has been extended to almost all

---

[a] myself - [b] Hermann Lopatin's - [c] world market

European countries; and must continue while the virgin черноземъ [a] of the Western American prairies remains unexhausted.

Very faithfully yours,

P. W. Rosher [363]

First published, in Russian, in *Minuvshiye gody*, No. 2, St Petersburg, 1908 and in the language of the original (English) in: K. Marx und F. Engels, *Ausgewählte Briefe*, Berlin, 1953

Reproduced from the original

208

ENGELS TO PAUL LAFARGUE [472]

IN PARIS

London, 14 November 1885

My dear Lafargue,

Thanks for the portrait—what a surly face they make me pull in France, a country where they nevertheless laugh from time to time, or so it is said. Perhaps they will laugh at me too. Nim says it makes me look ten years older, out of flattery no doubt.

The insurrections of May 1849 were provoked by the refusal of most of the German governments to accept the constitution for Germany as a whole approved by the National Assembly at Frankfurt. [473] This assembly, which never had any real power and neglected any steps to acquire some, also contrived to lose the last vestige of its moral power just at the moment when it had realised on paper its somewhat romantic 'constitution'. Nevertheless that constitution was then the sole banner under which it was still possible to try to launch a new movement—if they were not to deprive themselves of one after victory had been achieved. In the smaller states, therefore, they sought to compel the governments to recognise it. There followed the insurrections in Dresden (3 May) and, a few days later, in the Bavarian Palatinate and the Grand Duchy of Baden where the Grand Duke [b] took flight, the army having declared itself for the people.

The Dresden insurrection was put down after a heroic resistance— the fighting went on for four days—with the help of Prussian troops.

---

[a] (Russ.) black earth - [b] Leopold

(In Prussia reaction had gained the upper hand as a result of the coup d'état of November 1848; Berlin was disarmed and placed under a state of siege.) But to subdue the Palatinate and Baden an army was needed. So in Prussia they made a start by calling the *Landwehr* [474] to arms. At Iserlohn (Westphalia) and Elberfeld (Rhenish Prussia) men refused to march. Troops were sent, who found the towns barricaded and were repulsed. About a fortnight later Iserlohn was taken after two days' resistance. Elberfeld offered relatively few opportunities for defence and so, with troops bearing down on them from every side, the defenders, about a thousand in number, resolved to fight their way through to the states that had risen in the south. They were cut to pieces en route, but a fair number managed to get down there with the help of the population. I was aide-de-camp to Mirbach, the commandant at Elberfeld. Before carrying out his plan he sent me on a mission to Cologne, in other words into the enemy's camp, where I hid in Daniels' house. The truth is that he did not want to have a known communist in his corps for fear of alarming the bourgeoisie of the regions through which he was to pass. He made a rendezvous with me in the Palatinate but failed to turn up, having been taken prisoner (acquitted by the Elberfeld jury a year later). Mirbach had gone through the campaigns in Greece from 1825 to 1829 and Poland from 1830 to 1831; he later again returned to Greece where he died.

Meanwhile the insurrection in the south was gathering strength, but it made the fatal blunder of not attacking. The troops of the small adjacent states were only looking for a pretext to join the insurrection, at that time they were determined not to fight against the people. A pretext was then provided, namely that they should advance on Frankfurt in order to protect the assembly against the Prussian and Austrian soldiers who were surrounding the place. After the suppression of the *Neue Rheinische Zeitung* Marx and I had gone to Mannheim to recommend this move to the leaders. But they produced all manner of excuses — that the army was disorganised by the flight of their former officers, that they were short of everything, etc., etc.

About the beginning of June the Prussians on the one hand and the Bavarians on the other, reinforced by those same troops from the smaller states whom we could have won over with greater daring, but who saw themselves drowned in an ocean of reactionary armies, advanced on the insurgent areas. It took them no more than a week to clear the Palatinate — there were 36,000 Prussians against 8-9,000 insurgents, and the two fortresses of the country were in reactionary hands. We withdrew to the troops in Baden, some 8,000 men of the line and 12,000 irregulars, themselves beset by 30,000 reactionary troops. There were four general engagements in which numerical superiority and the violation of Württemberg territory, a move that enabled them to outflank us at the decisive moment, gave the reactionaries the advantage. After six weeks of fighting the remains of the rebel army had to cross over into Switzerland.

During this war I was aide-de-camp to Colonel Willich who commanded a corps of irregulars of marked proletarian character. I took part in three minor engagements and also in the last decisive battle of the Murg.

That, I trust, will enable you to sum the whole thing up in a few lines if you absolutely insist on writing a commentary on Citizen Clarus' fine work.

I trust your interesting furuncle will discharge its purulent contents before long. Wash the sore with 2% carbolic acid in 98% water; it's a capital way of killing suppurating cells.

A kiss for Laura.

Yours ever,
F. E.

First published in: Marx and Engels, *Works*, Second Russian Edition, Vol. 36, Moscow, 1964

Printed according to the original

Translated from the French

Published in English for the first time

209

ENGELS TO AUGUST BEBEL

IN BERLIN

London, 17 November 1885

Dear Bebel,

Just another word or two before you take your seat in the Reichstag. [475]

In answer to Schumacher's long letter defending his attitude to the Steamship Subsidies, [476] I have written to him at equal length [39] to say that I adhere to my old standpoint, namely, that if in order to respect the alleged prejudices of certain voters, you do not want to vote *unconditionally* against state aid paid to the bourgeoisie out of the workers' and peasants' pockets, you may, in my view, vote in favour only if a like amount of state aid is directly allocated for the benefit of the workers, both urban and rural — primarily for agricultural workers' cooperatives on state-owned land.

To avoid misunderstandings I have asked him, in the event of his discussing this letter with other comrades, always to show them *the whole letter.*

Liebknecht has certainly come most bravely to the fore all of a sudden. His 'collection' written in jail, [477] his study of the all but forgotten *Capital,* and the prospect, suggested to him by the Right, of falling between two stools, seem to have proved extremely beneficial. I shall be very happy if only it lasts. He will certainly be in the right place when the crucial moment comes, but until then he will cause the rest of us an appalling amount of trouble with that habit he has of hushing things up, which he regards as diplomacy and at which he is, it is true, far more adept than the rest of us.

War in Europe is beginning to pose a serious threat to us. So those miserable remnants of what once were nations, the Serbs, Bulgarians, Greeks and other rapacious riff-raff on whose behalf your liberal philistine enthuses in the interests of Russia, are begrudging one another the very air they breathe and must inevitably slit each other's greedy throats. That would be marvellous and would serve the philistine nationality-mongers right, were it not for the fact that each of these pigmy tribes holds the key to peace or war in Europe. The first shot has been fired at Dragoman, [478] but when and where the last will be fired, no one can say.

Our movement is getting on so splendidly, everywhere and without exception circumstances are turning out so much in our favour and our need for another few years of undisturbed development and consolidation is so great, that the last thing we want is a big political row. It would consign our movement to the background for years on end, after which we should doubtless have to start belatedly all over again, as after 1850.

On the other hand, a war might bring about a revolution in Paris which in turn would indirectly provide fuel for the movement in the rest of Europe, and in that case the French — no doubt violently chauvinist in the circumstances — would assume the leadership, a role for which their level of theoretical development qualifies them least of all. A few peaceful years of Radical rule [429] would be the very thing for the French who, since 1871, have made very good progress politically thanks to the instinctive, logical consistency that is peculiar to them. For these Radicals have adopted in its entirety the current middle-of-the-road, jumbled-up socialism deriving from Louis Blanc, Proudhon, etc., and it would be of inestimable value to us were they to be given the opportunity to demolish such empty verbiage in practice.

On the other hand, should a major war break out, it will place six million men in the field and cost an unprecedented amount of money. There will be bloodshed, devastation and, finally, a state of prostration such as has never been known before. That's why all these gentlemen are so afraid of it. One may further predict that if this war comes, it will be the last one; it will mark the end of the class state politically, militarily, economically (as also financially) and morally. It could lead to a situation in which the war machine turns rebellious and refuses to engage in prolonged mutual slaughter for the sake of the lousy Balkan nations. The watchword of the class state is *après nous le déluge* [436]; but after the deluge it's we who shall come and only we.

So everything remains as it was: whatever happens, it will ultimately provide a means for bringing our party to power and putting paid to all the old nonsense. But I must say I hope it will happen without this massacre; there's no need for it. If it's got to be, however, I only hope that when the moment arrives my old disability won't prevent me mounting a horse.

Your old friend
F. E.

First published, in Russian, in *Marx-Engels Archives*, Vol. I (VI), Moscow, 1932

Printed according to the original

Published in English for the first time

210

ENGELS TO MINNA KAUTSKY [479]

IN VIENNA

London, 26 November 1885

Dear Mrs Kautsky,

(You will, I hope, permit me to use this simple form of address, for why should two people like ourselves continue to stand on ceremony?) First of all, very many thanks for your kind references to myself. [480] I was very sorry not to have been able to spend more time with you while you were here; it gave me infinite pleasure, I do assure you, to meet for once a German authoress who had also remained a simple woman — in this respect it has been my misfortune to meet only affected, 'eddicated' [a] Berlin ladies of the kind one would not urge to take up the kitchen spoon again, if only because they would eventually wreak more havoc with it than with the pen. So I hope that it won't be too long before you cross the Narrow Seas again, when you and I shall be able to ramble gently round London and its purlieus, exchanging light-hearted banter lest our conversation should become altogether too serious.

That London didn't please you, I can readily believe. Some years ago I used to feel much the same. It is difficult to accustom oneself to the gloomy atmosphere and, for the most part, gloomy people, to the reserve, the class distinctions in social life, to living shut up indoors as the climate demands. One has to temper somewhat the animal spirits imported from the Continent and let the barometer of *joie de vivre* fall from, say, 760 to 750 millimetres, until one finally becomes acclimatised. Then one gradually reconciles oneself to the whole thing, discovering that the place has its good points, that people are on the whole more straightforward and reliable than elsewhere, that no city is better suited to the writing of learned works than London, and that the absence of harassment by the police makes up for a great deal. I know and love Paris but, given the choice, I would rather settle permanently in London than there. Paris can only be enjoyed properly if you become a Parisian yourself, with all the prejudices of a Parisian, if

---

[a] In the original 'jebildete' (Berlin dialect).

you confine your interests primarily to things Parisian and accustom yourself to believing that Paris is the centre of the world, the be-all and end-all. London is uglier yet more grandiose than Paris, and is the true centre of world trade; it also offers a far greater variety. But London also permits one to maintain a completely neutral attitude towards one's surroundings as a whole, as is essential to scientific and, indeed, artistic impartiality. One adores Paris and Vienna, detests Berlin, but towards London one's feelings are those of neutral indifference and objectivity. And that also counts for something.

Apropos Berlin. I am glad to hear that that wretched place is at last succeeding in becoming a metropolis. But as Rahel Varnhagen said as much as 70 years ago: In Berlin everything becomes *shabby*, so that Berlin would seem to be trying to show the rest of the world just how shabby a metropolis can be. Only poison all eddicated Berliners, conjure up at least tolerable surroundings there, and rebuild the whole place from the foundations up, and something decent might be made of it. But not, I think, so long as *that* dialect continues to be spoken there.

I have now also read *Die Alten und die Neuen*,[a] for which many thanks. The descriptions of the life of the salt miners are as masterly as were those of the peasants in *Stefan*.[b] Again, your descriptions of life in Viennese society are also very good on the whole. Vienna is, after all, the only German city that has a society, whereas Berlin has only 'certain circles' and even more uncertain ones, which is why it is productive only of novels about literati, civil servants and actors. Whether the action in this part of your book does not move rather too rapidly in places you are better able to judge than I; much that appears to do so to the likes of us, may seem perfectly natural to you in Vienna because of that city's peculiarly international character with its admixture of southern and east European elements. In both spheres, too, I find your customary clear-cut individualisation; each character is a type but at the same time a definite individual, a 'This One' as old Hegel puts it, and that is how it ought to be. But now, if only for the sake of impartiality, I really must find something to criticise, and this brings me to Arnold. The latter is indeed altogether too well-behaved and, when he is finally killed in a landslide, one can only reconcile it with poetic justice by telling oneself, for instance, that he was too good for this world. It is always a bad thing, however,

---

[a] a novel by Minna Kautsky - [b] M. Kautsky, *Stefan vom Grillenhof*.

for an author to dote on his own hero, and you would seem to me to have erred somewhat in this direction. With Elsa, individualisation is still in evidence, if not altogether devoid of idealisation, but with Arnold the man tends rather to be absorbed into the principle.

The source of this failing, however, may be discovered in the novel itself. In this book you obviously felt impelled to take sides openly, to testify to your convictions before the whole world. Now that you have done so, it is something you can put behind you and have no need to repeat again in the same form. I am not at all opposed to tendentious poetry as such. The father of tragedy, Aeschylus, and the father of comedy, Aristophanes, were both strongly tendentious poets, as were Dante and Cervantes, and the best thing about Schiller's *Kabale und Liebe* is that it was the first politically tendentious drama in Germany. The Russians and Norwegians of today, who are producing first-rate novels, are all tendentious writers. But I believe that the tendency should spring from the situation and action as such, without its being expressly alluded to, nor is there any need for the writer to present the reader with the future historical solution to the social conflicts he describes. Furthermore, in present circumstances, the novel is mainly directed at readers in bourgeois — i. e. not our own immediate — circles and, such being the case, it is my belief that the novel of socialist tendency wholly fulfils its mission if, by providing a faithful account of actual conditions, it destroys the prevailing conventional illusions on the subject, shakes the optimism of the bourgeois world and inexorably calls in question the permanent validity of things as they are, even though it may not proffer a solution or, indeed, in certain circumstances, appear to take sides. Your detailed knowledge and your wonderfully true-to-life descriptions, both of the Austrian peasantry and of Viennese 'society', provide ample material for this, and you have already shown in *Stefan* that you are also capable of handling your protagonists with a nice irony which testifies to the command an author has over his creatures.

But now I must desist, otherwise you'll think me altogether too prolix. Over here everything goes on much as usual; Karl and his wife[a] are learning physiology at Aveling's evening classes and are also busily engaged in other respects; I, too, am up to my eyes in work; Lenchen, Pumps and her husband[b] are going to the theatre tonight to see a melodrama and meanwhile old Europe is beginning to bestir herself

---

[a] Karl and Louise Kautsky - [b] Percy White Rosher

again, and high time too. I only hope I shall have time to complete the third volume of *Capital* and then the fun can begin.

Assuring you of my cordial feelings and sincere regard, I remain, Madam,

Yours,
F. Engels

First published, in Russian, in *Marx-Engels Archives*, Vol. I (VI), Moscow, 1932

Printed according to the original

Published in English in full for the first time

211

ENGELS TO PAUL LAVIGNE [481]

IN PARIS

[Draft]

[London,] 1 December 1885

Citizen,

When I received your letter of 8 August, [466] together with your manuscript, I was on the point of leaving for Jersey, whence I did not return until 14 September. [421] Since then I have had so much urgent work to deal with that I was unable to revert to the French translation of the *18th Brumaire*. Now, having at last had time to come back to it, I find myself placed between two rival mss. [482]

To begin with, it is impossible for me to set myself up as judge in a dispute when I am unable to make a careful investigation either of its causes or of its substance. All I know is that Fortin had been in correspondence with Marx for a number of years prior to the death of the latter, [483] that he asked me to revise his translation, that I promised him I would do so and that I have already attended to the revision of part of his ms. Accordingly I feel I am committed to him. Such being the position, I do not consider that I have the right to use your work in any way. I shall take good care not to read a single page, for were it to prove better than Fortin's, I should be unable to prevent myself from introducing some of your turns of speech into his ms. And that would be unfair to you and also, perhaps, to Fortin, since the two of you no longer get on with one another. Much to my regret, the need for me to be impartial prevents my familiarising myself with your work.

I am holding the ms. at your disposal.

The translation of the 2nd volume of *Capital* is an extremely difficult business. Moreover it will be absolutely impossible for me to undertake any revision at all next year. And then there are still many other things to consider. At the moment I cannot commit myself to anyone; that must lie in the future.

Yours sincerely

First published in: Marx and Engels, *Works*, First Russian Edition, Vol. XXVII, Moscow, 1935

Printed according to the original

Translated from the French

Published in English for the first time

212

ENGELS TO WILHELM LIEBKNECHT [484]

IN BERLIN

London, 1 December 1885

Dear Liebknecht,

As regards Russia's finances, [485] see Kolb's *Statistik*, 1875 ed.,[a] p. 499 et seq. The last loan shown therein is that of November 1873 for 15 million pounds. After that a further loan of 15 million pounds was raised with great difficulty in 1875, but the Russians were also advised by the bankers that this would be the last time, failing a guarantee by a representative assembly. For after provisional arrangements had been made in 1869 in respect of the funds appropriated for railway purposes, there were further borrowings:

---

[a] G. Fr. Kolb, *Handbuch der vergleichenden Statistik — der Völkerzustands- und Statenkunde.*

1870 — 12 million pounds
1871 — 12 ”   ”
1872 — 15 ”   ”
1873 — 15 ”   ”
1875 — 15 ”   ”

---

i. e between 1870 and 1875, six years, *69 million* pounds = *1,380 million* marks. They now had to think up some new dodges. Hence, 1) an *internal* loan. Though this was in fact a forced loan, it proved an almost complete flop. For there was little capital available in the country and the government was therefore compelled to lend its own money (paper money) to itself so as to give the impression that the loan had nevertheless been over-subscribed. 2) The Transcaucasian Railway Loan of £8,904,200. This was raised (1880 or 1881?) abroad on the security of the Poti to Baku line, but most of it had to be expended on the construction of the line itself; hence the financial straits persisted. Throughout this time repeated approaches were made to the bankers, all of them in vain. Finally the Minister for Finance[a] set off for the West in person — Paris, Berlin, Amsterdam; London was omitted from the itinerary as being quite hopeless. Everywhere he met with a rebuff; even Mendelssohn, the court banker in Berlin, is said to have asked for a parliamentary guarantee point-blank; in any case he, too, turned him away. The only remaining question was whether the Russian Duma ought to be convoked a year sooner or a year later; there was no other way out. Giers then visited Friedrichsruh and abased himself, whereupon Bismarck got hold of 15 million pounds for him in Germany, thereby postponing the evil day a little longer. [182]

(One of the conclusions we may draw from the above is that Russia won't be able to start a war without Bismarck's permission, for it can only raise money under his protection and the 15 million have long since been frittered away. So if it starts a war after all, or seriously threatens to do so, Bismarck will be directly responsible.)

I don't read *The Economist*, nor do I know where a run of them is to be found, for the many clubs have been the ruin of nearly all the reading-rooms here. I shall ask Kautsky to try and see if he can lay his hands on the *Economist, Statist, Bullionist* and *Money Market Review* and make extracts for you.

---

[a] Nikolai Bunge

Although your letter of 26 November was posted between 11 and 12 in the morning, it didn't reach me until the morning of 28 November; moreover the gum had been tampered with, as you will see from the envelope which I return herewith. It ought to have arrived here on the evening of 27 November. A bible is surely placed on the altar for the sole purpose of being *opened*. [455]

Your speech at the first budget reading was sent to me by Bebel from Dresden. It was very good; I'm only surprised that you had so few interruptions. After all, you did elicit the obligatory call to order. [486]

Your

F. E.

The seal on this letter is a count's coronet and the monogram JC intertwined.

The elections here are going very nicely. [487] For the first time the Irish in England have voted *en masse* for *one* side, to wit the Tories. In doing so they have shown the Liberals to what extent they can tip the scales, even in England. The 80 or 85 HOME RULERS over here — one of them has actually been elected in Liverpool! — correspond to the Centre [229] in the Reichstag and are capable of rendering any government powerless. Parnell must now show what he is worth.

Incidentally, the *new* 'Manchesterism' is also proving victorious, in other words the theory of retaliatory tariffs, which is, of course, even more senseless in this country than in Germany, but has been taken up by the new generation of manufacturers after eight years of rotten trade. [488] Next there is Gladstone's opportunist weakness and then, too, Chamberlain's inept manner, first aggressive, then ingratiating, which evoked the cry THE CHURCH IN DANGER! [489] Lastly Gladstone's deplorable foreign policy. The Liberals would have us believe that the new COUNTY VOTERS will vote liberal. These are of course an unknown quantity but, if the Liberals are to obtain an absolute majority, they will have to win more than 180 of the 300 seats still to be decided and there's no likelihood of that. Parnell will almost certainly become dictator of Great Britain and Ireland.

First published, in Russian, in *Marx-Engels Archives*, Vol. I (VI), Moscow, 1932

Printed according to the original

Published in English in full for the first time

213

ENGELS TO KARL KAUTSKY [490]

IN LONDON

[London,] 2 December 1885

Dear Kautsky,

Ad vocem[a] Adler:

1) Re the pistol business, don't forget to point out that the NCOs were wearing their *sabres*. They complained of an affront to the NCO caste. [491]

2) Hess. It is not of course possible to confirm — for I never saw him again after May 1848, when he disappeared for good — whether or not he spent a few days in Baden or the Palatinate. But he didn't 'take part'; he was neither orator, nor journalist, nor official, nor soldier, so it's inconceivable that some government or other — Adler certainly ought to have said which one — should have condemned him to death. [492]

Ad vocem Liebknecht. Before you post the letter, give me a chance to enclose a word or two of explanation; there was something I forgot to tell him yesterday. [b]

Your

F. E.

First published, in Russian, in *Marx-Engels Archives*, Vol. I (VI), Moscow, 1932

Printed according to the original

Published in English for the first time

---

[a] As regards - [b] See previous letter.

214

ENGELS TO JOHANN PHILIPP BECKER [484]

IN GENEVA

London, 5 December 1885

Dear Old Man,

As it's so long since I heard from you, I am reminding you of my existence by advising you of the despatch of a £ 5 money order which I hope will arrive at the same time as this letter and perhaps help to lighten the transition from the old year to the new. I trust you are still in the best of health and that you will send me a line or two before long acknowledging receipt.

I have been slogging away hard of late, as no doubt you will learn from the Zurich booksellers' publishing side, and in particular have seized the opportunity of reviving various pieces from the golden days of our youth in 1848-49. [493] This is damned important, for the younger generation, which has forgotten all about it, if indeed it ever knew, is beginning to want to find out what went on at that time and, in view of the many inaccurate sources and accounts, it's important to provide them with as much accurate information as possible. What is absolutely vital is that you should finish your memoirs; years ago the *Neue Welt* published some really charming pieces. [a] You're a wonderfully skilful narrator and on top of that your memory goes back at least 10 or 15 years further than mine and embraces the period 1830-40, which is also very important where later developments are concerned. Some money might also be made out of it, and that's not to be sneezed at.

I still have to revise the *Peasant War* [213] which is badly in need of it and shall then go on to Volume III of *Capital*, this having now been dictated in the rough from the original draft and set down in a legible hand. It will be the devil of a task, but a splendid one. Unfortunately a mass of translations into French, English, Italian and Danish keep intervening, which I have to go over—all too necessary in most

---

[a] J. Ph. Becker, 'Abgerissene Bilder aus meinem Leben', *Die Neue Welt*, Nos. 17-20, 23, 24, 26, 28 and 29; 22 and 29 April, 6 and 13 May, 3, 10 and 24 June, 8 and 15 July 1876.

cases. [494] Fortunately my knowledge of Russian, let alone Polish, doesn't extend to this sort of job, otherwise it would never end. But from that you will see how extensive is the international field our communism has now conquered and it is always a pleasure when one can do one's bit towards extending that field still further.

I hope the wretched business in the Balkans [445] will pass off peacefully. We are making such splendid progress everywhere that a world war would be inopportune just now—too late or too early. But ultimately it would also work in our favour by putting an end to militarism once and for all—at the cost of the massacre of $1\frac{1}{5}$ million men and the squandering of 1,000 billion francs. After that there could be no more war.

The elections in France have provided the Radicals with the immediate prospect of coming to power and have thus been of considerable help to us, too. [447] The elections over here have temporarily made the Irish masters of England and Scotland; without them neither party can govern. [487] There are still about 100 results to come in, but they'll make little difference to the outcome. Thus the Irish question will at last be settled—if not at once, at any rate in the immediate future and then the decks will be cleared over here as well. Some 8 or 10 working men have likewise been elected—some of them bought by the bourgeoisie, others trade unionists pure and simple—who will doubtless make thorough fools of themselves and be of enormous assistance in the creation of an independent labour party by banishing the inherited self-deceit of the workers. History moves slowly over here, but move it does.

Warm regards.

Your old friend
F. Engels

First published in: F. Engels, *Vergessene Briefe (Briefe Friedrich Engels' an Johann Philipp Becker)*, Berlin, 1920

Printed according to the original

Published in English in full for the first time

215

ENGELS TO WILHELM LIEBKNECHT [485]

IN BERLIN

London, 5 December 1885

Dear Liebknecht,

Herewith excerpts from the *Economist* and *Bullionist*. [a]

The amounts shown in my letter of the 1st inst. are those of the Russian loans quoted on the London STOCK EXCHANGE. The 1884 (Bismarck) loan [182] *is not dealt in over here at all* and is *excluded* from the list of securities negotiable on the STOCK EXCHANGE. Likewise the smaller hand-to-mouth loans which have been raised off and on since 1878; most of these were taken up internally and are quoted on the Berlin stock exchange. I have found the following in the latter's list of prices:

Orient Loan	5% I, II and III
Loan 1880	4%
Bonds 1883	6%

as well as other stuff about which I'm not clear. You'll have to get more information on the subject from someone on the Berlin stock exchange. Several also appear in the enclosed excerpts, but only with the net amount the government claims to have received.

The Russian paper rouble, which ought to be worth 39d. at par, is now standing at 23d., i. e. 16d. or 41% below the full value in gold.

If the Russian government is still managing to place its paper at home, this is simply because the colossal slowdown in trade makes it more advantageous for Russian manufacturers to invest their surplus cash in paper yielding 6-7% rather than in such currently ruinous activities as extensions to factories or speculative trading. The interest coupons are circulating as currency, especially for the payment of wages. Thus coupons, which are not payable until 1891-92, are now passing from hand to hand, and these the Russian worker must ac-

---

[a] See this volume, p. 360.

cept at face value in payment of his wages, though they can only be disposed of for half this amount (much the same thing happened in Germany not long ago). I have this *direct from Russia*.

Your

F. E.

First published, in Russian, in *Marx-Engels Archives*, Vol. I (VI), Moscow, 1932

Printed according to the original

Published in English for the first time

216

ENGELS TO EDUARD BERNSTEIN [495]

IN ZURICH

London, 7 December 1885

Dear Ede,

Here too we've had a storm in our socialist tea-cup. Kautsky will already have written and told you something about it; 2 *Echoes* (Liberal) enclosed herewith. Also some other stuff, and a document (letter from Bland, based on the minutes of the Executive of the SOCIAL DEMOCRATIC FEDERATION, sent you by Aveling), which will give you the substance. [496]

This time Hyndman has given himself the coup de grâce. He took money from the Tories for socialist candidatures in order to filch votes from the Liberals. He has admitted to taking £340, but since the official expenses of the 3 candidatures amounted to about £600, it must have been something in the region of £1,000, if not more.

Taking money from another party may, in certain circumstances and by way of an exception, be admissible if, 1) the money is given unconditionally and 2) the transaction does not do more harm than good. In this instance the very opposite was the case. 1) The condition was that socialist candidates be put up in districts where they could only be made to look ridiculous—as, indeed, happened: Williams, 27 votes out of 4,722, Fielding, 32 out of 6,374; only Burns got 598 votes out of 11,055 in Nottingham. 2) Hyndman, however, knew that to take money from the Tories would spell nothing less than irreparable moral ruin for the socialists in the eyes of the *one and only* class from which they could draw recruits, namely the great, radical working masses. It's almost a replica of the Stoecker alliance against the Party of Progress once proposed in Berlin. [497]

Well, not content with this heroic deed, Hyndman already saw himself as a second Parnell holding the scales between the two parties, though forgetting that, unlike Parnell, he does not command 80 votes in Parliament and 200,000 Irish votes in the elections in England and Scotland. [487] He got the Executive of the Federation to empower him to go to Birmingham with Champion and call on Chamberlain, the leader of the Radicals. [415] With Tory money in his pocket, he offered the latter his support if he, Chamberlain, would cede him a seat in Birmingham, assure him of Liberal votes and agree to introduce an Eight Hours' Bill. Not being such a mug as the Tories, Chamberlain showed him the door.

In the meantime the affair, arranged on the qt by the Federation's Executive, became known in the branches and caused a great furore. Of which more in Bland's letter; it was written for publication, but you should not mention the fact that it is based on the minutes. A general meeting is to be called and whether the Federation will survive it seems doubtful; not, at any rate, as a viable organisation.

Herewith Hunter Watts' statement in *The Pall Mall Gazette*. [498] It was written with Hyndman's connivance, yet he had to let the expression 'ILL-ADVISED', used of himself, stand. By contrast, Williams' statement in *The Echo* [496] is nothing less than a slap in the face, its attitude being, and not without reason, one of outright hostility to all socialist MIDDLE-CLASS MEN. So that's what Mr Hyndman has brought about with his pushfulness. The man is nothing but a caricature of Lassalle, totally indifferent to the nature of the means even when *not* conducive to the end, provided Hyndman himself gets something out of it; add to that his perpetual craving for instantaneous success, so that he kills the goose that lays the golden egg; and finally, the way he considers himself the centre of the universe, being utterly incapable of seeing the facts in any light other than that which is gratifying to him.

And, for good measure, a political adventurer *comme il faut*.[a] All Lassalle's bad points magnified, and not a single one of his good ones.

What do things look like in your parliamentary tea-cup?

Your

F. E.

First published, in Russian, in *Marx-Engels Archives*, Book I, Moscow, 1924

Printed according to the original

Published in English in full for the first time

217

ENGELS TO PAUL LAFARGUE [499]

IN PARIS

London, 7 December 1885

My dear Lafargue,

I shall speak to Tussy about Davitt. She may be able to get you what you want.

In opposition to your Social Studies Group [179] the good Malon and the no less celebrated Élie May have just set up a Republican Social Economy Society with ready-made rules. [500] Let's hope this 'research group' will be confined to Malon who will do his research in May's bosom, and to May who will do his research in Malon's heart. They are petty panjandrums whom you would be well advised to ignore completely; that would infuriate them most of all. It's Karl Blind to the life.

Why are you making such a splash in the *Socialiste* with Williams and the Social Democratic Federation? [501] You ought to know what attitude to take with respect to Hyndman, and this time you have fallen into a fine old trap. In the first place, Hyndman has contrived to make his party a laughing-stock second to none. Williams collected *27* votes out of 10,000, Fielding in North Kensington *32* out of 10,000,

---

[a] proper

Burns in Nottingham 598 out of 11,000.[a] Whereupon the liberal press kicked up an almighty fuss, alleging that the money needed for these foolish candidatures had been provided by the TORIES, and that the socialists had so lowered themselves as to do that party's dirty work for it. Williams then wrote to *The Echo* on 5 December[496] saying that all this had been arranged while he was in Liverpool, that they had recalled him by telegram without giving details, that he had been treated by the leaders as a mere tool and that he now saw

* 'that we cannot trust the middle class men of our movement any longer. I am not prepared to be made the tool of middle class men. I call upon my fellow wage-slaves to meet me as soon as possible and to say good-bye to the middle class men and to shut them out from what must be a real working men's organisation', * etc.

—in short he has now adopted a stance directly opposed to Hyndman, Champion, etc.

Now for what has been happening in the SOCIAL DEMOCRATIC FEDERATION (by the same post you will be getting a lettter via Aveling from Bland, one of its members). Hyndman was given money by the TORIES to put up candidates against the Liberals — £340 has been admitted. But it must have been in the region of £1,000, since the *official* expenses of the 3 candidates amounted to more than £600.— With the exception of Burrows, the Executive Committee sanctioned Hyndman's action. However opposition arose within the main body of the federation. But before this could make itself felt, Hyndman, already seeing himself in the role of political arbitrator *à la* Parnell, left with Champion for Liverpool to offer his services to — *Chamberlain*, the Radical leader[415]! The proposal they made the latter was that they would support the Liberals if Chamberlain was prepared to withdraw a Liberal candidate in Birmingham in favour of Hyndman and thus secure him the Liberal vote. Chamberlain showed them the door.

Opposition within the federation is increasing. At the last Committee meeting, at which many other members of the federation were present, the correspondence relating to the Tory money was read out, despite opposition from Hyndman who wished to suppress it. Great rumpus. Why had the sections not been consulted on so vital a mat-

---

[a] Cf. the relevant figures in the previous letter.

ter? In short there is to be a general meeting and we shall have to see whether the federation survives it.

Obviously one may accept money from another party if that money is given unconditionally and if it does not do more harm than good. But Hyndman has acted like an idiot. In the first place he ought to have known that his candidatures couldn't help but manifest the ridiculous weakness of socialism in England. Again, he ought to have known that, by accepting money from the TORIES, he has damned himself once and for all in the eyes of the radical working men who form the vast majority and *to whom alone socialism can look for support*. In short, if one does such things, one advertises them, one boasts about them, but one doesn't make a secret of them. Hyndman, however, is a caricature of Lassalle; to him all means are good, even if *not* conducive to an end. He is in such a hurry to play the political panjandrum that he has no time to consider his real position. He combines all the bad qualities of your English PROFESSIONAL POLITI-CIAN — your ADVENTURER — with a quality common enough in France but rare over here, of seeing facts not as they are but as he would like them to be.

All this has come so soon after his infamous behaviour towards Aveling [502] that he has not yet been forgiven — even within his own party — and he is bound to have a pretty hard time of it if he is to survive the affair. In any case, if the Social Democratic Federation continues, it will no longer have any substance.

A kiss for Laura.

Yours ever,

F. E.

First published in: Marx and Engels, *Works*, Second Russian Edition, Vol. 36, Moscow, 1964

Printed according to the original

Translated from the French

Published in English for the first time

218

ENGELS TO HERMANN SCHLÜTER

IN HOTTINGEN-ZURICH

London, 7 December 1885

Dear Mr Schlüter,

My best thanks for the 2 copies of *Dühring*. [208] If I can have 20 copies all told, that will do for the time being. Please also send me 4 copies of the *Peasant War*, 3rd edition. I haven't a single copy left and so cannot get to work on the new edition. [213]

I have no connections whatever with Eccarius and neither can nor wish to renew them. I shall see if the address is obtainable through Lessner. But I would at most advise you simply to reprint without alterations, etc.— for, having gone completely to the dogs, Eccarius is in fact unlikely to make any; moreover, in view of his bad conscience, any such addenda would most likely be used by him to introduce extenuating circumstances for the many ill-deeds he has perpetrated since 1873, and thus materially impair the book which was written with much prompting by and help from Marx (towards the end, entire pages were literally written by Marx), if not render it completely useless for our propaganda. I would even advise you to insist on printing it as it stands. [503]

You will have had the bill for the photographs. [a]

In my *Dühring* I continue to suffer at the printer's hands even in the list of misprints where I find hopeless 'error' [Verirrung] for 'confusion' [Verwirrung].

Kind regards.

Yours,

F. E.

First published in: Marx and Engels, *Works*, First Russian Edition, Vol. XXVII, Moscow, 1935

Printed according to the original

Published in English for the first time

---

[a] of Marx (see this volume, p. 309)

219

ENGELS TO FERDINAND DOMELA NIEUWENHUIS

IN THE HAGUE

London, 19 December 1885

Dear Comrade,

I have despatched per PARCELS CONTINENTAL EXPRESS a package addressed to you containing the three Parliamentary Reports for which you asked. As you will see from the enclosed intimation, the first HOUSE OF LORDS report on prostitution is no longer to be had.

You are perfectly right in refraining from any kind of violent rebellion over there. This would only entail unnecessary sacrifice and set the movement back by decades. Next year it will be a hundred years since the Prussians first plundered Holland, [504] and nothing would please Bismarck more than to celebrate the centenary by a repetition of that 'epic deed'. The thirst for annexation, as yet no more than a harmless and impotent desire, might in that case assume more tangible form.

I shall send you by post the second edition of my *Anti-Dühring* which has just come out. [208]

Always at you service in the common cause, I remain

Yours very sincerely,

F. E.

First published, in Russian, in *Istorik-marksist*, No. 6 (40), Moscow, 1934

Printed according to the original

Published in English for the first time

220

ENGELS TO PASQUALE MARTIGNETTI

IN BENEVENTO

London, 21 December 1885

Dear Citizen,

I should be very pleased if you would undertake the translation of Marx's work *Wage Labour and Capital*. The information in the *Socialiste*[505] will barely suffice for the biography and I have therefore asked our friends in Zurich to send you a copy of the Brunswick *Kalender*,[a] which contains a more complete biography written by myself.[b]

Yours truly,
F. Engels

I shall of course be happy to carry out the revision, should you so desire.

First published in *La corrispondenza di Marx e Engels con italiani. 1848-1895*, Milano, 1964

Printed according to the original

Translated from the Italian

Published in English for the first time

221

ENGELS TO HERMANN SCHLÜTER

IN HOTTINGEN-ZURICH

London, 21 December 1885

Dear Mr Schlüter,

20 *Dührings* (in all) and 4 of the *Peasant War* received with thanks.[c]

Kindly tell Mrs Wischnewetzky that, *as agreed*, I shall be prepared to go over the ms. of her translation[349] and write the preface[d] as soon

---

[a] See this volume, p. 374. - [b] F. Engels, 'Karl Marx', *Volks-Kalender*, Brunswick, 1878. - [c] See this volume, p. 371. - [d] F. Engels, 'The Labor Movement in America. Preface to the American Edition of *The Condition of the Working Class in England*'.

as she has made a *firm arrangement* with a publisher. I'm so snowed under with work that it's downright impossible to take on anything else unless it's urgently required.

I shan't be able to turn my mind to a new German edition[a] until I have shed considerable part of my present load of work. In January I have to revise the English translation of *Capital*, negotiate with the publishers, etc. After that there's the *Peasant War*[213] and numerous other incidental jobs. Then comes the very urgent matter of the *Capital*, Volume III. Once I've cleared the decks to that extent, I'll be able to turn my mind to the old book.[a]

I cannot recall the pamphlet mentioned by Bucher.[506] Peel died in 1850. Marx's PAMPHLETS[b] appeared in 1855. Nor is it likely that Palmerston would have given some writer or other 100 guineas and a cask of sherry to provide proof that Palmerston was a Russian agent. It is possible that Tucker, when alluding to the earlier piece, suggested the same title for one of Marx's PAMPHLETS; that would explain everything. Nor were there any woodcuts in Marx's PAMPHLETS.

Kindest regards.

Yours,

F. Engels

Martignetti wants to translate *Wage Labour and Capital*[c] into Italian along with a biography of Marx which he hasn't got, as the few scrappy items in the *Socialiste*[505] are inadequate. Could you send him Bracke's *Volks-Kalender* containing my biography of Marx[d]? I think it's in the 1878 volume, but you'll find it easily enough. The address is

Paolo[e] Martignetti
Benevento, Italia.

First published in: Marx and Engels, *Works*, First Russian Edition, Vol. XXVII, Moscow, 1934

Printed according to the original

Published in English for the first time

---

[a] F. Engels, *The Condition of the Working-Class in England*. - [b] *Lord Palmerston* - [c] by Marx - [d] F. Engels, 'Karl Marx'. - [e] Should be Pasquale; see also this volume, p. 421.

222

ENGELS TO LAURA LAFARGUE

IN PARIS

London, 22 December 1885

My dear Laura,

Herewith I hand you the cheque Paul wrote about [507] to which I have added a trifling *étrenne*[a] for yourself. The box with the plum-pudding and cake was forwarded last Saturday[b] but would not leave here before Monday so that you will at best have received it today.

When Jollymeier came from Paris he told me you were sorely in want of dictionaries for your translating work. Among Mohr's books the only one that could have suited you was Mozin's French and German, but it was so dilapidated that it will be no use to any one for regular work; Tussy took it at the time. English and German there were none. So I tried to find out what were the best and ordered Williams and Norgate to have them delivered to you, *bound*. They are

Flügel's English-German and German-English

Mozin-Peschier French-German and German-French.

They will be delivered I expect before Christmas. Now as I had no opportunity to look at them, I want you to examine and report upon them. Flügel is the best to be had, though it might be better; so if it is both English-German and German-English, it will be all right. But about the Mozin-Peschier I am not so sure that it is not an abbreviation of what I intended to send you, namely: *Dictionnaire c o m p l e t des langues française et allemande*, 2 volumes French-German and 2 volumes German-French. If it should not be the latter work, please let me know and I will have it exchanged, as not being sent to order.

On Saturday night Jollymeier arrived here, his holidays last till 12th January; and this morning who should jump in but the inevitable Meyer, fresh from Winnipeg where his first crop of wheat was frozen to death last August. He left again and will be in Paris to-morrow morning—but, he says, *ich sehe die Lafargue's nicht—warum nicht?—Weil Lafargue einen nie besucht*[c]—which he seems to have

---

[a] Christmas gift - [b] 19 December - [c] I don't see the Lafargues.—Why not?—Because Lafargue never comes to see anyone.

taken very much to heart, and which I told him was rather foolish for him to do. I merely state this to you as it was said, so that you may console you in case the illustrious stranger does not call upon you.

I will try and get a copy of *Justice* for Paul,[508] it is not so easy just now, as Tussy and Edward are at Kingston on Thames for a few days and will not be back before Friday. Johnny[a] is with us in the meantime, he has picked up his English again rather quickly, especially since he goes to school. He is a very good boy and reads an awful deal of, to him, unintelligible books.

I hope Paul is all right again, sound at the core and solid at the base, *plus solide que le Pont Neuf*[b] which seems also subject to pimples and boils.[509] By the bye, his last letter does not say a word about the final solution of the Labruyère-Séverine-Lissagaray affair, the last was the assertion of Labruyère that Lissagaray *a menti.*[c] Has it all ended in smoke, as most scandals are apt to do now-a-days?

There is no doubt Hyndman has done for himself this time. If he manages to keep together a show of the Social Democratic Federation,[300] it will be only a shadow. The provincial branches are sure to fall off and here in London his own people have remembered how at the time of the Morris-Aveling separation,[d] he packed the general meeting by showing in a lot of new members, created for the occasion. They have therefore resolved that only those are to vote who were members at the time of the general election and of his exploits.[496]

Nim, Pumps and Jollymeier are gone to the West End, Christmas shopping as they pretend, but in reality for a dinner at the Vienna Beer Hall. As I am still a little under restraint, I have stopped at home and use the time to write to you. But now the dinner bell rings — for me and Johnny — and so good-bye. Health and spirits and a sound foundation for Paul!

Yours affectionately,
F. Engels

First published in: Marx and Engels, *Works*, Second Russian Edition, Vol. 36, Moscow, 1964

Reproduced from the original

Published in English for the first time

---

[a] Jean Longuet - [b] stronger than the Pont Neuf - [c] had lied - [d] See this volume, pp. 236-38 and 245.

223

ENGELS TO WILHELM LIEBKNECHT

[IN BORSDORF NEAR LEIPZIG [34]]

London, 28 December 1885

Dear Liebknecht,

Borkheim died in Hastings on Wednesday, 16 December, and was buried on the following Monday. An attack of pneumonia on the previous Sunday swiftly brought about his end. He had had tuberculosis for 12 years and during the final ten years, after the whole of his left side had become paralysed, he never left his bed save for a few brief intervals each day. He bore his sufferings with exceptional resilience and indomitable cheerfulness, always kept up with the political and social movement, and was a subscriber to the *Sozialdemokrat* until the very end. Up till a year ago he received a pension, first from two, then from one, of the houses for whom he had previously worked as salesman and/or buyer. Last year we collected amongst his friends here a subscription big enough to ensure that he had what he needed. You might perhaps put a short obituary in the *Sozialdemokrat* [510]; I prefer not to thrust myself to the fore on an occasion like this. There is no objection to your doing it and, besides, you are better acquainted with his activities in Baden.

As regards Russia's finances, [485] herewith a further word on the latest critical turn the affair has taken:

A fortnight ago the Russian government obtained through Bleichröder and the Russian Bank a further loan, but only of 20 million roubles, which was, according to reports, heavily over-subscribed in Berlin. Depending on whether this is taken to mean roubles in specie or in paper, and that's something you can ascertain over there, it represents roughly either 60 million marks or else a mere 40 million. The loan was intended to secure the advances made by the Russian Bank to the government. As usual, the same old hollow excuse. How hollow became evident a few days later! About a week ago it was reported in the English papers that the Russian government had ordered the Russian Bank to sell the Russian aristocracy's (doubtless the Credit Bank's) mortgage bonds for 100 million roubles. The German press, enlarging on this, stated that in return the Bank was to advance the government 75 million of the proceeds. Thus the government is paying the Bank at best 20 million roubles in gold and is borrowing in return 75 million roubles extra. But since the realisation of 100 million mortgage notes is a highly tedious operation, especially in Russia, this means, in other words, that 75 millions in new paper money are to be created and loaned to the government. Before the holidays the rouble was standing at $23^1/_8d$. (instead of 39d.) over here and is bound to go even lower — as it will also do internally; in their present financial predicament the device they have to use to give some support to their ruined currency (the 20 millions in gold, when the Bank gets it) serves only to bedevil their paper currency even further. 1789 is on its way — even without the Nihilists [356] — expedited by the government itself.

One may further conclude from the above that Bismarck is holding his Russians on a short rein and will not authorise the release of German funds other than on a hand-to-mouth basis lest the Russians should get too uppish and do the dirty on him in the Balkans. [445]

I can only suggest the main points for you to work on, but you will have little difficulty in finding out further details in Berlin.

This Christmas we — the Avelings, the Kautskys, Pumps and her husband,[a] Schorlemmer, Lenchen and I — sat up drinking to our hearts' content and making merry until four in the morning.

A Happy New Year to you.

Your

F. E.

Schorlemmer sends his best wishes.

First published, in Russian, in *Marx-Engels Archives*, Vol. I (VI), Moscow, 1932

Printed according to the original

Published in English for the first time

---

[a] Percy White Rosher

224

ENGELS TO JOHANN PHILIPP BECKER

IN GENEVA

London, 28 December 1885

Dear Old Man,

This is to notify you that our friend Borkheim died of pneumonia at Hastings on the 16th of this month after a three days' illness. He had had tuberculosis for twelve years and for the last ten years the whole of his left side had been paralysed. According to the doctor he had enough ailments to kill three other men. All this he bore with indomitable cheerfulness and, so far as he was able, kept up with the movement to the end. I have asked Liebknecht to publish a short obituary in the *Sozialdemokrat*.[510]

At the beginning of this month I sent you a money order which I trust you have received.

For the rest—as the post is about to go and I get little time for writing in what is for me a period of turbulence—I wish you a Happy New Year and continuing good health; our movement is in no particular need of good wishes, since it is forging ahead everywhere—at a pace which varies according to place and people—, but everywhere splendidly, while the dirty business in the Balkans[445] actually seems to be petering out without a world war.

With my very kindest regards,

Your old friend

F. Engels

First published in: F. Engels, *Vergessene Briefe (Briefe Friedrich Engels' an Johann Philipp Becker)*, Berlin, 1920

Printed according to the original

Published in English for the first time

1886

225

ENGELS TO WILHELM LIEBKNECHT

[IN BORSDORF NEAR LEIPZIG [34]]

London, 2 January 1886

Dear Liebknecht, [511]

Borkheim's wife died some 8 years ago. No great loss to him — she drank. His son,[a] aged 19, is a clerk in Dunkirk. To begin with he himself was in business in Liverpool; during the Crimean War a speculative trip to Balaklava with a load of bits and pieces earned him £15,000 all at one go, which, however, he lost because he did the same thing again and peace supervened [512]; became a wine merchant and discovered that his palate for Bordeaux was probably the finest in London; became the agent of a Bordeaux house, built up a clientèle for them, but was insufficiently circumspect and, when he sought a partnership, was given the push — they no longer needed him. No wiser for the experience, he tried to repeat this brilliant performance with another house, the result being the same, hence had to start from the beginning once more. Again promptly discovered two good connexions, lived like a lord as always, while at Badenweiler had an apoplectic fit (about 10 years ago), which completely paralysed his left side, whereupon it transpired that, rather than possessing money, he had been borrowing from his friends in order to support his madly extravagant mode of life. But in spite of it all he was so much liked that people calmly put up with their losses, while the two houses for which he had worked paid him a pension to live on. His housemaid, with whom there had undoubtedly been some highly intimate goings-on, looked after him up till his death — she was able to furnish

---

[a] F. Borkheim

a boarding-house in Hastings [239] and still do pretty well out of it during the season. A year ago, when the last of his pensions was stopped, we succeeded in persuading his City friends, all of whom were owed money by him, to provide a new and adequate pension. Absurdly ostentatious in his conduct while his luck was in, he behaved like a hero when suddenly assailed by the most atrocious ill-fortune. Never a word of complaint, unfailingly cheerful, no sign of his having been affected by this sudden downfall. Rarely have I met such resilience. He spent his time writing his autobiography, first in English, then in German; the latter is probably not quite finished. [248] If you could find a publisher for it as well as some money for the boy, who earns a wage of £70 after an upbringing that might almost suggest his having been born in the purple, you would be doing a good turn. The address is F. Borkheim, *aux soins de*[a] Messieurs Bourdon & Cie, Dunkerque, France.

You are on the wrong track with your suppositions about the secret insinuations concerning you that have come to my ears. The only good friend who might possibly have managed to find some fault with you, the one 'who told you' this, 'who told you' that? — is called Wilhelm Liebknecht[b] and his insinuations have appeared in writing in his letters and in print in the *Sozialdemokrat* and any number of German newspapers. Thanks to this source I have known for years that you have a pleasing and insuperable weakness for all the 'eddicated' elements that hover round the fringes of the party and that you wish to win them over, even though 95 per cent of them can only do us harm. I further understand from this source that last year you only noticed personal differences within the parliamentary group [49] whereas now you are already discovering 'backsliders'. I am also indebted to the above source for the knowledge that this same Wilhelm Liebknecht is on occasion inclined to forget what has been written if, at that moment, it doesn't suit his book and that he hopes others will be good-natured enough to do him a similar favour. Which is not, unfortunately, always possible. But as to your passion for picking up 'eddicated' elements and glossing over all differences, one must put up with such things and does so fairly readily for their being unavoidable. But don't ask that they be overlooked. And their inevitability causes me all the less concern because I know, and shall say as much

---

[a] care of - [b] See this volume, p. 387.

at every opportunity, that, come the moment of decision between the conflicting elements, you will be on the right side. [513]

And now a Happy New Year.

Your
F. Engels

First published in *Leipziger Volkszeitung*, Nr. 218, 15. September 1983

Printed according to a photocopy of the original

Published in English for the first time

226

ENGELS TO FLORENCE KELLEY-WISCHNEWETZKY [27]

IN ZURICH

London, 7 January 1886
122 Regent's Park Road, N. W.

Dear Mrs Wischnewetzky,

I have received your ms. [349] but have not as yet been able to look at it, so cannot say how long it will take me. Anyhow I shall lose no time, you may be sure.

As to those wise Americans who think their country exempt from the consequences of fully expanded capitalist production, they seem to live in blissful ignorance of the fact that sundry States, Massachusetts, New Jersey, Pennsylvania, Ohio, etc., have such an institution as a Labour Bureau from the reports of which they might learn something to the contrary. [514]

Yours very truly,
F. Engels

First published abridged, in the language of the original (English), in *Briefe und Auszüge aus Briefen von Joh. Phil. Becker, Jos. Dietzgen, Friedrich Engels, Karl Marx u. A. an F. A. Sorge und Andere*, Stuttgart, 1906 and in full in: Marx and Engels, *Works*, First Russian Edition, Vol. XXVII, Moscow, 1935

Reproduced from the original

227

ENGELS TO WILHELM LIEBKNECHT

IN BERLIN

London, 7 January 1886

Dear Liebknecht,

Your conjecture re 'Blos'[a][515] merely provides me with further proof that the 'nervousness' you complain of is once again entirely of your own making. Still, as you say, NEVER MIND.

Borkheim was born in Glogau in 1825, studied at Greifswald and Berlin, was a three-year artillery volunteer in Glogau in 1848, came under investigation as a result of democratic meetings and bolted; subsequently spent some time in Berlin, fled, I believe, after the storming of the arsenal[516] and went, if I'm not mistaken, to Switzerland, whence he returned with Struve. I don't remember the exact details.

I shall be writing about the biographical note.[517]

Tussy will be given your message on Sunday.[b]

If you and Bebel, both of you, go to America together, you will certainly be able to raise money; should either of you not go or be replaced by someone else, that would make a difference of 25%-30% in the money you would receive.[518] Besides, you yourself will be particularly needed, since at least one of you will, from time to time, have to make a speech in English.

As regards the Baltic Canal I'm all for its being at least 8 metres deep.[519] The size and draught of merchant STEAMERS are constantly increasing (5,500 tons is already quite usual), and new docks are being increasingly taken to a depth of 9 or 10 metres, so that a shallower canal would become obsolete within a few years, just like the Eider Canal now, which became completely so 30 years ago (as to some extent it always had been).

Your trip might be brought forward by a dissolution occasioned by the dissolution of old William[c] which may happen at any moment.

---

[a] Bloß in the original. -[b] 10 January -[c] William I

But that would mean we should have the pleasure of seeing you here all the sooner.

Schorlemmer is still with us and sends his best wishes.

Otherwise everything is going well, but not for the SOCIAL DEMOCRATIC FEDERATION[300] which Mr Hyndman would seem to have ruined good and proper this time. [a] Though he may win a spurious victory at his PACKED GENERAL MEETING next Sunday, *he's done for in the provinces*, and here all he's left with is a *steadily dwindling number of supporters*.

Kindest regards.

Your old friend

F. E.

First published, in Russian, in *Marx-Engels Archives*, Vol. I (VI), Moscow, 1932

Printed according to the original

Published in English for the first time

228

ENGELS TO LAURA LAFARGUE

IN PARIS

London, 17 January 1886

My dear Laura,

Glad the dictionaries have arrived at last. [b] They were promised to be sent from here more than a week before Christmas.

Yesterday I received a post-card from Dr Max Quarck informing me that as a good extract from the *Capital* is wanted, he intends to translate Deville's [c]:

'*Herr Deville hat mir nun eben auf mein Nachsuchen die alleinige Autorisation zur Übersetzung seines Auszuges ins Deutsche gegeben*' [d];

the great Quarck has offered it to Meissner and desires me to favour him with a preface.

---

[a] See this volume, pp. 366-70. - [b] Ibid., p. 375. - [c] G. Deville, *Le Capital de Karl Marx. Résumé...* - [d] '*In reply to my request Mr Deville has just granted me the unreserved right to translate his brief exposition into German.*'

Now if Deville has really done so, I cannot but consider that he has acted very unwisely and moreover contrary to all the international obligations practically existing amongst the lot of us. How in the world could he commit himself with a man of whom he knew nothing? This Quarck is one of half a dozen young literati who hover about the boundary land between our party and the *Katheder-Sozialismus*,[54] take jolly good care to keep clear of all the risks involved by being connected with our party, and yet expect to reap all the benefits that may accrue from such connection. They make a lively propaganda for *das soziale Kaisertum der Hohenzollern*[a] (which Quarck has dithyrambically celebrated), for Rodbertus against Marx (Quarck had the cheek to write to me that he honoured the *Capital* by placing it in his library *neben die Werke des grossen Rodbertus*[b]) and especially for each other. The fellow is so utterly impotent that even Liebknecht who has a certain tenderness for these fellows, has agreed with Kautsky that he is not fit to write in the *Neue Zeit*.[520]

This moment Kautsky enters with Paul's letter,[c] according to that Deville has *not* replied and Quarck lies. I should be very glad if this was so, because then I should have that little scamp completely on the hip.

But now as to the translation itself. First of all, an extract from the *Capital* for our German workmen must be done from the German original, not from the French edition.[59] Secondly Deville's book is too big for the working men, and would in the translation, especially of the second half, be as difficult as the original, as it is composed as much as possible of literal extracts.[81] It does well enough for France where most of the terms are *not Fremdwörter*,[d] and where there is a large public, not exactly working men, who all the same wish to have some knowledge — of easy access — of the subject, without reading the big book. That public, in Germany, ought to read the original book. —

Thirdly, and chiefly, if Deville's book appears in German, I do not see how I can consistently with my duty towards Mohr let it pass unchallenged as a faithful résumé. I have held my tongue while it was published only in French, although I had distinctly protested against the whole second half of it, before publication.[e] But if it comes to be put before the German public that is quite a different thing. I cannot allow, in Germany, Mohr to be perverted — in his *very words*. If there

---

[a] *the social empire of the Hohenzollerns* - [b] *beside the works of great Rodbertus* - [c] Lafargue's letter to Engels of 10 January 1886 - [d] *foreign words* - [e] See this volume, pp. 61, 63.

had not been that absurd hurry at the time, if it had been revised as I suggested, there would not be that objection now. All I can say, I reserve my full liberty of action in case the book is published in Germany; and I am the more bound to do so as it has got abroad that I looked it over in the ms.

I cannot this moment ask Kautsky about his intentions as to Deville's book, because all the people for Sunday's dinner have come in, and I must conclude. Kautsky must write himself. As far as I know Kautsky and Bernstein intend making a fresh extract themselves which would be decidedly the best thing to do, and where they may make use of Deville's work and *acknowledge it with thanks*. [137]

Tussy, Edward, the Pumps' and Kautskys, all send their loves, kind regards and kisses and I don't know what more, ditto Johnny [a] and the other little ones.

Yours affectionately but hungry,
F. E.

First published, in the language of the original (English), in: F. Engels, P. et L. Lafargue, *Correspondance*, t. I, Paris, 1956

Reproduced from the original

229

ENGELS TO AUGUST BEBEL [521]

IN BERLIN

London, 20-23 January 1886

Dear Bebel,

So the great bolt has been fired. Schramm did me the honour of sending me a copy of the magnum opus [b]; but it is, I must say, a very *pauvre* [c] affair and the prompt reference to it in the *Sozialdemokrat* [d] did him too signal an honour. Ede will undoubtedly give him a good

---

[a] Jean Longuet - [b] C. A. S[chramm], *Rodbertus, Marx, Lassalle. Sozialwissenschaftliche Studie.* - [c] miserable - [d] 'Zur Aufklärung', *Der Sozialdemokrat*, No. 50, 10 December 1885.

dressing-down; I have, through Kautsky, drawn his attention to a number of points — the essentials can safely be left to him. [522] For Kautsky this controversy with Schramm has been salutory in every way. [523] Schramm, being unable to say anything about the actual matter in hand, is skilful enough to pick on all the errors of form perpetrated by Kautsky, partly out of youthful impetuosity, partly out of the habits acquired at university and in literary practice, and this has been a very salutory lesson to him. In this respect Ede already has a considerable advantage over Kautsky because, though neither a university man nor a professional littérateur, he is, through being on the *Sozialdemokrat*, always in the thick of the fray, besides which he's a business man and, last but not least, a Jew. For after all it's only in war that you learn the art of war.

What you tell me about the parliamentary group's frame of mind is most encouraging. Provided the party remains sound — and here the petty bourgeoisie will surely not gain the upper hand — the blunders of the deputy gentlemen can only serve to give these last a rude lesson. As you yourself say — and this is also my opinion — we shall never get the right kind of people into the Reichstag in time of peace and here the help afforded us by the party through bringing pressure to bear on the deputy gentlemen is absolutely invaluable; it shows that they must avoid any serious conflict, and the knowledge that this is so might, at a crucial moment, be of the utmost importance, since it would enable us to make a resolute stand in the certainty that we should emerge unscathed.

Of late Liebknecht has been positively bombarding me with letters asking for information about this and that. I took the opportunity of telling him, briefly and unequivocally, if in an altogether friendly way, just what I thought of his inconsistent conduct; and when, as usual, he tried to attribute this to some piece of gossip I must have heard, I told him that there was only one person who could harm him in my eyes, and that was Wilhelm Liebknecht who was for ever forgetting what he had said in his letters and published in the press. However that might be, I went on, we should simply have to put up with his foibles, and would do so all the more readily for the knowledge that, when things really came to a head, he would be found in the right place. [a] Whereupon, contrary to his usual customary insistence upon having the last word, he calmed down again.

---

[a] See this volume, pp. 381-82.

As he mentioned the matter of the Schleswig-Holstein Canal, I took the opportunity of telling him that it would be stupid to vote for a shallow canal less than 8 or 9 metres deep, [a] allegedly out of opposition to its use by the Fleet. The tonnage of large merchant ships is steadily on the increase, 5,000 or 6,000 tons being already the norm, and ever more ports are being adapted to accommodate vessels of corresponding draught. Those that cannot do so become obsolete and fall into decay, as will also happen in the Baltic. If the Baltic is to have its share of overseas trade, deep water harbours will accordingly have to be built there, and this will happen as surely as it has happened elsewhere. But to build the canal in such a way that, within the next 10 or 20 years, it will become as useless and obsolete as the old Eider Canal is now, would be throwing money down the drain.

As regards my proposal for productive cooperatives on state-owned land, [b] its sole purpose was to show the majority — which was, after all, then *in favour* of the Steamship Subsidies [342] — how they could decently vote against it and thus emerge from the impasse in which they found themselves. But in my view, the principle of the thing was altogether correct. It is perfectly true that, when we propose something positive, our proposals should always be *practicable*. But practicable *as such*, regardless of whether the present government can implement them. I would go even further and say that, if we propose socialist measures conducive to the downfall of capitalist production (as these are), we should restrict them to such as are *essentially feasible*, but could *not* be implemented by *this* government. For this government would tamper with and ruin any such measure, and put it through merely with a view to sabotaging it. This particular proposal, however, would not be implemented by any Junker or bourgeois government. To point the way for the rural proletariat in the Baltic provinces, if not set it upon the path that would enable it to put an end to exploitation by the Junkers and big farmers — to attract into the movement the very people whose servitude and stultification supplies the regiments upon which Prussia entirely depends, in short, to destroy Prussia from within, from the root up, is something that would never occur to them. The measure for which we must press, come what may, so long as big estates continue to exist there, and which we must ourselves put into practice the moment we come to the helm, is as fol-

---

[a] See this volume, p. 383. - [b] Ibid., pp. 239, 240.

lows: the transfer—initially on lease—of large estates to autonomous cooperatives under state management and effected in such a way that the State retains ownership of the land. But the great advantage of this measure is that it is perfectly feasible as such, although no party except ours would embark upon it, and thus no party can bedevil it. And it alone would suffice to put paid to Prussia, so that the sooner we popularise it the better for us.

The matter has nothing whatever to do either with Schulze-Delitzsch or with Lassalle. Both supported small cooperatives, in one case with, in the other without, state aid; but in neither were the cooperatives to take possession of the *already extant* means of production; rather they were to introduce new cooperative production *alongside* already extant capitalist production. My proposal envisages the introduction of cooperatives into existing production. *They are to be given land which would otherwise be exploited along capitalist lines*; just as the Paris Commune demanded that the workers should manage cooperatively the factories closed down by the manufacturers. [a] Therein lies the great distinction. Nor have Marx and I ever doubted that, in the course of transition to a wholly communist economy, widespread use would have to be made of cooperative management as an intermediate stage. [b] Only it will mean so organising things that society, i. e. initially the State, retains ownership of the means of production and thus prevents the particular interests of the cooperatives from taking precedence over those of society as a whole. The fact that the Empire is not a land-owner is neither here nor there; you will find some formula, just as you did in the Polish debate, for here again the expulsions were no immediate concern of the Empire's. [524]

Precisely because the government cannot envisage anything of the sort, there would be no harm in demanding the grant I propose as a counterpart to the steamship grant. Had there been any possibility of the government's assenting to it, you would, of course, have been right.

The disintegration of the German Free Thinkers [231] in the sphere of economics tallies exactly with what is happening among the English Radicals. [415] The old Manchester School men *à la* John Bright are dying off and, just like the Berliners, the younger generation is

---

[a] See K. Marx, *The Civil War in France* (present edition, Vol. 22, pp. 328-35). - [b] See *Resolutions of the Congress of Geneva, 1866...* 4. Co-operative labour.

dabbling in piecemeal social reform. Save that here the bourgeois wish to help not so much the industrial worker as the agricultural labourer who rendered them such signal service during the late elections [487] and, in true English fashion, are demanding intervention not so much by the State as by the local authorities. For rural workers, allotments and potato patches, for those in the towns, sanitary improvements and the like, such is their programme. It is an excellent sign that the bourgeois should already be having to sacrifice their pet classical economic theory, partly on political grounds and partly because they themselves have lost faith in it as a result of its practical consequences. The same thing is evident in the growth of armchair socialism [54] which, in one form or another, is increasingly supplanting classical economics in academic faculties on both sides of the Channel. The real contradictions engendered by the mode of production have in fact become so glaring that no theory will now serve to conceal them save the hotch-potch of armchair socialism which, however, is not a theory but sheer drivel.

Six weeks ago there were said to be indications that business was looking up here. Now all that is over and done with; poverty is worse than ever before, as is the mood of hopelessness and, on top of that, the winter is an exceptionally severe one. This is already the eighth year in which overproduction has exerted pressure on the markets and, instead of improving, the situation is getting steadily worse, nor can there be any doubt that it is essentially different from what it used to be. Since the appearance of serious rivals to Britain on the world market, the era of crises, in the old sense of the term, has come to an end. If, from being acute, the crises become chronic yet lose nothing of their intensity, what is likely to happen? There is bound to be another, if brief, period of prosperity after the vast stocks of goods have been run down, but I am curious to see what will come of it all. Of two things, however, we may be sure: We have entered a period which poses a far greater threat to the existence of the old state of society than did the period of ten-year crises; and, secondly, prosperity, if it comes, will affect Britain to a much lesser extent than before, when it alone used to skim the cream off the world market. The day when this is clearly realised in this country will be the day when the socialist movement will begin here in real earnest — and not before.

I shall have to leave the composition of the English Liberals to another time. It is a complex subject because it involves depicting a state of transition.[430]

This morning I received from Dresden the debate on the Polish motion (1st day). No doubt the 2nd day will follow shortly.[a] It is all the more essential for me to be sent these things now that I see only the weekly edition of the *Kölnische Zeitung* which contains only brief excerpts from the debates. How are the short-hand reports sold? I will gladly pay for those of all debates in which our people take a serious part.

Whatever happens, it's essential that you should also go on the American tour.[518] On the one hand, its success greatly depends on your presence. On the other, the party will not be properly represented unless you are there. If you don't go, the first-comer will be sent along with Liebknecht, and who knows what might not happen then. Thirdly, you should not miss the opportunity of seeing with your own eyes the most progressive country in the world. Life in Germany exerts an oppressive and constricting influence on anyone, even the best, as I know from my own experience, and one ought to get out of the place — from time to time at any rate. And in that case we might also see you over here again. Had I been able to get away from my work, I should long since have slipped across to America, as I was always hoping to do with Marx. Anyway, to people abroad, you and Liebknecht represent the party and there is no substitute for either of you. Should you not go, it will mean a loss of anything between 5,000 and 10,000 marks, if not more.

It might, in fact, be a very pleasant experience. For Tussy and Aveling have been corresponding with American free-thinkers about the possibility of a trip to that country, and would like to combine it with yours. They expect to hear within the next 3 or 4 weeks. If it comes off, the four of you would make agreeable travelling companions.

But now, good-bye for the present. Apropos, Ede exceeded my expectations in his first anti-Schramm article.[522] Absolutely splendid.

---

[a] *Stenographische Berichte über die Verhandlungen des Reichstags. VI. Legislaturperiode. II. Session 1885/86*, Vol. I. 25th sitting on 15 January 1886, 26th sitting on 16 January 1886.

He has indeed learnt to make war in accordance with the rules of strategy and tactics.

Your
F. E.

First published abridged in: F. Engels, *Politisches Vermächtnis. Aus unveröffentlichten Briefen*, Berlin, 1920 and in full, in Russian, in *Marx-Engels Archives*, Vol. I (VI), Moscow, 1932

Printed according to the original
Published in English in full for the first time

230

ENGELS TO EDWARD PEASE [525]

IN LONDON

[Draft]

[London,] 27 January 1886

Dear Sir,

In answer to your kind note of yesterday I regret to say that my time is so entirely taken up by urgent work on hand, that I cannot possibly for at least a year to come undertake any fresh engagements whatever.

Having said this much, I need not enter upon other considerations which might stand in the way of my writing the article you desire. But I may state at all events that the party to which I belong, has no fixed ready-made proposals to submit. Our views as to the points of difference between a future, non-capitalistic society and that of to-day, are strict conclusions from existing historical facts and developments, and of no value — theoretical or practical — unless presented in connection with these facts and developments. The economical aspect of these points of difference I have tried to establish and to explain in my book *Herrn E. D. Umwälzung der Wissenschaft* 2nd ed. p. 253 to 271; reprinted in my pamphlet *Die Entwicklung des Sozialismus etc.* 3rd ed. p. 28-48. [a] Shorter I cannot possibly do even this partial

---

[a] The reference is to Engels' *Anti-Dühring* and *Socialism: Utopian and Scientific* (see present edition, Vol. 25, pp. 254-71 and Vol. 24, pp. 306-25).

abstract, where neither political nor non-economic social questions are even touched. To give you a résumé in 600 words is therefore a task utterly beyond my powers.

I am yours faithfully

First published in: Marx and Engels, *Works*, First Russian Edition, Vol. XXVII, Moscow, 1935

Reproduced from the original

Published in English for the first time

231

ENGELS TO FRIEDRICH ADOLPH SORGE [521]

IN HOBOKEN

London, 29 January 1886

Dear Sorge,

At last I have some time to spare and hence shall hasten to write to you before anything else comes to claim it.

I hope your Adolf[a] has made a success of his new business. For he understands it and is a hard worker; besides, it's not a particularly speculative business — a great danger, in America as here — so I don't see why all should not be well. I therefore wish him every success.

I should *greatly* like to have Marx's comments re an English translation. [526] At last I have with me, here under my roof, the *complete* ms. of the English translation upon which I shall set to work next week. As soon as I know approximately how long the revision is going to take, and can thus determine the date when printing may begin, I shall make definite arrangements with the publisher. You will have seen (in *To-Day*) how Mr Hyndman, alias Broadhouse, endeavoured to put a spoke in my wheel. [527] This has forced me to get a move-on so as not further to impair my position vis-à-vis the publisher, but otherwise no harm has been done.

An American woman[b] has translated my book on the working

---

[a] Adolf Sorge jun. - [b] Florence Kelley-Wischnewetzky

class [a] into English, and has also sent me the ms. for revision—parts of which will be very time-consuming. Its publication in America is assured, but what this lady sees in the old thing I cannot imagine.

I further have in hand—to mention only revisions: 1) *The Eighteenth Brumaire*, [b] French—about $^1/_3$ already done. 2) *Wage Labour and Capital* by Marx—Italian. 3) *The Origin of the Family*—Danish. 4) *Manifesto* [c] and *Socialism: Utopian and Scientific*, etc., Danish; these two already in print but stiff with mistakes. 5) *The Origin of the Family*, French. [403] 6) *Socialism: Utopian and Scientific*, English. [528] PLENTY MORE LOOMING IN THE DISTANCE. As you can see, I'm turning into a mere schoolmaster correcting exercise-books. It's lucky that my knowledge of languages is not more extensive, for if it were, they'd be piling Russian, Polish, Swedish, etc., stuff on to me as well. But it is work of which one easily tires—in any case all these nice little bits and pieces (at any rate Nos. 2 to 5) will have to give way before Volume III of *Capital* which I have finished dictating from the ms., though the editing of some of the most important chapters will involve a *great* deal of work, these consisting in little more than an assemblage of building blocks. That is the only task to which I look forward.

I have *not* yet had the *New Yorker Volkszeitung*. I shall, if possible, send off *To-Day*, September, by the same post as this. You've no idea how difficult these things are to get hold of here—the slovenliness of the publishers is quite disgraceful.

If you haven't yet seen it, get Dietzgen to give you Hubert Bland's piece on Hyndman's simultaneous machinations with the Tories and Liberals over the elections. [496] It is absolutely true. After this, and provided it doesn't disintegrate, the SOCIAL DEMOCRATIC FEDERATION [300] will be morally defunct. Hyndman must be mad to act as he does. You will have read all about his insane attack on Aveling, and will also have seen the relevant documents in *Justice* and *Commonweal*. [502] Unfortunately, none of the other leaders of the FEDERATION are worth much more than he, being literati and political speculators. Indeed, the movement in this country has hitherto been quite bogus, but should it prove possible to educate within the SOCIALIST LEAGUE [346] a nucleus with an understanding of theoretical matters, considerable progress will have been made towards the eruption, which cannot be long in coming, of a genuine mass movement.

[a] F. Engels, *The Condition of the Working Class in England in 1844*. - [b] K. Marx, *The Eighteenth Brumaire of Louis Bonaparte*. - [c] K. Marx and F. Engels, *Manifesto of the Communist Party*.

Give my regards to Dietzgen. It's uphill work for him, but he'll manage all right.[529] AFTER ALL, the movement in America has made tremendous strides. True, the Anglo-Americans want to do things their *own* way with a total disregard for reason and science, nor could one expect anything else, yet they are drawing closer and will end up by coming all the way. Over there capitalist centralisation is going ahead like a house on fire — unlike here.

I trust your health is completely restored. I'm pretty well on the whole, otherwise I should never get through my work.

I've been working on Bebel with a view to his visiting the States with Liebknecht.[a] Tussy and Aveling might go too. But that remains to be decided.

My kindest regards to Adolf.

Your

F. Engels

First published abridged in *Briefe und Auszüge aus Briefen von Joh. Phil. Becker, Jos. Dietzgen, Friedrich Engels, Karl Marx u. A. an F. A. Sorge und Andere*, Stuttgart, 1906 and in full in: Marx and Engels, *Works*, First Russian Edition, Vol. XXVII, Moscow, 1935

Printed according to the original

Published in English in full for the first time

232

ENGELS TO FLORENCE KELLEY-WISCHNEWETZKY[530]

IN ZURICH

London, 3 February 1886

My dear Mrs Wischnewetzky,

To-day I forwarded to you, registered, the first portion of the ms. up to your page 70, incl. I am sorry I could not possibly send it sooner. But I had a job on hand which must be finished before I could start with your ms. Now I shall go on swimmingly; as I proceed I find we get better acquainted with each other, you with my peculiar,

---

[a] See this volume, p. 391.

old-fashioned German, I with your American. And indeed, I learn a good deal at it. Never before did the difference between British and American English strike me so vividly as in this *experimentum in proprio corpore vili.*[a] What a splendid future must there be in store for a language which gets enriched and developed on two sides of an ocean, and which may expect further additions from Australia and India!

I do not know whether this portion of the ms. will arrive in time to reach Miss Foster before her sailing, but I hope you will not be put to any particular inconvenience through my delay which was indeed unavoidable. I cannot be grateful enough to all the friends who wish to translate both Marx's and my writings into the various civilised languages and who show their confidence in me by asking me to look over their translations. And I am willing enough to do it, but for me as well as for others the day has but 24 hours, and so I cannot possibly always arrange to please everybody and to chime in with all arrangements made.

If I am not too often interrupted in the evenings I hope to be able to send you the remainder of the ms. and possibly also the introduction in a fortnight. This latter may be printed either as a preface[b] or as an appendix.[c] As to the length of it, I am utterly incapable of giving you any idea. I shall try to make it as short as possible, especially as it will be useless for me to try to combat arguments of the American press with which I am not even superficially acquainted. Of course if American workingmen will not read their own States' Labour Reports,[514] but trust to politicians' extracts, nobody can help them. But it strikes me that the present chronic depression which seems endless so far, will tell its tale in America as well as in England. America will smash up England's industrial monopoly—whatever there is left of it—but America cannot herself succeed to that monopoly. And unless *one* country has the monopoly of the markets of the world, at least in the decisive branches of trade, the conditions—relatively favourable—which existed here in England from 1848 to 1870, cannot anywhere be reproduced, and even in America the condition of the working class must gradually sink lower and lower. For if there are three countries (say England, America and Germany) competing on comparatively equal terms for the possession of the *Welt-*

---

[a] experiment upon one's own worthless body - [b] F. Engels, 'The Labor Movement in America. Preface to the American Edition of *The Condition of the Working Class in England*'.-[c] F. Engels, 'Appendix to the American Edition of *The Condition of the Working Class in England*'.

markt,[a] there is no chance but chronic overproduction, one of the three being capable of supplying the whole quantity required. That is the reason why I am watching the development of the present crisis with greater interest than ever and why I believe it will mark an epoch in the mental and political history of the American and English working classes—the very two whose assistance is as absolutely necessary as it is desirable.

Yours very truly,

F. Engels

First published, in the language of the original (English), in *Briefe und Auszüge aus Briefen von Joh. Phil. Becker, Jos. Dietzgen, Friedrich Engels, Karl Marx u. A. an F. A. Sorge und Andere,* Stuttgart, 1906   Reproduced from the original

---

233

ENGELS TO FERDINAND DOMELA NIEUWENHUIS [531]

IN THE HAGUE

London, 4 February 1886

Dear Comrade,

I am reading your work *Hoe ons land geregeerd wordt* with great pleasure, firstly because I am relearning a great deal of conversational Dutch therefrom and secondly because I am learning so much about the internal administration of Holland. Along with England and Switzerland, Holland is the only West European country *not* to have had absolute monarchy in the period between the 16th and 18th centuries, and in consequence enjoys a number of advantages, notably a residue of local and provincial self-government and an absence of any real bureaucracy in the French or Prussian sense. This is a great advantage both as regards the development of a national character and as regards the future; for only a few changes will have to be

---

[a] world market

made to establish here that free self-government by the working [people]ª which will necessarily be our best tool in the reorganisation of the mode of production. All this is lacking in Germany and France and will have to be built up from scratch. May I congratulate you on your success in producing a popular exposition.

Your translation of my pamphletᵇ places me most deeply in your debt. In this instance it will not be so easy to employ popular language throughout, as in your little opus, but this should present no problem to someone with so good a command of both languages as yourself.

'*Gewanne*' are the strips of land of roughly the same quality into which common agricultural and pasture land is first divided; maybe ten or twenty in all. Then each commoner with full rights is given an equal share of each strip. Thus, if there are ten strips and a hundred commoners, there will be 1,000 parcels of land all told, each commoner getting 10 parcels, one in each strip. Subsequently commoners may often swap parcels so that though they may have fewer individual plots, their holdings are more compact. The same thing was still happening until quite lately in Ireland in the 'RUNDALE' ⁵³² villages, and in the Highlands of Scotland (cf. *Fortnightly Review*, November 1885, an article on VILLAGE COMMUNITIES in Scotlandᶜ).

G. L. Maurer has written:

1) *Einleitung in die Geschichte der Mark-, Hof-, Dorf- und Städteverfassung in Deutschland.*

2) *Geschichte der Markenverfassung in Deutschland.*

3) *Geschichte der Hofverfassung   "   " 4 vols.*

4) ditto   " *Städteverfassung   " " 2 "*

5) ditto   " *Dorfverfassung   " " 2 "*

Nos. 1 and 2 are the most important, but the others are not without importance either, particularly as regards German history. Repetitiveness, poor style and lack of method make these otherwise excellent books difficult to study. *On n'est pas Allemand pour rien!* ᵈ

The best works on the great French Revolution are indubitably those of Georges Avenel who died round about 1875. *Lundis révolutionnaires*, a collection of feuilletons which came out in the *République*

ªThe manuscript is damaged here.- ᵇ F. Engels, *De ontwikkeling van het socialisme van utopie tot wetenschap.*- ᶜ J. Rae, 'The Scotch Village Community', *The Fortnightly Review*, Vol. XXXVIII, No. CCXXVII, 1 November 1885.- ᵈ One's not a German for nothing.

Française; also, *Anacharsis Cloots*, this last a survey, forming part of the biography, of the course of the Revolution up till Thermidor 1794. It's melodramatically written and, if one is not to lose the thread, one has continually to refer to Mignet [a] or Thiers [b] for the exact dates. But Avenel has made a close study of the archives and also produces a vast amount of new and reliable material. He is indisputably the best source for the period from September 1792 to July 1794. Then there is a very good book by Bougeart [c] on Jean Paul Marat, *L'Ami du peuple*; also another about Marat, said to be good, the name of whose author eludes me—it begins with Ch. [d] Some other good stuff also appeared in the final years of the Empire; the Robespierrites (Hamel, *St.-Just etc.*) not, on the whole, so good—mostly mere rhetoric and quotations from speeches.

Mignet still remains the bourgeois historian of my choice.

The Kautskys, Avelings, and Lenchen send their kindest regards. What is the position about your coming over here in the summer? With kindest regards from

Yours,
F. Engels

First published, in Russian, in *Istorik-marksist*, No. 6, Moscow, 1934

Printed according to the original

Published in English in full for the first time

234

ENGELS TO PYOTR LAVROV [533]

IN PARIS

[London,] 7 February 1886

My dear Lavrov,

Please tell me what meaning you attach to the word '*WORTHIES*'. When uttered by you I should hesitate to assign to it the philistine

---

[a] F. A. Mignet, *Histoire de la révolution française, depuis 1789 jusqu'en 1814.*
[b] A. Thiers, F. Bodin, *Histoire de la révolution française...*, Vols. 1-2; A. Thiers, *Histoire de la révolution française...*, Vols. 3-10.   Bougeard in the original. - [d] F. Chèvremont, *Jean-Paul Marat.*

meaning which is virtually the official meaning over here and which embraces a whole gamut ranging from a Faraday to a Peabody or a Lady Burdett-Coutts. However I shall try and find what you want.

The manuscript of the English translation of Volume I is at last to hand; I shall revise it straight away.[56] After that I shall start final editing of Volume III.[a] This will be hard, but I shall manage it in the end.

Yours ever,

F. E.

Энгельса[b]

First published in: Marx and Engels, *Works*, First Russian Edition, Vol. XXVII, Moscow, 1935

Printed according to the original

Translated from the French

Published in English for the first time

235

ENGELS TO NIKOLAI DANIELSON

IN ST PETERSBURG

London, 8 February 1886

My dear Sir,

I have received your kind letters 18/30 November, 19/31 December, 26 [December]/7 January and 8/20 January; also the four copies of the translation[c] one of which has gone to the British Museum, another to the Colonel[d] and a third to a lady well known[e] who has also translated several works of the Author[f] into your language. If you would be good enough to send another copy to Mr Otto Meissner, Hamburg, our German publisher, you would very much oblige me.

I have read your excellent preface[534] with much pleasure, and

---

[a] of *Capital* - [b] (Russ., gen. case) Engels - [c] into Russian of the second volume of *Capital* - [d] Pyotr Lavrov - [e] Vera Zasulich - [f] Karl Marx

that I have done so attentively, I should like to prove to you by stating that on page X, line 17, the printer seems to have left out a word; should it not read as follows: что и перемѣнная часть *капитальной* стоимости, [a] etc.? The omission is not of much consequence for any one who is used to the author's terminology, but would perhaps be puzzling to one who is not.

I thank you very much for your observations on the economical condition of your country. [535] Anything of this class is always of the highest interest to me. The last 30 years have shown, all over the world, in how little time the immense productive powers of modern industry can be implanted and take a firm root even in countries hitherto purely agricultural. And the phenomena accompanying this process repeat themselves everywhere. What you tell me about payments in coupons not yet due occurred all over Germany ten or fifteen years ago and may occasionally occur still; but especially before the introduction of the new coinage the complaints about the circulation of such coupons, not yet due, and originally given in payment of wages were universal. The rapid development of German manufactures has now passed beyond that stage, and if it still occurs it will be an exception; but fifteen years ago it was the rule, especially in Saxony and Thuringia. But that your economists should consider this as a proof of a deficiency of circulating medium, and that in the face of a paper currency depreciated by over-issue at least 36%, that is on a level with the views of the American greenbackers [536] who demanded, too, an increased issue of paper money because that paper money was no longer depreciated and therefore evidently under-issued!

I am glad to learn that our friend [b] is recommended a change of climate—I suppose it will be about the same where the doctors sent him to before and which seemed to agree well enough with his state of health. At all events this is proof to me that all danger of a sudden crisis in his malady is now over. [362]

I have now at last the whole manuscript of the English translation of Volume I [c] in my hands and shall go into the revision of it next week, and when I may have an idea how soon I can finish, conclude at once with a publisher. [56] There are two translators, the one a barrister and old friend of ours [d] (you and he are the two men living who know the book most thoroughly) but his professional occupations do

___

[a] that the variable part of *capital* value, too - [b] Hermann Lopatin - [c] of *Capital* - [d] Samuel Moore

not allow him to do it all in time, so Dr Aveling, the husband of the author's youngest daughter,[a] offered his services; but both the economic theories and the language of the author are rather new to him and I know the portion done by him will give me more work. As soon as that is in a fair way of getting ready for the press, I shall start again with Volume III[b] and do it to the end, not allowing any other work to interrupt it.

Here the industrial crisis gets worse instead of better, and people begin to find out more and more that England's industrial monopoly is at an end. And with America, France, Germany for competitors in the world's market, and high duties excluding foreign goods from the markets of other rising industrial countries, it becomes a simple matter of calculation. If one great monopolist industrial country produced a crisis every ten years, what will four such countries produce? Approximatively a crisis in 10/4 years, that is to say practically a crisis without end. *Uns kann recht sein.*[c]

Very faithfully yours,
P. W. Rosher[363]

First published, in Russian, in *Minuvshiye gody*, No. 2, St Petersburg, 1908

Reproduced from the original

Published in English for the first time

236

ENGELS TO FRIEDRICH ADOLPH SORGE[537]

IN HOBOKEN

[London,] 9 February 1886

Dear Sorge,

You have no doubt received my letter of 30 January,[d] also *To-Day* and the new edition of the *Communist Trial.*[e] Have had *New Yorker*

---

[a] Eleanor Marx-Aveling - [b] of *Capital* - [c] It might be helpful to us.
[d] See this volume, pp. 393-95. - [e] K. Marx, *Revelations Concerning the Communist Trial in Cologne.*

Volkszeitung, weekly edition[a] of 23 January, *but nothing else*. You should also have had the September number of *To-Day*.

Yesterday the gentlemen of the SOCIAL DEMOCRATIC FEDERATION were yet again responsible for a fearful public gaff—as you will already have heard by telegraph.[538] With any luck they will now be played out.

How is Adolf[b] getting along with his business?

Your
F. E.

First published abridged in *Briefe und Auszüge aus Briefen von Joh. Phil. Becker, Jos. Dietzgen, Friedrich Engels, Karl Marx u. A. an F. A. Sorge und Andere*, Stuttgart, 1906 and in full in: Marx and Engels, *Works*, First Russian Edition, Vol. XXVII, Moscow, 1935

Printed according to the original

237

ENGELS TO LAURA LAFARGUE

IN PARIS

London, 9 February 1886

My dear Laura,

Our clever folk of the Social Democratic Federation[300] scorn to rest on their laurels. Yesterday they must needs interfere in a meeting of the unemployed—who count now by hundreds of thousands—in order to preach *La Révolution*—revolution in general, and ask the mass to hold up their hands, those who were ready to follow Mr Champion to—well to what he does not know himself. Hyndman who can only overcome his personal cowardice by deafening himself by his own shouts, went on in the same strain.[538] Of course you know what a meeting at 3 p. m. in Trafalgar Square consists of: numbers of the poor devils of the East End who vegetate in the borderland between working class and lumpen proletariat, and a sufficient admix-

---

[a] *Wochenblatt der N. Y. Volkszeitung* - [b] Adolf Sorge jun.

ture of roughs and 'Arrys to leaven the whole into a mass ready for any 'lark' up to a wild riot *à propos de rien*.[a] Well just at the time when this element was getting the upper hand (Kautsky who was there [539] says *das eigentliche Meeting war vorbei; die Keilerei ging los und so ging ich weg*[b]) the wiseacres above-named took these roughs in procession through Pall Mall and Piccadilly to Hyde Park for another and a truly revolutionary meeting. But on the road the roughs took matters into their own hands, smashed club windows and shop fronts, plundered first wine-stores and baker's shops, and then some jewellers' shops also, so that in Hyde Park our revolutionary swells had to preach '*le calme et la modération*'[c]! While they were soft-sawdering, the wrecking and plundering went on outside in Audley St. and even as far as Oxford Street where at last the police interfered.

The absence of the police shows that the row was *wanted*, but that Hyndman and Co. *donnaient dans le piège*[d] is impardonable and brands them finally as not only helpless fools but also as scamps. They wanted to wash off the disgrace of their electoral manoeuvres [496] and now they have done an irreparable damage to the movement here. To make a revolution — and that *à propos de rien*,[e] when and where they liked — they thought nothing else was required but the paltry tricks sufficient to 'boss' an agitation for any vile fad, packing meetings, lying in the press, and then, with five and twenty men seemed to back them up, appealing to the masses to 'rise' somehow, as best they might, against nobody in particular and everything in general, and trust to luck for the result. Well I don't know whether they will get over it so easily this time. I should not wonder if they were arrested before the week is out. English law is very definite in this respect: you may spout as long as you like, so long as nothing follows; but as soon as any 'overt acts' of rioting ensue, you are held responsible for them, and many a poor devil of a Chartist, Harney and Jones and others, got two years for less. [540] Besides, *n'est pas Louise Michel qui veut*.[f][74]

At last I have got nearly the whole of the ms. of the English translation of Volume I[g] in my hands, the small remnant Edward has promised for Sunday. [h][56] I shall go at it this week — the only thing that keeps me from it is the revision of a translation (English) of my old book on

---

[a] over nothing -[b] the meeting proper was over; the fight started, so I went away -[c] calmness and moderation -[d] fell into the trap -[e] for nothing -[f] not everyone who wishes to can be Louise Michel -[g] of *Capital* -[h] 14 February

the English working class[a] by an American lady[b] who has also found a publisher for it in America — strange to say! This I do in the evenings and shall — unless much interrupted — finish this week. As soon as I see my way to fix a date for the printing to begin, I shall go and see Kegan Paul, and if we do not come to terms with him, go somewhere else, we have hints and offers from more than one. Our position in this respect is much improved. After that, — Volume III,[c] and no more interruptions tolerated.

We thought it very strange that Bernstein should have recommended a fellow like Quarck[d] and asked him. Here is his reply which I give you literally so that there can be no mistake:

'Von einer Quarck-Empfehlung bin ich mir gar nichts bewusst, wie sollte ich einen Mann empfehlen *den ich gar nicht kenne?* Es ist möglich dass ich auf eine Anfrage einmal geantwortet, *der Mann sei kein Parteigenosse,* aber es liege nichts gegen ihn vor, aber auch nur möglich... Sollte da nicht eine Verwechslung vorliegen? Ich selbst *kenne Quarck gar nicht,* habe auch noch *nie* mit ihm korrespondiert. Also wie gesagt, ich bestreite nicht absolut, über Quarck einmal Auskunft erteilt zu haben, aber *empfohlen habe ich ihn nicht.*[e]

Pardon me that I bother you again with this affair, but I wish to have this extract forwarded to Paris in the original German. As to the rest I write to Paul about it. Otherwise I wish Deville every happiness in his new *ménage*[f] and hope it will not interfere too much with his regularity of habits. If once settled down in a new routine, he promises to be the best and happiest of husbands.

The people here go on much as usual. Edward has taken a hall in Tottenham Court Road where he preaches twice every Sunday to an attentive and on the whole reasonably well paying audience — it interferes rather with his after-dinner port, but it's a good thing for him as it defeats Bradlaugh's plan *to ruin him as a public lecturer;* he also goes now and then to provincial towns for 3 lectures on a Sunday! and one the Saturday evening. Bax is something like Paul, writes

---

[a] *The Condition of the Working-Class in England* - [b] Florence Kelley-Wischnewetzky - [c] of *Capital* - [d] See this volume, pp. 384-85. - [e] 'I am totally in the dark about Quarck's recommendation. How could I give a recommendation to a person *of whom I know nothing at all?* It is possible that I could have answered a query to the effect that *the man is not a party member,* but nothing can be held against him, but this is only a possibility... Hasn't there been a mix-up? I myself *do not know Quarck at all* and have *never* corresponded with him. So, as I've already said, I cannot say for certain that I haven't given some information about Quarck, but *I have never recommended him.*' - [f] marriage

charming articles often enough in *The Commonweal*, but utterly unaccountable when an idea runs away with him. For practical agitation poor Bax is most dangerous, being utterly inexperienced; throws the ideas of the study, quite raw, into the meeting-room; has the feeling that something must be done to set the ball rolling, and does not know what; withal very nice, very intelligent, very industrious, so that we may hope he will outlive his zeal.

Yours affectionately,

F. E.

First published, in the language of the original (English), in: F. Engels, P. et L. Lafargue, *Correspondance*, t. I, Paris, 1956

Reproduced from the original

238

ENGELS TO AUGUST BEBEL [541]

IN BERLIN

London, 15 February 1886

Dear Bebel,

Your letter could not have arrived at a more opportune moment; I was in any case about to send you some further gladsome news to-day—of which more below.

Now as to the rumpus on the 8th inst. [a]

Despite publicity to the contrary, the SOCIAL DEMOCRATIC FEDERATION is an exceedingly weak organisation which comprises some good elements but is led by literary and political adventurers who, by a stroke of genius, had brought it to the very verge of dissolution on the occasion of the November elections. [496] At the time, Hyndman (pronounced Heindman), head of the society, had accepted money from the Tories (Conservatives) and used it to put up Social Democratic candidates in two London boroughs. Since they had not a single adherent in either constituency, the consequent débâcle might have been foreseen (one of them got 27 and the other 32 votes, each out of

---

[a] See this volume, pp. 403-04.

a possible 4-5,000!). But hardly had Hyndman touched the Tories' money than his head began to swell inordinately, and he departed forthwith for Birmingham where he called on Chamberlain, now a Minister, and offered him his 'support' (amounting, for the whole of England, to barely 1,000 votes) if he, Chamberlain, would secure him, Hyndman, a constituency in Birmingham with the help of the Liberals, and also introduce an Eight Hours' Bill. Chamberlain, being no fool, showed him the door. Despite all attempts to hush up the matter, there was a great rumpus about it in the Federation, and dissolution was imminent. So something had to be done to get things going again.

In the meantime unemployment was steadily rising. As a result of the collapse of Britain's monopoly of the world market, a state of crisis has persisted uninterruptedly since 1878 and is growing worse rather than better. Poverty, particularly in London's East End, is appalling. The winter which, since January, has been exceptionally severe, combined with the abysmal indifference of the propertied classes, has given rise to great unrest among the mass of the unemployed. As always, political wire-pullers have sought to exploit that unrest for their own ends. The Conservatives, recently deprived of office, [542] blamed unemployment on foreign competition (rightly) and foreign protective tariffs (for the most part wrongly), and advocated 'FAIR TRADE', i. e. retaliatory tariffs. There is also a labour organisation which is predominantly in favour of such tariffs. [543] This last called the meeting of the 8th inst. in Trafalgar Square. [538] Meanwhile the SOCIAL DEMOCRATIC FEDERATION had not been idle; having already demonstrated in a minor way, they now sought to take advantage of the aforementioned meeting. Thus two meetings took place, that of the retaliatory tariffs men, round Nelson's Column, the other addressed by the SOCIAL DEMOCRATIC FEDERATION men from a street next to the NATIONAL GALLERY, some 25 feet above the north side of the square. Kautsky was present [539]; he left before the rumpus began and told me that practically all the genuine working men attended the other meeting, while Hyndman & Co. had a mixed audience who were out for a lark, and in some cases were already half seas over. If this was evident to Kautsky who has been here barely a year, it must have been even more so to the gentlemen of the Federation. Nevertheless, when things seemed to be already subsiding, they put into practice an idea long cherished by Hyndman, namely a procession of 'unemployed' along Pall Mall, the street of the great political, aristocratic and ultra-capitalist clubs which are the hubs of political intrigue in Britain. The unemployed who followed them to another meeting in Hyde Park were mostly of the kind who do not wish to work — barrow-boys, idlers, police spies and rogues. Jeered at by the aristocrats from the club windows, they smashed the latter, likewise shop windows, and looted wineshops, the better to set up an impromptu consumers' club in the street so that, once in Hyde Park, Hyndman and Co. had hastily to swallow their bloodthirsty slogans and preach moderation. But by now the thing had gathered momentum. During the procession and this further little meeting as well as after it, most of the lumpen proletariat Hyndman had taken for unemployed poured along several of the grander streets nearby, looting jewellers' and other shops, and using the loaves of bread and legs of mutton thus looted solely for the purpose of smashing windows until eventually they scattered without encountering any resistance. Only a few stragglers were dispersed in Oxford Street by four (sic!) policemen.

Otherwise the police were nowhere to be seen, and so conspicuous were they by their absence that it was not only *we* who believed it to have been intentional. Evidently the chiefs of police are Conservatives and not averse to seeing a bit of a rumpus in these days of Liberal rule. However, the government immediately set up a Committee of Inquiry and this may cost more than one of these gentry his position.

In addition, very half-hearted proceedings have been instituted against Hyndman & Co. which, to all appearances, will be allowed to peter out, although English law provides for very stiff sentences the moment inflammatory speeches give way to overt acts. True, the gentlemen talked a lot of bunkum about social revolution which, having regard to their audience and in the absence of any organised support amongst the masses, was sheer lunacy, but I can hardly believe that the government would be so stupid as to make martyrs of them. These socialist gents are determined to conjure up overnight a movement which, here as elsewhere, necessarily calls for years of work,— though, once it has got going and has been imposed on the masses by historical events, it will admittedly advance far more rapidly here than on the Continent. But men of this type cannot wait—hence these childish pranks such as we are otherwise wont to see only among the anarchists.

The alarm of the philistines lasted four days and has now finally abated. One good thing about it is that the existence of poverty, which the Liberals simply denied and the Conservatives tried to exploit solely for their own ends, has now come to be recognised, and people see that something has got to be done, if only for appearances' sake. But the subscription fund started by the LORD MAYOR amounted, by Saturday,[a] to barely £ 20,000 [544] and, given the number of unemployed, would barely last out 2 days! But of one thing at least we have again received proof: Until something happens to frighten them, the propertied classes are totally indifferent to the destitution of the masses and I'm not at all sure they don't need rather more of a ·fright.

Now for France. Last week saw an event of an epoch-making kind, namely *the constitution of a workers' party in the Chamber*. It has only three members, and two Radicals besides,[429] but a start has been made and the split is definitive.

Basly (pronounced Bali), a miner and then a landlord (because disciplined) from Anzin, carried out an investigation on the spot of the killing of the infamous pit manager Watrin in Decazeville. [545] On his return, he first communicated his findings to a big meeting held on the 7th in Paris, in the course of which the Radicals from the Chamber came off very badly. [b] On Thursday in the Chamber he made a really splendid speech when he questioned the Ministry. [c] *He was left in the lurch by the whole of the extreme Left.* The only ones to speak in support of him were the two other working men, Boyer (of Marseilles, ex-anarchist) and Camélinat (ex-Proudhonist, Communard refugee), besides which he was applauded by Clovis Hugues and ·Planteau, while the other extreme Radicals were as if thunderstruck by this first bold, independent move on the part of the French proletariat in the Chamber.

(Between ourselves, Basly is completely under the influence of our men, Lafargue, Guesde, etc., of whose theoretical advice he is greatly in need and which he gladly accepts.)

I am sending you the *Cri du Peuple* with a full account of this historic sitting which I suggest you study. It's well worth the trouble. The importance of the rupture has been confirmed by Longuet who has just been over here and who, as Clemenceau's friend and fellow-editor, spoke with some disapproval of this unparliamentary behaviour on the part of the workers.

---

[a] 13 February.- [b] See E.J.Basly's speech at a meeting in Théâtre du Château d'Eau on 7 February 1886 (*Le Socialiste*, No. 25, 13 February 1886). - [c] See Basly's speech in the Chamber of Deputies on 11 February 1886 (*Le Cri du Peuple*, No. 837, 12 February 1886).

So in Paris, too, we now have our people in parliament, and of this I am glad, not only for the sake of the French to whose progress it will give a tremendous impetus, but also for the sake of our parliamentary group, some of whose members might yet learn much about boldness of approach from the above; for now we also have foreigners whom we can hold up as an example to the faint-hearts and weaklings.

The best part of it is that the Radicals proposed these chaps in the hope of being able to manipulate them, and now their trouble has been for nothing. I, too, felt very doubtful about Camélinat as a former Proudhonist, but a point in his favour was that, when he came here as a refugee, he immediately sought work in Birmingham (he is one of the best engravers) and had nothing to do with refugee politics.

Time for the post.

Your
F. E.

First published, in Russian, in *Marx-Engels Archives*, Vol. I (VI), Moscow, 1932

Printed according to the original

Published in English in full for the first time

239

ENGELS TO PAUL LAFARGUE [546]

IN PARIS

[Excerpt]

[London,] 16 February 1886

My dear Lafargue,

My congratulations. The sitting of the French Chamber on the 11th was an historical event. [a] The ice — the parliamentary omnipotence of the Radicals [429] — has been broken and it matters little whether those who dared to break it numbered three or thirty. And it was this superstition amongst the Parisian working men — this belief that by going further than the Radicals they would endanger the Republic or

---

[a] See previous letter.

зас 674 Clemes. 70г контур

Miners on strike in Decazeville, January 1886

at least play the Opportunists' game [236] by dividing the 'revolutionary party' — which lent strength to the Radicals.

This is the definitive defeat of utopian socialism in France. For the Radicals were all 'socialists' in the old sense of the term. What survived of Louis Blanc's and Proudhon's theses served them as socialist trappings; they represent French utopian socialism stripped of the utopias and hence reduced to a phrase pure and simple. On 11 February this antiquated French socialism was crushed by the international socialism of today. The Poverty of Philosophy!

So far as your propaganda in Paris and in France generally is concerned, this is an event of prime importance. The effect will be felt very quickly. The Radicals — whether they make a clean break with the workers or whether they temporise by granting them more or less sterile concessions — will lose their influence over the masses and, along with that influence, such little potency as is left in traditional socialism will be lost, and people's minds will become more receptive to a new order of ideas...

Z... [a] has left me in no doubt that Clemenceau and the rest of his gang, embroiled as they are in ministerial intrigues, have caught the parliamentary disease, that they no longer see clearly what is going on outside the Palais Bourbon and the Luxembourg, that it is here that, for them, the pivot of the movement lies and that, in their eyes, extra-parliamentary France is of no more than secondary importance. All this has given me the measure of these gentlemen.

In short I have seen that *flectere si nequeo superos, Acheronta movebo* [b] is not to their taste. Their backsides are seated on the same chute as that down which Ranc, Gambetta & Co. once slid. What frightens them is the proletarian Acheron.

I told Z...: So long as the Radicals allow themselves to be frightened, as for example at the inconclusive elections, by the cry 'The Republic is in danger', they will be nothing more than the servants of the Opportunists, will act as their cat's paw. But give each workman a gun and 50 cartridges and the Republic will never again be in danger!

First published in *Le Socialiste*, No. 115, Paris, 24 novembre 1900

Printed according to the newspaper

Translated from the French

---

[a] Presumably Charles Longuet. - [b] If Heaven be inflexible, Hell shall be unleashed (Virgil, *Aeneid*, VII, 312).

240

ENGELS TO EDUARD BERNSTEIN [547]

IN HOTTINGEN-ZURICH

[London, 24 February 1886]

Dear Ede,

Your articles[a] on the subject of C. A. Schramm[b] were very nice and caused us much glee. The man's pretty well done for. The new turn things have taken in France is most significant. See *Cri du Peuple*. On the 7th, Château d'Eau meeting[c] at which Basly disassociated himself from the Radicals. [429] On the 11th, in the Chamber, Basly's interpellation re Decazeville,[d] seconded by Camélinat and Boyer, applauded by Clovis Hugues and Planteau — separation from the Radicals, *formation of parliamentary workers' party*.[e] Splendid *entrée en scène*. Great chagrin of the Radicals over these highly unparliamentary goings-on. The three working men are to be punished by a vote of no confidence on the part of the bourgeois constituents. Meeting called at Château d'Eau for 21 inst. but cancelled upon the three declaring their intention to attend. Instead a meeting *du commerce*[f] at the Château d'Eau announced, to discuss public works for the benefit of the unemployed, in fact for the purpose of obtaining a vote of censure against the 3. But instead a great victory for the working men, Basly in the chair, the bourgeois walk out, brilliant speech by Guesde. See *Cri du Peuple* of 23rd inst. [g]

The French parliamentary workers' party is a great historic event and a great stroke of luck for Germany. Will make certain persons in

---

[a] [E. Bernstein,] 'Ein moralischer Kritiker und seine kritische Moral', *Der Sozial-demokrat*, Nos. 4-7, 21 and 28 January, 5 and 12 February 1886. - [b] C. A. S[chramm], *Rodbertus, Marx, Lassalle*. - [c] See E. J. Basly's speech at a meeting in Théâtre du Château d'Eau on 7 February 1886 (*Le Socialiste*, No. 25, 13 February 1886). - [d] See Basly's speech in the Chamber of Deputies on 11 February 1886 (*Le Cri du Peuple*, No. 837, 12 February 1886). - [e] See this volume, p. 409. - [f] of business people - [g] J. Guesde's speech at a meeting of business people (*Le Cri du Peuple*, No. 848, 23 February 1886).

Berlin stir their stumps. Moreover, wholly international; chauvinistic heckling fell completely flat.

Your

F. E.

First published, in Russian, in *Marx-Engels Archives*, Book I, Moscow, 1924

Printed according to the original

Published in English for the first time

241

ENGELS TO FLORENCE KELLEY-WISCHNEWETZKY [548]

IN ZURICH

London, 25 February 1886

Dear Mrs Wischnewetzky,

To-day mailed to you, *registered*, the rest of the ms. with my—introduction or postscript [360] — according to where it may suit you to place it. I believe the title had better be a simple translation: The Condition of the Working Class in England *in 1844*, etc.

I am glad that all obstacles to publication have been successfully overcome. Only I am sorry that Miss Foster has applied to the Executive of the Sozialistische Arbeiterpartei in New York, [549] as appears from their report of meeting in *Der Sozialist*, New York, 13th February. Neither Marx nor myself have ever committed the least act which might be interpreted into asking any Working Organisation to do us any personal favour — and this was necessary not only for the sake of our own independence but also on account of the constant bourgeois denunciations of 'demagogues who coax the workmen out of their hard-earned pennies in order to spend them for their own purposes'. I shall therefore be compelled to inform that Executive that this application was made entirely without my knowledge or authority. Miss Foster no doubt acted in what she thought the best way, and this step of hers is in itself no doubt perfectly admissible; still, if I could have foreseen it, I should have been compelled to do everything in my power to prevent it. [550]

The revision of your translation has delayed that of the English translation of *Das Kapital*[56] by three weeks—and at a most critical period of the year too. I shall set about it to-night and it may take me several months. After that, the German 3rd volume must be taken in hand; you see, therefore, that for some time it will be impossible for me to undertake the revision of other translations, unless few and far between and of small volume. I have at this moment waiting here an Italian translation of Marx's *Lohnarbeit und Kapital*[a] which must wait some weeks at least. But if you will translate that into English (it was recently republished at Zurich) and will not be too pressing for time, I shall be glad to revise it, and you cannot have a better popular pamphlet than that. My *Entwicklung*[b] Aveling intends to translate, and as the subject is in part rather difficult, I could not well give it to anyone except he be here on the spot, accessible to verbal explanation.[528] As to my *Anti-Dühring* I hardly think the English speaking public would swallow that controversy and the hostility to religion which pervades the book. However we may discuss that later on, if you are of a different opinion. At present Marx's posthumous manuscripts must be dealt with before anything else.

The semi-Hegelian language of a good many passages of my old book is not only untranslatable but has lost the greater part of its meaning even in German. I have therefore modernised it as much as possible.

Yours very truly,

F. Engels

First published, in the language of the original (English), in *Briefe und Auszüge aus Briefen von Joh. Phil. Becker, Jos. Dietzgen, Friedrich Engels, Karl Marx u. A. an F. A. Sorge und Andere*, Stuttgart, 1906

Reproduced from the original

---

[a] *Wage Labour and Capital* - [b] *Socialism: Utopian and Scientific*

242

ENGELS TO WILHELM LIEBKNECHT

IN BORSDORF NEAR LEIPZIG [34]

London, 25 February 1886

Dear Liebknecht,

It's really quite impossible to do anything about getting your Russian speech [a][551] published in this country for, as you know, the *big* newspapers are barred to us and the monthly *Commonweal* is too small to take on that sort of thing. You will have to see to the matter yourselves, e. g. by getting in touch with the *Standard* correspondent as Longuet, for instance, did in Paris with Mother Crawford, the *Daily News* correspondent. Knowing that the Reichstag has no real say in anything, the British press very rarely mentions it, save for quite short telegrams. If you had not virtually confined yourself to Faerber's view of the harm suffered by German capitalists,[b] but had introduced the present eastern imbroglio [445] and blamed it on Bismarck as the man who, because of the loan, has the Russians eating out of his hand, your speech could not have been passed over in complete silence. But what you say about the worthlessness of Russian paper is common knowledge even in this country.

Now as regards those charming German literati who infest the neutral border zone between ourselves and the armchair [54] and state socialists, and want to pocket all the advantages to be derived from our party while carefully shielding themselves against any disadvantage arising out of intercourse with us — I've just had another demonstration of what shits the said literati are. An importunate fellow by the name of Max Quarck — *nomen est omen* [c] — wrote to me saying that Deville in Paris had given him *exclusive rights* to translate his abridgment of *Capital*, and asking me to recommend him to Meissner and write a *preface* for him.[d] It was all a lie, a fact of which I have received confirmation from Paris and as he himself informed Kautsky in a letter the *selfsame day*. And now the wretch has the effrontery to suggest

---

[a] Liebknecht's speech in the Reichstag on 8 February 1886 (*Stenographische Berichte über die Verhandlungen des Reichstags. VI. Legislaturperiode. II. Session 1885/86*, Vol. II).- [b] See this volume, p. 338. - [c] the name tells all (Quark = curd or cottage cheese in German; fig. rubbish) - [d] See this volume, pp. 384-85 and 405.

that *I* should beg his pardon for *his* having lied to me! Just let him try that again, the scoundrel.[520]

You people will find you have competitors in France. The three working men, Basly, Boyer and Camélinat, since joined by Clovis Hugues, have set themselves up in the Chamber as a socialist labour group[a] in opposition to the Radicals,[429] and when, at a meeting last Sunday, the Radicals tried to inveigle the constituents into passing a vote of no confidence, they met with a resounding defeat — so much so that at the meeting they themselves had convened, the Radicals did not dare to open their mouths.[b] These three French working men will make more of an impact in Europe than your 25 because they sit in a Chamber which, unlike the Reichstag, is not a debating society, and because they have shaken themselves free of the milk-and-water petty-bourgeois following which hangs like a millstone round your necks. Clemenceau is now faced with a last crucial decision, but we can be almost sure that he will not hesitate to join the bourgeois camp, in which case, though he will indeed become a minister, he will be done for.

Your
F. E.

First published, in Russian, in *Marx-Engels Archives*, Vol. I (VI), Moscow, 1932

Printed according to the original

Published in English for the first time

243

ENGELS TO HERMANN SCHLÜTER

IN HOTTINGEN-ZURICH

[London,] 3 March 1886

Dear Sir,

Would you kindly send Williams & Norgate, 14 Henrietta St., Covent Garden, London — 1 copy of *Socialism: Utopian etc.* together

---

[a] See this volume, pp. 409-10. - [b] Ibid., p. 414.

with bill (incl. postage) in a wrapper — these people applied to me (they are my booksellers and, incidentally, publishers, a big firm) and I wrote and told them that my things are always to be had from the Volksbuchhandlung.[a]

Mrs Wischnewetzky played you a rotten trick with her ms.[349] For upon her insisting it was a matter of life and death, I had to buckle to straight away, and now the English translation of *Capital* has got to be done without delay, competition having cropped up (see *To-Day*)[527] in a menacing form. So if all is not to be lost, I must forge ahead and drop everything else, including the *Peasant War*.[213] The rival translation is, by the way, quite shocking, but so much the worse if it's not elbowed out forthwith.

Kindest regards,

Yours,

F. E.

First published in: Marx and Engels, *Works*, First Russian Edition, Vol. XXVII, Moscow, 1935

Printed according to the original

Published in English for the first time

244

ENGELS TO FLORENCE KELLEY-WISCHNEWETZKY[27]

IN ZURICH

London, 12 March 1886

Dear Mrs Wischnewetzky,

Deep buried as I am in the English *Capital*,[56] I have only the time to write a few lines in haste. It did not require all your exposition of the circumstances to convince me that you were perfectly innocent of what had been done in America with your translation.[b] The thing is done and can't be helped, though we both are convinced that it was a mistake.[c]

---

[a] a Social Democratic bookshop in Zurich - [b] the English translation of Engels' *The Condition of the Working-Class in England* - [c] See this volume, pp. 415-16.

I thank you for pointing out to me a passage in the appendix [552] which indeed is far from clear. The gradation from the Polish Jew to the Hamburger, and from the Hamburger again to the Manchester merchant does not at all come out to the front. So I have tried to alter it in a way which may meet both your and my own objection to it and hope I have succeeded.

And now I cannot conclude without expressing to you my most sincere thanks to you for the very great trouble you have taken to revive, in English, a book of mine which is half-forgotten in the original German.

Ever at your service as far as my time and powers allow, believe me, dear Mrs Wischnewetzky

Yours very faithfully,
F. Engels

The dedication to the English working men should be left out. [359] It has no meaning to-day.

First published abridged, in the language of the original (English), in *Briefe und Auszüge aus Briefen von Joh. Phil. Becker, Jos. Dietzgen, Friedrich Engels, Karl Marx u. A. an F. A. Sorge und Andere*, Stuttgart, 1906 and in full in: Marx and Engels, *Works*, First Russian Edition, Vol. XXVII, Moscow, 1935

Reproduced from the original

245

ENGELS TO PASQUALE MARTIGNETTI

IN BENEVENTO

London, 12 March 1886

Dear Citizen,

Please excuse the belated reply.

I have received your kind letter of 8 February and the manuscript, [a] which I shall deal with as soon as possible. But at the moment I am

---

[a] of the Italian translation of Marx's *Wage Labour and Capital*

obliged before anything else to check through the English translation of *Capital*, Volume I, which is most pressing and must be printed without delay [56]; it is no easy task. When I have a free moment I shall devote it to your work.

I have also received, and I thank you for them, the 6 copies of the *Origin etc.* [302]

I am sorry that my error 'Paolo' caused you inconvenience. [553] I shall not repeat it.

I must get hold of the calendar in order to restore the passage that was stuck and illegible [554]; I hope to find it here in London at a friend's house; this is another cause of delay.

I am sorry I cannot do better and more quickly than this, but the English *Capital* must take precedence; in any case I am committed by a deadline to the publisher. [a]

With respect I remain

F. Engels

I hope to spare some time in April on *Wage Labour and Capital*.

First published in *La corrispondenza di Marx e Engels con italiani. 1848-1895*, Milano, 1964

Printed according to the book

Translated from the Italian

Published in English for the first time

246

ENGELS TO HERMANN SCHLÜTER

IN HOTTINGEN-ZURICH

London, 12 March [b] 1886

Dear Mr Schlüter,

If I am to send you a speedy reply, I shall have to be brief.
1) The man with the money has not yet turned up.
2) We have Lexis [c] here. Thanks for the hint.

---

[a] William Swan Sonnenschein - [b] May in the original. - [c] W. Lexis, 'Die Marx'sche Kapitaltheorie', *Jahrbücher für Nationalökonomie und Statistik*, Vol. 11, Jena, 1885.

3) *Origin.* [a] This business of the '2nd edition' has its dubious aspects, but when I consider that the two markets are completely different and that the '1st edition' is therefore unlikely to get in the way of the '2nd', it's unlikely to do much harm. [555] Admittedly I should have been happier had Dietz consulted us first. He has behaved very arbitrarily in the past over other matters. This time it was quite unnecessary; he could, e. g., easily have informed me about the matter through Kautsky. But he likes *faits accomplis* and I shall get someone to tell him as much.

4) Reports of the International. [556] I was in Manchester at the time and can't really remember the details. The General Council did, at any rate, send a MESSAGE to all the congresses, but Marx's papers and pamphlets are all of them still in the unsorted state they were in when I lugged them over here and it will take about 6 weeks to put them in order. However I've asked Kautsky to make inquiries from Lessner; I should be very surprised if he hasn't collected everything.

5) Stephens' Speech. [557] Yes, the thing is by Weerth.

As to the introduction, I shall be glad to go through your ms. But here too there are few sources and the bourgeois have been responsible for some serious falsification. Last year Harney scoured the whole of Yorkshire, Lancashire and London for one copy of *The Northern Star*, the paper which he had edited and which had had a circulation of 100,000 copies. In vain. Evanescence — such is the curse that afflicts all proletarian literature not included in official literature. Thus Owen's works are nowhere to be had and the BRITISH MUSEUM would pay a great deal of money for a complete collection. A genuine account will therefore be difficult. The Brentanos and Co. know *nothing*. The Charter [101] was drawn up in 1835, *not* 1838, and O'Connel [b] was also involved if I'm not mistaken. What Brentano says about the petition is utter nonsense [c]; after 10 April the bourgeois of *both* parties stuck together and in such a case lies are always disseminated, it being impossible to refute them either in Parliament or in the press. Even if a House of Commons Committee did scrutinise the petition (which I very much doubt), it would have been quite incapable of distinguishing the genuine from the bogus. [558] But in the spring of 1848, no one was able to take much interest in such dirty

---

[a] F. Engels, *The Origin of the Family, Private Property and the State.* - [b] O'Connell in the original. - [c] L. Brentano, 'Die englische Chartistenbewegung', *Preußische Jahrbücher*, Nos. 5, 6, Berlin, 1874.

goings-on; there were other things to do. Besides, we weren't in England.

With kindest regards,

Yours,

F. Engels

First published in: Marx and Engels, *Works*, First Russian Edition, Vol. XXVII, Moscow, 1935

Printed according to the original

Published in English for the first time

247

ENGELS TO LAURA LAFARGUE

IN PARIS

London, 15-16 March 1886

My dear Laura,

You complain of the weather, and you are in Paris! Look at us here — nothing above freezing-point for the last ten days, a cutting east wind, of which you don't know which is the worst, the north-east or the south-east, — and to-night a fresh *couche de neige*[a] on streets and roofs. Nim is at her second cold, but it's getting better, I had one too, Pumps and Percy are in the same boat too, fortunately the children are well. However there must be an end to this some time, only I wish it would come.

The English *Capital* is at last getting into shape and form.[56] I have the whole ms. here and begun revising. Saving the 1st chapter which will require a severe overhauling, the first 200 pages of the original German are ready to go to press. I saw Kegan Paul last week, declined his proposals of two years ago and submitted mine. They were accepted in principle. This, with a man like Kegan Paul who is on all hands described as extremely slipping, means very little, and I expect there will be a tussle with him yet. But that matters nothing at all, because our position in the market has improved wonderfully and we have at least one other good firm who will be glad to take it on

---

[a] cover of snow

very favourable terms. As soon as the thing is concluded I will let you know.

The book will be published end of September so as not to come out in the dead season, and this gives me time to do the revising work thoroughly. Practically 300 pages of the original are revised, but the last 500 I have not as yet looked at, and there are some very difficult chapters there. And it would never do to hurry over them.

Broadhouse-Hyndman goes on translating 'from the original German' in *To-Day*. [527] He has in the sixth monthly number just finished Chapter I. But his 'original German' is the *French translation* now, and he insists on proving that with French he can play ducks and drakes quite as much as with German. The thing does so little harm, so far, that Kegan Paul never even mentioned it. But it ‛has done this good that I have got Moore and Edward to finish their work. You have no idea how difficult it is to get hold of this *To-Day*. I have paid in advance but have to dun them almost every month for my copy, moreover it comes out at all times of the *next* month. Tussy last year went and paid for a copy to be sent to you but as far as I have heard it was never sent! However there is nothing whatever in it except — Christian Socialism!

You will have seen from *Justice* — that at least you do receive in exchange for the *Socialiste* — how Hyndman keeps up his alliance with Brousse and even ignores the new proletarian party in the Chamber. [559]

To me, this appearance of a *parti ouvrier* [a] in the Palais Bourbon, is *the* great event of the year. The ice is now broken with which the Radicals [429] had so far succeeded to cover the working masses of France. These Radicals are now forced to come out in their true colours, or else follow the lead of Basly. The latter they will not do for long, nor willingly. Whatever they do, they must alienate the masses and drive them to us, and that quick. Events move rapidly, the Decazeville affair could not come more opportunely than it has done.[545] *C'est coup sur coup.* [b] And a very good thing it is that this takes place not in Paris but in one of the darkest and most reactionary and clerical corners of *la province*. I am exceedingly curious to learn how the affair has terminated to-day in the Chamber. [c] But whatever is done, must turn out to our benefit.

---

[a] workers' party - [b] One follows upon another. - [c] See this volume, p. 428.

The reappearance of France on the scene of the proletarian movement 'comme grande puissance'[a] will have a tremendous effect everywhere, especially in Germany and America; in Germany I have done
my best to let them know the full importance of the event, and sent
Basly's speech[b] to Bebel; Camélinat[c] will follow as soon as I get it
back from Kautsky. How furious Longuet must be that his old friend
and as he believed protégé Camélinat has turned his back upon
him!

At the same time, our Paris friends have done whatever they
could to pave the way so that the event, when it came, found a terrain
préparé.[d] Their action since the elections has been perfectly correct —
their attempt to rally all revolutionary proletarian elements, their
forbearance towards the Possibilists,[237] their limiting their attacks to
those points and facts which showed Brousse and Co. as simple obstacles to union — all this was just what it should have been. And they
are now reaping the fruits: Brousse has been driven into a position
where he must find fault with Basly and Co. and thereby sever the
last bond which still united him to the movement of the masses. Savoir
attendre[e] — that is what our friends have learnt at last, and that will
carry them through. Paul will be, if he likes, in the Palais Bourbon before Longuet.

A citoyen Hermann has applied to me for an addressed adhesion to
what I suppose is your meeting on the 18th.[560] I send it[f] to you herewith 1) to be sure that it falls into the proper hands and 2) that you
and Paul may look over and mend my rickety French.

Now good night, it's one o'clock and I must look over some papers
yet to get them out of the way of to-morrow. Kind regards to Paul.

Yours most affectionately,

F. Engels

16th March. Just seen the ordre du jour[g] adopted by the Chamber.[h]
It sounds rather different to all previous ordres du jour voted under
similar circumstances. It is a decided victory for us, and Freycinet too

---

[a] 'as a great power' - [b] E.J. Basly's speech in the Chamber of Deputies on
11 February 1886 (Le Cri du Peuple, No. 837, 12 February 1886).- [c] Z.R. Camélinat's speech in the Chamber of Deputies on 11 March 1886 (Le Cri du Peuple,
No. 866, 13 March 1886).- [d] fertilised soil - [e] To be able to wait - [f] F. Engels,
'On the Anniversary of the Paris Commune'. - [g] Order of the Day - [h] 'Réglement de l'ordre du jour', Le Cri du Peuple, No. 867, 14 March 1886.

pfeift aus einem andern Loch als früher.[a] *La situation devient sérieuse pour MM. les Radicaux.*[b]

First published, in the language of the original (English), in: F. Engels, P. et L. Lafargue, *Correspondance*, t. I, Paris, 1956

Reproduced from the original

248

ENGELS TO AUGUST BEBEL[521]

IN PLAUEN NEAR DRESDEN

London, 18 March 1886

Dear Bebel,

I am up to my eyes in the revision of the English translation of *Capital*, Volume I, which is at last on the point of coming out,[56] but since the business of Liebknecht's fund is urgent, I shall have to take a moment or two so as to be able to answer your letter quickly. Herewith, then my contribution,—a cheque for £10 on the Union Bank of London.[561]

Many thanks for the Anti-Socialist Law and spirits monopoly debates[c] and the *Bürger-Zeitung*.

It is indeed striking how faithfully the Anti-Socialist Law debate reflects the mood of the majority in the parliamentary group. Unable, presumably, to do as they wished they had, willy-nilly, to voice relatively correct opinions, and the impression made by the debate is, on the whole, very good, particularly since Singer was compelled by the Ihring case[562] to speak pretty sharply. In general these people, not excepting even Frohme, are not too bad when they have to come out against the police, either in their own interests or in those of their constituents and hence keep the worthy citizen well out of sight, for one of their besetting sins is this very worthiness which seeks to convince an opponent rather than fight him because 'our cause is, after all, so noble and so just' that any other worthy citizen is bound to come over

---

[a] sings another tune than before - [b] The situation is getting grave for Messrs the Radicals. - [c] See *Berliner Volksblatt*, Nos. 42, 43, 54-56; 19 and 20 February and 5-7 March 1886 (Supplement).

to us if only he can be made to understand it aright. This appeal to worthy sentiments, which neither recognises nor wishes to recognise the interests by which those sentiments are unconsciously motivated, is one of the chief characteristics of the philistinism which is peculiar to Germany and would be impossible over here or in France, either in parliament or in literature.

Never have I come across anything so tedious as the spirits debate; even Bamberger's jokes were as bad as ever, if not worse. So what matter if, after that, Schumacher also spoke tediously, proceeding to make what amounted to a naked appeal for 'etatisation' [*Verstaat-lichungs*]. Richter's speech, based on statistics, was quite the best.

I would not venture to pass judgment on Liebknecht's speech as reported in the *Bürger-Zeitung*. So much depends on nuances and the manner in which something is said and, in a summarised report, all that gets lost.[563]

I have not seen the account by Kautsky of which you speak. But as regards Hyndman, his behaviour in Trafalgar Square and Hyde Park on 8 February did far more harm than good.[538] Revolutionary ranting, which in France would be seen as the outmoded rubbish it is and do no harm, is sheer folly over here, where the masses are totally unprepared; it puts off the proletariat, encouraging only the worthless elements and, in this country, lends itself to but one interpretation, namely incitement to looting which in fact ensued, so that we shall be lastingly discredited over here, even in the eyes of the working class. As for its having drawn attention to socialism, you over there cannot know the extent to which, after centuries of freedom of the press and of assembly and its accompanying publicity, the public has become completely impervious to such methods. True, the initial alarm of the middle classes was quite funny, and brought in a subscription of some £40,000 for the unemployed—in all about £70,000—but that has already been spent, nothing else is forthcoming and poverty is as before. What has been achieved is to equate socialism with looting in the minds of the bourgeois public and, while this may not have made matters much worse, it has certainly got us no further. You might think that Hyndman showed great courage and so it might seem. But Hyndman, as I have learnt from Morris and others, is a coward and has behaved as such on crucial occasions. This doesn't prevent him, having once got himself into a dangerous fix, from drowning his cowardice in his own clamour and giving vent to the most bloodthirsty utterances. But this only makes him all the more of a menace to his colleagues — for no one, neither he nor they, can tell beforehand what he is going to do. Fortunately the whole business has been pretty well forgotten over here.

I wholly agree with your view that periods of prosperity of over 6 months will cease to recur. The only prospect of a reactivation of trade — directly where iron, at any rate, is concerned and otherwise indirectly — lies in the possible opening up of China to railway construction and hence the destruction of the only remaining closed and self-sufficient civilisation based on a combination of agriculture and handicrafts. But 6 months will be enough to discount that, after which we shall, perhaps, experience yet another *acute* crisis. Apart from destroying Britain's monopoly of the world market, the new methods of communication — the electric telegraph, the railways, the Suez Canal and the supplanting of sail by steam — have gone some way towards breaking down the ten-year industrial cycle. If China is opened up, not only will overproduction risk losing its last safety-valve, but emigration from China will assume such massive proportions that this alone will suffice to revolutionise conditions of production throughout America, Australia and India, even to the extent of affecting Europe — if it lasts itself till then.

Bismarck's folly is indeed becoming excessive. But it has one recurring theme — *more money!* His craziest schemes always and infallibly involve the voting of subsidies, and the National-Liberal gents [243] seem to have a positive passion for providing him with yet more cash.

Another victory in France. Camélinat's question[a] about Decazeville [545] provoked a three-day debate, while on Saturday,[b] 7 motions to proceed to the Order of the Day were thrown out, until finally the government and the Radical gents[429] agreed a resolution[c] unprecedented in French parliamentary history and which was passed on Monday [564]: That this Chamber proceed to the Order of the Day, confident that the Government will move all the necessary amendments to mining legislation and that its conduct in Decazeville will be dictated by the rights of the State and the interests of Labour.

The rights of Labour — it's absolutely unheard-of! And as if that was not enough, a decision unfavourable to the company which is wholly dependent on a *state concession* and now sees the terms of that concession turned against itself. All this, of course, is still on paper,

---

[a] See Z. R. Camélinat's speech in the Chamber of Deputies on 11 March 1886 (*Le Cri du Peuple*, No. 866, 13 March 1886). - [b] 13 March - [c] 'Réglement de l'ordre du jour', *Le Cri du Peuple*, No. 867, 14 March 1886.

but for a first step it's enough. The whole political situation in France has been revolutionised by the initiative of the three working men. The Radicals, who also call themselves socialists and who are, in fact, the representatives of French national socialism, of what survives of Proudhon and Louis Blanc, but who, as ministerial candidates, must make sure of keeping in with the republican bourgeoisie, are now compelled to show themselves in their true colours. The cool, almost hostile attitude they adopted from the outset towards the labour deputies, has shown the mass of the workers what is what; suddenly the latter see, alongside the 'eddicated' Radicals, *genuine* working-class socialists whom they joyously acclaim. The Radicals, incl. Clemenceau, must either temporarily renounce their ministerial aspirations and follow in Basly's and Camélinat's footsteps, or jeopardise their re-election. All of a sudden the question of capital and labour is included in the agenda, albeit as yet in very elementary form (rates of pay, the right to strike and, possibly, mining on a cooperative basis), but nevertheless it's there and there to stay. Since the workers of France, however, had received such a first-rate grounding from their history and from the altogether outstanding behaviour of our people during the past 2 years, nothing more was required to spark off the explosion but an event such as the Decazeville strike, combined with the stupidity of the Radicals in including 3 working men in their list of candidates. Now things will move fast in France. You'll have seen how afraid the Radicals are from the resolutions taken by the municipal councils of Paris, Lyons, etc., to vote money for the Decazeville strikers.[a] This again is unprecedented.

If that's the state your voice is in, don't go to America.[518] The demands made on the vocal chords by what is universal practice there far exceed anything you can imagine. But anyway we shall look forward to seeing you over here in the autumn.

Time for the post, too late for registration. Please send me a postcard acknowledging receipt of the cheque.

Your
F. E.

First published, in Russian, in *Marx-Engels Archives,* Vol. I (VI), Moscow, 1932

Printed according to the original

Published in English in full for the first time

---

[a] See *Le Socialiste,* Nos. 28 and 29, 6 and 13 March 1886.

249

ENGELS TO PAUL LAFARGUE [196]

IN PARIS

London, 20 March 1886

My dear Lafargue,

Herewith the cheque for £12. Yesterday I was again disturbed. It always happens when there is an urgent task to be done.

Monday's [a] vote in the Chamber was a great victory. [b] For the first time a French Chamber has sided with labour against capital — greatly against its will! But Basly & Co. have been valiantly supported by the monarchist gents who, after their relative victory at the polls, [447] are in a state of high excitement and evidently believe — notably in their capacity as capitalists, shareholders, etc.—that they can do anything they please. Placed as they are between an ultra-monarchist group and the revolutionary workers, they had to plump for the latter. At least they are Republicans and, after all, low finance, as represented by the Opportunists and Radicals, [429] has no desire to restore the régime of high finance that was toppled with MacMahon and Thiers. [463]

It was what I suspected—this reappearance of Malon's behind the scenes. [565] A parliamentary party embracing every shade of possibilism with Malon for secret leader—what a beautiful dream! The same old Bakuninist tactics which, so far as these intriguers are concerned, are now much more deeply ingrained than the bombastic language of anarchism! A firm stand must be made against these endeavours. If you can ensure that Basly and Camélinat—even on their own—carry on as they have begun and refuse to let themselves be persuaded to join a party *where they would form an impotent minority*, then the game is won. Any negotiations on their part would be the ruin of them and could only further the Radical cause. So long as they go forward with a firm tread and pay no heed to the honeyed words of the moderators

---

[a] of 15 March - [b] See previous letter.

and mediators, all this confusion will be swept away, like it or not. It is not good will that activates these gentry; rather it is fear and fear alone that has created such little good will as they have and this, when all is said and done, is the good will to spoil what Basly has begun and nothing else. Moreover such a party is out of the question. Either Basly or Camélinat will turn traitor, which I don't believe, or they will be forced to part company with these gentry as soon as the first important problem arises. It would therefore be better not to enter into an alliance with them.

Your article in the *Revue nouvelle*[a] gave me much pleasure. Obviously one makes some 'ALLOWANCE' for what you are permitted to say in a periodical of that kind. Even so, I was surprised at the number of risqué allusions you were allowed to get away with—but she [b] is a woman, she has a definite standpoint. Had the editor-in-chief been a man, you would have found yourself up against a much more ferocious brand of morality.[566] What with the *Journal des Économistes*, the *Revue philosophique* and Juliette, you are now well launched in literature of a primarily official nature.[567] And since you write better French (because more 16th-century and less Parisian) than others, you ought to succeed.

Juliette amused me much with her high foreign policy.[568] This is Blowitz to the life, though less grotesque in form.

Fortunately the SOCIALIST LEAGUE [346] is dormant for the time being. Our good Bax and Morris, craving to do something (if only they knew what?), are restrained only by the fact that there is absolutely nothing to do. Moreover they have far more truck with the anarchists than is desirable. Their celebrations on the 18th were held in concert with the latter [569] and Kropotkin spoke there—twaddle, or so they tell me. All this will pass, if only because there is absolutely nothing to be done over here just now. But with Hyndman, who is well versed in political imposture and capable of all sorts of folly when his self-advancement is at stake—with the said Hyndman on the one hand and our two political babes in arms on the other, prospects are by no means bright. Yet now we have socialist papers abroad proclaiming at the top of their voices that socialism in England is

---

[a] P. Lafargue, 'Le Matriarcat. Étude sur les origines de la famille', *La Nouvelle Revue*, Vol. 39, March-April 1886, pp. 301-36. - [b] Juliette Adam

marching forward with gigantic strides! I am very glad to say that what passes for socialism here in England is not on the march— far from it.

Yours ever,
F. E.

By the way, Bax has published a short history of philosophy that has some very good stuff in it.[a]

First published in: F. Engels, P. et L. Lafargue, *Correspondance*, t. I, Paris, 1956

Printed according to the original

Translated from the French

250

ENGELS TO VERA ZASULICH

IN GENEVA

London, 31 March 1886

Dear Citizen,

Many thanks for sending me the translation of *The Poverty of Philosophy*, which has been safely received.[185]

When opening the parcel I tore the part showing the sender's address. After a good deal of trouble I managed to reassemble the pieces well enough to decipher the address I am using today. But since I don't know whether I have read it correctly, I would ask you to advise me of your address once again, as I should like to send you a copy of the Russian translation of Volume II of *Capital*, which has arrived from St Petersburg.[570]

---

[a] E. B. Bax, *A Handbook of the History of Philosophy for the Use of Students.*

Please accept my apologies for the inconvenience caused by my clumsiness.

Yours sincerely,

F. Engels

First published, in Russian, in *Gruppa 'Osvobozhdeniye truda'*, No. 1, Moscow, 1924

Printed according to the original

Translated from the French

Published in English for the first time

251

ENGELS TO AUGUST BEBEL

IN LEIPZIG

London, 12 April 1886

Dear Bebel,

Thank you for the debate on the Anti-Socialist Law—it pleased me tremendously.[571] Here again we have something that does credit to the movement and this is the impression it gives from beginning to end. Even Liebknecht was quite his old self again; competition from the French seems to have had a good effect on him.[a] I like the spectacle of the whole gang—or pack of dogs rather—crowding round you barking and snapping, only to be beaten off by the lash of a whip. What a mercy that, apart from you and Liebknecht, only Vollmar spoke a word or two, and that Singer, the victim of a concerted attack, was compelled to hit back hard, while the tractable majority held their tongues.

The gentlemen's fears about regicide are too ludicrous. Surely they or their fathers have all of them sung:

> Has ever man had such hard luck
> As our poor Burgomaster Tschech,
> He shot at Fatty two paces away
> And yet his bullet went astray.

---

[a] See this volume, pp. 424-25.

True, the German bourgeoisie still had some vitality in those days; another example of the difference is that 1844 saw the appearance of *Das Lied von Freifrau von Droste-Vischering*,[572] whereas now the *Kulturkampf*[462] is being waged with the most humdrum weapons wielded by the most flaccid hands.

The socialists here have been acquitted.[538] I am sending you today's copy of the highly Conservative *Standard* (also a *Cri du Peuple*) containing an account of the final hearing.[a] You will be able to see from it how a judge goes about his business in England (though admittedly not in *Ireland*!). Translated from legal jargon, what he said was: The law on seditious speeches applies to the accused, but the law is outdated and invalid in practice. Otherwise you would have to convict every radical spokesman and minister. All you have to ask yourselves, therefore, is this: Was it, or was it not, the intention of the accused that there should be looting on 8 February?[b] And Cave is one of England's 16 principal judges.

The verdict is a fine advertisement for Hyndman, but it has come too late. He has contrived to ruin his organisation beyond hope of repair; in London it's fizzling out, while in the provinces the various organisations have adopted a neutral, wait-and-see attitude to the rifts down here. *Summa summarum* the two organisations—FEDERATION and LEAGUE[346]—have a combined paid-up membership of less than 2,000 and their papers[c] a combined readership of less than 5,000—the majority being sympathisers in the persons of bourgeois, priests, literati, etc. As things are now, it is truly fortunate that these immature elements are failing to penetrate the masses. They must first complete the process of fermentation, after which all may be well.

For the rest, one might almost be back in the days of the International. Only this morning a whole stack of German, French, Spanish and Belgian papers arrived and are taking up time I ought to be devoting to the English translation of *Capital*.[56] I only hope there isn't a bust-up before I've managed to finish the 3rd volume—after that it can come, so far as I'm concerned.

Things are going splendidly in Decazeville.[545] You will see from the report *(Cri du Peuple)* of last Sunday's meeting[d] (a week ago yes-

[a] *Le Cri du Peuple*, No. 888, 4 April 1886. - [b] See this volume, pp. 403-04, 406-08. - [c] *Justice* and *The Commonweal* - [d] *Le Cri du Peuple*, No. 888, 4 April 1886.

terday) which I am sending you today how skilfully those Parisians, who have been decried as revolutionary braggarts, contrive without relinquishing their revolutionary posture to advocate calm and lawfulness during the strike. It is indicative of the progress the French have made, thanks to the revolutionary soil on which they stand, that in their case there is a complete absence of that mass of sophistries and second thoughts which still confuse the minds of so many people in Germany. That one should proceed lawfully or unlawfully, depending on the circumstances, is taken entirely for granted over there and no one sees anything inconsistent in it. As to Paris, it is significant that up till yesterday the *Cri du Peuple* had raised 35,000 frs for Decazeville, but Rochefort's *Intransigeant* less than 11,000.

Bismarck, who appears to have been in a frightful rage, though obviously speaking for the benefit of the Crown Prince,[a] will doubtless get a reply from Laura and Tussy to the ludicrous insinuations he made about Marx.[573] Of the other speeches, Hänel's[b] was the best from a legal viewpoint; he came out with the absurd demand that a citizen should conform to the law not only outwardly but also *inwardly*—that such a thing should be called for, that the mere *intention* and the public expression thereof, could be held punishable by deprivation of rights shows how debased all middle-class concepts of legality have become in Germany—not that they have ever prevailed over there save in the case of the oppositional bourgeoisie; what has, in fact, always prevailed is the illegality of a police state, which in other countries (always excepting Ireland) could only assert itself shamefacedly and in the guise of a *coup de main*.

Must close because registration time (5 o'clock) draws near.

Your
F. E.

First published, in Russian, in *Marx-Engels Archives*, Vol. I (VI), Moscow, 1932

Printed according to the original

Published in English for the first time

---

[a] Frederick William - [b] A. Hänel's speech in the Reichstag on 31 March 1886 (*Stenographische Berichte über die Verhandlungen des Reichstags. VI. Legislaturperiode. II. Session 1885/86*, Vol. III, Berlin, 1886, pp. 1766-1770).

252

ENGELS TO PHILIPP VICTOR PAULI [a]

IN RHEINAU

London, 12 April 1886

Heartiest congratulations on Clara's engagement.

Friedrich Engels

First published in: Marx and Engels, *Works*, Second Russian Edition, Vol. 50, Moscow, 1981

Printed according to the original

Published in English for the first time

253

ENGELS TO LAURA LAFARGUE

IN PARIS

London, 28 April 1886

My dear Laura,

The English translation of *Capital* is awful work.[56] First they[b] translate. Then I revise and enter suggestions in pencil. Then it goes back to them. Then conference for settlement of doubtful points. Then I have to go through the whole again, to see that everything is made ready for the press, stylistically and technically, and all the quotations, which Tussy has looked up in the English originals, fitted in properly. So far I have finished 300 pages of the German, and shall soon have about 100 more. But then there is another hitch. Edward has missed translating some 50 pages of his share, and these I hope to get by the end of the week. As soon as I have got these, I shall stir up

---

[a] Written on Engels' visiting card. - [b] Samuel Moore and Edward Aveling

Kegan Paul's drowsiness.[a] The wily Scot who still fancies that we do not know our favourable position in the market, plays a waiting game, but will find himself awfully mistaken one fine morning. It is we that can afford to wait, and we intend to wait until we are quite ready to begin to print, say in a week. And as we have a written offer from another firm, we can stick to our terms.

This must serve as an excuse for my last short letter [39] and the delay that has taken place since. The fact is we must begin to print by middle of May so as to be ready to publish by end of September. And that we can, though it will keep me hard at work till far into June at least.

Your *billet-doux* to Bismarck [573] is making great stir in Germany. Bebel writes[b]:

'Die Erklärung von Laura und Eleanor Marx ist famos, der grösste Teil der deutschen Presse nimmt davon Notiz, hütet sich selbstverständlich sie abzudrucken. Otto wird wütend sein, für dergleichen Angriffe ist er sehr empfindlich.'[c]

The effect of the new departure in France [574] is plainly visible in the debate on the Socialist Law in Berlin.[571] Library [d] would hardly have ventured to come out so strongly again in his best old manner, had it not been that events in Paris and Decazeville [545] had stirred him up again a bit. This competition is invaluable for our people in Germany. The split and dissensions in Paris gave the philistine section amongst them a pretext for looking down, *de haut en bas*, upon the French, as if they, themselves, had not wallowed for years in splits, quarrels and dissensions; and they began to talk as if they, the German *kleinbürgerliche*[e] *section* of the party, were the leaders of the universal movement. That precious bit of chauvinism has now been effectually knocked on the head. Unfortunately the Socialist Law has this one effect that it excludes pretty effectually the circulation of such papers as the *Socialiste* and *Cri du Peuple*, and that the daily, *current* information about France has to be taken from the vile

---

[a] See this volume, p. 423. - [b] in his letter to Engels of 23 April 1886 - [c] 'Laura and Eleanor Marx's statement is excellent. The greater part of the German press have published notices about it but understandably take care not to reprint it. Otto [Bismarck] will be furious, for he is sensitive to such attacks.' - [d] Wilhelm Liebknecht's nickname given to him by Marx's daughters. - [e] *petty-bourgeois*

bourgeois papers. I have sent on the *Cris* and *Intransigeants* you sent me, to Bebel and Liebknecht but that does not go much further and may not always reach them.

It strikes me as very curious that I see nothing of the Villefranche judgment being appealed against.[575] As far as I know there is a double appeal 1) on account of the alleged incompetency of the court, 2) against the judgment as such; and then a final *pourvoi en cassation*[a] on both these issues. It seems to me well worth while to go in for that, if only to expose the infamy of the courts and keep the thing before the public.

I scarcely dare hope that Roche will get in next Sunday.[576] Not having read any *Cris* for about a week, I do not know what other candidates besides Gaulier are in the field. But anyhow the poll will show a great progress and be enough to frighten the Radicals[429] still more.

Here all is muddle. Bax and Morris are getting deeper and deeper into the hands of a few anarchist phraseurs, and write nonsense with increasing intensity. The turning of *The Commonweal* into a 'weekly' — absurd in every respect — has given Edward a chance of getting out of his responsibility for this now incalculable organ.[577] Bax *à la recherche*,[b] by means of half-digested Hegelian dialectic, of extreme and paradox propositions, and Morris going head foremost, bull fashion, against 'parliamentarism', will have to learn by experience what sort of people their anarchist friends are. It would be ridiculous to expect the working class to take the slightest notice of these various vagaries of what is by courtesy called English Socialism, and it is very fortunate that it is so: These gentlemen have quite enough to do to set their own brains in order.

Schorlemmer who is here, and Nim have taken little Lily to the Zoo, Pumps is going to Manchester for a few days. In our evening chats we talk a good deal of your promised coming over to London. When is that to be? Schorlemmer says you had mentioned something about Paul coming over at the same time. That would be all the better. Anyhow it is getting time that these good intentions set about developing into more or less tangible plans and projects, the season for execution is not too long in this blessed climate.

Did you see in last *Sozialdemokrat* the affair about Kalle and the *Weibergemeinschaft*[578]? That fellow was nicely caught. He is a great

---

[a] appeal - [b] in search

light among the National Liberals [243] and has large chemical (dye-stuff) works at Wiesbaden.

Love from Schorlemmer and Nim and yours affectionately,

F. Engels

Paul I hope will excuse if I do not write to him as often as I should like.

First published in: Marx and Engels, *Works*, Second Russian Edition, Vol. 36, Moscow, 1964

Reproduced from the original

Published in English for the first time

254

ENGELS TO FRIEDRICH ADOLPH SORGE [521]

IN HOBOKEN

London, 29 April 1886

Dear Sorge,

Have received your letters of 15 and 28 February and 8 March, and postcard of 21 March.

In most cases the notes contained in the ms. are the same as those Marx made in his copy for the 3rd edition.[526] In the case of those which provide for more insertions from the French, I would not commit myself unequivocally 1) because the work done for the 3rd edition is of much later date and hence, for me, more authoritative, 2) because, in respect of a translation to be made in America, i. e. outside his own orbit, Marx might have preferred some of the passages to be translated correctly from the simplified French version rather than incorrectly from the German — a consideration which no longer applies. Nevertheless, it has provided me with very useful tips which will, in due course, also come in handy for the 4th German edition. As soon as I have finished with it I shall return it to you by registered post.

The *Volkszeitung* and *Sozialist* are now arriving regularly. Over the past fortnight I have sent you *To-Day* and *Commonweal*, March and April. Also yesterday *To-Day*, May, the delay being due solely to the slovenliness of the publishers. Should you require anything else let me know.

Broadhouse (Hyndman)'s translation of *Capital* is a complete farce.[527] The 1st chapter was from the German, full of mistakes to the point of absurdity.[a] Now he's translating from the French, and making the same mistakes. At the rate it's now going, the thing won't be finished before 1900.

Thanks for the *Kalender*. I certainly had no idea that Douai was so grossly neglected a great man.[579] May he take with him to the grave the knowledge of his greatness as of its total neglect, without first seeing it compressed into a sugar mould. But he was the right man for America and, had he remained an ordinary Democrat, I should have wished him the best of luck. As it was, however, he went whoring after false gods.

As for the purist who quibbles about our style and our punctuation he doesn't know either German or English, otherwise he could not discover Anglicisms where there aren't any.[580] The German of which he's so enamoured and which was drummed into us at school, with its frightful periodic structure whereby the verb is put right at the end and is separated from its subject by ten miles of subclauses, is a German which it has taken me thirty years to *un*learn. This bureaucratic, pedagogical German, which completely ignores the fact that Lessing ever existed, is now on its last legs even in Germany. What would this worthy say were he to hear our people speaking in the Reichstag? Having done away with this horrible syntax because forever getting bogged down in it, they expressed themselves in that place like Jews[b]: 'Faced with this dilemma, Bismarck chose to kiss the pope's behind rather than the lips of the revolution', etc. Little Lasker was responsible for this improvement and it's the only good thing he ever did. Were the purist gent to go to Germany with his pedagogical German, he would be told that he spoke American. 'You know how petty your educated German philistine is'—especially so in America, it would seem. German syntax and punctuation, as taught at school 40 or 50

---

[a] See this volume, p. 424. -[b] Engels is referring to the more straightforward German syntax frequently employed by Jews, as exemplified in the sentence he then proceeds to quote.

Eleanor Marx-Aveling. 1886

years ago, are fit only for the scrap-heap to which, in Germany, they're being well and truly consigned.

I think I wrote and told you that an American lady[a] married to a Russian[b] has taken it into her head to translate my old book.[c] I have looked over the translation and this entailed a lot of work. But she had written to say that publication was assured and that I must do it at once, so I had to buckle to. It now transpires that she had entrusted the negotiations to a Miss Foster, secretary of a WOMEN'S RIGHTS society, who had been foolish enough to give the thing to the Socialist Labor Party.[550] I told the translator what I thought of this,[d] but the damage had been done. For the rest, I am glad that these folk aren't translating anything of mine—a fine mess they'd make of it. Their German is bad enough, let alone their English!

The *Volkszeitung* people must be pleased with themselves. They have gained complete control over the movement amongst the Germans, and business must be flourishing. That a man like Dietzgen should go to the wall is understandable enough.[529] Playing around with the boycott and minor STRIKES is, of course, far more important than theoretical guidance. But despite all this, the cause is making enormous strides in America. For the first time there is a real mass movement amongst the English-speaking population. That it should still be feeling its way, awkwardly, at random and in ignorance, is inevitable. But all this will right itself; the movement must and will evolve by learning from its own mistakes. Theoretical ignorance is an attribute of all young nations, but so is speedy practical development. In America as in England no amount of exhortation will help until the need is really there. And in America it is there, as is a growing awareness of it. The entry of the indigenous working masses into the movement in America is for me one of the great events of 1886.[581] As for the Germans over there, let the presently prosperous kind gradually assimilate with the Americans—they'll still be a step or two ahead of the latter and a nucleus will nevertheless remain which will still retain a theoretical grasp of the nature and progress of the movement as a whole, will keep the process of fermentation going and, eventually, rise to the top again.

The second great event of 1886 is the formation of a workers' party in the French Chamber by Basly and Camélinat, two working-class deputies who, for appearances' sake, were included in the list and given a leg up by the Radicals,[429] but failed to play the game and, in-

___
[a] Florence Kelley-Wischnewetzky - [b] Lazar Wischnewetzky - [c] *The Condition of the Working-Class in England*; see this volume, pp. 393-94. - [d] See this volume, p. 415.

stead of becoming the servants of the Radical gents, took the floor as working men. The Decazeville STRIKE[545] brought to a head the split between them—they were joined by 5 other deputies—and the Radicals.[a] The latter were thus forced to spell out their policy to the workers and, since it is only thanks to the Radicals that the government exists, this was highly distasteful, for it meant that they were rightly held responsible by the workers for everything done by the government. In short, the Radicals, Clemenceau et al, behaved contemptibly, with a result which no amount of exhortation had hitherto succeeded in bringing about, namely *the defection of the French workers from the Radicals.* And a further result was the uniting of all socialist groups for the purpose of joint action. Only the miserable Possibilists[237] held aloof, in consequence of which they are steadily going to pieces. This NEW DEPARTURE has been tremendously helped along by the government's foolishness, notably its attempt to raise a loan of 900 million frs for which purpose it needed the big financiers, while the latter, being also shareholders in Decazeville, refused their money unless the government broke the STRIKE. Hence the arrest of Duc and Roche[575]; the workers' riposte was to put up Roche in Paris as a candidate (for the Chamber) in next Sunday's elections and Duc (Quercy) as a candidate for the municipal council, where he is certain to get in.[576] In short, France can again boast a splendid movement, and this is making spanking progress but, best of all, our men, Guesde, Lafargue and Deville, are its theoretical leaders.

Nor has it been without repercussions in Germany. The revolutionary language and actions of the French have shown how lacklustre are the jeremiads of your Geisers, Auers & Co., which is why, in the recent Anti-Socialist Law debate, only Bebel and Liebknecht spoke, and very well too.[571] After this debate we can show our faces in decent company again, which is something we can by no means do after all of them. On the whole, it's a good thing that German pre-eminence should not remain altogether unchallenged, especially now that so many philistine elements have been elected (inevitable though this may have been). In Germany, when times are quiet, there is a general tendency to philistinism, and then the spur of French competition is absolutely indispensable. Nor will it be lacking. From being a sect, French socialism has suddenly become a party and

---

[a] See this volume, p. 409.

only now and because of this has it become possible for the workers to join *en masse*, for the latter are sick to the teeth of sectarianism, which explains why they adhered to the extreme bourgeois party, the Radicals. Next Sunday's elections should already see a great step forward, although we can hardly expect Roche to get in.

I believe that the printing of the English translation of *Capital*, Volume I, will begin in 2 or 3 weeks' time. I haven't nearly finished revising it, but 300 pages are completely ready for the press, and another 200 very nearly so.

One more thing. Not long ago a Mr J. T. McEnnis interviewed me for the purpose of seeking my advice on labour legislation, ostensibly on behalf of the State of Missouri. I soon smelt a journalistic rat and, indeed, he admitted working for THE LEADING DEMOCRATIC PAPER OF St Louis,[a] but promised on his word of honour that he would first submit the whole thing to me for revision. The fellow was sent to see me by a Russian, Stepnyak. That was nearly a fortnight ago and I am afraid he may not have kept his word. I have forgotten the name of the St Louis paper, but if anything should appear about the interview, I would ask you to insert the following statement[b] in the *Sozialist*, the *Volkszeitung* and anywhere else you think fit. If, however, the fellow comes back after all and abides by his word, I shall naturally let you know at once, and then you can tear up the statement.

Luckily the movement in this country has come to a *complete standstill*. Hyndman & Co. are political careerists who wreck everything and in the SOCIALIST LEAGUE[346] the anarchists are making enormous strides. Morris and Bax — the former as a sentimental socialist, the latter as a searcher after philosophical paradoxes — are presently as clay in their hands and must now find this out *in corpore vili*.[c] From the next *Commonweal* you will see that, thanks largely to Tussy's efforts, Aveling will no longer be responsible for this simulacrum, which is a good thing.[577] And it's these addlepates who propose to

---

[a] *Missouri Republican* - [b] F. Engels, 'A Statement to the Editorial Board of the *New Yorker Volkszeitung*'. - [c] in their own persons

lead the British working class! Fortunately the latter refuse to have anything to do with them.

Kindest regards,

Your

F. E.

First published in *Briefe und Auszüge aus Briefen von Joh. Phil. Becker, Jos. Dietzgen, Friedrich Engels, Karl Marx u. A. an F. A. Sorge und Andere*, Stuttgart, 1906

Printed according to the original

Published in English in full for the first time

255

ENGELS TO PAUL LAFARGUE [196]

IN PARIS

[Excerpt]

[London,] 7 May 1886

I congratulate you on Sunday's victory which has indeed confirmed the severance of the Parisian working man from radicalism.[576] What idiots those Radicals are! But it is the fatal idiocy that seizes hold of any bourgeois party as soon as it finds itself on the threshold of power and thus loses the characteristics of an opposition party. They are impatient to take over the administration, although they know that the moment has not yet come; they play at running a shadow government, but nevertheless become responsible for the follies and faults of the government of the day. At the same time they are confronted by the Workers' Party [201] growing from day to day as a result of the follies of the government the responsibility for which they can only partially disclaim. The Workers' Party will no longer accept fine words and promises; it will call upon them to act and this they cannot do. While wanting to retain it, they are compelled to act against it. Being not, as yet, in power and finding that the masses are deserting them in increasing numbers, *they are reduced to pointing a finger at the monarchist conspirators, to representing them as a real danger, to uttering the cry: Let us unite to save the Republic*, in short, *to becoming Opportunists*.[236]

Any party is lost if tries to assume power before the time is ripe for the imple-mentation of its own programme. But the impatience of the bourgeois par-ties to arrive is such that all founder prematurely on this rock. That gives us even less time in which to develop.

On the other hand our movement in Paris has entered a phase in which even a blunder would do it no great harm. There can be no doubt that the rate of progress in the future will largely depend upon the group leaders. But once the masses are on the move, they will be like a healthy body that is strong enough to eliminate traces of dis-ease and even a modicum of poison.

First published in *Le Socialiste*, No. 115, Paris, 24 novembre 1900

Printed according to the newspaper
Translated from the French

256

ENGELS TO WILHELM LIEBKNECHT [521]

[IN BORSDORF NEAR LEIPZIG [34]]

London, 12 May 1886

Dear Liebknecht,

The French papers (of which I have sent at least 3 parcels) were simply intended to give you an opportunity of reading at first hand some of the news about the brilliant turn things have taken in France. Since you take the *Cri du Peuple,* I need only send you the *Intran-sigeant,* etc. Lafargue sends me one now and again, when something happens, and I thought that in this way they could be turned to further account.

As regards Clemenceau, the moment may very well come when you would do better to drop *La Justice.* He is being pushed over onto the conservative, markedly bourgeois, side by, on the one hand, the immediate prospect of a ministerial post, and, on the other, by the to him unexpectedly rapid growth of the Workers' Party. [201] Even from his own point of view he is behaving stupidly. But that's how all these bourgeois are, even the most progressive. Longuet will soon have to choose, if he doesn't want to ruin himself utterly. Gaulier's candida-ture, supported solely by the press unaided by the *comités radicaux-socialistes,* cost the Radicals [429] 50,000 voters who have come over to us and are now the loudest in their denunciation of their one-time chiefs. [576] In the absence of colossal blunders — the movement is already strong enough now to absorb minor errors without damage to itself — we shall obtain between $1/4$ and $1/3$ of the seats at the next elections in Paris. And, now that they have something real to do, our people are behaving in quite exemplary fashion.

But to write for *Justice* without being paid is stupid. The paper is perfectly well able to pay; after all, its chief editors — deputies — are paid by the State.

Bebel has written to say that his voice is apt to give out after several days of exertion, and needless to say I told him that for an American STUMP tour the very first prerequisite was a voice that is proof against anything. [a] Whether he's not making too much of the business, I naturally cannot say, but it would in any case be quite a risk; once you're over there, you yourself will discover soon enough what the Yankees demand in return for their good money. If he doesn't go, you must at any rate make sure that no one of the tame, petty-bourgeois breed is sent with you. [518]

No doubt the Chicago affair [582] will put paid to the anarchist farce in America. The chaps can shout their heads off if they want, but pointless rowdyism is something the Americans refuse to put up with, now they have become an industrial nation.

There's nothing favourable to report of the so-called 'movement' over here. Hyndman loses more ground every day, having completely forfeited the confidence of his own people, and the LEAGUE [346] is increasingly coming under anarchist leadership. Since *The Commonweal* became a weekly — without adequate supplies either of money or talent — Aveling has had to resign his (honorary) editorship in favour of Bax who, like Morris, is strongly influenced by the anarchists. [577] The two gentlemen will have to learn *in corpore vile*[b]; they'll soon be sick of it and it's a real stroke of luck that these teething troubles will have been left behind before the masses join the movement, which at present they obstinately refuse to do. It's just as it was in France; a really big working class cannot be got moving by exhortation, but when things have reached the right stage, the least impulse is enough to precipitate an avalanche. And that's what will happen over here as well, and soon. Most probably it will be the financial collapse of the big TRADES UNIONS under the pressure of chronic

---

[a] See this volume, p. 429. - [b] from bitter experience

overproduction that will mark the moment when the eyes of the English are opened to the inadequacy of 'self-help' and of Radicalism. So [see you] here this autumn!

Your

F. E.

Tomorrow week Mrs Pfänder will be sailing for America to stay with her brother-in-law in New Ulm, Minnesota.

First published, in Russian, in *Marx-Engels Archives*, Vol. I (VI), Moscow, 1932

Printed according to the original

Published in English in full for the first time

257

ENGELS TO F. H. NESTLER & MELLE'S VERLAG [583]

IN HAMBURG

[Draft]

[London,] 13 May 1886

Dear Sirs,

Greatly flattered though I am by the offer you made me in your kind note of the 10th inst., I regret that I must nevertheless decline it on the grounds that I cannot spare the time.

I am responsible for editing the mss. left by Marx and for turning to account all the other papers he left. It is a responsibility that will occupy my time for several years to come and must take precedence over everything else.

In addition, I am responsible for revising the translations of our works into foreign languages — an essential task in the majority of cases. Not only is there the English translation of *Capital*, which I must now finish and which goes to the printers next month, [56] but also a constant influx of mss. of the kind that call for revision, translations of shorter works into French, Italian, Danish, Dutch, etc.,[a] and these take up all that remains of my spare time.

---

[a] See this volume, p. 394.

But once I have put all this behind me, I shall, assuming I live so long, first have to turn my mind to the completion, once and for all, of my own independent works which have been totally neglected for the past three years.

Among those whose views correspond to my own, my friend Karl Kautsky would no doubt be suitable for such a position, especially as he now lives here, and I should be glad to give him all the help I could. Moreover the relevant English literature, most of it quite unknown, is obtainable nowhere save in the BRITISH MUSEUM. Yesterday, therefore, I took the liberty of informing him of your proposal. But his commitments — apart from editing the *Neue Zeit* — are so many and extend so far ahead that he was unable to authorise my suggesting him to you as a candidate.

I am, as you can see, most interested in your scheme and hence am all the sorrier for being unable to participate in its execution. Meanwhile I would thank you for honouring me with your proposal, and remain

Yours faithfully

First published in: Marx and Engels, *Works*, First Russian Edition, Vol. XXVII, Moscow, 1935

Printed according to the original
Published in English in full for the first time

258

ENGELS TO EDUARD BERNSTEIN [484]

IN ZURICH

London, 22 May 1886

Dear Ede,

I am sending you the (*Daily News*) report of Thursday's parliamentary debate on the Irish Arms Bill [584]: Restrictions on the right to carry or possess arms, hitherto aimed at the Nationalists in Ireland, are now to be extended to the Protestant braggarts in Ulster; rebellion is

Eleanor Marx-Aveling and Wilhelm Liebknecht. 1886

in the offing. Remarkable speech by Lord Randolph Churchill,[a] brother of the Duke of Marlborough, democratising Tory, Secretary for India in the last Tory Cabinet, and as such a life member of the PRIVY COUNCIL. In view of our petty-bourgeois socialists' insipid and pusillanimous protests and assurances to the effect that, whatever the circumstances, they will pursue their objectives by peaceful means, this is surely the moment to point out that English ministers — Althorp, Peel, Morley, and even Gladstone — are advocating the right to revolt as a theory consistent with the Constitution, though admittedly only *for such time as they remain in opposition*, as Gladstone's subsequent vapourings have borne out,[b] though in none of them did he dare deny that right as such — and especially, too, because this emanates from England, the land of legality *par excellence*. Our Vierecks could hardly have had shorter shrift.

I'm glad to see from the *Sozialdemokrat*'s renewed verve that you are in good shape again.

I'm up to my eyes in the English translation of *Capital*. Aveling fixed up everything with the publishers this morning and the contract will be signed in a day or two, after which comes the printing, 5 sheets a week minimum.[56] Unfortunately I haven't finished revising it, but pp. 1-450 of the original are ready for the press; ditto, *almost*, pp. 450-640. But please don't make any announcement yet, as nothing has been signed so far.

Our Frenchmen are doing splendidly. Over here, on the other hand, everyone is playing about like a bunch of amateurs. The anarchist follies in America[582] may prove advantageous; it is undesirable that the American workers, given their present wholly bourgeois level of thinking — high wages and short hours — should win victories *too quickly*. That might unduly reinforce the biassed TRADES UNION spirit.

The most powerful TRADES UNION over here, the AMALGAMATED ENGINEERS, had to allocate from its reserve funds more than £43,000 for its unemployed members, bringing the reserves down from approx. £165,000 to approx. £122,000. Not until this fund is exhausted, and only then, will it be possible to do something with those chaps.

Your
F. E.

---

[a] R. Churchill's speech in the House of Commons on 20 May 1886 (*The Daily News*, No. 12515, 21 May 1886). - [b] W. E. Gladstone's speech in the House of Commons on 20 May 1886 (*The Daily News*, No. 12515, 21 May 1886).

I am sending this to Schlüter as I don't know the new number of your house.

First published, in Russian, in *Marx-Engels Archives*, Book I, Moscow, 1924

Printed according to the original

Published in English in full for the first time

259

ENGELS TO LAURA LAFARGUE

IN PARIS

London, 23 May 1886

My dear Laura,

I think I can to-day announce to you that the affair about the English edition of the *Kapital* is at last settled. [56] With Kegan Paul and Co. it was impossible to come to a satisfactory conclusion, so we arranged terms with Swan Sonnenschein and Co. I saw Swan Sonnenschein yesterday, with Edward, and there is now only the agreement to be signed formally and then the ms. will go to press at once. Swan Sonnenschein and Co. pay us 10% of gross selling price first 500 copies sold and $12^1/_2\%$ all following copies. First edition to be a library one, at 32/- in 2 volumes: the type to be clichéd at once but so that alterations for 2nd edition can be made within certain limits; then second edition in one volume say from 7/6 to 10/-, and this plan will suit us much better than Kegan Paul's who would have kept the price up at 28/- and thus excluded the book from general circulation.

As I have 450 pages (of the original German) ready to go to press, and about 200 more that can be got ready in 14 days, and all the rest done in the rough, there is no reason why we should not print 5 sheets a week and have done altogether by middle of August, and the book to be brought out 1st October.

I think Paul does not quite see why they wanted a letter from him on the Paris election for *The Commonweal*. The people here do not want directly to attack *Justice* and moreover their assertion would not go half as far as an authoritative statement from Paris. [585] But it's no great matter, as the League [346] is in a complete muddle through their having let the anarchists creep in. They will have their conference of delegates on Whit Sunday, [586] and then we shall see what comes of it.

I cannot make out why Decazeville collapsed so suddenly, [587] especially as Paul, like Napoleon after the burning of Moscow, all at once ceased to supply *Cris du Peuple* to me, at the critical moment. Is it so absolutely impossible for the Parisian mind to own to unpleasant things that can't be helped? The victory of Decazeville would have been exceedingly nice, but after all the defeat may be more useful to the movement in the long run. So I do believe, too, that the anarchist follies of Chicago will do much good. [582] If the present American movement — which so far as it is not exclusively German, is still in the Trades Union stage — had got a great victory on the 8 hours question, Trades Unionism would have become a fixed and final dogma. While a *mixed* result will help to show then that it is necessary to go beyond 'high wages and short hours'.

Yours affectionately,

F. Engels

First published, in the language of the original (English), in: F. Engels, P. et L. Lafargue, *Correspondance*, t. I, Paris, 1956

Reproduced from the original

260

ENGELS TO FLORENCE KELLEY-WISCHNEWETZKY [588]

IN ZURICH

[London,] 3 June 1886
122 Regent's Park Road, N. W.

Dear Mrs Wischnewetzky,

I have looked over the proofs and corrected in pencil a few additional mistakes.

That the set-up of the work would be anything but elegant, I foresaw as soon as I knew who had it in charge, and am therefore not much surprised. I am afraid there is no help now, so it's no use grumbling.

Whatever the mistakes and the *Borniertheit*[a] of the leaders of the movement, and partly of the newly-awakening masses too, one thing is certain: the American working class is moving, and no mistake. And after a few false starts, they will get into the right track soon enough. This appearance of the Americans upon the scene I consider one of the greatest events of the year. [581] What the downbreak of Russian Czarism would be for the great military monarchies of Europe — the snapping of their mainstay — that is for the bourgeois of the whole world the breaking out of class war in America. For America after all was the ideal of all bourgeois: a country rich, vast, expanding, with purely bourgeois institutions unleavened by feudal remnants or monarchical traditions, and without a permanent and hereditary proletariat. Here every one could become, if not a capitalist, at all events an independent man, producing or trading, with his own means, for his own account. And because there were not, *as yet*, classes with opposing interests, our — and your — bourgeois thought that America stood *above* class antagonisms and struggles. That delusion has now broken down, the last Bourgeois Paradise on earth is fast changing into a Purgatory, and can only be prevented from becoming, like Europe, an Inferno by the go-ahead pace at which the development of the newly fledged proletariat of America will take place. The way in which they have made their appearance on the scene, is quite extraordinary: six months ago nobody suspected anything, and now they appear all of a sudden in such organised masses as to strike terror into the whole capitalist class. I only wish Marx could have lived to see it!

I am in doubt whether to send this to Zurich or to the address in Paris you give at foot of your letter. But as in case of mistake Zurich is safest, I forward this and the proofs to Mr Schlüter, who no doubt will forward wherever it may be necessary.

Ever sincerely yours,

F. Engels

First published, in the language of the original (English), in *Briefe und Auszüge aus Briefen von Joh. Phil. Becker, Jos. Dietzgen, Friedrich Engels, Karl Marx u. A. an F. A. Sorge und Andere*, Stuttgart, 1906

Reproduced from the original

---

[a] stubborn narrowness

261

ENGELS TO HERMANN SCHLÜTER

IN HOTTINGEN-ZURICH

London, 3 June 1886

Dear Mr Schlüter,

Mrs Wischnewetzky has sent me some printed sheets [a] which I have got to return; she also gave me a Paris address, which I can't decipher properly, and without telling me whether they should be sent there. For safety's sake I am taking the liberty of posting my reply and corrections to you, with the request that you kindly forward them. You may perhaps know the Paris address, or else you could make inquiries at the Pension Tiefenau — it looks like c/Drexel, Harjes & Co., Paris. [589] I apologise for putting you to this trouble.

Your Chartism's [557] turn will come round as soon as the English translation of *Capital* allows me a free moment. Printing has just begun and, as only the first half is ready for the press, I absolutely must attend to the remainder first. [56] Hence I *cannot* allow anything more to stand in its way just now.

Regards to Ede.

Yours,

F. Engels

First published in: Marx and Engels, *Works*, First Russian Edition, Vol. XXVII, Moscow, 1935

Printed according to the original

Published in English for the first time

---

[a] F. Engels, 'Appendix to the American Edition of *The Condition of the Working Class in England*'.

262

ENGELS TO KARL KAUTSKY

IN LONDON

[Eastbourne, [590]] Friday, 2 July 1886

Many thanks for all the trouble you've taken. Please don't send me, apart from *Nature*, *any* English papers, or the Manchester paper which arrives on Saturdays, or, after Saturday, *any more* papers at all, apart from the *Sozialdemokrat*, or, after Monday, any more letters, for we shall be home again on Wednesday [a] afternoon. The weather continues magnificent—I await with interest the first election results from the larger towns [591] tomorrow morning. Best wishes from my family to yours.

Your
F. E.

First published, in Russian, in *Marx-Engels Archives*, Vol. I (VI), Moscow, 1932

Printed according to the original

Published in English for the first time

263

ENGELS TO KARL KAUTSKY

IN LONDON

[Eastbourne, 4 July 1886]

Dear Kautsky,

I would naturally prefer not to have any more visitors here, [590] as Schorlemmer will in any case probably be arriving tomorrow; however, what has to be has to be. Besides, I shall be back in London on Wednesday [a] and hope that Mrs Guillaume-Schack will find enough

---

[a] 7 July

to do in town until then. [592] Since yesterday it has been oppressively hot here too, though all the same there has been a bit of a breeze — on Friday it was actually chilly and I couldn't sit outside in the evening without my overcoat. Best wishes to your wife. Pumps, Percy and Moore have taken a boat and gone out to catch fish for supper, provided, that is, *le bon dieu*[a] doesn't object to their breaking the Sabbath and visit sea-serpents upon them. The Pilsener beer is also good here.

Your
F. E.

First published, in Russian, in *Marx-Engels Archives*, Vol. I (VI), Moscow, 1932

Printed according to the original

Published in English for the first time

264

ENGELS TO KARL KAUTSKY

IN LONDON

[London, 8 July 1886]

Safely home [590] — today called to see Guillaume-Schack, but she was out — hence, so far have not had the pleasure of making her acquaintance. [592] Schorlemmer is with us — shall you be coming over here tomorrow evening?

Your
F. E.

First published, in Russian, in *Marx-Engels Archives*, Vol. I (VI), Moscow, 1932

Printed according to the original

Published in English for the first time

---

[a] God

265

ENGELS TO JOHANN PHILIPP BECKER

IN GENEVA

London, 9 July 1886

Dear Old Comrade,

I put off answering your letter for a few days as I wanted to wait and see whether I could find some way of entering into your Paris scheme.[593] I couldn't, alas, if only because

1) I am tied down in England through having to attend to the proof-correction and publication of the English translation of *Capital* which is now printing[56]; nor could I leave this to anyone else even if I were not bound by my contract.

2) For the past 3 months, however, I have again become an invalid, 200 or 300 paces being the most I can manage, and am dependent on all sorts of medical persons; the business is just *gênant*,[a] no more, but at any moment complications might set in if I didn't take things easy, so there can be no question of a long journey. And even if, as I hope, I am more mobile this autumn, I really must do my utmost this time to rid myself for good of this old trouble by which I have been crippled off and on during the past three years, and that means doing nothing that might bring about a relapse. I simply must get to the stage of being able to walk for 2 or 3 hours on end, otherwise I shall be done for and unable to do any sustained work. I had thought that, during the past fortnight, I might get to the stage of being able to register a positive improvement, but it's taking longer than I imagined.

Well, with luck we might be able to make some other arrangement. For once in Paris, you might just as well cross the Channel and spend a little while here. I would gladly bear the cost, and your stay over here wouldn't cost you a penny. In August I am being sent to the seaside to recuperate and in September I shall have visitors from the provinces, from Germany and most likely also the Lafargues from Paris and, since I only have one spare room, putting up all these people will

---

[a] inconvenient

be none too easy. But in October it will all be over and I shall be able to let you have the room any time you like, and should be delighted to see you here. Then we could also talk things over and exchange all our news at greater leisure than in Paris where, after all, one is never on one's own.

So make up your mind. By October, too, my *urgent* work will be so far advanced that I shall be able to shelve everything else; I also hope to have made sufficient progress to tipple again. If, by the by, you would rather come here in September, let me know; either way, I'm sure it can be managed. There are all sorts of things that still remain to be discussed and, above all, you have so much information — known, as you say, to no one else — about the historical origins of the movement to pass on to me, that it would be a crying shame if we didn't do our utmost to foregather once again and get all this off our chests.

I haven't yet had a chance to put Marx's papers in order, a job that would take me at least a month. Perhaps I shall get round to it in the autumn, for done it has got to be, and done before the days grow too short.

I am taking out another five pound money order for you which I hope will reach you soon after, or at the same time as, this letter.

So do make up your mind. I look forward immensely to seeing you again and discussing things with you face to face. If I were as steady on my pins as you, I should come to Geneva — but as it is! Well, I expect you to do it in my stead, and come over here.

Your old friend

F. Engels

First published in: F. Engels, *Vergessene Briefe (Briefe Friedrich Engels' an Johann Philipp Becker)*, Berlin, 1920

Printed according to the original

Published in English for the first time

266

ENGELS TO KARL KAUTSKY

IN DEAL [594]

London, 26 July 1886

Dear Baron,

I have today sent you a *Volkszeitung* and shall tomorrow send off the one that arrived today; also *Deutsche Worte*, wherein the first instalment of an article on Gustav Cohn [595] — so far quite delightful. You really must get hold of the chap[a] for the *Neue Zeit*.

Yesterday we were more or less on our own — Tussy was ill as well so that Aveling had to leave early — it's nothing much, but nevertheless troublesome. On top of that it was raining cats and dogs — I hope you are having better weather down in the south-east where the climate is more continental than anywhere else in England.

So Dilke has providentially gone into political exile — *requiescat in pace!*[b] That's what comes of protestant hypocrisy. None of this business could ever have happened in a Catholic country — either in Vienna or in Rome or in Paris — nor yet in Petersburg; such whited sepulchres are possible only in two centres — London and Berlin. In fact, if Berlin is becoming a metropolis, this is only because London is increasingly deteriorating into a Berlin. What could be more typical of Berlin than gallant Captain Forster escorting his lady-friend to a brothel? [596]

No other news to speak of — Schorlemmer has gone to Germany; I am getting better every day. Nim has just finished reading *Märtyrer der Phantasie*[c] aloud (end has come!!) and is knitting stockings. Kindest regards to you and your wife from us both.

Your
F. E.

If there should be anything you want doing at home, I have once more reached the stage at which I can perfectly well walk as far as

---

[a] Julius Platter - [b] may he rest in peace - [c] *The Martyrs of Imagination*

that, and hope this will continue; so if I can do you any service, don't hesitate to let me know.

First published, in Russian, in *Marx-Engels Archives*, Vol. I (VI), Moscow, 1932

Printed according to the original

Published in English for the first time

267

ENGELS TO KARL KAUTSKY

IN DEAL [594]

London, 31 July 1886

Dear Kautsky,

I shall retain the POST OFFICE ORDER here as there would be no point in trying to cash it with the moron in Southampton Road. It will be kept at your disposal and, should you not return before, I shall leave it with Mrs Parker, alias Sarah, in an envelope addressed to you.

Instead, herewith a POST OFFICE ORDER for £4 in your name, *Karl* Kautsky, taken out by me Frederick Engels. If you could do with a few more pounds sterling, I will gladly let you have them.

Weather's improving — with you, too, I hope. So that there may be a chance of this letter's arriving today, I shall close. Kindest regards to your wife and yourself from Nim and

Your
F. E.

First published, in Russian, in *Marx-Engels Archives*, Vol. I (VI), Moscow, 1932

Printed according to the original

Published in English for the first time

268

ENGELS TO FRIEDRICH ADOLPH SORGE

IN MOUNT DESERT [597]

[London,] 3 August 1886

Interview [598] received with thanks; amused me greatly. Of course the idiot[a] puts into *my* mouth all the silly things *he himself* said. *Commonweal*, 1 May-17 July, will follow in 2 parcels tomorrow. I now get them through Lessner at intervals, but complete. *To-Day* will follow as soon as I have got the *July* no. which is still missing.

Translation of ms.[b] will be finished the day after tomorrow and last part handed over to publishers.[c] 320 pages have been printed, almost the same as 3rd German edition. Hope it will be finished by end of September and published in October. Am also going to the seaside this Saturday,[d] hope it will do us both and also your wife good.

Your

F. E.

First published in *Briefe und Auszüge aus Briefen von Joh. Phil. Becker, Jos. Dietzgen, Friedrich Engels, Karl Marx u. A. an F. A. Sorge und Andere*, Stuttgart, 1906

Printed according to the original

Published in English for the first time

269

ENGELS TO KARL KAUTSKY

IN DEAL [594]

London, 6 August 1886

Dear Kautsky,

We leave tomorrow for Eastbourne. [599] Address 4 Cavendish Place, as before.

---

[a] John T. McEnnis - [b] the English translation of the first volume of *Capital* (see Note 56) - [c] William Swan Sonnenschein - [d] 7 August

Have just booked a passage for Liebknecht on the Cunard STEAMER *Servia* and sent him the receipt. [600]

You will find your MONEY ORDER here in an addressed envelope. Also sundry American *Sozialists* for yourself and sundry American *Volkszeitungs* along with the *Missouri Republican* containing the outrageous interview [598] — please keep these *Volkszeitungs* and the *Republican* for me.

Will you please — when you get back — continue to forward my letters, etc., at regular intervals, i. e. *at most* every other day, but as a rule twice a week, just as you did before?

The translation of the ms.[a] was finally completed yesterday; 23 sheets have been set up and the proofs are in hand.

Liebknecht is sailing from Liverpool on 4 September, the Avelings on 31 August. [601] We shall be staying here until 28 August for certain and if possible a week longer; it depends on Liebknecht's arrival and other possible visitors.

You will have read about the sentences in Freiberg[b] — 6 months for Dietz, Heinzel and Müller, 9 for the others. [602] Typically German.

Thank you for your news from Vienna. [603] Otherwise all is tranquil while the world takes a breather, the one exception being the Russians who are surreptitiously intriguing away for all they are worth. Giers evidently intends to wangle something worthwhile out of Bismarck this year, but I don't imagine he will succeed.

Kindest regards to your wife.

Your
F. E.

First published, in Russian, in *Marx-Engels Archives*, Vol. I (VI), Moscow, 1932

Printed according to the original

Published in English for the first time

---

[a] the English translation of the first volume of *Capital* (see Note 56) - [b] Freiburg in the original.

270

ENGELS TO KARL KAUTSKY

IN LONDON

Eastbourne, 11 August 1886
4 Cavendish Place

Dear Baron,

I shall gladly do my best as regards your ms. [604] But to promise that it will be seen to by a specific date in the near future is utterly impossible: 1) everything depends upon the pressure of printed sheets, [a] each of which I must read through carefully at least 3 times for proof-correcting and the lst and 2nd revisions; 2) I have accumulated such a pile of urgent correspondence—which has been completely neglected for the past 3 months—that I shall have to dispose of that first; 3) 2 mss. have been lying about here for 7 months awaiting revision; however, I shall set them aside if needs must. [605]

So send me the ms. and *nous verrons*. [b] In any case he [c] only needs the *first* instalment, so *send* me *that*.

Dietz *must not hear a word* about my going through it. I am only too familiar with the way he casts all discretion to the winds as soon as he senses that some commercial benefit may be in the offing. If necessary, therefore, you will have to find another source of information.

Changeable weather since yesterday.

As regards papers, etc., please send me only the French, Spanish and German-American *Socialists*, [d] the *Sozialdemokrat*, the *Volkszeitung*, *Volksfreund* and *Nature*; the others can wait. All company prospectuses and reports can likewise wait.

I shall now get back to the printed sheets. I trust the sea air did you both good, especially your wife. Every night between 9 and 11 we have a hectic game of cards; so far I have been marvel-

---

[a] of the English translation of the first volume of *Capital* (see Note 56) - [b] we shall see - [c] J. H. W. Dietz - [d] *Le Socialiste*, *El Socialista*, *Der Sozialist*

lously lucky—as a loser. Nim and the Roshers send their best wishes.

Regards to your wife.

Your

F. E.

First published, in Russian, in *Marx-Engels Archives*, Vol. I (VI), Moscow, 1932

Printed according to the original

Published in English for the first time

271

ENGELS TO FLORENCE KELLEY-WISCHNEWETZKY

IN ZURICH

Eastbourne, 13-14 August 1886
4 Cavendish Place

Dear Mrs Wischnewetzky,

My reply to your kind letter of the 9th June was delayed for the simple reason that overwork compelled me to suspend *all* my correspondence (such as did not command immediate despatch) until the ms. of the translation of *Das Kapital* was finally ready for the printer. [56] Such is now the case, and I can at last attend to the heap of unanswered letters before me; and you shall have the first chance. Had you told me in the above letter that you had spare time on your hands for party work, I should at once have sent you a short reply; I am sorry if through my fault you were prevented from doing some useful work.

I quite forgot, when proposing to you *Lohnarbeit und Kapital*,[a] that an English translation had already appeared in London. As this is offered for sale in New York it would be useless to translate it over again.

---

[a] K. Marx, *Wage Labour and Capital*.

Now about *Der Ursprung*.[a] The thing is more difficult to translate than *Die Lage*,[b] and would require comparatively greater attention and more time per page on your part. But if I had time left to me for the looking it over, that would be no obstacle, provided you could devote that time and attention to it, and leave me a larger margin of blank paper to suggest alterations. There is however another matter to consider. If the thing is to come out in English at all, it ought to be published in such a way that the public can get hold of it through the regular book-trade. That will *not* be the case, as far as I can see, with *Die Lage*. Unless the trade arrangements are very different in America from those in Europe, the booksellers will not deal in works published by outside establishments belonging to a working men's party. This is why Chartist and Owenite publications are nowhere preserved and nowhere to be had, *not even in the British Museum*; and why all our German party publications are — and were, long before the Socialist Law[37] — not to be had through the trade, and remained unknown to the public outside the party. That is a state of things which sometimes cannot be avoided, but ought to be avoided wherever possible. And you will not blame me if I wish to avoid it for English translations of my writings having suffered from it in Germany for more than 40 years. The state of things in England is such that publishers can be got — either now or in the near future — for socialist works, and I have no doubt that in the course of next year I can have an English translation published here and the translator paid; and as I have, moreover, long since promised Dr Aveling the translation of the *Entwicklung*[528] and *Ursprung*,[606] if he can make it pay for *himself*, you see that an American edition, brought out outside the regular book-trade, would only spoil the chance of a London edition to be brought out in the way of the regular trade and therefore accessible to the public generally and everywhere.

Moreover I do not think that this book is exactly what is wanted at the present moment by the American working men. *Das Kapital* will be at their service before the year is out, that will serve them for a *pièce de résistance*.[c] For lighter, more popular literature, for real propaganda, my booklet will scarcely serve. In the present undeveloped state of the movement, I think perhaps some of the French po-

---

[a] F. Engels, *The Origin of the Family, Private Property and the State*. -[b] F. Engels, *The Condition of the Working-Class in England*. -[c] special dish

pularisations would answer best. Deville and Lafargue have published two series of lectures, *Cours d'économie sociale*, about two years ago, Deville taking the economic and Lafargue the more general, historic side of the Marxian theory.[179] No doubt Bernstein can let you look at a copy and get one from Paris, and then you might judge for yourself. Of course I do not mean Deville's larger work, the extract from *Das Kapital*, which in the latter half of it is very misleading.[a]

14th August

To return to the *Ursprung*. I do not mean to say that I have absolutely promised Aveling to let him have it, but I consider myself bound to him in case a translation is to come out in *London*. The final decision, then, would depend very much upon the nature of the publishing arrangements you can make in America. To a repetition of what Miss Foster has done with *Die Lage* I decidedly object.[b] When I see my way to an English edition, brought out by a firm known in the bourgeois trade, and not only of this book, but probably of a collection of various other writings, with the advantage of having the translation done here (which saves to me a deal of time) you will admit that I ought to look twice before sanctioning the bringing out, in America, of this little book alone and thereby spoiling the whole arrangement. And with the present anti-socialist scare in America, I doubt whether you will find regular publishers very willing to associate their names with socialist works.

A very good bit of work would be a series of pamphlets stating, in popular language, the contents of *Das Kapital*. The theory of surplus value No. 1; the history of the various forms of surplus value (cooperation, manufacture, modern industry) No. 2; accumulation and the history of primitive accumulation No. 3; the development of surplus value making in colonies (*last chapter*) No. 4—this would be especially instructive in America, as it would give the economical history of that country, from a land of independent peasants to a centre of modern industry, and might be completed by specially American facts.

In the meantime you may be sure that it will take some time yet

---

[a] G. Deville, *Le Capital de Karl Marx. Résumé...* - [b] See this volume, p. 415.

before the *mass* of the American working people will begin to *read* socialist literature. And for those that *do* read and will read, there is matter enough being provided, and least of all will *Der Ursprung* be missed by them. With the Anglo-Saxon mind, and especially with the eminently practical development it has taken in America, theory counts for nothing until imposed by dire necessity, and I count above all things upon the teaching our friends will receive by the consequences of their own blunders, to prepare them for theoretical schooling.

Yours very sincerely,

F. Engels

I shall be in this place until 27th inst. [599]; after that, in London.

First published, in the language of the original (English), in *Briefe und Auszüge aus Briefen von Joh. Phil. Becker, Jos. Dietzgen, Friedrich Engels, Karl Marx u. A. an F. A. Sorge und Andere*, Stuttgart, 1906

Reproduced from the original

272

ENGELS TO EDUARD BERNSTEIN [607]

IN ZURICH

Eastbourne, 14 August 1886
4 Cavendish Place

Dear Ede,

A fortnight ago I sent you a *Standard* containing a Bulgarian report on Russian intrigues in the Balkans which was very important. [a]

---

[a] 'Russia and Bulgaria', *The Standard*, No. 19359, 30 July 1886.

Meanwhile the situation has been getting more and more critical, for Alexander III is in need of a success after his many setbacks and, in view of the multifarious intrigues, it might well happen that matters get beyond the gentlemen's control and war breaks out. In this connection I wanted to pass on to you the story sent in by the *Daily News* correspondent in St Petersburg, which he insists is true despite all disclaimers, that between the 18th and the end of this month six Russian army corps, opposed by six ditto, will be engaged on manoeuvres in the neighbourhood of Vilna, i.e. close to the Prussian border; an assemblage, that is, of 12 army corps (the whole German army has only 18 of them) or, at a very modest estimate, 240,000 men. We may be sure that the vast sum of money involved isn't being chucked down the drain out of sheer bravado. Moreover Alexander III has forbidden *all* foreign officers to attend, even *Werder*, the Prussian. While these 240,000 men are concentrated on the border, Mr Giers will arrive in Germany to negotiate with Bismarck. It is a very bold stratagem, especially having regard to old William,[a] for he is being tackled precisely on this, his most sensitive flank. So things may go wrong and war break out. It may equally well be settled on the quiet, for we may be sure that Giers will not willingly be a party to such outrageous pranks. However I thought it as well to draw your attention to this curious business.

Tell Schlüter that I shall attend to his piece[557] as soon as I get back to London. I may possibly see old Harney before that, in which case I shall be able to glean a good deal of information that will be of interest to him.

Kindest regards. Back in London on the 28th of this month.[599]

Your

F. E.

First published, in Russian, in *Marx-Engels Archives*, Book I, Moscow, 1924

Printed according to the original

Published in English for the first time

---

[a] William I

273

ENGELS TO AUGUST BEBEL [608]

[IN PLAUEN NEAR DRESDEN]

Eastbourne, 18 August 1886
4 Cavendish Place

Dear Bebel,

It is a long time since I sent you word of myself, but on the one hand nothing in particular had happened that seemed to call for an exchange of opinions and, on the other, the ms. of the translation of *Capital* [a] was giving me such an immense amount of work that I had, quite literally and on principle, to let slide all correspondence that did not require immediate attention for about 10 weeks. Now that, too, has been dealt with, so that all that is pursuing me down to the seaside here are the very troublesome proofs and this means that I shall at last be able to make good my omissions, especially since various things have happened that are worth writing about.

First and foremost the Freiberg verdicts. [602] It would seem that your German, and notably Saxon, magistrate still deems himself insufficiently depraved. His case is like that of Eccarius in the days of the International, of whom Pfänder once said: 'You have absolutely no idea what Eccarius is like; he intends to become far worse than he already is.' And the Saxons are no exception. In Germany everything official is corrupt, but a petty state gives rise to a particular brand of corruption. For its semi or wholly hereditary official class is so small and at the same time so jealous of its caste privileges that its judiciary, police, administration and army, all brothers and relatives, come to one another's aid and play into one another's hands, and to such good purpose that the legal norms, indispensable in larger countries, are completely lost to view, and what is utterly impossible becomes possible. I myself have seen what can happen in this way, not only in Germany but also in Luxembourg and, quite recently, in Jersey, not to mention Switzerland in the bad old Bonapartist days. [b] And I am convinced that Bismarck could have achieved the same end in any

---

[a] the English translation of the first volume of *Capital* (see Note 56) - [b] The reference is to Engels' stay in Switzerland in 1849-50.

other petty German state as soon as the Court, the chief of the robber band, ceased to oppose him. In the largest of the petty states, in Prussia itself, this mutual aid society is formed by the military and official élite and is capable of any infamy in the real or purported interest of the caste.

Just now the ruling clique has more than enough to do. The death of old William [a] will usher in a period of uncertainty and indecision for them — hence, or so they believe, the need to consolidate their position as much as possible beforehand. Hence, too, the sudden furious hue and cry which is raised to an even higher pitch by their fury over the complete failure of all their previous machinations against us, and their hope of [provoking] minor disturbances which would make it possible to tighten up the law. [b] And that is why you people have got to spend nine months in jug.

I hope you will return from your travels this summer so fortified that those 9 months will not be deleterious to your health. This, your enforced retirement, will prove extremely deleterious to the party; true, the tractable members will at last be made to realise that mildness is no safeguard against imprisonment, yet they are unlikely to change their spots and their endeavour to pass themselves off as the genuine representatives of the party will be facilitated by everything that impedes the organisation, and hence the organised expression of opinion, of our masses. And once they know you're safely under lock and key, they'll really start to give themselves airs. Much will then depend on Liebknecht, but upon what will he depend? He will be coming over here in a fortnight's time and will pass on to me a vast amount of party gossip, or as much of it as he thinks fit. But of one thing you may be sure — my view of the German movement as a whole, of the tactics it should adopt, and of its individual members including Liebknecht himself, will remain what it has always been. Come to that, I am greatly looking forward to seeing him again, although I know from experience that reasoning with him is a complete waste of time — at most he may take some account of my opinion while in America, where Tussy Aveling will be able to give him an occasional nudge and so keep him on the straight and narrow. [600] As regards the fund-raising success of the tour, I have my doubts. Now that the American movement is acquiring reality, it is bound to become an ever less productive source of funds for Germany. This it could only

---

[a] William I - [b] See this volume, pp. 472-73.

be while still a completely academic proposition. But now that the Anglo-American workers have been roused from their lethargy, it is essential that in speeches and the press they be helped to take their first, still tentative steps, that a truly socialist nucleus be formed in their midst, and this costs money. Nevertheless, this time there may still be some pickings to be had.

The entry of the Americans into the movement and the revival of the French movement by the three labour deputies and by Decazeville [545] — these are the two events of world historic importance this year. In America there's all sorts of tomfoolery going on — here the anarchists, there the KNIGHTS OF LABOR [609] — but no matter; the thing has got going and will make rapid progress. There are still many disappointments in store — the wire-pullers of the old political parties are preparing covertly to take over the leadership of the budding workers' party — and colossal blunders will be made, but nevertheless, things will go faster there than anywhere else.

In France the 108,000 votes obtained by Roche [576] prove that the Radicals' spell [429] is broken and the Paris workers are beginning to disown them, and to do so on a massive scale. To consolidate this victory, this new-won position, our men have managed to transform the temporary organisation set up for Roche's election into a permanent one [610] and in this way have become the theoretical teachers of the working men who are turning away from the Radicals. Though they all describe themselves as socialists, these people are learning from bitter experience that the threadbare remnants they have inherited from Proudhon and Louis Blanc are mere bourgeois and pettybourgeois dross; hence they are proving quite accessible to Marx's theory. This is a consequence of the Radicals being *partially* at the helm; once wholly so, they will lose their entire working-class following and I maintain that the victory of Radicalism, i.e. of old, threadbare French socialism, in the *Chamber* will spell victory for Marxism, to begin with in the Paris *municipal council*. Oh, had Marx but lived to see his thesis vindicated in France and America,— his thesis that today's democratic republic is no more than the battleground upon which the decisive struggle between bourgeoisie and proletariat will be fought out!

For all that,[a] practically nothing is yet happening in this country.

---

[a] In the original 'trotz alledem und alledem'—a line from a poem by Ferdinand Freiligrath *Trotz alledem!*

Not even a socialist *sect*, as in Owen's day, can be said to exist. There are as many sects as there are heads. The SOCIAL DEMOCRATIC FEDERA- TION [300] does at least have a programme and a certain amount of dis- cipline, but no backing whatever from the masses. Its bosses are polit- ical adventurers of the most ambitious kind, and their paper, *Justice*, is one long lie about the historic power and importance of the FEDERA- TION. Even the worthy Ede occasionally forgets this and inoppor- tunely cites the paper, thus doing the *genuine* movement over here more harm than he can make good; from where he is it is difficult for him to assess the way in which *Justice* exploits this. The LEAGUE [346] is going through a crisis. Morris, a sentimental dreamer pure and simple, the personification of good will with so good an opinion of itself that it turns into ill will if ever there's a question of learning anything, has been taken in by the catchword 'Revolution' and fallen victim to the anarchists. Bax is very talented and no fool but, philosopher-fashion, has concocted his own brand of socialism which he regards as true Marxian theory and with which he does a great deal of harm. How- ever, in his case these are merely teething troubles and will soon dis- appear; only it's a pity the process should have to take place in pub- lic. Nor can Aveling learn very much, taken up as he is with working for his livelihood; he is the only one I see regularly. However, the publication of *Capital* in English [56] will clear the air enormously over here.

And with that I must close if I want to finish this letter. It is 6.45, tea is about to be served and the last post goes at 8. So take care of yourself and mind you don't pay my long silence back in kind. And above all, let me assure you that any gossip that might perhaps con- cern you yourself will make no impression on me whatever.

Your old friend
F. E.

I am sure to be here until the 28th of this month, [599] after which you had better write to London.

First published, in Russian, in *Marx- Engels Archives*, Vol. I (VI), Moscow, 1932

Printed according to the original

Published in English in full for the first time

274

ENGELS TO KARL KAUTSKY [611]

IN LONDON

Eastbourne, 20 August 1886
4 Cavendish Place

Dear Baron,

I return Dietz's letter herewith. [612] Provided you are given an assurance that Blos will not be allowed to put in anything whatever unless previously sanctioned by you, the mechanics could be left to him. If the worst came to the worst you might slip over to Stuttgart for a day or two and settle the matter. Anyhow that would be preferable to an attempt to spend 6 months there which would end in your being expelled after only 3 weeks, whereupon Mr Blos would have a completely free hand. But one thing you yourself should do is to exercise somewhat stricter censorship throughout that period, so that Blos should have no pretext for introducing anything slipshod.

It goes without saying that you may mention me in the prospectus as a contributor. Similarly, I will gladly let you have the introduction to the English translation of *The Condition of the Working-Class*[a] as soon as I myself have got it. It is not long. I am not at present in a position to promise you anything definite, particularly since the enterprising Schlüter wishes to republish *The Housing Question* which will require revision and an introduction[b]; also Borkheim's *Mordspatrioten*, for which I shall have to write a biographical note on Borkheim.[c] So you see, I need not bother about finding work; others do the bothering for me.

Your plan to settle into a house is a very sensible one, but in the long run you would find that the evening trains to Harrow leave too early and I would advise you to look round somewhere else. But it is more or less the same everywhere.

The sudden spate of prosecutions is clearly due to the impending demise of old William. [d] For the gang now in power it will usher in

---

[a] See present edition, Vol. 26, pp. 399-405. - [b] F. Engels, 'Preface to the Second Edition of *The Housing Question*'. - [c] F. Engels, 'Introduction to Sigismund Borkheim's Pamphlet *In Memory of the German Blood-and-Thunder Patriots. 1806-1807*'. - [d] William I

a period of uncertainty, and hence they are anxious in so far as possible to consolidate their position, partly by *faits accomplis* in domestic policy, partly, if they can, by provoking disturbances and thus yet greater alarm amongst the philistines.[a] What wouldn't the gang give for a bit of eel-snatching in Berlin, as in Amsterdam.[613] In addition there is the personal ire of Puttkamer who, like the true Prussian he is, regards every setback to one of his follies as an insult to his own august person.

On Tuesday,[b] Percy, Pumps and Lily went to pay a visit to the old Roshers at Walmer near Deal. They are supposed to return today, but I haven't heard anything. Yesterday was terribly close and humid, but marvellous weather today. Nim is well and sends her kindest regards, as I do mine. I trust your wife is well.

Your
F. E.

Thanks for Sonnenschein; the parcel had been addressed to Regent's Park Road by mistake; it contained something I needed and for which I had already dunned them.[614]

First published, in Russian, in *Marx-Engels Archives*, Vol. I (VI), Moscow, 1932

Printed according to the original

Published in English in full for the first time

275

ENGELS TO EDUARD BERNSTEIN

IN ZURICH

[Eastbourne,] 20 August 1886

Dear Ede,

I hope you have received a note from me via Mrs Schack.[c] The Russians have eaten humble pie but are quietly going on with their

---

[a] See this volume, p. 469. - [b] 17 August - [c] Gertrud Guillaume-Schack; see this volume, pp. 455, 466-67.

intrigues, mainly directed against Britain in Asia—Turkestan and China. That eliminates the risk of war this year. It is now improbable that the *Daily News* correspondent's 240,000 men will march[a]... This for your information. The aspect of things has changed so rapidly that people like us are mostly too late with our news. The poor Baron's[b] in despair at not having heard from you.

Your
F. E.

First published, in Russian, in *Marx-Engels Archives*, Book I, Moscow, 1924

Printed according to the original

Published in English for the first time

276

ENGELS TO HERMANN SCHLÜTER

IN HOTTINGEN-ZURICH

Eastbourne, 20 August 1886
4 Cavendish Place

Dear Mr Schlüter,

Now it's your turn at last. I had to give up writing letters until the English ms.[c] had been finished.

Firstly, therefore, your letter of 10 March.

1) Funds received at last. Receipt made out in duplicate.[d]

2) Have read Lexis.[e] The man is far from stupid, but he's an out-and-out rascal and knows it.

3) *The Origin*[f]—Dietz's way of going about things gave me fresh proof of how arbitrarily he behaves in business matters and I shall be guided by this in future dealings with him. Apart from that, the out-

---

[a] See this volume, p. 467.- [b] Karl Kautsky- [c] of the first volume of *Capital* (see Note 56) - [d] See this volume, pp. 418-19. - [e] W. Lexis, 'Die Marx'sche Kapitaltheorie', *Jahrbücher für Nationalökonomie und Statistik*, Vol. 11, Jena, 1885. - [f] F. Engels, *The Origin of the Family, Private Property and the State*.

come has been satisfactory and has enabled the thing to reappear in the bookshops.[555]

4) General Council's Addresses. Whether I have them all I shall only know when my friends give me sufficient time to put Marx's letters, etc., in order. So until then I shan't be able to help you.[615]

5) Chartist ms.[557] will be finished as soon as I get back to London *after the 28th*.[599] I shall probably have a chance to consult our old friend Harney about doubtful points; he is sure to be in London now. The article in the *Rheinische Jahrbücher* is by Weerth and you may name him.[a]

Postcard of 8/6.—You might send me the letters from the late Heß' papers when convenient, though they're unlikely to amount to more than tittle-tattle. After 1848 the good Moses ceased to be connected with any real movement and merely did a bit of Lassalling for a time under Schweitzer.

Letter 16/8.—I shall be glad to look over *The Housing Question*; the thing can be reprinted pretty well as it stands (so far as I am able to judge from memory). A word or two will be necessary by way of introduction.[b]

A re-issue of the *Mordspatrioten* would certainly be a very good idea. The thing is by Borkheim and I would write a short biographical note[c] to go with it. But as I have only one copy, likewise of *The Housing Question*, and as both of them will probably call for notes, I should be grateful if you would send me one copy of each (to London).

Would you kindly give the enclosed line to Ede.

Yours,

F. Engels

First published in: Marx and Engels, *Works*, First Russian Edition, Vol. XXVII, Moscow, 1935

Printed according to the original

Published in English for the first time

---

[a] G. W[eerth], 'Joseph Rayner Stephens...', *Rheinische Jahrbücher zur gesellschaftlichen Reform*, Vol. II, 1846. - [b] F. Engels, 'Preface to the Second Edition of *The Housing Question*'. - [c] F. Engels, 'Introduction to Sigismund Borkheim's Pamphlet *In Memory of the German Blood-and-Thunder Patriots. 1806-1807*'.

277

ENGELS TO KARL KAUTSKY [616]

IN LONDON

[Eastbourne,] 23 August 1886

As you wrote to tell me you would be forwarding my letters, etc., on Saturday, I simply wanted to inform you that I got nothing either on Saturday or yesterday, nor had anything arrived by 7 p. m. today (Monday); I had at least counted on getting the *Sozialdemokrat*.

Liebknecht has written to say he will probably be here this week. I shall come up for the day to collect him and shall write beforehand. Regards to your wife from Nim and

Your
F. E.

First published, in Russian, in *Marx-Engels Archives*, Vol. I (VI), Moscow, 1932

Printed according to the original

Published in English for the first time

278

ENGELS TO KARL KAUTSKY

IN LONDON

Eastbourne, 24 August 1886
4 Cavendish Place

Dear Kautsky,

I have been completely crushed, smothered, squashed and stultified by your avalanche of letters this morning. I shall have to see how I can manage to answer them. Very many thanks.

Liebknecht has written to say he may set off for London as early as tomorrow, taking the direct route via Flushing—I am expecting more definite word any day; as soon as I know the day he's arriving,

I shall come up for the day and bring him back here. I shouldn't buy him an *Esel*[617] if I were you, he can write perfectly well on board ship without an *Esel*. Or is he expecting to be seasick all the time? But so far no *Esel* has been able to cope with seasickness.

Old Becker[a] will be arriving from Geneva on the 12th-13th to stay with me in London.

Mother Schack has announced her intention of coming to London in the middle of September along with the Wischnewetzkys.[618]

If Schorlemmer and the Lafargues turn up as well — postcard arrived 16th August from Schorlemmer in Bellaggio, Lake of Como — it will be pretty hectic.

We shall be staying here until 4 September[599] — a week on Saturday.

Nim and the Pumpses send their best wishes to your wife and yourself, as does

Your
F. E.

First published, in Russian, in *Marx-Engels Archives*, Vol. I (VI), Moscow, 1932

Printed according to the original

Published in English for the first time

279

ENGELS TO LAURA LAFARGUE

IN PARIS

Eastbourne, 24 August 1886
4 Cavendish Place

My dear Laura,

This morning I receive your letter of the 20th from London with a perfect avalanche of other letters and papers — I cannot therefore do to-day more than send you the cheque £15. -

Old Becker[a] writes that he will be here (in London) with the van Kols' by 12th September.

---

[a] Johann Philipp Becker

Countess Guillaume-Schack who was here only a month ago writes she will be here about 15 September with the Wischnewetzkys [618] (male Russian, female Yankee).

Liebknecht writes he may leave for London to-morrow. As soon as he lets me know date of arrival, I shall go to London to see Edward and Tussy before their departure [601] and bring Liebknecht over here for a few days — we return to London 4 September. [599]

Glad to see that Vierzon [619] is exploited again like Decazeville. [a] [545]

The other day a postcard came from Schorlemmer from Bellaggio, Lake of Como.

Love from Nim, the Pumpses and yours affectionately,

F. Engels

First published, in the language of the original (English), in: F. Engels, P. et L. Lafargue, *Correspondance*, t. I, Paris, 1956

Reproduced from the original

280

ENGELS TO KARL KAUTSKY

IN LONDON

Eastbourne, 25 August 1886
4 Cavendish Place

Dear Baron,

Your letter sent to Offenbach will arrive in plenty of time, as Lieb-knecht doesn't leave Borsdorf until the evening of the 26th, i. e. will be in Offenbach on the 27th and won't leave Cologne until 1.40 p. m. on the 29th, assuming he is travelling via Flushing as he previously said he would. [600]

So I shall be arriving in London on Sunday evening [b] between 9 and 10 [599] and hope to see you both that same night. I have asked

---

[a] See also this volume, p. 489. - [b] 29 August

Liebknecht to take a CAB straight to my house, so what more could he want? You would greatly oblige me if you would call round on Friday evening to see whether any letters have arrived for me, in particular one from the *UNION BANK OF London*, and if so send them on, as I want to attend to one or two business matters on Saturday if possible.

Kindest regards.

Your

F. E.

First published, in Russian, in *Marx-Engels Archives*, Vol. I (VI), Moscow, 1932

Printed according to the original

Published in English for the first time

281

ENGELS TO KARL KAUTSKY

IN LONDON

Eastbourne, 26 August 1886

Dear Kautsky,

Liebknecht is arriving on Monday[a] at a station to be specified by you — via Flushing; if he hasn't got your letter, then at *Holborn*. So he has no need of advice. If he finds no one at the station, he will take a CAB to my house.

I shall be arriving in London on Saturday afternoon or, at the latest, evening[599] — I hope if possible to get to Regent's Park Road by 4 or 5. Harney will probably visit me on Sunday.[620] More when we meet. Should there be a letter for me from the UNION BANK on Friday and you could send it on *before* 5.30, I should be most grateful; other-

---

[a] 30 August

wise it can wait until I arrive, just as all the rest can wait; there is time enough.

Kindest regards to your wife.

Your
F. E.

First published, in Russian, in *Marx-Engels Archives*, Vol. I (VI), Moscow, 1932

Printed according to the original

Published in English for the first time

282

ENGELS TO FRIEDRICH ADOLPH SORGE [621]

IN HOBOKEN

[London,] 6 September 1886

The translation of *Capital*[a] is being published by W. Swan Sonnenschein, Lowrey & Co., Paternoster Square, London; 23 sheets have already been printed and the whole ms. is in the hands of the printers. Unfortunately I can't find the relevant article anywhere, otherwise I could doubtless have given you further information.[622] No doubt you will already have seen Liebknecht before receiving this; he sailed day before yesterday on the *Servia*.[600] As soon as I have disposed of the more urgent tasks — that is to say by the end of this week — I shall write you a longer letter.

Your
F. E.

First published in *Briefe und Auszüge aus Briefen von Joh. Phil. Becker, Jos. Dietzgen, Friedrich Engels, Karl Marx u. A. an F. A. Sorge und Andere*, Stuttgart, 1906

Printed according to the original

Published in English for the first time

---

[a] the English translation of the first volume of *Capital* (see Note 56)

283

ENGELS TO F. H. NESTLER & MELLE'S VERLAG

IN HAMBURG

[Draft]

[London, about 11 September 1886]

Dear Sirs,

I must categorically reject the insinuation in your favour of the 9th inst.[623]

Even had it occurred to Kautsky and, via him, to Dietz, to bring out a similar collection of excerpts simply as a result of the proposal you made me, you could have no cause for complaint, since in your postcard of 15 May you told me:

'We must frankly admit that w i t h o u t you we shall n o t be able to bring our idea to fruition.'

When you withdrew, they were fully entitled to step in. And why I should be considered in any way blameworthy in this matter is utterly incomprehensible to me.

However the above assumption is not even correct. The need for such a collection has long been discussed in socialist circles and preparations to bring one into being have often been all but completed. I know that Dietz, in particular, has had this in mind ever since he started his firm. When I spoke to Kautsky about your proposal, one of the reasons he gave for his refusing was that he was already corresponding with Dietz about a very similar offer and had *committed himself to Dietz to the extent* of being unable to entertain any proposition of a similar nature from elsewhere. I intimated as much when replying to you,[a] *in so far as it was permissible for me to do so*; I was not entitled to say more. In fact the matter had by then progressed so far that, at the time you wrote to me, Kautsky had already been engaged for several weeks in finishing off the first instalments (on Marx)[137] and hence needed no prompting from you.

Moreover, the appearance of Dietz's advertisement at this precise moment is in no way the result of your letter to me, of which Dietz, so

---

[a] See this volume, pp. 447-48.

far as I know, is not even aware. It is solely the result of the fact that Dietz, following his conviction in Freiberg,[602] feels impelled to get various schemes of his to a stage at which they can go ahead without his supervision during his six months' detention.

When I was in business I grew accustomed to hearing overhasty criticisms based on insufficient information. It is one of those philistine German customs which make it virtually impossible for Germans to play a really prominent role in the world of business. But I must confess I am somewhat surprised that a firm of your repute could be capable of this sort of thing.

Yours faithfully

First published in: Marx and Engels, *Works*, First Russian Edition, Vol. XXVII, Moscow, 1935

Printed according to the original

Published in English for the first time

284

ENGELS TO LAURA LAFARGUE

IN PARIS

London, 13 September 1886

My dear Laura,

Here we are again in London [599] — it's the same thing over and over again, jobs of all sorts. The last week I had to revise a German extract of the *Kapital* by Kautsky,[137] and it wanted revising very much. Two other mss. are in my desk and have been there for more than six months. Hope to clear them off this week. Fortunately for *me*, proof-sheets [a] have been few and far between, else it would have been but a poor holiday for me. Anyhow I shall now cut this sort of work completely, else I should never get to my chief work.

Tussy and Edward's ship the *City of Chicago* arrived in New York on the 10th, and Liebknecht's, the *Servia*, must be there by this time too, as she sailed 4th September. They will have a severe job to go

---

[a] of the English translation of the first volume of *Capital* (see Note 56)

through with travelling and speechifying.[600] Liebknecht was four days with us at Eastbourne, he is quite fat and carries a deal of weight in front of himself, no doubt the Yankees will take some of that out of him. Otherwise he was very jolly and confident as usual: '*alles geht famos*'.[a]

I wrote to you that I had a postcard from Schorlemmer about 18th August from the Lake of Como,[b] since then I have not heard from him. Anyhow he is now soon due in Paris whence he has sworn to bring you, and if possible Paul too, over to London. I sincerely trust that he will succeed, Nim is already busying her mind with the few necessary arrangements which indeed will not require great exertions. Paul's trial will not I hope prevent him from coming over,[624] the old shop where he likes to buy drawers at 1/6d. a pair is still there if that is an inducement. And if he cannot get off, surely you are bound to take a holiday too and see your old friends in London once more. You know what Meyer said: '*wenn sie im Zimmer kommt, ist es als wenn die Sonne aufginge*'[c] — so do let the sun rise once more over London!

Nim has had her photograph taken in Eastbourne, it was very good and is paid for, this is perhaps the reason why the copies are not yet sent.

Please thank Paul for his letter on the wine manufacture — it not only confirmed, but also *completed* what I had heard from other sources. It is very satisfactory to know that in these latter days of capitalist production the phylloxera has smashed up the Château Laffite, Lagrange and other *grands crus*,[d] as we that know how to appreciate them, do not get them, and the Jews and parvenus that get them, do not know [how] to appreciate them. Having thus no longer a mission to fulfil, they may as well go to smash, our successors will soon restore them when they are wanted for grand popular holidays.

What Mohr said in the Circular to the International in 1870,[e] that the annexation of Alsace, etc., had made Russia *l'arbitre de l'Europe*, is now at last becoming evident. Bismarck has had to cave in completely, and the will of Russia has to be done.[625] The dream of the Ger-

---

[a] 'everything is going swimmingly' - [b] See this volume, p. 478. - [c] 'when she comes into the room, it is as if the sun rises' - [d] famous vineyards - [e] K. Marx, 'Second Address of the General Council of the International Working Men's Association on the Franco-Prussian War'.

man Empire, the guardian of European peace, without whose leave not a cannon-shot can be fired, is dispelled, and the German philistine finds he is as much the slave of the Czar[a] as when Prussia was 'der fünfte Rad am europäischen Wagen'.[b] And now he falls foul of Bismarck who after all does only what he is compelled to do. The rage is great in Germany, not only among the philistines, but also in the army. Liebknecht says since 1866 there has not been such an outcry against an act of the government. But there it will not stop. If the Balkan drama enters its second act, a war between Russia and Austria will break out and then *vogue la galère*[c] — all Europe may burst out in flames. I should be rather sorry — no doubt it would be the *last* war, and no doubt this as anything else must turn out ultimately to our advantage. But it may after all delay our victory and the other road is safer. For that however there is scarcely another road than a revolution in Russia, and as long as Alexander[a] follows the lead of the Pan-Slavists, that is a very unlikely event. In fact, the decisive argument of Giers with Bismarck was this: we are between Pan-slavists and Nihilists,[356] if we keep the peace they will unite and the palace revolution will be a *fait accompli* — so we must go on towards Constantinople, and this will be less harmful to you, Bismarck and William,[d] than a Russian revolution. This winter will decide matters, so I am bound to get the 3rd volume[e] ready by next spring.

Had several visits from Bax and one from Morris lately — Bax sees the impasse he has got himself into, and would get out if he could do so without a direct recantation, and no doubt will find some way or other. Morris is a settled sentimental socialist, he would be easily managed if one saw him regularly a couple of times a week, but who has the time to do it, and if you drop him for a month, he is sure to lose himself again. And is he worth all that trouble even if one had the time? In the meantime Hyndman fortifies his position more and more, because he has a definite programme and a definite line of political action, to both of which Morris seems to object, his ideal is a debating club uniting all shades. In all this confusion I expect the principal help from the English *Kapital*.[f] 23 sheets are printed and revised, but there is something wrong with the printer, I do not receive any fresh proofs and cannot get any information as Sonnenschein is away for his holiday and nobody can or will tell where the hitch lies.

---

[a] Alexander III - [b] 'the fifth wheel in the European waggon' - [c] come what may -
[d] William I - [e] of *Capital* - [f] the first volume

Splendid weather to-day—hope it will last while you come.

Yours affectionately,

F. Engels

First published, in the language of the original (English), in: F. Engels, P. et L. Lafargue, *Correspondance*, t. I, Paris, 1956

Reproduced from the original

285

ENGELS TO AUGUST BEBEL

[IN PLAUEN NEAR DRESDEN]

London, 13-14 September 1886

Dear Bebel,

What I find odd about this whole Bulgarian and oriental business [445] is the Russians having only just realised that, as a result of the annexation of Alsace, etc., they have become the arbiters of Europe, as indeed was pointed out to the members of the International by Marx as long ago as 1870.[a] The only possible explanation for this is the universal adoption since the war (in Russia in 1874) of the Prussian *Landwehr* system which takes between 10 and 12 years to produce a commensurately powerful army.[474] Russia and France now also possess such an army, hence the fun can now begin. And that is precisely why the Russian army, which supplies the hard core of Pan-Slavism, is now exerting such tremendous pressure on the government that the Tsar[b] is faced with only two possibilities—he must either overcome his old animosity to the French Republic and enter into alliance with it, or he must persuade Bismarck to endorse Russia's oriental policy. For Bismarck and William,[c] the alternatives were, either resistance to Russia and the prospect of a Franco-Russian alliance and world war, or the certainty of a Russian revolution as a result of an alliance between the Pan-Slavs and the Nihi-

---

[a] K. Marx, 'Second Address of the General Council of the International Working Men's Association on the Franco-Prussian War'. - [b] Alexander III - [c] William I

lists,[356] or again submission to Russia, i. e. betrayal of Austria. That from their *own* standpoint Bismarck and William could not have acted otherwise, seems obvious to me, and this represents a great leap forward, in that the incompatibility of the Hohenzollerns' interests and those of Germany has now been made plainly and overwhelmingly manifest. The very existence of the German Empire is being imperilled by its Prussian foundations.

Temporarily — until after the winter, that is, — the affair will probably be glossed over, but the Pan-Slavs' appetite grows with eating, and they will never have such a favourable opportunity again. If the Russians succeed in occupying Bulgaria, they will also go on to attack Constantinople, unless insuperable obstacles — say an Austro-German-British alliance — intervene. Hence Bismarck's desperate plea for an actively anti-Russian policy on Britain's part, a plea he now gets *The Standard* to re-echo almost daily in the hope that *Britain* will avert a world war.

At all events, Austrian and Russian rivalry in the Balkan Peninsula is becoming so acute that war is more likely than the preservation of peace. And that will be the end of localised warfare. But what the outcome will be — who will win — we cannot say. The German army is certainly the best and the best-led, but is only one amongst many. The Austrians are an unknown quantity, both numerically and militarily, especially as regards leadership, and have always been dab-hands at getting their best troops beaten. The Russians, as always, are deluding themselves as to their strength which, on paper, is enormous; though exceedingly weak in attack, they are strong in the defence of their own country. Their weakest point, aside from the high command, is a lack of suitable material to officer the vast masses; the country does not produce the required number of educated people. The Turks are the best soldiers, but the high command is invariably execrable, if not suborned. Finally, the French are also short of officers, because too politically advanced to tolerate an institution such as that of one-year volunteers; also because the French bourgeois is (personally) utterly unwarlike. Lastly, the new organisation has never been put to the test anywhere save in Germany. Hence these quantities are very difficult to estimate, either numerically or qualitatively. Of the Italians, it may be said with certainty that, given equal numbers, they would be beaten by any other army. But how these various quantities will group themselves, either with or against each other, in a world war is equally incalculable. Britain's importance —

that of her Navy and that of her vast resources — will grow as the war goes on and, if she withholds her troops at the start, it may, in the end, be a British corps of 60,000 men which finally turns the scales.

All this presupposes that nothing happens inside the countries concerned. But in France a war might well bring revolutionary elements to the helm, while in Germany a defeat or the death of the Old Man [a] might result in a violent change of régime, which in turn might lead to a regrouping of the belligerents. In short, there will be chaos of which the *only* certain outcome will be wholesale slaughter on a hitherto unprecedented scale, the exhaustion of the whole of Europe to a hitherto unprecedented degree and, finally, the complete collapse of the old system.

Immediate victory for ourselves could only be produced by a revolution in France, which would confer on the French the role of liberators of the European proletariat. I do not know whether this would be the best thing for the latter; however it would raise *ideal* French chauvinism to the nth degree. A revolution in Germany following a defeat would be of use only if it led to peace with France. Best of all would be a Russian revolution which, however, can only be expected after severe defeats have been inflicted on the Russian army.

This much is certain: A war would above all retard our movement all over Europe, completely disrupt it in many countries, stir up chauvinism and xenophobia and leave us with the *certain* prospect, amongst many other uncertain ones, of having to begin all over again after the war, albeit on a basis far more favourable even than today.

Whether or not there is war, this much has been gained. Your German philistine has been shocked out of his lethargy and at last finds himself compelled to intervene actively in politics. Since numerous intermediary stages will have to be gone through between today's Prussian Bonapartism with its semi-feudal foundations and the socialist republic which will be our first stage, it can only be to our advantage that your German citizen should at last be forced to resume his political responsibilities and oppose the present régime, if only to

---

[a] William I

make it get some sort of move-on. And so I look forward keenly to seeing what happens during the coming session of the Reichstag. Since I do not get any German papers at the moment, I should be greatly obliged if you would send me some from time to time, when they carry reports of important sittings, particularly those concerned with foreign policy.

Liebknecht, too, had a great deal to say about the indignation provoked in Germany by Bismarck's kow-towing to the Russians.[625] He spent several days with me at the seaside in Eastbourne,[599] was in very good spirits and, as always, 'everything was going swimmingly'. Since the gentlemen of the right wing are no longer stirring up any trouble to speak of and have had to knuckle under, Liebknecht could again give vent to quite revolutionary utterances and do his best to pass himself off as the most resolute of men. I intimated pretty plainly that I knew more about these goings-on than he might, perhaps, care for but, since he was completely on the right track, there was absolutely no reason why our intercourse should be other than exceedingly cordial. I am unaware of, and hence not responsible for, anything he may have told you in his letters about the matters he and I discussed.

14 September

Having again been interrupted, I must make sure that I finish this in time for the evening post so that you get this letter by Thursday[a] morning at the latest. The Hungarian parliament will also be convening in the near future when the Bulgarian affair[445] is sure to be brought up. The best thing for us would be for Russia to be peacefully or forcibly repulsed, in which case the stage would be set for revolution there. The Pan-Slavs would join in, only to find next morning that they had been duped. This was a point upon which Marx always expressed himself with the greatest conviction — and I know of no one who understood Russia, both as regards internal and external matters, as well as he. He maintained that, as soon as the old régime had been destroyed in Russia, no matter by whom, and a representative assembly had convened, no matter of what kind, Russia's policy of aggression would cease and domestic questions take precedence over everything else.[b] And the repercussions on Europe, once this last

---

[a] 16 September - [b] See K. Marx, 'The Question of the Abolition of Serfdom in Russia', present edition, Vol. 16, pp. 51-53.

stronghold of reaction had been destroyed, would, he said, be tremendous; we in Germany would be the first to feel them.

Liebknecht's ship arrived in New York yesterday morning at 3 o'clock, that of the Avelings several days earlier.[600] If it's as hot there as it is here—now, at 4 in the afternoon it's 25 degrees Centigrade[a] here in my room—their tub-thumping is going to make them sweat a bit.

In France the good work still goes on. The method of agitation that was tried out at Decazeville[545] is now being repeated at Vierzon where there is a strike on.[619] Vaillant, whose home it is, is taking a leading part there. In Paris, the Radicals[429] are working for us, as is Bismarck in Germany. They have got themselves into a frightful mess over the bucket-shops, and Clemenceau, though he had no need to do so, has nevertheless become too deeply involved with that crew to be able to keep out of it altogether. Thus the rift between him and the erstwhile radical working men yawns ever wider, and his loss is our gain. Our people are behaving with great address and I am surprised at the amount of discipline shown by the French. It was just what they lacked, and now they are acquiring it, but against a background of a wholly revolutionary tradition which, in France, is taken for granted and is innocent of all those philistine misgivings which are the bane of our Geisers and Vierecks. Next time, even with the *scrutin de liste*,[375] we shall score considerable successes in France. And it is precisely because everything's going so marvellously, both there and in Germany, and because a couple of years of uninterrupted *internal* development, helped along by the events inevitable in the circumstances, would contribute so enormously to our progress—it is precisely because of all this that I wouldn't exactly wish for a world war— but history recks little of that! It pursues its course and we have to take it as it comes.

There's one thing you people should learn from the French. For 50 years all revolutionaries there have subscribed to the rule that the accused should *refuse* to give the examining magistrate *any information whatsoever*. The latter has the right to ask, the accused has the right not to answer, not to incriminate himself and his comrades. This— once it has been generally accepted to the extent that any deviation from it ranks as quasi betrayal—is of enormous advantage in all trials. One is still free to say what one likes at the public proceedings.

---

[a] 77 degrees Fahrenheit

But at the preliminary investigation all records are so worded as to falsify the statements made by the accused who is browbeaten into signing by all manner of subterfuges. You should see for yourselves sometime.

Your
F. E.

First published, in Russian, in *Marx-Engels Archives*, Vol. I (VI), Moscow, 1932

Printed according to the original

Published in English for the first time

286

ENGELS TO FRIEDRICH ADOLPH SORGE [608]

IN HOBOKEN

London, 16-17 September 1886

Dear Sorge,

I am forcing myself to take an hour off in order to write to you. For weeks I have been kept so busy with the proofs (in triplicate) of the translation of *Capital*, [a] that I have been unable to do anything else, and now they are coming thick and fast. Allegedly I am to get 6 sheets a week (i. e. 18 sheets a week to be corrected), and the whole thing is supposed to be finished in 4 weeks' time. We shall see. But I'm going to have a lively time of it since, apart from anything else, old Becker [b] is arriving tomorrow from Geneva to stay with me, the following week I shall have Schorlemmer and probably the Lafargues, not to mention other people from Switzerland who are proposing to come over here. So I know that, if I don't get a letter written today, there'll be no chance of doing so later on.

Many thanks for the trouble you have gone to over the interviewer. [c] He shall be the last. Now the chap has broken his word and I shall be justified in sending them packing, unless it's to our advan-

---

[a] the English translation of the first volume; see also this volume, pp. 462, 506.-
[b] Johann Philipp Becker - [c] John T. McEnnis

tage to impose upon some liar of this ilk. You are right in saying that I haven't, on the whole, any cause for complaint; the man does at least try to be decent from the personal point of view, and not he, but the American bourgeoisie, is to blame for his stupidity. [598]

A fine crew they'd seem to be at the head of the party in New York [549] and as for the *Sozialist*, it's a model of what a paper ought *not* to be. But nor can I congratulate Dietzgen on his article re anarchists [626]; it's an odd way he has of going about things. If, for instance, a person takes a somewhat narrow-minded view of a particular point, Dietzgen is at pains — often undue pains — to stress that there are two sides to every question. But now, because of the New Yorkers' abject behaviour, he suddenly takes the other side and tries to make us all out to be anarchists. This may be excusable as things are now, but even at a crucial juncture he should not, after all, entirely forget his dialectics. However, he has probably long since worked all this out of his system and is certainly back on the right track again, so there's no cause for alarm.

In a country as unsophisticated as America which, though wholly without a feudal past, has evolved along purely bourgeois lines yet has uncritically taken over from England a mass of ideology deriving from feudal times, such as English common law, religion, sectarianism, and where the exigencies of practical work and of the concentration of capital have engendered a general contempt, only now diminishing amongst the most highly educated and learned circles, for all theory — in such a country, the people will have to find out what their own *social* interests are by making one blunder after another. Nor will the workers be spared this experience; the confusion of the TRADES UNIONS, the socialists, the KNIGHTS OF LABOR, [609] etc., will persist for some time yet, until wisdom is born of their own misfortunes. But the main thing is that they are now in motion, that they are actually progressing, and that the spell has been broken; things will move fast, faster than anywhere else, even though the course they take may seem erratic and, from the theoretical standpoint, almost demented.

Your letter arrived too late for me to speak to Aveling about Brooks [627] — I only saw him, Aveling, for a couple of hours on 30 August, and I had left your letter behind in Eastbourne. [599] Anyhow, you will have seen him meanwhile in New York, also Liebknecht.

It would seem that your Adolf[a] has already dissolved his PARTNER-

---

[a] Adolf Sorge jun.

SHIP with the agent in Rochester; I trust he has not burnt his fingers in the process, as may happen even to the best of men on such occasions. I shall shortly be sending you the missing numbers of *To-Day*, in so far as I myself receive them, also *Commonweals*. It's not possible to subscribe to them direct. I shall send you some French papers when I myself get any from Paris. A few went off from Eastbourne. You should be able to obtain the *Socialiste* over there; the editorial and administrative offices are at 17 rue du Croissant, Paris, and the paper comes out weekly. *Abonnement étranger*[a] 4 frs a half year, incl. postage. I myself get it very irregularly and often have to write, but I have to keep it for REFERENCE.

I am also sending you some surplus proof-sheets of the *Capital* translation so that you can see how the thing's progressing and what it looks like.

I hope your health is improving; I *seem* robust enough, but for 3 years now my mobility has been restricted, sometimes very considerably and always to a *certain extent* by an internal ailment, so that I am, alas, no longer fit for active service.

The first thing I shall have to do, as soon as the translation is finished, is rid myself of the minor jobs that have been foisted on me — revising other people's work, notably translations — and avoid getting myself saddled *with any more*, so that I can return to the 3rd volume.[b] The whole thing's there, ready dictated, but there's still a good 6 months' hard slogging to be done. This confounded English translation has taken up the better part of a year. But it was absolutely essential and I don't regret it.

17 September

The proof-sheets went off yesterday and the *Commonweals* up to 18 September will follow today. I have got to look out the copies of *To-Day*.

The movement over here is still in the hands, on the one side of adventurers (DEMOCRATIC FEDERATION [300]) and, on the other, of hobby-horse riders and sentimental socialists (SOCIALIST LEAGUE [346]); the masses are still holding aloof, although here too *beginnings* of a movement are perceptible. But it will be some time before the masses are in full spate, which is a good thing because it means that there will be time for proper leaders to emerge.

---

[a] Overseas subscription - [b] of *Capital*

In Germany, some kind of movement will, presumably, at last come into being again among the *bourgeoisie*, whose cowardly inertia is becoming harmful to us; on the one hand the now imminent change of monarch [a] will induce a general state of instability, on the other Bismarck's kow-towing to the Tsar [b] is arousing even the most lethargic from their slumbers. [625] In France things are going famously. Our people are learning discipline, in the provinces from the STRIKES, in Paris from their opposition to the Radicals. [429]

Kindest regards,

Your
F. E.

First published abridged in *Briefe und Auszüge aus Briefen von Joh. Phil. Becker, Jos. Dietzgen, Friedrich Engels, Karl Marx u. A. an F.A. Sorge und Andere*, Stuttgart, 1906 and in full in: Marx and Engels, *Works*, First Russian Edition, Vol. XXVII, Moscow, 1935

Printed according to the original

Published in English in full for the first time

287

ENGELS TO PASQUALE MARTIGNETTI

IN BENEVENTO

[Excerpt]

[London,] 17 September 1886

...May [I th]ank [c] you for being so patient with [me] in the matter of your manuscript. [d] As soon as the English translation of *Capital* [56] has been done — in October, I hope — your ms. will be the first thing

---

[a] William I - [b] Alexander III - [c] The beginning of the letter is missing, and the manuscript is damaged. - [d] the Italian translation of Marx's *Wage Labour and Capital*

to which I shall turn my attention. I have found the *Kalender* and shall fill in the missing passage. [554]

Yours very sincerely,

F. E.

First published, in the language of the original (German), in *La corrispondenza di Marx e Engels con italiani. 1848-1895*, Milano, 1964

Printed according to the original

Published in English for the first time

288

ENGELS TO LAURA LAFARGUE

IN PARIS

London, 24 September 1886

My dear Laura,

I suppose you are at this moment at the Assize Court watching Paul's trial, [624] I hope it will end in an acquittal. In the meantime I have a bit of agreeable news for you. Meissner sends this morning account for last seasons sales, and the result is a profit of 2,600 marks or about £130 for us, after deducting all expenses of the second volume [a]; so your share will be above £40-. I have told him to remit the money, and as soon as received I shall send you a cheque for your share. There were sold 320 copies of Volume I and 1,260 of Volume II.

The English edition [b] will hardly be out before the New Year. [56] It looks as if Sonnenschein had more pressing things on hand, and in the hands of the same printer, by which our book was pushed back. The thing is proceeding, but rather slowly.

I had a letter from Tussy on her arrival in New York, [601] she had a very pleasant voyage, but was rather disappointed at the live American bourgeois she met on board, it rather dampened her enthusiasm for America, but prepared her for the realities of American

---

[a] of *Capital* - [b] of the first volume of *Capital*

life.

Old Becker[a] has been with me this last week, he is very jolly but getting rather rickety in body. He will leave for Paris next Tuesday[b] and hopes to see you there. [628] He is a splendid old chap, seventy-eight and still quite abreast of the movement.

No news from Schorlemmer here. How about your journey to London? You will be able to come to a resolution, if that be still necessary, after to-day's verdict. But even if Paul should be sent to Pélagie again, [402] that is not so pressing, surely they will give him a few weeks leave and so you and he might still come over for a bit.

Ever yours affectionately,

F. Engels

First published, in the language of the original (English), in: F. Engels, P. et L. Lafargue, *Correspondance*, t. I, Paris, 1956

Reproduced from the original

289

ENGELS TO NATALIE LIEBKNECHT

IN BORSDORF NEAR LEIPZIG [34]

London, 25 September 1886
122 Regent's Park Road

Dear Mrs Liebknecht,

At Liebknecht's behest, I am sending you herewith an Imperial bank-note for 100 marks, No. 1236179[d], Berlin, 3 September 1883, which he left with me on his departure. He also gave me reason to hope that you might come over in December, to welcome him here at my house. We should all be delighted if this were to happen, in which case I trust you will share our humble board and look upon my house as your own.

---

[a] Johann Philipp Becker - [b] 28 September

From what we have heard so far, out friends' tour has been most successful. [600]

With sincere regards to you and the children,

Yours truly,

F. Engels

First published, in Russian, in *Marx-Engels Archives*, Vol. I (VI), Moscow, 1932

Printed according to the original

Published in English for the first time

290

ENGELS TO LAURA LAFARGUE

IN PARIS

London, 2 October 1886

My dear Laura,

To begin with the beginning, I enclose cheque for £42,13.4, being one-third part of Meissner's remittance of £128.- [a] which I hope you will receive and get cashed all right.

I am sorry you cannot come just now while the weather is fine, but if you feel such a decided home-sickness after London fogs and our beautiful winter, you can be suited too. Nim undertakes to accommodate you at any time, Christmas or otherwise, and if we have other visitors at the same time, she undertakes to accommodate them too. So that is settled, and we shall this time not be disappointed.

I also forward 2 *Volkszeitungen which please return, as they belong to Edward* and he will expect to find them here on his return (his papers, etc., are forwarded to me in his absence). [601] From these you see that *la république cosaque*— Mohr's solution of Napoléon's [b] alternative: *ou république ou cosaque* [629] — flourishes in New York as luxuriantly as

---

in Paris. It is lucky for them that the first attempt at intimidation came so soon and was so clumsily executed.

I am afraid Paul exaggerates the significance of the Paris verdict in so far as it is a symptom of the accessibility of the industrial bourgeoisie for socialist ideas. [630] The struggle between usurer and industrial capitalist is one within the bourgeoisie itself, and though no doubt a certain number of petty bourgeois will be driven over to us by the certainty of their impending expropriation *de la part des boursiers*, [a] yet we can never hope to get the mass of them over to our side. Moreover this is not desirable, as they bring their narrow class prejudices along with them. In Germany we have too many of them, and it is they who form the dead weight which trammels the march of the party. It will ever be the lot of the petty bourgeois—as a mass—to float undecidedly between the two great classes, one part to be crushed by the centralisation of capital, the other by the victory of the proletariat. On the decisive day, they will as usual be tottering, wavering and helpless, *se laisseront faire*, [b] and that is all we want. Even if they come round to our views they will say: of course communism is the ultimate solution, but it is far off, maybe 100 years before it can be realised—in other words: we do not mean to work for its realisation neither in our, nor in our children's lifetime. Such is our experience in Germany.

Otherwise the verdict is a grand victory and marks a decided step in advance. The bourgeoisie, from the moment it is faced by a conscious and organised proletariat, becomes entangled in hopeless contradictions between its liberal and democratic general tendencies *here*, and the repressive necessities of its defensive struggle against the proletariat *there*. A cowardly bourgeoisie, like the German and Russian, sacrifices its general class tendencies to the momentary advantages of brutal repression. But a bourgeoisie with a revolutionary history of its own, such as the English and particularly the French, cannot do that so easily. Hence that struggle within the bourgeoisie itself, which in spite of occasional fits of violence and oppression, on the whole drives it forward—see the various electoral reforms of Gladstone in England, [299] and the advance of Radicalism in France. [429] This verdict is a new *étape*. And so the bourgeoisie, in doing its own work, is doing ours.

---

[a] on the part of the stock-brokers - [b] letting events follow their own course

But now I must conclude. I want this letter to be registered and have still to write to Tussy by first post.

Yours affectionately,

F. Engels

First published, in the language of the original (English), in: F. Engels, P. et L. Lafargue, *Correspondance*, t. I, Paris, 1956

Reproduced from the original

291

ENGELS TO AUGUST BEBEL [61]

[IN PLAUEN NEAR DRESDEN]

London, 8 October 1886

Dear Bebel,

I am writing to you today because of the conversations I have had with old Johann Philipp Becker who spent 10 days with me here and is now doubtless back in Geneva, having returned via Paris (where he discovered that his daughter had died suddenly). [628] It was a great pleasure to see the old colossus again; though he has aged physically, he's still as merry and pugnacious as ever. He is one of the characters out of our Rheno-Franconian saga that are personified in the *Nibelungenlied* — Volker the Fiddler to the life.

I had been asking him for years to set down his reminiscences and experiences [a] and he told me that, having also been encouraged by you and others, he himself felt very much inclined to do so and had actually made a start on several occasions, though he had met with little real encouragement when his work was published piecemeal (as in the *Neue Welt* to which he sent some quite splendid stuff [b] years ago, which was, however, considered insufficiently 'novelistic' as Liebknecht informed him via Motteler). A more formidable obstacle, however, was the need to work for his keep and earn 25 frs per week

---

[a] See this volume, p. 363. - [b] J. Ph. Becker, 'Abgerissene Bilder aus meinem Leben', *Die Neue Welt*, Nos. 17-20, 23, 24, 26, 28 and 29; 22 and 29 April, 6 and 13 May, 3, 10 and 24 June, 8 and 15 July 1876.

as correspondent to a Viennese paper. [631] For that he has to read a vast number of papers and periodicals and, since he has suffered from weak eyesight ever since the explosion during his experiment in Paris, [632] this alone is more than he can cope with. I have now promised him that for a start I shall write to you and Ede.

I feel that in so far as its resources permit — as they now do, according to what I have been told by Liebknecht and have heard from Zurich — the party is under an obligation to admit this old veteran, at least partially, to its pension fund, and not to allow him to ruin his eyes for the sake of 25 frs per week. At present Becker gets 25 frs a month from van Kol, a similar amount from a friend in Basle, while I myself have undertaken to pay him £5 = 125 frs a quarter, making 1,100 frs a year in all. I may have made a mistake about the amounts paid by the other two; it may only be 20 frs, in which case the total would come to 980 frs. The balance to be made up by the party would therefore be of no great significance and could doubtless be raised without difficulty by private subscription, so that in the case of payments the party treasury would simply act as intermediary. As to what the balance should amount to, this would be best determined by Ede with the help of the old man himself.

If this can be arranged, he would have time to write and/or dictate his memoirs which, since they are of the utmost importance as regards the history of the revolutionary movement in Germany, i. e. our party's antecedents, and to some extent the actual history of the party since 1860, would make an extremely valuable and saleable addition to the Volksbuchhandlung's [a] list. I consider this work highly necessary, for otherwise a whole mass of the most valuable material will go down with old Becker to the grave, or at best these things will be preserved and presented exclusively by those wholly or partially opposed to us, vulgar democrats, etc. Besides, the old man played quite an important political and military role. During the 1849 campaign he was the only commander who was a genuine product of the people and he achieved more with the crude, homespun strategy and tactics taught him by the Swiss army than any of the officers from Baden or Prussia, while at the same time he never deviated from the correct political course. Moreover he was a natural commander of a people's army, had remarkable presence of mind and was possessed of rare skill in the handling of young troops.

---

[a] a Social Democratic bookshop in Zurich

It was in fact my intention to write to Ede first about the bookselling aspect of the matter, because there would have been much I could have discussed in a more positive vein after receiving his reply, but that damned Freiberg verdict [602] may put paid to my plans at any moment and that is why I am approaching you straight away. If you take a favourable view of the matter, perhaps you would tell me whom I should deal with while you are in retreat, so that I can pursue this further — the old chap is somewhat mistrustful of Liebknecht, nor do I feel he is the right man, though I shall discuss it with him on his return; but the very fact of his being absent means that someone else will now have to deal with the business.

I must now close if this letter is to go off. I shan't forgive the court for depriving me of your visit and you of your trip to Paris. But could you, perhaps, come over here next summer before the elections and accompany me on a visit to the seaside so as to build up your strength for the campaign? Will it be more or less possible to contact you while you're in prison?

Liebknecht and the Avelings have been given a fairly, indeed unexpectedly, decent reception by the Anglo-American press. [600]

Kindest regards.

Your
F. E.

First published, in Russian, in *Marx-Engels Archives*, Vol. I (VI), Moscow, 1932

Printed according to the original

Published in English in full for the first time

292

ENGELS TO EDUARD BERNSTEIN

IN ZURICH

London, 9 October 1886

Dear Ede,

Having perused with some perplexity your 3 pages of painstaking argument [633] — perplexity as to what you could actually be driving at — I couldn't help laughing out loud when I finally got to the nub of the matter and realised that all this was intended to explain your marriage which, after all, calls for no explanation whatsoever. If all proletarians were to be so hesitant, either the proletariat would become extinct or it would reproduce itself only through illegitimate children, a method we are unlikely to resort to *en masse* until the proletariat has ceased to be. So please accept my heartiest congratulations on having at last overcome your grave hesitations and given free rein to the promptings of your heart. You will find that living as a couple, even when times are bad, is better than living alone; I myself put it to the test long enough, sometimes under the most wretched conditions, and never had cause to rue it. So give your fiancée [a] my kindest regards and jump into *thalamus* [b] with a will.

But it is already four o'clock and my letter must go off before 5.30, so now to business.

Old Becker has been here [628] and there was much talk about the necessity of his recording his reminiscences and experiences. It is something I and, he says, others as well, had often proposed to him, but how is he to do it? In order to live, he contributes to Schneeberger's *Korrespondenz* in Vienna [631] in return for 25 frs a week, and for this he must laboriously collect material. The toll on his strength and eyesight is such that he is able to do nothing else. [632] It is therefore essential that he be put in a position which will enable him to live while devoting all his time to the thing. Now van Kol, if I remember aright, gives him 25 frs a month and another friend the same amount. That makes 600 frs a year. I have undertaken to send him £5 = 125 frs a quarter. Total 1,100 frs. In my view, it is up to the party to supply the remainder, provided it has the means which, according to what Liebknecht told me, it does have. In fact, it ought really to provide wholly for the old veteran out of its pension fund. But I don't suppose there would be much difficulty about raising from well-to-do party comrades the few hundred francs still required, and this would mean that the party would merely act as intermediary for the regular payments.

The memoirs as such would be a highly valuable addition to the Volksbuchhandlung's [c] list, a new source on our party's antecedents (the revolutionary movement from 1827 to 1860) and its history

---

[a] Regina Schattner - [b] nuptial bed - [c] a Social Democratic bookshop in Zurich

(from the '50s up till the present), a document that no real historiographer could afford to overlook. And, what's more, a magnificently vivid account — genuine popular literature, if the samples published years ago in the *Neue Welt* are anything to go by.[a] And the sooner he gets down to it the better, for when a chap has already totted up a total of 77 years, his verbosity tends to outstrip his ability to assess what is important and what is not — such is the course of nature.

I wrote to August[b] about this yesterday; I had meant to write to you first and find out what you people at the publishing end thought about it, but since he is shortly due to go into jug,[602] there was no time to waste. I myself consider the thing to be of the utmost importance. An account of what happened by an active participant,— indeed *the only survivor from the thirties* whose standpoint is the same as *our own* — is an absolute necessity; it will cast a new light on the whole of the period between 1827 and 1840 and, unless done by Becker, will be lost forever. Or else it will be undertaken by people who are hostile to us — members of the People's Party[203] and other vulgar democrats, and that would serve no good purpose. It is an opportunity such as will never again present itself and to miss it would, I believe, be a crime.

I told August it would be best — once matters have got to that stage — if the details regarding the balance to be paid and the mode of publication were to be arranged personally between yourself and Becker. And in this connection there's another point which I thought it unnecessary to raise with August at this juncture, namely that the balance should be regarded simply as a pension and not as an advance on the fee. This last might be suggested by some of the 'leaders' but would be an exceedingly shabby way to treat the old warrior. Hence my proposal that as much of the balance as possible be raised by private subscription, when any such suggestion would be automatically precluded.

If all this should be settled and you enter into negotiations with Becker re publication, you should take no notice of his ideas about sales, etc., prospectus, and so forth. So far as his ideas about the sale of banned books are concerned, he might still be living in the '40s,

---

[a] J. Ph. Becker, 'Abgerissene Bilder aus meinem Leben', *Die Neue Welt*, Nos. 17-20, 23, 24, 26, 28 and 29; 22 and 29 April, 6 and 13 May, 3, 10 and 24 June, 8 and 15 July 1876. - [b] August Bebel; see previous letter.

and he has no inkling of the way this has now changed into a big industry.

So consider the matter and let me know what you think.

So far the Bulgarians have indeed done unexpectedly well and, if they hold out another 8 or 10 days, either they will win through or, should the Russians march against them, it will be only at the risk of a European war. [634] This they owe to the circumstances of having been so long subject to the *Turks*, who were content to preserve what remained of their gentile institutions, while only preventing — through the depredations of the pashas — the rise of the middle classes. The Serbs, on the other hand, who had been free of the Turks for 80 years, wrecked their old gentile institutions by introducing Austrian legislation and an Austrian-trained bureaucracy, hence their inevitable drubbing at the hands of the Bulgarians. Give the Bulgarians 60 years of bourgeois evolution — when they would certainly accomplish nothing — and of bureaucratic rule, and they would go to wrack and ruin just as the Serbs have done. It would have been infinitely better for the Bulgarians as for us had they remained Turkish until the European revolution; their gentile institutions would have provided a first-rate point of departure for their further evolution along communist lines, just as would the Russian *mir*, [a] which is now likewise being destroyed under our very noses.

As things are now I take the view that:

1) The southern Slavs should be supported if, and for as long as, they *oppose Russia*, for then they will go *along with* the European revolutionary movement.

2) If, however, they oppose the *Turks*, i. e. demand the annexation *à tout prix* [b] of the few Turkish Serbs and Bulgarians that still remain, then they will, consciously or unconsciously, be doing Russia's work for it, and we cannot go along with them. This could only be achieved at the risk of a European war, and isn't worth the candle. The chaps will have to wait, just like the Alsatians and the Lorrainers, the Trentini, etc. Moreover, the result of any renewed attack on the Turks could — in present circumstances — only be that the victorious small nationalities — victorious solely thanks to Russia — would come directly under the Russian yoke, or — cf. the linguistic map of the peninsula — become hopelessly embroiled with one another.

3) As soon as revolution breaks out in Russia, however, the chaps

---

[a] village commune - [b] whatever the cost

can do as they like. But then, too, they will realise that they are no match for the Turks.

Time for the post.

Your

F. E.

First published, in Russian, in *Marx-Engels Archives*, Book I, Moscow, 1924

Printed according to the original

Published in English for the first time

293

ENGELS TO EDUARD BERNSTEIN

IN ZURICH

London, 22 October 1886

Dear Ede,

This is to inform you that our friend Belfort Bax will probably be visiting you towards the end of this month. He is a thoroughly good sort, very erudite, especially in German philosophy, and speaks German, though in all political matters he's of a childlike innocence that can drive one to despair and is also much in evidence in *The Commonweal*. But among the 'eddicated' here he and Aveling are the only ones who not only are in earnest where the cause is concerned, but also devote some study to it.

Kautsky will have informed you about the legal niceties involved in getting married over here; I hope it can be arranged.

As regards Becker,[a] August writes[635] to say he has asked you to clarify matters with the old man. I trust you have already written to him — the old man —, as it is something he has very much at heart. August says that Becker is already getting an annual allowance of 200 frs from the party — I know I had omitted one item from the amounts I had stated[b]; this was it. I merely raise the point lest the impression

---

[a] Johann Philipp Becker - [b] See this volume, p. 501.

should have been given that Becker had concealed it from me, which was not the case.

If the stories put about by the Zankovists in Sofia are true[636] Alexander III can safely recall his discredited Kaulbars,[634] for he will then have everything he wants. It will be an improved version of the treaty of Unkiar-Skelessi[637] (1839, see Louis Blanc, *Dix ans,*[a] where it is set out in the last volume). The Black Sea will then belong to him and Constantinople will be his for the asking. This would be the result of the appropriation of parts of Turkey, namely Bosnia and Egypt, by Austria and Britain respectively, who thus revealed themselves in Constantinople as Russia's equals when it came to plundering Turkey. That was why the peace-loving Gladstone had to bombard Alexandria and wage war in the Sudan.[638]— However the story is being contested and it is probable that no formal agreement has yet been concluded; but at all events we must watch out for further news of the affair. For even *if* it were true, Austria in particular would try to hush it up lest it be compelled to attack before the Russians *really* showed signs of occupying the Dardanelles, i. e. when it was too late.

Meanwhile Alexander seems to have gone really insane — he is said to have taken one of his aides-de-camp for a Nihilist[356] and shot him —, while old William[b] is going rapidly downhill. The Russian revolution — be it ushered in by a palace revolution — is becoming more necessary than ever and would at once help to clear up the whole wretched business.

Your
F. E.

First published, in Russian, in *Marx-Engels Archives*, Book I, Moscow, 1924

Printed according to the original

Published in English for the first time

---

[a] L. Blanc, *Histoire de dix ans. 1830-1840*, in 5 volumes. - [b] William I

294

ENGELS TO LAURA LAFARGUE

IN PARIS

London, 23 October 1886

My dear Laura,

To-day I have a bit of a holiday that is to say no proof-sheets, [a] and the prefaces are as good as done. So I profit of it to write to you. Proofs are now up to sheet 40, or p. 644 of German 3rd edition. But there is a hitch again, otherwise I should be busy to-day at them again. It's awful work, every sheet 3 proofs, and a good many alterations to make in the text; the latter part of the manuscript was anything but *ausgefeilt*, [b] when we had to cede to pressure and hand it in to the printer. Sam Moore, in the polishing of the text, is invaluable to me, he has a capital eye for these things and a very ready hand. But I shall be glad when it's done, as it is I cannot take anything else in hand and there are about 5 jobs awaiting in my desk.

I certainly do hope that you will not again put off your journey till some other time which may be less foggy meteorologically but which after all would leave us both in a fog of fresh uncertainty. As to Schorlemmer he arrived here quite knocked up, had been laid up at home for a week with indigestion (it was the Vaterland I suppose he could not digest) and was in an awfully down-in-the-mouth mood here all the time — since then I have not heard a word from him.

I send you herewith two more letters from our transatlantic travellers, [c] please keep the lot for me until you come over, unless you return them before. They were yesterday in Providence (Rhode Island) and are now on the road from New England to the Great Lakes, stopping half way to-morrow at Albany and Troy (New York State) on the Hudson. [601] The press in the New England manufacturing districts has been almost cordial in its reception, thus showing not only its own dependence upon the working people, but also an evident sympathetic feeling towards socialism on the part of the latter. I am very glad of this and also of the favourable effect they have made on the bourgeois press generally, more particularly on account of their im-

---

[a] of the English translation of the first volume of *Capital* (see Note 56) - [b] polished - [c] Eleanor Marx-Aveling and Edward Aveling

pending arrival in Chicago where the bourgeois, six weeks ago, seemed inclined to get up police rows on their arrival. But they will hardly attempt anything of the kind in the face of the decided change in public opinion down East.

The Vienna anarchist plot is a pure police affair.[639] The best proof is in the self-inflaming bottles the poor fools were told to put in timber yards to set them on fire. A bottle with nitric acid, stopped with cotton impregnated with sulphuric acid. This latter was to percolate and on reaching the nitric acid, was expected to cause an explosion and fire!! Thus the same police which excited the anarchist jackasses to this plot, took damned good care that the fire bottles were perfectly harmless. But the present anti-proletarian jurisprudence will there as everywhere find means to convict them of arson.

Yesterday I had a card from an unknown place in Canada 'Rolandrie, P.O. Whitewood': '*Verehelicht*[a]: Dr R. Meyer, Mathilda Meyer, *geb.*[b] Trautow.' This must be a cousin of his whom he left on his farm last winter to mind it. On the back a few words in French from a Comte Ives de Rossignac or Prossignac that Meyer has had an accident and cannot use his right hand for a short time, and therefore cannot write himself. That is the end of another of your adorers. The grapes being sour, people take to crab-apples.

The successful issue of the Lyons Congress I read in the *Cri*,[c] but nevertheless Paul's comments and details were very welcome to me.[640] Things seem everywhere ripe for us and we have only to gather in the fruit; all old-fashioned forms of socialism are exploded while nothing can touch our theory, and so the working people need only stirring up — whenever they get into movement, no matter how, they are sure to come round to us.

Altogether things are going on bravely in France. Vierzon[619] continues Decazeville,[545] and rightly so. The government must be taught to respect their own laws and to get used to strikes. And on the other hand the discipline of a strike is most useful to the French working men; a movement in which strict legality is the first condition of success, and where all revolutionary brag and explosion necessarily brings on defeat. This discipline is the first condition of successful and lasting organisation, and the thing most feared by the bourgeoisie. And as it has brought on one ministerial crisis,[641] it may bring on more. As matters stand, it looks as if the present Chamber would soon

[a] married - [b] née - [c] *Cri du Peuple*

become impossible and have to be dissolved. I believe it will be very necessary to prepare for that event, for in the next general election the Socialists ought to force the Radicals [429] to place at least 20 of our people on the list for Paris; and the next Chamber ought to abolish *scrutin de liste*. [375] Paul ought to get into Parliament next time, he has effaced himself a good deal in favour of Guesde, Deville and others, taken the hard anonymous work upon himself and left to the others not only all the pay but also the greater part of the credit. I think the time is approaching when he ought to assert himself a little more. He is decidedly the best writer amongst the lot — now that he has once found his happy vein and sticks to it — and also the most studious. And he is far more than all the rest in constant touch with the international movement. He and Guesde at the very least ought to get in next time and shape for it from now. Guesde may be more flashy as an orator but Paul would be far better in bringing out *facts*.

However by next spring we may have a European war which upsets all our calculations being incalculable in its results. About that I shall write Paul [a] as soon as I find time. Now I must conclude, having just time enough left to send a few words to Tussy by to-day's mail.

Nim is very jolly and sends her love.

Yours affectionately,

F. E.

Liebknecht's wine-revolution is not very formidable, considering that he finds the most horrid wine '*famos*'. [b]

First published in: Marx and Engels, *Works*, Second Russian Edition, Vol. 36, Moscow, 1964

Reproduced from the original

Published in English for the first time

---

[a] See this volume, pp. 512-20. - [b] 'fine'

295

ENGELS TO AUGUST BEBEL

[IN PLAUEN NEAR DRESDEN]

London, 23 and 25 October 1886, Saturday

Dear Bebel,

The *Sozialdemokrat* containing your statement [642] arrived just now, at 9.30 p. m., and I am hastening to write to you although my letter cannot go off until 5.30 on Monday, when I shall have it registered. But on Monday, I may again have a whole lot of proofs [a] requiring my immediate attention.

Your statement is so worded that no exception whatever can be taken to it — assuming the necessity of such a step. As to this, I cannot rightly judge but, even in the absence of Freytag's opinion, it would seem to me justified. From the viewpoint both of the cause in general and of the newspaper in particular, it was, to my mind, most fortunate that the verdict enabled you to take this step in a seemly way. To have conferred an official character on the paper in the first place was, in my view, a great mistake, and so, indeed, it has proved to be in the Reichstag and elsewhere; but once it had been done, you could hardly go back on it without appearing to disown the paper and beat a retreat. The verdict gave you an opportunity of going back on it without producing that impression and you did right in making use of it. Nor, as Liebknecht saw it, was there any question of beating a retreat, and the paper will now be able to express the views of the great bulk of the party far more freely and with far less regard for the gentlemen of the right wing.

The *Neue Zeit* has not yet arrived. [643] I too take the view that Bismarck has got far more involved with the Russians than he need have done on France's account, and for this the main reason — besides those adduced by you, and overshadowing them all — is his having been told by the Russians what he knows to be true, namely: 'Either we must have decisive and resounding victories on the road to Constantinople, or else — we shall have *revolution*.' Without making sacrifices, neither Alexander III nor yet the Russian diplomats can exor-

---

[a] of the English translation of the first volume of *Capital* (see Note 56)

cise the Pan-Slav and chauvinist spirit they have conjured up, for otherwise Alexander III will be bumped off by the generals and then, whether they like it or not, they'll get a national assembly. And a Russian revolution is what Bismarck fears above all else. The collapse of Russian tsarism would entail that of the Prusso-Bismarckian economy. And hence everything possible must be done to postpone the crash, despite Austria, despite the indignation of the middle classes in Germany, and despite Bismarck's knowledge that, either way, he will eventually undermine his system—which, after all, depends on German hegemony in Europe—and that, on the day old William [a] dies, both Russia and France will rattle their sabres in quite different fashion.

The worst of it is that, given the rascality of those in power, no one can say how, in case of war, the belligerents will assort themselves, who will side *with*, and who *against* whom. That the eventual outcome will be revolution is plain, but at the cost of what sacrifices, of what general prostration—and after who knows how many changes.

In the meanwhile there'll be a respite until the spring, and during that time much can happen. In Russia the fun might begin without more ado, old William might kick the bucket and Germany change its policy, the Turks (having been deprived of Bosnia by Austria and of Egypt by Britain, they will, of course, now regard these their former allies merely as traitors) may again get out of the Russian furrow, etc.

Your opinion of the German bourgeoisie cannot be worse than mine. But it remains to be seen whether historical circumstances won't compel them actively to intervene willy-nilly, just like their French counterparts. The latter's performance is wretched enough and that of our lot would be even worse, but all the same they'd be forced to take a hand in their own history again. At the time, I read Berger's pronouncement with some pleasure, but as you say it's applicable only to Bismarck's lifetime. That it's their *intention* to drop their own 'liberal' slogans for good, I do not for a moment doubt. [644] It remains to be seen whether they can do so once they no longer have a Bismarck to rule for them and find themselves face to face with nothing but imbecile squireens and dim-witted bureaucrats—people of their own moral calibre. For come war or peace, Germany's hegemony has, during the past few months, gone for a burton and she has

---

[a] William I

again become the humble servant of Russia. And it was only the chauvinist satisfaction of being the arbiter of Europe that held the whole bag of tricks together. Fear of the proletariat will certainly help things along. And if these chaps gain admittance to the government, they will certainly start off by adopting the very attitude you describe, but will soon be forced to change their tune. I would go still further and say that even were the spell to be broken by the Old Man's death and the same people to remain at the helm as now, they would either be forced to resign as a result of renewed clashes—not only with the Court—or have to act in accordance with bourgeois views. Not at once, of course, but very soon. Political stagnation such as now obtains in Germany—a genuine Second Empire—can only be a transitory and exceptional state of affairs; large-scale industry will not allow its laws to be dictated by the cowardice of industrialists. Economic development will give rise to repeated clashes, each more severe than the last, nor will it suffer itself to be governed for any length of time by semi-feudal Junkers with feudal proclivities.

Come to that, there is also the possibility that in the spring they will all gird up their loins for war and, armed to the teeth, confront one another, each fearing to begin, until one of them puts forward a solution involving mutual compromise and the swallowing up of small states, whereupon they'll all grab their share. That Bismarck is presently adumbrating such an expedient seems probable enough.

25 October

Your remarks about Liebknecht's speeches presumably relate mainly to what he told the correspondent of the *New Yorker Volkszeitung* (little Cuno); this shouldn't be taken too literally—since interviewers always distort things. I agree that his other remarks about the *Kulturkampf*[462] are somewhat misguided, but as you know, Liebknecht is very dependent on atmosphere and tends to chance his hand with his audiences (not always successfully), while he never has more than two colours—black and white—on his palette. Not that very much harm will have been done, since it will all have been long since forgotten in America.

Goodbye, then, and mind you keep fit and send us occasional news of yourself during your imprisonment. [602] I hardly imagine that you will have to stay there for the full term, and in 9 months' time everything may have changed.

Your

F. E.

First published, in Russian, in *Marx-Engels Archives*, Vol. I (VI), Moscow, 1932

Printed according to the original

Published in English for the first time

296

ENGELS TO PAUL LAFARGUE [645]

IN PARIS

London, 25-26 October 1886

My dear Lafargue,

The Eastern affair is rather lengthy, and I shall be obliged to enter into a mass of detail in view of the absurdities which the French press, including the *Cri*,[a] has been disseminating on the subject, under the Russian patriotic influence.

In the winter of 1878[b] Disraeli sent 4 ironclads into the Bosphorus, this being sufficient to halt the Russian advance on Constantinople and to tear up the Treaty of San Stefano.[646] For a time the Treaty of Berlin stabilised the situation in the Orient. Bismarck succeeded in effecting a settlement between the Russians and the Austrians, in accordance with which Austria was tacitly given dominion over Serbia, while Bulgaria and Eastern Roumelia were to be left exposed to the predominant influence of Russia. In other words, if the Russians were later permitted to take Constantinople, Austria would get Salonika and Macedonia.

But on top of that, Bosnia was allotted to Austria, just as the greater part of Poland proper had been handed over to the Prussians and Austrians by Russia in 1794, only to be taken back by the latter in 1814.[647] Bosnia represented a constant drain on Austria, a bone of

---

[a] *Cri du Peuple* - [b] 1879 in the original

contention between Hungary and Western Austria and, in particular — *proof, where Turkey was concerned, that the fate awaiting it at the hands of Austria no less than at those of Russia, would be that suffered by Poland.* Henceforward there could be no question of mutual trust between Turkey and Austria — a tremendous victory, this, for Russia.

Though Serbia's sympathies were Slavophil and, consequently, Russophil it had, since its emancipation, looked to Austria for all its means of bourgeois development. Its young men went to university in Austria, its bureaucratic system, its statute books, its judicial procedure and its schools all conformed to the Austrian model, as was only natural. But Russia thought it necessary to prevent the same thing happening in Bulgaria and, besides, had no desire to act as Austria's cat's paw there. Thus, from the very outset, Bulgaria was organised along the lines of a Russian satrapy. The administration was Russian, as were the officers and non-commissioned officers in the army, the whole body of government officials and, indeed, the entire system, while Battenberg, imposed upon it as satrap, was a cousin of Alexander III's.

Russian domination, direct at first, then indirect, succeeded in stifling, within less than 4 years, all the sympathy Bulgaria had once felt for Russia, whole-hearted and enthusiastic though that sympathy had been. The people increasingly jibbed at the insolence of their 'liberators', so that even Battenberg, a man of weak character and devoid of political ideas, who asked nothing better than to serve the Tsar on condition that he himself was accorded some measure of respect — even Battenberg was becoming increasingly rebellious.

In the meantime things were taking their course in Russia. The government had succeeded, by draconian measures, in temporarily dispersing and disorganising the Nihilists. [356] But this could not last forever; what was needed was to gain the support of public opinion and to distract people's minds from social and political miseries at home — in other words, a bit of chauvinist phantasmagoria. And just as, under Louis Napoleon, the left bank of the Rhine had served to divert revolutionary fervour to foreign policy matters, so, too, in Russia the image of a Constantinople subdued, of oppressed Turkish Slavs 'liberated' to form part of a great federation under Russian leadership, was conjured up before the eyes of the anxious and restive people. But merely to evoke that phantasmagoria was not enough; something would have to be done to make it enter the domain of reality.

Circumstances were favourable. The annexation of Alsace-

Lorraine had thrown an apple of discord between France and Germany so that those two powers appeared to cancel each other out. Austria on her own was scarcely in a position to fight Russia, since her most effective offensive weapon — an appeal to the Poles — must, thanks to Prussia, remain permanently in the scabbard. And the occupation — or theft — of Bosnia constituted another Alsace between Austria and Turkey. Italy fell to the highest bidder, that is to say Russia, whose stake was the Trentino and Istria, if not also Dalmatia and Tripoli. And England? Gladstone, that peaceable Russophil, had hearkened to Russia's siren call and *had occupied Egypt* in time of peace, [648] thus ensuring not only continual discord between England and France, but also and into the bargain *the impossibility of any alliance between the Turks and the English who had just despoiled them* by appropriating Egypt, a Turkish fief. Moreover, Russia's preparations in Asia were sufficiently advanced to keep the English, in case of war, fully occupied in India. Never had the moment presented so many and such favourable opportunities to the Russians; their diplomacy was proving victorious all along the line.

The revolt of the Bulgarians against Russian domination provided the pretext for instituting a campaign. In the summer of 1885 a carrot was dangled before the Bulgarians of North and South — the possibility of unification, as pledged by the Peace of San Stefano and revoked by the Treaty of Berlin. They were told that, if they again entrusted themselves to the liberating arms of Russia, that country would accomplish her mission by accomplishing the said unification, but the Bulgarians, for their part, must first rid themselves of Battenberg. Duly forewarned, the latter reacted with unwonted promptitude and vigour. Off his own bat and on his own account he effected the unification which the Russians had intended to bring about in his despite. From that moment it was implacable war between him and Russia.

To begin with, that war was conducted covertly and by indirect means. The small Balkan states were reminded of Louis Bonaparte's splendid doctrine which held that, when a nation hitherto disunited — say Italy or Germany — constituted itself a nation, other powers — say France — were entitled to territorial compensation. Serbia swallowed the bait and went to war with Bulgaria. Russia's triumph was the greater in that the war, instigated by her in her own interests, appeared to the rest of the world to be taking place under the auspices of Austria, which had failed to prevent it for fear this should bring the Russian party to power in Serbia.— Russia, for her part, disrupted the Bulgarian army by recalling all its senior officers, including battalion commanders.

But contrary to all expectations the Bulgarians, deprived of Russian officers and with two men to the enemy's three, inflicted a resounding defeat on the Serbs and won the respect and admiration of an astonished Europe. [478] For those victories there were two reasons. In the first place Alexander Battenberg, though a weak politician, was a good soldier who waged war as he had learned to do in the Prussian school, whereas the Serbs, in both strategy and tactics, turned to Austria for their model. Secondly, the Serbs had lived for 60 years under a bureaucratic Austrian régime which, while failing to give them a strong middle class and an independent peasantry (by now all their property was mortgaged), had succeeded in undermining and disorganising what remained of the *gentile* communism which had lent them strength in their struggles against the Turks. In Bulgaria, on the other hand, these more or less communist institutions had been left intact by the Turks, and this is the explanation for their superior courage.

So Russia was foiled again and had to make a fresh start. And the Slavophil chauvinism which had been encouraged in the hope that it would counterbalance the revolutionary element, continued to grow day by day and had already begun to pose a threat to the government. So the Tsar betook himself to the Crimea [a] where, or so the Russian press maintained, he would achieve great things. He attempted to entice the Sultan [b] there so as to involve him in an alliance by demonstrating that his erstwhile allies—Austria and England— were traitors and robbers and that France was in tow to, and at the mercy of, Russia. But the Sultan did not come and, for the time being, there was no employment for the vast armaments Russia had accumulated in the west and the south.

The Tsar returned (last June) from the Crimea, [c] but in the meantime the tide of chauvinism had continued to rise and the government, far from controlling this upward surge, found itself increasingly carried away by it. So much so that, on the Tsar's return to Moscow, there was no preventing the mayor, [d] in his address, [e] of speaking loud

---

[a] on 1 April 1886 - [b] Abdul-Hamid II - [c] Alexander III returned to Gatchina (near St Petersburg) on 30 May 1886 (see *Правительственный вѣстникъ*, No. 108, 20 May (1 June) 1886). - [d] Nikolai Alexeyev - [e] See *Новое время*, No. 3666, 15 (27) May 1886.

and clear about the conquest of Constantinople. [649] Under the influence of the generals, *and under their aegis*, the press openly expressed the expectation that the Tsar would take action against Austria and Germany which were hampering him, nor did the government have the courage to muzzle it. In short, Slavophil chauvinism was stronger than the Tsar. Either the latter must give way or else—the Slavophils would rebel.

All this was compounded by a shortage of cash. No one was willing to lend money to a government which between 1870 and 1875 had borrowed 70 million pounds sterling (1,750 million frs) in London and was posing a threat to the peace of Europe. Only three years before, in Germany, Bismarck had raised a loan of 375 million frs on its behalf, but that had been frittered away long since; and without Bismarck's signature the Germans wouldn't give another farthing. But that signature was no longer to be had save at the cost of humiliating conditions. At home, the government paper-mill had already been producing to excess; the rouble in silver was worth 3 fr. 80, but in paper-money only 2 fr. 20. And armaments were diabolically expensive.

Finally action became imperative. Either a successful move against Constantinople, or revolution. Which is why Giers went to call on Bismarck to explain the situation to him. And Bismarck understood him perfectly. He would have restrained the Russians, first because of their insatiability and secondly out of consideration for Austria. But revolution in Russia *might involve the fall of Bismarck's régime in Germany*. Without the large reserves of the reactionary army, the rule of the cabbage Junkers in Prussia would not last a day. Revolution in Russia would, at a stroke, change the situation in Germany; it would put an end to that blind faith in Bismarck's omnipotence which had rallied to his standard all the propertied classes; it would foment revolution in Germany.

Bismarck, who had no illusions but that the existence of tsarism in Russia was the base upon which the whole of his system rested, understood very well; he hastened to Vienna to tell his Austrian friends that, in the face of such a danger, it would not be opportune either for him or for them to place undue insistence on questions of *amour-propre*; that the Russians must be allowed at least a semblance of victory, and that it was in their own interests that Germany and Austria should bow the knee before the Tsar. Moreover, were his esteemed friends the Austrians to insist on meddling in Bulgarian affairs, he would wash his hands of them and then they'd see what would happen. Kálnoky finally gave way, Alexander Battenberg was sacrificed, and Bismarck went in person to announce the fact to Giers.

There followed the kidnapping of Battenberg by military conspirators in circumstances which could not but shock any monarchically-minded conservative, in particular those princes *who had armies of their own*. But at this point Bismarck proceeded to the next item on the agenda, glad to have got off at so little cost.

Unfortunately, the Bulgarians gave evidence of a political aptitude and an energy which, in the circumstances, were highly inopportune, not to say intolerable in a Slav nation 'liberated' by Holy Russia. They arrested the conspirators and nominated an efficient government, energetic and — incorruptible (a quality wholly intolerable in a nation as yet barely emancipated!) which reinstated Battenberg. The latter thereupon proceeded to exert all his weakness by taking to his heels. But the Bulgarians proved incorrigible. Battenberg or no Battenberg, they resisted the supreme orders of the Tsar and forced even the heroic Kaulbars to make an ass of himself in the eyes of all Europe. [634]

Imagine the fury of the Tsar! Having curbed Bismarck, having broken the resistance of Austria, to find oneself brought up short by this runt of a nation, weaned only yesterday, which owes its 'independence' to oneself or to one's father [a] and fails to see that the aforesaid independence means nothing more than blind obedience to the 'liberator'! The Greeks and Serbs have not shown themselves wanting in ingratitude, but the Bulgarians exceed all possible bounds. Taking their independence seriously — has such a thing ever been heard of before?

To save himself from revolution, the hapless Tsar was compelled to take another step forward. But with every new step the peril increased, for it brought closer the risk of European war — something Russian diplomacy had always been at pains to avoid. There could be no doubt that, if Russia intervened in Bulgaria, and if such intervention subsequently led to complications, the moment would come when the mutually inimical interests of Russia and Austria would lead to an open clash. And this time there could be no question of localising the affair. There would be general war. And, given the rascals who were at that juncture governing Europe, there was no foreseeing what the

---

[a] Alexander II

composition of the two camps might be. Bismarck was capable of allying himself with the Russians against Austria if that was the only way of postponing revolution in Russia. What seemed more probable, however, was war between Austria and Russia, and that Germany would come to the help of Austria only in case of need, to prevent her being crushed.

While waiting for the spring — for before April the Russians cannot embark on a major war on the Danube — they did everything they could to lure Turkey into their snare, and Austria and England, by their treachery towards Turkey, furthered this ploy. Their object was to gain the right to occupy the Dardanelles, thus turning the Black Sea into a Russian lake, an unassailable haven for the organisation of powerful fleets which would sail out of it to dominate the French lake, as Napoleon called the Mediterranean. But in this they never succeeded, even though the cat had been let out of the bag by the few adherents they had in Sofia.

Such was the situation. To avoid revolution in Russia, the Tsar must have Constantinople. And Bismarck prevaricated, wishing to find some way of avoiding one or the other eventuality. And what of France?

For those Frenchmen whose thoughts, for 16 years, had centred solely on revenge, it would seem natural enough to seize on what might be a possible opportunity. But for our party it is not so simple, nor yet even for Messrs the chauvinists. War against Germany in alliance with Russia might lead to either revolution or counter-revolution in France. If a revolution were to bring the socialists to power, the alliance with Russia would collapse. In the first place, *the Russians would immediately conclude peace with Bismarck so that they might together fall upon revolutionary France.* And in the second, France would not put the socialists in power so that they might fight to prevent revolution in Russia. But such an eventuality is unlikely to arise. What is far more likely is *a monarchist counter-revolution,* promoted by the Russian alliance. You know how greatly the Tsar desires the restoration of the house of Orleans, and that this alone would enable him to conclude a good, stable alliance with France. Well, the war once embarked upon, good use would be made of the monarchist officers in the army who would help pave the way for the said restoration. For any partial defeat, however slight — and such there would be — they would blame the Republic, saying that, if victories were to be achieved and the whole-hearted cooperation of their Russian ally secured, there must be a stable, monarchical government — in short, Philippe VII [a]; the monarchist generals would themselves act irresolutely so that their failures could be laid at the door of the republican government — and hey presto, you've got your monarchy! And, Philippe once installed, all those kings and emperors would suddenly be of one mind and, instead of killing each other, share out Europe between them, swallowing up the smaller states. Once the French Republic had been killed there'd be another Congress of Vienna [650] at which France's republican and socialist sins might, perhaps, be made a pretext for refusing her Alsace-Lorraine, whether in whole or in part, and at which the princes would deride the stupidity of the republicans for believing in the possibility of a genuine alliance between tsarism and anarchy.

Is it true, by the bye, that General Boulanger is saying to anyone who chooses to hear *that war is to France a necessity, in that it is the only way to kill social revolution?* If so, let it be a warning to you. The good Boulanger has a swashbuckling air, excusable perhaps in a soldier, but which gives me a low opinion of his political nous. It is not he who will save the Republic. If he had to choose between the socialists and the house of Orleans he would, if needs be, come to terms with the latter, especially if it secured the Russian alliance for him. Whatever the case, *the bourgeois republicans in France are in the same boat as the Tsar in Russia; they see before them the spectre of revolution and can see only one means of salvation: war.*

In France as is Germany things are going so well for us that all we can wish for is the continuation of the *status quo.* And if revolution were to break out in Russia it would create a combination of circumstances which could hardly be more favourable. Whereas if there were to be general war, we should find ourselves back in the realm of uncertainty and of unpredictable events. Revolution in Russia and France would be averted, our party's splendid development in Germany would be violently interrupted, and the monarchy would probably be restored in France. Doubtless all this would eventually redound in our favour, but what a waste of time, what sacrifices, what fresh obstacles to be overcome!

---

[a] Louis Philippe Albert d'Orléans

The temptation to go to war is everywhere great. In the first place the Prussian military system, universally adopted, takes some 12 to 16 years to complete its development; after that period, all reserve formations are made up of men trained in the handling of weapons. Everywhere the 12-16-year period has elapsed; everywhere there are 12-16 classes which have passed through the army each year. Thus everywhere people are prepared, and the Germans no longer enjoy any particular advantage in that respect. And in the second place, old William [a] is probably about to die; then the system will undergo certain changes. Bismarck will see his position to some extent undermined and *may himself press* for *war as the only means of maintaining it*. For others this would represent a further temptation to attack Germany which would seem to them less strong and less stable at a time when internal affairs were in a state of flux. Indeed, the Stock Exchange everywhere believes there will be war as soon as the Old Man has closed his eyes.

As for myself, I believe we must take for granted the fact that the war, if war there be, will be conducted simply with a view to preventing revolution: in Russia, to forestall common action by all malcontents—Slavophils, Constitutionals, Nihilists [356] and peasants; in Germany to keep Bismarck in power; in France to stem the victorious progress of the socialists and (or so all the big bourgeoisie hopes) to re-establish the monarchy. Hence I am for 'peace at any price', seeing that it is not we who will pay that price.

Yours ever,

F. E.

I return *La France Juive.* [b] What a tiresome book!

26 October, Tuesday, 3.30 p. m.

So this letter will reach you tomorrow morning.

First published in: F. Engels, P. et L. Lafargue, *Correspondance*, t. I, Paris, 1956

Printed according to the original

Translated from the French

---

[a] William I - [b] É. Drumont, *La France Juive. Essai d'histoire contemporaine.*

297

ENGELS TO LAURA LAFARGUE

IN PARIS

London, 2 November 1886

My dear Laura,

I am sorry you gave yourself the trouble to copy out the Menger balderdash. [651] The fellow is a simple *Streber*[a] who knows that, the thicker he lays it on, the better will be his chance of promotion. We have got the book here and I shall give Kautsky notes enough to enable him to smash the cheeky devil up. The position he takes is so utterly ridiculous that it will nowhere be accepted unless in national-liberal newspapers, and there we must expect to have it served up again and again, but that is of the utmost indifference. The Rodbertus scare was far more serious and that we have already smashed up so completely that it is quite forgotten by this time. [b]

I don't think even Hyndman will venture to make capital out of this, except perhaps in a very small way.

Now I must begin writing my preface, [c] as Swan Sonnenschein and Co. are asking for it, so this looks like coming to a conclusion!

Very affectionately yours,

F. E.

First published, in the language of the original (English), in: F. Engels, P. et L. Lafargue, *Correspondance*, t. I, Paris, 1956

Reproduced from the original

---

[a] pusher - [b] See F. Engels, 'Marx and Rodbertus'; F. Engels, Preface to the first German edition of Volume II of *Capital*. - [c] Preface to the English edition of Volume I of *Capital*

298

ENGELS TO NIKOLAI DANIELSON

IN ST PETERSBURG

London, 9 November 1886

Dear Sir,

All this time I have been busy with the English translation of Volume I [56] which I hope will now be finished in a few weeks as I have read the *first* proof-sheets of the whole and only now have to read 2nd and 3rd corrections of the last 10 sheets. It was very hard work, as after all I shall be held responsible for the text. I have not been able to do anything else during that time, and thus a heap of other little matters have accumulated which I now shall clear off and then return to the 3rd volume. This, as I believe I told you, I have dictated from the original ms. into a legible handwriting, [a] and the greater part of it will not require much revision, but the chapter on the transformation of the rate of surplus value into the rate of profit, and that on banking capital, and to some extent — also that on the rent of land [652] will take a deal of working out yet. I hope to bring the whole out next year, but shall not send anything off to the printer until the whole is completed.

The sale of Volume II up to March 1886 was 1,300 copies. [4]

As soon as the English translation is out, I shall forward you a copy.

The reviews of Volume II in the German press have been exceedingly stupid. One, by a Dr Gross in Vienna, was very decent, [b] but the man is an idiot. Another by Professor Lexis in Breslau [c] is very clever in its way, the man understands the book perfectly, and knows that nothing can be said against it; but he is a '*Streber*' [d] and therefore disguises himself as a *Vulgärökonom*. It is in Hildebrand's *Jahrbücher für Nationalökonomie und Statistik*, XI. Band, 1885, 5tes Heft (5 Dezember 1885).

---

[a] See this volume, p. 348. - [b] G. Groß, 'Marx, Karl: *Das Kapital. Kritik der politischen Oekonomie*. Zweiter Band, Buch II', *Jahrbuch für Gesetzgebung, Verwaltung und Volkswirthschaft im Deutschen Reich*, No. 2, 1886. - [c] W. Lexis, 'Die Marx'sche Kapitaltheorie'. - [d] 'pusher'

I shall be only too glad when I can bring out the 3rd volume for as you say only then will the whole system of the author be completely understood and many stupid objections made at present will fall completely to the ground.

Yours faithfully,

P. W. Rosher [363]

First published, in Russian, in *Minuvshiye gody*, No. 2, St Petersburg, 1908

Reproduced from the original

Published in English for the first time

299

ENGELS TO E. T. [653]

IN LONDON

[London, about 13 November 1886]

In answer to above I have got a translator for the pamphlet in question, [528] and as it is rather difficult to translate, I should certainly not like any translation to be published without my first having revised it.

Yours faithfully,

F. Engels

First published in *The Commonweal*, Vol. 2, No. 44, 13 November 1886

Reproduced from the magazine

300

ENGELS TO LAURA LAFARGUE

IN PARIS

London, 23 November 1886

My dear Laura,

I intended to write to you today but had to write to Edward [39] first to catch the steamer, and that has taken me till now 5 p. m. So I must delay till to-morrow.

Prefaces, etc., [654] corrected in 14 proofs, so by end of week *my* share of the work will probably be done. Damned glad, it has worried me more than a little. How soon Swan Sonnenschein & Co. will now bring it out I cannot tell.

In the meantime I enclose the two American letters [655] I have just replied to.

Thanks for 'Fergus' [656] — they do decline then to take his name?

Cyon has orders to start a large French paper (or to buy an existing one) in Paris in the interest of Russia, that was what he went home and brought the money for.

Yours affectionately,

F. E.

First published in: Marx and Engels, *Works*, Second Russian Edition, Vol. 36, Moscow, 1964

Reproduced from the original

Published in English for the first time

301

ENGELS TO LAURA LAFARGUE

IN PARIS

London, 24 November 1886

My dear Laura,

I hope you have received the American letters I sent you yesterday, [655] to-day I can keep my word and write. Our people have indeed hit upon a lucky moment for their journey, [601] it coincides with the first formation of a real American working men's party and what was practically an immense success, the Henry George 'boom' in New York. [657] Master George is rather a confused sort of a body and being a Yankee, has a nostrum of his own, and not a very excellent one, but his confusion is a very fair expression of the present stage of development of the Anglo-American working class mind, and we cannot expect even American masses to arrive at theoretical perfection in six or eight months — the age of this movement. And considering that the Germans in America are anything but a fair and adequate sample of the workmen of Germany, but rather of the elements the movement at home has eliminated — Lassalleans, disappointed ambitions, sectarians of all sorts — I for one am not sorry that the Americans start independently of them, or at least of their leadership. As a ferment the Germans can and will act, and at the same time undergo, themselves, a good deal of useful and necessary fermentation. The unavoidable starting point, in America, are the Knights of Labor, [609] who are a real power, and are sure to form the first embodiment of the movement. Their absurd organisation and very slippery leaders — used to the methods of corrupt American partisanship — will very soon provoke a crisis within that body itself, and then a more adequate and more effective organisation can be developed from it. All this I think will not take very long in Yankeeland; the great point gained is that the political action of the working class as an independent party is henceforth established there.

From America to Russia *il n'y a qu'un pas.* [a] Tussy told me last summer that Lawroff had asked her to write something about Lopatine, and to ask me to do the same, as he was to publish something about him. I told her that as far as I knew, Lopatine was still awaiting his trial, [362] and that surely under those circumstances Lawroff would not publish anything to aggravate his position; would she therefore again write to Lawroff to know how this was (for it led me almost to conclude Lawroff must have been informed that Lopatine was dead) and what he desired me to say about him. Since then I have not heard anything more with respect to this matter. I now see in the papers that a fresh Nihilist [356] trial is coming on in Petersburg, and from the way it is worded, it looks likely that this concerns Lopatine too if he be still alive. Would you be good enough to ask Lawroff next time

---

[a] is but a step

you see him how all this is, and what he wishes me to do with regard to Lopatine as I shall be always ready and willing to contribute my testimony in confirmation and acknowledgment of the great services he has done to the cause, provided I know what is wanted and what is his position at the present moment.

Thanks to the stupidity of all its rivals and opponents, the Social Democratic Federation [300] is beginning to become a power. The government saved them from a *four*[a] by forbidding their procession on Lord Mayor's Day, and prepared them a nominal triumph by allowing them to hold what they called a meeting the same afternoon on Trafalgar Square. And when after that, the Social Democratic Federation called a meeting for last Sunday on Trafalgar Square, [658] the same government made it a real triumph by first announcing that artillery should be brought out to St. James Park in readiness to act, and then countermanding this ridiculous plan. So the meeting—the first where the Social Democratic Federation had announced they would proceed orderly and peaceably—was puffed by the government into a great event, and when it did come off orderly and peaceably, the bourgeois and *Spiessbürger*[b] found that whatever the strength of the Social Democratic Federation itself might be, it had a very powerful tail behind it. The fact is that as the Socialist League [346] is too deeply engaged in discussing its own rules and regulations with its anarchist members, to have a moment to spare for events outside No. 18 Farringdon Road, and as the Radical Clubs of the East End [659] take no initiative whatever with regard to the unemployed, the Social Democratic Federation have no competitor, are alone in the field, and work this question, which springs up afresh as soon as winter comes on, entirely to their own liking. And they have certainly of late been far more sensible in their doings—of late, that is to say for the last fortnight. How long that will last, of course nobody can tell. Hyndman *est capable de tout.*[c]

That Professor Menger who seems to have frightened people all over the continent by his brazen impudence, is a vulgar *Streber*[d] who aspires to the Ministry of Justice. I have given Kautsky the necessary materials and partly worked them out myself as far as necessary, and if we can manage it, *bekommt er sein Fett schon in der ersten Nr. de N. Z. Ja-*

---

[a] *failure* - [b] philistines - [c] is capable of anything - [d] pusher

nuar 87.[a] Of course the Liberal papers have made an awful fuss about his discoveries, just as they did about Vogt's. Only times have changed and we can hit back now, and with effect. The conspiracy of the bourgeois press in 1859 against us[660] was 1,000 times more effective than Bismarck's contemptible Socialist Law.[37]

You have no idea how glad I am that the book[b] is at last through the press. It was impossible to do anything else while it was going on. The arrangements were of necessity very complicated, proofs being sent to Edward, Moore, and myself, which naturally caused delay and constant pegging on the part of Swan Sonnenschein and Co. Then, as I only lately found out, the book was printed in — *Perth!* And considerable neglect of business in Swan Sonnenschein and Co.'s office through which everything had to pass. Finally, the usual course of things: neglect and delay, on the part of the printers, in summer, then, towards end of September, hurry and worry, just over that part of the ms. which wanted most careful final revisal, and constant attempts to saddle the delay on us.[56] *Grosse Industrie*[c] in the publishing trade is all very well for periodicals, novels and *Tagesliteratur,*[d] but for works like this it won't do, unless your ms. is perfect to the dot on every i; otherwise, woe to the Author!

Well now, and how about your journey to London, you and Paul? Tussy will sail from New York 25 December, X-mas day, which brings her here about 6th January. But that is no reason why you should stay away so long, on the contrary we hope to have you here on Christmas day. And Paul this time has no excuse and I won't take any either, everything in France is nice and quiet, no trials, no prison, no great meetings, no excitement, and perfectly hopeless to get any during *la saison des étrennes.*[e] And you, as you have let the summer and autumn pass, you will have to face the fogs — don't you feel a little home-sick for them? — which fogs by the way so far treat us very well, for we have it clear and bright, while since Monday[f] not only the City but even Kilburn are benighted and murky. So please make your minds and let us be knowing how many days before Christmas you will make your appearance here. Nim is getting very impa-

---

[a] he'll get it hot already in the first number of *Die Neue Zeit*, in January 1887 (see Note 651) - [b] the English edition of the first volume of *Capital* - [c] big industry - [d] topical literature - [e] the holidays - [f] 23 November

tient and quite capable of going over to fetch you if there is any further delay. And herewith

Yours affectionately,

F. Engels

First published, in the language of the original (English), in: F. Engels, P. et L. Lafargue, *Correspondance*, t. I, Paris, 1956

Reproduced from the original

302

ENGELS TO HERMANN SCHLÜTER [661]

IN HOTTINGEN-ZURICH

London, 26 November 1886

Dear Mr Schlüter,

Very many thanks for your communication re J. Ph. Becker. [662] As to his moving to Zurich, that is a matter I would rather leave to you to deal with direct. You say that the need for it is perfectly obvious; to you in Zurich that may seem entirely right, but to me here in London, where I am less able to weigh up the pros and cons, the case looks different. And for that reason I cannot possibly persuade him to move, at the drop of a hat, to Zurich from Geneva to which, after forty years, he has grown accustomed, having become, so to speak, part and parcel of the place. Accordingly I have so far said not a word about the matter.

The English translation[a] is all but done and once I have paid off my most pressing debts in the shape of letters owed to correspondents, I shall at last be able to attend to the items in suspense reposing in my desk. In order of seniority these are as follows:

1) Italian translation of *Wage Labour and Capital*,[b] 10 months old,
2) French ditto of the *18th Brumaire*,[482] 8 months old,
3) your Chartist ms.,[557]
4) and 5) my *Housing Question*, etc., and the *Mordspatrioten*.[c] To these you have now added 6) and 7).

---

[a] of the first volume of *Capital* (see Note 56) - [b] by Marx - [c] F. Engels, 'Introduction to Sigismund Borkheim's Pamphlet *In Memory of the German Blood-and-Thunder Patriots. 1806-1807*'.

6) *Theory of Force.* [663] You are welcome to go ahead, but what do you mean by 'correspondingly altered'? The purely positive part amounts to no more than a few pages while the anti-Dühring polemic is itself positive and indispensable both factually and technically. However if you simply mean the deletion of individual passages having no particular relevance to the question of force and merely serving to link together the rest of the text, then I agree. This will amount to about 25 pages and is rather little. In my view the 2 chapters, Morality and Law: *Eternal Truths* and *Equality*, could be similarly revised and added on, since these also revolve round the materialist-economic view of history, in which case the whole could be entitled *On Law and Force in World History* or something of the kind.

7) *On Social Relations in Russia.* [664] If you reprint the little pamphlet as it stands I have no objection; a preface to it would mean my embarking on further Russian studies, for which I have absolutely no time; a preface *without* further studies would provide nothing new and would therefore best be omitted. The articles relating to it in the *Volksstaat* would also best be omitted. No. 3 was an attack on Lavrov who since then has given us no cause to bring up the old business again and, like the beginning of No. 4 (attacking Tkachov),[a] it contains nothing, save for one or two perhaps tolerable jokes, that could be of any interest today, let alone have any effect as propaganda.

If Ede is not wholly engrossed in the Eternal Feminine,[b] kindly tell him that in my view the SOCIAL DEMOCRATIC FEDERATION [300] ought now to be handled somewhat differently. The stupidity of the government, the inaction of the working men's Radical Clubs [659] vis-à-vis the enormous growth in the number of 'unemployed' and, finally, the wisdom of the SOCIALIST LEAGUE, [346] whose constant preoccupation with its own rules and regulations leaves it time for nothing else, have provided the SOCIAL DEMOCRATIC FEDERATION with so splendid a pitch that not even Hyndman & Co. have yet managed to queer it. The SOCIAL DEMOCRATIC FEDERATION is beginning to be something of a power, since the masses have absolutely no other organisation to which they can rally. The facts should therefore be recorded impartially, in particular the most important fact of all, namely that a genuinely socialist labour movement has come into being over here. But one must be very careful to draw a distinction between the masses and their tem-

---

[a] In the original mistakenly articles Nos. 1 and 2. - [b] See this volume, p. 501.

porary leaders and, in particular, make sure you don't identify your-selves with the latter in any way, for it is virtually certain that before very long these political adventurers will, with the impatience that is born of ambition, again commit the most appalling blunders. As soon as the movement has acquired substance, either it will keep these gen-tlemen in check or they will destroy themselves. Hitherto the irrita-tion felt by the majority has simply taken the form of dull, uncon-scious dissatisfaction, but it is in this way that the ground has been prepared for sowing.

In America, *apart from New York*, the real movement is running ahead of the Germans. The Americans' real organisation is the KNIGHTS OF LABOR [609] which is as muddle-headed as the masses them-selves. But it is from this chaos that the movement will evolve, not from the German sections—the Germans, that is, who, for the past 20 years, have proved incapable of extracting from their theory what America needs. [549] But this is just the moment when the Germans might exert a very enlightening influence—if only they had learnt English!

Kindest regards to everyone.

Yours,

F. Engels

First published in: Marx and Engels, *Works*, First Russian Edition, Vol. XXVII, Moscow, 1935

Printed according to the original

Published in English in full for the first time

303

ENGELS TO KARL KAUTSKY

IN LONDON

London, 29 November 1886

Dear Kautsky,

This morning a letter from Mrs Liebknecht wherein, on her hus-band's advice, she informs me that she will be arriving day after tomorrow at Victoria Station via Flushing. As this question cropped up yesterday, I hasten to let you know and leave it to you to decide whether, as the only person acquainted with her, you are under any compulsion to go and meet her at the station in the middle of the night. Far be it from me to put any kind of pressure on you — I merely thought fit to acquaint you with this weighty Victorian fact.

We have got some more beer in, if only I were allowed to drink it! Regards to your wife.

Your

F. E.

First published in *Friedrich Engels' Brief-wechsel mit Karl Kautsky*, Wien, 1955

Printed according to the original

Published in English for the first time

304

ENGELS TO FRIEDRICH ADOLPH SORGE [665]

IN HOBOKEN

London, 29 November 1886

Dear Sorge,

Today I have delivered the last corrected proofs of the Preface [a] to the publishers, thus finally ridding myself of this incubus. I hope to be able to send you a copy of the translation in a fortnight's time. Mrs Liebknecht arrives here the day after tomorrow to await her husband who left New York only the day before yesterday. [600]

The Henry George boom [657] naturally brought a vast amount of dirty business to light, and I'm glad I wasn't there. Nevertheless, it was an epoch-making day. The Germans simply have not realised how they can use their theory as a lever that will set the American masses in motion; they themselves do not for the most part understand the theory and treat it in doctrinaire and dogmatic fashion as something which, having once been learnt by rote, is sufficient as it

---

[a] F. Engels, Preface to the English edition of Volume I of *Capital*.

stands for any and every need. To them it is a credo, not a guide to action. Besides which, they refuse to learn English on principle. Hence the American masses have had to find a way of their own and would appear to have done so for the time being in the KNIGHTS OF LABOR [609] whose muddle-headed principles and ridiculous organisation would seem to match their own muddle-headedness. From all that I hear, the KNIGHTS OF LABOR are a real power, particularly in New England and the West, and are daily becoming more so as a result of the brutality of the capitalist opposition. It is, I believe, necessary to work in their midst, to form, within this still fairly malleable mass, a nucleus of men who know the movement and its aims and will thus automatically take over the leadership of at least some part of it when, as is inevitable, the present 'Order' disintegrates. The worst aspect of the KNIGHTS OF LABOR is their political neutrality whose only result is the sharp practice of the Powderlys, etc. But this last has had its sting drawn by the response of the masses in the November elections, more especially in New York. In a country that has newly entered the movement, the first really crucial step is the formation by the workers of an independent political party, no matter how, so long as it is distinguishable as a labour party. And this step has been taken far sooner than we might have expected, and that's the main thing. That the first programme of this party should still be muddle-headed and extremely inadequate,[a] that it should have picked Henry George for its figurehead, are unavoidable if merely transitory evils. The masses must have the time and the opportunity to evolve; and they will not get that opportunity until they have a movement of their own — no matter what its form, providing it is *their own* movement — in which they are impelled onwards by their own mistakes and learn by bitter experience.

The movement in America is at the same stage as it was at home before 1848; the really intelligent chaps will at first play the same role over there as did the Communist League before 1848 among the working men's associations.[b] Save that in America things will move infinitely faster; for it is completely unprecedented for a movement to achieve such electoral successes after an existence of barely eight months. And what is still lacking, the bourgeois will make good; nowhere else in the world do they behave so outrageously and tyranically

---

[a] See *Der Sozialist*, No. 40, 2 October 1886. - [b] See F. Engels, 'Preface to the 1888 English Edition of the *Manifesto of the Communist Party*'.

as there, and your judges knock Bismarck's imperial pettifoggers into
a cocked hat. When the struggle is conducted by the bourgeois with
weapons such as these, it will rapidly come quickly to a head and, unless we in Europe bestir ourselves, the Americans will soon steal
a march on us. But just now it is doubly necessary to have a few chaps
on our side who are thoroughly versed in theory and in well-tried
tactics and who can also speak and write English, since the Americans, for good historical reasons, lag far behind in all theoretical matters; true, they did not bring with them from Europe any medieval institutions, but instead a mass of medieval traditions — religion, English common (feudal) law, superstition, spiritualism — in short,
every kind of balderdash that was not immediately harmful to business and now comes in very handy for the stultification of the masses.
And if people are available whose clear grasp of theory enables them
to tell the Americans what the consequences of their mistakes are likely to be, and make them see that any movement which does not
constantly bear in mind that the ultimate goal is the destruction of
the wage system, must necessarily go astray and come to nothing,
then much silliness can be avoided and the process be considerably
curtailed. But it must be done in English, the specifically German
character must be sloughed off, and this the gentlemen of the *Sozialist* are hardly qualified to do, while those of the *Volkszeitung* may be
shrewder, but only in regard to *business*.

The American elections this month made a tremendous impact on
Europe. The absence up till now of a labour movement in England,
and more especially in America, has been the great trump card of
radical Republicans everywhere, notably in France. Now these chaps
are utterly dumbfounded — Mr Clemenceau in particular who, on
2 November, witnessed the collapse of all that his policy was based
on. 'Just look at America,' he never tired of saying, 'that's a real republic for you — no poverty and no labour movement!' And it's the
same with the men of Progress [93] and 'democrats' in Germany and
over here — where they are just experiencing an incipient movement
of their own. What has completely stunned these people is the fact
that the movement is so strongly accentuated as a labour movement,
and that it has sprung up so suddenly and with such force.

Over here it was the absence of all competition on the one hand
and the stupidity of the government on the other that enabled the
gentlemen of the SOCIAL DEMOCRATIC FEDERATION [300] to assume a position to which they would never have ventured to aspire 3 months ago.

The hoo-hah that was created about the plan — never seriously contemplated — to form a procession behind the LORD MAYOR's [a] Show on 9 November, and the similar hoo-hah later on, about the Trafalgar Square meeting of 21 November [b] when, despite talk of bringing up the artillery, the government eventually had to back down — all this at long last compelled the gents of the SOCIAL DEMOCRATIC FEDERATION to hold a quite ordinary meeting on the 21st, without any hollow rhodomontade or pseudo-revolutionary demonstrations with their obbligato plebeian accompaniment,— and all of a sudden the philistines began to feel respect for the men who had stirred up so much dust and yet behaved so reputably. [658] And, since no one except the SOCIAL DEMOCRATIC FEDERATION bother about the UNEMPLOYED whose numbers, in these days of chronic stagnation of trade, increase substantially every winter and who suffer extreme want, the SOCIAL DEMOCRATIC FEDERATION can hardly fail to win. In this country we now have the beginnings of a labour movement, AND NO MISTAKE, and if the SOCIAL DEMOCRATIC FEDERATION is the first to reap the reward, this will be due to the cowardice of the Radicals and the stupidity of the SOCIALIST LEAGUE [346] which is bickering with the anarchists, is unable to shake them off and hence has no time to spare for the real live movement that is taking place there under its very nose. How long, for that matter, Hyndman & Co. will continue to act in this relatively rational way remains to be seen. I anticipate that, being in too much of a hurry, they will before long again perpetrate the most colossal blunders, whereupon they'll discover that, in a serious movement, this simply won't do.

In Germany things are getting nicer and nicer — sentences in Leipzig of up to 4 years' *hard labour* for 'insurrection'! [666] They are absolutely determined to provoke a rumpus.

I now have 7 lesser jobs in my desk — Italian and French translations, prefaces, new editions, etc.[c]— and then inexorably on to Volume III.[d]

Your old friend
F. E.

First published in *Briefe und Auszüge aus Briefen von Joh. Phil. Becker, Jos. Dietzgen, Friedrich Engels, Karl Marx u. A. an F. A. Sorge und Andere*, Stuttgart, 1906

Printed according to the original

---

[a] John Staples - [b] 31 November in the original; see also this volume, p. 526. - [c] See this volume, p. 528. - [d] of *Capital*

305

ENGELS TO HERMANN SCHLÜTER [667]

IN HOTTINGEN-ZURICH

[London,] 7 December 1886

Please send me a copy of *The Bakuninists at Work* [668]; the only one I've got was in a bundle with other stuff. The thing is badly crumpled and requires close scrutiny. On Sunday[a] afternoon the soldier[b] turned up here, where his wife had already been for several days—he's very satisfied with his success. [600] Yesterday Paul, the Berliner,[c] also turned up. Since I cannot easily apply myself to any really big jobs while they are here, I shall see if I can't get something or other ready for press for you; however, I would prefer to write my prefaces myself.
Kindest regards.

Yours,

F. E.

First published in: Marx and Engels, *Works*, First Russian Edition, Vol. XXVII, Moscow, 1935

Printed according to the original

Published in English for the first time

306

ENGELS TO HALLIDAY SPARLING

IN LONDON

[London,] 7 December 1886
122 Regent's Park Road, N. W.

Dear Sir,

For your *private* information I beg to say that *at present* there is no English translation published of the work alluded to by you. [669]

---

[a] 5 December - [b] Wilhelm Liebknecht - [c] Paul Singer

I make this information private as I cannot see the use of having such things published in *The Commonweal*.

Yours truly,
F. Engels

[At the bottom of the letter]

H. H. Sparling Esq.

First published in: Marx and Engels, *Works*, Second Russian Edition, Vol. 50, Moscow, 1981

Reproduced from the original

Published in English for the first time

307

ENGELS TO LAURA LAFARGUE

IN PARIS

London, 13 December 1886

My dear Laura,

Well, here we have you at last nailed to a date,[670] and I hope you will make it the 23rd, so as to be able to go a bit about town with Nim before Christmas and look at the Christmas shops. And to cut short any further excuses, I enclose a check for £20.- to enable you to perform your promise.

Also a letter from Tussy, who was yesterday in Williamsport, Pennsylvania, and will have meetings after that in Baltimore, Wilmington and New York — but in New York a whole series from 19th to 23rd, and leave on 25th.[601] Another letter from Edward will be sent tomorrow, I have to make a note or two out of it. Please bring all these letters with you when you come for I have a strong suspicion that they were written with *one* eye to business, for I find that Liebknecht also wrote almost daily his *impressions de voyage* to his wife, not so much for her sake as for that of forming the material basis of a book already contracted for.

Last Wednesday week [a] Mrs Liebknecht arrived here, an extremely German lady, and before 24 hours had passed, she began to unbosom herself to Nim with an eagerness that was almost too much for Nim. The household seems to be a model German one, *Sentimentalität und häuslicher Zwist*,[b] but considerably more of the latter. Nim will tell you more anon. On Sunday afternoon Liebknecht dropped in, more hungry than usual, fortunately there was a boiled leg of mutton to appease his craving. He is quite the old Liebknecht, only Nim who has got the deepest inside in his household mysteries affirms that he is somewhat more of a Philistine. What Tussy says of him is quite correct, his notion of his own importance, capacities and absolute invincibility is astounding; but at the same time there is an undercurrent of a dim apprehension that after all he is not the stupendous man that he would like the people to believe him to be; which undercurrent drives him to be more in want of other people's admiration than he otherwise would be, and in order to obtain that, to manipulate facts considerably in all his tales about himself. But his wife says with truth that if he was not so immensely satisfied with himself, he would never be able to do the work he does. So we must take him as he is and be satisfied with a quiet laugh at much of what he says; he will create much mischief in a small way by his diplomatising ways *pro aris et focis*,[c] but at the decisive moment he will always take the right side. They left on Friday for Leipzig.

Percy is quite well again, he always has these violent attacks, but if once over the first assault, he is soon right again.

The Kautskys are taking a house beyond the Archway — not the Archway Tavern but the real Archway farther on. That is to say, Scheu takes the house for three years, and takes part of it with his daughter, a rather silly girl of about 18 whom he has got over from Hungary; and the Kautskys take the other part. They are beginning to move into it to-day and hope to have done with it by Saturday.

I had a letter last week from old Harney, he sailed 12th October, much too late for his condition of body, and of course arrived rheumatic and gouty all over. But he could not leave England which he adores while he hates America, and if he lives, he says he will come

---

[a] 1 December - [b] sentimentality and household quarrels - [c] for our altars and firesides (Cicero, *De natura deorum*, III, 40, 94)

across again next spring and live and die in England! Poor fellow—
when the Chartist movement broke down he found himself adrift and
the glorious time of free-trade prosperity in England was indeed
enough to drive a fellow to despair. Then he went to Boston, only to
find there, in an exaggerated form and ruling supreme, those very
things and qualities he had hated most in England. And now when
a real movement begins on both sides of the Atlantic amongst the English speaking nations, he is too old, too decrepit, too much an out-
sider, and—too patriotic to follow it. All he has learnt in America is
British chauvinism!

Now Nim comes and brings me the out-of-the-way stamps to affix
to this uncommon heavy letter, while Anni is getting the dinner
things into shape and so I must conclude. Nim sends her love to both
of you. As to Paul you will perhaps after all succeed in bringing him
with you on the 23rd, what in the name of dickens is he going to
mopse in Paris in Christmas week, not even the chambers sitting?

Ever affectionately yours,
F. Engels

First published, in the language of the   Reproduced from the original
original (English), in: F. Engels, P. et L.
Lafargue, *Correspondance*, t. I, Paris, 1956

308

ENGELS TO EMIL ENGELS Jun.

IN ENGELSKIRCHEN

London, 22 December 1886

Dear Emil,

I was very pleased to hear from you again and through you from
your mother[a] and all the others.

As to your request, it occurs to me that it would be considered gross
inconsistency on my part if *I* wished to contribute 150 marks to the
Protestant Institute in Barmen because the aims it pursued were, as

---

[a] Charlotte Engels

a rule, generally worthy. I believe your father-in-law [a] would likewise think it inconsistent were he to make a donation to an avowedly Social Democratic workers' fund on account of its generally worthy aims. But where there's a will there's a way and since in any case it always strikes me as somewhat comical whenever I see myself listed in the books as a shareholder of the Protestant Institute, I hereby present *you* with both the shares to do with as you please. I enclose a note for Hermann [b] who will, I trust, attend to the matter.

I am glad to hear that you are all well and especially that your mother's solicitude for her children and grandchildren is giving her a new lease of life. All of you will indeed miss your father [c] for a long time to come, both in the family and in the business. He was every inch a man and such a one will never be replaced in the family and only with difficulty in the business. However it will be a great help to you young people to step into positions of responsibility early on; unfortunately it was rare enough in Germany in my day, yet it is absolutely essential to the formation of the mind and particularly of the character. So let the elderly gentlemen amuse themselves in Barmen and in summer use Engelskirchen more for recuperation than for business. If you can run the firm on your own, so much the better; it will give you self-confidence.

But now I must close; Schorlemmer will be arriving from Manchester in a few minutes and tomorrow I expect more visitors from Paris [d]; we shall therefore have a full house and that will put paid to my work and also to my correspondence. However I was anxious to settle the matter of the shares beforehand and have used my last free moment for this purpose.

So my particularly fond regards to your mother and to your wife, [e] your boy, [f] Hermanns [g] and Moritz [h] and regards to yourself

From your Uncle
Friedrich

And in particular a very Merry Christmas and prosperous New Year to you all.

First published in *Deutsche Revue*, Jg. 46, Bd. 3, Stuttgart-Leipzig, 1921

Printed according to the original

Published in English for the first time

---

[a] Friedrich Wilhelm Röhrig - [b] Hermann Engels jun.- [c] Emil Engels sen. - [d] Laura and Paul Lafargue - [e] Johanna Klara Engels - [f] Emil Engels - [g] Hermann Engels sen. and his son Hermann- [h] Rudolf Moritz Engels

309

ENGELS TO FLORENCE KELLEY-WISCHNEWETZKY

IN NEW YORK

London, 28 December 1886
122 Regent's Park Road, N. W.

Dear Mrs Wischnewetzky,

Your letter of November 13th never reached me, of which I am very sorry; it would have suited me much better to write a preface *then*, and moreover would have left me more time.[671]

But let me first congratulate you on the happy family event in which you have been the principal actor and add my best wishes for your own health and that of the little one newly arrived.

Of course the appendix[a] is now a little out-of-date, and as I anticipated something of the kind, proposed that it should be written when the book was ready through the press. Now a preface will be much wanted, and I will write you one; but before, I must await the return of the Avelings[601] to have a full report of the state of things in America; and it seems to me that my preface will not be exactly what you desire.

First you seem to me to treat New York a little as the Paris of America, and to overrate the importance, for the country at large, of the local New York movement with its local features. No doubt it has a great importance, but then the North-West with its background of a numerous farming population and its independent movement will hardly accept blindly the George theory.

Secondly the preface of *this* book is hardly the place for a thoroughgoing criticism of that theory, and offers even not the necessary space for it.

Thirdly I should have to study thoroughly Henry George's various writings and speeches[672] (most of which I have not got) so as to render impossible all replies based on subterfuges and side-issues.

My preface will of course turn entirely on the immense stride made by the American working-men in the last ten months, and naturally

---

[a] F. Engels, 'Appendix to the American Edition of *The Condition of the Working Class in England*'.

also touch Henry George and his land scheme. But it cannot pretend to deal extensively with it. Nor do I think the time for that has come. It is far more important that the movement should spread, proceed harmoniously, take root and embrace as much as possible the whole American proletariat, than that it should start and proceed, from the beginning, on theoretically perfectly correct lines. There is no better road to theoretical clearness of comprehension than to learn by one's own mistakes, '*durch Schaden klug werden*'. And for a whole large class, there is no other road, especially for a nation so eminently practical and so contemptuous of theory as the Americans. The great thing is to get the working-class to move *as a class*; that once obtained, they will soon find the right direction, and all who resist, Henry George or Powderly, will be left out in the cold with small sects of their own. Therefore I think also the Knights of Labor [609] a most important factor in the movement which ought not to be pooh-poohed from without but to be revolutionised from within, and I consider that many of the Germans there have made a grievous mistake when they tried, in the face of a mighty and glorious movement not of their creation, to make of their imported and not always understood theory a kind of *alleinseligmachendes Dogma*,[a] and to keep aloof from any movement which did not accept that dogma. Our theory is not a dogma but the exposition of a process of evolution, and that process involves successive phases. To expect that the Americans will start with the full consciousness of the theory worked out in older industrial countries is to expect the impossible. What the Germans ought to do is to act up to their own theory—if they understand it, as we did in 1845 and 1848,—to go in for any real general working-class movement, accept its *faktische*[b] starting point as such, and work it gradually up to the theoretical level by pointing out how every mistake made, every reverse suffered, was a necessary consequence of mistaken theoretical views in the original programme: they ought, in the words of the *Kommunistischen Manifest*: '*in der Gegenwart der Bewegung die Zukunft der Bewegung zu repräsentieren*'.[c][673] But above all give the movement time to consolidate, do not make the inevitable confusion of the first start, worse confounded by forcing down people's throats things which, at present, they cannot properly understand, but which they will soon learn. A million or two of working-men's votes next November for

---

[a] the only saving dogma - [b] actual - [c] 'in the movement of the present to represent the future of the movement'.

a bona fide working-men's party is worth infinitely more at present than a hundred thousand votes for a doctrinally perfect platform. The very first attempt — soon to be made if the movement progresses — to consolidate the moving masses on a national basis — will bring them all face to face, Georgites, Knights of Labor, Trade-Unionists and all; and if our German friends by that time have learnt enough of the language of the country to go in for a discussion, then will be the time for them to criticise the views of the others and thus, by showing up the inconsistencies of the various standpoints, to bring them gradually to understand their own actual position, the position made for them by the correlation of capital and wage labour. But anything that might delay or prevent that national consolidation of the working-men's party — on no matter what platform — I should consider a great mistake, and therefore I do not think the time has arrived to speak out fully and exhaustively either with regard to Henry George or the Knights of Labor.

I did not wire 'yes' because I could not exactly make out what you might make out that 'yes' to mean.

As to the title: *I* cannot omit the 1844, because the omission would give an entirely false idea of what the reader has to expect. And as I, by the preface and appendix, take a certain responsibility, I cannot consent to its being left out. You may add: 'With preface and appendix by the Author', if you think proper.

The proofs I return corrected by same mail.

Yours very faithfully,

F. Engels

First published abridged, in the language of the original (English), in *Briefe und Auszüge aus Briefen von Joh. Phil. Becker, Jos. Dietzgen, Friedrich Engels, Karl Marx u. A. an F. A. Sorge und Andere*, Stuttgart, 1906

Reproduced from the original

Published in English in full for the first time

310

ENGELS TO ELEANOR MARX-AVELING [674]

[IN LONDON]

[London,] 25 March 1886
122 Regent's Park Road, N. W.

My dear Tussy,

You know I would do anything in my forces to please our friend Donkin, but I am afraid I cannot do so in this case.

The work I have had in hand for the last few years is so urgent and of such dimensions [675] that I have had to give up, once for all, attending meetings and societies and taking part in discussions or preparing for such. If I am to accomplish my work, I cannot break through this rule, and the less so, as having given way once, I could not plead the same reason again for refusing in other cases.

Moreover the subject I am asked to discuss, has been lost sights of by me for more than a year, [676] and I should therefore be compelled to read it up again and to look at whatever has been published since with respect to it, which would take me more than a week to be exclusively devoted to that purpose, and that week, I am sorry to say, I cannot spare.

And therefore, highly flattered as I feel by the invitation, I very much regret that circumstances will not allow me to avail myself of it.

Yours affectionately,
F. Engels

Kindest regards to Dr Donkin!

First published in *Die Wahrheit*, Nr. 39, 1./2. Oktober 1988

Reproduced from the original

Published in English for the first time

APPENDIX

1

ELEANOR MARX-AVELING
TO HORATIO BRYAN DONKIN [677]

IN LONDON

[London,] 8 February 1886
35 Great Russell St., W. C.

My dear Dr Donkin,

I have heard of the Club — and I am much obliged to Mr Pearson
for asking me to join it.[678] But I cannot — for these reasons. First,
I think many members of the Club would decidedly object to my belonging to it. You see, it is a very different matter to advocate certain
things, in theory, and to have the courage to put one's theory into
practice. Probably, many of the good ladies in the Club would be
much shocked at the idea of my becoming a member of it, and
I should only be giving Mr Pearson trouble if I accepted his friendly
suggestion. But there is also another reason. I have, as it is, hardly
a moment of time for real study, a half the work I *ought* to do I don't
do. And apart from this, any time not taken up in trying to earn
bread (and it is *so* difficult for a woman to do like that!) I feel I must
give to what seems to me the highest and most important work
I could do — i. e. the propaganda of Socialism.

It would not be right to join this Club well knowing that I could
not undertake to 'wilt progress' for it, or attend its meetings regularly,
or even take such an interest in it as a member ought to take. If, however, mere 'visitors' are admitted, and no one objects to me, I shall be
very glad to go to any meeting and take part in any discussion on
a question of which I know something.[679] — Please thank Mr Pear-

son very much for asking me. I have often wished to meet him, but have always, somehow, missed doing it. If I went to the Club on an evening, I should be glad if it could be when you are there!

Yours very sincerely,

Eleanor Marx-Aveling

First published in *Die Wahrheit*, Nr. 39, 1./2. Oktober 1988

Reproduced from the original

Published in English for the first time

NOTES
AND
INDEXES

NOTES

[1] This letter was first published in English in an abridged form in: K. Marx and F. Engels, *Letters on 'Capital'*, New Park Publications, London, 1983.— 3, 6, 87, 92, 125, 137, 186, 188, 193, 261, 267, 306, 318

[2] Engels was busy sorting out Marx's library and archives. Apart from extensive economic manuscripts (including the manuscripts of the second and third books of *Capital*; see Note 4), he found a large number of diverse conspectuses, excerpts, letters and documents on the working-class movement (see notes 57, 72, 174). It took Engels until late March 1884 to put the archives in order, whereupon he moved all the manuscripts which had survived and the correspondence to his own house. He was faced with tasks of enormous dimensions, namely preparing for the press Marx's unfinished works, notably volumes II and III of *Capital*.— 3, 6, 33

[3] On 31 March 1883 Pyotr Lavrov informed Engels from Paris that he was sending him a postal order which he had received from the students of Technological Institute and Russian women students with the request that it be used to buy a wreath to be laid on Marx's grave. Engels had an announcement printed in *Der Sozialdemokrat* of 3 May 1883 to the effect that the request had been carried out (see F. Engels, 'On the Death of Karl Marx', present edition, Vol. 24, p. 473).— 3

[4] Engels is referring to the manuscripts of the second and third books of *Capital*, written by Marx. As he studied Marx's manuscripts, Engels was able to establish within certain limits the time span in which they must have been written (see Engels' prefaces to volumes II and III of *Capital*, present edition, vols 36 and 37). By the spring of 1884 Engels became convinced of the need to change Marx's original plan according to which the second volume of *Capital* was to consist of two books and decided to publish the manuscripts of these books as volumes II and III of *Capital* (see this volume, pp. 121, 122). When preparing Volume II for the press, Engels used the later versions of the drafts (see Note 17) which came to his notice afterwards (see Engels' letters to Johann Philipp Becker of 22 May, to Friedrich Adolph Sorge of 29 June and to Karl Kautsky of 18 September 1883).

The second volume of *Capital*, edited by Engels, appeared in 1885, and the third in 1894.— 3, 6, 26, 29, 88, 121, 348, 522

5 The idea of writing a study of dialectics came to Marx in late 1857 or early 1858 when Ferdinand Freiligrath gave him — most probably after 22 October 1857 — an incomplete set of Hegel's *Works*. On 16 January 1858, Marx wrote to Engels: 'If ever the time comes when such work is again possible, I should very much like to write 2 or 3 sheets making accessible to the common reader the *rational* aspect of the method which Hegel not only discovered but also mystified' (see present edition, Vol. 40, p. 249). Marx was going to call the study 'Dialectic' (see his letter to Joseph Dietzgen of 9 May 1868, present edition, Vol. 43, p. 31), but this plan failed to materialise.— 3

6 On 24 February 1883 Hermann Lopatin fled from exile in Vologda to Paris, whence he proceeded to London in September 1883.— 4

7 Engels is referring to the sister of Paul Lafargue's mother. It is clear from Laura's letter to Engels of 4 May 1883 that Lafargue's mother lived together with her sister and the latter's children in Bordeaux.— 4

8 The family of Jenny, Marx's eldest daughter who died in January 1883 — her husband Charles Longuet and their four children — lived in Argenteuil near Paris.— 4

9 Paul Lafargue, Jules Guesde and Jean Dormoy were tried by a jury in Moulins in late April 1883 for their actions in the province of Montluçon and elsewhere in the autumn of 1882; the charges brought against them were conspiracy and incitement to civil war. The court sentenced each of them to six months' imprisonment as well as imposing fines. Guesde and Lafargue served their sentences in Ste Pélagie prison, Paris, from 21 May to 21 November 1883 (see Note 402).— 5, 20, 28, 30, 41, 46, 48, 59, 61, 64, 115

10 No information is available on the French edition of the *Manifesto* mentioned by Engels. In all probability it never materialised.— 5

11 In his letter of 17 March 1883, Ferdinand Domela Nieuwenhuis, on behalf of the Dutch Socialist Workers' Party, asked Engels to 'pass on our homage and grateful acknowledgement, to the Marx family and to all those who join us in mourning at the grave of the master'. Nieuwenhuis also informed Engels that he planned to translate his work *Socialism: Utopian and Scientific* into Dutch, which he actually did in 1886. Nieuwenhuis further enquired about Engels' plan with regard to Volume II of Marx's *Capital*, further study of the English labour movement after 1845 and the reissue of Engels' *The Condition of the Working-Class in England*.— 6

12 Engels is referring to the *Social-Democratic Association of the Netherlands* which was formed in 1881 and united in a single party the Social-Democratic associations of Amsterdam, The Hague, Haarlem and Rotterdam. The associations had been formed in 1878-81 with the active involvement of former members of the Dutch section of the First International. Nieuwenhuis was among the founders of the new organisation.— 6

13 The London monthly *The Republican* carried a short obituary entitled 'Karl Marx' in its issue of April 1883 containing a reference to the November issue of 1882 which had published a biography and photo of Marx.— 7

14 In his letter of reply to Engels of 16 April 1883, Eduard Bernstein confirmed that the wood block of Marx's portrait was in the possession of the editorial board of *Der Sozialdemokrat*.— 7

15 The reference is to the third congress of the Socialist Workers' Party of Germany which was held illegally in Copenhagen from 29 March to 2 April 1883, with 60 delegates taking part. The congress was to work out the *German Social Democrats'* political line on the social reforms being carried out by the bourgeois government, to decide on the party's tactics and the position to be taken by *Der Sozialdemokrat*, its printed organ, given the Anti-Socialist Law in Germany (see Note 37). The congress unanimously called on the party to expose the demagogy of Bismarck's domestic policy, endorsed the stance of the main printed organ and the general line of conduct of the parliamentary group (see Note 49). It further made it incumbent on every party member, including the Social-Democratic representatives in the Reichstag, to observe party discipline and help carry out party decisions (see also Note 16).— 7, 14, 21

16 Engels is probably referring to the first report on the Copenhagen Congress of the Socialist Workers' Party of Germany carried by *Der Sozialdemokrat* of 12 April 1883. ('Kongreß der deutschen Sozialdemokratie. Abgehalten in Kopenhagen vom 29. März bis 2. April 1883'.) Subsequent reports were printed by the newspaper on 19 and 26 April.— 7

17 Eight of Marx's draft manuscripts for Volume II (Book II, as he originally intended) of *Capital* have survived. The longest of them, consisting of three lengthy chapters, is Manuscript I. It was completed in the spring of 1865, and Engels subsequently turned it into parts of Volume II. Since he did not regard the said manuscript as the final version of Book II, as he was preparing Volume I of *Capital* for the press Marx wrote Manuscript III (in which he gave a conspectus of works apparently intended for quotation in Volume II) and Manuscript IV, which Engels later described as 'an elaboration, ready for the press, of Part I and the first chapters of Part II of Book II' (see present edition, Vol. 36, Preface). In 1868-70 Marx wrote a completely new version of the second book, i. e. Manuscript II. The reason why manuscripts III and IV appeared earlier than Manuscript II is that, when he was numbering the drafts of Volume II in the late seventies, Marx started with the two complete versions and followed them with the outlines of individual parts. In the latter half of the 1870s Marx resumed work on Book II, having realised that it was not complete; although he had examined the simple reproduction of capital in great detail in Manuscript II, he had not analysed its extended reproduction. Manuscripts V, VI and VII appeared between April 1877 and July 1878 and were an attempt to turn the text into a suitable form for printing. The final version of the second book of *Capital* was Manuscript VIII on which Marx seems to have worked between the autumn of 1879 and early 1880. Later it was used in full by Engels when preparing Part III of Volume II.— 8, 14, 18, 26, 33, 43, 53, 58, 88, 154, 160, 244

18 This letter is the reply to the letter by the editor of *The Nineteenth Century*, Thomas James Knowles, of 7 April 1883 in which the latter requested Engels to send him a short résumé in English of Volume I of Marx's *Capital* for an article his journal was planning to publish on the subject.— 8

[19] This letter was written by Engels in reply to that by Philipp Van Patten of 2 April 1883. In it the latter informed Engels that at a meeting dedicated to Marx's memory Johann Most' and his supporters had claimed Most had been on intimate terms with Marx, that he had helped to popularise *Capital* in Germany and his propaganda work had enjoyed Marx's support. Engels' letter and an excerpt from that by Van Patten were published in German in Engels' article 'On the Death of Karl Marx' carried by *Der Sozialdemokrat*, No. 21 of 17 May 1883 (see present edition, Vol. 24). Engels made several changes in the German text of his letter the most important of which are given in the footnotes.

This letter was first published in English in an abridged form in: K. Marx and F. Engels, *Correspondence. 1846-1895*, Martin Lawrence, London, 1934, and in full in: K. Marx and F. Engels, *Letters to Americans. 1848-1895. A Selection*, International Publishers, New York, 1953.— 9

[20] The reference is to the disruptive activities in the International of Mikhail Bakunin and his supporters. In the autumn of 1868 in Geneva they founded the International Alliance of Socialist Democracy, an organisation with its own programme and rules that contradicted those of the International (see present edition, Vol. 21, pp. 207-11).

Following the refusal by the General Council of the International Working Men's Association to admit the Alliance to the International, in 1869 Bakunin, in violation of the promise he had given to disband his organisation, secretly introduced the Alliance into the International with the aim of seizing its leadership. Posing as sections of the International, sections of the Alliance publicised their anarchist programme, claiming it was the programme of the International. In November 1871, the Bakuninists' congress in Sonvillier, Switzerland, called for a revision of the International's Rules, notably the articles on the importance of the political struggle by the working class and its party.— 10, 108

[21] At the Hague Congress of the First International (2-7 September 1872) a special commission was formed to investigate the secret activities of the Alliance. On the strength of the materials it studied, the commission concluded that the activities of the Alliance were incompatible with membership in the International, as were the activities of the leaders of the former, Bakunin and Guillaume. Having generally accepted the commission's proposals, the Hague Congress decided to publicise the documents at the commission's disposal concerning the Alliance and expelled Bakunin and Guillaume from the International.— 10

[22] In his reply of 18 April 1883 to Engels' letter of 17 April (see this volume, pp. 8-9), Thomas James Knowles wrote that he was intending to include in the journal *The Nineteenth Century* the English translation of Engels' *Synopsis of Volume One of 'Capital' by Karl Marx* (see present edition, Vol. 20, pp. 263-308) complete with the author's name. Knowles intended to publish in the same issue an article about Marx written by Maltman Barry, who had been a member of the International.— 12

[23] In mid-November 1850 Engels joined the Manchester branch of the German textiles firm Ermen & Engels. The German side of the enterprise was run by Fr. Engels (Senior) with the assistance of Anthony Ermen. The firm's office was in Barmen. Following the death of his father in 1860, Engels received £ 10,000 from his brothers as compensation for renouncing his rights to the factory in Engelskirchen, which bolstered his financial and legal status in the Manchester firm.

Engels was a co-owner of the Manchester firm of Ermen & Engels for five years between June 1864 and June 1869. At the end of this period he left the firm to concentrate on party, academic and journalistic work.— 12

²⁴ Engels wrote this letter on a postcard. The address, also in his hand, reads: Herrn Ed. Bernstein, 137, alte Landstraße, *Riesbach-Zürich*, Switzerland.— 12, 72

²⁵ The reference is to Engels' *Socialism: Utopian and Scientific* (see present edition, Vol. 24) which in 1883 was published in three German editions running to a total of 10,000 copies. The work was composed of three revised chapters by Engels from his work *Herr Eugen Dühring's Revolution in Science (Anti-Dühring)* (see present edition, Vol. 25).— 12, 15, 37, 60

²⁶ The article by Engels which is referred to in this letter was published in *Der Sozial-demokrat*, Nos. 19 and 21, 3 and 17 May 1883, under the heading 'On the Death of Karl Marx' (see present edition, Vol. 24). It was written in reply to the articles about Marx and Engels by Brousse, a Possibilist leader (see Note 237), which had been carried by *Le Prolétaire*, Nos. 234 and 237, 24 March and 14 April 1883.— 12

²⁷ This letter was first published in English in: K. Marx and F. Engels, *Letters to Americans. 1848-1895. A Selection*, International Publishers, New York, 1953.— 13, 382, 419

²⁸ The *New Yorker Volkszeitung*, No. 68, 20 March 1883 reported that, on 19 March, after a meeting of New York workers in memory of Marx, Engels had been sent the following telegram: 'The proletariat of New York, assembled at the Cooper Institute, honours the memory of its immortal Karl Marx and calls on its brothers: Workers of all countries, unite!' — 14

²⁹ The trip was planned for the spring of 1884 with the aim of collecting funds from the workers to finance the election campaign for the Reichstag in the autumn of that year. However, Wilhelm Liebknecht was not able to go to the United States until the autumn of 1886, and with a different aim in mind (see Note 600).— 14, 114

³⁰ Engels attached a great deal of importance to publicising Marx's theoretical and practical revolutionary activity. With this aim in mind, he wrote three biographies of Marx at different times—in 1869, 1877 and 1892—and for different publications (see present edition, Vol. 21, pp. 59-64, Vol. 24, pp. 183-95 and Vol. 27, pp. 332-43). The new biography which Engels planned, taking account of the extensive correspondence and other materials which had survived, and to which he refers in this letter, was not written.— 14, 17, 26, 40, 79

³¹ On 19 March 1883 Friedrich Adolph Sorge informed Engels that Henry George's propaganda in America was leading the labour movement astray and suggested the publication of the letter Marx had written to him on 20 June 1881 (see present edition, Vol. 46). This letter contained a critique of Henry George's book *Progress and Poverty* which had been published in New York in 1880. However, Engels considered that it would be rather premature to publish Marx's letter in the American press (see this volume, p. 42, and Engels' letter to Sorge of 18 June 1887, present edition, Vol. 48). Engels gave a critical exposé of George's views of the nationalisation of land in the Preface to the American edition of his book *The Condition of the Working-Class in England* (see present edition, Vol. 26, pp. 437-39).— 14, 114

³² When he learned that Engels' pamphlet *Socialism: Utopian and Scientific* (present edition, Vol. 24; see also Note 25) was about to appear, Sorge wrote on 19 March 1883 that he could request Otto Weydemeyer to translate it into English and have it published in the United States. The publication failed to materialise.— 15

³³ Eduard Bernstein was returning to Switzerland from Copenhagen where he had been a delegate to the congress of the Socialist Workers' Party of Germany (see Note 15).— 15

³⁴ Following the introduction of a local state of siege in Leipzig in 1881 (see Note 67), Wilhelm Liebknecht, August Bebel and other German socialists had been forced to leave the city. They settled in the village of Borsdorf near Leipzig.— 16, 19, 20, 47, 52, 80, 83, 147, 258, 377, 380, 417, 445, 495

³⁵ Engels was unable to carry out these plans due to the enormous demands made on him by the preparation for the press of volumes I and II of *Capital* and the publication of translations of Marx's and his own works. At the same time, he was working on his book *The Origin of the Family, Private Property and the State* (see Note 174).— 17

³⁶ On 17 March 1883, August Bebel informed Engels that at the forthcoming congress of the Socialist Workers' Party of Germany in Copenhagen (see Note 15) he intended to put up for discussion the question of the party erecting a monument to Marx. It seems that the stance taken by Marx's family, about which Engels informed Bebel in this letter, long remained an obstacle to the erection of a monument in Highgate Cemetery where Marx was buried. In 1954 the Marx grave was moved to a better place in the cemetery. Lawrence Bradshaw was commissioned by the Communist Party of Great Britain to sculpt a bronze head of Marx, and the monument which incorporated it was unveiled in 1956 by Harry Pollit, then General Secretary of the British Communist Party.— 17

³⁷ The *Exceptional Law Against the Socialists* (Gesetz gegen die gemeingefährlichen Bestrebungen der Sozialdemokratie — the Law against the Harmful and Dangerous Aspirations of Social Democracy) was introduced by the Bismarck government, supported by the majority in the Reichstag, on 21 October 1878 to counter the socialist and workers' movement. This law, better known as the Anti-Socialist Law, made the Social-Democratic Party of Germany illegal, banned all party and mass workers' organisations, and the socialist and workers' press; on the basis of this law socialist literature was confiscated and Social Democrats subjected to reprisals. However, during its operation the Social-Democratic Party, assisted by Marx and Engels, uprooted both reformist and anarchist elements and managed to substantially strengthen and widen its influence among the people by skilfully combining illegal and legal methods of work. Under pressure from the mass workers' movement, the Anti-Socialist Law was abrogated on 1 October 1890. For Engels' assessment of this law, see his article 'Bismarck and the German Working Men's Party' (present edition, Vol. 24, pp. 407-09).— 17, 21, 26, 32, 50, 93, 100, 114, 124, 125, 129, 132, 145, 147, 164, 187, 199, 213, 216, 220, 242, 268, 271, 275, 285, 290, 295, 300, 303, 305, 307, 313, 464, 527

³⁸ The materials used by the prosecution in the trial of Wilhelm Liebknecht, August Bebel and Adolf Hepner for high treason in Leipzig in March 1872 included the

Manifesto of the Communist Party by Marx and Engels. It was carried by the book *Leipziger Hochverrathsprozess. Ausführlicher Bericht über die Verhandlungen des Schwurgerichts zu Leipzig in dem Prozeß gegen Liebknecht, Bebel und Hepner wegen Vorbereitung zum Hochverrath vom 11-26. März 1872*, Leipzig, 1872, pp. 97-119.— 18

[39] The letter mentioned has not been found.— 18, 23, 62, 80, 108, 124, 147, 201, 204, 210, 211, 212, 249, 257, 293, 353, 437, 524

[40] The reference is to Engels' *The Condition of the Working-Class in England. From Personal Observation and Authentic Sources* (see present edition, Vol. 4) which was put out in early 1845 by Otto Wigand's publishing house in Leipzig. In 1872-73 Engels discussed with Liebknecht the plan for a second edition of his book since the latter was planning to publish it in a socio-political literature series with the participation of the editorial board of *Der Volksstaat* (see present edition, Vol. 44, pp. 375, 477). It is clear from the letters which Wilhelm Liebknecht and Adolf Hepner wrote to Engels in early 1873 that they helped to sort out Engels' legal relations with the Leipzig publishing house. However, this matter was not clarified for the next 12 years (see Engels' letter of 19 January 1885 to August Bebel, this volume, p. 253). The second authorised edition of *The Condition of the Working-Class in England* was not published until 1892 by Dietz.— 19, 248, 251, 253, 263

[41] A short quote from this letter was first published in English in: R. H. Dominick III, *Wilhelm Liebknecht and the Founding of the German Social Democratic Party*, The University of North Carolina Press, Chapel Hill, 1982.— 20

[42] On 6 June 1879 Wilhelm Bracke wrote to Engels, 'I admire Bebel; he is the only one among us with the skills for life in parliament.'— 20

[43] August Bebel failed to obtain election to the Reichstag at the 1881 poll. In April 1883 Social Democrats in Hamburg nominated Bebel as a candidate at the additional elections being held then. On 2 May 1883 Bebel wrote to Engels that, given the relatively poor effect of campaigning and particularly parliamentary work against the background of the Anti-Socialist Law, he had requested the voters in Hamburg not to nominate him as a candidate. However, this letter did not arrive until after he had been elected to the Reichstag on 29 June.— 20

[44] The *half-and-halfs* — representatives of the Right wing of the Socialist Workers' Party of Germany grouped at that time around Wilhelm Blos and Bruno Geiser. The decision of the Copenhagen Congress (see Note 15) of Social-Democratic candidates nominated for the elections to the Reichstag was directed against them. It stated that the candidates should fully endorse the party programme, observe party discipline and help implement party decisions (see *Der Sozialdemokrat*, No. 17, 19 April 1883).— 21

[45] When the question of the merger of the Social-Democratic Workers' Party (Eisenachers) and the Lassallean General Association of German Workers was being discussed in the early 1870s, Marx and Engels considered this step to be premature. They believed that joint political activity 'against the common foe' should precede the establishment of a united party and the elaboration of its programme (see K. Marx, *Critique of the Gotha Programme*, F. Engels to A. Bebel, 18-28 March 1875, present edition, Vol. 24, p. 78). At the Gotha Unity Congress (22-27 May 1875) the Lassallean Wilhelm Hasenclever was elected a co-chairman of the party Executive Committee, and in June 1875 Wilhelm Hasselmann joined the board of the party-

owned national German co-operative printing office in Berlin which had been formed by decision of the Congress.— 21

[46] On 2 May 1883, Bebel wrote to Engels that 'Liebknecht, instead of showing the toughness [against Right-wing and the half-and-half members of the Socialist Workers' Party of Germany] he ought, is doing his utmost to blur and hush up the conflicts. He has the half-and-halfs for protection.'
On the *half-and-halfs*, see Note 44.— 21

[47] The reference is to Friedrich Wilhelm Fritzsche's and Louis Viereck's journey around the USA from February to May 1881 on an assignment for the Socialist Workers' Party of Germany. The purpose of the journey was to engage in propaganda work and collect money for the election campaign to the Reichstag. The elections were due to take place that autumn. On Wilhelm Liebknecht's and August Bebel's trip to the USA planned for 1884, see Note 29.— 22, 80

[48] In the latter half of April and early May 1883 the Reichstag discussed a bill on workers' health insurance and one providing for changes in trade regulations; the two bills were part of Bismarck's so-called social reform (see Note 312). On 2 May 1883 Bebel informed Engels that some of the Social-Democratic deputies — including Moritz Rittingshausen and Max Kayser — had intended to vote in favour of these bills. However, they had submitted to party discipline and voted against them along with the remainder of the Social-Democratic group in the Reichstag on 31 May and 2 June 1883, respectively.— 22

[49] The reference is to the Social-Democratic group in the Reichstag which in 1880 was officially recognised as the party centre at the illegal congress in Wyden, Switzerland, against the background of the Anti-Socialist Law (see Note 37). Prior to that the party centre was in fact the Relief Committee for the repressed Social Democrats set up in 1878.— 22, 145, 381

[50] Wilhelm Blos was expelled from Hamburg in late 1880 in connection with the introduction of a so-called local state of siege (see Note 67) in some places in Germany. His letter to Engels from Bremen of 4 February 1881 showed that he was disturbed at the reaction which had ensued and was in a liquidationist mood, which was manifested in particular by his proposal to dissolve the Socialist Workers' Party of Germany.— 23

[51] On 2 May 1883 Bebel wrote to Engels that symptoms were apparent in various branches of the German economy which suggested the approach of a crisis.— 23

[52] This letter by Engels is his reply to the Italian economist Achille Loria whose article 'Karl Marx' had been carried by the journal *Nuova antologia di scienze, lettere ed arti*, ser. 2, Vol. 38, fas. 7, Rome, 1883, pp. 509-42. Engels' letter was published in German by *Der Sozialdemokrat*, No. 21, 17 May 1883 in the article 'On the Death of Karl Marx' (see present edition, Vol. 24).
For a critique of Loria's article, see also Engels' Preface to Volume III of *Capital* (present edition, Vol. 37).— 24

[53] Engels is referring to Loria's quotation in his article 'Karl Marx' of the expression Alphonse de Lamartine used with regard to Proudhon in his work *Histoire de la révolution de 1848*, Brussels, 1849, Vol. 1, Book VII, Ch. 5.— 24

[54] The *armchair socialists* — representatives of a trend in German bourgeois political economy which emerged in the last third of the 19th century in response to the growth of the workers' movement and the spread within it of the ideas of scientific socialism. They preached bourgeois reformism at universities, passing it off as socialism. They alleged that the state, specifically the German Empire, was above all classes and could help achieve improvements in the condition of the working class by way of social reforms.— 24, 138, 184, 226, 348, 385, 390, 417

[55] A fragment from this letter was first published in English in: K. Marx and F. Engels, *Correspondence. 1846-1895*, Martin Lawrence, London, 1934.— 25, 98

[56] The idea of translating *Capital* into English occurred to Marx as early as 1865, when he was working on the manuscript (see Marx's letter to Engels of 31 July 1865, present edition, Vol. 42). The British journalist and member of the International's General Council, Peter Fox, was to help Marx find a publisher. However, this matter was not settled due to Fox's death in 1869. The English translation of the first volume of *Capital*, edited by Engels, did not appear until after Marx's death, in January 1887, and was published by Swan Sonnenschein, Lowrey & Co., London. The translation was done by Samuel Moore and Edward Aveling between mid-1883 and March 1886. Eleanor Marx-Aveling took part in the preparatory work for the edition (see also this volume, pp. 33 and 127-28).— 29, 31, 33, 52, 83, 122, 124, 130, 133, 143, 153, 202, 245, 261, 291, 306, 313, 348, 400, 401, 404, 416, 419, 421, 423, 426, 434, 436, 447, 449-50, 453, 456, 460-63, 468, 471, 474, 480, 482, 493-94, 506, 509, 522, 527-28

[57] Engels is referring to the extracts from statistical reports and specialised studies of the various forms of land ownership and the history of the village commune in Russia which Marx wrote down in the 1870s. He intended to use this material for the section on ground rent in Book III of *Capital*. However, this plan did not materialise (see Engels' Preface to Volume III of *Capital*, present edition, Vol. 37).— 29, 88

[58] The reference is to Marx's economic manuscripts: 1) *Outlines of the Critique of Political Economy (Rough Draft of 1857-58)*, and 2) the Manuscripts of 1861-63, which Marx entitled *A Contribution to the Critique of Political Economy* (see present edition, Vols. 28-29 and 30-34).— 29

[59] The first volume of *Capital* was translated into French in full by Joseph Roy and appeared in Paris in 1872-75 as individual instalments which were then put together to form a book. Marx gave an assessment of the translation and the work which had been done in connection with it in the Preface and Afterword to the French edition (see present edition, Vol. 35) and also in his letter to Nikolai Danielson of 28 May 1872 (present edition, Vol. 44). The changes and additions which Engels made to the third German edition of Volume I of *Capital* (1883) on the basis of the French edition were pointed out by him in the Preface to the said edition (see present edition, Vol. 35).— 29, 33, 41, 42, 385

[60] The reference is to Marx's and Engels' joint work on the manuscript of *The German Ideology* and to Engels' work *The True Socialists* (see present edition, Vol. 5) between 1845 and 1847. Not long before his death Engels dictated to Eduard Bernstein a list

of manuscripts from his own and Marx's literary legacy and of other materials stored in his archives. The list contained the following note, '... manuscript of *The German Ideology*' ('Stirner, 1845/46, Moor and I', 'Feuerbach and Bauer, 1846/47, Moor and I', '*True Socialism*, 1847, Moor and I').— 31

⁶¹ An excerpt from this letter was first published in English in: K. Marx, F. Engels, *On Literature and Art*, Progress Publishers, Moscow, 1976.— 32, 90, 159, 498

⁶² The surviving page of the draft manuscript of chapter two of the *Manifesto of the Communist Party* is reproduced in the present edition, Vol. 6, p. 579.— 34

⁶³ On 7 June *Der Sozialdemokrat*, No. 24 carried a biographical outline of Georg Weerth written by Engels and accompanied by Weerth's poem 'Song of the Apprentices' (see present edition, Vol. 26, pp. 108-11).

Weerth's poem referred to in this letter, namely 'Die rheinischen Weinbauern', was published in *Der Sozialdemokrat*, No. 29, 12 July 1883.— 34

⁶⁴ Following the assassination of Alexander II by members of the Narodnaya Volya (People's Will) group on 1 March 1881, liberal reforms were expected in Russia; however, in a manifesto published on 29 April 1881 Alexander III stated that he intended to strengthen autocratic rule.

When King Frederick William IV of Prussia ascended the throne in 1840 the Prussian liberal bourgeoisie had hoped he would carry out the constitutional reforms promised by his father, Frederick William III. However, these hopes proved to be unfounded, and the judicial persecution of liberal bourgeois writers and officials was begun as early as 1841.— 34

⁶⁵ In the 1870s and 1880s the French government pursued an active colonialist policy: in 1876 Franco-British financial control had been established in Egypt, and interference in the country's internal affairs continued until 1882, in 1881-83 a French protectorate was established in Tunisia. In 1882 came the provocation of an armed conflict in Madagascar and the beginning of a colonial war in North Vietnam (Tongking) which grew to become a war with China and led to the setting up of a French protectorate in Vietnam in June 1884.— 34, 57

⁶⁶ Here Engels quotes a thesis from the Programme of the Socialist Workers' Party of Germany adopted at the Gotha Congress in 1875 (see Note 45). It read, 'The emancipation of labour must be the work of the working class, in relation to which all other classes *are only one reactionary mass*.' For comment of this thesis see Marx's *Critique of the Gotha Programme* (present edition, Vol. 24, p. 88).— 35

⁶⁷ The reference is to the '*local (lesser) state of siege*' envisaged by paragraph 28 of the Anti-Socialist Law (see Note 37); in certain districts and places, usually centres of the labour movement, a state of siege was introduced, as a rule, for a year. During this period meetings were allowed only with police permission, the distribution of printed material in public places was prohibited and persons considered politically unreliable were expelled from the places concerned. However, the implementation of these measures led to a growth in the influence of the Socialist Workers' Party and increased activity on the part of the workers' and Social-Democratic movement in parts of Germany that were well away from its traditional centres.— 35, 81, 98

⁶⁸ Engels is referring to the English Revolution in the 17th century and the French Revolution of 1789. Between 1642 and 1646 England witnessed its first civil war

which ended in the defeat of the monarchy and the victory of Parliament relying on the support of the big, middle and petty bourgeoisie and the new nobility.

The years 1789 to 1793 cover the three periods of the French revolution when power was transferred from the hands of the big bourgeoisie and the liberal nobility (Feuillants) to the commercial, industrial and landowning bourgeoisie (Girondists) and finally to the Jacobins who expressed the interests of the revolutionary-democratic petty bourgeoisie that had allied themselves with the peasantry and the lower urban strata.— 35

⁶⁹ Engels is referring to Volume II of *The German Ideology* (present edition, Vol. 5; see also Note 60).— 37, 38

⁷⁰ On 12 June 1883 Pasquale Martignetti wrote to tell Engels that he had read his work *Socialism: Utopian and Scientific* and intended to publicise it in Italy. With this in mind, Martignetti made an Italian translation from the French one by Paul Lafargue and sent it to Engels for the latter to look through. Apart from minor insertions, Engels made major additions to the text which had not featured in the French version.— 37

⁷¹ On 20 June 1883 Laura Lafargue wrote to Engels reminding him that, during her stay with Marx at the Swiss spa town of Vevey in August-September 1882 he had informed her of his plans for future work and promised to give her all the documents and papers she required to write a history of the International Working Men's Association. He further requested her to start work on an English translation of the first volume of *Capital*.— 39

⁷² As he was sorting through Marx's literary legacy, Engels found a number of works relating to Marx's preoccupation with mathematics. Marx's interest in mathematics had emerged in the early 1850s and had grown as he worked on *Capital* (see Marx's letter to Engels of 11 January 1858, present edition, Vol. 40). The first signs of Marx's mathematical endeavours date back to 1846 and are to be found in his initial notebooks on political economy. In the 1850s and 1860s this work was of an auxiliary nature and connected with his studies of political economy, but in the latter half of the 1870s it became systematic and more independent. Marx's most complete mathematical manuscripts were first published in full in the language of the original (German) with a parallel Russian translation in: К. Маркс, *Математические рукописи*, Nauka, Moscow, 1968 (see Note 79).— 39

⁷³ In his article 'On the Death of Karl Marx' carried by *Der Sozialdemokrat* in May 1883 (see present edition, Vol. 24, p. 476) Engels announced that Marx's works would be published by his literary executors, Marx's youngest daughter Eleanor and Engels himself.— 39

⁷⁴ Louise Michel, a French revolutionary and participant in the Paris Commune, was sentenced in June 1883 to six years' imprisonment and ten years' stringent police surveillance for taking part in a Paris unemployed demonstration in March 1883. She was amnestied in January 1886.— 41, 404

⁷⁵ The reference is to Marx's surviving personal copy of the first volume of the second German edition of *Capital* (Hamburg, 1872). All the changes and additions which Marx made to the text are given in *Marx/Engels Gesammtausgabe* (MEGA²), Abt. II, Bd. 8, Berlin, 1988.— 41, 42

[76] This letter was first published in English with minor abridgements in *Science and Society*, Vol. 2, New York, 1938, No. 2.— 42

[77] Engels learned from Adolf Hepner, editor of the *New-Yorker Volkszeitung*, that an English translation of the *Manifesto of the Communist Party* was being prepared in the United States. On 7-12 May 1883 Hepner wrote to Engels, 'The Mostians and Schewitsch, i. e. the Marx Memorial Committee, organised an English translation of the *Communist Manifesto* ... naturally, without asking you or showing you the translation... A few days ago I happened to go to the print shop and saw the proofs of the Introduction. They included the words, "It was written by K. Marx, assisted by Fr. Engels...".'— 42

[78] The *Manifesto of the Communist Party* appeared twice in Russian in Geneva: in 1869, it was published by the Volnaya russkaya tipografiya publishing house and issued for a second time in 1882. It is not quite certain whether the first translation was by Mikhail Bakunin or Nikolai Lyubavin. The second Russian edition, supplied with a preface specially written by Marx and Engels (see present edition, Vol. 24, pp. 425-26), was prepared by Georgi Plekhanov and appeared in the Russian Social-Revolutionary Library series.— 42, 89

[79] This apparently refers to Marx's mathematical manuscripts which he sent to Engels in 1881 ('Über den Begriff der Abgeleiteten Funktion' and 'Über das Differential') (see Engels' letters to Marx of 18 August 1881 and 21 November 1882, present edition, Vol. 46; see also Note 72).— 43

[80] From the late 1860s Marx studied agrarian relations in the United States, Belgium and Russia in the intention of using this material in the third book (Volume II) of *Capital* when examining the emergence of ground rent. It is clear from Marx's correspondence that he obtained some of the materials he used on agrarian relations in the United States from his friends there (see Marx's letters to Sigfrid Meyer of 4 July and 14 September 1868, and to George Julian Harney of 21 January 1871; present edition, Vols. 43 and 44).

On Marx's notes from Russian sources see Note 57.— 43, 88, 264

[81] Following the appearance in 1875 of the French edition of Volume I of *Capital* (see Note 59), the French socialist Gabriel Deville considered issuing a short conspectus of this work (see Marx's letter to Deville of 23 January 1877, present edition, Vol. 45). On 2 August 1882 he met Marx in Paris where the latter looked through part of his manuscript. On 10 August 1883 Deville wrote to Engels that Paul Lafargue had told him he (Engels) was willing to read the rest of the work. He sent Engels the manuscript with the request that he make the necessary corrections. Deville's book was published that year under the title *Le Capital de Karl Marx. Résumé et accompagné d'un aperçu sur le socialisme scientifique*. In the Preface the author wrote that he had done the work 'at the courteous request and benevolent encouragement of Karl Marx'. Deville sent Engels a copy with his own dedication. For Engels' assessment of the book see this volume, pp. 61, 76-77.— 44, 50, 52, 59, 61, 63, 94, 112, 385

[82] Between 17 August and 14 September 1883 Engels was on holiday in Eastbourne on the south coast of England.— 44, 45, 47, 50, 58

[83] Engels is referring to his previous stay in Eastbourne from 5 to 27 August 1879.— 46

[84] The reference is to a winning lottery ticket (see this volume, p. 178).— 46

[85] In his letter of 10 August 1883 Wilhelm Liebknecht asked Engels to let him have the exact dates of death of Marx's wife and eldest daughter. He further enquired about Heinrich Heine's links with the Paris *Vorwärts!* as well as Marx's cooperation with the same newspaper and the *Deutsche-Brüsseler-Zeitung*. Liebknecht intended to use this information in his article 'Karl Marx' which was later published in *Die Neue Zeit*, No. 10, 1883.— 47

[86] It is clear from Heinrich Heine's letter to Marx of 21 September 1844 that on the same day he also sent Marx some of the proofs of his book *Neue Gedichte*. It included the poem 'Deutschland. Ein Wintermärchen', which Heine intended to publish as a separate edition. He further requested Marx to write an introduction to this poem to appear in *Vorwärts!* In October 1844 the newspaper started to publish the poem, preceded by an editorial article probably written by Karl Ludwig Bernays.— 47

[87] In a letter to Engels of 25 June 1883 Pasquale Martignetti thanked the recipient for endorsing his Italian translation of *Socialism: Utopian and Scientific* (see Note 70). Expressing his regret that he had not been able to translate from the German original, Martignetti asked Engels to advise him of a textbook which might help him to learn German; he also requested Engels to let him know where he might find works by Marx, Engels and other authors which the recipient could recommend as reading material. On 30 July Martignetti informed Engels that, as the latter had requested (see this volume, p. 37), he was sending him copies of the Italian translation of the above-mentioned work by Engels which had just appeared in Benevento.— 48

[88] This letter was first published in English in an abridged form in: K. Marx, F. Engels, *Selected Correspondence*, Foreign Languages Publishing House, Moscow, 1955.— 49, 101, 131, 139, 147

[89] In 1872 Johann Philipp Becker was a delegate to the Hague Congress of the International Working Men's Association.— 49

[90] Eduard Bernstein recommended Engels the Austrian Social Democrat Emil Kaler-Reinthal as a secretary to prepare Marx's works for publication.— 50

[91] The question of a republic in France was raised in *Der Sozialdemokrat*, No. 27, 28 June 1883, which carried an article entitled 'Louise Michel vor Gericht' containing excerpts from her speech for the defence (see Note 74), and in No. 28, 5 July 1883, in an article on the same subject under the title 'Republik oder Monarchie? Zum Jahrestag des Bastillesturmes'.— 51

[92] On 4 September 1870 in Paris, following the routing of the French army by Prussian forces at Sedan, a mass revolutionary uprising took place which led to the fall of the Second Empire and the proclamation of the Third Republic headed by a bourgeois government (see K. Marx, *The Civil War in France*, present edition, Vol. 22, p. 307).— 51, 324

[93] The *Party of Progress (Fortschrittspartei)* — a bourgeois-liberal party formed in Prussia in 1861. It represented the interests of the petty bourgeoisie and the section of the middle bourgeoisie that was involved in foreign trade. The party supported the idea of German unification under Prussian supremacy but demanded the establishment of a parliamentary system. In 1866 its Right wing split away to form the National Liberal Party. In 1884 the men of Progress merged with the Left wing which had broken away from the National Liberals to form the German Party of Free Thinkers (Deutsche Freisinnige Partei).— 51, 140, 147, 533

[94] An excerpt from this letter was first published in English in *The Labour Monthly*, London, 1933, Vol. 15, No. 9, IX.— 52, 73, 80, 85, 118

[95] In the Preface to Volume II of *Capital* (see present edition, Vol. 36) Engels described in detail the state of Marx's surviving manuscript and recalled that shortly before his death Marx had told his daughter Eleanor that he (Engels) should 'make something' out of the manuscript.— 53

[96] The reference is to the second ballot to the Reichstag held on 29 June 1883 at which Bebel, obtaining 11,711 votes, gained a victory over the candidate from the Party of Progress (see Note 93) who received 11,608 votes. In this way he became the thirteenth Social-Democratic deputy to the Reichstag (see Note 43).— 53

[97] A hint at the statement made by Bismarck with reference to his aggressive policy towards France.— 53

[98] In January 1883 agreements were signed between Germany and Serbia on trade and the establishment of consular relations. On 12 July 1883 an agreement on trade and shipping was signed between Germany and Spain.
   In August 1883 talks were held on Romania's accession to the Triple Alliance (made up of Austria-Hungary, Germany and Italy); the talks ended with the conclusion of a defensive alliance between Romania and Austria-Hungary which reinforced Romania's subordination to the Triple Alliance.— 53

[99] *Democratic Federation* — an association of various British workers' and radical-democratic societies formed on 8 June 1881 by a group of radical intellectuals headed by Henry Mayers Hyndman. The Federation's programme was limited to bourgeois-democratic demands like adult suffrage, the nationalisation of land and a parliamentary reform. However, as it was joined by socialist intellectuals (Ernest Belfort Bax, William Morris and others) and advanced workers (Harry Quelch, John Elliot Burns), the leadership of the Federation adopted noticeably more socialist positions.
   The Federation's conference in June 1883 adopted a Manifesto drawn up by Hyndman and setting out its fundamental principles. It was soon put out as a separate pamphlet entitled *Socialism Made Plain, being the Social and Political Manifesto of the Democratic Federation*. It contained a demand for 'nationalisation of the means of production and distribution'. In August 1884 the Democratic Federation became the Social Democratic Federation (see Note 300).— 54, 106, 114, 118, 123, 165

[100] In 1881 Henry Mayers Hyndman published the pamphlet *England for All* which he intended to serve as a commentary on the programme of the Democratic Federation (see Note 99). In two of its chapters Hyndman gave an interpretation of several sections of Volume I of *Capital*, in many cases failing to correctly express their content and referring neither to the author nor the book itself. Marx expressed his resolute protest at this in a letter to Hyndman of 2 July 1881 (see present edition, Vol. 46).— 54, 114

[101] The reference is to the *Chartist movement* in England, the first mass political and revolutionary movement of the English proletariat in the 1830s and 1840s. Its slogan was the struggle for a 'People's Charter'. This document contained six points: universal suffrage (for men of 21 and over), annual Parliaments, vote by ballot, equal electoral districts, abolition of the property qualification for MPs, and payment of

MPs. Petitions urging the adoption of the People's Charter were turned down by Parliament in 1839, 1842 and 1848.— 54, 422

[102] The reference is to a series of concessions the British bourgeoisie made to the working class in the 1870s. In 1871 the Liberal government under Gladstone adopted the Trade Union Act which improved the judicial status of the unions. Trade unions were thus recognised for the first time, it was no longer possible to proclaim them illegal, they were able to register their rules and determine their internal structure and procedure of their activities without interference from the judiciary. In 1875 Disraeli's Conservative cabinet enacted legislation permitting 'peaceful picketing', thus giving the workers a right to strike.

1867 saw the second electoral reform in England under which the property requirement for voters in the counties was reduced to £12 in rent for tenants, whilst in the towns the right to vote was accorded to homeowners and tenants of flats and houses who had lived in the same place for not less than a year and paid rent of not less than £10. Some of the skilled workers also received the right to vote. However, this law did not extend to Scotland or Ireland.— 55

[103] A fragment from this letter was published in English for the first time in: K. Marx and F. Engels, *On Colonialism*, Progress Publishers, Moscow, 1959.— 55

[104] In his letter of 14 September 1883 Karl Kautsky sent Engels a leaflet apparently put out by Bruno Geiser and other adherents of the opportunist wing of the German Social Democrats. Kautsky wrote to Engels that the leaflet was a clear demonstration of how, against the background of the Anti-Socialist Law, petty bourgeois elements in the party were advancing not socialist, but petty bourgeois, slogans (the right to work and demand for a minimum wage); in order to counteract this, Kautsky suggested to Engels that he should without delay write a piece for *Der Sozialdemokrat* explaining that it was impossible to implement the demand for a 'right to work' under capitalist conditions.— 55

[105] The reference is to a series of articles by Karl Kautsky entitled 'Die Entstehung der Ehe und Familie' and carried by the magazine *Kosmos*, Stuttgart, Vol. XII (October 1882-March 1883). Engels set out his opinion of the initial articles in his letters to Kautsky of 10 February and 2 March 1883 (see present edition, Vol. 46).— 56

[106] The reference is to the attempt to annex Port Moresby in New Guinea staged by the British colonial authorities in Queensland, Australia, in April 1883; in November 1884 the British government proclaimed a temporary protectorate over the South-Eastern part of New Guinea and the adjacent island.— 57

[107] The regular trade union congress was held in Nottingham from 10 to 15 September 1883.— 57

[108] This is an allusion to a series of articles headed 'Die Trades Unions' which Wilhelm Liebknecht published anonymously in *Die Neue Zeit* in early 1883.— 57

[109] In the first three issues of *Die Neue Zeit* for 1883 the Austrian economist Emanuel Hans Sax (pseudonym Fritz Denhardt) published two reviews and a short article entitled 'Zur sozialen Statistik in Deutschland'.

Replying to Engels, Kautsky wrote on 3 October 1883, 'Other contributors I had been counting on are holding back out of cowardice. I can only ascribe it to this that Braun and Fritz Denhardt have ceased to deliver material. I am becoming increasingly distrustful of the "educated" socialists who have not broken with the past.'—57

¹¹⁰ Intending to become a factory inspector, Victor Adler took a trip around Germany, Switzerland and Britain in 1883 to familiarise himself with the work of the inspectors there. In Stuttgart he visited Kautsky, who gave him a reference for Engels.—57

¹¹¹ The postcard referred to has not been found.—59, 211

¹¹² Hermann Lopatin visited Engels on 19 September, several months after fleeing from exile in Vologda (see Note 6). They met for the second time on 23 September. On 20 September 1883 Lopatin wrote to Maria Oshanina, telling her about the substance of his first conversation with Engels (see present edition, Vol. 26, pp. 591-93).—59

¹¹³ The first volume of Marx's *Capital* (third German edition) was issued by the Meissner publishing house in Hamburg and printed on Otto Wigand's press in Leipzig.—60

¹¹⁴ During his prison sentence (see Note 9) Paul Lafargue worked on an article entitled 'Le blé en Amérique...' which was carried by the *Journal des Économistes* in 1884.—63, 71

¹¹⁵ The reference is to the international workers' conference held in Paris on 29 October 1883 by decision of the congress of the French Workers' Social-Revolutionary Party (Possibilists; see Note 237) which took place in late September and early October of that year. The Possibilists regarded its convocation as the first step towards the formation of a new International in which they would have the leadership. With this in mind, invitations to the congress were issued only to the British trade unions and the socialist movements in Italy and Spain. The decision to form an International, like others, did not yield any practical results.
    The anti-Broussists were opponents of the Possibilists.—64, 96

¹¹⁶ In early November 1883 Vera Zasulich asked Engels a number of questions with a view to ascertaining his attitude to the plans to publish the second volume of Marx's *Capital* in Russian in St Petersburg. She informed him that, if they were given the opportunity, Russian socialist émigrés were prepared to take on the translation. Together with the letter Zasulich sent Engels the announcement about the publication of the Library of Contemporary Socialism series (see Note 124) and the Russian translation of Marx's *Wage Labour and Capital* which had just appeared in Geneva. She further informed Engels that his work *Socialism: Utopian and Scientific*, which she had translated into Russian, was in the press. This book appeared in Geneva in 1884 under the title *Развитіе научнаго соціализма.*—65

¹¹⁷ Hermann Lopatin began translating the first volume of Marx's *Capital* into Russian during his stay in London in the summer and autumn of 1870. Before leaving for Russia at the end of the year he translated the second, third and beginning of the fourth chapter of the first German edition of Volume I of *Capital*. The translation in full was done by October 1871 by Nikolai Danielson and Nikolai Lyubavin, Professor of Chemistry at Moscow University. The first Russian edition of Volume I of *Capital* appeared in St Petersburg in 1872.
    The second volume of *Capital* was published in Russian in Danielson's translation in January 1886.—65

[118] The reference is to the German translation of Marx's *The Poverty of Philosophy. Answer to the 'Philosophy of Poverty' by M. Proudhon* which was written in French and appeared in Brussels and Paris in 1847. The translation into German was begun by Eduard Bernstein who was later joined by Karl Kautsky. Engels edited the translation, wrote a special preface for it and a number of notes, using the amendments made by Marx on a copy of the French edition of 1847. The book was published by Dietz in Stuttgart in January 1885.— 66, 67, 73, 90, 124, 126, 131, 133, 135, 138, 153, 176, 186, 189, 191, 195, 196, 261

[119] On 10 November 1883 Eduard Bernstein informed Engels that Max Quarck (literary pseudonym Freiwald Thüringer) was the author of a book about the Thuringian cottage industry; the book contained positive comments on the social reforms carried out by the German government.— 67

[120] Engels is referring to Georgi Plekhanov's translation of the *Manifesto of the Communist Party* by Karl Marx and Frederick Engels which appeared in 1882 (see Note 78) and also to Marx's *Wage Labour and Capital* which was published in Russian in Geneva in the autumn of 1883 as the fourth book in the Russian Social-Revolutionary Library. The cover carried the note 'translation from the German edition of 1880 (Breslau)'.— 67

[121] Engels wrote the essay 'The Mark' between mid-September and the first half of December 1882 as an appendix to the German edition of his work *Socialism: Utopian and Scientific* (see present edition, Vol. 24). 'The Mark' was published by *Der Sozialdemokrat* in March-April 1883 and as a separate edition in Hottingen-Zurich under the title *Der deutsche Bauer. Was war er? Was ist er? Was könnte er sein?* which was specially prepared by Engels for propaganda work among the peasants.—68

[122] On 10 November 1883 Eduard Bernstein informed Engels of his intention to publish in *Der Sozialdemokrat* Paul Lafargue's pamphlet *Le Droit à la Paresse* which Lafargue had prepared for publication as a separate edition in the summer of 1883, during his imprisonment in Ste-Pelagie (see Note 9). The pamphlet *Le Droit à la Paresse. Réfutation du 'Droit au Travail' de 1848* was published for the first time in 1880, in *l'Égalité*; a separate pamphlet appeared the same year in Paris. This was also published in German in *Der Sozialdemokrat* under the heading 'Das Recht auf Faulheit' in December 1883-January 1884.— 68, 86

[123] *Wailers* (Heuler) — the name the republican democrats in Germany in 1848-49 applied to the moderate constitutionalists; here Engels uses the label to describe adherents of the Right wing of the Socialist Workers' Party of Germany.— 68, 125, 140, 145

[124] Engels is quoting from the announcement of the publication of the Library of Contemporary Socialism series issued by Russian Social-Democratic émigrés in Geneva on 25 September 1883. The announcement set out the main aims and tasks of the first Russian Marxist organisation, the Emancipation of Labour group. It read in part, 'In now changing their programme to serve their struggle against absolutism and the organisation of the Russian working class in a separate party with a definite socio-political programme, the former members of the Black Redistribution group hereby form a new group — Emancipation of Labour — and definitively break with the old anarchist tendencies'. The group regarded the following as

its main tasks: 1) the translation into Russian and dissemination of the major works of K. Marx and F. Engels and their followers; 2) a critique of the Narodniks and efforts to deal with current problems of Russian life.— 68

125 Karl Kautsky was in London from late November to early December 1883. On 28 November, he attended Engels' birthday party together with Eleanor Marx and Edward Aveling.— 68, 80

126 In his letter of 26 November 1883 Johann Philipp Becker asked Engels to remind Laura Lafargue that she had promised, in the presence and with the agreement of Marx, to send him the letters of 1848 and 1849 which Becker had let Marx have for his work on the pamphlet *Herr Vogt*.— 69, 98, 152, 203, 301

127 In 1849 Engels and Johann Philipp Becker took part in the Baden-Palatinate uprising (see Engels' 'The Campaign for the German Imperial Constitution', present edition, Vol. 10, pp. 147-239 and also 'Johann Philipp Becker', present edition, Vol. 26, pp. 418-23).— 69

128 Engels wrote the lines below on a postcard which he addressed: 'Karl Kautsky. Esq., Wedde's Hotel, Greek St., Soho, W. C.'— 70

129 On 19 December 1883 the Paris newspaper *Le Cri du Peuple* published an article by Paul Lafargue headed 'L'Assassinat d'O'Donnell'. It denounced the hostile position adopted by George Shipton, editor of the English trade union newspaper *The Labour Standard*, to the trial, taking place in London at the time, of Patrick O'Donnell, a member of an Irish secret society. On 6 May 1882 members of this society had killed Lord Frederic Cavendish, Principal Secretary for Irish Affairs, and his deputy T. H. Burke. The main witness for the prosecution, James Carey, himself one of the murderers, had subsequently been killed by O'Donnell. Flying in the face of democratic public opinion, *The Labour Standard* sharply condemned O'Donnell.— 72

130 On 2 December 1883 Wilhelm Ludwig Rosenberg, editor of the *New Yorker Volkszeitung*, organ of the Socialist Labor Party of the USA, published an article signed 'von der Mark'. It alleged that the state was an abstract concept, a 'union of individuals'. Responding to this, Eduard Bernstein used the pseudonym 'Leo' when publishing in *Der Sozialdemokrat*, No. 52, 20 December 1883 an article entitled 'Der Sozialismus und der Staat' in which he quoted verbatim statements Engels had made in *Socialism: Utopian and Scientific* about the historical role of the state and his assessment of Lassalle's term 'free state' (see present edition, Vol. 24, pp. 320-21). Bernstein also stressed that, in contrast to the anarchists, the Marxists suggested beginning not with the abolition of the state, but with the transfer of power to the proletariat.

On 3 January 1884 Rosenberg continued the polemic by publishing another article in the *New Yorker Volkszeitung* with the title 'Herr Leo'. In it he tried to prove that Engels and Bebel were making a concession to the anarchists and alleged the Marxists believed that, following the withering away of the state, there would ensue a situation marked by an absence of authorities.— 72, 86, 91

131 Engels is referring to Johann Karl Rodbertus' letter to Rudolf Hermann Meyer of 20 September 1871. It was published in the book *Briefe und socialpolitische Aufsaetze von Dr Rodbertus-Jagetzow*. Published by Dr R. Meyer, Vol. 1, Berlin, [1882], p. 111.— 72

[132] In the 'Preface to the 1872 German Edition of the *Manifesto of the Communist Party*' Marx and Engels referred readers to the passage in Marx's work *The Civil War in France* where, on the strength of the experience gathered by the Paris Commune, he concluded that 'the working class cannot simply lay hold of the ready-made State machinery, and wield it for its own purposes' (see present edition, Vol. 23, p. 175).— 73

[133] By way of a reminder the appendix to the Russian edition of the *Manifesto of the Communist Party*, which appeared in Georgi Plekhanov's translation in Geneva in 1882 (see Note 78), contained an excerpt from Marx's *The Civil War in France*. Engels is further referring to the 1883 German edition of the *Manifesto* for which he wrote a special preface (see present edition, Vol. 26); this edition was published without an appendix.— 74

[134] On 21 December 1883 *The Times* reported that on 10 December 1883, when Tsar Alexander III had been out hunting, the horses had bolted and upturned the sled in which he was sitting.— 74

[135] On 16 December 1883 his chief and secret police inspector Lieutenant-Colonel Georgi Sudeikin was murdered in St Petersburg in the flat of Sergei Degayev (Yablonsky). The terrorist act was carried out on the decision of the Executive Committee of the Narodnaya Volya (People's Will) party which, on pain of his own death, had forced the exposed provocateur Degayev organise the murder.
The Standard, No. 18561, 11 January 1884, reported that the St Petersburg chief of police supposed the murderers were led from Paris by Lavrov and Tikhomirov.— 74, 79

[136] On 29 December 1883 Karl Kautsky wrote to Engels that the tsarist government had ordered from his father Johann Kautsky's workshop in Prague the scenery which was to capture various moments from the coronation of Alexander III in May 1883; the scenery was to be put on public display in various Russian cities and to be completed by May 1884.— 76

[137] On 29 December 1883 Karl Kautsky informed Engels that he was planning to publish in Germany Gabriel Deville's *Le Capital de Karl Marx. Résumé et accompagné d'un aperçu sur le socialisme scientifique* (see Note 81) which had just appeared in Paris. On Engels' advice, Kautsky decided not simply to publish a translation but wrote a work of his own in accordance with the instructions Engels gave him in this and subsequent letters (see this volume, pp. 101 and 462); Kautsky's work appeared under the title *Karl Marx's Oekonomische Lehren. Gemeinverständlich dargestellt und erläutert von Karl Kautsky*, Stuttgart, 1887.— 76, 78, 89, 101, 386, 481, 482

[138] The second, illegal, edition of August Bebel's book *Die Frau und der Sozialismus* was printed in Dietz's works in Stuttgart but appeared under the auspices of the Zurich publisher Schabelitz with the title *Die Frau in der Vergangenheit, Gegenwart und Zukunft* in 1883. The first editon was issued in Zurich-Hottingen in 1879.— 77, 81, 132, 164, 204

[139] *Der Sozialdemokrat*, No. 1, 1883 did not appear on Thursday, as usual, but on Monday, 1 January, whilst No. 2 was published the following Thursday, 4 January. The last issue for that year, No. 52, appeared on Thursday, 20 December, whilst on 27 December the newspaper was not published at all. The following issue, No. 1, did not appear until 3 January 1884.— 77

[140] In a letter to Engels of 7 January 1884 Paul Lafargue wrote about the 'German "goût"' (taste), illustrating it with such examples as pictures for children, toys and artificial flowers. Lafargue continued that German producers were planning to capture part of the French market from the domestic industrialists and, for this purpose, the goods they exported to France were being supplied with German labels, this serving to indicate that they were more competitive.— 78

[141] In a letter of 31 October 1883 August Bebel asked Engels to find a place in an English family for the daughter of his associé Ferdinand Issleib. But on the very next day Bebel apologised to Engels for the trouble he had caused him and sent him Issleib's urgent request that he return Bebel's letter of 31 October.

Engels' letter to Bebel, written in pencil, has not been found.— 80

[142] Engels is referring to the propaganda in favour of the introduction of the right to work carried on by the Right wing of the Socialist Workers' Party of Germany (see also Note 104).— 81

[143] During trips to England and Ireland in 1882 and 1884 the American economist Henry George gave lectures in which he attempted to prove that the nationalisation of land was a means of settling social contradictions under the capitalist system (see also Note 31).— 82

[144] The Archives of German Social Democracy were established by a decision of the Conference of the Socialist Workers' Party of Germany held in Zurich from 19 to 21 August 1882. They contained manuscripts by figures from the German workers' movement, including Marx and Engels, literature on the history of Germany and the international workers' movement as well as the workers' press. The archives were originally based in Zurich and the initial documents were collected by Eduard Bernstein. From April 1883 the archives were run by Hermann Schlüter. In June 1888, following its move from Switzerland to London, the editorial board of *Der Sozialdemokrat* also transferred the archives of German Social Democracy to the same place. They were moved to Berlin following the repeal of the Anti-Socialist Law.— 83, 85, 95, 107, 111, 328

[145] August Bebel's book *Die Frau und der Sozialismus* appeared in English translation in London in 1885 under the title *Woman in the Past, Present and Future.*— 83

[146] Engels made a draft of his reply on Charles L. Fitzgerald's letter to him of 25 January in which the latter asked Engels to write for the recently founded newspaper *Justice*. Fitzgerald's letter was written on paper belonging to the editorial board and carrying the address, 'The Editorial Office of *Justice*, Palace Chambers, 9, Bridge Street, Westminster, S. W.'.— 84

[147] In his letter of 23 January 1884 Ludwik Krzywicki requested Engels' permission to publish the first volume of Marx's *Capital* in Polish translation. The translation was the work of Stanisław Krusiński, Kazimierz Pławinski, Mieczysław Brzeziński, Jósef Siemaszko, Kazimierz Sosnowski, representatives of Polish revolutionary youth, as well as Krzywicki himself, who edited the entire translation. The first instalment appeared in 1884, the second in 1886 and the third in 1889. The book was published in full in 1890 in Leipzig, and one copy of this edition was sent to Engels.— 87

[148] Russian books from Marx's library were sent to Pyotr Lavrov on 3 March 1884.

On 7 March he acknowledged their receipt from Engels. It is not known what happened to Lavrov's library, including these volumes.— 88

[149] Engels used the manuscript when preparing the third volume of *Capital* (see present edition, Vol. 37).— 88

[150] In his letter of reply, written on 30 January 1884, Pyotr Lavrov recommended Kazimierz Sosnowski to Engels as 'a sincere and devout socialist and an excellent young man'. Lavrov also expressed his doubts 'as to where this pretty poor group will find enough money to publish something as large as the first volume of *Capital* in Polish'. On the translation of the first volume of *Capital* into Polish, see Note 147.— 89

[151] The reference is to Marx's article 'On Proudhon' which he wrote on 24 January 1865 at the request of the editorial board of *Der Social-Demokrat* (see present edition, Vol. 20). Engels planned to include it in full in the preface to the second French edition of *The Poverty of Philosophy*, which Laura Lafargue was preparing at the time. It appeared in 1896, following Engels' death. The article by Marx was included in the appendix under the title 'Proudhon jugé par Karl Marx'. In the German edition of *The Poverty*, which appeared in Stuttgart in 1885, this article by Marx came after Engels' preface.— 91, 102, 107, 206

[152] The *New Yorker Volkszeitung*, No. 12, 14 January 1884, carried an article entitled 'Ein paar Muster'. Its author advised the Social Democrats, particularly the French and the German, to follow the example of the Irish and Russian revolutionaries, who, as he put it, observed unity and displayed agreeability.

In *Der Sozialdemokrat*, No. 6, 7 February 1884, these views were criticised in an article entitled 'Toleranz, aber keine Indifferenz' (Tolerance, but not indifference).— 91

[153] It is clear from Eduard Bernstein's letter to Engels of 2 February 1884 that the editorial board of *Der Sozialdemokrat* intended to devote one of the March issues to the memory of Marx. The article 'Marx and the *Neue Rheinische Zeitung* (1848-49)', which Engels wrote for this issue, was included in *Der Sozialdemokrat*, No. 11, 13 March 1884 (see present edition, Vol. 26).— 92

[154] Engels is referring to the events in Vienna where Hlubek and Blöch, two secret police agents, were killed in December 1883 and January 1884. The murders were provoked by the government, which attributed them to the anarchists and used this as an excuse to introduce a state of siege in Vienna and its environs as well as adopting legislation against the anarchists which was actually directed against the socialist movement. Workers' organisations were subjected to police persecution, their leaders deported and their press prohibited.— 92

[155] In his letter of 30 January 1884 Pyotr Lavrov suggested to Engels the idea of publishing the second volume of *Capital* in Russia in instalments parallel to it being prepared for the press in Germany. He drew Engels' attention to the great Russian public interest in this edition. He also wrote that Hermann Lopatin had come to Paris for a few days and, intending to publish a Russian edition of this volume in St Petersburg, had expressed the hope that Engels would send the proofs of the German edition in preparation to Nikolai Danielson (see also Note 168).— 93

[156] On 30 January 1884 Pyotr Lavrov wrote to Engels about the need to reissue Marx's early works, which had already become a rarity; he further informed Engels that he had been given the chance to publish in *Вѣстникъ Народной Воли* the

translation of Marx's work *The Class Struggles in France, 1848 to 1850* (see present edition, Vol. 10) which had been carried in 1850 by the *Neue Rheinische Zeitung. Politisch-ökonomische Revue* under the title 'Von 1848 bis 1849'. Lavrov asked Engels for more detailed information about this work.— 93, 261

[157] The reference is to the propaganda trip Paul Lafargue, Jules Guesde, Simon Dereure and Jean Dormoy made around the northern districts of France in connection with the forthcoming congress of the French Workers' Party in Roubaix (29 March to 7 April 1884) (see Note 195). On 27 January 1884 Lafargue, Guesde and Dereure addressed a large rally in St Quentin. On 28 January they spoke in St-Pierre-Calais, not having arrived until ten o'clock in the evening since they had been forced to wait $3^1/_2$ hours for a train to Calais. The meeting had nevertheless passed off successfully, as Lafargue informed Engels on 6 February 1884.— 94, 96

[158] Engels is referring to a series of articles carried on 23 December 1883, 13 January and 3 February 1884 by the London weekly *The National Reformer* published by Charles Bradlaugh and Annie Besant. The author of the first and third articles, which appeared in the 'Daybreak' column was Annie Besant, whilst the second was unsigned and published in the 'Crowded Table' column.— 95

[159] From March 1864 to his death Marx lived with his family in North West London, first at 1 Modena Villas (renamed 1 Maitland Park Road in 1868), then in March 1875 they moved to 41 Maitland Park Road.— 95, 104, 118, 121

[160] Using the pseudonym 'Deux amis de la liberté' (Two friends of freedom), F. M. Kerverseau and G. Clavelin published a work in several volumes entitled *Histoire de la révolution de 1789...* in Paris between 1790 and 1803.— 95

[161] *Blue Books* — collected documents of the British Parliament and Foreign Office published since the 17th century.— 95, 128

[162] The reference is probably to the German Workers' Educational Society formed in London in 1840 by Karl Schapper, Johann Moll, Heinrich Bauer, and other members of the League of the Just. Marx and Engels took part in its activities in 1847 and 1849-50. The name of the society was changed in the following years, and from the 1870s it was called Communist Workers' Educational Society (Kommunistischer Arbeiterbildungsverein). Soon after the introduction of the Anti-Socialist Law (see Note 37), a group of extremist-minded members gained the upper hand in the society. They opposed the tactics employed by the German Social Democrats against the background of the Anti-Socialist Law, came out against a combination of legal and illegal methods of struggle, against the Social Democrats working in Parliament and for individual acts of terrorism. In March 1880 a considerable number of members left the society and formed their own organisation retaining the previous name. The refounded society announced that it intended to act in accord with the principles and tactics of the German Social Democrats. The remaining members, including the supporters of Most, continued to adhere to Leftist views and were active under the same name.— 95, 119, 210, 263

[163] The *Cercle international* of the fifth arrondissement was a workers' association in Paris belonging to the Federation of the Centre (the Paris association of the Possibilists) (see Note 237). The secretary of the association, Henri Leclère, was one of the Possibilist leaders; it included among its members a number of German and Russian émigrés.— 96

[164] It seems likely that the French journalist Paule Mink (Pauline A. Mękarska) went on a trip to the South of France, where she engaged in propaganda work. It is clear from Paul Lafargue's letter to Engels of 10 April 1884 that she later joined Lafargue and Jules Guesde (see Note 157) and visited a number of northern French cities together with them where Lafargue gave a report on the significance of the International Working Men's Association.— 96

[165] The reference is to the second French edition of Marx's *The Poverty of Philosophy* which was being prepared at that time by Laura Lafargue (see also Note 169). The preparatory work on this edition was protracted and it did not appear until 1896 (in Paris), after Engels' death.— 97, 104, 111, 115, 124, 133

[166] This letter was written by Engels in reply to Nonne's letter of 7 February 1884. Heinrich Nonne, an émigré from Hanover who was living in Paris and taught foreign languages, informed Engels of his plan to set up a kind of international centre in Paris with a view to bringing about a rapprochement between socialists in different countries. Nonne asked Engels to send him statistical notes and information about events in other countries. Later, in September 1884, it turned out that Nonne was in the pay of the Prussian police (see Note 303).— 97

[167] On 5 February 1884 Johann Philipp Becker wrote to Engels saying he believed there was a need to broaden the campaign for universal suffrage in Germany and that the masses there were not learning to act in a collective and coordinated manner. Becker wrote that this campaign was an excellent means of setting the masses in town and country in motion, notably young people between 21 and 25, who were deprived of the right to vote, and also of exposing the bourgeois parties.— 98

[168] Replying on 9 February to Engels' enquiry about the possibility of publishing a Russian translation of the second volume of *Capital* in Russia (see Note 155), Pyotr Lavrov wrote that the Russian revolutionaries had decided to bring out this translation 'by all means' and that, should it be confiscated, the book would be put out abroad.

The first Russian edition of the second volume of *Capital* appeared in St Petersburg on 11 January 1886 with a preface by Nikolai Danielson and in his translation. The year of publication printed on the title page was 1885.— 100

[169] Engels did not write a special preface to the second French edition of *The Poverty of Philosophy*. This led Laura Lafargue to include in the edition Engels' preface to the first German edition of the work ('Marx and Rodbertus') which had appeared in Stuttgart in 1885 (see present edition, Vol. 26).— 101, 104, 124

[170] The reference is to Rudolf Meyer's book *Der Emancipationskampf des vierten Standes*, Vol. 1, Berlin, 1874. Engels refers to this book in the preface to the second volume of *Capital* (see present edition, Vol. 36).— 101

[171] The reference is to Marx's manuscript *A Contribution to the Critique of Political Economy* (1861-63). Its central part is called *Theories of Surplus Value* (see present edition, vols 30-34). Marx planned to revise it and then publish as a separate book of *Capital* entitled 'The History of the Theory' (see Marx's preface to the first volume of *Capital,* present edition, Vol. 35). However, neither Marx nor Engels carried out this plan. Engels gave a detailed description of this manuscript in the preface to the second volume of *Capital* (see present edition, Vol. 36).

Marx gives a critique of Rodbertus' theory of rent in Notebooks X-XI of the *Theories* (present edition, Vol. 31).— 102, 104, 121, 122, 188, 244, 264, 278

[172] The reference is to Karl Kautsky's letter to Engels of 2 February 1884 in which, on behalf of the Volksbuchhandlung in Zurich, he asked for the right to publish a new edition of Engels' *The Condition of the Working-Class in England*.— 102

[173] The 'original cantons' was the name given to Switzerland's mountainous cantons which formed the original core of the Swiss Federation in the 13th and 14th centuries.— 103

[174] When sorting through Marx's manuscripts after his death, Engels discovered a detailed conspectus of *Ancient Society or Researches in the Line of Human Progress from Savagery, through Barbarism to Civilization*, London, 1877, written by the American scientist Lewis H. Morgan. The conspectus had been drawn up by Marx in 1880-81 and contained his critical remarks, conclusions of his own and some information from other sources (the conspectus is not included in the present edition). Believing that Marx had intended to write a work specifically devoted to the initial period in the history of human society, basing himself on Morgan as he did so, Engels, who had familiarised himself with Marx's conspectus and Morgan's book, thought it necessary to carry out Marx's plan. *The Origin of the Family, Private Property and the State*, on which Engels worked from early April to 26 May 1884, appeared in Zurich at the end of the same year.— 103, 121, 123, 131, 132, 135

[175] Engels' critical remarks about Taylor's and Lubbock's works are contained in his preface to the fourth German edition of *The Origin of the Family, Private Property and the State* which appeared in 1891 (see present edition, Vol. 27).— 103

[176] By 'later versions' Engels means the manuscripts of the first (1867) and third (1865) volumes of *Capital*.— 104

[177] In his capacity as a representative of the German Social Democrats, Eduard Bernstein visited Lyons and Rouen in February 1884; he gave a speech at the German Workers' Club in Paris. From 25 February to 2 March Bernstein stayed with Engels in London, whereupon he returned to Zurich.— 104, 109

[178] This letter by Engels was written in reply to John Darbyshire's letter of 17 February 1884. Reminding Engels of their meeting in 1872, Darbyshire informed him of his efforts to 'start the International again' and continued by saying that in Manchester he had 'at last succeeded in forming a Committee of English, Irish, Welsh and Scotch'. Darbyshire asked Engels to remind him of the names of members of the International so that he might resume correspondence with them and further promised to send him a copy of the 'Principles, Objects and Aims' of the future organisation.— 106

[179] The reference is to the cycle of lectures Paul Lafargue and Gabriel Deville gave ('Cours d'économie sociale') on Marx's doctrine which were organised on Sundays from 23 January 1884 by a circle at the Socialist Library of the French Workers' Party. The cycle of lectures given by Lafargue was called 'Le Matérialisme économique de Karl Marx'. He entitled his second lecture 'Le Milieu naturel. Théorie darwinienne'. Deville called his cycle of lectures 'L'Évolution du capital'. There were five in all, entitled 'Genèse du capital', 'Formation du prolétariat', 'Coopération et manufacture', 'Machinisme et grande industrie' and 'Fin du capital'. The lectures were published in the press and also as separate pamphlets in 1884.

Referring to 'bon dieu', Engels means the disproof of the idealist world view as developed by Lafargue in his first lecture 'Idéalisme et matérialisme dans l'histoire'.— 107, 115, 134, 143, 162, 368, 465

180 The reference is to the second congress of the *League of Peace and Freedom*— a bourgeois pacifist organisation formed in Switzerland in 1867 with the active involvement of Victor Hugo, Giuseppe Garibaldi and other democrats. Mikhail Bakunin took part in its work in 1867 and 1868. At the League's second congress, which took place in Berne on 21-25 September 1868, he proposed a resolution proclaiming the need for the economic and social equalisation of classes. Having failed to win the support of the congress, which voted by a majority against his resolution, Bakunin and his supporters left the League.— 108

181 Engels is referring to the declaration of 21 March 1871 ('République Française. Liberté, égalité, fraternité...') which Benoît Malon signed as assistant to the Mayor of the 17th arrondissement in Paris together with the Mayor himself and two other assistants. The document stated that, since the Mayor and his assistants were alienated from power by force, the validity of all acts of the municipality of the 17th arrondissement ceased from that day.

On Malon's activities in this period see also Marx's and Engels' *Fictitious Splits in the International* (present edition, Vol. 23, p. 94).— 108

182 In April 1884 Russia obtained a loan of 300 million marks from Germany.— 109, 112, 148, 338, 360, 365

183 Engels wrote the following on a postcard which he addressed: Monsieur Paul Lavroff, 328 rue St. Jacques, *Paris*, France.— 110

184 This letter was first published in English in: K. Marx and F. Engels, *Selected Correspondence*, Foreign Languages Publishing House, Moscow, 1955.— 111, 155, 311

185 In her letter of 2 March 1884, Vera Zasulich, writing on behalf of the Russian revolutionary émigrés in Switzerland, requested permission from Engels to put out a Russian edition of Marx's *The Poverty of Philosophy* (see present edition, Vol. 6). She also asked Engels to send her the text of the preface which he intended to write for the first German edition then in preparation (see Note 118) and expressed the hope that he would look through the proofs of the Russian edition and, if need be, make his remarks. The Russian edition of *The Poverty of Philosophy* appeared in Geneva in 1886 in the fifth issue of the Library of Contemporary Socialism series.— 111, 432

186 The 'reactionary socialists' was the name Engels gave to the armchair socialists (see Note 54) who spread the 'myth about Rodbertus' in their works. For a critique of them see Engels' preface to the second volume of *Capital* (present edition, Vol. 36).— 111

187 This false accusation against Marx is contained in Johann Karl Rodbertus' letters to Rudolf Meyer of 29 November 1871 (in *Briefe und socialpolitische Aufsaetze von Dr Rodbertus-Jagetzow*. Published by Dr R. Meyer, Vol. 1, Berlin, [1882], p. 134), and to J. Zeller of 14 March 1875 (in *Zeitschrift für die gesammte Staatswissenschaft*, Vol. 35, Tübingen, 1879, p. 219). Engels rebuffed Rodbertus' accusation in the preface to the first German edition of Marx's *The Poverty of Philosophy* ('Marx and Rodbertus', present edition, Vol. 26) and also in the preface to the second volume of Marx's *Capital* (present edition, Vol. 36).— 111, 166, 187

[188] After the assassination of Emperor Alexander II on 1 March 1881, Alexander III, his successor, was staying in Gatchina (the Russian tsars' country residence), fearing that new terrorist acts would be staged by the Narodnaya Volya (People's Will).— 112, 280

[189] Engels is probably referring to the terrorist activities of the members of the Narodnaya Volya (People's Will), a secret revolutionary Narodnik organisation, which continued even after 1 March 1881 (see previous note).— 112

[190] Engels is referring to the letter Marx wrote in the autumn of 1877 to the editorial board of the St Petersburg magazine *Otechestvenniye zapiski* (see present edition, Vol. 24, p. 196). In an effort to have it published in the Russian press after Marx's death, Engels made three handwritten copies of the letter. The first he gave in September 1883 to Hermann Lopatin, who was in London at the time (see this volume, p. 59), and the second he sent to Vera Zasulich, that being the subject of this letter. He seems to have made the third copy in connection with Nikolai Danielson's unsuccessful attempt in the autumn of 1885 to have Marx's letter published in the journal *Severny vestnik* (see this volume, pp. 322 and 347).

A Russian translation of Marx's letter was first published in Russia in 1885 in the form of a lithograph; the translation was most likely the work of Vera Zasulich. A large part of the edition was confiscated by the police, a fate it shared with another illegal hectographic version of the letter which appeared that December in St Petersburg.

Marx's letter was first published in Russian abroad in Geneva in *Вѣстникъ Народной Воли*, No. 5, 1886. The following year it appeared in German in the American newspaper *New-Yorker Volkszeitung* (3 May) and *Der Sozialdemokrat* (Zurich, 3 June).— 113

[191] An excerpt from this letter was first published in English in *The Socialist Review*, London, March 1908.— 113

[192] In the 1880 general election Henry Mayers Hyndman stood as an independent candidate for Marylebone constituency. However, his extremely moderate programme (he did not support the demand for the nationalisation of land and opposed universal suffrage) lost him votes among the workers and provided Gladstone, who was registered as a voter in the said constituency, with the occasion to denounce him as a Tory. Hyndman's attempt to be elected to Parliament failed.— 114

[193] On 10 February 1884 Friedrich Adolph Sorge informed Engels that George Stiebeling was about to criticise Marx's concept of history.— 114

[194] The reference is to the regular elections to the German Reichstag which took place on 28 October 1884.— 114, 150, 152, 185, 192, 198, 201

[195] The congress of the French Workers' Party met in Roubaix from 29 March to 7 April 1884. It was attended by 26 delegates representing about 60 groups, circles and trade unions. The delegates unanimously endorsed the programme adopted at Le Havre in 1880 (see also Note 201). Also present at the congress were Ernest Belfort Bax and Harry Quelch, representatives of the Democratic Federation (see Note 99). An address was read out from the Socialist Workers' Party of Germany, proclaiming solidarity between the workers of all countries. The reply to this address adopted at the congress expressed regret that no German delegation was pre-

sent and stated that no government measures could destroy the solidarity between the French and German proletariat.— 115, 118, 123, 125, 129

196 This letter was first published in English in: F. Engels, Paul and Laura Lafargue, *Correspondence*, Vol. 1, Foreign Languages Publishing House, Moscow, 1959.— 116, 129, 134, 179, 255, 444

197 In his letter to Laura and Paul Lafargue of 21 February 1884 (see this volume, p. 107), Engels asked them to look through his French translation of Marx's 'On Proudhon' (see present edition, Vol. 20). In this letter Engels examines the corrections they sent him to the translation. Marx's article was included in the appendix to the second French edition of his work *The Poverty of Philosophy* (see Note 165).— 116

198 The reference is to Proudhon's book *Si les traités de 1815 ont cessé d'exister? Actes du futur congrès*, Paris, 1863, in which he opposed a revision of the decisions on Poland taken by the 1815 Vienna Congress. He also spoke out against support for the Polish national liberation movement by European democrats and, in so doing, actually backed up the foreign policy of Russian tsarism.— 117

199 On 16 March 1884 London witnessed a workers' demonstration in connection with the anniversary of Marx's death and in commemoration of the Day of the Paris Commune. A meeting was held at Marx's grave in Highgate Cemetery.— 118

200 Engels is referring to the review of the March issue of *To-Day* published in *Justice*, No. 8, 8 March 1884. The author criticised the publication of Edward Aveling's article 'Christianity and Capitalism' and believed that the views it presented on religious and atheist issues were well known. The reviewer also considered Eleanor Marx's article 'Dr Marx and Mr Gladstone's Budget Speech of 1863' to be 'scarcely suited' to appear in the journal. In it, Eleanor Marx disproved the allegations made by the English economist Sedley Taylor who had accused Marx of citing Gladstone's 1864 budget speech in a distorted way. This accusation by Taylor was the continuation of the campaign of slander begun back in 1872 which Engels exposed in 1891 in his work *In the Case of Brentano Versus Marx* (see present edition, Vol. 27).— 118

201 Following the adoption of a programme based on Marxist positions at the 1880 Congress of the French Workers' Party in Le Havre (see K. Marx, 'Preamble to the Programme of the French Workers' Party', present edition, Vol. 24), the struggle between the Possibilists (see Note 237) and the Guesdists was aggravated; the latter represented the party's revolutionary wing and favoured the revolutionary transformation of society. The struggle led to a split in the party at its 1882 Congress in St Etienne. The Guesdists, who were in a minority, gathered together their representatives in Roanne and formed their own party, retaining the previous name.— 118, 444, 445

202 'Ex-President of Mankind' was the name Marx and Engels gave to Bernhard Becker, who had been President of the General Association of German Workers (Lassalleans). This was an allusion to Marx's article 'The "President of Mankind"' (see present edition, Vol. 20, pp. 92-96) containing a critique of Becker's activities.— 119

203 The *German People's Party* (Deutsche Volkspartei) appeared in Stuttgart in 1868. It consisted of democratic elements from the petty and middle bourgeoisie, mainly

from the South German states, and thus was also called South German and Swabian. Opposing the establishment of Prussian hegemony in Germany and advancing general democratic slogans, the German People's Party at the same time expressed the particularist aspirations of the bourgeoisie in a number of German states. This was manifested in its campaign against the unification of Germany to become a single centralised democratic republic, in favour of a federal German state and a republican form of government. From the late 1870s the party took a negative stance on the Anti-Socialist Law (see Note 37). In an effort to gain control of the workers' movement, the party repeatedly came out in favour of joint action with the German Social Democrats during the election campaigns to the Reichstag. The party's permanent leader and the chairman of its parliamentary group from its foundation up to the 1890s was Leopold Sonnemann. The party ceased to exist in 1910 when it merged with the People's Party of Progress (Fortschrittliche Volkspartei).— 119, 282, 502

204 Engels is probably referring to the part of Karl Kautsky's letter of 12 March 1884 dealing with the English socialist William Morris. Kautsky wrote that he had incorrectly understood Eleanor Marx's remark about William Morris and, in one of his articles, had therefore called him a 'Gefühlssozialist' (socialist by feeling). The offended Morris categorically rejected this opinion.— 121

205 Engels is referring to the newspaper *Révolutions de Paris* published by Élisée Loustalot, the newspaper *Feuille Villageoise* and Maurice Alhoy's and Louis Lurine's book *Les prisons de Paris. Histoire, types, moeurs, mystères*, Paris, 1846.— 122

206 The magazine *To-Day*, No. 4, April 1884, carried the articles by M. Davitt, 'The Irish Social Problem' and P. Lafargue, 'Peasant Proprietary in France'.

The newspaper *Justice*, No. 11, 29 March 1884, reported that *To-Day* was about to publish Lafargue's article 'On Peasant Proprietary in France' and described the author as 'perhaps the greatest living authority on the French peasantry'.— 122

207 The letter referred to by Marx was probably written in the spring of 1882 and has not been found. Engels quotes Marx's opinion of Richard Wagner in Chapter II of his work *The Origin of the Family, Private Property and the State* (see present edition, Vol. 26, p. 147).— 124

208 On 7 April 1884 Eduard Bernstein informed Engels that the second and third parts of his work *Anti-Dühring* ('Political Economy' and 'Socialism', see present edition, Vol. 25) were almost sold out and that 300 copies remained of the first part ('Philosophy'). He therefore suggested that a new edition of the work be prepared, but this time as a single volume and not in separate parts. The second German edition of *Anti-Dühring* appeared in Zurich at the beginning of December 1885 with additions made by Engels to the second chapter of the third part. The title page gave the year of publication as 1886.— 124, 126, 130, 131, 142, 249, 251, 263, 310, 324, 327, 346, 371, 372

209 On 11 October 1880 Heinrich Wilhelm Fabian, a German émigré living in the United States, wrote to Marx and Engels asking them to contribute to a weekly journal called *Einheit* which he planned to start publishing in an American city on 1 January 1881. The journal's programme was compiled by Fabian together with Wilhelm Ludwig Rosenberg and sent together with the letter.

On 6 November 1880 Fabian wrote to Marx about $\sqrt{-1}$ (on this, see Ch. XII of the first part of *Anti-Dühring*; present edition, Vol. 25, p. 112).

In April 1884 Fabian published in the *Freidenker* newspaper an article directed against Marx's and Engels' doctrine of the state.— 124, 295

210 On 22 March 1884, during a reception on the occasion of his birthday for a delegation made up of representatives from the Federal Council, the German Reichstag and Prussian Landtag, Emperor William I (nicknamed Lehmann) of Germany expressed his displeasure at the Reichstag's decision at the first reading to reject the prolongation of the Anti-Socialist Law. The Emperor made it plain that he regarded opposition to this law as opposition to him personally.— 124, 147

211 On 7 April 1884 Karl Kautsky informed Engels that on 1 April a legal newspaper called the *Berliner Volksblatt* had begun to appear in the German capital. Its first editor-in-chief, Wilhelm Blos, belonged to the Right wing of the Socialist Workers' Party. The members of the Social-Democratic group in the Reichstag, including Blos himself, opposed Liebknecht playing any part in the newspaper's publication.— 124

212 Engels is referring to the decision taken at the congress of the French Workers' Party in Roubaix (see Note 195) to call an international congress in London for spring 1885 to discuss factory law. The congress took place in Antwerp in August 1885.— 125

213 The reference is to Engels' plans to revise *The Peasant War in Germany* (see present edition, Vol. 10), which he failed to carry out. For the fragments which have survived and plans of the book see present edition, Vol. 26, pp. 554-55.—130, 131, 133, 142, 217, 244, 245, 249, 328, 363, 371, 374, 419

214 Legend has it that Martin Luther, speaking in the Diet of Worms on 18 April 1521, answered the question as to whether he stood by his works or rejected them as heresy by saying: 'Here stand I—I can do no other'.— 132

215 Apparently Ludwig Kugelmann sent Engels Leibniz' correspondence as published in Hanover, first in the journal *Zeitschrift des historischen Vereins für Niedersachsen* for 1881 and 1884 and later as separate offprints from this journal: *Leibnizens Briefwechsel mit dem Minister von Bernstorff und andere Leibniz betreffende Briefe und Aktenstücke aus den Jahren 1705-1716*, Hanover, 1882, and *Briefwechsel zwischen Leibniz und der Herzogin Elisabeth Charlotte v. Orléans in den Jahren 1715 und 1716*, Hanover, 1884.— 133

216 At the elections to the Paris municipal council, which were set for 4 May 1884, the French Workers' Party decided to put up its own candidates only in those constituences where no candidates were standing from the Possibilists (see Note 237) or from other socialist tendencies.— 134

217 Paul Lafargue's letter to Engels of 9 May 1884 gives reason to believe that the reference is to Engels' article on Marx's *Capital* which he (Lafargue) found at home ('Review of Volume One of *Capital* for *The Fortnightly Review*', present edition, Vol. 20). It is clear from Marx's correspondence with Engels that they intended to publish this review in Lafargue's French translation in *Le Courier français*, the newspaper of the Left-wing republicans (see Marx to Engels, 1 February 1868, present edition, Vol. 42, p. 532). However, the article was not published in Marx's and Engels' lifetimes.— 134

²¹⁸ Engels' work 'Prussian Schnapps in the German Reichstag' (see present edition, Vol. 24) was written in February 1876. The publication of this work, which exposed the Prussian Junkers, in *Der Volksstaat* and as a separate offprint caused consternation in government quarters.— 136

²¹⁹ Here Engels is apparently referring to several representatives of the Right wing in the Socialist Workers' Party of Germany such as Bruno Geiser, editor of the Stuttgart-based *Die Neue Welt*, and to journalists who were close to this trend, like Karl Frohme, Wilhelm Blos, Louis Viereck, etc.— 136, 145, 153, 160, 169

²²⁰ Eugen Richter, one of the leaders of the German Party of Free Thinkers (see Note 231) opposed the schnapps monopoly as lucrative for the Junkers.— 137

²²¹ In a letter of 29 April 1884 Karl Kautsky suggested to Engels that his work *The Origin of the Family, Private Property and the State* (see present edition, Vol. 26) should be published in Germany at what was, in his opinion, an opportune moment — during the Reichstag discussion on the prolongation of the Anti-Socialist Law. He believed that on the eve of the elections all parties would have to reckon with the voters' opinion and the government would therefore not risk banning *Die Neue Zeit* and the publication of Engels' work.— 137

²²² On 12 May 1884 the Reichstag voted by a majority of 189 to 157 at the third reading to prolong the Anti-Socialist Law (see Note 37) until 1886.— 137, 140

²²³ The Social-Democratic newspaper *Süddeutsche Post* was banned on 19 May 1884 because of its 'general tendency' and, in particular, for publishing a leader in No. 57 entitled 'Recht auf Arbeit' ('The Right to Work'). Under Paragraph 11 of the Anti-Socialist Law the newspaper was accused of attempting to overthrow the state and social system.— 137

²²⁴ At Engels' request (see this volume, pp. 85 and 95) he was sent the following materials from the Archives of the German Socialist Workers' Party (see Note 144): 1) Rodbertus, *Offener Brief an das Comité des Deutschen Arbeitervereins zu Leipzig*, Leipzig, 1863, and 2) *Der Social-Demokrat*, Nos. 16, 17 and 18 of 1, 3 and 5 February 1865 containing Marx's article 'On Proudhon' (see Note 151).— 138, 139

²²⁵ Engels is referring to the accusation made by Rodbertus-Jagetzow that in *Capital* Marx plagiarised his work *Zur Erkenntniss unsrer staatswirtschaftlichen Zustände*, Neubrandenburg and Friedland, 1842 (see also Note 187 and Engels' Preface to Volume II of *Capital*, present edition, Vol. 36).— 138, 319

²²⁶ Karl Kautsky gave a detailed critical analysis of Rodbertus-Jagetzow's views in 'Das "Capital" von Rodbertus', published in *Die Neue Zeit*, Nos. 8 and 9, August and September 1884 (see also Note 254).— 138

²²⁷ The reference is to a group of persons who took part in publishing Rodbertus-Jagetzow's literary legacy, notably his work *Das Kapital. Vierter socialer Brief an von Kirchmann*, Berlin, 1884. This work was published by Theophil Kozak who also wrote an introduction, a preface was written by the German economist Adolph Wagner.— 138

²²⁸ Given the fact that tighter controls on the Swiss-German border were causing difficulties in transporting the printed edition of *Der Sozialdemokrat* from Zurich to Germany, Eduard Bernstein went to Belgium with a view to organising the rerouting of the newspaper via the Belgian-German border.— 139

²²⁹ The *Centre*—a political party of German Catholics formed in June 1870; it expressed the separatist and anti-Prussian tendencies that were widespread in West and South-West Germany (the deputies representing this party had their seats in the centre of the chamber). The Centre Party united different social sections of the Catholic clergy, landowners, bourgeoisie, sections of the peasantry and, as a rule, occupied an intermediate position, manoeuvring between the parties which supported the government and the Left opposition groups in the Reichstag. The Centre was in opposition to the Bismarck government from the mid-1870s to the early 1880s but still voted for the measures it took against the workers' and socialist movement. Engels described the Centre in detail in *The Role of Force in History* and in 'What Now?' (see present edition, Vol. 26).— 140, 192, 216, 222, 343, 361

²³⁰ The *Conservatives* expressed the interests of the German Junkers, the aristocracy, the generals, the Lutheran clergy and senior officials. In the Reichstag they were represented by the German Conservative Party and the Free Conservative Party.— 140, 147, 192

²³¹ The reference is to the *German Party of Free Thinkers* formed in March 1884 through the merger of the Party of Progress with the Left wing of the National Liberal Party (see notes 93 and 243). Reflecting the interests of banking and trading capital, the middle and petty bourgeoisie, in the 1880s it was in opposition to the Bismarck government on a number of domestic policy issues and took a hostile stance towards the Social Democrats. The party fell apart in 1893.— 140, 149, 389

²³² During the ballot on the prolongation of the Anti-Socialist Law held in the Reichstag on 10 May 1884 (see Note 222) the majority of deputies—including 27 members of the German Party of Free Thinkers and 39 deputies of the Centre (see Note 229)—voted in favour of its prolongation. The total vote in favour was 189, with 157 against. Fearing a possible dissolution of the Reichstag (see Note 244) and the calling of new elections, the leaderships of the German Party of Free Thinkers and the Centre, by supporting Bismarck's domestic policy, weakened the liberal opposition to the government.— 140

²³³ When the bill to prolong the Anti-Socialist Law was being discussed in the Reichstag on 9 May 1884 Bismarck declared that he recognised the 'right to work'. On 17 May, the *Norddeutsche Allgemeine Zeitung*, the mouthpiece of the government, declared in its evening edition by way of explanation that Bismarck had meant the use of unemployed labour in workhouses (like those in Britain) or in places of detention. It was planned to use the unemployed in Germany to carry out.physically arduous work—repairing the roads, breaking up stones, chopping wood, etc.— and to pay them in money or food.— 140, 150

²³⁴ *Phalanstère*—palaces in which, according to the French utopian socialist, Charles Fourier, members of producer and consumer associations were to live and work in an ideal socialist society.

The ideas which Engels goes on to advocate in this letter were used in an editorial article probably written by Eduard Bernstein and carried by *Der Sozialdemokrat*, No. 22, 29 May 1884 under the heading 'Reklame und Wirklichkeit'.— 141

²³⁵ The *national workshops (ateliers)* were instituted by the Provisional Government immediately after the February revolution of 1848. By this means the government

sought to discredit Louis Blanc's ideas on 'the organisations of labour' in the eyes of the workers and, at the same time, to utilise those employed in the national workshops, organised on military lines, against the revolutionary proletariat. For an assessment of the national workshops, see K. Marx, *The Class Struggles in France, 1848 to 1850* (present edition, Vol. 10, p. 63).— 141

236 *Opportunists* was the name given in France to the party of moderate bourgeois republicans after its split in 1881 and the formation of a radical party based on the Left wing and headed by Georges Clemenceau.

The reason for this name, introduced in 1877 by the journalist Henri Rochefort, was the statement by Léon Gambetta, the party's leader, that reforms should be carried out 'at an opportune time'.— 141, 314, 413, 444

237 *Possibilists*— followers of a reformist trend in the French socialist movement between the 1880s and the beginning of the 20th century. It was led by Paul Louis Marie Brousse and Benoît Malon who caused a split in the French Workers' Party in 1882 by forming their own party called the Workers' Social-Revolutionary Party (see Note 201). Its ideological basis was the theory of municipal socialism. The Possibilists proclaimed the 'policy of possibilities' to be their principle; at the beginning of the 20th century they became part of the French Socialist Party.— 141, 320, 425, 442

238 In connection with Wilhelm Liebknecht's trip to Paris in mid-May 1884 German newspapers reported that preparations were underway there for a conference of socialists from several European countries.— 144

239 From 29 May to 4 June 1884 Engels stayed in Hastings with Sigismund Borkheim, a participant in the revolution of 1848-49 in Germany.— 144, 152, 381

240 On 29 May 1884 Kautsky informed Engels of the differences of opinion which had arisen on the editorial board of *Die Neue Zeit* between himself and the publisher Johann Heinrich Wilhelm Dietz. The latter thought it essential to make the journal more up to date by introducing a new column headed 'Politische Rundschau' which, he intended, should be run by Wilhelm Blos in Stuttgart. Then Dietz insisted on Blos being appointed editor of *Die Neue Zeit*. This situation prompted Eduard Bernstein, in a letter to Engels of 29 May 1884, to suggest that for the time being no chapters should appear there from Engels' work *The Origin of the Family, Private Property and the State*.— 145, 153

241 The reference is to the 'Programm der sozialistischen Arbeiterpartei Deutschlands' adopted at the unification congress in Gotha in May 1875. On this document see K. Marx, *Critique of the Gotha Programme* (present edition, Vol. 24).— 146

242 Engels is referring to the system of provocation, espionage, false evidence and forgeries employed by the Prussian police officer Wilhelm Stieber, who organised the Cologne trial of members of the Communist League in 1852.— 147

243 The reference is to the *National Liberals*, a Prussian, and from 1871 all-German, Right-wing bourgeois party which existed from 1867 to 1918. It was one of the pillars of the Junker-bourgeois bloc. The party's programme called for civil equality and bourgeois-democratic freedoms, but as the workers' movement in Germany strengthened it abandoned these demands and contented itself with Bismarck's half-hearted reforms. Following the unification of Germany it definitively took shape as a party of the big, mainly industrial, bourgeoisie and for all practical purposes disavowed the demands it had made earlier.— 147, 192, 428, 439

[244] On 9 May 1884, during the discussion on the prolongation of the Anti-Socialist Law (see Note 37) Bismarck read out to the Reichstag a letter written by William I in March 1884 following the assassination of Tsar Alexander II of Russia (see Note 188). The author referred to the need for joint action by the great powers to combat 'the threat of assassination attempts hanging over the whole of Europe'. Bismarck then announced his intention to dissolve the Reichstag immediately in the event of the bill being defeated.— 147

[245] In late February 1884 a major strike began at the coal mines in Anzin, Denain district, department Nord, France. Involving more than 10,000 workers, the strike was in protest at the prohibition of trade unions and lasted until mid-April when the employers reversed their decision to introduce harder working conditions.— 149

[246] Under the English *Act for the Reliefs of the Poor* (43rd Elizabeth) (1601) a special tax was levied in each parish to help the poor. Those residents who were unable to provide for themselves and their families received help from the poor fund.

An *Act for the Amendment and Better Administration of the Laws Relating to the Poor in England and Wales* (1834) provided for only one form of assistance to the poor, namely their accommodation in workhouses, otherwise known as 'bastilles for the poor'. The aim of the act was to force the poor to agree to harder working conditions and, in this way, to provide the industrial bourgeoisie with a more plentiful supply of cheap labour.— 150

[247] The reference is to the Act against the Criminal Use of Explosives. It was introduced in response to the unsuccessful assassination attempt organised by a provocateur in Niederwald on 27-28 September 1883. During the discussion of the bill in May 1884 the Social-Democratic deputies announced their refusal to discuss or vote on it. The act was passed by the Reichstag on 15 May 1884 and subjected to police surveillance the production, use, storage and import of explosive substances. Violations of the act were punished by long terms of imprisonment or even the death sentence.— 150

[248] Sigismund Ludwig Borkheim's autobiography was published posthumously in *Die Neue Zeit*, Nos. 3, 5, 6 and 7 for 1890 under the heading 'Erinnerungen eines deutschen Achtungvierzigers'.— 152, 381

[249] This letter was published in English for the first time in *The Labour Monthly*, London, 1933, Vol. 15, No. 10, X.— 153

[250] In Salzburg Karl Kautsky met some Austrian Social Democrats who told him that the anarchists did not wield any appreciable influence among the masses. He informed Engels about the details of this meeting on 23 June 1884.— 153

[251] A number of explosions occurred in London on 30 May 1884, including one at Scotland Yard when a dynamite charge was set off in a public convenience. Irish nationalists claimed responsibility for the explosions.— 154

[252] An anarchist newspaper called *L'Explosion* began to appear in Carouge near Geneva in April 1884. One of the men behind it was the former Bakuninist Carlo Terzaghi (see also K. Marx and F. Engels, *The Alliance of Socialist Democracy and the International Working Men's Association*, present edition, Vol. 23).— 154

[253] The reference is to the anarchists who were expelled from Vienna and its surround-

ings due to the introduction of a state of siege there on 30 January 1884 (see Note 154). Some of them emigrated to Britain.— 154

²⁵⁴ On 23 June 1884 Karl Kautsky sent Engels the beginning of his article 'Das "Kapital" von Rodbertus' (see also this volume, p. 138) so that the latter might familiarise himself with its contents. The article was published in *Die Neue Zeit*, Nos. 8 and 9 for 1884. It marked the start of Kautsky's polemic with Carl August Schramm (see Engels to Bebel, 20-23 January 1886, this volume, pp. 386-87).— 155

²⁵⁵ The reference is to the work: J. K. Rodbertus-Jagetzow, *Zur Erkenntniss unsrer staatswirtschaftlichen Zustände*, Neubrandenburg and Friedland, 1842. Rodbertus' treatment of the constituted value as referred to in this letter is examined by Engels in the article 'Marx and Rodbertus' which he wrote by way of a preface to the first German edition of Marx's *The Poverty of Philosophy* (see present edition, Vol. 26).— 156

²⁵⁶ Engels is replying to Evgenia Papritz's letter of 26 June 1884 in which she wrote that, with a view to spreading the ideas of scientific socialism in Russian society, a start had been made in Moscow on publishing the lithographed journal *Социалистическое знание*. The journal was to publish translations of works by West European authors and articles on socio-political issues. Informing Engels that she was translating his work *Outlines of a Critique of Political Economy* (see present edition, Vol. 3), Papritz enquired where she could obtain little-known works by Marx and himself for translation and asked where she might find 'the last manifesto to the English workers' as well as Engels' work *Anti-Dühring. Herr Eugen Dühring's Revolution in Science* (see present edition, Vol. 25).— 157

²⁵⁷ In the 1880s a number of works by Marx and Engels were published in Russian in Geneva: in 1882, the *Manifesto of the Communist Party* (see present edition, Vol. 6 and this volume, Note 120), and also the *Provisional Rules of the Association*, written by Marx (Vol. 20); in 1883, Marx's *Wage Labour and Capital* (Vol. 9), and in 1884, Engels' *Socialism: Utopian and Scientific*. Marx's *The Poverty of Philosophy* (see Note 185) appeared in 1886. The second volume of *Capital* by Marx was published in St Petersburg in 1885 (see Note 155).— 158

²⁵⁸ Marx's work *Wage Labour and Capital* (see present edition, Vol. 9) was first published in 1849 as a series of leading articles in the *Neue Rheinische Zeitung*. The first separate edition of the work appeared in Breslau (Wrocław), Silesia in 1880 without Marx's involvement. The second edition was published in the same place in 1881. In 1884, with Engels' participation and a short Introductory Note written by him on the history of its publication (see present edition, Vol. 26), the work was published in Hottingen-Zurich.— 159

²⁵⁹ In his letter of 20 June 1884 Eduard Bernstein asked Engels to send him a photograph of Marx for a chromolithograph a comrade of his was planning. For the original Bernstein wished to have either the drawing in chalk which he had seen at Engels' home in his study, or else a photograph of Marx.— 159

²⁶⁰ On 20 June 1884 Eduard Bernstein wrote to Engels saying that the Zurich publishing house Die Volksbuchhandlung was planning to publish a collection of socialist poetry. Bernstein enquired in this conjunction about previous editions of verse by Georg Weerth. Engels is probably referring to the collection of Weerth's poems selected from two previous editions, *Jahrbuch für Kunst und Poesie*, Barmen, 1843, and

Album. Originalpoesien von Georg Weerth, Borna, 1847. Moreover, Weerth completed another collection of poems in 1848, which was not, however, published in his own lifetime. It was included in Georg Weerth's *Sämtliche Werke* published in Berlin in 1956-57.— 160

[261] Hermann Schlüter, the keeper of the Archives of German Social Democracy (see Note 144) asked Bernstein to remind Engels that he had agreed to send him a number of materials for the archives. Bernstein did this in his letter to Engels of 20 June 1884, remarking that Schlüter had 'a real mania for collecting things'.— 160

[262] A draft of this letter was written by Engels on the back of Sarah Allen's letter to him of 5 July 1884.— 161

[263] An excerpt from this letter was published in English for the first time in *The Labour Monthly*, London, 1933, Vol. 15, No. 10, X.— 164, 176, 197, 206, 212, 244, 299, 315, 340

[264] Following prolonged and unsuccessful talks with the publisher Dietz on printing Engels' work *The Origin of the Family, Private Property and the State* in Stuttgart, Karl Kautsky wrote to Engels on 16 July 1884 that this work could be issued by the Social Democratic publishing house Die Volksbuchhandlung in Hottingen-Zurich where Hermann Schlüter was a member of staff. Of the total edition of 5,000 copies, 1,000 would be passed on to the publisher Jakob Schabelitz for distribution in Germany.— 164, 172

[265] In their letters to Engels of 16 July 1884 Karl Kautsky and Eduard Bernstein informed him that the Stuttgart publisher Johann Heinrich Wilhelm Dietz was planning to cease issuing *Die Neue Zeit* because of financial difficulties. However, a month later, on 18 August, Kautsky wrote to tell Engels that he and Dietz had discussed plans for moving the journal's place of publication to Hamburg. This plan was not carried out and *Die Neue Zeit* continued to appear in Stuttgart up to 1923.— 164, 189

[266] Nos. 20, 21 and 22 of *Die Neue Welt* for 1884, the editor being Bruno Geiser, published an article by Karl du Prel called 'Der Somnambulismus'.— 165, 170

[267] The 'Sozialpolitische Rundschau' column of *Der Sozialdemokrat*, No. 28, 10 July 1884, carried a report about the spread of cholera among the poor in Europe. In a note on the report the author severely criticised 'the scholars from the *Volkszeitung* and other German papers' for using the word 'bacillum'. Among others, this note was directed against Bruno Geiser. *Die Neue Welt*, of which he was the editor, had used the word in its report on the cholera epidemic.— 166

[268] Given the fact that a cholera epidemic was expected in Paris in the summer of 1884, Engels and Paul Lafargue agreed to persuade Laura Lafargue to move to England for some time. However, Laura did not arrive at Engels' home until the autumn of 1884.— 167, 171, 224

[269] *Le quart d'heure de Rabelais* — the moment of settling accounts, an unpleasant interlude. This expression originates from an episode which allegedly happened to the French author Rabelais and was retold by Voltaire. On his way from Rome to Paris, Rabelais stopped off at a hotel in Lyons and, not having any money to live on, thought up an original way of solving his problem. With the assistance of the son of the hotel's owner, he made some labels on which he wrote 'Poison to kill the

King' and 'Poison to kill the Queen' to be attached to bottles. After that Rabelais, having now eaten his fill for free, was taken to Paris in the company of two police-men.— 167

²⁷⁰ The editorial board of the *Journal des Économistes*, which carried Paul Lafargue's article 'Le blé en Amerique', added an accompanying note to the article express-ing regret that Lafargue had not 'devoted his excellent enquiring mind and good style to political economy'.— 168

²⁷¹ On 16 July 1884 Eduard Bernstein wrote to Engels that the voters' mood did not favour the Social Democrats in the constituencies where August Bebel and Wil-helm Liebknecht were standing at the forthcoming elections (see Note 194) and that the Right-wing Social Democrats Bruno Geiser and Louis Viereck had the better constituencies.— 169

²⁷² Engels is referring to Bruno Geiser's attacks on atheism in his article 'Das Innere der Erde. Eine Auseinandersetzung über den gegenwärtigen Stand einiger Fragen der Wissenschaft' which was published in *Die Neue Welt*, Nos. 14 and 15, 1884.— 170

²⁷³ In a letter of 25 July 1884 Paul Lafargue asked Engels to look through his résumé of P. P. Leroy-Beaulieu's book *Le Collectivisme*... in which the author set out to disprove some of the propositions of Marx's economic theory. For Engels' remarks on Lafargue's work 'La théorie de la plus-value de Karl Marx et la critique de M. Paul Leroy-Beaulieu' see this volume, pp. 179-83.— 171, 175, 178

²⁷⁴ In Eduard Bernstein's correspondence published by the International Institute of Social History, Amsterdam, this excerpt from Engels' letter is dated: [Hastings, c. 5 July 1884?] (see *Eduard Bernsteins Briefwechsel mit Friedrich Engels*, herausgege-ben von H. Hirsch, Assen, Van Gorcum, 1970, pp. 282-83). However, since the date and place of writing are doubted by the publishers themselves, the present edition has retained the traditional dating.— 173

²⁷⁵ *Epistolae obscurorum virorum* (Letters of obscure men) — a collection of satirical let-ters in two parts (Part I—1515, Part II—1517), probably written by members of a humanists' club in Erfurt who supported Reichlin. A major role in the second (and perhaps also the first) part of the *Letters* was played by Ulrich von Hutten. The letters were directed against Cologne-based theologians.— 173

²⁷⁶ This letter was first published in the language of the original (English) in: Fried-rich Engels, Paul et Laura Lafargue, *Correspondance*, t. I, 1868-86, Paris, Editions sociales, 1956.— 174

²⁷⁷ Engels vacationed in Worthing on the South coast of England from about 5 Au-gust to 1 September 1884.— 174, 176, 178, 190

²⁷⁸ The annual conference of the Democratic Federation (see Note 99) was held in London in early August 1884; the conference resolved to rename the Democratic Federation and call it the Social Democratic Federation (see Note 300).— 177

²⁷⁹ The beginning of the letter has not been found.

In this letter Engels sets out his remarks on the manuscript of Paul Lafargue's résumé of the book *Le Collectivisme. Examen critique du nouveau socialisme* by the French economist and sociologist Paul Leroy-Beaulieu. Part of the book was devot-ed to a denial of Marx's economic doctrine, particularly his theory of surplus value. Taking account of Engels' remarks, Lafargue's article was published in the *Journal des Économistes*, No. 9, 1884 under the heading 'La théorie de la plus-value de Karl Marx et la critique de M. Paul Leroy-Beaulieu'.— 179

280 Here, the direct form of the circulation of commodities means the form: commodity—money—commodity, and the second form: money—commodity—money.— 180

281 The editor-in-chief of the *Journal des Économistes*, Gustave Molinari, assured Paul Lafargue that he would be given the opportunity to make a reply should Paul Leroy-Beaulieu raise objections to his résumé (see Note 279), whereupon the discussion would be considered finished. However, the one to raise objections was not Beaulieu, but Maurice Block, who published an article in the *Journal des Économistes* entitled 'Le Capital, de Karl Marx, à propos d'une anticritique'. Lafargue replied to him in the *Journal des Économistes*, No. 11, 1884, with an article called 'Le "Capital" de Karl Marx et la critique de M. Block'.— 183, 224

282 In a letter of 6 August 1884 Georg Heinrich von Vollmar asked Engels to advise him of a suitable higher educational establishment for Miss Kjellberg who was planning to embark on a thorough study of the social sciences.— 184

283 *Manchesterism — the Manchester School* — a trend in economic thought which reflected the interests of the industrial bourgeoisie. Its supporters, known as Free Traders, advocated freedom of trade and non-interference by government in economic life. The centre of the Free Traders' agitation was Manchester.

   Marx dealt in detail with Frédéric Bastiat's views in the *Economic Manuscripts of 1857-58* (see present edition, Vol. 28, pp. 5-16).— 184

284 On 12 August 1884, Marya Jankowska (pseudonym Stefan Leonowicz), the representative of a Polish Social-Democratic group in Geneva, wrote to Engels requesting permission to publish a Polish edition of his work *The Origin of the Family, Private Property and the State*. Engels wrote a draft of his reply on the back of the letter from Jankowska.— 185

285 In a letter of 18 August, 1884 Karl Kautsky suggested to Engels that he should advertise the forthcoming publication of his work *The Origin of the Family, Private Property and the State* and include its preface in *Die Neue Zeit* with a view to preventing the book being banned in Germany. The September issue of the journal carried an announcement that this work was to appear shortly together with excerpts from Engels' preface (see present edition, Vol. 26, pp. 129-276).— 187

286 On 18 August 1884 Eduard Bernstein wrote to inform Engels that translation work had been completed on Marx's *The Poverty of Philosophy* (see Note 118). He also offered to compile an index to *Capital* together with Karl Kautsky.— 188

287 Engels wrote this letter on a postcard. The address it bears is also in his handwriting and reads: 'Herrn K. Kautsky, 38, Berglistr.; Riesbach-Zürich, Switzerland.'— 189, 200, 205

288 In his letter of 26 August 1884 Karl Kautsky drew Engels' attention to the fact that, in his work *Rodbertus, der Begründer des wissenschaftlichen Sozialismus*, Georg Adler described as mistaken Engels' claim that Rodbertus had borrowed his doctrine of crises from Sismondi (see present edition, Vol. 25, p. 273, Engels' footnote).— 189

[289] The reference is to a number of polemical articles in *Der Sozialdemokrat*. In No. 36, 3 September 1884 there was a leading article called 'Höheres Blech' directed against an article praising Rodbertus by the Austrian journalist Hermann Bahr which had appeared in the Viennese *Deutsche Wochenschrift* in August.

In the same issue of *Der Sozialdemokrat*, Eduard Bernstein, using his pseudonym Leo, published an article ('Ein Ketzerriecher') against Heinrich Wilhelm Fabian, a German socialist living in the United States who had published articles against Marx's and Engels' doctrine of the state in the April issue of *Der Freidenker* and the *New Yorker Volkszeitung*.

Der Sozialdemokrat, No. 37, 11 September 1884 carried an article called 'Wie stellen wir uns zur Börsensteuer?' evidently written by Abraham Gumbel. The article said that the German Social Democrats should support the bill on the stock exchange tax proposed by Bismarck. Taking up the polemics on this issue, the editorial board of *Der Sozialdemokrat* declared that, in its opinion, the bill accorded merely with the interests of the big landowners' party (see 'In Sachen der Börsensteuer', *Der Sozialdemokrat*, No. 39, 25 September 1884).— 191

[290] Engels' reply to the editors of *To-Day* has not been found.— 192, 195

[291] The *Kölnische Zeitung*, No. 241, 30 August 1884 (first edition) carried an article headed 'Professor Schweifurth über den Congo' on the activities of the Association Internationale Africaine which had been founded in Brussels in 1876 by King Leopold II of Belgium. The organisation was renamed the Comité d'Études du Haut-Congo in 1878. Among those taking part in its work was the famous explorer Henry Morton Stanley. The actual aim of the association was to seize and exploit the Congo basin. The article reported that, alongside their philanthropic and scientific work, the Belgian settlers were buying slaves in the Congo, employing the slave labour of the indigenous population, buying ivory, palm oil and other local commodities for export.— 192

[292] German colonial policy became much more active in 1884. The first congress of the German Colonial Union took place on 5 January in Frankfurt-am-Main. The same year saw the organisation of the first German trading station on the South-West coast of Africa, which served as a base for expanding the role played by German capital in Africa.— 192, 199

[293] The reference is to the manuscripts of Carl Schramm's and Karl Kautsky's articles. Engels goes on in the letter to examine the latter's article against Schramm. The German Social Democrat and reformist Carl Schramm sent the editors of *Die Neue Zeit* his manuscript 'K. Kautsky und Rodbertus' for publication in which he sharply attacked Kautsky's article 'Das "Kapital" von Rodbertus' which the journal had published previously. Schramm's article and Kautsky's reply, entitled 'Eine Replik', were carried by *Die Neue Zeit*, No. 11, 1884.— 193

[294] The neo-Malthusian Charles Robert Drysdale published an article entitled 'The State Remedy for Poverty' in the September issue of *To-Day*. Referring to Karl Kautsky's book *Der Einfluss der Volksvermehrung auf den Fortschritt der Gesellschaft* (Vienna, 1880), he wrote that the 'ardent Socialist' Kautsky 'fully admits the truth of the generalisation of Malthus and Darwin'.— 195

[295] This letter was written by Engels on a postcard. On it he wrote the following ad-

dress: 'Herrn H. Schlüter, Volksbuchhandlung, Hottingen-Zürich, Switzerland.'— 196

²⁹⁶ This letter was written by Engels on a postcard. He provided it with the following address: 'Herrn H. Schlüter, Volksbuchhandlung, Kasinostr. Hottingen-Zürich, Switzerland.'— 196

²⁹⁷ On 15-17 September 1884, a meeting took place in Skierniewice, Poland, between the emperors of Germany, Austria and Russia and their foreign ministers. The result was the prolongation for three years of the agreement reached between Russia and Germany in June 1881 on the maintenance of benevolent neutrality should the other country be attacked.— 198

²⁹⁸ Engels seems to be referring to the impression the results of the German Reichstag elections of 10 January 1874 had in Europe, when the Socialist Workers' Party of Germany scored a considerable victory: nine of its candidates (including August Bebel and Wilhelm Liebknecht) were elected and the party won over six per cent of the poll.— 198

²⁹⁹ In 1884 the third parliamentary reform was carried out in England, as a result of which the suffrage was extended to include small farmers and the farm workers who were homeowners or householders. Suffrage was not extended to the poorer rural and urban sections of the population (tenants and domestic servants), nor to women. The first elections under the new electoral law took place in November-December 1885, with the electorate having a numerical strength of two million higher than at the previous poll (see Note 487).— 198, 270, 304, 314, 317, 318, 320, 341, 497

³⁰⁰ *Social Democratic Federation* — an English socialist organisation founded in August 1884 and based on the Democratic Federation (see Note 99); it united different socialist elements, mainly drawn from the intelligentsia and part of the politically active workers. The Federation's programme stated that all the wealth should belong to labour — its only source, it called for the socialisation of the means of production, distribution and exchange, for the set-up of society of 'complete emancipation of labour'. It was the first socialist programme in England, which was on the main based on Marx's ideas. The leadership of the Federation was in the hands of Henry Mayers Hyndman, who was prone to use authoritarian methods, and his supporters, who denied the need to work in the trade unions. This doomed the organisation to isolation from the working masses. As a counter to Hyndman's line, a group of socialists within the Federation (Eleanor Marx-Aveling, Edward Aveling, Tom Mann, William Morris and others) campaigned for the establishment of close links with the mass workers' movement. The disagreements in the Federation over questions of tactics and international cooperation (attitude to the split in the French Workers' Party; see notes 201 and 348) led in December 1884 to a split and the foundation of an independent organisation called the Socialist League (see Note 346). In 1885-86 the local branches of the Federation took an active part in the unemployed movement, supported the strike campaign and the fight for an eight-hour working day.— 198, 207, 224, 236, 245, 341, 376, 384, 394, 403, 471, 492, 526, 529, 533

³⁰¹ The reference is to the German edition of Marx's *The Poverty of Philosophy*, which appeared in Stuttgart in January 1885 (see Note 118). The book included, in place of Marx's preface, his article 'On Proudhon' (see present edition, Vol. 20) and two

appendices: an excerpt from Marx's work *A Contribution to the Critique of Political Economy* on the theory of the English socialist John Gray (see present edition, Vol. 29, pp. 320-23), and a translation of the 'Speech on the Question of Free Trade' (Vol. 6).

At one time *Die Neue Zeit* was printed in a distinctive orthography proposed by Bruno Geiser.— 200, 205, 206, 208, 216

302 The Italian translation of Engels' work *The Origin of the Family, Private Property and the State* was done by Pasquale Martignetti and edited by Engels himself (see this volume, p. 215). The Polish edition appeared in Paris in 1885, and the Russian translation was published in St Petersburg in 1894.— 205, 421

303 In a note headed 'Exécution d'un agent provocateur' the Paris newspaper *Le Cri du Peuple*, No. 356, 18 October 1884 reported that Heinrich Nonne, a Hanoverian living in Paris, had been exposed as a provocateur and police spy and expelled from the Socialist Workers' Party of Germany (see also Note 166).— 207

304 When he visited his relatives in Darmstadt in the summer of 1884, Carl Schorlemmer was detained by the authorities on suspicion of bringing illegal literature into Germany. Being a British subject, however, he succeeded in avoiding punishment (see also F. Engels, 'Carl Schorlemmer', present edition, Vol. 27).— 209, 245

305 An excerpt from this letter was first published in English in: K. Marx, F. Engels, *On the Paris Commune*, Progress Publishers, Moscow, 1971.— 210

306 At the Reichstag elections on 28 October 1884— the outcome of which August Bebel telegraphed to Engels— and at the second ballots held in early November, the Socialist Workers' Party of Germany was able to increase its number of seats to 24 as against 13 at the previous elections. It received 549, 990 votes, or 238,029 more than at the 1881 elections.— 210, 216, 221

307 The election result meant that the Social-Democratic group was able to initiate legislation for the first time, since the Reichstag's rules accorded this right only to parliamentary groups with 15 or more seats.— 210, 217

308 Bebel was elected to the Reichstag in Hamburg I (12,282 votes) and Dresden I (8,620 votes at the first ballot and 11,106 at the second) constituencies. He did not receive the required number of votes in Leipzig and Cologne.— 211

309 The Reichstag elections of 28 October 1884 brought fresh success to the German Social Democrats when compared with the 1878 elections held before the Anti-Socialist Law came into force; their vote increased from 493,000 to 549,900.— 212

310 Wilhelm Liebknecht failed to obtain the required number of votes at the first ballot in Offenbach-Dieburg, but he was elected at the second ballot with 10,505 votes.— 212

311 Following August Bebel's failure at the first ballot in Cologne, representatives of the National Liberals and the Centre stood at the second ballot (see notes 229 and 243).

In its reports headed 'Die Stichwahlen...' (second edition), No. 307, 4 November 1884; 'Die Reichstags-Stichwahl in Köln...' (second edition), No. 309, 6 November 1884 and 'Noch einmal die Kölner Stichwahl...' (second edition), No. 311, 8 November 1884, the *Kölnische Zeitung* called upon the Social-Democratic electors to vote for the National Liberal candidate and demanded that they publicly disavow revolutionary principles.— 213, 231

³¹² Bismarck's social reform was a distinctive method employed by the ruling classes in their fight against the revolutionary workers' movement during the period when the Anti-Socialist Law (see Note 37) was in force in Germany. Having failed to destroy the Social Democrats in the initial years of this law (see notes 307 and 309), in late 1881 Bismarck set out to achieve his objective through a carrot and stick policy. On 17 November, a proclamation was published by the Emperor announcing a number of reforms (social insurance laws in cases of industrial accident, illness, old age and invalidity). Bismarck hoped that their introduction would split the Social Democrats and isolate the working class from the Socialist Workers' Party of Germany.— 213

³¹³ In this letter Pasquale Martignetti asked for Engels' permission to translate his work *The Origin of the Family, Private Property and the State* into Italian and for his agreement to look through the translation; the book appeared in Benevento in 1885.— 215

³¹⁴ In his reply to Engels of 18 November, Pasquale Martignetti informed him that he had conducted talks with the publisher Gennaro, who had issued the Italian translation of Engels' *Socialism: Utopian and Scientific*, and that the latter had agreed to publish *The Origin of the Family, Private Property and the State.*— 215

³¹⁵ On the back of this letter Engels wrote: 'London 11. Novbr. 1884 Friedrich beantw. 13 Novbr. wie immer' (London 11. Novbr. 1884 Friedrich repl. 13 Novbr. as always).— 218

³¹⁶ This letter was first published in English in an abridged form in: K. Marx and F. Engels, *Correspondence. 1846-1895*, Martin Lawrence, London, 1934.— 220, 231, 279

³¹⁷ As a result of the War of the Austrian Succession (1740-48) Frederick II of Prussia seized Silesia from Austria. Frederick II waged the war against Austria in alliance with France and Bavaria and twice during its course betrayed his allies by concluding a separate peace treaty with Austria (1742 and 1745).

Prussia was among the participants in the Seven Years' War from 1756 to 1763.

On 5 April 1795 Prussia concluded the separate Peace of Basle with the French Republic, thus betraying its allies in the first anti-French coalition.— 221

³¹⁸ *German Confederation* (der Deutsche Bund) was an ephemeral union of German states formed by decision of the Congress of Vienna in June 1815 and originally comprising 35 absolutist feudal states and four free cities. The central body of the German Confederation was the Federal Diet, which consisted of representatives of the German states. The Confederation sealed Germany's political and economic fragmentation and retarded her development. After the defeat of the revolution of 1848-49 and the failure of the attempts to establish a more stable political union, the German Confederation was restored in its old decentralised and amorphous form.

The German Confederation finally ceased to exist during the Austro-Prussian war of 1866. This war ended the long-standing rivalry for supremacy in Germany between Austria and Prussia in favour of the latter and marked an important stage in the unification of Germany from above under the hegemony of Junker-bourgeois Prussia.— 221

319 Engels is referring to the annexation and incorporation into Prussia of the King-dom of Hanover, the Electorate of Hesse-Kassel, the Duchy of Nassau and the free city of Frankfurt-am-Main. This occurred after Prussia's victory in the war with Austria, in which they had supported the latter, and were the subject of legislation adopted on 20 September 1866.— 221

320 Engels is apparently referring to the confiscation of the property and lands belong-ing to George V, the King of Hanover, who had fought on the Austrian side. This decision was adopted by the Prussian government on 2 March 1868.— 221

321 The *North German Confederation* (Norddeutscher Bund) — a federative state formed in 1867 after Prussia's victory in the Austro-Prussian war to replace the disintegrat-ed German Confederation (see Note 318). It initially included 19 states and three free cities, which were formally recognised as autonomous. In 1870 Bavaria, Baden and Württemberg joined the Confederation. The establishment of the North Ger-man Confederation and its Constitution securing Prussian domination, was a ma-jor step towards the national unification of Germany. The Confederation ceased to exist in January 1871, when the German Empire was formed.— 221

322 The reference is to the November coup d'état in Prussia which ended on 5 Decem-ber 1848 in the dispersal of the Prussian National Assembly and the publication of the so-called imposed constitution (see also present edition, Vol. 11, pp. 66-70).— 222

323 *Edda* — a collection of epic poems and songs about the lives of the Scandinavian gods and heroes. It has come down to us in a manuscript dating from the 13th cen-tury, discovered in 1643 by the Icelandic bishop Sveinsson — the so-called *Elder Edda* — and in a treatise on the poetry of the scalds compiled in the early 13th cen-tury by Snorry Sturluson (*Younger Edda*).— 224

324 *Der Sozialdemokrat*, No. 47, 21 November 1884 reported that the French socialists had held a major rally on 15 November 1884 in solidarity with the German work-ers. It also published excerpts from an article carried by the *Lyon-Socialiste*, No. 9, 9 November 1884 and welcoming the German Social Democrats' victory in the Reichstag (see Note 306).— 225

325 During the second ballot to the Reichstag, Philipp Heinrich Müller, the Social-Democratic candidate in Darmstadt constituency, issued a leaflet in response to one put out by the National Liberals (see Note 243). Müller declared that he and millions more Germans supported the Republic and resolutely defended the Paris Commune. The text of the leaflet was reprinted in *Der Sozialdemokrat*, No. 46, 14 November 1884.

Jules Guesde quoted Müller in the leading article carried by *Le Cri du Peuple*, No. 387, 18 November 1884, which was headed 'Nouvelle victoire'.

What Engels meant by the Hanoverian programme was the election leaflet is-sued in Hanover stating that the growth in reaction in Germany could be explained by the cowardice of the National Liberals and their grovelling to Bismarck. The text of the leaflet was carried by *Der Sozialdemokrat*, No. 47, 21 November 1884.— 225, 232

326 With regard to the preparations for a meeting of solidarity with the German Social Democrats scheduled to take place in Redoute (France) on 15 November 1884 (see

Note 324) Eduard Bernstein wrote to Paul Lafargue asking him to refrain from sharp criticism of Lassalle. Lafargue informed Engels of the same on 18 November 1884.— 225

[327] This letter was first published in the language of the original (English) in: Thompson E. P., *William Morris. Romantic to Revolutionary*, Lawrence and Wishart, London, 1955, p. 861.— 227

[328] The English worker and socialist John L. Mahon wrote to Engels on 26 November 1884 requesting that he receive him to discuss a number of issues concerning the English workers' movement, in particular, an opportunity of setting up a workers' party.— 228

[329] The reference is to the events of May 1860; see Engels' letter to Emile Engels of 11 April and Engels' letters to Marx of 7 and 10 May 1860 (present edition, Vol. 41, pp. 120-21, 134 and 137; see also this volume, Note 23).— 229

[330] Engels wrote this letter on a postcard which he addressed 'Herrn Karl Kautsky, Hungelbrunngasse, 14, Wien IV, Austria'.

In a letter of 2 December 1884, Karl Kautsky, who was preparing to move from Zurich to London and was to stop off in Vienna and Berlin, gave Engels his Vienna address and also asked him to receive his correspondence at his (Engels') London address for a start. Kautsky further inquired whether Engels thought it better to publish Marx's 'Speech on the Question of Free Trade' as a separate pamphlet or as an appendix to the German edition of *The Poverty of Philosophy* (see Note 301) being printed by Dietz's publishing house in Stuttgart at the time.— 230

[331] The original of this letter contains a number of changes written in an unknown hand, perhaps that of August Bebel. The present edition reproduces Engels' text and gives the changes in footnotes.— 231

[332] Speaking on 10 May 1884 in the Reichstag debate on the prolongation of the Anti-Socialist Law (see Note 37), Bruno Geiser stated that the Social Democrats did not seek to use violence to overthrow the existing state and society. He described Bismarck's statement in the Reichstag of 9 May 1884 in which the latter acknowledged the right to work (see Note 233) as evidence of a social revolution in progress.

Speaking in the debate on 12 May 1884, August Bebel declared, in contrast to Geiser, that the law's prolongation would not effect the development and implementation of socialist ideas and that 'sooner or later they will quite certainly come to play the dominant role in state and society'.

Geiser's and Bebel's speeches were published in a pamphlet entitled *Aus den Verhandlungen über die Verlängerung des Sozialistengesetzes* which appeared in Nuremberg in 1884.— 231

[333] The reference is to the five thousand millions of golden francs which France paid under the peace treaty it concluded with Germany on 10 May 1871 in Frankfurt-am-Main after losing the Franco-Prussian War of 1870-71.— 233

[334] The reference is to the representatives of the radical bourgeoisie in the Prussian National Assembly which met in Frankfurt-am-Main from 1848 to 1849 (see also Note 322).— 234

[335] The reference is to the party of moderate Republicans headed by Armand Marrast which formed around the newspaper *Le National* in the 1840s; it was supported by

the industrial bourgeoisie and a section of the liberal intellectuals connected with it.— 234

[336] The interim government formed on 24 February 1848 during the bourgeois-democratic revolution in France was a coalition of three political groupings: the bourgeois republicans, the petty bourgeois democrats and the petty bourgeois socialists. The representatives of the two latter groupings made up the 'Social-Democratic minority'—accounting for four of the 11 members of the government—and were unable to exert any influence in their own right on government decisions.— 234

[337] This excerpt from the letter was reproduced by Paul Lafargue in the article 'Descendre dans la rue' published in the *Lyon-Socialiste*, No. 15, 21 December 1884. The original has not been found.

The surviving fragment of the letter is published in English for the first time in the present edition, Vol. 26.— 235

[338] This letter was first published in an abridged form in *The Labour Monthly*, London, 1933, Vol. 15, No. 10, X.— 236

[339] This evidently refers to the trips to Scotland undertaken by Andreas Scheu (in November 1884) and Henry Mayers Hyndman (in early December 1884). In Edinburgh Scheu took part in the founding of the Scottish Land and Labour League from among the local socialists. In an effort to extend the organisation's influence to other Scottish cities, Scheu contacted socialists in Glasgow and called on them to form a branch of this League. However, a gathering of socialists took place in Glasgow on 1 December at which Hyndman was present and which proclaimed the formation of the Glasgow branch of the Social Democratic Federation. This was reported in *Justice*, No. 47, 6 December 1884.— 237

[340] At a meeting of the executive of the Social Democratic Federation chaired by H. Quelch on 27 December 1884 a vote of no-confidence in Hyndman was passed by ten to eight and the behaviour of Andreas Scheu was endorsed. Immediately after this, ten members (Eleanor and Edward Aveling, R. Banner, B. Bax, W. J. Clark, J. Cooper, J. Lane, J. L. Mahon, S. Mainwaring and W. Morris) declared that they were leaving the Federation.— 238

[341] The fragment below from Engels' letter was reproduced by Liebknecht in his article 'Zur Dampfersubvention' published in *Der Sozialdemokrat*, No. 2, 8 January 1885. The whereabouts of the original is unknown.— 239

[342] In late 1884, Bismarck, seeking to step up German colonial policy (see Note 292) demanded that the Reichstag approve annual subsidies for steamship companies to organise regular services to Eastern Asia, Australia and Africa. This demand led to disagreements within the Social-Democratic group in the Reichstag. The Left wing headed by August Bebel and Wilhelm Liebknecht came out against supporting the government's policy. The Right-wing majority in the group (Dietz, Frohme, Grillenberger, etc.) intended to vote for the subsidies under the pretext that they promoted international links. Under pressure from the majority, the parliamentary group decided to declare the subsidies issue to be of no major importance and give each member the right to vote as they thought fit (see *Der Sozialdemokrat*, No. 50, 11 December 1884).

The sharp criticism expressed in *Der Sozialdemokrat* and the resolutions adopted by the party leadership led the majority of the parliamentary group to somewhat modify their attitude to the government's project when it was discussed in the Reichstag in March 1885 and to make their support conditional on the Reichstag accepting a number of the group's proposals. It was not until after the Reichstag declined to endorse the proposals made by the Social-Democratic group that they voted against the subsidies.— 239, 240, 242, 245, 268, 295, 388

[343] The reference is to the speech made by Max Kayser on 17 May 1879 with the agreement of the entire Social-Democratic group in the Reichstag in support of the government plan to introduce protective customs tariffs. Marx and Engels sharply condemned Kayser's action in defending a proposal put before the Reichstag in the interest of large industrialists and big farmers and to the detriment of the masses. They further criticised the lax attitude shown to Kayser by a number of German Social-Democratic leaders (see present edition, Vol. 24, pp. 259-61).— 241

[344] In a letter written on 28 December 1884 Bebel informed Engels that on 31 December he intended to surrender his shares in the workshop producing door and window handles which had been formed in Berka a. W. in 1876.— 243

[345] In a letter of 18 November 1884 Pasquale Martignetti requested Engels' permission to publish in one volume two works, namely *The Origin of the Family, Private Property and the State* and *The Peasant War in Germany*, the former of which he was translating into Italian at the time.— 243

[346] The reference is to the Social Democratic Federation (see Note 300) and the Socialist League.

The *Socialist League* was formed in December 1884 by a group of English socialists who had left the Social Democratic Federation. Its organisers included Eleanor Marx, Ernest Belfort Bax, William Morris and others. 'The Manifesto of the Socialist League' (see *The Commonweal*, No. 1, February 1885) proclaimed that its members advocate 'the principles of Revolutionary International Socialism' and '...seek a change in the basis of Society ... which would destroy the distinctions of classes and nationalities'. The League set itself the task of establishing a national workers' party adhering to international stand, assisting the trade union and cooperative movements. In its initial years the League and its officials took an active part in the workers' movement. However, in 1887 the League's leadership split into three factions (anarchist elements, the 'parliamentarians' and the 'antiparliamentarians'); its links with the day-to-day struggles of the English workers were gradually weakened and there was a growth in sectarianism. In 1889-90 the League fell apart.— 245, 247, 265, 275, 321, 394, 431, 434, 443, 446, 451, 471, 492, 526, 529, 534

[347] The fragment below from Engels' letter to the editor of *Der Sozialist* Joseph Dietzgen was first published in the same, No. 4, 24 January 1885 (New York) in the column 'Sozial-politische Nachrichten der letzten Tage'. An editorial note placed before the fragment read as follows: 'In a communication from London of 31 December 1884, Fred. Engels tells us that Volume II of Marx's *Capital*, so long and eagerly awaited, is now ready to go to press, and likewise gives us the glad tidings that, exceeding all our expectations, the third and fourth volumes are also to be bestowed upon us.'

The whereabouts of the original letter is not known.— 246

348 The reference is to the rapprochement between the leadership of the Social Democratic Federation and the French Possibilists (see notes 300 and 237).
On 27 December 1884 the newspaper *Justice*, No. 50 published a letter from Adolphe Smith under the heading 'France and the International Congress'. The author considered it essential that the Social Democratic Federation, having proposed the convocation of an international socialist congress, should recognise the Possibilists as the main organisation of the French socialists and not maintain relations with the French Workers' Party.— 247

349 The reference is to the manuscript of the English translation of Engels' book *The Condition of the Working-Class in England* (present edition, Vol. 4) prepared by the American socialist Florence Kelley-Wischnewetzky for publication in the United States (see also Note 360).— 248, 257, 373, 382, 419

350 Engels is referring to the review of the pamphlet G. Groß, *Karl Marx*, Leipzig, 1885 being prepared by Karl Kautsky. The review was published in *Die Neue Zeit*, No. 6, 1885.— 250

351 On 9 January 1885 Kautsky wrote to Engels to say that the German Social Democrat Louis Viereck had offered him a temporary or permanent post with one of the newspapers he published.— 250

352 Hermann Schlüter asked Engels to send him a set of the *Neue Rheinische Zeitung. Politisch-ökonomische Revue* since he was intending to publish in the Sozialdemokratische Bibliothek series a number of works by Marx and Engels which the said journal had carried in 1850.— 251

353 *Reptiles* (grovellers) is a term which became widespread after Bismarck used it in his speech before the Prussian Chamber of Deputies on 30 January 1869 to describe the government's opponents. The left-wing press took up this expression and began to describe as reptilian the semi-official press which was in the pay of the government, labelling the relevant category of journalists as reptiles.— 253

354 Engels' negative attitude to Franz Mehring which he expresses in this letter had to do with the fact that from the mid-1870s Mehring started to criticise Social-Democratic theory and tactics in the bourgeois-democratic press. His position was summarised in the pamphlet *Die deutsche Sozialdemokratie, ihre Geschichte und ihre Lehre; eine historisch-kritische Darstellung*, three editions of which were issued in 1877, 1878 and 1879, respectively, by the publishing house belonging to the *Weser-Zeitung*, a National-Liberal (see Note 243) newspaper based in Barmen. Captivated by the Kantian philosophy, Mehring believed that the history was made by the 'strong personalities', while the workers' movement and, consequently, Social Democracy were not the natural result of the social development.
In the early 1880s Mehring had been revising his views on the socialist movement. Having joined the Socialist Party of Germany in 1891 he became one of its left-wing leaders. Engels' attitude to Mehring changed accordingly; right up to his death in 1895 Engels repeatedly praised Mehring's journalistic and academic endeavours.— 253, 316

355 This letter, which Paul Lafargue passed on to Jules Guesde, formed the basis for Guesde's leading article in the newspaper *Le Cri du Peuple*, No. 461, 31 January 1885. The excerpt published here was included in the article in full, where it was

stated that a letter written by 'one of the veterans of our great social battles' had been received from London. Engels examined the issue to which he refers in this excerpt in the article 'Real Imperial Russian Privy Dynamiters' carried by *Der Sozialdemokrat*, No. 5, 29 January 1885 (see present edition, Vol. 26). The whereabouts of the original letter are unknown.— 255

[356] *Nihilists*— a term used in the 1860s to describe the progressive-minded Russian intellectuals of different social estates. The Nihilists refused to recognise the dominant ideology and morality, rejected religion and demanded freedom of the personality. They advocated equality between the sexes and called for the study of the natural and exact sciences. Towards the end of the 1860s the term almost completely disappeared from polemic writing, although it was used later on occasions by reactionary political commentators as a label for revolutionaries. In West European writing, the term was applied to participants in the Russian revolutionary movement of the 1870s and 1880s, notably the members of the Narodnaya Volya (People's Will).— 256, 275, 279, 338, 378, 484, 486, 505, 513, 520, 525

[357] On 13 (1) January 1885 Russia and Prussia exchanged notes on the extradition of persons accused of criminal offences against the monarchs of the contracting parties or members of their families, as well as of persons found guilty of manufacturing or storing explosives. This was the subject of a report in *The Times*, 24 January 1885 (No. 31352) entitled 'Extradition by Russia and Prussia. Berlin, Jan. 23'.— 256

[358] The series of explosions which Engels is writing about took place on Saturday, 24 January 1885. The investigation showed that the man responsible for the explosion in the Tower was the same one who had organised the explosion on the underground railway two years previously, when bombs had been placed at Charing Cross and Praed Street stations. He was sentenced to 14 years' imprisonment and hard labour. See also Note 251.— 256

[359] The reference is to Engels' preface to the first edition of his work *The Condition of the Working-Class in England* (see present edition, Vol. 4, pp. 302-04) and his dedication of this book 'to the Working-Classes of Great-Britain' (ibid., pp. 297-301). The preface and dedication were not included in the edition of this work which appeared in the United States (see Note 349).— 257, 420

[360] In February 1886 Engels wrote an article as a preface or epilogue to the American edition of *The Condition of the Working-Class in England* (see present edition, Vol. 26). When publication was delayed, Engels considered it essential to write another preface in January 1887 (ibid.). The first article was included as an appendix in the American edition.— 257, 259, 415

[361] To speed up the Russian translation of the second volume of *Capital* Engels sent Nikolai Danielson the proofs of the German edition as they were printed. The volume appeared in January 1886.— 260, 265, 278, 289, 294, 303, 311

[362] Hermann Lopatin was arrested in St Petersburg on 6 October 1884 and was under investigation up to May 1887; on 4 June 1887 he was sentenced to death, later commuted to life imprisonment in Schlisselburg fortress. Lopatin was released on 28 October 1905.— 260, 319, 349, 401, 525

[363] Engels' pseudonym in his correspondence with Nikolai Danielson; Engels used the

name of the husband of his wife's niece—Percy White Rosher.—260, 278, 294, 319, 322, 350, 402, 523

364 Pyotr Lavrov enquired as to whether the information about Marx contained in Groß' pamphlet was correct (see Note 350) and whether Engels had made any additions or changes to the 1885 German edition of Marx's *The Poverty of Philosophy*.—261

365 Karl Kautsky lived in London from early 1885 to June 1888.—262, 265

366 To Engels' enquiry about the rumours regarding the prohibition in Germany of his work *The Origin of the Family, Private Property and the State* (see this volume, p. 252), Hermann Schlüter replied that, according to his information, the work had not been officially banned, but there had been a case of a large number of copies being confiscated in Leipzig. Although they had all been returned, booksellers refused to stock the book any longer and from that time it was being distributed directly from Zurich on advance order only.—263

367 In a letter published in *Der Sozialdemokrat*, No. 9, 26 February 1885, Karl Varenholz, a member of the Social Democratic Federation, came out in defence of Henry Hyndman's policy and attempted to disprove the reasons for the split in the Social Democratic Federation reported by the same newspaper, No. 3, 15 January 1885; the report reflected Engels' views (see this volume, pp. 236-38). Bernstein's letter to Engels of 15 January gives reason to believe that the report was written by Eleanor Marx-Aveling. Edward Aveling's reply to Varenholz was carried by *Der Sozialdemokrat*, No. 13, 26 March 1885. Aveling exposed Hyndman's activities in trying to take over the presidency of the Federation, his intrigues against Andreas Scheu and other members of the Federation and the authoritarian practices employed by the editors of *Justice*, which carried material for the most part reflecting the position of Hyndman and his supporters.—265

368 The reference is to Maitland Park Crescent, which led into Maitland Park Road. In the 1870s, this street, together with Modena Villas, Maitland Park Villas and Maitland Park Road was given the single name Maitland Park Road (see also Note 159).

Eleanor Marx-Aveling lived at 67, Maitland Park Road.—265

369 Jenny and Karl Marx were buried at Highgate Cemetery in London (see also Note 36). 14 March 1885 was the second anniversary of Marx's death.—265

370 The reference is to the group of French workers in the Montceau-les-Mines coalfield who were arrested in November 1884 on a charge of organising explosions in the mine and the town. The immediate reason for their arrest was the explosion of 7 November organised by the agent provocateur Claude Brenin, who was in the pay of local police commissar Thévenin. Those arrested included activists in the workers' movement who had no connection with these explosions. The role played by Brenin as a provocateur was exposed by the socialist newspaper *Le Cri du Peuple*, 16 February 1885. At the trial in late May the accused were sentenced to various terms of imprisonment.—265

371 On 21 March 1885 Richard Stegemann asked Engels to let him know where he could obtain personal information about Marx for inclusion in a work he was preparing for the press about the latter's economic doctrine. Stegemann requested

Engels, in the absence of printed sources for a biography of Marx, to send him his own thoughts about Marx as a man.— 266

[372] The French government under the leader of the moderate Republicans Jules Ferry, who had held the post since 1883, resigned on 30 March 1885 due to an unsuccessful colonial adventure in Indochina.— 267, 270

[373] Following the elections in 1884 (see Note 306), the Social-Democratic group in the Reichstag was made up of a right-wing majority led by Wilhelm Blos, Bruno Geiser, Karl Frohme, Wilhelm Hasenclever and others, and a left-wing minority led by August Bebel and Wilhelm Liebknecht.— 268, 300

[374] The majority of the Social-Democratic group in the German Reichstag, consisting of reformists, tried to dispute the right of the party newspaper — *Der Sozialdemokrat* — to criticise the action of the parliamentary group and its attitude towards the bill envisaging the payment of subsidies to steamship companies (see Note 342). They published a statement to this effect in *Der Sozialdemokrat*, No. 14, 2 April 1885.

However, the majority of the local Social-Democratic organisations resolutely supported the editors. The reformists were virtually forced to renounce their objections and, in a joint statement with the editors of *Der Sozialdemokrat* published on 23 April, they recognised the newspaper's status as the '*organ* of the whole party' (see also notes 380 and 390).— 268, 269, 275, 290, 300, 313, 323

[375] Until 1885, France was divided into 'small constituencies', each sending one representative to the Chamber of Deputies. In June 1885, on the initiative of the moderate bourgeois republicans, a system of voting by department lists was introduced. Under this system, which operated until 1889, small constituencies were combined to form larger ones each corresponding to a department. Now a voter received a ballot paper with names of candidates from different parties, but he was obliged to vote for the total number of candidates to be elected, with one deputy for every 70,000 people. A deputy was considered elected in the first ballot provided he had received an absolute majority of votes; a relative majority was sufficient in the second ballot.— 270, 314, 317, 320, 326, 330, 489, 508

[376] Engels is referring to Gladstone's Liberal administration which had formed the government in Britain from 1880 (see Note 414).— 270

[377] *Der Sozialdemokrat*, Nos. 2, 3, 5 and 7 of 8, 15 and 29 January and 12 February 1885 published articles and editorial comments criticising the attitude taken by the majority of the parliamentary group to the bill on subsidies to steamship companies (see Note 342). The first article was signed 'W. L.', the second was without a signature, the third carried the initials 'J. A.' and the fourth, 'H. R.'.— 271, 284

[378] In March and April 1885 there was a conflict between Britain and Russia caused by their rivalry over the area around the North-West frontier of Afghanistan. Following the annexation of Southern Turkestan by Russia there was a clash between Russian and Afghan forces, the latter supported by Britain, which threatened to escalate into an armed conflict between the two powers. However, the diplomatic isolation of Britain due to the position taken by Germany, forced the Gladstone administration to step down in its dispute with Russia about the division of spheres of influence in Central Asia.

The April issue of the organ of the Socialist League — *The Commonweal*

(No. 3) — carried an article by Ernest Belfort Bax entitled 'At Bay!' in which he set out his views on the foreign policies pursued by Britain and Russia, including those on the Anglo-Russian conflict.— 275

[379] In his letter to Engels of 27 March 1885 Paul Lafargue asked what the former thought of his hypothesis about the origin of certain legal terms.— 275

[380] With regard to the conflict between the Social-Democratic group in the Reichstag (see Note 49) and the editors of *Der Sozialdemokrat* (see Note 374) August Bebel sent the parliamentary group a note of protest on 5 April 1885 in which he reserved the right to appeal to the party should the parliamentary group continue to suppress the freedom of opinion.

The parliamentary group completed three days of debates on 15 April 1885.— 277

[381] Nikolai Danielson provided Engels with some figures about the length of the working day and the wages paid to workers in Russia as well as about the extent to which peasants had joined the ranks of the proletariat. He also was ready to send Engels the following books by Russian economists: Н. И. Зибер, *Давид Рикардо и Карл Маркс в их общественно-экономических исследованиях* (2nd edition, St Petersburg, 1885), И. И. Янжул, *Фабричный быт Московской губернии* (Moscow, 1882) and П. А. Песков, *Санитарное исследование фабрик по обработке волокнистых веществ в г. Москве* (Moscow, 1882).— 277

[382] A draft of this letter in Engels' handwriting has survived. All substantial variations are given in footnotes.— 279

[383] The reference is to the first Russian Marxist organisation, the Emancipation of Labour group (see Note 124).— 279

[384] In his book *Наши разногласія* (*Our Differences*), Geneva, 1884, Plekhanov repeatedly used the expression 'unstable balance' to describe relations in the Russian village commune.— 280

[385] The reference is to the following passage in Plekhanov's letter to Pyotr Lavrov of 22 July 1884, which appeared in place of a preface in Plekhanov's book *Our Differences*: 'I think that the Russian revolution has an enormous, invincible potential energy, and that reaction is raising its head only because we are unable to transform that energy from potential into kinetic.'— 280

[386] Here, Engels quotes Hegel from the second volume of his work *Vorlesungen über die Geschichte der Philosophie* (see *Werke*, Bd. XIV, Berlin, 1833, S. 62). Explaining the expression 'Socratic irony', Hegel wrote: 'All dialectics regard as valid what should be valid, as if it were valid, have the inner destruction develop of its own accord on this account — general irony of the world.' — 281, 348

[387] This letter is Engels' reply to Richard Stegemann's second request (see Note 371) that he write a short personal description of Marx for a work Stegemann was preparing on the latter's economic doctrine. Stegemann justified his request with a need to reply to the efforts being made by bourgeois authors in various countries to distort Marx's personality.— 282

[388] Tuileries documents is the name Engels gives to the lists of agents in the pay of Napoleon III found in the Tuileries in 1870 and published by the government of the Third Republic in September 1871. Under the letter 'V' was the note 'Vogt —

in August 1859 has been sent a remittance of 40,000 francs.' This bore out Marx's assumption that Karl Vogt was a Bonapartist agent (see K. Marx, *Herr Vogt*; present edition, Vol. 17, pp. 190, 212). Engels wrote about this document in the article 'Once Again "Herr Vogt"' published in May 1871 (see present edition, Vol. 22, p. 303).— 282

³⁸⁹ On the conflict between the parliamentary group and the editorial board, see Note 374. The original text of the parliamentary group's decision of 20 March 1885 carried by *Der Sozialdemokrat* contained a clause saying that the parliamentary group bore 'moral responsibility' for the newspaper's contents. This met with objections on the part of members of the editorial board, including Eduard Bernstein. The parliamentary group had sent Wilhelm Liebknecht to Zurich, the place of publication, to settle the conflict. The text published by *Der Sozialdemokrat* on 2 April 1885 contained, among other things, the following remark: 'the party organ must under no circumstances become opposed to the parliamentary group, which bears the moral responsibility for the contents of the same', and continued, 'It is not the paper which has to determine the stance of the parliamentary group, but the parliamentary group which has to monitor the stance of the paper.'— 284

³⁹⁰ The reference is to the statement by the Social-Democratic group in the Reichstag and the editors of the paper carried by *Der Sozialdemokrat*, No. 17, 23 April 1885, in which it was stated that any attempt to limit criticism in the party would be a violation of party principles and would shake it to the foundations. As for the relations between the parliamentary group and the editorial board, the statement represented a compromise. It pointed out, on the one hand, that *Der Sozialdemokrat* was the organ of the party as a whole but that, on the other hand, the parliamentary group was the party's representative body and had a right to monitor the work of the editorial board. On the parliamentary group's first statement, see Note 374.— 284

³⁹¹ The *protective tariffs system* was introduced by Bismarck in 1879 in the interest of the landowners and large industrialists and remained in force throughout the 1880s (in 1885 and 1887 it was supplemented by further rises in the duties payable on imported agricultural produce). To a certain extent it promoted the growth of German industry, but brought a major deterioration in the situation of the masses. This led to major discontent, not only among the proletariat, but also the middle and petty bourgeoisie.— 285

³⁹² This letter was first published in English in an abridged form in *Science and Society*, New York, 1938, Vol. 2, No. 3.— 286

³⁹³ In a letter of 13 May 1885 Hermann Schlüter asked Engels to help him select revolutionary poems and songs for inclusion in a collection from a series of poems for workers which he was preparing for the press. Among other things, Schlüter was interested in songs and poems originating from the period of peasant uprisings in the 15th and 16th centuries, the revolution of 1848 in Germany and the time of the English Chartists which had been in general circulation. (The collection appeared in Zurich in 1886 under the title *Vorwärts! Eine Sammlung von Gedichten für das arbeitende Volk.*) In the same letter Schlüter informed Engels of his intention to publish a number of minor works and articles by Marx, including some documents from the International, within the framework of the Sozialdemokratische Bibliothek series (see also Note 352).— 286

394 Engels is referring to Luther's choral 'Ein feste Burg ist unser Gott' ('God is our firm stronghold'), which Heine, in his *Zur Geschichte der Religion und Philosophie in Deutschland*, called the 'Marseillaise of the Reformation' (*Der Salon*, Vol. 2, Hamburg, 1835, p. 80).

In the Introduction to his *Dialectics of Nature* Engels calls this choral the 'Marseillaise of the sixteenth century' (see present edition, Vol. 25, p. 319).—286

395 The reference is to a song written in 1844 by Matthäus Friedrich Chemnitz and beginning with the words 'Schleswig-Holstein, meerumschlungen' (Schleswig-Holstein, surrounded by the sea). It was particularly popular in 1848-50, during the struggle for Schleswig-Holstein's liberation from Danish rule.

The *Heckerlied* is a revolutionary song about the Baden-Palatinate uprising of 1848 led, among others, by Friedrich Hecker, a prominent figure among the South German petty bourgeoisie. Engels gave the version of the chorus cited below in his work *The Campaign for the German Imperial Constitution* (present edition, Vol. 10, p. 149).—287

396 The *Marseillaise*—a French revolutionary song. The words and music were written in Strasbourg in 1792 by Claude Joseph Rouget de Lisle. Its original title was 'Chant du guerre pour l'armée du Rhin' ('War chant for the Rhine army'). Having become widespread in the Republican army, it made its way to Marseilles, thus receiving the name 'Marseilles March' or 'Marseillaise', and later became popular in Paris.—287

397 A conflict arose between Prosper Lissagaray, editor-in-chief of *La Bataille* and its publisher Périnet. With assistance from Paul Brousse and his supporters, Périnet staged an abortive attempt to gain control of the editorship and pocket 10,000 francs donated to the newspaper by Capoul, a former singer.—288

398 The article by Louis-Edouard Grimaux referred to below ('Les substances colloïdales et la coagulation', *Revue scientific*, Vol. XXXV, 1885) contains the following quote from Carl Schorlemmer, 'If chemists ever succeed in artificially obtaining proteins, they will be in the form of living protoplasm.' And later on, 'The enigma of life can only be resolved by protein synthesis.'—289

399 The reference is to sections 5 and 6 of Volume III of *Capital* (see present edition, Vol. 37).—290

400 An incomplete copy of this letter signed by Engels is to be found at the International Institute of Social History in Amsterdam. The copy carries the address of the sender and the date of writing ('London, 19 May 1885, 122, Regent's Park Road, N. W.'), the first paragraph of the draft and the following note by Engels: 'The original of this letter was sent to Nitti in Naples on 26.5.92.'—291

401 Engels wrote the note on *Mark* (see present edition, Vol. 26, p. 236) for Chapter VII ('The Gens Among the Celts and Germans') of the Italian translation of his work *The Origin of the Family, Private Property and the State*.—291

402 On 21 May 1885 Paul Lafargue was sent to Ste Pélagie prison, Paris, for two months for failing to pay a fine of 100 francs imposed on him in April 1883 by a jury in Moulins as punishment for his public speeches (see Note 9). To begin with, Lafargue was kept in the cell reserved for criminals, but later transferred to

the part of the prison where the political detainees were kept.— 292, 297, 301, 303, 310, 495

403 Paul Lafargue intended to translate Engels' *The Origin of the Family, Private Property and the State* into French, but failed to carry out this plan. The French translation was done by Henri Ravé from the fourth German edition edited by Laura Lafargue and looked through by Engels; it appeared in Paris in 1893.— 293, 394

404 On 24 May 1885 a demonstration was organised in Paris in memory of the members of the Paris Commune. Carrying red flags, the demonstrators made their way to the Mur des Fédérés in Père-Lachaise cemetery where 200 members of the Commune had been shot on 27 May 1871. The police attacked the demonstrators on the pretext that it was forbidden to carry red flags on demonstrations in Paris. A clash ensued in which a number of people were killed and injured.

Engels expected that the police would try to organise a similar act of provocation on 1 June during the funeral of Victor Hugo who had died on 22 May 1885.— 293, 297

405 This letter was first published in English in: K. Marx and F. Engels, *Letters on 'Capital'*, New Park Publications, London, 1983.— 294

406 Between 1869 and 1873 Marx maintained regular correspondence with Nikolai Danielson, who systematically sent him Russian books and articles in journals dealing with the agrarian question in Russia. In his letter of 24 April (6 May) 1885, Danielson enquired of Engels whether the statistics on the Russian economy had been included in the third volume of *Capital*.

The chapter on ground rent to which Engels refers forms part of Section 6 of Volume III of *Capital* (see present edition, Vol. 37).— 294

407 A fragment from this letter was first published in English in: K. Marx and F. Engels, *Letters to Americans. 1848-1895. A Selection*, International Publishers, New York, 1953.— 295

408 Here, Engels uses an expression from the speech made by the Prussian officer Prince Lichnowski in the Frankfurt Assembly on 31 August 1848. Lichnowski used a double negative ('With regard to historical right there does not exist no date'). See also present edition, Vol. 7, p. 369.— 296

409 The reference is to the work *De origine actibusque Getarum* by the Gothic historian Jordanes. It is a short conspectus of *Historia Gothorum* by Cassiodorus, which is not extant, and to which Jordanes added surviving oral pieces, legends of the Germanic tribes and material from other sources.— 296

410 This letter has survived in the form of an excerpt (the beginning of the letter and name of the addressee are missing). According to the International Institute of Social History in Amsterdam, where the original is kept, it was written on the letter which A. N. Davisson sent to Engels on 10 June 1885. The note 'Soc. League' on Engels' letter suggests that the addressee was John Lincoln Mahon, the secretary of the said organisation (see Note 346).— 298

411 Frederick Charles, Prince of Prussia and inspector-general of the cavalry, died on 15 June 1885.— 300, 302, 304

412 *Der Sozialdemokrat*, No. 17, 23 April 1885 published a statement adopted by a meeting of Social Democrats in Frankfurt-am-Main and sharply criticising the

position of the majority of the Social-Democratic group in the Reichstag and its attempts to impose this position on the party as a whole (see Note 374). On 7 May 1885 Karl Frohme, one of the leaders of the parliamentary group, published a letter attacking this statement in response to this in the bourgeois *Frankfurter Journal*. The editorial board of *Der Sozialdemokrat* reprinted Frohme's letter (No. 20, 14 May 1885) and in the next issue, 21 May 1885 published August Bebel's article in reply called 'Auch "ein Protest"' in which he criticised Frohme's position.— 302, 307

⁴¹³ The Hamburg party organisation, which supported the Social-Democratic group in the Reichstag in its conflict with the editorial board of *Der Sozialdemokrat* (see Note 374), donated 1,000 francs to the French socialists' election fund.— 303

⁴¹⁴ Engels is referring to the resignation in June 1885 of the Liberal cabinet under Gladstone due to the refusal of the majority in parliament (Conservatives and Irish members) to vote for the government proposal to increase taxes on spirits. The real reasons for the resignation were the failures in colonial policy — the concessions to Russia when it came to dividing up spheres of influence in Central Asia (see Note 378) and the major defeats inflicted on the British forces by rebels in the Sudan — as well as the government's refusal to grant Irish self-administration in the framework of the British Empire.— 303

⁴¹⁵ *Tories* — traditional name of the Conservative Party.
The *Whigs* were the right wing of the Liberal Party, and the *Radicals* its left wing. The Whigs expressed the interests of the landed, and in part, financial aristocracy, of the big and medium capitalist farmers, whilst the Radicals were the representatives of large sections of the trading and industrial bourgeoisie, the bourgeois intelligentsia and the rich trade unions. The Liberal Party exerted an influence on the trade unions through the Radicals, who recognised the need for democratic social reforms. The differences between the Whigs and the Radicals became particularly clear during the preparations for the electoral reform of 1884, when the Whigs opposed the extension of the suffrage to Irish peasants and the establishment of constituencies of equal size, thus backing the Conservatives. Most of the Radicals favoured Home Rule and improvements in the agrarian law. However some of them, headed by J. Chamberlain, wanted to keep the Union of 1801 intact. The rivalry between the Whigs and the Radicals became aggravated on the eve of the 1885 general election which the Radicals expected would bring them victory in the party and the country as a whole (see notes 299 and 487). It was at this time that the political outlook of the Radical movement took its final shape, as expressed in 'The Radical Programme with a Preface of J. Chamberlain', London, 1885 (see also Note 430).— 304, 326, 345, 367, 369, 389

⁴¹⁶ The trials of the *Neue Rheinische Zeitung* and the Rhenish district committee of Democrats took place in Cologne on 7 and 8 February 1849. The accused at the first trial were Karl Marx as editor-in-chief, Frederick Engels as co-editor and Hermann Korff as responsible publisher. Those indicted at the second trial were Marx, Karl Schapper and the lawyer Schneider II. The trials ended with the accused being acquitted. They were reported in the *Neue Rheinische Zeitung* — the first on 14 February and the second on 19, 25, 27 and 28 February 1849. In October 1885 the report on the trial of the Rhenish district committee of Democrats was published as a separate pamphlet in the Sozialdemokratische Bibliothek series in

Hottingen-Zurich. Entitled *Karl Marx vor den Kölner Geschwornen. Prozeß gegen den Ausschuß der rheinischen Demokraten wegen Aufrufs zum bewaffneten Widerstand*, it included a preface by Engels (see present edition, Vol. 26, p. 304).— 304

[417] There was no separate collected edition of Marx's and Engels' articles about the June insurrection (see present edition, Vol. 7, pp. 121, 123-28, 130-64).— 305, 309, 332

[418] The reference is to a separate edition of Wilhelm Wolff's series of articles on the situation of the Silesian peasants called *Die schlesische Milliarde* and printed in a number of issues of the *Neue Rheinische Zeitung* between 22 March and 22 April 1849. Engels included a preface in this edition, which came out in 1886. Its first section was a biography of Wolff which he had written back in 1876 (see F. Engels, 'Wilhelm Wolff', present edition, Vol. 24) but in a much abbreviated form, whilst the second section was the article 'On the History of the Prussian Peasants. Introduction to Wilhelm Wolff's pamphlet *The Silesian Milliard*' (Vol. 26) specially for that edition.— 309, 324, 328, 332, 346

[419] In his letter of 24 June 1885 Hermann Schlüter informed Engels that Meissner, whose publishing house had issued *Capital*, was offering *Der Sozialdemokrat* publishers in Zurich copies of the second volume of *Capital* to distribute on terms he considered unfavourable.— 309

[420] Engels is referring to the report in *Justice*, No. 73, 6 June 1885 that the publisher William Reeves intended to put out Gabriel Deville's book *Le Capital de Karl Marx. Résumé...* (see Note 81) in an English translation by John Broadhouse (Hyndman's pseudonym). At that time Engels was negotiating with the publishers Kegan Paul and Co. about publishing the English translation of the first volume of *Capital* (see Note 56). These negotiations ended without success. Marx's work was put out by another publishing house and Deville's book did not appear in English.— 310, 313

[421] Engels spent his holidays on the island of Jersey from 14 August to 14 September 1885.— 310, 315, 321-25, 328, 358

[422] The German socialist Gertrud Guillaume-Schack, who was preparing an article on the limitation of female labour, wrote to Engels on 1 July 1885 to ask whether it was true that he and Marx had been involved in drawing up the programme of the French Workers' Party, which contained the demand that equal pay be given for equal work.

Following the establishment of the French Workers' Party at a congress in Marseilles in October 1879, the French socialist Jules Guesde began work on the party programme and, through Paul Lafargue, requested Marx and Engels to help draw up a draft election manifesto for the French Workers' Party. The theoretical introduction was formulated by Marx and dictated to Guesde (see K. Marx, 'Preamble to the Programme of the French Workers' Party', present edition, Vol. 24, p. 340). The practical part of the programme (minimum programme, see Vol. 24, Note 384) was compiled by Guesde and Lafargue. The programme was endorsed at the party congress held in Le Havre in 1880.

On the Rouen tendency, or the Guesdists, see Note 201.— 311

[423] The whereabouts of the original of this letter are not known. The draft of the letter

was written by Engels on a letter which John Lincoln Mahon had written to him (on paper used by the editorial board of *The Commonweal*) on 11 July 1885.— 312

⁴²⁴ Under the heading 'The Parting of the Waters', *The Edinburgh Review*, No. 331, July 1885, contained a summary of the parliamentary debates for 1884-85. It sharply criticised the policies pursued by the Radical wing of the Liberal Party (see Note 415). The author of the summary called on the Whigs to split with the Radical wing, describing this act as a 'watershed'.— 314

⁴²⁵ In a letter of 10 July 1885 to the German Workers' Educational Society in London (see Note 162) Wilhelm Liebknecht objected to the Society's proposal that an extraordinary party congress be held due to the conflict between the reformist majority in the Social-Democratic group in the Reichstag and the editorial board of *Der Sozialdemokrat*. He supposed that the disagreements, including that between the Frankfurt organisation and Karl Frohme (see Note 412), were not of a major nature and could thus quickly be settled with his mediation.— 315

⁴²⁶ On 14 July 1885 Wilhelm Liebknecht spoke to a meeting of Social Democrats in Offenbach and criticised the letter by the group of Frankfurt Social Democrats which had been published in *Der Sozialdemokrat* (see Note 412). His words appeared in the *Berliner Volksblatt*, 18 July 1885. The dissatisfaction his speech created in the Frankfurt Social-Democratic organisation led to Liebknecht publishing a statement in *Der Sozialdemokrat*, No. 32, 6 August 1885, claiming that his criticism only related to the tone of the letter and that he rated highly the fight waged against the Anti-Socialist Law by the Social Democrats in Frankfurt.— 315

⁴²⁷ Engels is evidently referring to Karl Kautsky's book *Der Einfluss der Volksvermehrung auf den Fortschritt der Gesellschaft*, Vienna, 1880, which he sharply criticised for its Malthusian errors in a letter to Kautsky of 1 February 1881 (see present edition, Vol. 46) and also to a series of articles about marriage in primitive society with the general heading 'Die Entstehung der Ehe und Familie' published in *Kosmos*, Jg. VI, Stuttgart, 1882-83 (see Engels' letters to Laura Lafargue of 16-17 February and to August Bebel of 7 March 1883; present edition, Vol. 46, and also this volume, p. 56).— 316

⁴²⁸ Maybe this refers to Franz Mehring's articles on Rodbertus in *Demokratische Blätter*, Nos. 19, 20 and 21, 13, 20 and 28 May 1885, or his article 'Der soziale Beruf des Adels' in *Volks-Zeitung*, Nos. 155 and 156, 7 and 8 July 1885.— 316

⁴²⁹ The *Radicals*—in the 1880s and 1890s a parliamentary group which had split away from the party of moderate republicans in France ('Opportunists', see Note 236). The Radicals had their main base in the petty and, to some extent, the middle bourgeoisie and continued to press for a number of bourgeois-democratic demands: a single-chamber parliamentary system, the separation of the Church from the State, the introduction of a system of progressive income taxes, the limitation of the working day and settlement of a number of other social issues. The leader of the Radicals was Clemenceau. The group formed officially as the Republican Party of Radicals and Radical Socialists (*Parti républicain radical et radical-socialiste*) in 1901.— 317, 326, 330, 343, 354, 409-10, 414, 418, 424, 428, 430, 438, 441, 445, 470, 489, 493, 497, 508

⁴³⁰ Engels is referring to the disagreements within the Liberal Party (see Note 415) and the noticeable rapprochement between its right wing — the Whigs — and the

Conservatives. In 1886 this wing, which opposed the granting of Irish self-administration, split off and a Liberal-Unionist bloc headed by Joseph Chamberlain was formed of supporters of the 1801 Union of Ireland with Great Britain; the Liberal-Unionists backed the Conservatives on most issues. They constituted a political expression of a major regrouping among the British ruling classes and signified a shift to the right.— 317, 391

⁴³¹ In 1688-89, as a result of the coup d'état which brought William III (of Orange) to power in England, absolutism was abolished as the form of government and replaced by a constitutional monarchy. Parliament became the supreme organ of state power, carrying out the will of the bourgeoisie and the new nobility.— 317

⁴³² The envelope has survived and carries in Engels' handwriting 'N. F. Danielson Esq., Moika 27, *St. Petersburg*, Russia'. The name of the street and of the addressee have been written by an unknown hand in Cyrillic script.— 318

⁴³³ Engels did not write a special preface for the Russian translation of the second volume of *Capital*. The Russian edition contained an abbreviated version of his preface to the first German edition of the second volume. The second half of the preface, including the criticism of Rodbertus, was omitted.— 318

⁴³⁴ Paul Lafargue was planning to visit his mother in Bordeaux.— 320

⁴³⁵ In connection with Engels' fears about the planned publication in England of Deville's book *Le Capital de Karl Marx. Résumé...* (see Note 420), Laura Lafargue wrote to Engels on 7 August 1885 saying that the French publisher Henri Oriol had said he could prevent the book being translated into English.— 320

⁴³⁶ '*Après moi* (or *nous*) le déluge!'—words uttered to Louis XV and attributed to Mme Du Barry or to Mmle Pompadour.— 320, 354

⁴³⁷ Engels wrote this letter on a postcard. It carries the following address in his handwriting: 'K. Kautsky Esq., care of Mrs Huggetts' Dew House, Camden Road, Eastbourne.'— 321

⁴³⁸ In this letter (see present edition, Vol. 26) written on the advice of Nikolai Danielson, Engels suggested to the editors of *Severny vestnik* that they print Marx's unpublished letter to the editorial board of *Otechestvenniye zapiski* which he had written in response to Nikolai Mikhailovsky's article 'Карлъ Марксъ передъ судомъ г. Ю. Жуковскаго' (see Note 190).— 322, 347

⁴³⁹ Engels wrote this letter on a postcard carrying the following address in his handwriting: 'Herrn H. Schlüter, Volksbuchhandlung, Kasinostr. 3, Hottingen-Zürich, Switzerland.'— 322, 324

⁴⁴⁰ A hint that Louis Viereck was the illegitimate son of Emperor William I of Germany. Engels is referring to Viereck's speech on 8 August at a workers' meeting in Munich in which he said that the emperor would give the workers much more if he knew how poorly they lived. The Munich Social Democrats protested at Viereck's speech (see *Der Sozialdemokrat*, No. 34, 20 August 1885). In his reply, published in the Munich-based *Deutsches Wochenblatt*, No. 30, 30 August and *Der Sozialdemokrat*, No. 36, 3 September 1885, Viereck, to all intents and purposes, supported Bismarck's social reform (see Note 312).— 324, 328

⁴⁴¹ Engels is referring to the conflict which emerged between Germany and Spain in August-September 1885 as a result of Germany's attempts to seize the Caroline is-

lands to which Spain laid claim. The German government sent a gunboat to one of the islands, where the German flag was raised. This led to tension in the relations between the two states. Pope Leo XIII, who acted as arbitrator, supported the Spanish claims.— 324

442 On 20 September 1885 in Paris, during the funeral of Antoine Jules Arnaud, a member of the Paris Commune, the police used the excuse that processions with red banners were prohibited to attempt to seize the red cover which had been placed over the deceased and attacked those attending the funeral.— 326

443 The reference is to the English socialists' free speech struggles against the police suppression of outdoor meetings. Between July and September 1885 the London police on several occasions arrested socialist speakers at meetings in the East End. One of them, John E. Williams, a member of the Social Democratic Federation, was sentenced to a month's hard labour. This prompted the Social Democratic Federation, the Socialist League, the Labour Emancipation League and the London Radical Clubs (see Note 659) to organise a joint meeting on 20 September in the area of Dod Street, which was attended by several thousand people. The police tried to arrest the speakers, but met with resistance. Several people were detained, but released the next day. This was reported in *The Daily News* of 21 and 22 September.— 326

444 Laura Lafargue's French translation of the *Manifesto of the Communist Party* was published in *Le Socialiste*, Nos. 1-11, from late August to early November 1885. It was published with Engels' changes as an appendix to Mermeix (pseudonym), *La France Socialiste*, Paris, 1886.— 326, 328, 333, 342

445 The reference is to the so-called Bulgarian crisis which began in September 1885. In the night of 5-6 September an uprising of Bulgarian patriots occurred in Plovdiv, the capital of Eastern Roumelia (Southern Bulgaria), which, according to the 1878 Treaty of Berlin, was under the control of Turkey (see present edition, Vol. 45, Note 430). The Turkish governor was overthrown. Roumelia was reunited with Bulgaria and Grand Duke (formerly Prince) Alexander Battenberg of Bulgaria proclaimed himself ruler of the united Bulgaria on 8 September. Russia, showing its displeasure at the rapprochement between Battenberg and Austria-Hungary which had begun some time previously, recalled its officers from the Bulgarian army. Reports on this were carried by the *Kölnische Zeitung*, Nos. 276, 277, 278 and 279, 5, 6, 7 and 8 October 1885.

On the subsequent course of the Bulgarian crisis, see Engels' article 'The Political Situation in Europe' (present edition, Vol. 26, and also this volume, pp. 512-20 and notes 478 and 634).— 329, 364, 378-79, 417, 485, 488

446 The reference is to the trial of a group of German Social Democrats at the Saxon provincial court in Chemnitz between 28 and 30 September 1885. Auer, Bebel, Dietz, Müller, Ulrich, Viereck, Vollmar, Frohme and Heinzel were charged with belonging to a secret society seeking by illegal means to hinder the implementation of laws and regulations issued by the authorities. The reason for the indictment was their participation in the 1883 congress of the Socialist Workers' Party of Germany in Copenhagen (see Note 15). In the absence of proof of their guilt, the court acquitted them. The government appealed to the imperial court which passed on the case for re-examination at the provincial court in Freiberg, Saxony (see Note 602).— 330

[447] At the elections held on 4 October 1885 to the French Chamber of Deputies, numerous candidates failed to receive the number of votes required for election, so that a second ballot was scheduled for 18 October. This ballot brought a republican majority, comprising representatives of the party of moderate republicans ('Opportunists') and the party of Radicals (see notes 236 and 429). The Chamber of Deputies was made up of 382 republicans (including 180 Radicals) and 202 monarchists.— 330, 364, 430

[448] The views about the elections in France which Engels sets out in this letter were reflected in the leading article in *Der Sozialdemokrat*, No. 42, 15 October 1885.— 330

[449] The results of the first ballot gave rise to´particular disappointment among the French socialists. This prompted Engels to explain to Paul Lafargue the essence of the situation in France. An excerpt from his letter was printed in *Le Socialiste* with the title 'The Situation' (see present edition, Vol. 26, pp. 331-32). The whereabouts of the full text of the letter are not known.— 331

[450] Apart from the works mentioned in the text, Engels also included in the new edition of Marx's pamphlet *Revelations Concerning the Communist Trial in Cologne* a fourth appendix— 'The Communist Trial in Cologne'— to Marx's work *Herr Vogt* (see present edition, Vol. 17, pp. 305-11) and his afterword to the second German edition of the pamphlet (see present edition, Vol. 24, pp. 51-54).— 332

[451] This letter was written on a postcard and carries the following address in Engels' handwriting: 'Monsieur P. Lavroff, 328 rue St. Jacques, *Paris*, France.'— 337

[452] In a letter of 19 October 1885 Pyotr Lavrov asked Engels to let him know what materials he might use for a work he was planning to write on Chartism.— 337

[453] Engels attached great importance to publicising the experience of Chartism as the first political movement of the British working class. It is thought that in the 1880s he wrote special notes for inclusion in *Die Chartistenbewegung in England* by the German democrat Sigismund Borkheim, although Engels' text has not yet been found. *Die Chartistenbewegung in England* (Zurich, 1887) by the German socialist Hermann Schlüter was based on a chronology of Chartism compiled in August 1886 by Engels at the request of the author (see present edition, Vol. 26).— 337

[454] The Social Democrat Salo Faerber from Breslau suggested that Engels write an article on the financial position of Russia in the *Volks-Zeitung*, Berlin, with a view to hindering subscriptions to Russian loan bonds in Germany.— 337

[455] Here, Engels is alluding to the following statement in the Reichstag by Heinrich von Stephan, head of the postal and telegraph service: 'The secrecy of the mail rests just as firmly on the conscience of the German Empire's postal officials as the Bible does on the altar.'— 337, 361

[456] The reference is to the Russo-Turkish war of 1877-78 which was caused by a growth in the activities of the national liberation movement in the Balkans and the exacerbation of international conflicts in the Middle East. The war ended in victory for Russia.

In 1806, Prussia joined the fourth anti-French coalition, and its army was soon routed by the Napoleonic forces at the battles of Jena and Auerstedt.— 339

[457] The reference is to Wilhelm Liebknecht's reply to Salo Faerber's letter requesting him to shed light on the state of Russian finances in his Reichstag speech during

the third reading of the budget. In the letter Liebknecht explained the reasons why he had not made any speech.— 339

⁴⁵⁸ At the elections to the Saxon Provincial Diet on 15 September 1885 Liebknecht, who was standing for the rural district around Leipzig, lost at the hands of a candidate jointly nominated by the Conservatives (see Note 230) and the National Liberals (see Note 243).

The poll was held in line with the electoral qualifications set out in the law of 1868; the vote extended to persons of 25 and over who had paid at least three marks in direct taxes, whilst to stand as a candidate it was necessary to be not less than 30 years of age, to have paid at least 30 marks in direct taxes and have been a Saxon citizen for a minimum of three years.— 340

⁴⁵⁹ The French utopian socialist Étienne Cabet tried to organise a communist colony in North America made up of several hundred of his followers drawn from among the French workers. The colony existed from 1848 to 1856. The last communist community in the United States, which had been formed by adherents of Cabet, ceased to exist in 1895.— 342

⁴⁶⁰ In 1880, at the request of Paul Lafargue, Engels transformed three chapters of his *Anti-Dühring* (Chapter I of the 'Introduction' and Chapters I and II of Part three — see present edition, Vol. 25, pp. 16-27 and 244-71) into a popular work in its own right. Entitled *Socialism: Utopian and Scientific*, it was published under the heading 'Socialisme utopique et socialisme scientifique' in the French journal *La Revue socialiste*, Nos. 3, 4 and 5, 20 March, 20 April and 5 May 1880, and later that year under the same heading as a separate pamphlet in Paris.— 342

⁴⁶¹ The words by Reichstag deputy Ludwig Bamberger which became a standard phrase were uttered at one of the 1876 sittings to describe the manner in which Bismarck dealt with the National Liberals.— 342

⁴⁶² Engels is referring to the *Kulturkampf*, a word which has come to describe the measures taken by the Bismarck government in the 1870s against the Catholic Church and the Party of the Centre, which was closely associated with it (see Note 229). Between 1871 and 1875 a number of laws were passed which were designed to weaken the Party of the Centre and the Catholic clergy who supported it. However, the Church refused to submit. In the latter half of the 1870s and the early 1880s, given the growth of the labour movement, Bismarck sought to rally all reactionary forces and steered a course of reconciliation with the Catholic Church, as a result of which most of these laws were repealed.— 343, 434, 511

⁴⁶³ The reference is to an attempted coup aimed at restoring the monarchy in France and staged in 1877 by Marshal Mac-Mahon, President of the Third Republic. However, Mac-Mahon failed to gain support not only from large sections of the general public but also from a section of the officers and rank-and-file soldiers, who reflected the republican sentiments among the French peasantry. The parliamentary elections of October 1877 brought victory for the republicans and the formation of a government made up of bourgeois republicans; Mac-Mahon resigned in January 1879.— 343, 430

⁴⁶⁴ The reference is to the following passage contained in the preface to the 1872 German edition of the *Manifesto of the Communist Party*: '... in view of the practical experience gained ... in the Paris Commune, where the proletariat for the first time held

political power for two whole months, this programme has in some details become antiquated. One thing especially was proved by the Commune, ... that "the working class cannot simply lay hold of the ready-made state machinery, and wield it for its own purposes"' (see present edition, Vol. 23, p. 175).— 344

[465] *Olivia*, written by the English playwright W. G. Wills, is an adaptation of Oliver Goldsmith's *The Vicar of Wakefield.*— 345

[466] In a letter of 8 August 1885 the French socialists Paul Lavigne asked Engels to look through the manuscript of his translation of Marx's *The Eighteenth Brumaire of Louis Bonaparte.*— 345, 358

[467] This is the number of votes Paul Lafargue received at the election to the French Chamber of Deputies in October 1885 (see Note 447).— 345

[468] Engels is referring to the passage in his work *On the History of the Communist League* where he deals with the activities of Stephan Born, a member of the League; at this point he also indicates that Born's real surname was Buttermilch (see present edition, Vol. 26, pp. 325-26). Born does not figure among the list of names Georg Adler thanks for their assistance in the preface to the said book by Adler.— 346

[469] The *Thirty Years' War* (1618-48) — a general European war in which the Pope, the Spanish and Austrian Habsburgs and the Catholic German princes fought against the Protestant countries: Bohemia, Denmark, Sweden, the Republic of the Netherlands, and a number of German states. The Treaty of Westphalia (1648) sealed political dismemberment of Germany.— 348

[470] Nikolai Danielson attached to his letter of 25 August 1885 several excerpts from letters which Marx had written to him on 12 December 1872, 15 and 28 November 1878, 10 April 1879, 12 September 1880 and 19 February and 13 December 1881 (see present edition, Vols. 44, 45 and 46).

Danielson believed that these excerpts — which contained a description of the economic, notably the financial and agrarian, crisis in Britain and several other countries, as well as advice on translating the first volume of *Capital* into Russian — might be of use to Engels in his work on the third volume of *Capital* and the preface to the second volume. In his letter of 10 April 1879 Marx also explained why he had not yet completed the second and third volumes of *Capital.*— 348

[471] The reference is to the economic crisis in Britain and other capitalist countries which Marx dealt with in his letter to Nikolai Danielson of 10 April 1879 (see present edition, Vol. 45).— 349

[472] This letter is Engels' reply to Paul Lafargue's request (voiced in his letter of 13 November 1885) for information on his involvement in the May 1849 uprising in Dresden and the Rhine Province. Lafargue intended to include the information in a biography of Engels he was preparing for publication between 14 November 1885 and 28 August 1886 in the 'Galerie socialiste internationale' column of *Le Socialiste*. Engels' letter formed the basis for the second part of the biography which appeared unsigned in No. 13 of the newspaper, 21 November 1885. The same issue carried a portrait of Engels by the artist Clarus; Lafargue sent Engels a copy of this portrait together with the letter mentioned.— 350

[473] Engels gives a detailed analysis of the reasons behind the movement in support of the Imperial Constitution and the course of armed hostilities in Rhenish Prussia,

Baden and the Palatinate in *The Campaign for the German Imperial Constitution* (see present edition, Vol. 10).— 350

⁴⁷⁴ *Landwehr* — the army reserve formed in Prussia during the struggle against Napoleon. In the 1840s it consisted of men under forty who had done three years active service and not less than two years in the reserve. In contrast to the regular army, conscription to the army reserve took place in cases of extreme necessity (war, or threat of war).— 351, 485

⁴⁷⁵ The sitting of the Reichstag opened on 19 November 1885.— 352

⁴⁷⁶ The German Social Democrat and Reichstag deputy Georg Schumacher wrote to Engels on 14 August 1885 in an attempt to justify the position taken by those who had voted in favour of state subsidies for steamship companies in the Reichstag (see Note 342). On Engels' attitude to this issue, see this volume, pp. 240-42.— 353

⁴⁷⁷ Wilhelm Liebknecht served a four-week prison sentence in Leipzig beginning on 29 September 1885. It is roughly during this period that *Der Sozialdemokrat* carried a series of his articles headed 'Ueber den Normalarbeitstag' (22 and 29 October, 5, 12 and 19 November 1885).— 353

⁴⁷⁸ The reference is to the first battle of the Serbian-Bulgarian war, which took place on 16 November 1885. The war was caused by the so-called Bulgarian crisis (see notes 445 and 634). Under the influence of Austria-Hungary, Serbia declared war on Bulgaria on 14 November 1885, demanding territorial compensation for the growth in Bulgarian territory. The Bulgarian forces inflicted a crushing defeat on the Serbian army in the very first month and entered Serbia. Bulgaria ceased its advance under pressure from Austria-Hungary and, on 3 March 1886, a peace treaty was concluded in Bucharest under which Serbia recognised the borders of the reunited Bulgaria.— 353, 515

⁴⁷⁹ An excerpt from this letter was published in English for the first time in: K. Marx and F. Engels, *Literature and Art*, International Publishers, New York, 1947.— 355

⁴⁸⁰ This letter is the reply to that of 15 October 1885 from Minna Kautsky, Karl Kautsky's mother, who had got to know Engels during her stay in London in the summer of 1885. She described her impressions of London and Berlin to Engels and asked his opinion of her book *Die Alten und die Neuen*.— 355

⁴⁸¹ It follows from Paul Lafargue's letter to Engels of 4 November 1885 that Engels asked Lafargue for information on Paul Lavigne. Lafargue wrote: 'The question you ask concerning Lavigne is difficult to answer. One fine day he appeared in our midst saying that he had translated Marx's *18th Brumaire* and *The Holy Family*, that Fortin did not know the ABC of German.... Believing him to be a giant refreshed in German we commissioned him to translate the *Manifesto*. But after going over the translation for the first number, we decided it had to be thrown into the waste-paper basket. ...Lavigne seems to me slightly mad....'
   Lavigne wrote to Engels on 8 August 1885 saying, among other things, that he intended to translate the second volume of Marx's *Capital*.— 358

⁴⁸² Apart from Paul Lavigne's manuscript, this refers to the translation of Marx's *The Eighteenth Brumaire of Louis Bonaparte* (present edition, Vol. 11) done by Édouard Fortin (see this volume, p. 345). This translation, edited by Engels, was published

in *Le Socialiste*, January-November 1891 and appeared as a separate volume during the same year in Lille.— 358, 528

[483] Édouard Fortin repeatedly wrote to Marx in 1881 in connection with his study of the first volume of *Capital* (see K. Marx to Charles Longuet of 4 January 1881; present edition, Vol. 46).— 358

[484] An excerpt from this letter was first published in English in: K. Marx and F. Engels, *Ireland and the Irish Question*, Progress Publishers, Moscow, 1971.— 359, 363, 448

[485] Liebknecht wrote to Engels on 26 November 1885 asking his assistance in obtaining material in English on the financial situation of Russia for a speech he was to make in the Reichstag about the granting of a German loan to Russia. Liebknecht made use of Engels' recommendations during his Reichstag speech of 8 February 1886 (see also Note 551).— 359, 365, 377

[486] The speech by Wilhelm Liebknecht to which Engels refers was made in the Reichstag on 24 November 1885. In it, Liebknecht sharply criticised Bismarck's home and foreign policy, for which he was called to order.— 361

[487] The British general election took place from 23 November to 19 December 1885. The Liberals obtained 335 seats of which 4 belonged to the 'independents', the Conservatives 249 and the supporters of Irish Home Rule, 86 seats. These were the first elections held after the parliamentary reform of 1884 (see Note 299).— 361, 364, 367, 390

[488] At the beginning of the 1880s, the English bourgeoisie started to call for protective tariffs due to growing competition on the world market from the United States and Germany, thus departing from the principles of free trade as advocated by the Manchester school (see Note 283).— 361

[489] The slogan *The Church in danger*! was advanced by the Conservatives during the British election campaign in the autumn of 1885. It was prompted by the fact that the Liberals supported the demand raised by bourgeois-radical elements and Irish Catholics for the separation of the Anglican Church from the state. When the Conservative propaganda attracted a favourable response among a large number of voters, the Liberals to all intents and purposes ceased to support this demand.— 361

[490] This letter was written in connection with the preparatory work Karl Kautsky was doing— at Engels' initiative and on his instructions (see this volume, p. 344) — on a résumé of *Die Geschichte der ersten Sozialpolitischen Arbeiterbewegung in Deutschland* by the German journalist Georg Adler. The book depicted the history of the Communist League and Marx's revolutionary activities in a distorted manner. The résumé was published in *Die Neue Zeit*, No. 2, February 1886.— 362

[491] In his book Georg Adler wrote that, as editor of the *Neue Rheinische Zeitung*, Marx had allegedly been constantly subjected to insults and physical attacks which posed a serious threat to his life. In his résumé of the book, Karl Kautsky ridiculed this allegation as instructed by Engels. By way of proof he cited an episode recalled to him by Engels. Two armed non-commissioned officers had appeared at Marx's home demanding retribution for his alleged derision of the title of non-commissioned officer. Marx had greeted them in a dressing gown with the butt of

an unloaded pistol protruding from the pocket. At the sight of this, the NCOs had quickly taken their leave (see present edition, Vol. 38, pp. 192-93).— 362

[492] Georg Adler claimed in his book (see Note 490) that Moses Hess had taken part in the South German uprising of May 1849, for which he had been sentenced to death. In his résumé, Karl Kautsky refuted this unsubstantiated claim on Engels' instructions.— 362

[493] The reference is to the works by Marx which were prepared for republication and issued with Engels' prefaces by the German Social-Democratic publishing house in Hottingen-Zurich in 1885-86: 'The Preface to the Pamphlet *Karl Marx Before the Cologne Jury*'; On the History of the Communist League (see present edition, Vol. 26), and also Engels' work 'On the History of the Prussian Peasants. The Introduction to Wilhelm Wolff's Pamphlet *The Silesian Milliard*' (see present edition, Vol. 26).— 363

[494] In the course of 1884 and 1885 Engels edited the German translation of *The Poverty of Philosophy* (present edition, Vol. 5), the English translation of *The Condition of the Working-Class in England* (Vol. 2), the Italian and Danish translations of *The Origin of the Family, Private Property and the State* (Vol. 26) as well as the translations of *The Eighteenth Brumaire of Louis Bonaparte* (Vol. 11) and the *Manifesto of the Communist Party* (Vol. 6) into French and other languages.— 364

[495] This letter was first published in English in an abridged form in *The Labour Monthly*, London, 1933, Vol. 15, No. 11, XI.— 366

[496] Henry Mayers Hyndman and Henry Hyde Champion, the leaders of the Social Democratic Federation (see Note 300) received money from the Conservative Party to put up their candidates at the 1885 general election (see Note 487). The Federation fielded candidates in London constituencies — Hampstead and Kensington — where they had no prospects of winning but could capture a proportion of the Liberal vote to the benefit of the Conservatives. The Federation's leadership attempted to justify their agreement to these conditions by claiming that the election campaign merely served as propaganda for the future revolution. This created displeasure among many of the Federation's members, as a result of which a number of them resigned and several local organisations split from the Federation. *The Echo*, Nos. 5285 and 5287, 5 and 7 December 1885 carried a statement from John Edward Williams, one of the Federation's candidates, claiming he was not aware of the receipt of any money from the Tories, an editorial giving details of how the money had been received and a note by Federation member Charles L. Fitzgerald criticising the leadership. *Der Sozialdemokrat*, No. 51, 17 December 1885, published an editorial based on this letter by Engels, material from *The Echo* and a letter by Hubert Bland, one of the Federation officials, dealing with the meetings of the Executive Committee on 9 and 12 November at which Hyndman and Champion had been censured for their actions.— 366-67, 369, 376, 394, 404, 406

[497] The reference is to the attempt made by the leaders of the German Conservative Party (see Note 230) and the Christian-Social Party, Adolph Wagner and Adolf Stoecker, to conclude an electoral alliance with the Social Democrats against the candidates of the Party of Progress (see Note 93) during the Berlin elections of November 1881. They agreed to support Social-Democratic candidates (August Bebel and Wilhelm Hasenclever) in two Berlin constituencies on condition that the

Socialist Workers' Party acknowledged the 'social reforms' being carried out by Bismarck's government and backed the implementation of these 'reforms' with a view to warding off a revolution. On behalf of the party, Bebel and Liebknecht sharply rebuffed these manoeuvres on the part of the reactionaries. Their statement was published in the *Volks-Zeitung*, 19 November 1881.— 367

498 In a statement headed 'The Socialists and the General Election' and carried by *The Pall Mall Gazette*, 4 December 1885, John Hunter Watts, the treasurer of the Social Democratic Federation (see Note 300), tried to justify the actions of 'an ill-advised few London Socialists' by claiming that they intended 'to take ammunition from the enemy in order to blaze it in their faces'.— 367

499 The substance of this letter formed the basis for the editorial 'Angleterre' published in *Le Socialiste*, No. 16, 12 December 1885.— 368

500 The *Republican Social Economy Society* (Société Républicaine d'Économie sociale) was founded on 7 November 1885 at the initiative of the Possibilist (see Note 237) leader Benoît Malon. The society set itself the aim of studying the social question and putting forward plans for imminent reforms.— 368

501 In its leading article 'En Angleterre', dealing with the results of the elections to the House of Commons, *Le Socialiste*, No. 15, 5 December 1885 quoted from the election platform put forward by John Edward Williams, a candidate for the Social Democratic Federation (see Note 300), and also mentioned other candidates from this party.— 368

502 The reference is to two notes by Henry Mayers Hyndman published in *Justice*, No. 90, 3 October and No. 92, 17 October 1885 where he accuses Edward Aveling of offending against an agreement concluded between various socialist organisations about speeches to be made by socialists at the Dod Street demonstration of 27 September 1885. Hyndman's accusation was refuted in a statement signed by 31 members of socialist organisations. The statement together with both notes from *Justice* was carried by *The Commonweal*, No. 10, November 1885 in an article entitled 'Free Speech and the Police'.— 370, 394

503 On 16 November 1885 Hermann Schlüter wrote to Engels asking for the address of Johann Georg Eccarius, the former secretary of the General Council of the First International. He intended to reissue the latter's book *Eines Arbeiters Widerlegung der national-ökonomischen Lehren John Stuart Mill's* in the Social-Democratic publishing house in Zurich; Schlüter believed that Eccarius would revise his book. It appeared in 1888, without any changes on Engels' advice.— 371

504 Engels is referring to the Prussian armed intervention of 1787 in the Netherlands, which was aimed at crushing the uprising by the opposition party of 'patriots'. The party had used the defeat of the Dutch in the war with Britain (1784) to seize power and expel Stadtholder William V. The Prussian forces invaded the country and restored him to power.— 372

505 The reference is to the short biography of Marx carried by *Le Socialiste*, No. 12, 14 November 1885 and probably written by Paul Lafargue.— 373, 374

506 Hermann Schlüter wrote to Engels on 19 December 1885 that Lothar Bucher, in his pamphlet *Der Parlamentarismus wie er ist* claimed a journalist in the pay of Palmerston had written a pamphlet entitled *Palmerston, What Has He Done?* at the latter's

bidding. Schlüter asked Engels whether Bucher was not perhaps alluding to Marx's pamphlet *Lord Palmerston* (present edition, Vol. 12).— 374

507 The reference is to Paul Lafargue's letter to Engels of 21 January 1885 in which he asked Engels to send him a cheque for £12 (see F. Engels, Paul and Laura Lafargue, *Correspondence*, Vol. 1, Foreign Languages Publishing House, Moscow, 1959, p. 322).— 375

508 In his letter of 21 December 1885 Paul Lafargue asked Engels to send him *Justice*, No. 100, 12 December 1885 containing a statement by Henry Mayers Hyndman and other leaders of the Social Democratic Federation in which they sought to refute the accusations levelled at Hyndman for his having received money from the Conservatives to finance the election campaign (see this volume, pp. 366-68).— 376

509 Engels is playing on the fact — of which Paul Lafargue informed him — that the oldest of all bridges in Paris, the Pont Neuf, which became proverbial for its strength, was partly destroyed when the Seine burst its banks. It is an allusion to Lafargue's illnesses.— 376

510 The obituary to Sigismund Borkheim was carried by *Der Sozialdemokrat*, No. 3, 15 January 1886 under the heading 'In memoriam!'. It was probably written by Wilhelm Liebknecht. The factual inaccuracies it contained were corrected by the author in the following issue in a note headed 'Sigismund Borkheim' (*Der Sozialdemokrat*, 21 January 1886). The date, year and place of Borkheim's birth were put right, as were the years he attended school and a number of facts associated with the events of 1848.

Engels wrote a short biographical sketch of Borkheim by way of an introduction to S. Borkheim, *Zur Erinnerung für die deutschen Mordspatrioten. 1806-1807*, Hottingen-Zurich, 1888. It was published on Engels' initiative and with his assistance (see present edition, Vol. 26, pp. 446-51).— 377, 379

511 Engels wrote this letter by way of a supplement to his letter of 28 December 1885 to Wilhelm Liebknecht in which he had requested Liebknecht to place the obituary of Borkheim in *Der Sozialdemokrat* (see this volume, p. 377).— 380

512 The *Paris Peace Treaty*, which ended the Crimean War of 1853-56, was signed by representatives of Russia, Austria, France, Great Britain, Sardinia, Turkey and Prussia on 18 (30) March 1856.— 380

513 The reference is to the clashes of ideas which occurred under the Anti-Socialist Law (see Note 37) in the Socialist Workers' Party of Germany between December 1884 and mid-July 1885. The question was whether it was possible for two ideological tendencies — revolutionary-proletarian and opportunist — to coexist within the framework of a single party in the German workers' movement. Differences of principle on a wide range of issues emerged between the representatives of these two tendencies within the Socialist Workers' Party: the strategy and tactics of the workers' movement, inner-party discipline, the significance of parliamentary activity by socialist deputies, the role of the bourgeois state and the social reforms being carried out by the government, etc.

Engels wrote to Bebel setting out his attitude to Liebknecht's position in the conflict as described in this letter (see this volume, p. 387).— 382

514 The reference is to the annual reports of the Bureau of Statistics of Labor. From

1869 onwards these bureaus were set up in numerous US states under pressure from workers' organisations.— 382, 396

515 An allusion to Wilhelm Blos' speech in the Reichstag on 9 January 1886 during the first reading of the bill on the construction of a Baltic canal (see Note 519).— 383

516 The reference is to the attempt of 14 June 1848 by German workers and artisans during the revolution to seize an arsenal in Berlin.— 383

517 Engels provided Liebknecht with additional brief biographical details of Borkheim for the obituary (see this volume, pp. 379 and 381).— 383

518 The reference is to Bebel's and Liebknecht's planned trip to the United States to raise funds for the German Social Democrats' election campaign (see this volume, pp. 14 and 114). Liebknecht departed alone on the trip, which lasted from September to December 1886, whilst Eleanor Marx-Aveling and Edward Aveling stayed in the United States almost concurrently with him (see Note 600).— 383, 391, 429, 446

519 The reference is to the project for the construction of a ship canal in Schleswig-Holstein connecting the harbour of Kiel with the mouth of the River Elbe near Brunsbüttel, subsequently called the Kiel Canal (alternatively, the North Sea-Baltic Canal, Kaiser Wilhelm Canal). The bill providing for its construction was presented to the Reichstag by Bismarck on 12 December 1885 and discussed on 9 January and 20 February 1886. It was enacted at the third reading on 25 February 1886.

On Engels' attitude to the bill, see also this volume, p. 388.— 383

520 In 1884 and 1885 *Die Neue Zeit* carried a number of articles by Max Quarck. Engels vehemently protested against Quarck contributing to the journal (see this volume, pp. 164 and 258).— 385, 418

521 A fragment from this letter was published in English for the first time in *The Labour Monthly*, London, 1933, Vol. 15, No. 11, XI.— 386, 393, 426, 439, 445

522 This letter is Engels' reply to August Bebel's letter of 7 December 1885 in which Bebel insisted on publishing in the press a critique of C. A. Schramm, *Rodbertus, Marx, Lassalle. Sozialwissenschaftliche Studie* and asked Engels to assist Karl Kautsky with the same.

Schramm's book was the continuation of the polemic between Kautsky and himself (see Note 523). In it the author once again tried to play down the significance of Marx's theoretical and practical work. Eduard Bernstein provided a critical analysis of this work in a series of articles headed 'Ein moralischer Kritiker und seine kritische Moral' and published in *Der Sozialdemokrat*, Nos. 4-7, 21, 28 January, 5 and 12 February 1886.— 387, 391

523 Kautsky began the polemic with Schramm by publishing a critique of Rodbertus' *Das Kapital von Rodbertus* in *Die Neue Zeit*, Nos. 8 and 9, 1884. This was occasioned by the attempts of the armchair socialists (see Note 54) to set Rodbertus against Marx and depict him as the most outstanding theoretician of political economy. Engels looked through the article (see this volume, pp. 193-94). Schramm defended Rodbertus in the article 'K. Kautsky und Rodbertus' carried by *Die Neue Zeit*, No. 11, 1884. The same issue contained Kautsky's reply, 'Eine Replik'. Following the inclusion under the heading 'Marx und Rodbertus' in the January issue of *Die Neue Zeit* of Engels' preface to the German translation of Marx's *La Misère de la*

philosophie, the polemic continued in *Die Neue Zeit*, No. 5, 1885 with the publication of Schramm's 'Antwort an Herrn K. Kautsky' and Kautsky's reply headed 'Das Schlusswort'. That marked its end.— 387

524 The reference is to the expulsion of 30,000 Poles who were not German subjects from the Eastern provinces of Prussia. This prompted Dr Ludwig von Jazdzewski to request an explanation on behalf of the Polish faction in the Reichstag on 28 November 1885, a move supported by the Social-Democratic deputies. At the Reichstag sitting of 1 December 1885 Bismarck made use of a message from William I in an attempt to prevent the matter being discussed. He claimed that it came under the jurisdiction of the Prussian government and could not therefore be debated by the Reichstag. However, the Social Democrats successfully insisted on a discussion, which took place on 15-16 January 1886.— 389

525 This is Engels' reply to a letter from Edward R. Pease, a member of the Executive Committee of the Fabian Society, who had requested him to write a brief résumé of the most important economic, social and political proposals of the party for a pamphlet called *What Is Socialism?* that was in preparation.

The *Fabian Society*—an organisation founded in 1884 by democratically-minded intellectuals. The society took its name from a Roman general who lived in the third century B. C., viz. Quintus Fabius Maximus, surnamed Cunctator ('the delayer') for his cautious tactics in the war against Hannibal. A leading role in the society was played by Sidney and Beatrice Webb, George Bernard Shaw and others. The branches of the society included among their members workers attracted by the sharp criticism of capitalist relations contained in the Fabians' publications. The Fabians rejected Marx's and Engels' doctrine of class struggle and the revolutionary transformation of bourgeois society, considering it possible to carry out the transition from capitalism to socialism by way of a number of reforms within the framework of what they called municipal socialism.— 392

526 Marx's comments on the English translation of Volume I of *Capital* in the margins of the manuscript in 1877 were occasioned by the planned publication of the book in the United States, which failed to materialise. Marx then sent the manuscript to Friedrich Adolph Sorge. Having discovered that Engels was editing the English translation of the first volume, Sorge wrote to him on 3 August 1885 offering to send him the manuscript. Engels received it in early 1886.— 393, 439

527 In October 1885 *To-Day* began to publish the English translation of the first volume of *Capital* done by Henry Mayers Hyndman (pseudonym John Broadhouse). Engels criticised the beginning of this translation (of the first and a part of the second sections of Chapter One) carried by *To-Day*, vol. 4, No. 22, in his article 'How Not to Translate Marx' (see present edition, Vol. 26). The translation was published in the journal up to May 1889 inclusive; it covered the first seven chapters and a large part of Chapter Eight of the first volume.— 393, 419, 424, 440

528 The English edition of Engels' *Socialism: Utopian and Scientific* was published in Edward Aveling's translation in London in 1892.— 394, 416, 464, 523

529 Engels is referring to Joseph Dietzgen's contributions to the American newspapers *Der Sozialist* and the *New Yorker Volkszeitung*, organs of the Socialist Labor Party (see Note 549) in which the Lassalleans held leading positions at the time. Sorge

repeatedly informed Engels that Dietzgen's articles in these newspapers were being altered and distorted.— 395, 441

530 This letter is Engels' reply to that from Florence Kelley-Wischnewetzky of 10 January 1886 in which she asked him to send her the corrected manuscript of her English translation of *The Condition of the Working-Class in England* for dispatch to the United States via R. M. Foster.— 395

531 Engels is replying to a number of questions Nieuwenhuis posed in his letter of 28 January 1886 in connection with his work on the Dutch translation of the pamphlet *Socialism: Utopian and Scientific*; the pamphlet also included Engels' article 'The Mark' as an appendix (see present edition, Vol. 24).
    A fragment of this letter was first published in English in: K. Marx, F. Engels, V. I. Lenin, *On Scientific Communism*, Progress Publishers, Moscow, 1967.— 397

532 Under the *rundale* system Irish tenant farmers each paid rent separately for his plot of the land which had formerly belonged to the entire gens but later had been seized by the British invaders. However, they then put all the arable and grazing land together and divided it into strips according to location and quality, with each farmer receiving a share of each lot. For Engels' description of this system, see present edition, Vol. 26, p. 234.— 398

533 Engels wrote this letter on a postcard addressed as follows: 'Monsieur P. Lavroff, 328 rue St. Jacques, Paris, France.' It is his reply to Lavrov's request, voiced in a letter of 23 January 1886 for a publication in which he might find a description of the external appearance, habits, etc., of the 'foremost English worthies'.— 399

534 The reference is to Nikolai Danielson's preface to the first Russian edition of Volume II of *Capital* (see notes 155 and 168). In his letter to Engels of 31 December 1885 Danielson informed the recipient that he had completed the Russian translation of the second volume of *Capital* and was waiting for the third volume to appear.— 400

535 It is probable that Nikolai Danielson's remarks about the economic situation in Russia were contained in his letters of 30 November, 7 January and 20 January whose whereabouts are unknown.— 401

536 *Greenbackers* — a political party in the Western American states formed in March 1875 and chiefly composed of farmers. It opposed the removal from circulation of the paper money (bills with a green reverse) issued during the Civil War of 1861-65, a measure carried out due to its devaluation. The Greenbackers wrongly thought that the retention of a large volume of paper money would bring about a rise in the price of agricultural produce. Following the inclusion of a number of working-class demands in the party programme, a considerable number of workers joined the party, which became known as the Greenback Labor Party. The party fell apart after 1884.— 401

537 Engels wrote this letter on a postcard addressed: 'F. A. Sorge Esq., Hoboken N. Y., U. S. America.'
    On its first publication in English, see Note 27.— 402

538 The supporters of protective tariffs, including pro-Conservative trade union officials (S. Peters, T. M. Kelly, W. Kenny and T. Lemon, who were expelled at the Trades Union Congress in Manchester in 1882) held a meeting in Trafalgar Square on 8 February 1886. The Social Democratic Federation (see Note 300) or-

ganised a meeting and unemployed demonstration in opposition to the Conservative campaign for protective tariffs. This demonstration (see this volume, pp. 403-04 and 406-08) was joined by the lumpenproletarian elements, who began to behave in an unruly manner and loot shops. The police subsequently arrested Henry Mayers Hyndman, John Burns, Henry Hyde Champion and John Edward Williams, the leaders of the Federation, on a charge of making 'inciting speeches'. The trial ended on 10 April with their acquittal.— 403, 407, 427, 434

539 Karl Kautsky published a report on the events of 8 February 1886 in *Der Sozialdemokrat*, No. 8, 19 February under the heading 'Der anarchistisch-sozialistische Aufruhr in London' and in the Viennese newspaper *Die Deutsche Wochenschrift*, No. 8, 21 February under the heading 'Arbeiterunruhen in London'.— 404, 407

540 The reference is to the conviction of E. Jones, J. Fussell, I. Williams, A. Sharpe and T. Vernon, who were arrested in early June 1848 in connection with a Chartist demonstration planned for 12 June in London; they were each sentenced to two years' imprisonment and fined on a charge of incitement to revolt and overthrow the government. Harney was not among those arrested; it was at his initiative that a special fund was set up to assist the convicted and their families.— 404

541 On 12 February 1886 Bebel requested Engels to provide him with information on the activities of the Social Democratic Federation (see Note 300) and on the events in London (see Note 538), since the German reactionary press was using them as an excuse in support of the need to prolong the Anti-Socialist Law (see Note 37). Bebel intended to take part in the discussion of this matter in the Reichstag.
On the letter's first publication in English, see Note 521.— 406

542 The Conservative government of Lord Robert Arthur Salisbury resigned on 26 January 1886; it was replaced in early February by a Liberal government formed by William Ewart Gladstone.— 407

543 *Fair Trade*— the name given in 1881 in Great Britain to a movement to protect industry from foreign competition by means of import duties. The movement was organised by certain quarters from the Conservative Party who founded the Fair Trade League that same year. The League was joined by a small group of trade union officials.— 407

544 According to *The Annual Register: A Review of Public Events at Home and Abroad, for the year 1886*, New Series, London, 1887, the subscription fund amounted to £ 78,000, or £ 28,000 more than the official estimation of the damage.— 409

545 3,500 miners went on strike in *Decazeville* (department of Aveyron) on 26 (27?) January 1886 in response to the ruthless exploitation to which they were exposed by the owners of the Aveyron Association of Coalmines and Foundries. At the beginning of the strike, the miners killed Watrin, the manager of the collieries, who had refused to heed their demands. The government sent troops to Decazeville. The strike continued until mid-June and evoked a broad response in France; the events led to the formation in the Chamber of Deputies of a workers' group which supported the miners' demands. The strike ended in the surrender of the company to the miners; an increased rate was promised, and the obnoxious officials dismissed.— 409, 424, 428, 434, 437, 442, 470, 478, 489, 507

546 An excerpt from this letter has survived only as a newspaper publication in *Le Socialiste*, No. 115, 24 November 1900 with the heading 'Engels et les radicaux'. On the letter's first publication in English, see Note 196.—410

[547] This letter was written by Engels on a postcard addressed: 'Herrn E. Bernstein, Asylstr. 43, Hottingen-Zürich, Switzerland.'

It was used in the editorial note 'Aus Frankreich', *Der Sozialdemokrat*, No. 10, 5 March 1886.— 414

[548] This is Engels' reply to Florence Kelley-Wischnewetzky's letter of 22 February in which she wrote about the forthcoming publication in America of the English translation of his *The Condition of the Working-Class in England*, the major importance of this publication for the American workers and the need for translations of other works by Engels.— 415

[549] The *Socialist Labor Party* of the United States (originally called the *Workingmen's Party*) was founded at the unification congress held in Philadelphia on 19-22 June 1876 as a result of the merger between the American sections of the First International, led by Friedrich Adolph Sorge and Otto Weydemeyer, and the Labor Party of Illinois and Social Democratic Party, led by Adolph Strasser, A. Gabriel and Peter J. McGuire. However, the party failed to become a mass organisation throughout the country due to the sectarian policies pursued by the leadership which neglected to form links with the mass organisations of the indigenous American proletariat, and due to the predominance of the Lassallean influence in a number of local organisations.— 415, 491, 530

[550] On the instructions of Florence Kelley-Wischnewetzky, the translator of Engels' *The Condition of the Working-Class in England*, R. Foster — secretary of the National Women Suffrage Association — sought a publisher to put out the book in the USA. She turned to the Executive Committee of the Socialist Labor Party (see Note 549) for help, and on 8 February 1886 the latter set up a special commission for the purpose of negotiating with publishing houses. However, the negotiations were protracted, and the book was issued in May 1887 without any involvement on the part of the Committee.— 415, 441

[551] On 8 February 1886 Wilhelm Liebknecht took part in the Reichstag discussion of the imperial budget, which provided for financial assistance to the Russian government. Relying on advice from Engels and the material he had sent him, Liebknecht analysed the state of the Russian Empire's finances and stressed that Bismarck was rendering it financial assistance in order to help government overcome economic difficulties and prevent them growing into a domestic political crisis (see this volume, pp. 360, 365).— 417

[552] For the appropriate passage in Engels' 'Appendix to the American edition of *The Condition of the Working Class in England*', see present edition, Vol. 26, p. 400.— 420

[553] When addressing his letter of 21 December 1885 to Martignetti, Engels mistakenly gave his name as Paolo instead of Pasquale (see this volume, p. 374), which delayed delivery.— 421

[554] The *Volks-Kalender* published in Brunswick in 1878 contained Engels' work 'Karl Marx' (see present edition, Vol. 24) which Pasquale Martignetti was translating into Italian for publication in one volume together with Marx's *Wage Labour and Capital*. Since two pages were stuck together in Martignetti's copy of the

Volks-Kalender, he was not able to translate them in full and asked Engels to fill in the missing text in the manuscript sent to him for editing.— 421, 494

555 On 10 March 1886 Schlüter informed Engels that Dietz had received 1,000 copies of his *The Origin of the Family, Private Property and the State* from the Social-Democratic publishing house in Zurich and provided them with a new title page for sale as the second edition in Germany.— 422, 475

556 Hermann Schlüter intended to publish as a separate volume the reports of the General Council to the congresses of the International Working Men's Association and therefore enquired of Engels when and where they had been printed. He further informed him that 'a translation into Armenian of Marx's *Wage Labour and Capital* recently appeared in Constantinople'.— 422

557 On 10 March 1886 Hermann Schlüter informed Engels that he intended to publish as a separate pamphlet a speech by the Reverend Joseph Stephens, one of the leaders of the Chartist movement, which had been printed in Georg Weerth's article 'Joseph Rayner Stephens, Prediger zu Staleybridge, und die Bewegung der englischen Arbeiter im Jahre 1839' contained in *Rheinische Jahrbücher zur gesellschaftlichen Reform*, Herausgegeben unter Mitwirkung Webserer von Hermann Püttmann, Vol. II, Belle-Vue, near Constanz, 1846. Schlüter asked Engels to look through the introduction he had written for this publication. He later changed his plans and published the manuscript anonymously after Engels had looked through it under the title *Die Chartistenbewegung in England*, Hottingen-Zürich, 1887 (see also Note 453).— 422, 453, 467, 475, 528

558 Engels is replying to Hermann Schlüter's question about when the People's Charter was drawn up.

The purpose of the mass demonstration planned for 10 April 1848 was to present to Parliament the Chartists' third petition supporting the admission of the People's Charter. Unconfirmed reports said the petition was signed by some five million people. However, the demonstration was prohibited by the government and did not take place.— 422

559 Engels is probably referring to the article 'French Socialists at the Ballot Box' by A. S. Headingley, carried by *The Justice*, No. 113, 13 March 1886. The article describes the Possibilists (see Note 237) as the main socialist organisation in France but fails to mention the formation of a workers' group in the Chamber of Deputies (see this volume, pp. 409-10).— 424

560 On 18 March 1886 two thousand people gathered in Paris to commemorate the fifteenth anniversary of the Paris Commune. The meeting was addressed by Paul Lafargue, Jules Guesde, Louise Michel, Gabriel Deville and Oury. Engels sent a letter of greetings which was published in *Le Socialiste*, No. 31, 27 March 1886 (see present edition, Vol. 26, pp. 406-07).— 425

561 In connection with Wilhelm Liebknecht's forthcoming 60th birthday, on 29 March 1886, a group of Social-Democratic deputies in the Reichstag (Ignaz Auer, August Bebel, Paul Singer and others) proposed setting up a fund to assist him and his family. Bebel attached the group's appeal to his letter to Engels of 9 March and requested him to make his contribution.— 426

562 At the sitting of 18 February 1886 in the Reichstag Paul Singer exposed Ferdinand Ihring, an employee of the police criminal investigation department, who had in-

filtrated a workers' society in Berlin under the name of Mahlow and incited the workers to carry out acts of terrorism for the purpose of provocation.— 426

563 This probably refers to Wilhelm Liebknecht's speech at the workers' meeting on 8 March 1886 in Berlin. Liebknecht rebuffed the claims by government circles that the Anti-Socialist Law was of an 'educative significance' for the Social Democrats and exposed the attempts to pass off the introduction of a state monopoly on spirits as a 'socialist' measure.— 427

564 The Chamber of Deputies passed the resolution on 15 March 1886 by 379 votes to 100.— 428

565 On 17 March 1886 Paul Lafargue wrote to Engels that Benoît Malon, one of the Possibilist (see Note 237) leaders, was seeking to set up a parliamentary group made up of socialists of all complexions except those who were 'too red'.— 430

566 On 1 March 1886 *La Nouvelle Revue*, whose editor-in-chief was Juliette Adam, published Paul Lafargue's article 'Le Matriarcat...'. On 17 March 1886 he wrote to Engels, 'You will have received the copy of *La Nouvelle Revue* which I sent you yesterday. So as to correspond to the magazine's level of publications I have made the theoretical part much shorter; in the proofs Mme Adam has abridged it even more... However one should not blame her since she has dropped rather serious things which would have shocked brave philistines who subscribe to it. The prudery of the Parisian journals is incredible...'— 431

567 In 1884 the *Journal des Économistes. Revue de la science économique et de la statistique* carried the following articles by Lafargue: in Nos. 7 and 8, 'Le blé en Amérique, production et commerce'; in No. 9, 'La théorie de la plus-value de Karl Marx et la critique de M. Paul Leroy-Beaulieu'; in No. 11, 'Le "Capital" de Karl Marx et la critique de M. Block'. The *Revue philosophique de la France et de l'étranger*, Vol. XX, September 1885, published Lafargue's article 'Recherches sur les origines de l'idée du bien et du juste'.— 431

568 Each issue of *La Nouvelle Revue* contained a section headed 'Lettres sur la politique extérieure' and signed 'J. Adam'.— 431

569 On 18 March 1886 South Place Chapel in London was the venue for a meeting to commemorate the anniversary of the Paris Commune. The meeting was addressed by representatives of the Socialist League (see Note 346) (Eleanor Marx-Aveling, Frank Kitz and others), the Social Democratic Federation (see Note 300) (Tom Mann, Harry Quelch and others), Friedrich Lessner from the German Workers' Educational Society (see Note 162) and also a number of anarchists, including Pyotr Kropotkin.— 431

570 In her letter of reply written in April 1886, Vera Zasulich thanked Engels for sending her the Russian translation of the second volume of *Capital* and gave her precise address: 'Madame Beldinsky, Maison Goss-Renevier, Chemin de la Queue d'Arve, Plain palais, Genève.'— 432

571 The reference is to the Reichstag repeated debates on the prolongation of the Anti-Socialist Law held on 30 and 31 March and 2 April 1886. Engels is alluding to the bold interventions by the leaders of the German Social Democrats. Speaking on 31 March, for example, August Bebel stated that the government would not require any anti-socialist law if it was in a position to halt the proletarianisation of the

masses but—since it was not in a position to do so—no anti-socialist laws would help it. In his speech of 2 April Wilhelm Liebknecht severely criticised Bismarck's speech in which he had accused Bebel of advocating terror, and compared Bismarck's regime with that of the Second Empire in France.

On 2 April 1886 the Anti-Socialist Law was prolonged for two years at the third reading by 169 votes to 137.— 433, 437, 442

572   Engels is quoting from a popular satirical song dating from 1844-45. *Tschech's Attentat* relates to the unsuccessful attempt on the life of Frederick William IV staged on 26 July 1844 by H. L. Tschech, the mayor of Storkow.

The second song, *Freifrau von Droste-Vischering*, is a parody directed against the Catholic clergy in Trier.— 434

573   In the Reichstag discussion on the prolongation of the Anti-Socialist Law on 31 March 1886, Bismarck turned to August Bebel and said that, although he could not prove that Marx had engaged in 'training murderers', Ferdinand Blind—who had made an attempt on his life on 7 May 1866—was a pupil of Marx. At Engels' insistence, Laura Lafargue and Eleanor Marx-Aveling made a statement on the matter in which they categorically rejected this false allegation. The statement was published in *Der Sozialdemokrat*, No. 16, 15 April 1886 and reprinted in *Le Socialiste*, No. 35, 24 April 1886.— 435, 437

574   Engels is referring to the formation of a workers' group in the French Chamber of Deputies (see this volume, pp. 409-10 and 413).— 437

575   The reference is to the sentence passed by the criminal court in Villefranche on 17 April 1886 on the socialists Ernest Roche and Albert Duc-Quercy. As special correspondents of *L'Intransigeant* and *Le Cri du Peuple* during the strike at Decazeville (see Note 545), they had been arrested there on a charge of inciting acts of violence and the organised downing of tools. Roche and Duc-Quercy were each sentenced to 15 months' imprisonment.— 438, 442

576   The reference is to the by-elections to the Chamber of Deputies held in Paris on 2 May 1886. The socialist parties and groups (with the exception of the Possibilists, see Note 237) put forward Ernest Roche as their candidate, whilst the Radicals nominated Alfred Nicholas Gaulier. Roche received 100,000 votes, and Gaulier 146,000. At the previous elections on 4 October 1885 the socialist vote had been over 35,500.

At the poll to elect part of the Paris municipal council on 31 October 1886 the socialist candidate Duc-Quercy received 901 votes, whilst Faillet collected 988 votes for the Possibilists.— 438, 442, 444, 446, 470

577   In May 1886, *The Commonweal* started to appear weekly instead of monthly. Edward Aveling used this as an occasion to leave the editorial board which was increasingly being influenced by anarchist ideas. Aveling's letter of resignation was made public in the first weekly issue (No. 16) of 1 May 1886. The letter merely said that 'the necessary demands of a weekly on an editor's time can only be met by those in relatively more fortunate positions'. Thereafter Aveling contributed to *The Commonweal* from time to time on a freelance basis.— 438, 443, 446

578   In the article 'Ein Musterbourgeois ist Herr Kalle...' published in the 'Sozialpolitische Rundschau' column, *Der Sozialdemokrat*, No. 16, 15 April 1886 carried a report on the speech made in the Reichstag on 2 April by manufacturers' association

president Fritz Kalle during the debate on the prolongation of the Anti-Socialist Law (see Note 571). Kalle claimed that the Social Democrats aspired to the 'communality of wives' (Weibergemeinschaft) and quoted in a distorted manner from the *Manifesto of the Communist Party* to back up his claim. At the same sitting Wilhelm Liebknecht sharply rebuffed Kalle and provided documentary evidence to show that the quotation was not from Marx, but from Pastor Schuster.— 438

579 Engels is referring to *Pionier. Illustrirter Volks-Kalender für 1886*, New York, which carried a biographical article entitled 'Aus dem Leben eines alten Sozialdemokraten' about Carl Daniel Adolph Douai, a German socialist who had participated in the 1848 revolution and was living as an émigré in the United States.— 440

580 The reference is to the critical remarks about the style of the second volume of *Capital* which Friedrich Adolph Sorge received from a German socialist émigré in the United States and communicated to Engels in his letter of 28 February 1886.— 440

581 Engels is referring to the mass campaign for the eight-hour working day which developed in major centres of US industry (Chicago, New York, Pittsburgh, Cincinatti, St Louis, Boston, Baltimore, Milwaukee) in the spring of 1886. The campaign culminated in a general strike and mass demonstrations on 1 May 1886 involving over 350,000 people. Almost 200,000 workers secured a shorter working day as a result.— 441, 452

582 In the spring of 1886 the United States witnessed a mass proletarian campaign for the eight-hour working day (see Note 581). Up to 65,000 people went on strike in Chicago in the first days of May. Workers clashed with police at a meeting held on 3 May. During the following day's protest meeting in Haymarket Square an agent provocateur threw a bomb which exploded and killed seven policemen and four workers. The police opened fire on the crowd, as a result of which a number were killed and over 200 wounded. Mass arrests were carried out and the leaders of the Chicago Labor Union brought before the court. Despite the broad campaign in defence of the accused in the United States and a number of European countries, four of them — Albert R. Parsons, August Spies, Adolph Fischer and George Engel — were hanged on 11 November 1887 on the decision of the US Supreme Court.

In memory of the events of 1886 in Chicago, the International Socialists' Congress held in Paris in 1889 resolved to proclaim 1 May International Workers' Day.— 446, 449, 451

583 This letter is Engels' reply to that of 10 May 1886 from the Hamburg publishers F. H. Nestler und Melle asking him to edit the 'Handbibliothek der Sozial-Oekonomie' which they were planning to issue. The edition was to be a series of pamphlets containing statements on social issues by prominent academics.

The letter was first published abridged in English in: K. Marx, F. Engels, V. I. Lenin, *The Communist View on Morality*, Novosti Press Agency Publishing House, Moscow, 1974.— 447

584 The debates on the *Irish Arms Bill* to which Engels refers occurred at the second reading in the House of Commons on 20 May 1886. The purpose of the bill was to prolong the ban on the sale, carrying and importation of arms for certain areas of

Ireland which had been instituted with *The Peace Preservation (Ireland) Act* of 1881. In his substantiation of the bill, John Morley, Secretary of State for Ireland, said that it was particularly important in the North of Ulster, where an overt campaign for the organisation of resistance to the introduction of Irish Home Rule was being carried on among the Protestant population (Englishmen). Randolph Churchill set out to show that these steps were legitimate by referring to Lord Althorp and Sir Robert Peel, who in 1833 had spoken of a possible justification for civil war should a threat emerge to the integrity of the British Empire. In his reply, Gladstone accused Churchill of supporting resistance to government measures. The bill was adopted in the House of Commons by 303 votes to 89.

The material which Engels sent and the ideas expressed in his letter formed the basis for the leading article 'Das Recht zur Rebellion' in *Der Sozialdemokrat*, No. 22, 27 May 1886.— 448

585 On the eve of the by-elections to the Chamber of Deputies in Paris (see Note 576) *Justice*, No. 120, 1 May 1886 carried an item by A. S. Headingley headed 'The Socialists and the Paris Elections' in support of the position taken by the Possibilists (see Note 237). They had declined to support the candidature of Ernest Roche which had been put forward by the Workers' Party (see Note 201) together with all the other socialist groups and had nominated their own candidate in the shape of a working miner named Soubrié. In response to this, Eleanor Marx-Aveling published a short note in *The Commonweal*, No. 18, 15 May 1886 stating that one of its coming issues would carry an article by Lafargue about the strike in Decazeville (see Note 545) and the Paris elections. Lafargue did, indeed, write such an article, which was carried by *The Commonweal*, No. 22, 12 June 1886 under the heading 'The Decazeville Strike'; the article explained that the Possibilists' position had facilitated the victory of the bourgeois candidate.— 450

586 The second annual conference of the Socialist League, held at 13 Farringdon Road on 13 June 1886 with 19 delegates attending, revealed a growth in disagreements between the anarchist-influenced supporters of 'direct action' and the proponents of a struggle by parliamentary means.— 451

587 Engels' reference to the collapse of the Decazeville strike (see Note 545) is evidently based on incorrect sources, possibly the report by *Le Socialiste*, No. 38, 15 May 1886 that the strike was nearing its end. In reality the strike did not end until mid-June.— 451

588 Engels is replying to Florence Kelley-Wischnewetzky's letter of 31 May 1886 in which she informed him that she had sent him the manuscript and proofs of the 'Appendix to the American Edition of *The Condition of the Working Class in England*', wrote about the quality of the print of Engels' book and the importance for the American reader of its publication.— 451

589 Schlüter replied to Engels' letter on 8 June 1886. He wrote out Florence Kelley-Wischnewetzky's address on a postcard: 'Drexel, Haryes & Co., Paris'.— 453

590 Engels was on holiday in Eastbourne approximately from 25 June to 7 July 1886.— 454, 455

591 The British parliament was dissolved on 26 June 1886. The elections to the House of Commons began on 2 July and were not completed before 20 July 1886. They brought defeat for the Liberals, who obtained 191 seats as against 316 for the Con-

servatives, 78 for the Liberal Unionists (see Note 430), and 85 for the supporters of Home Rule in Ireland.— 454

⁵⁹² On 3 July 1886 Kautsky wrote to tell Engels that he had been visited by Mrs Guillaume-Schack who wished to see him in Eastbourne. She obtained Engels' address and wrote the same day asking him to receive her.— 455

⁵⁹³ Becker wrote to Engels on 18-22 June 1886 suggesting that they meet in the autumn in Paris where he intended to visit the family of his eldest daughter.— 456

⁵⁹⁴ Karl Kautsky was on holiday in Deal near Dover from the latter half of July to the beginning of August.— 458-60

⁵⁹⁵ The reference is to the unsigned article 'Die Kathederweisheit der "christlich-ethischen" Nationalökonomie', a résumé of Gustav Cohn's book *System der National-ökonomie*, Vol. 1, Stuttgart, 1885, published in *Deutsche Worte*, Nos. 7, 8 and 9, 1886. Its author was the Zurich economist Julius Platter.— 458

⁵⁹⁶ In August 1885, the British Liberal politician Charles Dilke — Deputy Foreign Secretary in Gladstone's Cabinet — was forced to surrender his seat in Parliament and undertake to refrain from political activity due to his involvement in the divorce proceedings of Donald Crawford, Liberal M. P. for Lanark. A certain Captain H. Forster likewise figured amongst those involved in the proceedings.— 458

⁵⁹⁷ Engels wrote this letter on a postcard addressed: 'F. A. Sorge, Esq. in *Hoboken, N. Y.*, U. S. America.' The address was crossed out by an unknown hand and replaced with 'Mt. Desert, Maine'. It follows from Sorge's letter to Engels of 20 July 1886 that at this time Sorge and his wife were on holiday in Mount Desert (Maine), a small island in the north-east of the United States.— 460

⁵⁹⁸ The reference is to the interview which Engels gave to J. T. McEnnis, a correspondent for *The Missouri Republican* (see this volume, p. 443). Following the publication of the interview, Sorge placed in the *New Yorker Volkszeitung*, No. 162, 8 July 1886 the statement sent to him by Engels (see present edition, Vol. 26, p. 408).— 460-61, 491

⁵⁹⁹ Engels was on holiday in Eastbourne from 7 August to 4 September 1886.— 460, 466-67, 471, 475, 477-79, 482, 488, 491

⁶⁰⁰ At the invitation of the Executive Committee of the Socialist Labor Party (see Note 549) Wilhelm Liebknecht took part in a campaign tour of the United States to raise money for the German Social Democrats' election fund. Eleanor Marx-Aveling and Edward Aveling made a trip around the United States at approximately the same time (see Note 601). Liebknecht stayed in Eastbourne with Engels for four days, left Liverpool on 4 September and arrived in New York on 13 September where he met the Avelings. In New York, Philadelphia, Boston, Detroit, Chicago, Pittsburgh, Washington and other cities he gave talks and lectures on the theory and history of socialism, the state of the workers' movement in Europe and other subjects. This trip, which he completed on 26 November, raised 16,000 marks for the German Social Democrats' election fund. On his way back to Germany, Liebknecht stayed with Engels in London from 5 to 10 December, following which he set off on his way home to Borsdorf near Leipzig.— 461, 469, 478, 480, 483, 489, 496, 500, 531, 535

⁶⁰¹ Like Wilhelm Liebknecht, Eleanor Marx-Aveling and Edward Aveling toured the

United States giving lectures and talks at the invitation of the Executive Committee of the Socialist Labor Party (see Note 549). They left Liverpool on 31 August and arrived in New York on 10 September. Their trip was a great success, ending on 25 December. On 4 January 1887 the Avelings returned to London. In early 1887 they gave numerous lectures and talks on the labour movement in the United States to a working-class audience in London.— 461, 478, 494, 496, 506, 525, 536, 540

602 As a re-examination of a sentence passed by a court in Chemnitz (see Note 446), a new trial began on 25 July 1886 in Freiberg (Saxony) of a group of leading figures in the Socialist Workers' Party of Germany. On 4 August 1886 the local provincial court sentenced Ignaz Auer, August Bebel, Carl Ulrich, Louis Viereck, Georg Heinrich von Vollmar and Karl Franz Egon Frohme to nine months', as well as Johann Heinrich Wilhelm Dietz, Philipp Heinrich Müller and Stefan Heinzel, to six months' imprisonment on a charge of belonging to a 'secret society'. Bebel served his prison sentence in Zwickau from mid-November 1886 to 14 August 1887.— 461, 468, 482, 500, 502, 511

603 On 3 August 1886 Karl Kautsky informed Engels that from that autumn Victor Adler was planning to publish a socialist weekly in Vienna which he wished to put at the party's disposal. Adler published the socialist weekly *Gleichheit* from December 1886 to June 1889.— 461

604 This is Engels' reply to the request made by Kautsky in his letter of 9 August 1886 that Engels look through the manuscript of the book *Karl Marx's Oekonomische Lehren* which he was preparing for the press at the time (see also Note 137). Engels read the manuscript in the first half of September and made a number of remarks which the author took into account when publishing the book.— 462

605 This evidently refers to the Italian translation of Marx's *Wage Labour and Capital* and Hermann Schlüter's work on the history of the Chartist movement (see Note 557).— 462

606 There was no English translation of *The Origin of the Family, Private Property and the State* made during Engels' lifetime.— 464

607 The substance of this letter by Engels was used in the editorial carried by *Der Sozialdemokrat*, No. 34, 18 August 1886.— 466

608 This letter was first published in English abridged in *The Labour Monthly*, London, 1934, No. 2.— 468, 490

609 The *Knights of Labor* (The Noble Order of the Knights of Labour) is the name of an American workers' organisation founded in Philadelphia in 1869 and constituting a secret society until 1881. The bulk of the members of the 'Order' were unskilled workers, including a large number of Blacks. Its aims were to set up cooperatives and organise mutual assistance, and it took part in a considerable number of working-class campaigns. However, the leadership of the 'Order' to all intents and purposes rejected the idea of workers' taking part in political struggle and advocated cooperation between classes. In 1886 the leadership worked against the general strike, forbidding its members to take part. Rank-and-file members of the 'Order' nevertheless did so, and after this the 'Order' began to lose influence among the working masses, falling apart by the end of the 1890s.— 470, 491, 525, 530, 532, 541

610 During the run-up to the elections for the Chamber of Deputies on 2 May 1886 (see Note 576) the socialist organisations and groups who had put forward Ernest Roche set up an election committee. After the elections, the leadership of the Socialist Federation of the department of Seine published an official report on the meeting of 9 May 1886 in *Le Socialiste*, No. 38, 15 May. It was announced in the report that the committee members had decided to maintain the coalition of these organisations and groups and had set up a standing commission including among its members Paul Lafargue from the Paris organisation of the Workers' Party.— 470

611 A fragment of this letter was first published in English in: K. Marx, F. Engels, *On Reactionary Prussianism*, Foreign Languages Publishing House, Moscow, 1943.— 472

612 In the letter referred to Johann Heinrich Wilhelm Dietz suggested to Kautsky that, for the duration of the six months' imprisonment to which he had been sentenced by the court in Freiberg (see Note 602), Wilhelm Blos should be entrusted with editing *Die Neue Zeit* in Stuttgart (Kautsky had just done the general editing of the journal from London). Kautsky sent this letter to Engels on 19 August, asking his opinion on the matter and requesting permission to publish his name on the list of the journal's regular contributors in the prospectus for 1887.— 472

613 Engels is referring to the following event: On 25 July 1886 the police in Amsterdam had tried to break up a traditional fete on the grounds that its participants were playing a forbidden game known as 'eel-snatching'. The police action met with considerable resistance, and clashes continued until the following day. Several dozen people were killed and an even greater number injured. Government bodies and the press used these events to launch a provocative campaign against the Socialist Party. Persecution began on a massive scale, a number of socialists were arrested and brought before the court.— 473

614 The reference is to the parcel from Swan Sonnenschein & C° publishers which was addressed to Engels in London and forwarded by Karl Kautsky to the recipient in Eastbourne.— 473

615 Engels is evidently referring to the General Council reports which Schlüter planned to publish as a separate volume (see Note 556).— 475

616 Engels wrote this letter on a postcard addressed: 'K. Kautsky Esq., 50, Maitland Park Road, N. W. London.'— 476

617 On 23 August Karl Kautsky wrote to Engels that Wilhelm Liebknecht had asked him to purchase an easel which he could hang around his neck by means of a belt and on which he could write whether standing or walking. (Play on words: *Esel* meant both 'ass' and 'easel'.) — 477

618 On 16 August 1886 Gertrud Guillaume-Schack informed Engels that she intended to come to London in mid-September in the company of the Wischnewetzkys.— 477, 478

619 The reference is to the strike by the workers at the *Vierzon* (department of Cher) factory of the Société française de construction de matériel agricole which began on 4 August 1886 in response to the dismissal of some of them due to the crisis in the engineering industry. The events in Vierzon were widely reflected in the

French press, as Laura Lafargue wrote in her letter to Engels of 20 August 1886.—
478, 489, 507

620 On 25 August 1886 George Julian Harney informed Engels that he had intended
to visit him in Eastbourne on 29 August but was no longer able to do so due to
changed circumstances. On 26 August, Harney sent two consecutive letters to let
Engels know he would visit him in London.— 479

621 Engels wrote this letter on a postcard addressed: 'F. A. Sorge Esq., *Hoboken N. Y.*,
U. S. America.'— 480

622 The *New Yorker Volkszeitung*, No. 200, 21 August 1886 carried an item headed
'Ein Bedürfniß und eine Schmach' expressing surprise at the lack of a complete
English translation of Volume I of *Capital*. It stated that the translation being
printed by *To-Day* (see Note 527) could not meet with the readers' satisfaction
since it was being published in numerous short parts. The author of the item described this situation as disgraceful and suggested that the funds for an English edition of *Capital* might be obtained from some well-to-do Social Democrat.— 480

623 In the letter referred to, the Hamburg publishers F. H. Nestler und Melle accused Engels, once he had refused to edit the 'Handbibliothek der Sozial-Oekonomie' (see this volume, p. 448 and Note 583), of having passed on the offer to Karl
Kautsky and then *Die Neue Zeit*. Dietz's publishing house was advertising the
forthcoming appearance of a series called 'Klassiker der Nationalökonomie
und des Sozialismus', whilst Kautsky had also been planning a similar edition
for some considerable time.— 481

624 Engels is referring to the trial of Jules Guesde, Paul Lafargue, Etienne Suisini and
Louise Michel for the speeches they had made in the Théâtre du Château-d'Eau
on 3 June 1886. The trial took place on 12 August 1886, but Guesde, Lafargue and
Suisini refused to appear before the court, so that only Louise Michel was present.
All four of them were sentenced to terms of imprisonment between four and six
months and fined 100 francs. On 24 September 1886 Guesde, Lafargue and Suisini
appealed against the court's decision and all four were acquitted.— 483, 494

625 Engels analysed Bismarck's relations with Russia in his letter to Paul Lafargue of
25-26 October 1866 (see this volume, pp. 512-18) which was subsequently published as an article entitled 'The Political Situation in Europe' (see present edition,
Vol. 26).— 483, 488, 493

626 Engels is apparently referring to the article 'Haben wir etwas mit den Anarchisten
gemein?' carried by *Vorbote*, the weekly supplement to the *Chicagoer Arbeiter-Zeitung*,
on 9 June 1886.— 491

627 In his letter of 10-11 August 1886 Sorge informed Engels that the Reverend
J. G. Brooks from Brockton near Boston (Massachusetts) had asked for Edward
Aveling and Eleanor Marx-Aveling to visit him during their tour of the United
States. Brooks promised them the opportunity to address a large working-class au-
dience.— 491

628 From 17 to 28 September 1886 Johann Philipp Becker stayed with Engels in London, and from 29 September to 4 October with the Lafargues in Paris.— 495, 498,
501

629 An allusion to the following passage in Marx's *The Eighteenth Brumaire of Louis Bo-*

naparte: 'The French bourgeoisie had long ago found the solution to Napoleon's dilemma: "Dans cinquante ans, l'Europe sera républicaine ou cosaque." It had found the solution to it in the "république cosaque"' (the words are taken from the book: Las Cases, *Mémorial de Sainte-Hélène, ou journal où se trouve consigné, jour par jour, ce qu'a dit et fait Napoléon durant dix-huit mois*, Paris, 1823-24) (see present edition, Vol. 11, p. 182).— 496

630 In his letter to Engels of 30 September 1886 Paul Lafargue described the acquittal at his trial (see Note 624) as a manifestation of the fact that 'the bourgeois have ripened to appreciate some part of our theories'.— 497

631 At that time Johann Philipp Becker was a contributor to *Deutsch-Italienische Korrespondenz* published by Franz Julius Schneeberger in Vienna.— 499, 501

632 As an émigré in Paris, in 1857 Becker engaged in applied chemistry; an explosion occurred during one of his experiments.— 499, 501

633 The reference is to Eduard Bernstein's letter to Engels of 17 September 1886.— 500

634 The reference is to the political crisis which emerged in Bulgaria in the autumn of 1886 after Prince Alexander Battenberg was toppled from the throne by a group of military conspirators associated with the secret service of the Russian government. The interim government set up on 9 August survived for just a few days and was replaced by a pro-Austrian regency. An attempt to restore Alexander Battenberg to the throne was unsuccessful, meeting with overt Russian resistance. In September 1886, the Russian government sent Major-General Nikolai Kaulbars to Sofia with the mission of preparing the ground for the installation of a Russian candidate on the Bulgarian throne. The mission was unsuccessful, partly due to the position taken by the West European powers, notably Britain. On 5 November Kaulbars was recalled and the government of the Russian Empire broke off diplomatic relations with Bulgaria (see also Note 445).— 503, 505, 517

635 The reference is to August Bebel's letter to Engels of 12 October 1886.— 504

636 Several newspapers reported that the supporters of Dragan Zankoff, the leader of Bulgaria's liberal party, had spread rumours to the effect that the Russian government had concluded a secret agreement with Turkey. They alleged that the agreement guaranteed the inviolability of the Sultan's possessions and reduced the outstanding war debt to be paid by the Turks in return for the right to set up Russian fortifications in the Dardanelles.— 505

637 The *Treaty of Unkiar-Skelessi* was signed by Russia and Turkey on 8 July 1833. It provided for mutual aid in the event of war with a third power. A secret article in the treaty freed Turkey from the obligation to give military aid to Russia in return for an undertaking to close the Straits to all foreign men-of-war on Russia's demand.— 505

638 The reference is to the bombardment of Alexandria by the British Navy under Admiral Beauchamp Seymour on 11 July 1882. It represented one of the crucial actions carried out by the British in their quest to colonise Egypt. Following the seizure of Alexandria on 2 August, units of the Anglo-Indian army occupied the Suez Canal zone, and on 15 September Cairo was taken. Whilst nominally remaining a part of the Ottoman Empire, Egypt was actually turned into a British colony.

The British colonisers' penetration into the Sudan from the early 1870s met with stiff resistance from the local people; an uprising of national liberation in 1881 drove British forces from almost the entire country. An independent centralised state was formed in the course of the uprising, and the British did not manage to break the Sudanese until 1899.— 505

[639] It was announced in Vienna in early October 1886 that the police had uncovered an 'anarchist conspiracy', allegedly to organise fires and explosions in various parts of the city with the aim of creating panic among the public. It was also reported that the police had found a number of caches with explosives and side-arms; some 20 people were arrested as a result.— 507

[640] The first national congress of the French trade unions was held in Lyons from 11 to 17 October 1886, with representatives of more than 700 trade councils (chambres syndicales) taking part. The congress adopted a resolution recognising that the genuine liberation of the proletariat was not to be had by way of cooperation, profit-sharing for workers and similar measures, as proposed by the bourgeoisie, but only through the abolition of private property and its replacement by collective, social property, through the socialisation of the means of production. The congress also adopted a resolution on the need to campaign for an eight-hour working day and on the establishment of a National Federation of Trade Unions (*La Fédération nationale des Syndicats*).

Commenting on the outcome of the congress in his letter to Engels of 22 October 1886, Paul Lafargue wrote that 'the congress in Lyons will be a crucial means for attracting the French workers to communism'.— 507

[641] The events in Vierzon (see Note 619) and Henry Maret's interpellation about the dispersal of a strikers' demonstration by gendarmes on 5 October and the arrest of demonstrators meant that Internal Affairs Minister Jean Sarrien was forced to resign on 18 October 1886. This coincided with the announcement of Finance Minister Sadi Carnot's resignation and raised the danger of a government crisis. However, President Jules Grévy and Prime Minister Charles de Freycinet were successful in persuading both ministers to withdraw their resignations.— 507

[642] The reference is to the statement by the Social-Democratic group in the Reichstag that *Der Sozialdemokrat* was no longer to be called the party's official printed organ; on 5 November 1886 the newspaper started to appear with the subheading 'Organ der Sozialdemokratie deutscher Zunge' (Organ of Social Democracy in the German tongue).

This decision was occasioned by the confirmation on the part of the criminal chamber of the imperial court of the sentence imposed by the Saxon provincial court in Freiberg against a group of German Social-Democratic leaders on 4 August 1886 (see Note 602). They were accused of belonging to a 'secret society', the grounds behind the accusation including their links with *Der Sozialdemokrat* which carried the subheading 'Zentral-Organ der deutschen Sozialdemokratie' (Central Organ of German Social Democracy).— 509

[643] Engels is referring to *Die Neue Zeit*, No. 11, 1886, which carried August Bebel's article 'Deutschland, Rußland und die orientalische Frage'.

In his letter of 12 October 1886 Bebel expressed the view that one of the reasons for Bismarck's efforts to achieve a rapprochement with Russia was his fear that a European war might give rise to social upheavals.— 509

⁶⁴⁴ In his speech of 20 May 1886 to the Prussian Chamber of Deputies, the National Liberal Louis Berger stated that he and his friends did not expect the establishment of a liberal cabinet and were prepared to content themselves with a moderate conservative one. August Bebel wrote to Engels on 12 October that, if the liberals came to power, all their 'opposition' to the present regime would come to an end.— 510

⁶⁴⁵ This letter was published slightly abridged and with editorial alterations as an article headed 'Situation politique de l'Europe' in *Le Socialiste*, No. 63, 6 November 1886 (see present edition, Vol. 26, pp. 410-17).
On its first publication in English, see Note 196.— 512

⁶⁴⁶ The preliminary *Peace Treaty of San Stefano*, which ended the Russo-Turkish war of 1877-78, was concluded on 3 March (February 19) 1878 at the place of the same name near Constantinople. It provided for the establishment of an autonomous Bulgarian principality with nominal dependence on Turkey; for state independence for Serbia, Montenegro and Romania and their territorial enlargement, etc. The treaty considerably strengthened Russian influence in the Balkans and gave rise to sharp opposition from Britain and Austria-Hungary with the tacit support of Germany. Under diplomatic and military pressure, the Russian government was forced to agree to an international congress to reconsider the treaty, given that it concerned 'general European' issues. The congress was held in Berlin from 13 June to 13 July 1878 and attended by representatives of Russia, Germany, Austria-Hungary, France, Britain, Italy and Turkey. The outcome was the Treaty of Berlin, which represented a major deterioration in the conditions of the Treaty of San Stefano for Russia and the Slavs of the Balkan Peninsula. The size of self-governing Bulgaria was reduced to less than half that specified in San Stefano; an autonomous province — Eastern Rumelia — was set up under the Sultan's rule in the parts of Bulgaria located south of the Balkans; the size of Montenegro was considerably reduced. The Treaty of Berlin endorsed the return to Russia of that part of Bessarabia which had been cut off from it in 1856 and at the same time sanctioned the occupation of Bosnia and Herzegovina by Austria-Hungary.— 512

⁶⁴⁷ The suppression of the Polish national insurrection (1794) was followed, in 1795, by the third partition of Poland between Austria, Prussia and Russia, and the final abolition of the Polish state. By a decision of the Vienna Congress (1814-15), the Kingdom of Poland was established as part of the Russian Empire and included a large part of the lands seized by Prussia and Austria in the third partition of Rzecz Pospolita.— 512

⁶⁴⁸ In the 1870s, Britain and France, Egypt's main creditors, used the Egyptian government's financial difficulties, notably its large external debts, to impose their financial control on the country. This led in the 1880s to a growth in the national liberation movement and efforts by the Egyptians to free themselves from dependence on foreign powers. In the summer of 1882, Britain provoked a conflict with Egypt, took military action and seized the country, turning it into a British colony to all intents and purposes (see also Note 638).— 514

⁶⁴⁹ Welcoming Alexander III back from the Crimea at a meeting in Moscow on 25 May 1886, Nikolai Alexeyev, the mayor of the city, stated: 'Our hope gains wings,

and strength is imparted to our belief that the Cross of Christ will shine upon St Sophia' (Alexeyev was referring to St Sophia's Church in Constantinople).— 516

650 The *Congress of Vienna* was held by European monarchs and their ministers in September 1814-June 1815. They established the borders and status of the European states after the victory over Napoleonic France and sanctioned, contrary to the national interests and will of the peoples, the reshaping of Europe's political map and the restoration of the 'legitimate' dynasties.— 519

651 In *Das Recht auf den vollen Arbeitsertrag in geschichtlicher Darstellung*, which appeared in 1886, the Austrian sociologist and lawyer Anton Menger set out to prove the 'unoriginality' of Marx's economic theory, claiming he had borrowed some of his conclusions from the English utopian socialists of the Ricardian school (Thompson, etc.). Laura Lafargue wrote to Engels on 30 October 1886, informing him of the book's appearance. Feeling that if he personally was to oppose Menger in public, the latter might use this to boost his image, Engels thought it expedient to rebuff Menger with an editorial in *Die Neue Zeit* or a résumé of the book in the name of Karl Kautsky, the editor of the said journal. Engels originally intended to write the bulk of the article himself, but was unable to continue his work on it due to illness. The article was completed by Kautsky in line with Engels' instructions. It appeared unsigned in *Die Neue Zeit*, No. 2, 1887 and was headed 'Juristen-Sozialismus' (see present edition, Vol. 26, pp. 597-616).— 521, 527

652 The reference is to I, Part I; I, Part V; II, Part VI of the third volume of *Capital* (see present edition, Vol. 37).— 522

653 This letter is Engels' reply to a certain E. T. who had published in *The Commonweal* an item called 'Socialisme utopique et socialisme scientifique' containing the following: 'Please say if there is an English translation of Engels' "Socialisme Utopique et Socialisme Scientifique". If not, do you know if Engels has given permission to any particular person to translate it; and is there any likelihood in that case of its being issued shortly? Or is it open to any one who wishes to translate it into English, to do so?' — 523

654 Engels is probably referring to Marx's prefaces to the first and second editions of Volume I of *Capital*, which were included in the English edition, and also his own preface to this edition.— 524

655 This seems to refer to letters by Eleanor Marx-Aveling and Edward Aveling who were on a tour of the United States with Wilhelm Liebknecht at the time (see Note 601).— 524

656 Paul Lafargue signed his articles in *La Nouvelle Revue* with the pseudonym 'Fergus'.— 524

657 Engels is referring to the election for the mayor of New York which took place on 2 November 1886. Henry George, the candidate from the United Labor Party, received 68,110 votes, or 31 per cent of the poll. Workers' candidates were elected in Chicago, Milwaukee, Stanton and other cities.

The *United Labor Party* was formed in the run-up to the New York municipal elections in the autumn of 1886 to promote joint political action on the part of the working class. The initiative for its foundation was taken by the *Central Labor Union of New York*, an association of the city's trade unions established in March 1882.

Following the New York example, similar parties were set up in other cities, including Baltimore, Milwaukee, Detroit, Chicago, etc.— 525, 531

⁶⁵⁸ A special meeting of the General Council of the Social Democratic Federation on Tuesday (October 5) decided to call on the unemployed of London to follow the Lord Mayor's Show on 9 November 1886. The authorities banned all demonstrations in the vicinity of the procession and deployed a large number of police in the area. The leadership of the Federation nevertheless held a meeting in Trafalgar Square on 9 November without any of the rioting and disorder the authorities did so much to provoke. On 21 November the greatest working-class demonstration ever seen in London was held in Trafalgar Square. The demonstration, with tens of thousands participating, passed off without any incidents and contributed to a certain growth in the authority the Federation enjoyed among working people in London.— 526, 534

⁶⁵⁹ The *Radical Clubs* began to appear in London and other cities during the 1870s. They united bourgeois radicals and workers. The proletarian element was predominant in the poorest areas of the capital, like the East End. The clubs were distinctive for the fact that they criticised Gladstone's policy on Ireland and called for greater democracy (extension of the suffrage and other reforms). Socialist ideas were spread in the Radical Clubs from the early 1880s. In 1885 the Radical Clubs in London merged to form the Metropolitan Radical Federation.— 526, 529

⁶⁶⁰ Engels is referring to the bourgeois press' attacks on Marx which were directly occasioned by the pamphlet: K. Vogt, *Mein Prozess gegen die Allgemeine Zeitung. Stenographischer Bericht. Dokumente und Erläuterungen.* Published in Geneva in December 1859, it was directed against Marx and his associates in the Communist League. Marx exposed Vogt's attacks in his work *Herr Vogt* (see present edition, Vol. 17).— 527

⁶⁶¹ A fragment of this letter was first published in English in: K. Marx, F. Engels, *On the United States*, Progress Publishers, Moscow, 1979.— 528

⁶⁶² On 4 November 1886 Schlüter wrote to Engels informing him of the successful conclusion of talks with Johann Philipp Becker on the granting of material assistance in return for his writing his memoirs (see this volume, pp. 498-500). The plan did not materialise as Becker died on 7 December 1886.— 528

⁶⁶³ This is Engels' reply to the suggestion made by Schlüter that he revise three chapters from the second part of *Anti-Dühring* for publication as a separate pamphlet under the title *The Theory of Force*. They contain an exposition of the materialist views of the correlation between economics and politics. Engels subsequently changed his plans and decided to add a fourth chapter giving concrete form to the main propositions using the example of the history of Germany from 1848 to 1888 and analysing them from the viewpoint of a critique of Bismarck's policies. The pamphlet was to be called *The Role of Force in History*. Engels worked on the fourth chapter at a later date, between late December 1887 and March 1888, but did not complete it. The unfinished work, as well as various plans and fragments, were not published until after Engels' death (see present edition, Vol. 26, pp. 452-510, 511, 578-80).— 529

⁶⁶⁴ The reference is to the article 'On Social Relations in Russia' from the Refugee Literature series, published in *Der Volksstaat* from 1874 to 1875 (see present edition,

Vol. 24, pp. 3-50); this article also appeared as a separate pamphlet in late June-
early July 1875 in Leipzig. The third and fourth articles of the series to which Engels refers did not have any titles of their own.
Schlüter's plans to publish a pamphlet *Soziales aus Rußland* were not carried
out at the time. The first, second and fifth articles in the series, together with an
afterword specially written by Engels ('Afterword (1894) to *On Social Relations in
Russia*', present edition, Vol. 27) appeared as a collection of articles by Engels
published in Berlin in 1894 as *Internationales aus dem 'Volksstaat' (1871-75)*.— 529

665   A fragment of this letter was first published in English in *The Socialist Review*, London, 1908, III-VIII, and in full in: K. Marx, F. Engels, *Selected Correspondence*,
Foreign Languages Publishing House, Moscow, 1955.— 531

666   In late November 1886 a Leipzig jury court sentenced the joiner and Social Democrat Karl Schumann to four years' and several others to various terms of imprisonment on a charge of 'insurrection'. They were accused on the strength of the seeing-
off ceremony which Leipzig workers organised for Schumann on 25 September
1886 in connection with his expulsion from the city under the Anti-Socialist Law
(see Note 37).— 534

667   Engels wrote this letter on a postcard addressed: 'Herrn H. Schlüter, Volksbuchhandlung, Casinostraße, Hottingen-Zürich, Switzerland.' — 535

668   Schlüter wrote to Engels on 4 December 1886 describing his plans to reissue Engels' pamphlet *The Bakuninists at Work* together with his article 'On Social Relations in Russia' as an issue in the Sozialdemokratische Bibliothek series (see Note
664). Schlüter further wrote about Eduard Bernstein's proposal that this issue
be supplied with a preface from the publishers.— 535

669   This apparently refers to the English translation of Engels' *The Condition of the
Working-Class in England* made by Florence Kelley-Wischnewetzky (see Note
550).— 535

670   On 28 November 1886 Laura Lafargue wrote to Engels saying that she would be
arriving in London on 23 or 24 December.— 536

671   Florence Kelley-Wischnewetzky wrote to Engels on 10 December 1886 asking
him to write a preface to the American edition of her translation of *The Condition of
the Working-Class in England in 1844* (see Note 550). She explained that the afterword Engels had written for this edition in February 1886 had become outdated
and asked him to concentrate in the new preface on a critique of Henry George's
doctrine, notably his plan for land reform. In the same letter Florence Kelley-
Wischnewetzky asked Engels whether he was agreeable to omitting 'in 1844' from
the title.— 540

672   Engels may have meant the following works by Henry George: *Our Land and Land
Policy* (1871), *Progress and Poverty* (1880), *The Irish Land Question* (1881), *Social
Problems* (1883), *Protection or Free Trade* (1886).— 540

673   Engels is referring to the following passage from the *Manifesto of the Communist
Party*: 'The Communists fight for the attainment of the immediate aims, for the en-
forcement of the momentary interests of the working class; but in the movement of
the present, they also represent and take care of the future of that movement' (see
present edition, Vol. 6, p. 518).— 541

[674] This is Engels' reply to the invitation to join Karl Pearson's Club (see Note 678) which Dr Horatio Bryan Donkin passed on to him via Eleanor Marx-Aveling (see Eleanor Marx-Aveling's letter to Horatio Bryan Donkin of 8 February 1886, this volume, pp. 547-48).

The original is kept in the library at University College, London (Pearson Papers, 10/36). It was found by the German scholar Erhard Kiehnbaum and published in German translation in *Die Wahrheit*, 1/2 October 1988. We were kindly presented with a x-copy of the original for publication in Marx's and Engels' *Collected Works*.— 543

[675] The reference is to Engels' editing of the English translation of Volume I of Marx's *Capital* (see this volume, Note 56).— 543

[676] Engels is probably referring to the discussions at Pearson's Club of issues relating to the family and the social emancipation of women (see Note 678). He dealt with these questions in *The Origin of the Family, Private Property and the State* (see notes 174, 264 and 555).— 543

[677] The original of this letter is kept in the library at University College, London (Pearson Papers, 10/37). It was published in German translation by the German scholar Erhard Kiehnbaum in *Die Wahrheit*, 1/2 October 1988. We were kindly presented with a x-copy of the original for publication in Marx's and Engels' *Collected Works*.— 547

[678] The reference is to the Club established by Karl Pearson, an English biologist and philosopher, to encourage free and unbridled discussions on questions connected in some way or another with relations between men and women. Its members were 15-20 intellectuals, among them Horatio Bryan Donkin, a doctor who had treated Marx, and Olive Schreiner, a friend of Eleanor who had written a book entitled *Woman and Labour*. The discussions centred on Pearson's books *The Woman Question* and *Socialism and Sex*. Pearson, who sympathised with the workers' and socialist movement, wished to recruit Engels and Eleanor Marx-Aveling as members of the Club; in the summer of 1885 the latter had published a review of Bebel's book *Die Frau und der Sozialismus* (see Note 145).— 547

[679] It is clear from the correspondence between Donkin and Pearson that Eleanor Marx-Aveling intended to visit the Club in April 1886 but never carried out this plan. The Club's minutes contain no record of any contributions made by Engels or Eleanor.— 547

NAME INDEX

Social Democratic Federation from 1884, later a founder of the Socialist League, an organiser of the mass movement of unskilled workers and unemployed in the 1880s-90s, delegate to the international socialist workers' congress of 1889 in Paris; husband of Eleanor Marx.— 7, 74, 78, 94, 119, 122, 127, 129, 143, 155, 161, 165, 167, 168, 172, 177, 191, 202, 207, 214, 224, 237-38, 245, 247, 248, 261, 265, 274, 275, 297, 303, 320, 323, 326, 345, 366, 369, 370, 376, 378, 386, 391, 394, 395, 399, 402, 404, 405, 416, 424, 436, 438, 443, 446, 449, 450, 458, 461, 464, 465, 471, 478, 482, 489, 491, 496, 500, 504, 506, 524, 540

Aveling — see *Marx, Eleanor*

Avenel, Georges (1828-1876) — French historian and journalist, author of works on history of the French Revolution.— 398-99

B

Bachofen, Johann Jakob (1815-1887) — Swiss historian of law, author of works on ancient history.— 189, 205, 207

Bahr, Hermann (1863-1934) — Austrian journalist, critic, novelist and playwright.— 191

Bakunin, Mikhail Alexandrovich (1814-1876) — Russian revolutionary and journalist; participant in the 1848-49 revolution in Germany; subsequently an ideologist of Narodism and anarchism; opposed Marxism in the First International; was expelled from the International at the Hague Congress (1872) for his splitting activities.— 10, 108, 198, 430

Balzac, Honoré de (1799-1850) — French realist writer.— 71, 320

Bamberger, Ludwig (1823-1899) — German democratic journalist; took part in the 1849 Baden-Palatinate uprising; emigrated to France in the 1850s, returned to Germany in 1866, later National Liberal and deputy to the Reichstag (1871-93).— 427

Baron — see *Kautsky, Karl Johann*

Basly, Émile Joseph (1854-1928) — French miner, socialist, trade unionist, member of the Chamber of Deputies several times.— 409, 414, 418, 424-25, 429-31, 441

Bastiat, Frédéric (1801-1850) — French economist and politician.— 184

Battenberg, Alexander (1857-1893) — son of Prince Alexander of Hesse; first Prince of Bulgaria (1879-86), pursued pro-Austrian and pro-German policy.— 329, 513-15, 517

Bax, Ernest Belfort (1854-1926) — English historian, philosopher and journalist, socialist, an editor of *The Commonweal* from 1884, member of the Social Democratic Federation, a founder of the Socialist League in 1884; was on friendly terms with Engels from 1883.— 74, 105, 114, 122-23, 127-29, 155, 165, 172, 177, 207, 224, 236, 238, 245, 248, 275, 405, 406, 431, 432, 438, 443, 446, 471, 484, 504

Bebel, Ferdinand August (1840-1913) — a leading figure in the German and international working-class movement; turner; President of the Union of German Workers' Associations from 1867; member of the First International; deputy to the Reichstag from 1867; a founder (1869) and leader of the Socialist Workers' Party of Germany; opposed the Lassalleans; took an internationalist stand during the Franco-Prussian war of 1870-71; came out in support of the Paris Commune; friend and associate of Marx and Engels.— 14, 20, 22-23, 32, 47, 52-55, 68, 77, 80-83, 99, 114, 146-48, 150, 151, 153, 162, 164, 169, 187, 195, 197-202, 204, 209-13, 220-23, 225, 231, 234, 235, 240-43, 245, 253-55, 268-71, 285, 306-09, 315-17, 329, 340-44, 352-54, 361, 386, 387, 391, 395, 406, 409, 410, 425-29, 433-

1893) — German financier, Bismarck's personal banker and his unofficial adviser on financial matters.— 109, 112, 377

Blenker, Ludwig (Louis) (1812-1863) — German ex-officer; democrat; took part in the Baden-Palatinate uprising of 1849; emigrated to the USA and fought in the Civil War on the side of the Union.— 287

Blind, Karl (1826-1907) — German democratic journalist; took part in the Baden revolutionary movement in 1848-49; a leader of the German petty-bourgeois refugees in London in the 1850s-early 1860s; later National Liberal.— 368

Block, Maurice (1816-1901) — French statistician and economist.— 224, 225

Blos, Wilhelm (1849-1927) — German journalist; member of the Socialist Workers' Party of Germany from 1872; an editor of *Der Volksstaat* (1872-74), sided with the reformist wing of German Social Democrats from the 1880s; deputy to the Reichstag (1877-1918).— 21, 23, 34, 150, 173, 296, 383, 472

Blowitz, Henri Georges Stephan Adolphe Opper de (1825-1903) — French journalist, Austrian by birth; correspondent of *The Times* in Paris from 1871.— 431

Blum, Robert (1807-1848) — German democrat; journalist; leader of the Left wing in the Frankfurt National Assembly; participated in the defence of Vienna in October 1848, court-martialled and executed after the fall of the city.— 287

Bödiker, Tonio (Anton) Wilhelm Laurenz Karl Maria (1843-1907) — German government official, adviser of the Imperial Home Ministry from 1881, was engaged in trade and insurance legislation, delivered reports in the Reichstag on behalf of the ministry on these mat-

ters, headed the Imperial Insurance Ministry in 1884-97.— 34

Boelling, Hedwig (née Engels) (1830-1904) — Frederick Engels' sister, wife of Friedrich Boelling.— 220

Bonaparte — see *Napoleon III*

Borde, Frédéric — French journalist; socialist.— 36

Borkheim, F. — Sigismund Ludwig Borkheim's son.— 380, 381

Borkheim, Sigismund Ludwig (1825-1885) — German democratic journalist; took part in the 1849 Baden-Palatinate uprising, emigrated after its defeat; merchant in London from 1851; was on friendly terms with Marx and Engels.— 152, 203, 269, 377, 379, 380, 383, 472, 475

Born, Stephan (real name *Buttermilch, Simon*) (1824-1898) — German typesetter; member of the Communist League; leaned towards reformism during the 1848-49 revolution; turned his back on the workers' movement after the revolution.— 346

Bougeart, Alfred (1815-1882) — French Left journalist; author of several works on the French Revolution.— 399

Boulanger, Georges Ernest Jean Marie (1837-1891) — French general, War Minister (1886-87); strived to establish his own military dictatorship.— 519

Boyer, Antoine Jean Baptiste (Antide) (1850-1918) — French potter; member of the Chamber of Deputies several times.— 409, 414, 418

Bracke, Wilhelm (1842-1880) — German Social Democrat; publisher of socialist literature in Brunswick; a founder (1869) and leader of the Socialist Workers' Party of Germany (Eisenachers); member of the Social-Democratic parliamentary group in the Reichstag (1877-79); represented the revolutionary wing of German Social Democracy.— 20, 374

Bradlaugh, Charles (1833-1891) — English journalist and politician, bourgeois Radical; editor of *The National Reformer* from 1860.— 94, 115, 405

Bray, John Francis (1809-1895) — English economist, utopian socialist, follower of Robert Owen; supporter of the theory of labour money.— 156

Brenin, Claude (b. c. 1851) — French miner, an organiser of the provocative explosions in Montceau-les-Mines in 1884.— 265

Brentano, Clemens (1778-1842) — German romantic poet.— 286

Brentano, Lujo (Ludwig Joseph) (1844-1931) — German economist, professor, armchair socialist.— 422

Bright, John (1811-1889) — English manufacturer and politician, a leader of the Free Traders and founder of the Anti-Corn Law League; M. P. (from 1843); leader of the Left Wing of the Liberal Party from the early 1860s, held several ministerial posts.— 389

Broadhouse, John — see *Hyndman, Henry Mayers*

Broadhurst, Henry (1840-1911) — English bricklayer, a trade union leader, secretary of the parliamentary committee of the Trades Unions Congress (1875-90), Liberal M. P. from 1880, Under-Secretary of State for the Home Department (1886).— 57

Brocher, Gustave (1850-1931) — teacher, French by birth, lived in Russia in the late 1860s-early 1870s and took part in the Narodnik movement; lived in London in 1874-93, sided with the anarchists; moved to Switzerland in 1893; atheist.— 13

Brooks, J. G. — American clergyman, advocated socialist views.— 491

Brousse, Paul Louis Marie (1844-1912) — French socialist, physician; member of the First International (up to 1872); participant in the Paris Commune, after its defeat lived in Spain and Switzerland; sided with the anarchists; returned to France in 1880 and

became a member of the French Workers' Party; a Possibilist leader.— 68, 107, 123, 225, 289, 425

Bucher, Lothar (1817-1892) — Prussian official and journalist; deputy to the Prussian National Assembly (Left Centre) in 1848; after the defeat of the 1848-49 revolution emigrated to London, later National Liberal, supporter of Bismarck.— 374

Bückler, Johann (1780-1803) — German robber nicknamed *Schinderhannes* (Hans the Skin-flint); in a number of literary works depicted as a 'noble robber' and defender of the poor.— 198

Bunge, Nikolai Kristianovich (1823-1895) — Russian lawyer, economist and politician, professor at Kiev University from 1850, Minister of Finance in 1881-86, Chairman of the Committee of Ministers in 1887-95.— 360

Buonarroti, Filippo Michele (1761-1837) — Italian revolutionary, utopian communist, a leader of the revolutionary movement in France at the end of the 18th and the beginning of the 19th centuries, Babeuf's comrade-in-arms.— 226

Burdett-Coutts, Angela Georgina, Baroness (1814-1906) — English aristocrat, philanthropist.— 400

Burns, John Elliot (1858-1943) — English worker, activist of the English working-class movement, a leader of the new trade unions (late 1880s-early 1890s), organiser of the London dock strike (1889), M. P. from 1891, minister in the Liberal cabinets in 1905-14.— 366, 368

Burrows, Herbert (1845-1922) — English official, a founder of the Social Democratic Federation; helped found trade unions of the unskilled workers.— 195, 238, 245, 369

C

Cabet, Étienne (1788-1856) — French journalist, utopian communist, author of

95, 104-06, 107, 115, 118, 120, 122, 123, 126, 130, 131, 135, 144, 167, 168, 175, 178, 224, 226, 248, 265, 272, 274, 276, 289, 292, 293, 304, 315, 321, 327, 345, 350, 357, 376, 378, 399, 423, 438, 439, 458, 459, 463, 473, 477, 478, 483, 496, 508, 527, 536-38

Denhardt, Fritz — see *Sax, Emanuel Hans*

Dereure, Louis Simon (1838-1900) — French shoemaker, prominent figure in the French and international working-class movement, Blanquist, member of the Paris section of the First International, member of *La Marsellaise* editorial board; member of the Paris Commune, emigrated to the USA after its suppression, member of the General Council of the International elected by the Hague Congress, member of the French Workers' Party from 1882.— 141

Deville, Gabriel Pierre (1854-1940) — French journalist, socialist, member of the French Workers' Party, author of the popular exposition of Volume I of Marx's *Capital* and some other works on philosophy, economy and history; withdrew from the working-class movement in the early 20th century.— 44, 46, 50, 59-63, 76-78, 89, 90, 94, 96, 101, 112, 113, 115, 134, 144, 162, 183, 310, 313, 320, 384-86, 405, 417, 442, 465, 508

Dietz, Johann Heinrich Wilhelm (1843-1922) — German Social Democrat, founder of the Social-Democratic publishing house in 1881, deputy to the Reichstag (1881-1918).— 17, 20, 27, 36, 58, 77, 102, 162-64, 200-01, 204-07, 210, 212, 230, 249, 251, 346, 422, 461, 462, 472, 474, 481, 482

Dietzgen, Joseph (1828-1888) — German leather-worker, philosopher, Social Democrat, member of the First International, delegate to the Hague Congress (1872).— 246, 297, 394, 395, 441, 491

Dilke, Sir Charles Wentworth, Baronet (1843-1911) — English politician and writer, a leader of the Radical wing of the Liberal Party; M. P.— 268, 458

Disraeli, Benjamin, 1st Earl of Beaconsfield (1804-1881) — British statesman and writer; leader of the Conservative Party in the second half of the 19th century; Chancellor of the Exchequer (1852, 1858-59, 1866-68); Prime Minister (1868, 1874-80).— 512

Dobrolyubov, Nikolai Alexandrovich (1836-1861) — Russian revolutionary democrat; literary critic and materialist philosopher; one of the predecessors of Russian Social Democracy.— 158

Donkin, Horatio Bryan (1845-1927) — English physician, doctor of the Marx family in 1881-83.— 274, 543

Dormoy, Jean (1851-1898) — French metal-worker, socialist, sentenced for a term in prison together with Guesde and Lafargue in 1883.— 115

Douai, Karl Daniel Adolph (1819-1888) — German journalist, pettybourgeois democrat, later socialist; French by birth; took part in the 1848-49 revolution in Germany, emigrated to the USA in 1852 and took part in its socialist movement; edited a number of socialist papers including the *New Yorker Volkszeitung* (1878-88); contributed to the *Vorwärts!* — 13, 296, 440

Drumont, Édouard Adolphe (1844-1917) — French politician and journalist, author of anti-Semitic books and articles.— 520

Drysdale, Charles Robert — English physician, supported neo-Malthusianism.— 195

Duc-Quercy, Albert (1856-1934) — French journalist, took part in the working-class and socialist movement, a founder of the French Workers' Party (1879), an editor of *Le Cri du Peuple*.— 442

Dühring, Eugen Karl (1833-1921) — German philosopher and economist; lecturer at Berlin University (1863-77).— 251, 289, 529

Dupont, Eugéne (c. 1837 (1831?)-1881) — prominent figure in the French and international working-class movement, musical instrument-maker; took part in the June 1848 insurrection in Paris; lived in London from 1862, member of the General Council of the First International (November 1864 to 1872), participant in all congresses (except the Basle Congress) and conferences of the International; member of the British Federal Council (1872-73); emigrated to the USA in 1874; associate of Marx and Engels.— 310

E

Eccarius, Johann Georg (1818-1889) — prominent figure in the German and international working-class movement; tailor, journalist; member of the Communist League; member of the First International and of its General Council (1864-72); took part in the British trade union movement.— 371, 468

Ede — see *Bernstein, Eduard*

Edward — see *Aveling, Edward Bibbins*

Eisengarten, Oskar — German typesetter, Social Democrat, emigrated to London, secretary of Engels in 1884-85.— 153, 160, 170, 177, 190, 279

Elisabeth I (1533-1603) — Queen of England and Ireland (1558-1603).— 150

Ely, Richard Theodore (1854-1943) — American economist, professor of political economy at the Wisconsin University.— 295

Engels, Charlotte (née *Bredt*) (1833-1912) — wife of Emil Engels, Frederick Engels' brother.— 228-30, 538

Engels, Elisabeth Franziska Maurita (née *van Haar*) (1797-1873) — Frederick Engels' mother.— 229

Engels, Emil (1828-1884) — Frederick Engels' brother; a partner in the Er-

men & Engels firm in Engelskirchen.— 218, 220, 228, 229, 538

Engels, Emil (1858-1907) — Emil Engels' son, nephew of Frederick Engels, employee, and from 1889 a partner in the Ermen & Engels firm in Engelskirchen.— 538-39

Engels, Emil (b. 1885) — son of Frederick Engels' nephew, Emil Engels.— 539

Engels, Emma (née *Croon*) (1834-1916) — Hermann Engels' wife.— 220

Engels, Friedrich (1796-1860) — Frederick Engels' father.— 219, 229

Engels, Hermann (1822-1905) — Frederick Engels' brother; manufacturer in Barmen, a partner in the Ermen & Engels firm in Engelskirchen.— 218-20, 228, 539

Engels, Hermann Friedrich Theodor (1858-1926) — Hermann Engels' son, nephew of Frederick Engels; manufacturer, a partner in the Ermen & Engels firm in Engelskirchen.— 219, 220, 539

Engels, Johanna Klara (b. 1862) — wife of Emil Engels, Frederick Engels' nephew.— 539

Engels, Rudolf (1831-1903) — Frederick Engels' brother; manufacturer in Barmen, a partner in the Ermen & Engels firm in Engelskirchen.— 219

Engels, Rudolf Moritz (1858-1893) — Frederick Engels' nephew, son of Rudolf Engels; employee, and from 1889 a partner in the Ermen & Engels firm in Engelskirchen.— 539

F

Fabian, Heinrich Wilhelm — German Social Democrat.— 124, 191, 295

Faerber, Salo — German Social Democrat, merchant in Breslau.— 337-39, 417

Faraday, Michael (1791-1867) — English physicist and chemist, founder of the teachings on the electromagnetic field.— 400

Reichstag (1881-1918).— 118, 119, 125, 296, 307, 315, 426

G

Gambetta, Léon Michel (1838-1882) — French statesman, bourgeois republican; member of the Government of National Defence (1870-71); founded the paper *Republique Française* in 1871; Prime Minister and Minister of Foreign Affairs (1881-82).— 413

Gartman, Lev Nikolayevich (1850-1913) — Russian revolutionary, Narodnik, took part in the terroristic act of the People's Will organisation against Alexander II after which emigrated to France and later to England, settled in the USA in 1881, withdrew from politics.— 13, 256

Gaulier, Alfred Nicolas (b. 1829) — French politician and journalist, Radical, member of the Chamber of Deputies (1886-89).— 438, 445

Geiser, Bruno (1846-1898) — German journalist, edited *Die Neue Welt* (1877-86), deputy to the German Reichstag (1881-87) where he belonged to the Right wing of the Social-Democratic group; expelled from the Socialist Workers' Party of Germany in the late 1880s.— 21, 34, 81, 124, 140, 150, 165-66, 173, 187, 204, 218, 231, 296, 307, 442, 489

Gendre — see *Nikitina, Varvara Nikolayevna*

George, Henry (1839-1897) — American economist and journalist; favoured nationalisation of land by the state.— 14, 42, 74, 82, 114, 237, 525, 531-32, 540-42

Gerville-Réache, Gaston Marie Sidoine Théonile (b. 1854) — French lawyer and politician, member of the Chamber of Deputies for Guadeloupe.— 180

Giers, Nikolai Karlovich (1820-1895) — Russian diplomat, envoy to Teheran (from 1863), Berne (from 1869), and Stockholm (from 1872); Deputy Minister for Foreign Affairs (1875-82), Minister for Foreign Affairs (1882-95).— 461, 467, 484, 516, 517

Giffen, Sir Robert (1837-1910) — English economist and statistician, specialist on finances, publisher of the *Journal of the Statistical Society* (1876-91); head of the statistical department at the Board of Trade (1876-97).— 5

Gladstone, William Ewart (1809-1898) — British statesman, first Tory, later a leader of the Liberal Party in the latter half of the 19th century; Chancellor of the Exchequer (1852-55, 1859-66) and Prime Minister (1868-74, 1880-85, 1886 and 1892-94).— 109, 227, 267, 281, 303, 361, 449, 497, 505, 514

Goethe, Johann Wolfgang von (1749-1832) — German poet.— 30, 48, 92, 253

Gray, John (1798-1850) — English economist, utopian socialist; follower of Robert Owen; an author of the labour money theory.— 208

Grévy, François Paul Jules (1807-1891) — French statesman, bourgeois republican; President of the Republic (1879-87).— 41, 303

Grillenberger, Karl (1848-1897) — German worker, later journalist; deputy to the German Reichstag from 1881, where belonged to the Right wing of the Socialist Workers' Party of Germany.— 231

Grimaux, Louis Edouard (1835-1900) — French chemist.— 289

Gronlund, Laurence (1846-1899) — American journalist, Dutch by birth, a member of the Executive of the Socialist Labor Party from 1887.— 192, 295

Groß, Gustav (1856-1935) — Austrian politician, economist and journalist, lecturer at Vienna University.— 250, 261, 522

Guesde, Jules (pen-name for *Mathieu Jules Bazile*) (1845-1922) — prominent figure in the French and international socialist movement; a founder (1880) and leader of the French Workers' Party up to 1901; for some years on, a leader of the revolutionary wing in the French socialist movement.— 28, 30, 41, 61, 64, 74, 94, 115, 141, 225, 409, 414, 442, 508

Guillaume-Schack, Gertrud (née *countess Schack*) (1845-1903) — German socialist, took part in the women workers' movement in Germany.— 311, 454, 455, 473, 477, 478

Guizot, François Pierre Guillaume (1787-1874) — French historian and statesman; Orleanist; Foreign Minister (1840-48); in 1847-48 also Prime Minister; virtually directed France's home and foreign policy from 1840 to the February revolution of 1848; expressed the interests of the big financial bourgeoisie.— 95

Gumbel, Abraham — German Social Democrat, émigré in France in the early 1880s, bank employee in Paris in 1883.— 191

Gumpert, Eduard (d. 1893) — German physician in Manchester; friend of Marx and Engels.— 62

H

Haeckel, Ernst Heinrich (1834-1919) — German biologist, follower of Darwin, adherent of materialism in natural science, atheist; formulated the biogenetic law of the relationship between phylogenesis and ontogenesis; ideologist of 'social Darwinism'.— 289

Hagen — correspondent of Engels in Bonn.— 252

Hamel, Ernest (1826-1898) — French historian and journalist, author of works on history of the French Revolution.— 399

Hänel, Albert (1833-1918) — German lawyer and politician, a leader of the Party of Progress, member of the Prussian Chamber of Deputies (1867-88)

and deputy to the German Reichstag (1867-93 and 1898-1903).— 435

Harney, George Julian (1817-1897) — prominent figure in the English labour movement, a Chartist leader (Left wing); editor of *The Northern Star* and other Chartist periodicals; an émigré in the USA in 1863-88; member of the First International, was on friendly terms with Marx and Engels.— 274, 289, 292, 293, 337, 404, 422, 467, 475, 479, 537

Hartmann — see *Gartman, Lev Nikolayevich*

Hasenclever, Wilhelm (1837-1889) — German Social Democrat, edited the *Neuer Social-Demokrat*, President of the General Association of German Workers in 1871-75, a chairman of the Socialist Workers' Party of Germany from May 1875; edited together with Liebknecht the *Vorwärts!* in 1876-78; deputy to the Reichstag (1874-88).— 21

Hasselmann, Wilhelm (b. 1844) — one of the leaders of the Lassallean General Association of German Workers; editor of the *Neuer Social-Demokrat* in 1871-75; member of the Socialist Workers' Party of Germany from 1875; expelled from the Party for his anarchist views in 1880.— 21

Haug — German Social Democrat.— 209

Haxthausen, August Franz Ludwig Maria, Baron von (1792-1866) — Prussian official and economist, conservative, author of works on the agrarian system and the peasant commune in Russia.— 179

Hecker, Friedrich Karl Franz (1811-1881) — German democrat, a leader of the Baden republican uprising in April 1848; after its defeat emigrated to Switzerland and later to the USA, took part in the Civil War on the side of the Union.— 287

Hegel, Georg Wilhelm Friedrich (1770-1831) — German philosopher.— 35, 126, 186, 189, 281, 348, 356, 438

I

Ihring, Ferdinand — officer of the German political police, agent provocateur in a Berlin workers' society under the name of Mahlow; was exposed in February 1886.— 426

Irving, Sir Henry (John Henry Brodribb) (1838-1905) — English producer and actor; engaged in some plays by Shakespeare.— 345

Issleib — daughter of Ferdinand Issleib, August Bebel's partner.— 80

J

Jagemann, Christian Joseph (1735-1804) — German philologist, wrote on the Italian literature history, composed an Italian-German dictionary.— 85

Jankowska, Marya (née *Zaleska*, pseudonym *Stefan Leonowicz*) (1850-1909) — Polish socialist, journalist, member of the First International; lived in emigration in the 1880s-90s, delegate to the international socialist congresses in Paris (1889), Brussels (1891) and Zurich (1893); took part in the foundation of the Polish Socialist Party in 1892; married Polish socialist Stanisław Mendelson in 1889.— 185-86

Joffrin, Jules François Alexandre (1846-1890) — French mechanic, socialist, an organiser of the mechanics' trade union; took part in the Paris Commune, after its defeat an émigré in England (1871-81); member of the French Workers' Party, a leader of the Possibilist wing; member of the town's council of the 18th arrondissement of Paris.— 134, 141-42

Johny — see *Longuet, Jean Laurent Frédéric (Johny)*

Jollymeier — see *Schorlemmer, Carl*

Jones, Ernest Charles (1819-1869) — proletarian poet and journalist, prominent figure in the English working-class movement, Left-wing chartist leader, friend of Marx and Engels.— 404

Jordanes (Jornandes, Jordanis) (b. c. 500) — historian, wrote a work on the Goths.— 296

Jornandes — see *Jordanes*

Joynes, James Leigh (1853-1893) — English journalist and translator, a leader of the Social Democratic Federation, an editor of the *To-Day*, contributed to the *Justice* and *The Commonweal*, translated Marx's *Wage Labour and Capital* into English.— 74, 105, 127, 129, 172, 207, 236

Juta, Johann Carl (Jaan Carel) (1824-1886) — Dutch merchant, husband of Karl Marx's sister Louise, bookseller in Capetown (South Africa).— 71

Juta, Louise (1821-1893) — Karl Marx's sister, Johann Carl Juta's wife.— 71

K

Kaler-Reinthal, Emil (1850-1897) — Austrian journalist, Social Democrat, withdrew from the workers' movement in the late 1880s, opposed Social Democracy.— 50

Kalle, Fritz (1837-1915) — German industrialist, National Liberal, deputy to the Reichstag in 1884-90.— 438, 439

Kálnoky, Gustav, Count von (1832-1898) — Austro-Hungarian statesman, ambassador to St Petersburg (1880-81), chairman of the Imperial Council of Ministers and Foreign Minister (1881-95).— 517

Kant, Immanuel (1724-1804) — German philosopher.— 114, 122

Kaulbars, Nikolai Vasilyevich, Baron (1842-1905) — Russian general, military attaché in Austria (1881-86), was on special diplomatic mission in Bulgaria in 1886.— 505, 517

Kautsky, Karl Johann (1854-1938) — German journalist, economist and historian, Social Democrat, edited *Die Neue Zeit* (1883-1917), wrote on

Marxist theory, later an ideologist of centrism in German Social Democracy and the Second International.— 17, 27, 55-58, 63-64, 68, 70, 72, 73, 75-78, 80, 81, 85, 86, 89, 90, 101-03, 109-10, 120-21, 123-25, 131-33, 135-39, 144, 147, 153-57, 160, 162-66, 170, 174-77, 186-87, 189-90, 192-95, 201, 203-08, 210, 212, 218, 230, 236, 250, 251, 262, 265, 270, 272, 274, 283, 285, 302, 303, 307, 316, 321-25, 329, 334, 344, 357, 360, 362, 366, 378, 385, 386, 399, 404, 407, 417, 422, 425, 427, 448, 454, 455, 458-59, 460-63, 472-74, 476-79, 481-82, 504, 521, 526, 530, 537

Kautsky, Louise (née Strasser) (1860-1950) — Austrian socialist, first wife of Karl Kautsky, secretary of Engels from 1890.— 262, 265, 273, 320-25, 357, 378, 386, 399, 454, 458, 459, 461, 463, 473, 477, 480, 531, 537

Kautsky, Minna (née Jaich) (1837-1912) — German writer of social novels; Karl Kautsky's mother.— 320, 321, 355-58

Kayser, Max (1853-1888) — German journalist, Social Democrat, deputy to the Reichstag (1878-84), sided with the Reformist wing of the Social-Democratic group.— 21

Kelley-Wischnewetzky, Florence (1859-1932) — American socialist, translated Engels' The Condition of the Working-Class in England into English; Lazar Wischnewetzky's wife.— 248, 256-59, 373, 382, 393, 395-97, 405, 415-16, 419, 420, 441, 451-53, 463-66, 477, 478, 540-42

Kjellberg, Julia — daughter of the Swedish industrialist, wife of Georg Heinrich von Vollmar.— 185

Klopfer, Ludwig — German Social Democrat, an émigré in Switzerland.— 25-28

Knowles, Sir James Thomas (1831-1908) — English architect, writer and publisher, founded and edited The Nineteenth Century (1877-1908).— 8, 12

Kock, Charles Paul de (1793-1871) — French novelist and dramatist.— 170

Kol, Henri Hubert van (1852-1925) — a founder and leader of the Dutch Social-Democratic Workers' Party.— 477, 499, 501

Kolb, Georg Friedrich (1808-1884) — German politician, journalist and statistician; democrat.— 359

Krantz — see Lavrov, Pyotr Lavrovich

Kravchinsky, Sergei Mikhailovich (pseudonym Stepnyak) (1851-1895) — Russian author and journalist, revolutionary Narodnik in the 1870s; an émigré after he took part in the revolutionary action against the police chief in St Petersburg in 1878; lived in England from 1884.— 256, 443

Kropotkin, Pyotr Alexeyevich, Prince (1842-1921) — Russian geographer, geologist and revolutionary; theoretician of anarchism, an émigré in 1876-1917.— 431

Krzywicki, Ludwik Joachim Franciszek (1859-1941) — Polish anthropologist, sociologist, economist and journalist; professor at Warsaw University; took part in the socialist movement in the 1880s, a translator into Polish and editor of the first volume of Capital; propagated Marxism in Poland.— 87, 89

Kugelmann, Ludwig (1828-1902) — German physician, took part in the 1848-49 revolution in Germany; member of the First International, Marx's regular correspondent (1862-74), friend of Marx and Engels.— 133, 134

Kuropatkin, Alexei Nikolayevich (1848-1925) — Russian general, took part in the Russo-Turkish war (1877-78) and campaigns to the Central Asia (1879-83).— 339

L

Labruyère, Georges de — French journalist, contributed to Le Cri du Peuple.— 376

272, 291-93, 298-99, 373-74, 420-21, 493-94

Marx, Eleanor (Tussy) (1855-1898) — Karl Marx's youngest daughter; took part in the British and international working-class movement in the 1880s-90s; wife of Edward Aveling from 1884; member of the Social Democratic Federation, a founder of the Socialist League (1884); was active in foundation of trade unions of unskilled workers in England in the late 1880s.— 3, 5, 6, 14, 31, 39-41, 53, 58-60, 63, 69-71, 74, 76-78, 83, 85, 87-89, 91, 92, 94, 111, 115, 120, 124, 128, 167, 175, 195, 214, 224, 237, 245, 247, 250, 261, 265, 274, 275, 297, 301, 303, 320, 323, 326, 368, 375, 376, 378, 383, 386, 391, 399, 402, 424, 435-37, 443, 458, 461, 469, 478, 482, 489, 494, 498, 500, 506, 508, 524, 525, 527, 537, 540

Marx, Heinrich (1777-1838) — Karl Marx's father, lawyer, Counsellor of Justice in Trier.— 29

Marx, Jenny (née von Westphalen) (1814-1881) — Karl Marx's wife.— 34, 39, 47, 152

Marx, Karl (1818-1883).— 3, 6-18, 24, 25, 29, 31, 33, 36, 39-44, 47-51, 53-54, 60, 67, 72, 73, 78, 79, 84, 88-94, 100, 103, 111, 114, 117, 122, 124, 128-29, 133, 138, 150, 152, 158-59, 163, 165, 166, 175, 181, 182, 184, 186, 192-94, 202, 204, 206, 214, 224, 226, 229, 233, 251, 258, 260, 262, 265, 266, 279-80, 282, 283, 287-88, 291, 295, 305-07, 309, 311, 316, 319, 328, 329, 332, 333, 344, 351, 358, 371, 373-75, 385, 389, 391, 393-94, 396, 400, 402, 416, 420, 422, 435, 439, 447, 452, 457, 465, 470, 475, 481, 483, 488

Maurer, Georg Ludwig von (1790-1872) — German historian, studied the social system of ancient and medieval Germany.— 179, 398

May, Élie Henri (1842-1930) — French socialist, Possibilist; a founder of La So-ciété républicaine d'économie sociale, later supported Boulanger.— 368

Mayall — photographer in London.— 15, 18

McEnnis, J. T.— correspondent of the Missouri Republican in Saint Louis (USA).— 443, 460, 490, 491

Mead, Edward P.— English workers' poet, contributed to the Chartist newspaper The Northern Star.— 92

Mehring, Franz (1846-1919) — German philosopher, historian and journalist, took part in the working-class and socialist movements; author of works on history of Germany and of Social Democracy; biographer of Karl Marx, member of the German Social-Democratic Party (from 1891); permanent contributor to Die Neue Zeit.— 253, 255, 316

Meissner, Otto Karl (1819-1902) — Hamburg publisher, published Capital and some other works by Marx and Engels.— 17, 20, 26, 40, 60, 76-78, 89, 92, 96, 101, 121, 122, 190, 309, 319, 328, 384, 400, 417, 494, 496

Mendelssohn — bank manager in Berlin.— 338

Menger, Anton (1841-1906) — Austrian lawyer and politician, sociologist, professor at Vienna University.— 521, 526

Meyer, Mathilde (née Trautow) — wife of Rudolf Hermann Meyer.— 507

Meyer, Rudolf Hermann (1839-1899) — German economist and journalist, conservative, biographer of Rodbertus.— 54, 79, 101, 138, 250, 375, 483, 507

Michel, Louise (pseudonym Enjolras) (1830-1905) — French teacher, was active in the Paris Commune; supported Blanquists during the Second Empire, was exiled to New Caledonia after the suppression of the Commune; after the 1880 amnesty took part in the working-class movement in France, Belgium and Holland, sided with the anar-

and secretary of the Fabian Society.—392, 393

Peel, Sir Robert (1788-1850) — British statesman, Tory; Home Secretary (1822-27, 1828-30); Prime Minister (1834-35, 1841-46).— 374, 449

Percy — see Rosher, Percy White

Peschier, Charles Jaques (nickname Adolphe) (1805-1878) — professor of French literature at Tübingen; a compiler of the French-German dictionary.— 85, 375

Petrarch or Petrarca, Francesco (1304-1374) — Italian poet of the Renaissance.— 48

Pfänder, Karl (c. 1819-1876) — German painter, took part in the German and international working-class movement; emigrated to London in 1845; member of the German Workers' Educational Society in London, of the Communist League and of the General Council of the International; friend and associate of Marx and Engels.— 468

Pfänder.— 447

Philippe VII — see Louis Philippe Albert d'Orléans, comte de Paris

Planteau, François Edouard (b. 1838) — French radical politician; member of the Chamber of Deputies (from 1885); sided with the socialists (1887-89); follower of Boulanger (from 1889).— 409, 414

Platter, Julius (1844-1923) — Swiss economist, professor at Zurich University (1879-84).— 458

Plekhanov (Plechanoff), Georgi Valentinovich (1856-1918) — Russian philosopher, propagated Marxism in Russia; founder of the first Russian Marxist organisation, the Emancipation of Labour group (1883).— 67, 264, 279-80

Potter, George (1832-1893) — British worker, carpenter; leader of the Amalgamated Union of Building Workers and of the trade union movement; member of the London Trades Council; founder, editor and publisher of The Bee-Hive Newspaper.— 320

Powderly, Terence Vincent (1849-1924) — mechanic, a leader of the working-class movement in the USA (1870s-90s); a leader of the Knights of Labor (1879-93); sided with the Republicans in 1896.— 532, 541

Proudhon, Pierre Joseph (1809-1865) — French writer, economist and sociologist; founder of anarchism.— 102, 105, 117, 156-57, 208, 342, 354, 413, 429, 470

Pumps — see Rosher, Mary Ellen

Pushkin, Alexander Sergeyevich (1799-1837) — Russian poet.— 48

Putnam, George Haven (1844-1930) — owner of a New York publishing house (from 1872); Liberal.— 259

Puttkamer, Robert Victor von (1828-1900) — Prussian statesman, Minister of Home Affairs (1881-88).— 138, 473

Q

Quarck, Max (pseudonym Freiwald Thüringer) (1860-1930) — German lawyer and journalist; Right-wing Social Democrat; deputy to the German Reichstag (1912-18).— 64, 67, 138, 164, 258, 384, 385, 405, 417

Quelch, Harry (1858-1913) — English worker; a leader of the new trade unions; socialist; delegate to international socialist congresses of 1891 and 1893.— 123

R

Rackow, Heinrich (d. 1916) — German Social Democrat; a refugee in London (from 1879); owner of a tobacco shop; member of the German Workers' Educational Society in London.— 118

Radford, Ernest — English lawyer.— 40

Rae, John (1845-1915) — English economist and sociologist; contributed to the

Assembly (Left wing) in 1848-49; one of the five imperial regents (June 1849); emigrated to Switzerland in 1849; received subsidies from Napoleon III in the 1850s-60s.— 282, 587

Vollmar, Georg Heinrich von (1850-1922) — German army officer; Social Democrat; a leader of the Right wing in German Social Democracy; an editor of *Der Sozialdemokrat* (1879-80); deputy to the German Reichstag (1881-87 and 1890-1918).— 184, 185, 433

W

Wagner, Adolph (1835-1917) — German economist and politician, professor of political economy and finance; a founder of socio-legal school in political economy; armchair socialist.— 138

Wagner, Richard (1813-1883) — German composer, conductor and musical writer.— 124, 174, 283

Walther — German physician, acquaintance of the Bebel family.— 316

Watrin (d. 1886) — French engineer, manager of the mines in Decazeville.— 409

Watts, John Hunter (1853-1923) — English socialist, a leader of the Social Democratic Federation; later member of the British Socialist Party.— 367

Weerth, Georg (1822-1856) — German proletarian poet and journalist; member of the Communist League; edited the *Neue Rheinische Zeitung* in 1848-49; friend of Marx and Engels.— 34, 160, 161, 422, 475

Wegmann — German confectioner, relative of A. Wegmann, a member of the First International.— 293

Wehner, J. G. — German refugee in Manchester; Treasurer of the Schiller Institute in the 1860s; Engels' acquaintance.— 204

Weiler, G. Adam (1841-1894) — German joiner; refugee in the USA and from 1862 in England; member of the First

International (from 1865) and of the British Federal Council (1872-73); member of London Trades Union Council (1872-73) and of the Social Democratic Federation (from 1883).— 57

Werder, Bernhard Franz Wilhelm von (1823-1907) — Prussian general and diplomat, military attaché in St Petersburg (1869-86), governor of Berlin (1886-88), ambassador to St Petersburg (1892-95).— 467

Wermuth, Karl Georg Ludwig (1804-1867) — chief of police in Hanover; an organiser of and witness for the prosecution at the Cologne Communist trial (1852); in collaboration with Stieber wrote the book *Die Communisten-Verschwörungen des neunzehnten Jahrhunderts.*— 305, 329, 344, 346

Westphalen, Johann Ludwig von (1770-1842) — Jenny Marx's father, Privy Councillor in Trier.— 332

Weydemeyer, Otto — son of Joseph Weydemeyer; took part in the US working-class movement.— 14

Wicksteed, Philip Henry (b. 1844) — British Unitarian minister, Christian socialist.— 192, 195

William I (1797-1888) — King of Prussia (1861-88) and Emperor of Germany (1871-88).— 34, 81, 124, 130, 140, 147, 268, 299, 304, 317, 318, 320, 324, 328, 329, 383, 467, 469, 473, 484, 486, 487, 493, 505, 510, 520

Williams, John Edward (1854-1917) — a founder and leader of the Social Democratic Federation (1881).— 366-69, 375

Willich, August (1810-1878) — Prussian army officer; member of the Communist League; took part in the Baden-Palatinate uprising of 1849; a leader of the sectarian group in the Communist League in 1850; emigrated to the USA in 1853, general in the Northern army during the Civil War.— 352

Willis, Edwin.— 118

Wills, William Gorman (1828-1891) — Irish dramatist.— 345

Wischnewetzky — see *Kelley-Wischnewetzky, Florence*

Wischnewetzky, Lazar — physician, Polish by birth; emigrated to the USA in 1886, member of the Socialist Labor Party, Florence Kelley-Wischnewetzky's husband.— 441, 477, 478

Woermann, Adolf (1847-1911) — big German merchant; National Liberal; deputy to the Reichstag (1884-90); active participant in the colonial expansionism in Africa.— 199

Wolff, Wilhelm (Lupus) (1809-1864) — German teacher, proletarian revolutionary; member of the Central Authority of the Communist League from March 1848; an editor of the *Neue Rheinische Zeitung* in 1848-49, took an active part in the 1848-49 revolution in Germany; emigrated to Switzerland and later to England; friend and associate of Marx and Engels.— 309, 324, 328

Wright — English socialist, member of the Social Democratic Federation.— 224

Y

Yanson, Yuli Eduardovich (1835-1892) — Russian statistician and economist, professor at St Petersburg University (from 1865) and at some other educational institutions, head of the statistical bureau of the Petersburg municipal board (from 1881); wrote fruitfully on the theory and history of statistics.— 339

Z

Zasulich (Zasoulitch), Vera Ivanovna (1849-1919) — participant in the Narodnik (from 1868) and later in the Social-Democratic movements in Russia; a founder (1883) and active member of the Emancipation of Labour group.— 63-67, 93, 111-13, 204, 264, 279, 281, 400, 432

Zhukovsky, Yuli Galaktionovich (1822-1907) — Russian economist and journalist; manager of the State Bank; author of the article 'Karl Marx and His Book on Capital'.— 112

Zitz, Franz Heinrich (1803-1877) — German lawyer, deputy to the Frankfurt Assembly (Left wing) in 1848; took part in the Baden-Palatinate uprising of 1849; emigrated to the USA.— 287

INDEX OF LITERARY AND MYTHOLOGICAL NAMES

Ahriman (Gr. myth.) — Greek name for the Persian source of all evil in the world, Angro Mainyush, contrasts with Good Spirit, Ahura Mazda (Greek Ormazd).— 13

Ahura Mazda (Ormazd, Ormuzd) — Persian god of Good Spirit.— 13

Arnold — a character in Minna Kautsky's *Die Alten und die Neuen.* — 356

Brunhild — the legendary heroine in the Old German and Scandinavian epic and in the German medieval poem, *Nibelungenlied*; Queen of Island, wife of Gunther, King of the Burgundians.— 224

Droste-Fischering — a character in a German satirical folk song.— 434

Elsa — a character in Minna Kautsky's *Die Alten und die Neuen.* — 357

Freya (Sc. myth.) — goddess of fertility

INDEX OF QUOTED
AND MENTIONED LITERATURE

WORKS BY KARL MARX AND FREDERICK ENGELS

Marx, Karl

Capital. A Critique of Political Economy. Vol. I, Book One: *The Process of Production of Capital* (present edition, Vol. 35).— 26, 56, 77, 107, 111, 115, 183, 184, 188, 194, 353, 385, 465

— Das Kapital. Kritik der politischen Oekonomic: Erster Band, Buch I: Der Produktionsprocess des Kapitals. Hamburg, 1867.— 8, 127, 154, 225, 264, 267, 278, 310

— Das Kapital. Kritik der politischen Oekonomie: Erster Band, Buch I: Der Produktionsprocess des Kapitals. Zweite verbesserte Auflage. Hamburg, 1872.— 11, 60, 124, 128

— Капиталъ. Критика политической экономіи. Сочиненіе Карла Маркса. Переводъ съ нѣмецкаго. Томъ первый. Книга I: Процессъ производства капитала. С.-Петербургъ, 1872.— 8, 65

— Le Capital. Traduction de M.J. Roy, entièrement revisée par l'auteur. [Vol. 1.] Paris, [1872-1875].— 8, 29-31, 33, 41-42, 182, 313, 342, 385, 424, 439, 440

— Das Kapital. Kritik der politischen Oekonomie. Erster Band, Buch I: Der Produktionsprocess des Kapitals. Dritte vermehrte Auflage. Hamburg, 1883.— 14, 20, 29, 32-33, 39, 41-44, 47-49, 52, 58, 60, 63, 65, 71, 76, 83, 89, 113, 125-26, 129-30, 153, 182, 385, 436, 439, 440, 450, 460, 494, 506

— Kapitał. Krytyka ekonomii politycznej. Tom pierwszy. Księga I: Wytwarzanie kapitału. Lipsk, 1884 [-1889].— 87, 89

— Capital. A Critical Analysis of Capitalist Production. By Karl Marx. Translated from the third German edition by Samuel Moore and Edward Aveling and edited by Frederick Engels. Vol. 1. [Parts 1-2]. London, 1887.— 29, 31, 33, 40, 46, 50, 52, 59, 83, 95, 122, 124, 127-30, 133, 143, 153, 191, 198, 202, 244, 261, 289-91, 306, 310, 313, 328, 348, 374, 393, 400-02, 404, 416, 419-21, 423, 426, 434, 436, 443, 447, 449-50, 453, 456, 460-64, 468, 471, 474, 480, 484, 490, 492-94, 506, 509, 522, 527-28, 531

Capital. A Critique of Political Economy. Vol. II, Book Two: *The Process of Circulation of Capital* (present edition, Vol. 36)
— Das Kapital. Kritik der politischen Oekonomie. Zweiter Band, Buch II: Der Cirkulationsprocess des Kapitals. Hamburg, 1885.— 3, 5-8, 14, 17, 25, 26, 29, 33, 39, 42-44, 53, 58-59, 65, 88, 92-93, 100, 102, 115, 121, 122, 130, 133, 138, 143, 151-54, 157, 160, 186-88, 190, 197, 202, 206, 217, 220, 244, 249, 260, 262-67, 271, 278, 283, 289, 292-93, 296, 303, 308-09, 316, 319, 328, 347-48, 359, 494, 522
— Капиталъ. Критика политической экономіи. Переводъ съ нѣмецкаго. Томъ второй. Книга II: Процессъ обращенія капитала. С.-Петербургъ, 1885.— 65, 93, 100, 260, 261, 266, 289, 294, 303, 311, 318, 400, 432

Capital. A Critique of Political Economy. Vol. III, Book Three: *The Process of Capitalist Production as a Whole* (present edition, Vol. 37)
— Das Kapital. Kritik der politischen Oekonomie. Dritter Band, Buch III: Der Gesamtprocess der kapitalistischen Produktion. Hamburg, 1894.— 3, 29, 88-89, 102, 121, 122, 152, 160, 179, 188, 224, 244, 249, 261-64, 267, 271, 277-78, 286, 289, 292, 296, 301, 304, 306, 308, 310, 316-17, 348-49, 358, 363, 374, 394, 400, 402, 405, 416, 434, 484, 492, 522-23, 534

The Civil War in France. Address of the General Council of the International Working Men's Association. London, 1871 (present edition, Vol. 22).— 158
— Der Bürgerkrieg in Frankreich. Adresse des Generalraths der Internationalen Arbeiter-Assoziation an alle Mitglieder in Europa und den Vereinigten Staaten. Separatabdruck aus dem Volksstaat. Leipzig, 1871.— 73-74, 287, 389
— [Extract from Chapter III]. In: *Манифестъ коммунистической партіи Карла Маркса и Фр. Энгельса.* Переводъ съ нѣмецкаго изданія 1872. Съ предисловіемъ авторовъ. Женева, 1882.— 73-74

The Class Struggles in France, 1848 to 1850 (present edition, Vol. 10)
— Die Klassenkämpfe in Frankreich, 1848 bis 1850 (published in 1850 under the title *1848 bis 1849*). In: *Neue Rheinische Zeitung. Politisch-ökonomische Revue*, Nr. 1, 2, 3, 5-6, Januar, Februar, März, Mai bis Oktober 1850.— 93, 251, 261, 305

A Contribution to the Critique of Political Economy. Part One (present edition, Vol. 29)
— Zur Kritik der politischen Oekonomie. Erstes Heft. Berlin, 1859.— 29, 195, 208
— [Extract from Chapter 2]. In: Marx, K. *Das Elend der Philosophie. Antwort auf Proudhons 'Philosophie des Elends'.* Stuttgart, 1885. Anhang I.— 208, 216

A Contribution to the Critique of Political Economy (1861-63) (present edition, vols 30-34).— 29, 102, 104, 122, 188, 244, 264, 278

Critical Marginal Notes on the Article 'The King of Prussia and Social Reform. By a Prussian'. ('Vorwärts!', No. 60) (present edition, Vol. 3)
— Kritische Randglossen zu dem Artikel: 'Der König von Preußen und die Socialreform. Von einem Preußen' ('Vorwärts!', Nr. 60). Paris, den 31. Juli 1844. In: *Vorwärts!*, Nr. 63, 64; 7., 10. August 1844.— 47

[Economic Manuscripts of 1857-58] (present edition, vols 28-29).— 29

The Eighteenth Brumaire of Louis Bonaparte (present edition, Vol. 11).— 51, 93, 251
— Der Achtzehnte Brumaire des Louis Bonaparte. Zweite Ausgabe. Hamburg, 1869.— 92-93

— Der Achtzehnte Brumaire des Louis Bonaparte. Dritte Auflage. Hamburg, 1885.— 292

— Le dix-huit Brumaire de Louis Bonaparte. In: *Le Socialiste,* janvier-novembre 1891.— 62, 310, 333, 345, 358-59, 394, 496, 529, 534

Epilogue [to 'Revelations Concerning the Communist Trial in Cologne'] (present edition, Vol. 24)

— Nachwort. In: Marx, K. *Enthüllungen über den Kommunisten-Prozeß zu Köln.* Neuer Abdruck. Leipzig, 1875.— 305

Excerpts from Lewis Henry Morgan 'Ancient Society'.— 103, 120

Herr Vogt (present edition, Vol. 17)

— Herr Vogt. London, 1860.— 282

Illustrations of the Latest Exercise in Cabinet Style of Frederick William IV (present edition, Vol. 3)

— (anon.) Illustrationen zu der neuesten Cabinetsstylübung Friedrich Wilhelm IV. In: *Vorwärts!,* Nr. 66, 17. August 1844.— 47

Inaugural Address of the Working Men's International Association, Established September 28, 1864, at a Public Meeting Held at St. Martin's Hall, Long Acre, London (present edition, Vol. 20)

— Address. In: *Address and Provisional Rules of the Working Men's International Association, Established September 28, 1864, at a Public Meeting Held at St. Martin's Hall, Long Acre, London.* [London], 1864.— 287

The June Revolution (present edition, Vol. 7)

— Französische Republik. In: *Neue Rheinische Zeitung,* Nr. 29, 29. Juni 1848.— 36, 287

[Letter to 'Otechestvenniye Zapiski'] (present edition, Vol. 24)

— À la rédaction de l' 'Отечественныя Записки'.— 112-13

Lord Palmerston (present edition, Vol. 12)

— Palmerston and Russia. Palmerston, What Has He Done? In: *Tucker's Political Fly-Sheets,* Nos. I, II. London, 1855.— 374

Marx to F. A. Sorge, 20 June 1881 (present edition, Vol. 46)

— In: Sorge, F. A. *Die Arbeiterbewegung in den Vereinigten Staaten. 1877-1885.* In: *Die Neue Zeit,* 1891-92, Jg. 3, Bd. 2, Nr. 33.— 42, 114

Математические рукописи, Москва, 1968.— 39, 43

Moralising Criticism and Critical Morality. A Contribution to German Cultural History. Contra Karl Heinzen (present edition, Vol. 6)

— Die moralisierende Kritik und die kritisierende Moral. Beitrag zur deutschen Kulturgeschichte. Gegen Karl Heinzen. In: *Deutsche-Brüsseler-Zeitung,* Nr. 86, 87, 90, 92, 94; 28., 31. Oktober, 11., 18., 25. November 1847.— 47

Mr. George Howell's History of the International Working-Men's Association (present edition, Vol. 24). In: *The Secular Chronicle, and Record of Freethought Progress,* Vol. X, No. 5, August 4, 1878.— 9

On Proudhon (present edition, Vol. 20)
— Ueber P.J. Proudhon. In: *Der Social-Demokrat*, Nr. 16-18; 1., 3., 5. Februar 1865.—91, 102, 104, 107, 110, 139, 206
— An Schweitzer. In: Marx, K. *Das Elend der Philosophie. Antwort auf Proudhons 'Philosophie des Elends'*. Stuttgart, 1885.—130, 206, 208, 261
— Карлъ Марксъ о Прудоне. In: *Карлъ Марксъ. Нищета философіи. Отвѣтъ на философію нищеты г. Прудона.* Съ предисловіемъ и примьчаніями Фридриха Энгельса и двумя приложеніями. Женева, 1886.—111
— Proudhon jugé par Karl Marx. In: *Misère de la philosophie. Réponse à la philosophie de la misère de M. Proudhon. Avec une préface de Friedrich Engels*. Paris, 1896. Appendice I.—102, 116, 130, 139

The Poverty of Philosophy. Answer to the 'Philosophy of Poverty' by M. Proudhon (present edition, Vol. 6)
— Misère de la philosophie. Réponse à la philosophie de la misère de M. Proudhon. Paris, Bruxelles, 1847.—64, 86, 101-02, 111, 163, 195
— Das Elend der Philosophie. Antwort auf Proudhons 'Philosophie des Elends'. Stuttgart, 1885.—64, 66-67, 73, 90, 101-02, 107, 111, 115, 124-26, 130, 134-35, 138, 176, 186, 189, 191, 195, 198, 201, 206, 211, 220, 250, 261
— Нищета философіи. Отвѣтъ на Философію Нищеты г. Прудона. Съ предисловіемъ и примьчаніями Фридриха Энгельса и двумя приложеніями. Женева, 1886.—112, 115, 158, 432
— Misère de la philosophie. Réponse à la philosophie de la misère de M. Proudhon. Avec une préface de Friedrich Engels. Paris, 1896.—96, 101, 104, 111, 115, 124, 130, 133

[*Preamble to the Programme of the French Workers' Party*] (present edition, Vol. 24)
— Programme électoral des travailleurs socialistes. In: *L'Égalité*, No. 24, 30 juin, 1880.—311

[*Preface to the First German Edition of the First Volume of 'Capital'*] (present edition, Vol. 35)
— Author's Prefaces. I.—To the First Edition. London, July 25, 1867. In: Marx, K. *Capital: a Critical Analysis of Capitalist Production*. Vol. I, London, 1887.—524, 534

[*Preface to the Second German Edition of the First Volume of 'Capital'*] (present edition, Vol. 35)
— Author's Prefaces. II.—To the Second Edition. London, February 24, 1873. In: Marx, K. *Capital: a Critical Analysis of Capitalist Production*. Vol. I, London, 1887.—524, 534

[*The Question of the Abolition of Serfdom in Russia*] (present edition, Vol. 16). In: *New-York Daily Tribune*, No. 5458, October 19, 1858.—488

Report of the General Council to the Fifth Annual Congress of the International Working Men's Association Held at The Hague, from the 2nd to the 7th September 1872 (present edition, Vol. 23)
— Offizieller Bericht des Londoner Generalraths, verlesen in öffentlicher Sitzung des Internationalen Kongress. Braunschweig, 1872.—287-88

Revelations Concerning the Communist Trial in Cologne (present edition, Vol. 11)
— Enthüllungen über den Kommunisten-Prozeß zu Köln. Basel, 1853.—288, 305
— Enthüllungen über den Kommunisten-Prozeß zu Köln. Neuer Abdruck. Leipzig, 1875.—288, 305-06, 332
— Enthüllungen über den Kommunisten-Prozeß zu Köln. Neuer Abdruck, mit Einleitung von Friedrich Engels, und Dokumenten. Hottingen-Zürich, 1885.—288, 305, 309, 328, 329, 331, 402

Second Address of the General Council of the International Working Men's Association on the Franco-Prussian War (present edition, Vol. 22)
— Second Address of the General Council of the International Working-Men's Association on the War. To the Members of the International Working-Men's Association in Europe and the United States. London, 1870.—483, 485

Speech on the Question of Free Trade (present edition, Vol. 6)
— Discours sur la question du libre échange, prononcé à l'Association Démocratique de Bruxelles, dans la Séance Publique du 9 janvier 1848 [Bruxelles, 1848.].—196, 208
— Rede über die Frage des Freihandels, gehalten am 9. Januar 1848 in der demokratischen Gesellschaft zu Brüssel. (The title mistakenly has: 1849). In: Marx, K. *Das Elend der Philosophie. Antwort auf Proudhons 'Philosophie des Elends'.* Stuttgart, 1885. Anhang II.—196, 216, 230, 261

Theories of Surplus Value (present edition, vols 30-33).—102, 104, 121, 122, 188, 226, 244, 278

Wage Labour and Capital (present edition, Vol. 9)
— Lohnarbeit und Kapital. In: *Neue Rheinische Zeitung*, Nr. 264-267, 269, 5.-8., 11. April 1849.—158, 159
— Lohnarbeit und Kapital. Breslau, 1880.—67, 159, 306
— Наемный трудъ и капиталъ. Переводъ съ ньмецкаго изданія 1880 г. съ двумя приложеніями. Женева, 1883.—67, 158
— Lohnarbeit und Kapital. Hottingen-Zürich, 1884.—158-59, 416
— Wage-Labour and Capital. London, 1886.—463
— Capitale e salario. Prima traduzione italiana di P. Martignetti. Milano, 1893.—373-74, 394, 416, 420, 421, 462, 493, 529, 535

Engels, Frederick

Anti-Dühring. Herr Eugen Dühring's Revolution in Science (present edition, Vol. 25)
— Herrn Eugen Dühring's Umwälzung der Wissenschaft. I. Philosophie. Leipzig, 1877.—126
— Herrn Eugen Dühring's Umwälzung der Wissenschaft. II. Politische Oekonomie. Sozialismus. Leipzig, 1878.—126
— Herrn Eugen Dühring's Umwälzung der Wissenschaft. Philosophie. Politische Oekonomie. Sozialismus. Leipzig, 1878.—126, 133, 138, 158-59, 194, 249, 289, 295
— Herrn Eugen Dühring's Umwälzung der Wissenschaft. Zweite Auflage. Zürich, 1886.—124, 126, 130-31, 133, 142, 217, 249, 251-52, 263, 288, 310, 322-24, 327, 346-47, 371-73, 392, 416, 529, 534

Appendix [to the American Edition of 'The Condition of the Working Class in England'] (present edition, Vol. 26)
— Appendix. In: Engels, F. *The Condition of the Working Class in England in 1844.* New York, 1887.— 259, 373, 396, 415, 419, 420, 451, 453, 540, 542

The Bakuninists at Work. An Account of the Spanish Revolt in the Summer of 1873 (present edition, Vol. 23)
— Die Bakunisten an der Arbeit. Denkschrift über den letzten Aufstand in Spanien. (Separat-Abdruck aus dem 'Volksstaat'). [Leipzig, 1873].— 535

The Campaign for the German Imperial Constitution (present edition, Vol. 10)
— Die deutsche Reichsverfassungs-Campagne. In: *Neue Rheinische Zeitung. Politisch-ökonomische Revue*, H. 1-3, Januar-März, 1850.— 251

The Condition of the Working-Class in England. From Personal Observation and Authentic Sources (present edition, Vol. 4)
— Die Lage der arbeitenden Klasse in England. Nach eigner Anschauung und authentischen Quellen. Leipzig, 1845.— 92, 102, 124, 248, 251, 263, 373, 415, 420, 441, 464
— The Condition of the Working Class in England in 1844. New York, 1887.— 249, 257, 259, 373, 382, 394-96, 405, 415, 419, 420, 464-65, 535, 540
— Die Lage der arbeitenden Klasse in England. Nach eigner Anschauung und authentischen Quellen. Zweite durchgesehene Auflage. Stuttgart, 1892.— 248-49, 253, 259, 273

Democratic Pan-Slavism (present edition, Vol. 8)
— Der demokratische Panslawismus. In: *Neue Rheinische Zeitung*, Nr. 222, 223; 15., 16. Februar 1849.— 287

Details about the 23rd of June (present edition, Vol. 7)
— Details über den 23. Juni. In: *Neue Rheinische Zeitung*, Nr. 26, 26. Juni 1848. Extrabeilage.— 287

Engels to Achille Loria, 20 May 1883 (this volume). In: *Der Sozialdemokrat*, Nr. 21, 20. Mai 1883.— 25

[Engels' telegram to Friedrich Adolph Sorge, 14 March 1883] (present edition, Vol. 46). In: *New Yorker Volkszeitung*, Nr. 64, 15. März 1883.— 13, 91

Herr Tidmann. Old Danish Folk Song (present edition, Vol. 20)
— Herr Tidmann. Altdänisches Volkslied. In: *Der Social-Demokrat*, Nr. 18, 5. Februar 1865.— 286

The Housing Question (present edition, Vol. 23)
— Zur Wohnungsfrage. In: *Der Volksstaat*, Nr. 51-53, 103, 104; 26., 29. Juni, 3. Juli, 25., 28. Dezember 1872; Nr. 2, 3, 12, 13, 15, 16; 4., 8. Januar, 8., 12., 19., 22. Februar 1873.— 51
— Zur Wohnungsfrage. Separatabdruck aus dem 'Volksstaat'. Leipzig, 1872-1873.— 472, 475
— Zur Wohnungsfrage. Separatabdruck aus dem 'Volksstaat' von 1872. Zweite, durchgesehene Auflage. Hottingen-Zürich, 1887.— 472, 475, 529, 534

Introduction to Sigismund Borkheim's Pamphlet 'In Memory of the German Blood-and-Thunder Patriots. 1806-1807' (present edition, Vol. 26)
— Einleitung. In: Borkheim, S. *Zur Erinnerung für die deutschen Mordspatrioten. 1806-1807.* Hottingen-Zürich, 1888.— 383, 472, 475, 528, 534

Jenny Longuet, née Marx (present edition, Vol. 24)
— Jenny Longuet, geb. Marx. In: *Der Sozialdemokrat*, Nr. 4, 18. Januar 1883.— 47

Jenny Marx, née von Westphalen (present edition, Vol. 24)
— Jenny Marx, geb. v. Westphalen. In: *Der Sozialdemokrat*, Nr. 50, 8. Dezember 1881.— 47

The June Revolution [The Course of the Paris Uprising] (present edition, Vol. 7)
— Die Junirevolution. In: *Neue Rheinische Zeitung*, Nr. 31, 32; 1., 2. Juli 1848.— 287

Karl Marx (present edition, Vol. 24)
— Karl Marx. In: *Volks-Kalender.* Braunschweig, 1878.— 373-74, 422, 494

The Labor Movement in America. Preface to the American Edition of 'The Condition of the Working Class in England' (present edition, Vol. 26)
— Preface. In: Engels, F. *The Condition of the Working Class in England in 1844.* New York, 1887.— 373, 396

Lawyers' Socialism (present edition, Vol. 26)
— Juristen-Sozialismus. In: *Die Neue Zeit*, 5. Jg., H. 2, Februar 1887.— 527

The Mark (present edition, Vol. 24)
— Die Mark. In: Engels, F. *Die Entwicklung des Sozialismus von der Utopie zur Wissenschaft.* Hottingen-Zürich, 1882. Anhang.— 68
— Der deutsche Bauer. Was war er? Was ist er? Was könnte er sein? ['Volksbuchhandlung und Expedition des *Sozialdemokrat*'. Hottingen-Zürich, 1883].— 68

Marx and the 'Neue Rheinische Zeitung' (1848-1849) (present edition, Vol. 26)
— Marx und die 'Neue Rheinische Zeitung' 1848-49. In: *Der Sozialdemokrat*, Nr. 11, 13. März 1884.— 92

Marx and Rodbertus. Preface to the First German Edition of 'The Poverty of Philosophy' by Karl Marx (present edition, Vol. 26)
— Marx und Rodbertus. In: *Die Neue Zeit*, 3. Jg., H. 1, 1885.— 250
— Vorwort. London, 23. Oktober 1884. In: Marx, K. *Das Elend der Philosophie. Antwort auf Proudhons 'Philosophie des Elends'.* Stuttgart, 1885.— 73, 101, 102, 111, 125, 138, 154, 187, 201, 203, 206, 208-09, 211, 216, 220, 250, 261, 521

On the Anniversary of the Paris Commune (present edition, Vol. 26)
— Lettre d'Engels. In: *Le Socialiste*, No. 31, 27 mars 1886.— 425

On the Death of Karl Marx (present edition, Vol. 24)
— Zum Tode von Karl Marx. In: *Der Sozialdemokrat*, Nr. 19, 21; 3., 17. Mai 1883.— 3, 12

On the History of the Communist League (present edition, Vol. 26)
— Zur Geschichte des 'Bundes der Kommunisten'. In: *Der Sozialdemokrat*, Nr. 46-48; 12., 19., 26. November 1885.— 331, 346
— Zur Geschichte des 'Bundes der Kommunisten'. London, 8. Oktober 1885. In:

Marx, K. *Enthüllungen über den Kommunisten-Prozeß zu Köln.* Hottingen-Zürich, 1885.— 288, 305-06, 309, 328-29, 331

On the History of the Prussian Peasants. Introduction to Wilhelm Wolff's Pamphlet 'The Silesian Milliard' (present edition, Vol. 26)
— Zur Geschichte der preußischen Bauern. In: Wolff, W. *Die schlesische Milliarde.* Hottingen-Zürich, 1886.— 309, 324, 332, 346

On Social Relations in Russia (present edition, Vol. 24)
— Soziales aus Rußland. Leipzig, 1875.— 529

The Origin of the Family, Private Property and the State. In the Light of the Researches by Lewis H. Morgan (present edition, Vol. 26)
— Der Ursprung der Familie, des Privateigenthums und des Staats. Im Anschluss an Lewis H. Morgan's Forschungen. Hottingen-Zürich, 1884.— 103, 121, 123, 131-32, 134-36, 143, 151, 153, 163-64, 171-72, 176, 185, 187, 191, 196-98, 201, 205, 207, 215, 243, 252, 346, 422, 464-66
— L'origine della famiglia, della proprietà privata e dello stato, in relazione alla ricerche di Luigi H. Morgan. Benevento, 1885.— 205, 215, 272, 279, 291, 293, 298, 421
— Początki cywilizacyi. Na zasadzie i jako uzupełnienie badań Lewisa H. Morgana. Paryż, Lipsk, 1885.— 185, 204
— Der Ursprung der Familie, des Privateigenthums und des Staats. Im Anschluss an Lewis H. Morgan's Forschungen. Zweite Auflage. Stuttgart, 1886.— 346, 422, 474
— Familjens, Privatejendommens og Statens Oprindelse. I Tilslutning til Lewis H. Morgans. Dansk, af Forfatteren gennemgaaet Udgave, besøerget af Gerson Trier. København, 1888.— 264, 279, 291, 394

Outlines of a Critique of Political Economy (present edition, Vol. 3)
— Umrisse zu einer Kritik der Nationaloekonomie. In: *Deutsch-Französische Jahrbücher,* 1., 2. Lieferungen. Paris, 1844.— 158

The Peasant War in Germany (present edition, Vol. 10).— 130-31, 133, 142, 217, 243-44, 249, 328, 363, 419
— Der deutsche Bauernkrieg. In: *Neue Rheinische Zeitung. Politisch-ökonomische Revue,* H. 5-6, Mai-Oktober 1850.— 251
— Der deutsche Bauernkrieg. Dritter Abdruck. Leipzig, 1875.— 371, 373-74

Preface [to 'The Condition of the Working-Class in England'] (present edition, Vol. 4)
— Vorwort. Barmen, den 15. März 1845. In: Engels, F. *Die Lage der arbeitenden Klasse in England.* Leipzig, 1845.— 257

Preface to the 1872 German Edition of the 'Manifesto of the Communist Party' (present edition, Vol. 23)
— Vorwort. London, 24. Juni 1872. In: Marx, K., Engels, F. *Das Kommunistische Manifest.* Neue Ausgabe mit einem Vorwort der Verfasser. Leipzig, 1872.— 73, 344

Preface to the 1892 English Edition of 'The Condition of the Working Class in England' (present edition, Vol. 27)
— Preface. January 11-th, 1892. In: Engels, F. *The Condition of the Working Class in England in 1844.* London, 1892.— 472, 540-42

Socialism: Utopian and Scientific (present edition, Vol. 24)
— Socialisme utopique et socialisme scientifique. Traduction française par Paul La-
fargue. Paris, 1880.— 115, 342
— Die Entwicklung des Sozialismus von der Utopie zur Wissenschaft. Hottingen-
Zürich, 1882.— 15, 37, 60, 133, 164, 288
— Socyjalism utopijny a naukowy. Genève, 1882.— 115
— Die Entwicklung des Sozialismus von der Utopie zur Wissenschaft. Zweite un-
veränderte Auflage. Hottingen-Zürich, 1883.— 12, 15, 37-38, 60, 115, 392, 418
— Die Entwicklung des Sozialismus von der Utopie zur Wissenschaft. Dritte un-
veränderte Auflage. Hottingen-Zürich, 1883.— 60, 68, 115, 392
— Il socialismo utopico e il socialismo scientifico. Benevento, 1883.— 37-38, 115
— Развитіе научнаго соціализма. Переводъ съ 2-го нѣмецкаго изданія 1883 г.
Женева, 1884.— 65, 113, 115
— De ontwikkeling van het socialisme van utopie tot wetenschap. Gravenhage,
1886.— 394, 398
— Socialism Utopian and Scientific. London, 1892.— 115, 172, 191, 207, 394, 416,
464, 523

A Statement to the Editorial Board of the 'New Yorker Volkszeitung' (present edition,
Vol. 26)
— An die Redaktion der N. Y. Volkszeitung. In: *New Yorker Volkszeitung*, Nr. 162,
8. Juli 1886.— 443

*Summary of Frederick Engels' Article 'Outlines of a Critique of Political Economy' pub-
lished in 'Deutsch-Französische Jahrbücher'* (present edition, Vol. 3).— 158
— Umrisse zu einer Kritik der Nationaloekonomie. In: *Deutsch-Französische Jahrbücher*, 1., 2. Lieferungen, 1844.— 158

[*Synopsis of Volume One of 'Capital' by Karl Marx*] (present edition, Vol. 20)
— Das Kapital von K. Marx. I. Band. I. Buch. Produktionsprozess des Kapitals.—
8, 12

[*The True Socialists*] (present edition, Vol. 5).— 31, 37-38, 50

The 23rd of June (present edition, Vol. 7)
— Der 23. Juni. In: *Neue Rheinische Zeitung*, Nr. 28, 28. Juni 1848.— 287, 305, 332

The 24th of June (present edition, Vol. 7)
— Der 24. Juni. In: *Neue Rheinische Zeitung*, Nr. 28, 28. Juni 1848.— 287, 305, 332

The 25th of June (present edition, Vol. 7)
— Der 25. Juni. In: *Neue Rheinische Zeitung*, Nr. 29, 29. Juni 1848.— 287, 305, 332

[*To the 'New Yorker Volkszeitung'*] [March 16, 1883] (present edition, Vol. 24). In:
New Yorker Volkszeitung, Nr. 66, 17. März 1883.— 13

[*To the Editors of the 'New Yorker Volkszeitung'*] [April 18, 1883] (present edition,
Vol. 24).— 13, 91

To the Editors of the 'Severny Vestnik' (present edition, Vol. 26).— 322, 347

To the Working-Classes of Great-Britain (present edition, Vol. 4)
— To the Working Classes of Great-Britain. March 15th, 1845. In: Engels, F. *Die
Lage der arbeitenden Klasse in England*. Leipzig, 1845.— 257, 420

WORKS BY DIFFERENT AUTHORS

Borkheim, S. *Erinnerungen eines deutschen Achtungvierzigers. Bearbeitet von Reinhold Rüegg.* In: *Die Neue Zeit*, 8. Jg., H. 3, 5-7, 1890.— 152, 381
— *Zur Erinnerung für die deutschen Mordspatrioten. 1806-1807.* Leipzig, 1871.— 475
— *Zur Erinnerung für die deutschen Mordspatrioten. 1806-1807.* Mit einer Einleitung von Fr. Engels. Hottingen-Zürich, 1888.— 472, 475, 529

Bougeart, A. *Marat, l'ami du peuple.* Tomes I-II. Paris, 1865.— 399

Boyer, [A.J. B.] [Speech in the Chamber of Deputies on 11 February 1886]. In: *Le Cri du Peuple*, No. 837, 12 février 1886.— 409

Brentano, L. *Die englische Chartistenbewegung.* In: *Preußische Jahrbücher*, Bd. 33, H. 5, 6. Berlin, 1874.— 422

Briefwechsel zwischen Leibniz und der Herzogin Elisabeth Charlotte von Orleans. 1715/1716. Herausgegeben von Eduard Bodemann. In: *Zeitschrift des historischen Vereins für Niedersachsen.* Herausgegeben unter Leitung des Vereins-Ausschusses. Jahrgang 1884. Hannover, 1884.— 133

Briefwechsel zwischen Leibniz und der Herzogin Elisabeth Charlotte v. Orléans in den Jahren 1715 und 1716. Herausgegeben von Eduard Bodemann. Hannover, 1884.— 133

Bucher, L. *Der Parlamentarismus wie er ist.* Berlin, 1855.— 374

[Buonarroti, Ph.] *Buonarroti's History of Babeuf's Conspiracy for Equality; with the Author's Reflections on the Causes & Character of the French Revolution, and His Estimate of the Leading Men and Events of that Epoch. Also, His Views of Democratic Government, Community of Property, and Political and Social Equality.* London, 1836.— 226

Camélinat, [Z. R.] [Speech in the Chamber of Deputies on 11 February 1886]. In: *Le Cri du Peuple*, No. 837, 12 février 1886.— 409
— [Speech in the Chamber of Deputies on 11 March 1886]. In: *Le Cri du Peuple*, No. 866, 13 mars 1886.— 424, 428

Campbell, G. *Modern India: a sketch of the system of civil government. To which is prefixed, some account of the natives and native institutions.* London, 1852.— 179

Cassiodorus. *Historia Gothorum.*— 296

[Chemnitz, M. F.] *Schleswig-Holstein.* In: *Kleine deutsche Liederhalle.* Leipzig, 1849.— 287

Chèvremont, F. *Jean-Paul Marat.* Tomes 1-2. Paris, 1880.— 399

Churchill, R. [Speech in the House of Commons on 20 May 1886]. In: *The Daily News*, No. 12515, May 21, 1886, in the column 'Last Night in Parliament'.— 449

Cicero, M. T. *De natura deorum.*— 537

[Danielson, N.] [Даниельсон, Н. Ф.] Предисловіе къ русскому изданію [of Volume II of *Capital*]. In: Марксъ, К. *Капиталъ. Критика политической экономіи. Переводъ съ нѣмецкаго.* Томъ второй. Книга II. Процессъ обращенія капитала. С.-Петербургъ, 1885.— 400

Darwin, Ch. *On the Origin of Species by Means of Natural Selection, or the Preservation of Favoured Races in the Struggle for Life.* London, 1859.— 226

Davitt, M. *The Irish Social Problem.* In: *To-Day*, Vol. 1, No. 4, April 1884.— 122

Defoe, D. *The Life and Strange Surprising Adventure of Robinson Crusoe of York.*— 194

Deville, G. *Le Capital de Karl Marx. Résumé et accompagné d'un aperçu sur le socialisme scientifique.* Paris, [1883].—44, 46, 50, 52, 59-61, 76-78, 89-90, 93, 96, 101, 112-13, 183, 310, 313, 384-86, 417, 465

— *L'Évolution du capital. Cours d'Économie Sociale.* Paris, [1884].—115, 134, 143, 161, 465

Dietzgen, J. *Haben wir etwas mit dem Anarchisten gemein?* In: *Chicagoer Arbeiterzeitung,* 9. Juni 1886.—491

Douai, A. *Eine Entgegnung auf Dr. Stiebeling's Artikel.* In: *Der Sozialist,* Nr. 13, 28. März 1885.—296

Drumont, É. *La France Juive. Essai d'histoire contemporaine.* Tomes I-II. Paris, [1885 or 1886].—520

Drysdale, Ch. R. *The State Remedy for Poverty.* In: *To-Day,* No. 9, September 1884.—195

Dühring, E. *Kritische Geschichte der Nationalökonomie und des Socialismus.* Dritte, theilweise umgearbeitete Auflage. Leipzig, 1879.—251

Eccarius, J. G. *Eines Arbeiters Widerlegung der national-ökonomischen Lehren John Stuart Mill's.* Berlin, 1869.—371

— *Eines Arbeiters Widerlegung der national-ökonomischen Lehren John Stuart Mill's.* Hottingen-Zürich, 1888.—371

Die Edda, die ältere und jüngere nebst den mythischen Erzählungen der Skalda, übersetzt und mit Erläuterungen begleitet von Karl Simrock. Stuttgart und Tübingen, 1851.— 224, 226

Ely, R. T. *French and German Socialism in Modern Times.* New York, 1883.—295

Epistolae obscurorum virorum.—173

Fabian, H. W. [Article against Marx's and Engels' doctrine of the state]. In: *Freidenker,* April 1884.—124, 191

Fleischmann, A. *Die Sonneberger Spielwaaren-Hausindustrie und ihr Handel. Zur Abwehr gegen die fahrenden Schüler des Katheder-Sozialismus in der National-Oekonomie.* Berlin, 1883.—64

Flügel, J. G. *A Complete Dictionary of the English and German and German and English Languages, containing all the words in general use.* In two volumes. *Vollständiges Englisch-Deutsches und Deutsch-Englisches Wörterbuch, enthaltend alle in beiden Sprachen allgemein gebräuchliche Wörter.* In zwei Theilen. Leipzig, 1830.—375

Freifrau von Droste-Vischering (song).—434

Freiligrath, F. *Abschiedswort der Neuen Rheinischen Zeitung.* In: *Neue Rheinische Zeitung,* Nr. 301, 19. Mai 1849.—52

— *Trotz alledem!*—470

Frohme, K. *Die Entwicklung der Eigentums-Verhältnisse.* Bockenheim, 1883.—125

— [Letter to the editors of *Frankfurter Journal.* 7 May 1885. In: *Der Sozialdemokrat,* Nr. 20, 14. Mai 1885, in the column 'Korrespondenzen'.—302, 307

— *Replik.* In: *Der Sozialdemokrat,* Nr. 21, 21. Mai 1885.—307

— [Speech in the Reichstag on 18 February 1886]. In: *Stenographische Berichte über die Verhandlungen des Reichstags. VI. Legislaturperiode. II. Session 1885/86.* Zweiter Band. Berlin, 1886.—426

Geiser, B. *Das Innere der Erde. Eine Auseinandersetzung über den gegenwärtigen Stand einiger Fragen der Wissenschaft.* In: *Die Neue Welt*, Neunter Band, Nr. 14-15, 1884.— 169, 173
— [Speech in the Reichstag on 10 May 1884]. In: *Aus den Verhandlungen des Sozialistengesetzes. Reden der Abg. Geiser und Bebel.* Nürnberg, Verlag von C. Grillenberger, 1884.— 231

George, H. *The Irish Land Question: What it Involves, and How Alone it Can Be Settled. An Appeal to the Land Leagues.* London, 1881.— 42
— *Progress and Poverty: an Inquiry into the Cause of Industrial Depressions, and of Increase of Want with Increase of Wealth. The Remedy.* New York, 1880.— 14, 42, 82

Gladstone, W. E. [Speech in the House of Commons on 20 May 1886]. In: *The Daily News*, No. 12515, May 21, 1886, in the column 'Last Night in Parliament'.— 449

Goethe, J.W. von. *Dichtung und Wahrheit.*— 253
— *Faust.*— 48
— *Klaggesang von der edlen Frauen des Asan Aga, aus dem Morlakischen.* Vermischte Gedichte.— 92
— *Wilhelm Meisters Lehrjahre.*— 30

Grimaux, É. *Les substances colloïdales et la coagulation.* In: *Revue scientifique.* Troisième série, T. IX, T. XXXV de la Collection, janvier à juillet 1885, No. 16, 18 avril.— 289

Gronlund, L. *The Cooperative Commonwealth in Its Outlines. An Exposition of Modern Socialism.* Boston, 1884.— 192, 295

Groß, G. *Karl Marx. Eine Studie.* Leipzig, 1885.— 250, 261
— *Marx, Karl: Das Kapital. Kritik der politischen Oekonomie. Zweiter Band, Buch II.* In: *Jahrbuch für Gesetzgebung, Verwaltung und Volkswirthschaft im Deutschen Reich*, H. 2, 1886.— 522

Guesde, J. *Nouvelle Victoire.* In: *Le Cri du Peuple*, No. 387, 18 novembre 1884.— 225
— [Speech at a meeting of business people]. In: *Le Cri du Peuple*, No. 848, 23 février 1886.— 414

Guizot, [F. P. G.] *Histoire de la civilisation en France, depuis la chute de l'Empire romain jusqu'en 1789. Cours d'histoire moderne.* Tomes 1-5. Paris, 1829-1832.— 95

Haeckel, E. *Die Perigenesis der Plastidule oder die Wellenzeugung der Lebenstheilchen. Ein Versuch zur mechanischen Erklärung der elementaren Entwickelungs-Vorgänge.* Berlin, 1876.— 289

Hamel, E. *Histoire de Saint-Just, député à la Convention nationale.* Paris, 1859.— 399

Hänel, [A.] [Speech in the Reichstag discussion on the prolongation of the Anti-Socialist Law on 31 March 1886]. In: *Stenographische Berichte über die Verhandlungen des Reichstags. VI. Legislaturperiode. II. Session 1885/86.* Dritter Band. Berlin, 1886.— 435

Haxthausen, A. Freiherr von. *Die ländliche Verfassung Rußlands. Ihre Entwickelungen und ihre Feststellung in der Gesetzgebung von 1861.* Leipzig, 1866.— 179

Headingley, A. S. *French Socialists at the Ballot Box.* In: *Justice*, No. 113, March 13, 1886.— 424
— *The Socialists and the Paris Elections.* In: *Justice*, No. 120, May 1, 1886.— 450

The Hecker song.— 287

Hegel, G. W. F. *Vorlesungen über die Geschichte der Philosophie*. Bd. 2. In: *Werke*, Bd. XIV. Berlin, 1833.— 281, 348

Heine, H. *Atta Troll*.— 167
— *Deutschland. Ein Wintermärchen*. In: *Neue Gedichte*. Hamburg, 1844.— 47
— *Deutschland. Ein Wintermärchen*. In: *Vorwärts!*, Nr. 85-88, 90, 92, 93, 96; 23., 26., 30. Oktober, 2., 9., 16., 20., 30. November 1844, in the column 'Feuilleton des Vorwärts'.— 47
— *Die schlesischen Weber*. In: *Album*. Originalpoesieen..., Hrsg. H. Püttmann, Borna, 1847.— 226

Howell, G. *The History of the International Association*. In: *The Nineteenth Century*, No. XVII, July 1878.— 8

Hyndman, H. M. *England for All*. London, 1881.— 54
— *The Historical Basis of Socialism in England*. London, 1883.— 163
— (anon.) *Karl Marx. Capital. Translated by J. Broadhouse* [pseud.] In: *To-Day*, Vol. 4-5, October 1885-May 1886.— 127, 313, 345, 393, 419, 424, 440
— *A Sad Anniversary. To the Editor of 'Justice'*. In: *Justice*, Vol. I, No. 8, March 8, 1884.— 118
— (anon.) *Socialism Made Plain, being the Social and Political Manifesto of the Democratic Federation*. [London], June 1883.— 54

Jagemann, C. G. *Dizionario italiano-tedesco e tedesco-italiano*. T. I-II. Weissenfels e Lipsia, 1790-91.— 85

Jordanes. *De origine actibusque Getarum*.— 296

Kaltenboeck, H. *Familie und Ehe. Eine völkerpsychologische Untersuchung*. In: *Frankfurter Zeitung und Handelsblatt*, Nr. 278, 4. Oktober 1884. Morgenblatt, in the column 'Feuilleton'.— 207

Karl Marx vor den Kölner Geschwornen. Prozeß gegen den Ausschuß der rheinischen Demokraten wegen Aufrufs zum bewaffneten Widerstand. (9. Februar 1849). Mit einem Vorwort von Fr. Engels. Hottingen-Zürich, 1885.— 304, 311, 328

Kautsky, K. (anon.) *Der 'anarchistisch-sozialistische Aufruhr in London'*. In: *Der Sozialdemokrat*, Nr. 8, 19. Februar 1886, in the column 'Sozialpolitische Rundschau'.— 404, 407
— *Arbeiterunruhen in London*. In: *Deutsche Wochenschrift*, Nr. 8, 12. Februar 1886.— 404, 407, 427
— *Aus dem Nachlasse von Carl Marx*. In: *Frankfurter Zeitung und Handelsblatt*, Nr. 263, 19. September 1884. Morgenblatt, in the column 'Feuilleton'.— 208
— *Auswanderung und Kolonisation*. In: *Die Neue Zeit*, 1. Jg., Hefte 8, 9, 1883.— 56
— *Der Einfluss der Volksvermehrung auf den Fortschritt der Gesellschaft*. Wien, 1880.— 195, 316
— *Die Entstehung der biblischen Urgeschichte*. In: *Kosmos. Zeitschrift für Entwickelungslehre und einheitliche Weltanschauung*. VII. Jahrgang. Bd. XIII, Juni 1883.— 56
— *Die Entstehung der Ehe und Familie*. In: *Kosmos. Zeitschrift für Entwickelungslehre und einheitliche Weltanschauung* VI. Jahrgang. Bd. XII, Dezember 1882-Februar 1883.— 316

— *Peasant Proprietary in France.* In: *To-Day,* Vol. 1, No. 4, April 1884.— 122 ⁻

— *Recherches sur les origines de l'idée du bien et du juste* [septembre 1885]. In: *Revue philosophique de la France et de l'étranger.* Dixième année, T. XX (juillet à décembre 1885), 1885.— 431

— *Das Recht auf Faulheit. Widerlegung des Rechtes auf Arbeit.* In: *Der Sozialdemokrat,* Nr. 51, 52; 13., 20. Dezember 1883; Nr. 1-5; 3., 10., 17., 24., 31. Januar 1884.— 68, 86

— *Socialism and Darwinism.* In: *Progress,* Vol. 2, December 1883.— 71

— *La théorie de la plus-value de Karl Marx et la critique de M. Paul Leroy-Beaulieu.* In: *Journal des Économistes.* T. XXVII, No. 9, 15 septembre 1884, in the column 'Correspondance'.— 171, 175, 179-83, 225, 431

— *The Tonkin War and Socialism.* In: *The Commonweal,* Vol. 1, No. 4, May 1885.— 275

Lamartine, A. de. *Histoire de la révolution de 1848.* Bruxelles, 1849.— 24

Lassalle, F. *Herr Bastiat-Schulze von Delitzsch, der ökonomische Julian, oder: Capital und Arbeit.* Berlin, 1864.— 188

Leibnizens Briefwechsel mit dem Minister von Bernstorff und andere Leibniz betreffende Briefe und Aktenstücke aus den Jahren 1705-1716. Mit einer Einleitung herausgegeben von Archivar Dr. Doebner. In: *Zeitschrift des historischen Vereins für Niedersachsen.* Herausgegeben unter Leitung 'des Vereins-Ausschusses. Jg. 1881. Hannover, 1881.— 133

— Ibid. Hannover, 1882.— 133

Leroy-Beaulieu, [P.] *Le Collectivisme. Examen critique du nouveau socialisme.* Paris, 1884.— 171, 174-75, 178-83

Lexis, W. *Die Marx'sche Kapitaltheorie.* In: *Jahrbücher für Nationalökonomie und Statistik.* Neue Folge, Elfter Bd., Jena, 1885.— 421, 474, 522

Liebig, J. von. *Die Chemie in ihrer Anwendung auf Agricultur und Physiologie.* In zwei Theilen. Siebente Auflage. Erster Theil: *Der chemische Proceß der Ernährung der Vegetabilien.* Braunschweig, 1862.— 107

Liebknecht, W. [Speech in the Reichstag on 24 November 1885]. In: *Kölnische Zeitung,* Nr. 327, 25. November 1885, Erstes Blatt. Under the general heading *Verhandlungen des deutschen Reichstages.* (Telegramm.) Berlin, 24. November.— 361

— [Speech in the Reichstag on 8 February 1886]. In: *Stenographische Berichte über die Verhandlungen des Reichstags. VI. Legislaturperiode. II. Session 1885/86.* Zweiter Band. Berlin, 1886.— 417

— (anon.) *Die Trades Unions.* In: *Die Neue Zeit,* 1. Jg., H. 2, 3, 1883.— 57

— *Ueber den Normalarbeitstag.* In: *Der Sozialdemokrat,* Nr. 43-47, 22., 29. Oktober, 5., 12., 19. November 1885.— 353

Lippert, J. *Die Geschichte der Familie.* Stuttgart, 1884.— 207

Loria, A. *Karl Marx.* In: *Nuova antologia di scienze, lettere ed arti.* Ser. 2, vol. 38, fas. 7. Roma, 1883.— 24, 25

— *La teoria del valore negli economisti italiani.* Bologna, 1882.— 24

— *La théorie de la valeur de Karl Marx.* In: *Journal des Économistes,* No. 10, octobre 1884.— 226

Luther, M. *Ein' feste Burg ist unser Gott...*— 286

Mably, L'Abbé de. *Oeuvres completes.* Londres, 1789.— 95

Malthus, T. R. *Essai sur le principe de population, ou exposé des effets passés et présens de l'action de cette cause sur le bonheur du genre humain; suivi de quelques recherches relatives a l'espérance de guérir ou d'adoucir les maux qu'elle entraîne.* 3^c Édition française très-augmentée. Tomes 1-4, Paris-Genève, 1836.— 95

Maurer, G. L. von. *Einleitung zur Geschichte der Mark-, Hof-, Dorf- und Stadt-Verfassung und der öffentlichen Gewalt.* München, 1854.— 398

— *Geschichte der Dorfverfassung in Deutschland.* Bd. I-II. Erlangen, 1865-1866.— 398

— *Geschichte der Fronhöfe, der Bauernhöfe und der Hofverfassung in Deutschland.* Bd. I-IV. Erlangen, 1862-1863.— 398

— *Geschichte der Markenverfassung in Deutschland.* Erlangen, 1856.— 398

— *Geschichte der Städteverfassung in Deutschland.* Bd. I-IV. Erlangen, 1869-1871.— 398

Mead, E. P. *The Steam King.* In: *The Northern Star,* Vol. VI, No. 274, February 11, 1843.— 92

Menger, A. *Das Recht auf den vollen Arbeitsertrag in geschichtlicher Darstellung.* Stuttgart, 1886.— 521

Meyer, R. *Der Emancipationskampf des vierten Standes.* Bd. I. Berlin, 1874.— 101

Mignet, F. A. *Histoire de la révolution française, depuis 1789 jusqu'en 1814.* Tomes I-II. Bruxelles, 1828.— 399

[Mikhailovsky] М[ихайловский], Н. [К.] *Карлъ Марксъ передъ судомъ г. Ю. Жуковскаго.* In: *Отечественныя записки,* No. 10, октябрь 1877, in the column 'Современное обозрѣніе'.— 112

Mommsen, Th. *Römische Forschungen.* Erster Band. Zweite unveraenderte Auflage. Berlin, 1864.— 207

Money, J. W. B. *Java; or, how to manage a colony. Showing a practical solution of the questions now affecting British India.* In two volumes. London, 1861.— 102, 179

Morgan, L. [H.] *Ancient Society or Researches in the Lines of Human Progress from Savagery, through Barbarism to Civilization.* London, 1877.— 103, 120, 123, 131-32

— Ibid. New York, 1877.— 103, 115, 120

Morris, W. *The Story of Sigurd the Volsung and the Fall of the Nibelungs,* 1877.— 224

Most, J. *Kapital und Arbeit. Ein populärer Auszug aus 'Das Kapital' von Karl Marx.* Chemnitz, [1873].— 11

— *Kapital und Arbeit. Ein populärer Auszug aus 'Das Kapital' von Karl Marx.* 2 verbesserte Auflage. Chemnitz, [1876].— 11

Mozin-Peschier. *Dictionnaire complet des langues française et allemande, résumé des meilleurs ouvrages anciens et modernes sur les sciences, les lettres et les arts, avec le concours de M. Guizot pour les synonymes.* Quatrième édition. Tomes 1-4. Stuttgart, 1863.— 85, 375

Müller, Ph. [Leaflet]. In: *Der Sozialdemokrat,* Nr. 46, 14. November 1884, in the column 'Sozialpolitische Rundschau'.— 225, 232

Nibelungenlied.— 498

Nieuwenhuis, F. D. *Hoe ons land geregeerd wordt op papier en in de werkelijkheid.* Graven-hage, 1885.—397, 398
— (anon.) *Karl Marx.* In: *Recht voor Allen,* No. 4, 24 maart 1883.—6

Novikova, O. *The Russification of England.* In: *The Pall Mall Gazette,* January 15, 1885.—256

Paquet, J. *Des institutions provinciales et communales et des corporations des pays de l'ancienne France à l'avénement de Louis XI.* Paris, 1860.—226

[Platter, J.] *Die Kathederweisheit der 'christlich-ethischen' Nationalökonomie.* In: *Deutsche Worte,* VI. Jg., Nr. 7, 8-9, 1886.—458

[Plekhanov] Плехановъ, Г. [В.] *Наши разногласія.* Женева, 1884.—264, 279-81
— *Соціализмъ и политическая борьба.* Женева, 1883.—67

Prel, K. du. *Der Somnambulismus.* In: *Die Neue Welt,* Neunter Band, Nr. 20-22, 1884.—165, 170

Proudhon, P. J. *Si les traités de 1815 ont cessé d'exister? Actes du futur congrès.* Paris, 1863.—117

[Quarck, M.] *Kommerzienrath Adolf Fleischmann als Nationalökonom und die Thüringer Hausindustrie. Soziale Studie in kritischen Anmerkungen.* Leipzig, 1883.—64, 67

Rae, J. *The Scotch Village Community.* In: *The Fortnightly Review,* Vol. XXXVIII, New Series. July 1 to December 1, 1885, No. CCXXVII, November 1, 1885.—398

Richter, [E.] [Speech in the Reichstag on 4 March 1886]. In: *Stenographische Berichte über die Verhandlungen des Reichstags. VI. Legislaturperiode. II. Session 1885/86.* Zweiter Band. Berlin, 1886.—427

Rodbertus-Jagetzow, [J. K.] *Briefe und Socialpolitische Aufsaetze.* Herausgegeben von Dr. R. Meyer. Bd. 1, Berlin, [1882].—188, 262, 301
— *Das Kapital. Vierter socialer Brief an von Kirchmann.* Herausgegeben und einge-leitet von Theophil Kozak. In: *Aus dem literarischen Nachlass von Dr. Carl Rod-bertus-Jagetzow.* II. Berlin, 1884.—138, 262
— [Letter to R. Meyer of 20 September 1871]. In: Rodbertus-Jagetzow, [J. K.] *Briefe und Socialpolitische Aufsaetze.* Herausgegeben von Dr. R. Meyer. Bd. 1, Berlin, [1882].—72
— [Letter to R. Meyer of 29 November 1871]. In: Rodbertus-Jagetzow, [J. K.] *Briefe und Socialpolitische Aufsaetze.* Herausgegeben von Dr. R. Meyer. Bd. 1, Berlin, [1882].—187
— [Letter to J. Zeller of 14 March 1875]. In: *Zeitschrift für die gesammte Staatswissen-schaft.* Bd. 35, H. 2. Tübingen, 1879.—111, 166, 187, 262
— *Der Normal-Arbeitstag. (Separat-Abdruck aus der 'Berliner Revue'.)* Berlin, 1878.—139, 166
— *Offener Brief an das Comité des Deutschen Arbeitervereins zu Leipzig.* Leipzig, 1863.—102, 124, 138
— *Sociale Briefe an von Kirchmann.* Briefe 1-3. Berlin, 1850-1851.—111
— *Zur Erkenntniss unsrer staatswirthschaftlichen Zustände.* Neubrandenburg und Fried-land, 1842.—156, 163, 166, 175-76, 206, 262

— *Zur Erkenntniss unsrer staatswirthschaftlichen Zustände*. 2. erhebliche erweiterte Auflage. Hrsg. von J. Zeller. Berlin, 1885.— 196

— *Zur Erklärung und Abhülfe der heutigen Creditnoth des Grundbesitzes*. Bd. I-II. Jena, 1869.— 204

Romance de la penitencia del roy Rodrigo.— 289

[Rosenberg, W. L.] [The article signed with a pseudonym *von der Mark*]. In: *New Yorker Volkszeitung*, 2. Dezember 1883.— 72, 91

Rouget de Lisle, C. J. *Chant de guerre pour l'armée du Rhin*. [Marseillaise.]— 287

Sax, E. *Hausindustrie in Thüringen. Wirtschaftsgeschichtliche Studien*. I. Theil. Jena, 1882.— 79

[Schäffle, A.] *Die Quintessenz des Socialismus. Von einem Volkswirth*. Separatabdruck aus den 'Deutschen Blättern'. Gotha, 1875.— 267

Schiller, F. von. *Kabale und Liebe. Ein bürgerliches Trauerspiel*.— 357

Schippel, M. *H. M. Hyndman. The Historical Basis of Socialism in England. London. 1883*. [Review]. In: *Die Neue Zeit*, 2. Jg., Nr. 7, 1884, in the column 'Literarische Rundschau'.— 163

[Schlüter, H.] *Die Chartistenbewegung in England*. Hottingen-Zürich, 1887.— 422, 453, 462, 467, 475, 528

[Schramm, C. A.] *Antwort an Herrn K. Kautsky*. In: *Die Neue Zeit*, 3. Jg., H. 5, 1885. Signed: *C. A. S.*— 387

— *K. Kautsky und Rodbertus*. In: *Die Neue Zeit*, 2. Jg., H. 11, 1884. Signed: *C. A. S.*— 193, 204, 387

— *Rodbertus, Marx, Lassalle. Sozialwissenschaftliche Studie*. München, [1885 or 1886]. Signed: *C. A. S.*— 387, 414

Schumacher, [G.] [Speech in the Reichstag on 5 March 1886]. In: *Stenographische Berichte über die Verhandlungen des Reichstags. VI. Legislaturperiode. II. Session 1885/86*. Zweiter Band. Berlin, 1886.— 426

Singer, [P.] [Speech in the Reichstag on 18 February 1886]. In: *Stenographische Berichte über die Verhandlungen des Reichstags. VI. Legislaturperiode. II. Session 1885/86*. Zweiter Band. Berlin, 1886.— 426

[Skrebitzky] Скребицкій, А. *Крестьянское дѣло въ царствованіе императора Александра II. Матеріалы для исторіи освобожденія крестьянъ. Губернскіе комитеты, ихъ депутаты, и редакціонныя комиссіи въ крестьянскомъ дѣлѣ*. Тома 1-4. Боннъ на Рейнѣ, 1862-68.— 339

Smith, A. *Recherches sur la nature et les causes de la richesse des nations*. Traduction nouvelle, avec des notes et observations; par Germain Garnier. Tomes I-V. Paris, 1802.— 95

Smith, A[dolphe]. *France and the International Congress. To the Editor of 'Justice'*. In: *Justice*, Vol. I, No. 50, December 27, 1884.— 247

Stiebeling, G. C. *'Reform oder Revolution'*. In: *Der Sozialist*, Nr. 7, 14. Februar 1885.— 296

Thierry, A. *Essai sur l'histoire de la formation et des progrès du tiers état.* 2-ed. Tomes I-II. Paris, 1853.— 226

Thiers, A. *De la propriété.* Paris, 1848.— 117

— *Histoire de la révolution française, accompagnée d'une histoire de la révolution de 1355, ou des États-généraux sous le roi Jean.* Tomes 3-10. Paris, 1824-1827.— 399

Thiers, A., Bodin, F. *Histoire de la révolution française, accompagnée d'une histoire de la révolution de 1355, ou des États-généraux sous le roi Jean.* Tomes 1-2. Paris, 1823.— 399

Tschech's Attentat [folk song].— 433

Varenholz, C. [Letter.] *London, 2. Februar.* [1885]. In: *Der Sozialdemokrat,* Nr. 9, 26. Februar 1885, in the column 'Korrespondenzen'.— 365

Vico, [G. B.] *La science nouvelle.* Paris, 1844.— 276

Viereck, L. [Reply to the Social-Democrats of Munich]. In: *Demokratisches Wochenblatt,* Nr. 30, 30. August 1885.— 328

Virgil. *Aeneid.*— 413

Vogt, K. *Mein Prozess gegen die Allgemeine Zeitung. Stenographischer Bericht, Dokumente und Erläuterungen.* Genf, 1859.— 527

Watts, J. H. *The Socialists and the General Election.* In: *The Pall Mall Gazette,* December 4, 1885.— 367

Weerth, G. *Handwerksburschenlied.* In: *Der Sozialdemokrat,* Nr. 24, 7. Juni 1883.— 34

— (anon.) *Joseph Rayner Stephens, Prediger zu Staleybridge, und die Bewegung der englischen Arbeiter im Jahre 1839.* In: *Rheinische Jahrbücher zur gesellschaftlichen Reform,* Bd. II, 1846. Signed: *G. W.*— 422, 475

— *Nichts Schönres gibt es auf der Welt...*— 161

— *Die rheinischen Weinbauern.* In: *Der Sozialdemokrat,* Nr. 29, 12. Juli 1883.— 34

Wermuth/Stieber. *Die Communisten-Verschwörungen des neunzehnten Jahrhunderts.* Th. I-II. Berlin, 1853-54.— 305, 329, 344, 346

Wicksteed, Ph. H. *Das Kapital. A Criticism.* In: *To-Day,* No. 10, October 1884.— 192, 195

Williams, H. E. *The Socialist Candidates.* In: *The Echo,* No. 5285, December 5, 1885.— 366-69

Wills, W. G. *Olivia.*— 345

Wolff, W. *Die schlesische Milliarde. Abdruck aus der 'Neuen Rheinischen Zeitung'. März-April 1849.* Mit Einleitung von Friedrich Engels. Hottingen-Zürich, 1886.— 309, 328, 332, 346

[Yanson] Янсонъ, Ю. Э. *Сравнительная статистика Россіи и западно-европейскихъ государствъ.* Тома I-II. С.-Петербургъ, 1878-1880.— 339

DOCUMENTS

An Act for the Amendment and Better Administration of the Laws Relating to the Poor in England and Wales (1834).— 150

An Act for the Reliefs of the Poor (43rd Elizabeth), 1601.— 150

Arms (Ireland) Bill (1886).— 448

[Debate on the Polish motion in the Reichstag on 15 and 16 January 1886.] In: *Stenographische Berichte über die Verhandlungen des Reichstags. VI. Legislaturperiode. II. Session 1885/86.* Bd. I. Berlin, 1886.— 389, 391

Der Entwurf eines Gesetzes, betreffend die Abänderung der Gewerbeordnung. In: *Stenographische Berichte über die Verhandlungen des Reichstages. V. Legislaturperiode. II. Session 1882/83.* Bd. 3-4. Berlin, 1883.— 22

Der Entwurf eines Gesetzes, betreffend die Krankenversicherung der Arbeiter. In: *Stenographische Berichte über die Verhandlungen des Reichstages. V. Legislaturperiode. II. Session 1882/83.* Bd. 3-4. Berlin, 1883.— 22

The Factory & Workshops Act 1878. By Alex. Redgrave, Her Maj. Inspector of Factories. 2nd ed. London, 1879.— 334

Gesetz gegen die gemeingefährlichen Bestrebungen der Sozialdemokratie. Vom 21. Oktober 1878. In: *Deutscher Reichs-Anzeiger und Königlich Preußischer Staats-Anzeiger.* Nr. 249, 22. Oktober. Abends. 1878.— 17, 21, 26, 32, 35, 50, 93, 98-99, 124-25, 129, 132, 138, 140-41, 145, 147, 160, 187, 199, 213, 216, 220, 231-32, 242, 268, 271, 275, 285, 290, 296, 300, 303, 305, 307, 313, 527

The People's Charter; being the Outline of an Act to Provide for the Just Representation of the People of Great Britain in the Commons' House of Parliament. Embracing the Principles of Universal Suffrage, No Property Qualification, Annual Parliaments, Equal Representation, Payment of Members, and Vote by Ballot. Prepared by a committee of twelve persons, six members of Parliament and six members of the London Working Men's Association, and addressed to the People of the United Kingdom. London, 1838.— 422

Programm der sozialistischen Arbeiterpartei Deutschlands. In: *Der Volksstaat,* Nr. 59, 28. Mai 1875.— 34, 146

Programme électoral des travailleurs socialistes. In: *L'Égalité,* No. 24, 30 juin, 1880, 2nd serie.— 311

[Programme of the United Labor Party]. In: *Der Sozialist,* Nr. 40, 2. Oktober 1886 (in the article 'Die Aufstellung Henry George's...').— 532

Proposal from the London District of the Communist League to the Central Authority in Cologne (present edition, Vol. 10).— 332

Protokoll über den Kongreß der deutschen Sozialdemokratie in Kopenhagen. Abgehalten vom 29. März bis 2. April 1883. Hottingen-Zürich, 1883.— 21, 32

Réglement de l'ordre du jour. In: *Le Cri du Peuple,* No. 867, 14 mars 1886.— 425, 428

République Française. Liberté, égalité, fraternité. Mairie du 17ᵉ Arrondissement. Paris, le 21 mars 1871. Signed: *Les Adjoints, Villéneuve, Cacheux, Malon. Le Maire, G. Favre.* — 108

Resolutions of the Congress of Geneva, 1866, and the Congress of Brussels, 1868. The International Working Men's Association. Office of General Council. London, [1869].— 389

Zwei politische Prozesse. Verhandelt vor den Februar-Assisen in Köln. I. Der erste Preßprozeß der Neuen Rheinischen Zeitung. II. Prozeß des Kreis-Ausschusses der rheinischen Demokraten. Köln, 1849.— 304

[Александр III.] *Высочайшій манифестъ. С.-Петербургъ. 29-го апрѣля.* In: *С-Петербургскія вѣдомости,* No. 88, 30 апреля (12 мая) 1881.— 34

Военно-статистическій сборникъ. Выпускъ IV. Россія. С.-Петербургъ, 1871.— 339

Сборникъ статистическихъ свѣдѣній по Московской губерніи. Тома I-IX. Москва, 1877-85.— 339

Сборникъ статистическихъ свѣдѣній по Тверской губерніи. Томъ I. Москва, 1885.— 339

Труды экспедиціи, снаряженной императорскими Вольнымъ экономическимъ и Русскимъ географическимъ обществами, для изслѣдованія хлѣбной торговли и производительности въ Россіи. Томъ II, Выпуски 1-4. С.-Петербургъ, 1870-1872.— 100

ANONYMOUS ARTICLES AND REPORTS PUBLISHED IN PERIODIC EDITIONS

Berliner Volksblatt, Nr. 42, 43, 54-56; 19., 20 Februar, 5.-7. März 1886. Beilage: [Debate in the Reichstag on the exceptional law and spirits monopoly], in the column 'Parlamentsberichte'.— 426

The Commonweal, Vol. 1, No. 10, November 1885: *Free Speech and the Police.*— 394

Le Cri du Peuple, No. 356, 18 octobre 1884: *Exécution d'un agent provocateur.*— 207
— No. 825, 31 janvier 1886: [On the strike in Decazeville].— 409
— No. 838, 13 février 1886: [Account of the debate in the Chamber of Deputies on 11 February 1886].— 409
— No. 888, 4 avril 1886.— 434

The Daily News, September 12, 1883: *London, Wednesday, September 12* (leader).— 57
— No. 12307, September 21, 1885: *The Socialist Meetings at the East End. Further Arrests.*— 326
— No. 12308, September 22, 1885: *The Socialists and the Free Speech Question.*— 326
— No. 12515, May 21, 1886: *Last Night in Parliament.*— 449

The Echo, No. 5287, December 7, 1885.— 366

The Edinburgh Review, or Critical Journal, No. 331, July 1885: *The Parting of the Waters. Parliamentary Debates, 1884-85.*— 314

Justice, Vol. I, No. 8, March 8, 1884: *To-Day.*— 118
— Vol. I, No. 11, March 29, 1884: *Peasant Proprietary in France.*— 122
— Vol. II, No. 73, June 6, 1885: [Report in the column 'Tell Tale Straws'].— 310
— Vol. II, No. 90, October 3, 1885: [Report in the column 'Tell Tale Straws'].— 370, 394
— Vol. II, No. 92, October 17, 1885.— 370
— Vol. II, No. 100, December 12, 1885: *Tory gold!* — 376

Kölnische Zeitung, Nr. 199, 20. Juli 1883, Zweites Blatt: *Köln, 20. Juli,* in the column 'Kölner Local-Nachrichten'.— 52

— Nr. 241, 30. August 1884, Erstes Blatt: *Professor Schweinfurth über den Congo.*— 192
— Nr. 307, 4. November 1884, Zweites Blatt: *Die Stichwahlen. Köln, 4. November.*— 213, 231
— Nr. 309, 6. November 1884, Zweites Blatt: *Die Reichstags-Stichwahl in Köln. Köln, 6. November.*— 213, 231
— Nr. 311, 8. November 1884, Zweites Blatt: *Noch einmal die Kölner Stichwahl. Köln, 8. November.*— 213, 231
— Nr. 314, 11. November 1884, Zweites Blatt: *Lübeck-Büchenbahn*, in the column 'Eisenbahn-Einnahmen'.— 219
— Nr. 276, 5. Oktober 1885, Erstes Blatt: *Der Orient. Sofia. 4. Oct. (Telegram).*— 329
— Nr. 277, 6. Oktober 1885, Zweites Blatt: *Der Orient. Sofia. 5. Oct. (Telegram).*— 329
— Nr. 278, 7. Oktober 1885, Zweites Blatt: *Der Orient.*— 329
— Nr. 279, 8. Oktober 1885, Erstes Blatt: *Der Orient.*— 329
— Nr. 279, 8. Oktober 1885, Zweites Blatt: *Der Orient.*— 329

Königlich privilegirte Berlinische Zeitung von Staats- und gelehrten Sachen. Nr. 235, 24. Mai 1883, 1. Beilage: *Zur Beurteilung von Karl Marx.* Signed: *H. V. T.*— 33

The Labour Standard, December 8, 1883: 'Shall O'Donnell hang?..'— 72

Londoner Zeitung. Hermann, Nr. 1316, 22. März 1884: *Die Märzfeier in London.*— 119

Lyon-Socialiste, No. 9, 9 novembre 1884: [Article about the German Social-Democrats' victory at the Reichstag elections].— 225

Neue Rheinische Zeitung. Organ der Demokratie, Nr. 221, 14. Februar 1849: *Preßprozeß der Neuen Rheinischen Zeitung. Verhandelt am 7. Februar vor den Assisen zu Köln,* in the column 'Deutschland. Köln, 13. Februar'.— 304
— Nr. 226, 231-233; 19., 25., 27., 28. Februar 1849: *Assisenverhandlung wegen Aufreizung zur Rebellion. Verhandelt zu Köln den 8. Februar,* in the column 'Deutschland. Köln'.— 304

New Yorker Volkszeitung, Nr. 68, 20. März 1883: *Zuschriften und Depeschen. IV.*— 14
— Nr. 12, 14. Januar 1884: *Ein paar Muster.*— 91
— Nr. 200, 21. August 1886: *Ein Bedürfniß und eine Schmach.*— 480

Norddeutsche Allgemeine Zeitung, 17. Mai 1884, evening edition: [Article about the 'right to work'].— 140

Новое время, No. 3666, 15 (27) мая 1886, in the column 'Утренняя почта. Среда, 14-го мая...'.— 515

Pionier. Illustrierter Volks-Kalender für 1886: Aus dem Leben eines alten Sozialdemokraten.— 440

Правительственный вѣстникъ, No. 108, 20 мая (1 июня) 1886.— 515

The Republican, Vol. VIII, No. 8, November 1882: *Dr. Karl Marx.*— 7
— April 1883: [Karl Marx. Obituary].— 7

Le Socialiste, No. 15, 5 décembre 1885: *Ein Angleterre.*— 368
— No. 28, 29; 6, 13 mars 1886: *France,* in the column 'Mouvement social'.— 429

Le Soir, 29 août 1883.— 53

INDEX OF PERIODICALS

Cologne under Marx's editorship from 1 June 1848 to 19 May 1849. Engels was among its editors.— 26, 36, 52, 92, 287, 288, 304, 305, 310, 332, 351

Neue Rheinische Zeitung. Politisch-ökonomische Revue — a theoretical journal of the Communist League founded by Marx and Engels in December 1849 and published from March to November 1850.— 93, 251, 261, 305

Die Neue Welt. Illustriertes Unterhaltungsblatt für das Volk — a German socialist fortnightly published in Leipzig from 1876 to 1881, then in Stuttgart and Hamburg till 1919; Wilhelm Liebknecht was its editor in 1876-80.— 7, 160, 165, 173, 174, 309, 324, 363, 498, 502

Die Neue Zeit — a theoretical journal of the German Social Democrats; published monthly in Stuttgart from 1883 to October 1890 and then weekly till the autumn of 1923; Engels contributed to it from 1885 to 1895.— 26, 27, 57, 103, 121, 132, 135, 137, 144, 153, 163, 164, 189, 204, 212, 220, 250, 274, 307, 385, 448, 458, 509, 527

New Yorker Volkszeitung. Den Interessen des arbeitenden Volkes gewidmet — a German-language socialist daily published in New York from 1878 to 1932.— 13-14, 91, 143, 165, 246, 394, 402-03, 440, 441, 443, 458, 461, 462, 496, 511, 533

The Nineteenth Century. A Monthly Review — a liberal review published in London from 1877 to 1900.— 8

The Northern Star — central organ of the Chartists, published weekly from 1837 to 1852, first in Leeds, and, from November 1844, in London. Its founder and editor was Feargus O'Connor. Engels contributed to the paper from 1843 to 1850.— 337, 442

La Nouvelle Revue — a French republican journal founded by Juliette Adam and published in Paris from 1879.— 431

The Pall Mall Gazette. An Evening Newspaper and Review — a daily published in London from 1865 to 1920, in the 1860s and 1870s pursued a conservative line; Marx and Engels maintained contacts with it from July 1870 to June 1871.— 256, 367

Pionier. Illustrierter Volks-Kalender — a German-language annual published by the Socialist Labor Party in New York in 1883-1904.— 440

Progress. A Monthly Magazine — a monthly on science, politics and literature published in London from 1883 to 1887; Eleanor Marx-Aveling and Edward Aveling contributed to it.— 7, 71, 74, 75

Recht voor Allen — a Dutch socialist newspaper founded by Ferdinand Nieuwenhuis in Amsterdam in 1879 and published till 1900.— 6

The Republican — British journal of radical trend published in London under this title between 1880 and 1886 and as *The Radical* from 1886 to 1889.— 7

La République Française — a radical daily founded by Léon Gambetta and published in Paris from 1871 to 1924.— 398-99

Révolutions de Paris — a revolutionary-democratic weekly published in Paris from July 1879 to February 1894; till September 1890 the paper was edited by Elisée Loustalot.— 95, 122

Revue philosophique de la France et de l'étranger — a monthly journal published in Paris from 1876.— 431

SUBJECT INDEX